MANAGEMENT ACCOUNTING

PRINCIPLES & PRACTICE

Alan Upchurch

FINANCIAL TIMES
PITMAN PUBLISHING

FINANCIAL TIMES
MANAGEMENT

FINANCIAL TIMES MANAGEMENT
128 Long Acre, London WC2E 9AN
Tel: +44 (0)171 447 2000
Fax: +44 (0)171 240 5771
Website: www.ftmanagement.com

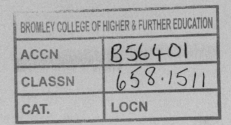

A Division of Financial Times Professional Limited

First published in Great Britain in 1998

© Financial Times Professional Limited 1998

The right of Alan Upchurch to be identified as Author of
this Work has been asserted by him in accordance with the
Copyright, Designs and Patents Act 1988.

ISBN 0 273 62226 9

British Library Cataloguing in Publication Data
A CIP catalogue record for this book can be obtained from the British Library

10 9 8 7 6 5 4 3 2

Typeset by Pantek Arts, Maidstone, Kent.
Printed and bound in Great Britain by William Clowes Ltd, Beccles.

The Publishers' policy is to use paper manufactured from sustainable forests.

MANAGEMENT ACCOUNTING

PRINCIPLES & PRACTICE

CONTENTS

Part 1 ■ FUNDAMENTALS

Part 3 ■ PLANNING, CONTROL AND PERFORMANCE EVALUATION

PREFACE

Aims of the book

The purpose of this book is to provide an introductory text which is neither overly technical nor unduly abstract, neither too superficial nor excessively detailed – and one which presents management accounting in an accessible manner. No small task. As an introduction to the subject, it is aimed principally at first- and second-year undergraduate courses, and will be particularly useful for courses which are 'non-specialist', in their accounting content. Although many readers will have some knowledge of financial accounting, this is in no way an essential prerequisite.

Principles and practice

Use of the words 'principles and practice' in the book's title indicates the approach taken with the subject matter: we need to know both *why* things are (or should be) done in a particular way, and *how* we (should) do them. The problem is that the how and why cannot be understood in isolation – so principles and practice cannot really be considered as separate issues and are dealt with in an integrated manner. Neither are they taken to extremes of abstraction in the case of principles or of *nth*-degree technical detail in the case of practice.

Management accounting techniques

Techniques are an important feature of management accounting; although many readers may not have to prepare management accounting information, they must nevertheless be sufficiently familiar with the operation of the techniques involved to make full use of the information they provide. Similarly, proper appreciation that management accounting does not offer a managerial 'quick fix' requires not only theoretical, but also technique-based knowledge. It is hard to imagine how any subject's scope and (equally importantly) its limitations can be grasped without a solid grounding in the methods which it employs to achieve its aims. When we are dealing with a subject which is as pervasive as management accounting – we are all, either directly or indirectly, in professional or private capacity, subject to some of its influence – understanding of 'why' and 'how' has increased significance.

Common themes

Certain themes occur regularly throughout the book:

- The need to provide different information for different purposes.
- The need for consistency between strategic, tactical and operational information.
- The likelihood that management accounting information (valuable though it is) will only provide a partial picture of complex wholes.

Although stated separately here (and at various points in the book) these issues are closely linked and the danger of ignoring them can be more clearly seen when principles and practice are understood.

A changing environment

The implications for management accounting of recent changes in its organisational/managerial environment (such as increasing awareness of quality management), will be stressed early in the book. But a balance must be struck between 'new' and 'traditional': on the one hand, emergence of philosophies like world class manufacturing, of advanced manufacturing technologies and of just-in-time systems presents a vigorous challenge to many of the received (at least in a UK context) wisdoms of management accounting; on the other hand, a book which purports to reflect 'principles and practice' cannot ignore how management accounting still operates in very many organisations.

Organisational setting

Management accounting functions occur in virtually every type of organisation: manufacturing, service, private and public sector, commercial and not-for-profit. Although details may differ between organisations, the broad aim of providing useful information to help management, and the general principles dealing with management accounting's inputs to planning, control and decision making are pretty much the same regardless of organisation. For this reason, a wide range of organisational settings has been used for in-chapter scenarios, questions and press extracts; specialist knowledge of specific types of organisation is not, however, required – the aim is to illustrate management accounting's breadth of applicability.

Student learning features

The advance of semesterisation and modularisation has meant a move to 'short and fat' course provision, and a learning culture is now the major focus for instructional effort; all of which places added onus on students for taking charge of their own learning. For this reason, I felt that the book should be as reader-friendly as possible, hence the following features:

■ *Chapter objectives and summaries* While these are fairly standard in most textbooks, chapter summaries are intended to be sufficiently detailed not only to fulfil their role as summaries, but also to provide quick reference, e.g. for revision purposes.

■ *Newspaper extracts* Extracts (mostly from the *Financial Times*) relevant to the topic under discussion are scattered throughout the text to underscore their practical application and to add a 'real world' dimension often lacking in accounting texts.

■ *In-text activities* Each chapter contains a number of brief activities to be undertaken by the reader. These offer the chance to practice, consolidate or evaluate subjects as they are presented, and in 'bite-size' chunks. Activities are indicated by the symbol ➪ and in all cases, feedback is provided within the text immediately following.

- *Glossary* A separate glossary of technical terms is included at the end of the book; this should be useful in its own right and may also be valuable to readers dealing with chapters in a piecemeal way.
- *Chapter-end questions* Each chapter concludes with a section comprising of several short self-test questions plus several 'exam style' questions which have their objectives stated at the outset; answers to both these categories of question are provided at the end of the book. There are additionally some questions whose answers are not given in the text, but in the accompanying *Lecturer's Guide*.
- *Chapter scenarios* Wherever practicable, a single example is used for illustrative purposes within each chapter, being progressively developed in line with the subject-matter. This avoids the distraction for readers of having to continually absorb new background information.

Support material for lecturers

Lecturing colleagues have not been forgotten; the following supplementary material is available for use with the text:

- *On-line back-up* A regularly updated Website containing advice and comment, relevant to the text can be found at **http://www.ftmanagement.com**. This address also has the facility for e-mail transmission of specific queries.
- *Password protected areas* In addition, lecurers who adopt this text can gain access to Password protected areas containing additional cases and questions. To request a registration form and password, send an e-mail to register@ftmanagement.com.
- *Lecturer's Guide* This manual includes, for each chapter, suggestions about points which may need to be stressed and/or areas of potential difficulty, answers to chapter-end questions not provided within the text, a substantial bank of MCQS, some additional 'exam-type' questions, plus answers.
- *PowerPoint® discs* Key chapter points are presented on a series of 3.5" discs prepared using Microsoft *PowerPoint®*, offering the facility for computerised slide/OHP master generation and provision of handout materials.
- *OHP masters* A full set of 'conventional' OHP masters is available, based around chapter summaries.

The book in outline

The book is divided into three sections:

- *Part 1 – Fundamentals* This comprises of Chapters 1–5 and describes the management accounting framework, changes to the environment within which it operates, and the basic techniques of cost estimation, overhead absorption, absorption costing and marginal costing.
- *Part 2 – Decision analysis* This section consists of Chapters 6–11 and extends the discussion in Part 1 to cover financial evaluation of decisions, both short term and long term.

■ *Part 3 – Planning, control and performance evaluation* Comprising of Chapters 12–16, this section deals with management accounting contributions to planning, control and performance evaluation, ending with consideration of some behavioural aspects of the subject.

These sections are not mutually exclusive – the management process which we are attempting to support is not neatly compartmentalised.

Suggestions on use of the book

The variety of management accounting content within different courses is such that it is almost impossible to be other than indicative as to what chapters may/may not be relevant in a given situation. For this reason, chapters have been written in as much a stand-alone manner as practicable, to facilitate a 'pick and mix' approach designed to meet the needs of specific courses. Some general suggestions are as follows:

■ 'specialist' accounting courses omit Chapter 11
■ non-'specialist' accounting courses omit Chapters 3, 9 (possibly 11) and Appendix A

Individual sections within chapters may also be omitted; for example, some non-'specialist' courses may cover price-setting, but not limiting factor decisions (omit the second section of Chapter 8); Chapter 11, which links management accounting with corporate finance, will not be necessary on courses with a separate finance module.

Alan Upchurch
December 1997

PLAN OF BOOK

PART 1 – FUNDAMENTALS

Chapter 1 Introduction	Chapter 2 The management accounting framework	Chapter 3 Cost estimation

Chapter 4 Absorption of overheads	Chapter 5 Absorption costing and marginal costing

PART 2 – DECISION ANALYSIS

Chapter 6 Cost/volume/profit analysis	Chapter 7 Relevant costs and benefits for decision making	Chapter 8 More decisions: price-setting, limiting factors
Chapter 9 Decision making under conditions of risk and uncertainty	Chapter 10 Capital investment appraisal	Chapter 11 Capital investment appraisal: further issues

PART 3 – PLANNING, CONTROL AND PERFORMANCE EVALUATION

Chapter 12 Budgetary planning	Chapter 13 Budgetary control	Chapter 14 Analysis of variances

Chapter 15 Performance appraisal	Chapter 16 Behavioural consideration

PLAN OF SUPPORT MATERIAL

LECTURER'S GUIDE

LECTURER'S INTRODUCTION
- Brief narrative approach to each chapter indicating important issues and/or areas of difficulty

ANSWERS
- To end of chapter questions not included in the main textbook

QUESTIONS
- 30 exam-style questions and answers

TEST BANK
- 75 photocopiable multiple choice questions arranged by section of book

POWERPOINT® PRESENTATION
- Notes on each chapter with diagrams on *PowerPoint*® for visual presentations

OVERHEAD PROJECTOR MASTERS
- Traditional OHP hard copy masters of diagrams and chapter notes

MANAGEMENT ACCOUNTING WEBSITE

For Lecturers and Students
- About the book
- Ordering information
- Questions and answers
- Links to other sites

For Lecturers only
- Facility to e-mail queries
- Additional questions and answers
- Additional cases
- *Lecturer's Guide*

Note: The *Lecturer's Guide* is available free to adopters of the main text. Please apply on the headed paper of your teaching institution to:

Pearson Profession Distribution Centre
Slaidburn Crescent
12–14 Fylde Road
Southport
PR9 9YF

Lecturers wishing to use the resources available on the website need to register. Please visit the Financial Times Management website (**http://www.ftmanagement.com**) for details of how to register.

ACKNOWLEDGEMENTS

Only one name appears as author – my own. In terms of responsibility for shortcomings in the text, this is only fair, but with regard to the help, support and advice so generously offered by others, it is grossly unfair. In an inadequate attempt to remedy this, may I record my sincere gratitude to: Marion, Aileen, Gillian (and Alba), for suffering more than their usual share of antisocial behaviour; Prof Alan Godfrey, HoD Accountancy and Finance, Glasgow Caledonian University, for his most tangible support; Denise Ashworth, Bruce Bowhill, Pat Coyle, David Crowther, Robert Greenhalgh, Rona O'Brien, Elaine Porter and Tim Thompson for their perceptive and valued comments on draft material; Mike Broadbent, Christine Cheong and Michael Wormald for review of the completed draft; Pat Bond, Grace Evans, Michelle Graham and Julianne Mulholland at Financial Times Management for their tolerance, help and advice; Anna Nicholl and Julie Godley and David Welch for their unflinching performance of thankless tasks; the *Financial Times, Guardian, Independent* and *Observer* newspapers for kind permission to quote from articles; and numerous students, past and present, without whom none of this would be possible.

If I have omitted anyone, please accept my assurance that this reflects a woefully inadequate memory, not lack of appreciation.

List of reviewers

The following people contributed to this book by commenting on the initial plan, or by providing detailed feedback on the entire manuscript:

Denise Ashworth	Manchester Metropolitan University
Bruce Bowhill	Portsmouth University
Michael Broadbent	Manchester Metropolitan University
Christine Cheong	Temasek Polytechnic, Singapore
Pat Coyle	Thames Valley University
David Crowther	Aston University
Robert Greenhalgh	University of Nottingham
Rona O'Brien	Sheffield Hallam University
Elaine Porter	Bournemouth University
Timothy Thompson	Humberside University
Michael Wormald	University of Cape Town

PART 1

Fundamentals

In this section, we introduce management accounting, consider its operating framework and the changes this is undergoing, and then examine some of its basic techniques. Chapters within this section are:

1 Introduction

2 The management accounting framework

3 Cost estimation

4 Absorption of overheads

5 Absorption costing and marginal costing

The issues we cover in these chapters are of fundamental importance to management accounting. Chapters 1 and 2 deal with the basic and broad questions of 'why?', 'what?' and 'how?'. Since management accounting is largely focused on the future, estimation is one of its key features; we discuss this subject in Chapter 3. Methodology for inclusion of overheads within cost per unit, along with the related question of whether such methodology is useful for management accounting purposes, are subjects of much debate; how this debate is resolved by individual organisations has major implications for the design and operation of their management accounting systems, and could also affect the usefulness of the information they provide. We describe and illustrate this debate in Chapters 4 and 5.

CHAPTER 1

Introduction

SUNK COSTS

Eurotunnel should be admired, at the very least, for its chutzpah. The Channel tunnel operator, announcing net losses of £925m in 1995, nearly two and a half times greater than in the previous year, called for the ferries to rationalise their services.

Cheeky, but right. Like many large infrastructure projects in the UK, the tunnel would never have been built had the costs and revenues been predicted more accurately . . .

Eurotunnel's statement that the first full year of operations was 'disappointing financially' is uncontentious. But the dominant feature of the figures is that financial charges accounted for £768m of the net loss, of which £118m represents interest unpaid since mid-September . . .

The legacy of its original financing aside, the operation of the tunnel represents a potentially healthy business. Last year's turnover, at £299m, was ahead of projections made in October. More significantly, Eurotunnel reports a positive operating cashflow in 1995 of £101m, which more than covered capital expenditure in the period of £69m. The outlook for operating cashflow – and hence for the value of the operations – remains unclear. Eurotunnel announced yesterday that it now has about 75 staff in the capitals it serves, compared with 275 in 1991; there is scope, however, to trim operating costs further. However, many factors remain beyond its control, such as the performance of the railway companies which are entitled to 50 per cent of the tunnel's capacity. Eurotunnel says they 'should contribute over 40 per cent of our total revenues in the years ahead' but has complained repeatedly that the companies have failed to develop their traffic in line with those predictions.

None the less, the tunnel is capable of fighting a tough battle with the ferry operators because its operating costs per passenger are always likely to be lower . . .

Source: Financial Times, 23 April 1996.

EXHIBIT **1.1 Different types of information about organisational activity**

INTRODUCTION

We live in the age of information: *information* technology, the *information* super-highway, management *information* systems, e-mail, fax – even 'junk' mail is information (of a sort). Exhibit 1.1 is full of information about Eurotunnel's past and predicted performance; all the quoted financial information will have its origin in the company's accounting system: historic figures such as the £925m loss announced for 1995 will be reflected in the period's profit and loss account, but what about the estimates and unit costs referred to in the quotation? Figures of the latter kind are the product of the organisation's management accounting system, and it is with provision of such figures that we are concerned. In this chapter, we will distinguish between two forms of accounting: *financial* (source of the reported £925m loss, £299m turnover and £101m operating cashflow) and *management* (source of all the predicted/estimated figures and of the unit costs). What we will see is that, although the two forms of accounting aim to provide information, the nature, purpose and users of that information differ. This is an important point, and one which is implicit in Exhibit 1.1; when reading the exhibit, you may have wondered how it is possible to claim that a company which has just reported a loss of £925m is a 'potentially healthy business'. The point is that the £925m loss occurred in the past, which is not necessarily a reliable guide to the future; a decision by Eurotunnel's creditors to demand immediate repayment because of this loss may, in light of predicted performance, be exactly the wrong decision to make. A recurrent theme of management accounting is the need for information which is appropriate to its use – Eurotunnel's past reported losses are, perhaps, an inappropriate basis for a decision about the future.

Since management accounting is concerned with provision of information, we must first make a general distinction between information and data in the context of organisations, their management and their management information systems. This will allow us to consider different classifications of information which a management information system can provide: classification by type (financial, non-financial, quantitative and qualitative) and classification by scope and span (strategic, tactical and operational). Information provision is not an end in itself, however, and should ultimately stem from desire to achieve organisational objectives (which may not be as simple as it appears).

Not only must information be provided for a purpose, but it must also be provided to an end user (or users), so we need to know in broad terms who these might be – and in particular whether they are external or internal relative to the organisation. Our distinction between internal and external users of information permits us to identify two subsets of accounting information – financial and management – and to define their purpose. The purpose of management accounting is to provide useful information, so we need to be aware of what attributes make information useful and of how management accounting seeks to provide such information.

In summary, management accounting is a medium of communication, requiring identification of the same parameters and suffering from the same barriers to effectiveness as any other such medium.

OBJECTIVES   When you have completed this chapter, you will be able to:

- distinguish between data and information;

- appreciate that management accounting forms part of a wider, integrated management information system;

- distinguish between financial, non-financial, quantitative and qualitative information;

- use Anthony's strategic–tactical–operational 'hierarchy' to classify information;

- explain how problems relating to objectives may impinge on information provision;

- identify potential users of accounting information;

- outline the different roles of financial accounting and management accounting, their similarities and differences;

- define the purpose of management accounting in terms of management activity;

- state the main characteristics of useful information along with the significance of the cost/benefit criterion in this context;

- appreciate management accounting's scorekeeping, attention-directing and problem-solving aspects and their interrelationship;

- suggest possible barriers to communication which may affect management accounting information.

DATA, INFORMATION AND THE MANAGEMENT INFORMATION SYSTEM

Although we tend to use the words 'data' and 'information' interchangeably, there is an important difference in meaning: **data** are the 'raw' facts and figures that, once processed, become **information**. For example, a pile of supplier invoices (data), after passing through the accounting system, will provide information about such things as purchase costs, range of goods/services purchased and sources of purchase. The **management information system (MIS)** is a set of interrelated systems which filters and processes data from a variety of internal and external sources so as to produce usable information relating to an organisation's activities. Figure 1.1 illustrates (*see* p. 6).

⇨ What 'other systems' might, along with accounting, form an organisation's MIS?

The precise constituents of an MIS will depend on the organisation concerned, but, in addition to accounting, we could see systems such as personnel, marketing, purchasing, production scheduling and quality control. The arrows with dotted lines in Figure 1.1 show that these 'subsystems' of an MIS do not exist in isolation: data (and possibly information) will frequently be shared between two or more systems. Employee data, for instance, will be input to both accounting and personnel

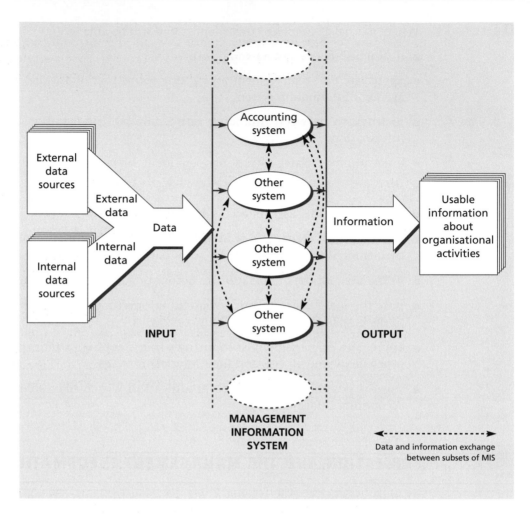

Figure 1.1
Data, MIS and information

systems, customer data to both marketing and accounting, supplier details to both purchasing and accounting. What should be clear from consideration of an MIS is the important role of accounting as a part of the wider management information system. Figure 1.1 also shows that data from sources external to the organisation (e.g. about the market conditions which it faces) are every bit as important as data from internal sources.

This, you may feel, is all very well and good for large organisations, but what about small ones? The general principles illustrated in Figure 1.1 are true for all organisations – large or small, private or public, commercial or non-profit – but the nature of an organisation will affect its MIS in the following ways:

1 *The degree of formality* Generally, larger organisations will require a much more formal MIS than smaller organisations; but you should note that a certain minimum accounting system is necessary in all organisations.
2 *The precise subsystems* The sophistication of the accounting system, along with what other subsystems exist within an MIS, will be determined by organisational circumstances (e.g. 'production' scheduling is irrelevant in a hospital, but a subsystem which schedules operating theatre usage is not).

Without an MIS to impose order on the mass of available data, organisational activity will at best be severely hampered, and at worst will be quite impossible. One way in which the MIS imposes such order is by classifying information according to type: financial, non-financial, quantitative, qualitative.

FINANCIAL, NON-FINANCIAL, QUANTITATIVE AND QUALITATIVE INFORMATION

Financial information, such as Eurotunnel's net loss of £925m, is merely a monetary expression of one or more aspects of organisational activity; non-financial information (like the number of staff employed by Eurotunnel in each capital) is stated in non-monetary terms. Information can be further split into:

- **quantitative information**: information expressed in numerical form; and
- **qualitative information**: information which is not (or which cannot be) expressed in numerical form.

Quantitative information abounds in Exhibit 1.1 – '£768m of the net loss', 'positive operating cashflow in 1995 of £101m', 'about 75 staff in the capitals which it serves'. Information of this sort is the principal output of an MIS, and of its accounting subsystem in particular, since financial information is almost exclusively quantitative. Non-financial information, however, may be either quantitative or qualitative.

▷ Is there any qualitative information in Exhibit 1.1?

The following qualitative information is contained in Exhibit 1.1:

- 'operation of the tunnel represents a potentially healthy business'
- 'outlook for operating cashflow . . . remains unclear'
- 'there is scope, however, to trim operating costs further'
- 'many factors remain beyond its control'
- 'the tunnel is capable of fighting a tough battle with the ferry operators'

Although these quotations may be based on analysis of quantitative evidence, they are essentially matters of *judgement*, or relate to factors external to the organisation. What should be clear from Exhibit 1.1 – and this is a point that we shall return to on several occasions in subsequent chapters – is that quantitative information may not present a complete picture, or may present one which is at variance with the totality of a situation.

Valuable as accounting/quantitative information may be, it cannot (and should not) be used to the exclusion of qualitative, since the process of management is fundamentally judgemental (see Exhibit 1.2). The role of accounting could be defined as:

provision of support for judgements about organisational activities past, present and future.

HIGHLAND TAPS INTO MACALLAN'S INDEPENDENT SPIRIT

For a product that takes a minimum of 10 years to make, life has moved with blinding speed recently for Macallan–Glenlivet, considered one of the best single malt Scotch whiskies . . .

And yet hardly anything has changed. Macallan still uses rare barley and the second-smallest stills in the world to produce a highly distinctive spirit but at a cost at least 10 per cent higher than other whiskies.

Add in sherry casks at £350 apiece to mature the spirit, against £60 bourbon casks used by others, store for a minimum of 10 years and the costs escalate rapidly.

'We don't know the full extra cost but we don't care because Macallan sells at a premium of at least 10 per cent,' said Mr Brian Ivory, chief executive of Highland Distilleries [the parent company]. 'We will make absolutely no change in the process.'

Highland's reputation as a distiller and marketer of Scotch rides on its Macallan acquisition . . .

Source: Roderick Oram, *Financial Times*, 26 November 1996.

EXHIBIT **1.2 Quantitative data is only part of the picture**

STRATEGIC, TACTICAL AND OPERATIONAL INFORMATION

In addition to classification by type, an MIS may also classify information according to its scope and span. These two classifications are not mutually exclusive: that which we are about to describe cannot meaningfully be used in isolation from the last classification – a point which should become apparent as our discussion continues. Anthony (1965) identified the information 'hierarchy' set out in Figure 1.2, each level being roughly equated with the different strata of organisational management.

Strategic information

Strategic information will be employed mostly by senior management to determine organisational objectives, along with the resources and policies necessary to achieve them. Such information relates to the organisation as a whole, over a medium- or long-term time horizon, and in the context of the wider environment within which the organisation operates. The need for, and thrust of, strategic information often derives from an organisation's **mission statement** (or 'mission'), which specifies its intended economic/social role over the long term; where it is explicitly stated, mission is most often expressed as a fairly generalised objective (e.g. 'provide high-quality domestic appliances to the retail market'). The purpose of strategic information can be seen as adding form and substance to such broad statements.

The decision about Halewood's role, as set out in Exhibit 1.3, is strategic, and will be based on an analysis, by senior Ford executives, of strategic information.

⇨ Suggest *three* examples of strategic information upon which Ford management's decision may have been based.

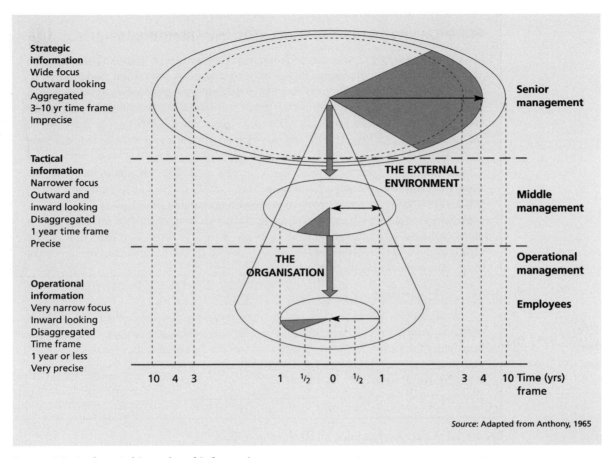

Strategic
information
Wide focus
Outward looking
Aggregated
3–10 yr time frame
Imprecise

Tactical
information
Narrower focus
Outward and
inward looking
Disaggregated
1 year time frame
Precise

Operational
information
Very narrow focus
Inward looking
Disaggregated
Time frame
1 year or less
Very precise

Senior
management

Middle
management

Operational
management

Employees

THE EXTERNAL
ENVIRONMENT

THE
ORGANISATION

10 4 3   1 ½ 0 ½ 1   3 4 10 Time (yrs)
frame

Source: Adapted from Anthony, 1965

FIGURE 1.2 Anthony's hierarchy of information

One important area of strategic interest would be the company's projected share of the UK/European market over the medium and long term. Management would also be likely to consider factors such as:

■ current and expected future developments (both by Ford and by its competitors) of new models of car;
■ current and expected future trends in production and distribution costs at each of the three plants mentioned;
■ any potential governmental/European Community action which might affect the company's market, its costs, or both; and
■ implications for the company of the possible redundancies referred to (in both cost and industrial relations terms).

Our list is far from being comprehensive, and you may well have made some different suggestions. Incomplete as it is, we can, however, use the list to make two points about strategic information, compared with tactical and operational information (which we discuss below):

9

FORD TO SHED THIRD OF HALEWOOD WORKFORCE

Ford, Britain's leading car company, yesterday put the long-term future of its Halewood plant on Merseyside into doubt by announcing the plant would not build the next-generation Escort car. The company sought 1,300 voluntary redundancies, about one-third of the Halewood workforce, before the move from double to single-shift working on Escorts in April. The news came as a blow to the government's attempts to promote the UK as a low-cost production centre and was taken particularly hard on Merseyside, where unemployment is at 11.4 per cent . . .

Ford blamed its move on the need to cut costs because of the decline in its UK market share and the severe overcapacity in the European motor industry. The company lost $203m (£121.5m) in the first nine months of last year and is expected to close 1996 at a loss.

Mr Tony Woodley, the Transport and General Workers Union's national secretary for the motor industry, said cuts should have been spread across Ford's European plants. The TGWU said workers' representatives would consider a co-ordinated response to Ford's move, raising the possibility of strike action.

Ford indicated production of the next generation Escort would be concentrated at its plants at Saarlouis in Germany and Valencia in Spain.

The company surprised analysts, however, by revealing that the current Escort would remain in production at Halewood exclusively for about two years after the launch of the new model. Ford also said that the plant would be the European source for an unspecified new vehicle, provided Halewood achieved 'competitive levels of performance' and there was sufficient demand . . .

Source: Haig Simonian, Stefan Wagstyl and Michael Peel, *Financial Times*, 17 January 1997.

Exhibit **1.3** **A decision requiring strategic information**

1 Strategic information draws much more heavily on sources external to the organisation – 'environmental' sources.
2 It is considerably less precise – witness the statement at the end of Exhibit 1.3 about the 'unspecified new vehicle'.

Gathering and using strategic information is vital to the continued wellbeing of an organisation, but there is evidence to suggest that this does not always happen. For example, a 1995 survey of 500 companies conducted by the Industrial Research Bureau concluded that there was 'a yawning gulf between organisations' growing recognition of the value of information as a strategic asset and their ability or inclination to manage it as an asset'.

Tactical information

Tactical information provides the conduit through which strategic objectives, plans and decisions are translated into action by middle management. The time horizon involved will be shorter than at the strategic level (commonly one year), there will be much greater precision, and the focus of information will be narrower. For example, management at Ford will prepare annual plans which, taken cumulatively over the relevant time horizon (say, two years in this instance), will result in achieving the

REXAM OFFERS BONUSES FOR SPEEDY DISPOSALS

Managers at Rexam, the packaging group, have been given incentives to sell subsidiaries quicker and for a higher price than set by internal targets.

Mr Rolf Börjesson, the Swedish chief executive who took over last year, said the unspecified bonuses would be paid if Rexam executives exceeded a 'target price' . . .

Mr Börjesson said he expected to complete Rexam's disposal programme by mid-1998. The group said last month that it had created a special, eighth sector within the company, called Rexam Octagon, which groups together businesses with total current annualised sales of about £300m which are to be sold . . . However, he indicated yesterday that other small businesses which are underperforming may still be added to Octagon . . . A final decision about the make-up of Octagon is expected within the next two months . . .

However, analysts have said that the timing of the disposals is not ideal, because the packaging industry has not properly emerged from its most recent recession . . .

While Octagon management is focusing on disposals, Mr Börjesson and the managers of the other sectors were discussing Rexam's longer-term prospects . . .

Source: Michael Lindeman, *Financial Times*, 16 January 1997

EXHIBIT **1.4 Strategic and tactical decisions**

strategic objective of redefining the Halewood plant's role. Exhibit 1.4 provides a further, slightly different, example of the link between strategic and tactical.

Rexam's strategy is evidently to improve long-term profitability by selling 'underperforming' subsidiaries, preferably sooner rather than later and certainly by mid-1998. The tactics adopted to achieve this are the setting up of Rexam Octagon, coupled with offering incentives to executives for quick sale above target price. Tactical information will therefore relate to Octagon and incentives.

⇨ Suggest *three* items of tactical information which may be relevant to Rexam's situation.

In order to expedite company strategy, management will be interested in information about such things as:

■ The subsidiaries comprising the group (e.g. their size, the market sector in which they operate, their past and anticipated performance).

■ The extent to which various subsidiaries trade with each other and their integration with broader group activities.

■ Possible purchasers for subsidiaries to be sold and means of generating interest in their purchase should this be lacking.

■ Specification of a criterion (or criteria) upon which to judge the performance of subsidiaries: for example, net profit percentage or return on capital employed (*see* Chapter 15).

Once again, our list is not exhaustive, but it is sufficient to illustrate the increased focus on internal factors, the narrower emphasis and need for greater precision characteristic of tactical (as opposed to strategic) information.

Exhibit 1.4 also refers, indirectly, to the potential conflict between tactical and strategic considerations: 'the timing of the disposals is not ideal'. A similar conflict could arise where strategy requires acquisition of an expensive asset, a requirement resisted because of the negative impact such acquisition may have at tactical level. (We shall explore this problem in Chapter 15.)

Operational information

Operational information is used by lower managerial echelons and employees to support the actions necessary to effect desired tactical outcomes (themselves aimed at achieving a given strategy). It can be defined as planning the economic, efficient and effective use of resources so as to achieve tactical plans.

BRITISH STEEL SHEDS 400 JOBS IN COST-CUTTING DRIVE

British Steel yesterday announced the loss of 400 jobs at its tinplate business in South Wales, as it took its first step towards implementing a company-wide cost-cutting programme launched earlier this month.

The group expects to announce further job cuts in the next few weeks as managers prepare detailed proposals to fulfil a plan to shed over 1,000 posts a year over the next five years. About 150 jobs are to go in the next 12 months at the tinplate plant at Ebbw Vale. A further 250 will be cut in the following year at Ebbw Vale and at a second plant at Trostre, Llanelli.

British Steel said the business, which employs 2,750 people, was responding to overcapacity in the European tinplate market. 'We want to raise efficiency and improve services to customers,' said the company . . .

Source: Stefan Wagstyl, Financial Times, 30 April 1997.

EXHIBIT **1.5 Strategic–tactical–operational decision spectrum**

British Steel's strategic plan in Exhibit 1.5 is to cut costs by shedding 1,000 jobs per year over the next five years; the 400 job losses referred to in the article's title are part of the tactics deemed necessary to achieve this. The operational thread will stem from these tactics: for example, estimating the costs/cost savings of the 150 jobs which 'are to go in the next 12 months', providing information to employees about voluntary redundancy or early retirement and assessing their potential take-up rate, and deciding which categories of employee will be subject to compulsory redundancy (should this prove necessary). Operational information is therefore much more narrowly focused, is very largely internal and more precise, and has a shorter time frame than tactical or strategic.

The distinction between strategic–tactical–operational may be somewhat blurred in practice, as may be the users of each kind of information; in many small organisations, the same person(s) may use all three types, as may also happen in large organisations (particularly those where management 'delayering' has occurred). Nevertheless, Anthony's 'hierarchy' emphasises two key issues:

1 Different information is required for different purposes.
2 Strategic, tactical and operational issues are inextricably linked.

Effective information provision should reflect these two points, and they will recur regularly in the chapters which follow.

If, as we have suggested, different information is required for different purposes, is there an overall purpose for all of an MIS's output?

ORGANISATIONAL OBJECTIVES

Our discussion of Exhibit 1.5 suggests that the ultimate purpose of all information is the desire to achieve an organisation's strategic objective(s) (which determine tactical and operational objectives).

⇨ What strategic objective(s) might be applicable to a commercially-operated passenger transport company?

Since we are dealing with a commercial concern, the most obvious answer is 'to earn sufficient profit to provide the company's shareholders with an acceptable return'. But there are plenty of other possibilities; for example:

- survival;
- growth (e.g. increasing market share, diversification);
- provision of quality service at reasonable price; and
- company 'image'.

If we consider a public sector or non-profit organisation, such as a university, the same diversity of objectives is possible: for instance, growth in student numbers, increased flexibility in modes of attendance/study, academic reputation of the institution, and so on. We are not attempting here to provide a definitive statement about what precise objectives organisations may (or should) have – this will depend on the nature of the organisation concerned and the environment within which it operates. The intention is to consider the following three features of objectives which have general relevance to information provision:

1 *Multiple objectives* As we have just seen, organisations may have several different objectives, and these may conflict (e.g. 'quality' and 'profit'). This may be further complicated by different subunits within the organisation having different objectives, and by the possibility of individual managers' aims being at odds with those of the organisation.
2 *Change over time* Organisations operate in dynamic environments, which means that objectives are likely to change, or that the weighting attached to different objectives will change. In addition, objectives which may conflict in the short term, such as 'profit' and 'quality' may, in the longer term, prove to be complementary.
3 *Quantification* Many objectives are not readily quantifiable. This is particularly true of quality-related objectives and in relation to provision of many services. How, for example, do we quantify an objective such as 'provision of quality education'?

These three factors, together and in isolation, can have a major effect on information provision – even more so when distilled from strategic through tactical to operational levels. As a minimum, they serve to reinforce the points we have already made that different information will be required for different purposes, and that a range of financial, non-financial, quantitative and qualitative information should be employed by management. Unclear objectives can result in conflicting information 'signals' to management (e.g. the possibility of contradiction between quantitative and qualitative or between strategic and tactical information).

Thus far, we have examined the nature of an MIS's output; what we must discuss now are the users of that output – and in particular users of the output of the MIS's accounting subsystem.

Users of accounting information

Because of its ability to provide a range of accessible, quantified, and comparatively simple indicators of organisational activity, accounting is an important element in every organisation's information system. Who are the users/potential users of accounting information? A short answer to this would be **stakeholders**: that is, those individuals, groups or other organisations who:

1 have an interest in the activities of the organisation producing the accounting information; and/or
2 are in some way affected by these activities.

⇨ Who are the likely stakeholders in a company which provides goods/services on a commercial basis?

Table 1.1 lists the potential stakeholders in such an organisation and suggests possible uses for which each might want accounting information. This is a wide-ranging

TABLE **1.1 Organisational stakeholders and possible uses of accounting information**

Stakeholder	Potential use(s) of accounting information
Owners/shareholders	Assessing their investment (e.g. dividends).
Management	Running the business.
Employees	Assessing security of employment, wage bargaining.
Government (national/local)	Taxation: income, corporation and value added (VAT); economic statistics.
Lenders	Assessing ability of borrower to repay.
Suppliers	Likelihood, volume and value of future orders.
Customers	Reliability of future supply.
'Specialists'	Provision of investment advice.
General public	Assessing impact on local economy.

list, with great diversity in the potential use(s) of accounting information; so much so that it is very debatable whether accounting can (or indeed should) address them all. What we can do with Table 1.1 is distinguish between *internal* users/uses of accounting information and *external*: management and employees comprise the former grouping, and all other stakeholders the latter. The only possibly 'grey' area is that of owners/shareholders, since these may also manage the organisation (in which case, they will be both internal and external users). Or there may be no 'owners' in the strict sense, as with charities or public sector organisations. Here, there would be no such stakeholder group, but others (e.g. the general public) would assume greater significance as potential users of accounting information.

FINANCIAL ACCOUNTING AND MANAGEMENT ACCOUNTING

The distinction which we have just drawn between internal and external users of accounting information can be extended to provide the basis for a distinction between different forms of accounting: **financial accounting** (primarily targeted at external users/uses); and **management accounting** (intended for internal users/uses, and management in particular). Despite their different emphases, financial and management accounting have some common characteristics, as follows:

1 They reflect organisational activities in quantitative, and predominantly (but not exclusively) in financial terms.
2 They share certain data sources: for example, personnel data may be used by both financial and management accounting, albeit in different ways and for different purposes.
3 There is a limited area of common ground between the two as regards users/uses: for example, budgets prepared for internal use may form the basis of published profit forecasts.
4 They are key elements within the MIS, and a degree of integration between the two is often present: for example, budgetary control (management accounting) requires the input of actual costs and revenues which have been recorded in the financial accounts (*see* Chapter 13).

However, there is a danger that these surface similarities could obscure the very marked differences between financial and management accounting, and that this might result in the wrong type of accounting information being used for the wrong purpose (with possibly serious consequences for the organisation).

The dispute described in Exhibit 1.6 may stem partly from the fact that the 'profit forecast' referred to is published by listed companies in compliance with Stock Exchange regulations (i.e. is financial accounting information), whereas figures provided to the company's bank are the product of its management accounting system. What should be clear from Exhibit 1.6 is that financial accounting and management accounting information (which presumably describe the same aspects of organisational activity) may differ quite markedly – hence the call for an investigation. We could take this further by suggesting that the root cause of the problem is provision to the bank (an external user) of accounting information meant for internal use.

DTI ASKED TO QUIZ WILLIAM COOK ON TRADING FORECASTS

The Department of Trade and Industry has been asked to investigate discrepancies between a downbeat trading statement issued by William Cook, the steel castings group, and financial information it gave to its bankers a month earlier . . .

A document passed to the DTI entitled 'Confidential Information Memorandum' prepared by William Cook to help secure a £22.5m credit facility, appears to show the company forecasting increases in turnover and profits to 29 March 1997. The letter [requesting the DTI to investigate] questions whether this is inconsistent with the information to shareholders on 25 October when William Cook published interim results . . .

Mr Cook [chairman of William Cook] said that the financial information prepared for the company's bankers, in September, was based on internal budgets, rather than profit forecasts . . .

Source: William Lewis and Richard Wolffe, *Financial Times*, 31 January 1997.

EXHIBIT **1.6 Wrong information for the purpose?**

Table 1.2 summarises the main areas of difference between the two forms of accounting. The differences shown in Table 1.2 are reflected in the definitions of financial and management accounting contained in the Chartered Institute of Management Accountants' (CIMA) *Official Terminology*:

1 **Financial accounting** 'The classification and recording of monetary transactions of an entity in accordance with established concepts, principles, accounting standards and legal requirements and presentation of a view of the effect of those transactions during and at the end of an accounting period.'
2 **Management accounting** 'An integral part of management concerned with identifying, presenting and interpreting information.'

TABLE **1.2 Main areas of difference between financial and management accounting**

	Financial	*Management*
Users/uses	Mostly external	Mostly internal
Externally regulated/published?	Yes (e.g. Companies' Act, Statements of Standard Accounting Practice, Financial Reporting Standards, external audit, Stock Exchange regulations)	No
Time orientation	Predominantly historic	Predominantly future
Scope and span	Tactical and operational; routine recording of transactions	Strategic, tactical and operational; routine and *ad hoc* information

CIMA's definition of management accounting proceeds to list potential uses of management accounting information, which we shall consider in the next section. 'Integral' is a crucial part of the management accounting definition: not only is it a significant component of the management *process*, but it is also one constituent of a multidisciplinary management whole. It is for these reasons that an understanding of the subject is vital to managers whose principal expertise lies in areas other than finance and accounting.

▷ Do the differences listed in Table 1.2 and encapsulated in the CIMA definitions have any implications for the *nature* of the information provided by management accounting compared with that provided by financial accounting?

The nature of information produced differs in two important respects:

1 Management accounting information will tend, on the whole, to incorporate more imprecision, as it largely concerns the future, rather than the past. Note, however, that this is a matter of degree – financial accounting is far from being a precise science.
2 Because of its lack of external regulation and its wider scope and span, management accounting information will tend to be much more organisation- and situation-specific.

These two points will recur frequently throughout our study of management accounting, and are worth bearing in mind.

Purpose of MANAGEMENT ACCOUNTING

We might make a 'broad brush' statement of the objective of management accounting as being:

the provision of information which is useful in the management of an organisation.

To render this more precise, we need to consider how managers manage.

▷ In general terms, what do managers do in order to manage?

In order to fulfil its function, management must, as a minimum: *plan and control*; and *make decisions*. We can therefore re-define management accounting as:

the provision of useful information to help management plan, control and make decisions.

In addition, management accounting should mirror the facts that planning, control and decision making occur at strategic, tactical and operational levels and that they are essentially concerned with the future.

Planning and control

It is difficult to imagine how any organisation could survive for long without some form of planning and control. We will consider the detailed planning and control process in Chapters 12, 13 and 14, but in outline form, the planning and control cycle might operate as illustrated in Figure 1.3.

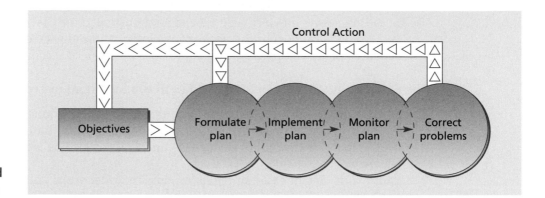

FIGURE 1.3
A simple
planning and
control cycle

The first aspect of Figure 1.3 which is worthy of note is the fact that plans stem from objectives, so that it is quite possible for difficulty with objectives to be transmitted into the planning and control process. The second feature is that planning and control cannot meaningfully exist in isolation: that is, planning implies control and vice versa. Finally, control is not passive: when problems arise in the achievement of plans, *action* ('control action') is needed.

Management accounting makes several contributions to planning and control: most notably **budgets** and **standard costs** (see Chapters 12 and 13), and **variance analysis** (Chapter 14).

Decision making

Decision making is an integral part of management; Figure 1.4 illustrates the essential components of the 'alternative choice' decision process.

⮕ At what stage(s) in the decision process will management accounting provide inputs?

Management accounting's principal inputs to the decision process occur at the evaluation and monitoring stages. As with planning and control, you will see that decisions stem from objectives – and again we must bear in mind the potential difficulties with objectives. The need to make a decision may become apparent from financial information available to management, but equally it may stem from another source, either internal and/or external to the organisation.

The third stage in the decision process – 'seek and identify options' – appears simple on paper, but is likely to be much more problematic in practice. One partic-

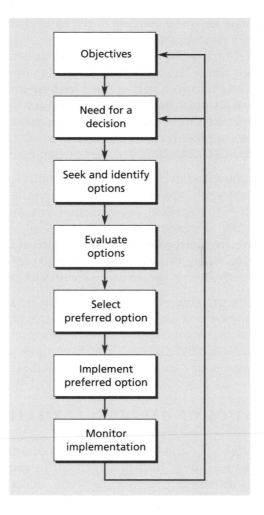

FIGURE **1.4**
The 'alternative choice' decision process

ular difficulty is that identification of *all* feasible options is unlikely because of what is referred to as 'bounded rationality': that is, the inability of any single person or group to know everything. To the extent that this is true, we could say that the decision-making process is flawed. However, the effect of bounded rationality can be mitigated, if not removed, by pooling knowledge across a range of individual managers and managerial disciplines.

Virtually every decision has some kind of financial consequence: management accounting (as we shall see in later chapters) offers a range of financial criteria against which strategic, tactical and operational decisions may be gauged. The attraction of such criteria is their ability to express complex realities concisely and comprehensibly. But there is the pitfall of overreliance on financial evaluation, to the detriment (or even exclusion) of other criteria; and, as with planning and control, quantified financial decision criteria may suggest a precision which does not truly exist, given that decisions (like plans) relate to the future. There is also the possibility that certain financial criteria may be misunderstood, or be misapplied, or that their limitations could be overlooked. It is therefore important that managers have an understanding of the nature, strengths and weaknesses of the financial information presented to them.

Once a particular course of action has been embarked upon, the success with which it meets its objective(s) must be monitored; at this stage, decision making effectively becomes part of the planning and control cycle. In practical terms, many of an organisation's routine decisions will be encapsulated within its budgetary procedures. There will also be decisions of a 'one-off' (*ad hoc*) nature, required to meet specific, perhaps unusual, circumstances. We can make the following broad distinction between categories of decision:

- **Programmed decisions** These are routine decisions, where financial and other variables are subject to comparatively little uncertainty and the outcome(s) are fairly easy to predict. Many tactical, and most operational decisions tend to fall into this category.
- **Non-programmed decisions** Decisions of a non-routine, possibly non-recurrent nature, where variables and outcome(s) are subject to considerable uncertainty. Virtually all strategic decisions are non-programmed.

Unlike programmed decisions (such as placing a replenishment order with a supplier), non-programmed decisions require the exercise of managerial judgement, often to a considerable extent. Supporting such judgement is management accounting's key role in organisational decision making. Note, however, that management accounting's role is that of *support* – ultimately, decision making is the responsibility of managers.

CHARACTERISTICS OF USEFUL INFORMATION

We defined the aim of management accounting as being the provision of useful information to support management in their planning, control and decision-making activities. In order to be useful, information should ideally possess certain characteristics.

⇨ Suggest *three* necessary features of useful information.

You may have thought of a variety of features including: *relevance; understandability; timeliness; comparability; objectivity; reliability*; and *completeness*. You should appreciate from the outset the potential for contradiction between these characteristics: for instance, the need for timely information may be at odds with its completeness or objectivity.

Relevance

Management accounting information must be relevant to the purpose for which it is provided. This will be of particular importance in non-programmed situations where inclusion of irrelevant information may distort the financial 'signal', thereby exacerbating existing uncertainty and possibly resulting in an incorrect decision being taken. Management accounting approaches the issue of relevance as primarily one of *classification* of costs and revenues, an issue which we will examine in the next chapter. Even in routine circumstances, care is needed – at the very least we must recognise that information which might be relevant to some/all external users is unlikely to be particularly relevant to management. Published accounts, for example, are typically based on historic transactions; management, as an essentially forward-looking activity, will be much more concerned with the future.

Understandability

Information will be of little use if it is incomprehensible to its user. This is a matter partly of explaining the nature of accounting information to managers in non-finance functions, and partly of accountants using appropriate, varied and imaginative methods of communication.

Timeliness

If it is received too late to be acted on, information has no value. For example, being published annually or bi-annually (and some time after the end of the relevant period as well), the published accounts of a limited company will be of little interest to management in their day-to-day activities. For tactical and operational purposes, management requires information much more quickly than this. A year-end comparison of budgeted cost with actual, for instance, and the discovery, at that point, of a significant overspend, will not help management – had budget and actual expenditure been monitored on an ongoing basis throughout the year (e.g. month by month), then the potential overspend might have been spotted sufficiently early to allow remedial action to be taken. Similarly, unforeseen circumstances may arise which require an almost instant response, with the accompanying requirement for support information.

Strategic information, however, is likely to be produced at less frequent intervals, since it relates to a longer time horizon. Progress towards a five-year strategic budget, for example, may be monitored on an annual basis.

Finally, the need for timely information may be so pressing as to override other considerations, such as completeness. The possible impact on information quality of extreme time pressure should therefore be appreciated.

Comparability

Management accounting information is frequently used to make comparisons: for example, of a department's performance over time, or of the performance of different departments within the same period. The success of such an exercise depends on our ability to compare like with like. This really means that management accounting information should be prepared consistently, or, where it is not, the fact (and the reason why) should be made clear. It may be necessary to restate figures previously provided to show the effect of changing the basis of preparation. There are two difficulties here:

1 restating previously provided figures may cause confusion and might possibly detract from the credibility of future figures and of the management accounting function; and
2 consistency may be impossible (e.g. between programmed and non-programmed situations).

Objectivity

Management accounting information should be as free from subjective elements as possible. Management is not an impersonal process. If the people involved in, and affected by, planning, control and decision making feel that these activities are occurring on an arbitrary basis, then we may expect some sort of adverse behavioural consequences. Since management accounting is principally concerned with the future, and since this is inherently uncertain, it would be unrealistic to expect total objectivity in management accounting information. It is therefore important to specify (and be able to justify) any underlying assumptions (e.g. an estimate of next year's sales volume).

Reliability

Like objectivity, complete reliability is unlikely in information which relates mainly to the future; again, statement of any underlying assumptions is important, as is specification of any areas of particular uncertainty in the information being provided. However, reliability does not necessarily mean 100 per cent accuracy, nor does it require that every conceivable detail be included. The information should be sufficiently accurate for its purpose: strategic information, for example, will be considerably less detailed and accurate than tactical or operational information, though this does not nullify its value to management. A balance must be struck between too much detail (which can confuse) and too little (which may be insufficient for the purpose). One way in which this balance can be achieved is by reference to the cost/benefit criterion (see below).

Completeness

Subject to the 'bounded rationality' factor which we mentioned above, there should be no material omission from information. At the same time, it will generally not be necessary to include everything that is (or can be) known; not only might this breach the concept of relevance, but it could prove counterproductive by clouding important issues.

The cost/benefit criterion

Information is a resource and, like all resources, has a cost, which can be either *explicit* or *implicit*. The explicit cost of information is exemplified by expenditure such as payment to an outside consultant to undertake a market survey, or acquisition of decision-support software. High as such costs may be, the implicit cost of information may be even higher.

⇨ What is the implicit cost of information?

Management must spend time collecting, collating and interpreting information. Although this is one of management's primary functions, we need to be careful that time is not wasted with superfluous information, or in dealing with the wrong information at the wrong time in relation to events. A point will eventually be reached where the cost of obtaining additional information is disproportionate to the benefit derived from having it, as Figure 1.5 shows.

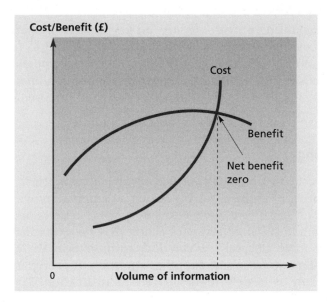

FIGURE 1.5
Costs and benefits of information

It is not practicable to place precise monetary amounts on the costs and benefits of different volumes of information. As a 'rule of thumb', we could approximate the net benefit of information (i.e. its benefit *less* its cost) by assessing the extent to which management acts upon it and whether those actions are preferable to what would have occurred without the information. If, for example, management complains about information overload and/or bypasses the formal MIS in favour of informal sources, then we can be reasonably confident that the cost/benefit criterion is not being met. The desirable characteristics of useful information which we have just discussed must effectively be governed by the cost/benefit criterion: for example, complete information may be available, but may be too late to be useful, and have a cost which cannot be justified. Similarly, accuracy is desirable, but striving for total accuracy (especially in future-oriented information) is to pursue the unattainable at a cost likely to prove prohibitive.

MANAGEMENT ACCOUNTING AS MANAGEMENT SUPPORT

Management accounting performs several identifiable, though not always clearly separable, functions in order to achieve its aim of providing useful information.

Scorekeeping

This is essentially an exercise in keeping tally of financial data so as to aid management. Arguably the most fundamental feature of management accounting, scorekeeping involves activities such as calculation of unit costs, for example as an aid to price-setting (*see* Chapter 8).

Attention directing

Management accounting provides reports on key aspects of operations, allowing managers to focus their attention on important issues and to take action sufficiently early for it to be effective. Budget control reports, comparing budgeted and actual costs/revenues for a period, are an important attention-directing mechanism (*see* Chapter 13), and *ad hoc* reports are also frequently prepared (e.g. monitoring installation and operation of a new item of equipment).

Problem solving

Most often associated with analysis of non-recurrent decisions or problems, management accounting in problem-solving 'mode' attempts to provide quantification of the positive and negative consequences of possible courses of action. Based on this quantification, a preferred course of action may be recommended to management (*see*, for example, Chapter 7, which deals with financial analysis of decisions).

The dividing-line between scorekeeping, attention directing and problem solving is often so fine as to defy their separate identification. Typically, all three elements will be present in any given item of management accounting information, but the balance between the three will depend on specific circumstances. Exhibit 1.7 provides a simple illustration.

Bilton Primary School

The school, which has responsibility for managing its own budget, is considering replacement of some outdated computer hardware which has an excessively high operating cost of £1,300 per unit per annum (there are 10 such units). Two mutually exclusive options are possible:

1 Purchase 10 desktop PCs with Internet connectivity built in, at a cost £1,200 each.
2 Purchase 10 desktop PCs with no Internet facility, at a cost £900 each.

In every respect save Internet connectivity, the two options are identical. Because of its lower purchase cost, the second option has been recommended to the school governors as being financially preferable.

EXHIBIT **1.7 Scorekeeping, attention directing and problem solving**

▷ From the information in Exhibit 1.7, identify the scorekeeping, attention-directing and problem-solving elements.

The operating costs of existing equipment and purchase costs of proposed replacements represent scorekeeping; the 'excessive' operating cost of the present hardware is also attention directing, as reporting this figure has presumably led to the judgement that the amount is excessive. The problem-solving element consists of the comparison of the cost of proposed replacements and the recommendation that the second option is cheaper. Simple though our example is, it allows us to stress three points which we have already mentioned at different points in this chapter:

1 Scorekeeping, attention directing and problem solving are interrelated (i.e. financial information such as unit costs must be prepared for a purpose).
2 Financial considerations may not give the whole picture. For instance, if the cheaper hardware is purchased, what are the implications of inability to connect with the Internet? Can these units be upgraded to provide such connection? If so, at what cost?
3 There may be a conflict between objectives: is the purpose of the replacement to reduce costs *only*, or to reduce costs *and* improve the quality of pupils' hands-on experience? If the former, the recommendation in Exhibit 1.7 may be acceptable, but if the latter, that is questionable.

And following from the last point:

4 There is often a need to compromise between objectives. In this case, the compromise is between maximum benefit to pupils and minimum cost. The school might achieve this compromise by, for example, investigating the possibility of having *some* machines with Internet connectivity.

Figure 1.6 presents a schematic view of the interrelationships between scorekeeping, attention directing and problem solving.

So central is scorekeeping to management accounting that it is frequently denominated by the separate term **cost accounting**, which the CIMA *Official Terminology* defines as: 'the establishment of budgets, standard costs and actual costs of operations, processes, activities or products'. In practice the terms 'cost accounting', 'management accounting' and 'cost and management accounting' are used interchangeably, which is further evidence of the closeness of the relationships illustrated in Figure 1.6.

MANAGEMENT ACCOUNTING AS COMMUNICATION

We can summarise our discussion in this chapter under the single heading of 'communication'; this is the essence of an MIS and its management accounting output. For this to be effective, we need to be clear about the following questions:

■ Why are we providing information?
■ To whom are we providing information?
■ When are we providing information?
■ What information are we providing?

The answers to these questions will define the 'how' of information provision. On paper, this appears to be straightforward, but, even if we can pinpoint the 'why–whom–when–what–how' of information, there are still difficulties in communicating effectively, often described as **barriers to communication**.

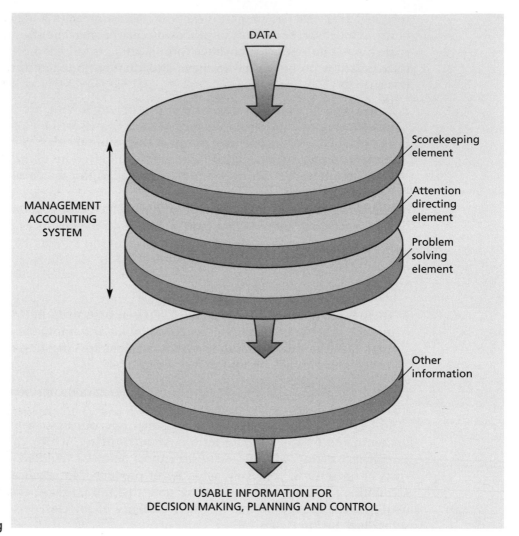

FIGURE 1.6
Scorekeeping,
attention
directing and
problem solving

⇨ Suggest *three* possible factors which might adversely affect communication
of information.

There are many possibilities; some of those more commonly encountered are given
below and are linked to certain of the characteristics of useful information which
we discussed earlier:

1 *Bias* This could be on the part of either/both sender and receiver of information. Hence the need for as much objectivity as possible in management
accounting information.

2 *Incomprehension* This relates not only to the recipient of information, but also to
the provider, who may fail to appreciate the needs or capabilities of the recipient. Information must therefore be understandable.

3 *Withholding information* This may be accidental, or may be by design (e.g. because
of the 'knowledge = power' syndrome). Completeness is therefore desirable.

4 *'Noise'* This term describes the existence, within a system of communication, of irrelevance and/or inaccuracy which will cause distraction from the meaning of the information. Relevance is therefore critical.

5 *Lack of immediacy* Urgent information which is received after a time-lag may be viewed by its recipient as unimportant, or might be displaced by unimportant information which, by speedy transmission, may acquire the trappings of urgency and significance.

We could continue this list of potential barriers to communication for some time. However, even the fairly abbreviated version given should indicate that, regardless of an information *system's* complexity or sophistication, it is *people* who will ultimately determine the effectiveness (or otherwise) of that system. We shall return to this point in Chapter 16, but you should bear it very much in mind as you progress through earlier chapters.

SUMMARY

In the course of this chapter, we have refined and narrowed our initial, fairly broad discussion of information and an organisation's MIS to the point where we were able to identify and define a particular part of that output – management accounting information. During this chapter, we have seen that:

- **Data** are unprocessed items of **information**.

- An organisation's **management information system (MIS)** consists of an integrated set of subsystems aimed at providing information about organisational activity.

- **Financial information** is stated in monetary terms, **non-financial information** is stated in non-monetary terms.

- **Quantitative information** is expressed in numerical form, **qualitative information** is not (or cannot be) expressed in numerical form.

- **Strategic information** is mainly the domain of senior managers, relating to organisational objectives and the policies/resources needed to achieve them.

- **Tactical information** is used principally by middle management and defines the resources/actions required to achieve, on a rolling basis, a given strategic objective.

- **Operational information** is the province of operational management and describes the specific actions needed to achieve desired tactical outcomes.

- Organisational objectives should be the ultimate determinant of information provision, but there may be problems in quantifying objectives, an organisation may have multiple objectives, and objectives may change over time.

- Potential users of accounting information are **stakeholders**: that is, those individuals/groups who have an interest in the activities of an organisation and/or who are affected by them.

- **Management accounting** is aimed at users internal to, **financial accounting** at users external to, the organisation.

■ Management accounting and financial accounting have certain broad similarities:
  - they are both predominantly quantitative;
  - they share certain data sources;
  - there is limited common usage; and
  - they are both key elements in the MIS and may be integrated.

■ There are major differences between management and financial accounting in the following areas:
  - external regulation;
  - time orientation; and
  - scope and span.

■ Management accounting aims to provide useful information to help management in its planning, control and decision making.

■ Management accounting's contributions to planning and control include **budgets**, **standard costs** and **variance analysis**.

■ Management accounting's major inputs to decision making are at the option evaluation and post-implementation monitoring stages.

■ The characteristics of useful information – which may conflict – are: relevance, understandability, timeliness, comparability, objectivity, reliability, and completeness.

■ The **cost/benefit criterion** stipulates that the cost (explicit and implicit) of obtaining information should not outweigh the benefit of possessing it.

■ Management accounting supports management activity by **scorekeeping**, **attention directing** and **problem solving**.

■ Management accounting may be affected by **barriers to communication** such as noise, bias, withholding of information, incomprehension and lack of immediacy.

In Chapter 2, we will discuss cost attribution, and describe developments in management philosophy and operational method, exploring the possible implications of these developments for management accounting as a whole.

FURTHER READING

Anthony, R., *Planning and Control Systems: A Framework for Analysis, Harvard University Press*, 1965.

Chadwick, L. and Magin, M., *Creative Cost & Management Accounting*, Hutchison Education, 1989. Chapter 1 provides some interesting introductory material.

Emmanuel, C., Otley, D. and Merchant, K., *Accounting for Management Control*, Chapman & Hall, 1990. Chapters 1 and 2 contain useful introductory material.

Wilson, D. A., *Managing Information*, Butterworth-Heinemann, 1993. Information management and the MIS is viewed from a wider managerial perspective in this text.

Self-test questions

1.1 KGK Building Society wishes, over the next four years, to upgrade the computer system in all of its branches. Although the proposal has been shown to be financially viable, management has still to reach a final decision.

Requirement
State *three* items of qualitative information which may have a bearing on this decision.

1.2 For each of the statements which follow, place a tick in the appropriate box to indicate whether it is true or false.

	True	False
(a) Management accounting is not subject to external regulation; financial accounting is.	☐	☐
(b) In order to be useful, information should always be 100 per cent accurate.	☐	☐
(c) Operational information should seek to achieve strategic aims.	☐	☐
(d) Management should be provided with all available information.	☐	☐
(e) A programmed decision requires the exercise of considerable managerial judgement because of the high level of uncertainty involved.	☐	☐
(f) Management accounting information is predominantly quantititive.	☐	☐
(g) Because of its predominantly future-oriented nature, management accounting information will not be wholly objective.	☐	☐

1.3 A domestic television company plans to enter into a joint venture with an overseas partner in order to expand its range of productions. In the first year of the joint venture, two costume dramas and one major documentary will be co-produced. To this end, employees of both companies are presently seeking locations for the first costume drama.

Requirement
Identify the strategic, tactical and operational elements in the scenario outlined above.

1.4 Management of an organisation will make little use of published accounting information because:

I   it is not sufficiently objective;
II it is not sufficiently reliable;
III it is not sufficiently timely.

Which of the statements above is correct?

A   I only;
B   II only;
C   III only; or
D   I and III only.

1.5 TPO Ltd's computerised management information system is capable of producing, and regularly does produce, complex and detailed reports for managers. At a recent meeting, the following statements were made about these reports:

I   'As the company owns the computer hardware and software, they are produced at zero cost.'

II 'The reports incur a cost in respect of the stationery on which they are printed.'

III 'The reports incur costs which are not recorded in the accounts.'

Which of these statements is correct?

A I only;

B II only;

C I and II only; or

D II and III only.

QUESTIONS WITH ANSWERS

1.6 This question tests whether you can:

- suggest a range of possible objectives for a given organisation;

- discuss the problems which may arise with these objectives both in general and in the specific context of management information;

- illustrate the potential impact of environmental change on organisational objectives.

The Touring Theatre Company, which is principally funded by an Arts Council grant, is based in Stratford, but spends almost the entire year touring the country presenting a wide variety of plays.

Requirements

(a) List *five* objectives which might apply to the Touring Theatre Company.

(b) Explain the general problems which may relate to the objectives in (a) and suggest how these problems may affect the provision of management accounting information.

(c) Give *one* example to illustrate how a change in the Touring Theatre Company's external environment may cause one or more of its objectives to change.

1.7 This question tests whether you can:

- assess the usefulness to management of a particular output from the MIS;

- suggest improvements which might be made to address any problems with this output.

Puckleys is a large retail store, selling goods ranging from clothing to electrical. The store is organised into 14 sales departments, plus goods inward/outward, accounts and administration. At the end of every quarter, the manager of each of these departments receives a copy of the same profit statement for the entire store. Exhibit 1.8 provides such a statement.

Senior management at the store has expressed concern that profit for Quarter III was lower than expected and feels that a major promotional campaign should be undertaken in selected sales departments in order to improve the situation. Accordingly, a meeting of all departmental heads has been called, with a view to:

Puckleys: Profit statement for Quarter III, 19X4

	£	£
Total sales revenue		850,000
Cost of sales		380,000
Gross profit		470,000
Selling and distribution costs	120,000	
Administration costs	160,000	280,000
Net profit		190,000

EXHIBIT **1.8 Quarterly profit report**

- explaining the lower-than-expected profit for the quarter; and

- suggesting how the promotional campaign might be undertaken.

Requirements

(a) Discuss the usefulness to management of statements such as that presented in Exhibit 1.8, with particular reference to the topics for discussion at the meeting of department heads.

(b) Suggest improvements which could be made to the store's internal reporting system, along with a brief supporting explanation.

1.8 This question tests whether you can:

- discuss the purpose and limitations of management accounting information.

Telec plc, an electronic engineering business, is redesigning its accounting system. At a recent board meeting, the company chairman insisted that, to be of real value, the management accounting function of the new system 'must be able to tell managers everything they need to know to do their jobs properly'.

Requirement
Draft a memorandum to the chairman explaining the extent to which his desired criterion for a management accounting system is/is not achievable.

QUESTIONS WITHOUT ANSWERS

1.9 The Board of TPN Ltd, which operates a countrywide chain of carpet retail stores, has been considering the possibility of diversifying the business, which at present is solely confined to sale of floor coverings.

Requirements

(a) Illustrate and explain the steps involved in the decision-making process, using the proposed diversification as an example.

(b) Assuming that diversification is to occur via takeover of another company, discuss the tactical and operational aims which might stem from this strategic objective and suggest what supporting information may be necessary at both tactical and operational levels.

(c) Explain the major areas of management accounting input to (a) and (b).

1.10 At a recent meeting between senior officials of Saltoun County Council, discussion centred on user department dissatisfaction with the new management accounting system. The following exchanges are fairly typical:

Ms I. CONN *(Director of Art Galleries and Museums)*: The system is worse than useless – my staff and I can't make head nor tail of the reports we receive, which in any case, are usually too late to be of any value.

MR M. PYRE *(Building Services Manager)*: The reports I receive seem to be full of information about Architectural Services, which is a different department, and detail of loan repayments and capital commitments. To make matters worse, I am constantly being hounded by staff from the Finance Department looking for information which I simply do not have and which the system seems to be incapable of providing me with.

MR R. E. CUMBENT *(Director of Leisure Services)*: Pounds and pence! Pounds and pence! What about the benefits our services offer? The quality of life?

Ms I. M. DUNN *(Deputy Director of Finance)*: I am surprised to hear your comments. The consultants employed by my department provided a detailed report which demonstrated beyond a shadow of a doubt that this system is at the cutting edge of technology and also represents the best possible value for the limited funds available.

Requirement
Discuss the issues raised at the meeting relative to the effectiveness of the new system.

CHAPTER 2

The management accounting framework

EXHIBIT 2.1 Just-in-time: a technique with implications for management accounting

INTRODUCTION

In Chapter 1, we described the broad aim of management accounting as being provision of useful information to aid management. We now need to consider the fundamental mechanisms which management accounting employs in order to achieve this aim, how these relate to organisational inputs and outputs, and how certain developments (such as the just-in-time approach referred to Exhibit 2.1) may have significant implications for management accounting.

Our starting-point is cost attribution – i.e. the linkage of costs to particular objectives; this activity is so central to management accounting that it is virtually impossible to produce meaningful management accounting information without it first having taken place. Having established that cost attribution is necessary to support the scorekeeping function of management accounting (itself necessary to support the problem solving and attention directing functions), we can examine the means by which cost attribution is effected – cost classification – and discuss some major classifications of cost.

The nature of an organisation's inputs, processes, procedures and outputs has a major bearing on cost attribution and classification. This is reflected in the costing methodologies which management accounting has developed to deal with different organisational environments. We have described these methodologies as 'traditional' because their relevance may arguably be diminishing as the result of developments such as world class manufacturing and total quality management. An outline of these developments, and their possible implications for management accounting forms the final section of this chapter.

OBJECTIVES   When you have completed this chapter, you will be able to:

- explain the need for cost attribution and the importance of the cost objective;

- distinguish between subjective and objective classification;

- define and identify direct and indirect costs, along with their subdivisions into labour, materials and expenses;

- define and identify variable, fixed, step and semi-variable costs;

- explain the significance and meaning of the relevant range;

- describe the main characteristics of specific order, continuous operation, job, contract, batch, process and service costing, citing examples of organisations/ output where each would be appropriate;

- outline the principles of world-class manufacturing and total quality management;

- identify value-added and non-value-added activities; and

- appreciate the benefits and potential problems of computerisation in the context of management accounting, along with the potential impact of advanced manufacturing technologies.

Why do we need to attribute costs?

A short answer to the question 'Why do we need to attribute costs?' is that it is necessary to permit effective scorekeeping, which in turn allows management accounting to perform its attention-directing and problem-solving functions. The key points to appreciate about cost attribution are, first, that it is unavoidable, and second, that the form which it takes should be governed by the reason for undertaking it. The starting-point for cost attribution is therefore identification of the **cost objective**: that is, the target or purpose at which such attribution is aimed. We need to know *what* is to be costed and *why* it is to be costed before we can proceed. Table 2.1 lists some common cost objectives, analysed into 'what' and 'why'. Table 2.1 is not intended to be – nor can it be – exhaustive, but it should serve to illustrate that:

- different cost objectives exist; and
- a variety of reasons for attribution of costs to a given objective is possible.

Of the cost objectives illustrated in Table 2.1, one will occur in virtually every organisation: the **cost unit**, i.e. the unit of the product or service which the organisation (or organisational subunit) produces. The cost unit (or units, where more than one product/service is produced) must be an accurate reflection of the nature of the output to which costs are being attributed; if the cost unit is wrongly (or inaccurately) defined, then there is every chance that the costs being attributed will also be wrong. Incorrect cost attribution could have serious consequences: e.g. where selling price is based on cost per unit (a topic we shall explore in Chapter 8).

TABLE 2.1 Common cost objectives

What is to be costed?	*Why* is it to be costed?
Units of product or service ('cost units')	<ul><li>stock valuation/profit measurement</li><li>basis of selling price</li><li>budgetary planning and control</li><li>*ad hoc* decisions (e.g. accept special order)</li></ul>
Organisational subunits (e.g. departments, sections)	<ul><li>departmental cost or profitability reporting</li><li>budgetary planning & control</li><li>*ad hoc* decisions (e.g. closure)</li><li>performance evaluation</li><li>*ad hoc* decisions (e.g. disinvestment)</li></ul>
Competitive goods/services	<ul><li>cost reduction, comparison with own costs</li></ul>
Other (e.g. specific proposal)	<ul><li>*ad hoc* decisions (e.g. acquire/dispose of)</li><li>budgetary planning and control</li></ul>

⇨ What is an appropriate cost unit for a business which manufactures computers?

If the business produces only one model of computer, that will be the cost unit; if more than one model is involved, each different model will be a cost unit. If the computers are produced in groups or batches, then each batch could be the cost unit. This is reasonably straightforward, but, as we shall see shortly, there are situations where definition of an appropriate cost unit may be less clear-cut.

We will discuss attribution of costs to the other cost objectives in Table 2.1 in later chapters – to organisational subunits, for example, in Chapters 4, 13 and 15; to specific proposals in Chapters 7, 8, 9 and 10. What this should underscore is the pervasive influence of management accounting's scorekeeping function (discussed in the last chapter).

Even from the limited variety in Table 2.1, we should appreciate that a uniform approach to cost attribution is inappropriate. Management accounting links the 'what' and 'why' from Table 2.1 by means of *classification* – and, in particular, classification of cost.

COST CLASSIFICATION

As with any kind of classification, the general objective of cost classification is to impose ordered structure – in this case on an organisation's cost data. Without such a structure, effective record keeping and linkage of costs to cost objectives are impossible. Although cost classification is necessary for the production of financial accounting information, the classification used here will not always be relevant to management's information needs; it may even give managers exactly the *wrong* information (*see*, for example, Chapter 5).

Cost classification is essentially a matter of grouping together costs which share the same attribute(s) *relative to a stated cost objective*. The words in italics are vitally important because:

1 the cost objective should determine the classification to be used; and
2 changing the cost objective may alter the categorisation of a specific cost within a given classification.

The statements above lead to a crucial conclusion: the classification(s) selected *must be appropriate to the purpose for which selected*. A large part of the discussion in subsequent chapters revolves around the issue of correct classification: in Chapter 7, for example, we will see that financial analysis of decisions requires that costs (and revenues) be classified into those which are relevant to the decision and those which are irrelevant; in Chapter 14, we will classify costs into standard costs and actual costs to facilitate financial control. As a corollary to this, later chapters will illustrate the potential hazards attendant on misclassification, or use of an inappropriate classification. In this chapter we will confine our discussions to the two major classifications which are essential to the remainder of Part 1 of the book: classification into direct and indirect cost and classification by behaviour.

Defining and grouping individual costs according to specified attributes (e.g. direct/indirect or fixed/variable) is termed **subjective classification**; linking a subjective classification to a stated cost objective is known as **objective classification**. You should note that neither type of classification can meaningfully exist in isolation: for example, a statement that 'the foreman's salary is indirect' (subjective classification) immediately prompts the response 'indirect *relative to what?*' (objective classification).

Classification into direct and indirect cost

This common classification makes a distinction between **direct costs** and **indirect costs**: direct costs can be unambiguously and quantifiably attributed to a single cost objective, indirect costs cannot (see Figure 2.1)

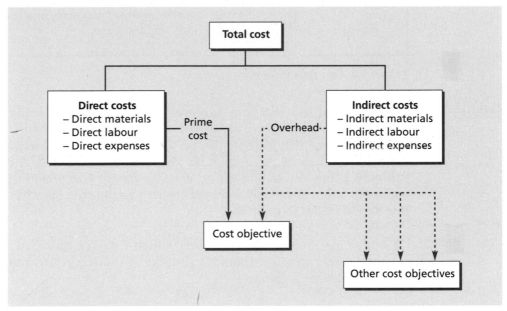

FIGURE 2.1
Classification of
costs according
to their nature

The terms **prime cost** and **overhead** respectively describe total direct costs and total indirect costs; materials and labour are self-explanatory, with 'expenses' referring to any cost which cannot be regarded as either of the first two. We use the term 'expenses' in a very narrow sense when describing cost attribution, and you should not confuse this with the wider, more everyday usage of the term. Exhibit 2.2 contains some information which we shall use to illustrate a direct/indirect classification.

In order to apply a direct/indirect classification to the costs in Exhibit 2.2, we must firstly define the cost objective: say, the particular job for which details are specified. In order to attribute direct costs to this job, we should identify those costs which can be unambiguously and quantifiably associated with it. From the exhibit, we can see, for example, that the job requires 150 hours of cover design employees' time; we know how many hours need to be spent on this specific job, so the associated cost meets the criteria for classification as direct.

NJ Graphic Design

The business has two main departments – book cover design and technical illustration – with Naheed supervising the former, and James the latter department. A list of the major costs incurred in running the business is given below:

> Naheed's salary · James's salary · salaries of employees engaged in cover design · salaries of employees engaged in technical illustrations · paper and stationery · computer diskettes · rent and rates on premises · telephone · electricity

In addition to the costs listed above, the business pays a flat-rate fee of £20 per job under a software licensing agreement. Different jobs are undertaken on behalf of various publishers, and details of one job are:

> 150 hours of cover design employees' time · 100 hours of technical illustration employees' time · 20 computer diskettes · assorted paper and stationery plus telephone calls as required · supervision as necessary by Naheed and James

EXHIBIT 2.2 Cost classification

If we look at rent and rates, however, we have no way of achieving the sort of direct linkage between cost and cost objective which we had for cover design employees' time. The best we can say is that this cost is necessarily incurred to allow the work to be performed; but this is true, not only of the specific job in Exhibit 2.2, but also of *all* jobs. So here, we have a cost which cannot be unambiguously and quantifiably associated with a single cost objective (job), and it is therefore classified as indirect.

⇨ Following the same methodology which we have just used, classify the remaining costs in Exhibit 2.2 as direct or indirect relative to the job for which details are given.

The remaining costs in Exhibit 2.2 are classified as follows in relation to the job:

- *Direct costs*:
  - 100 hours of technical illustrators' time;
  - 20 computer diskettes;
  - £20 per job payable under software licence.
- *Indirect costs*:
  - paper and stationery;
  - telephone;
  - Naheed's salary, James's salary;
  - electricity.

Your classification may be slightly different to ours. You may, for example, have treated paper and stationery, telephone, and Naheed's and James's salaries as direct. This would be correct if Exhibit 2.2 quantified consumption of these resources by the job to which we are attributing costs. Since it does not, however, we cannot establish the kind of relationship necessary to support classification of these costs as direct. A more sophisticated recording system for resources consumed by jobs would overcome this – but you should bear in mind the cost benefit criterion. The best we can do in the absence of additional information is to say that undertaking the job in question necessarily incurs overhead (i.e. indirect costs), and that overhead is incurred as a result of more than just this single job. In Chapter 4, we will describe how we can estimate an overhead cost per unit of product/service.

⮕ Of the direct and indirect costs listed above for the specific job, which represent materials, which labour, and which expenses (remembering the limited meaning of 'expenses' in a cost attribution context)?

Analysis of the direct and indirect costs of the job into materials, labour and expenses gives:

- *Direct costs*:
  - direct materials: 20 computer diskettes;
  - direct labour: 150 hours of cover design workers' time; 100 hours of technical illustrators' time;
  - direct expenses: £20 fee payable in respect of software licence.
- *Indirect costs*:
  - indirect materials: paper and stationery;
  - indirect labour: Naheed's salary, James's salary;
  - indirect expenses: rent and rates on premises; electricity; and telephone.

Suppose we wish to ascertain the cost of running the technical illustration department – how will this affect our cost classification? The cost objective has changed and we must be alert to the possibility of a change in classification for individual costs as a result:

- *Direct costs*:
  - direct labour: James's salary; technical illustrators' salaries.
- *Indirect costs*:
  - indirect materials: paper and stationery; computer diskettes;
  - indirect expenses: software licence fee; telephone; rent and rates; and electricity.

As in the case of the individual job, more detailed information might allow us to quantify usage of items such as paper and stationery in each department of the business, thereby permitting their classification as direct; or it might reveal that a proportion of Naheed and James's time is spent on general administration of the business – an indirect cost as far as operation of the two departments is concerned. The change in classification of the software licence fee is worthy of note: this is paid on a *per job* basis – and, assuming that jobs involve both design work and technical illustration, cannot be unambiguously and quantifiably associated with a single department (and is therefore indirect relative to this cost objective). Here again, additional information would be useful, and again the cost/benefit criterion needs to be borne in mind. As a final illustration of the relationship between objective and subjective classifications, think what would happen had the cost objective been the business as a whole: in this case, *all* costs would be direct.

A direct/indirect cost classification is the basis of costing methodology in virtually all UK organisations and underpins the absorption costing approach which we will describe in Chapters 4 and 5.

Another common – and important – classification of cost is according to behaviour, and it is this which we will now discuss.

Classification according to the behaviour of costs

This approach classifies costs according to their behaviour in relation to changes in volume of activity (e.g. number of units produced). Although output is an important and commonly used activity measure, we need to be aware that it is not the only possible measure. As we shall see, cost behaviour patterns are determined with reference to the cost objective in the same way as was the direct or indirect nature of a cost.

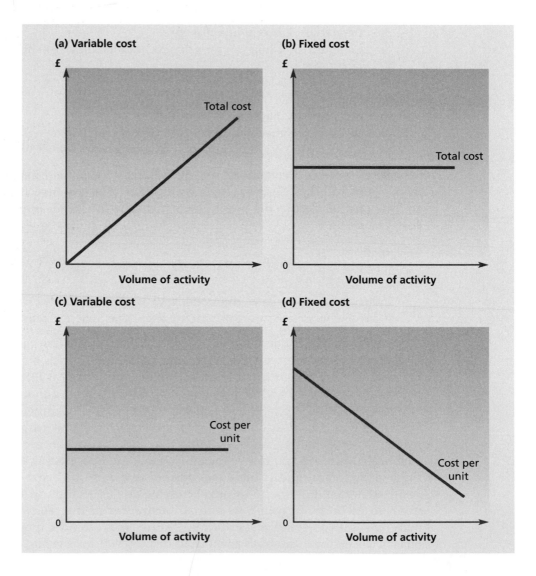

FIGURE 2.2
Variable and
fixed costs

As Figure 2.2(a) shows, the total amount of a **variable cost** increases and decreases in line with increases/decreases in the volume of activity. The total amount of the **fixed cost** in Figure 2.2(b), however, is unaffected by increases/decreases in the volume of activity. If we take the total number of jobs performed by NJ Graphic Design in Exhibit 2.2 (p. 38) as the measure of activity (cost objective), then the £20 per job software licence fee will exhibit a variable behaviour pattern, with the total associated cost increasing as the number of jobs increases, and decreasing as the number of jobs decreases.

⇨ Referring to Exhibit 2.2, can you identify one further variable cost relative to the number of jobs performed?

The total cost of computer diskettes is also variable relative to the number of jobs performed. You may have suggested salaries – either of Naheed and James, or of the cover design and technical illustration employees. It is much more likely, however, that these costs will be fixed in relation to the number of jobs, with the individuals concerned being paid a certain salary per annum (regardless of how much work is done during the year).

⇨ Apart from salaries, can you identify another fixed cost in Exhibit 2.2?

The amount paid for rent and rates will be fixed relative to volume of jobs, and it is possible that paper and stationery costs are fixed (if, say, sufficient quantity is purchased to cover all likely volumes of work).

The costs illustrated in Figure 2.2 have a **linear relationship** with the volume of activity : that is, the variable cost *per unit of activity* is constant at all volumes (as illustrated in Figure 2.2(c)), and the amount of total fixed cost is constant at all volumes, which results in a straight-line ('linear') plot. On a 'per unit' basis, fixed cost will decline (Figure 2.2(d)) as volume increases, since the same amount of total fixed cost is being spread over more and more units. If we combine the variable and fixed cost per unit, we have an average cost per unit which increases/decreases in an inverse relationship to increases/decreases in output in a manner not unlike the fixed cost per unit. This is easily illustrated by reference to two of the costs mentioned in Exhibit 2.2 – the software licence fee and rent and rates. Supposing rent and rates amount to £4,000 per annum, the total cost of licence fee plus rent and rates if 50 jobs are performed during the year is:

licence fee (50 jobs × £20)	£1,000
rent and rates	£4,000
	£5,000

This gives an average cost per job of:

$$\frac{£5,000}{50 \text{ jobs}} = £100$$

⇨ What is the average cost per job for licence fee plus rent and rates assuming 100 jobs are performed during the year?

The total cost is:

licence fee (100 jobs × £20)	£2,000
rent and rates	£4,000
	£6,000

So the average cost per job is:

$$\frac{£6,000}{100 \text{ jobs}} = £60$$

Awareness of these relationships may prevent incorrect decisions: for example about cost-based pricing (*see* Chapter 8).

Although it is possible for unit variable costs to be constant, it is equally possible that they are not, as shown in Figure 2.3.

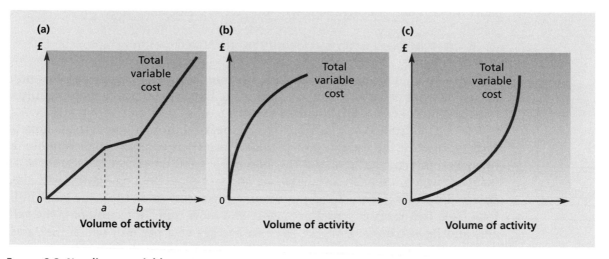

FIGURE 2.3 Non-linear variable costs

⇨ What pattern of variable cost behaviour is suggested by Figure 2.3(a)?

The variable cost illustrated in Figure 2.3(a) is at a constant amount per unit of activity over each of the volume ranges 0–*a*, *a*–*b* and above *b*. However, the amount per unit differs between volume ranges, being higher over 0–*a* than *a*–*b*, and higher above *b* than over *a*–*b*. We can tell that this is the case by examining the slope of the total variable cost line within each volume range: the steeper the slope, the higher the variable cost per unit of activity.

Figures 2.3(b) and 2.3(c) illustrate **curvilinear cost functions**, meaning that there is a continuous change in the variable cost per unit of activity as volume increases/decreases. In Figure 2.3(b), the slope of the total cost curve is flattening as volume increases, indicating a decreasing unit variable cost, with the steadily steepening curve in Figure 2.3(c) indicating an increase in unit variable cost. You

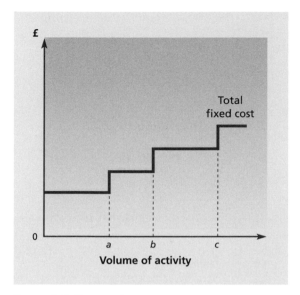

FIGURE 2.4 **Step cost**

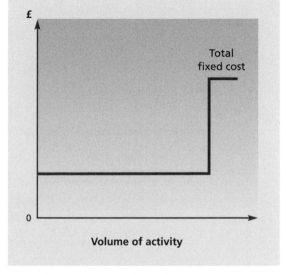

FIGURE 2.5 **Property costs relative to volume of activity**

should note that, in both Figures 2.3(b) and 2.3(c), the *rate* of increase/decrease in variable cost per unit is not constant. In the next chapter, we will discuss one possible reason for curvilinear cost behaviour – the learning curve.

It may have occurred to you that our representation of a fixed cost in Figure 2.2 is rather unrealistic; Figure 2.4 presents a more plausible version. A **step cost** is unchanged within a certain volume range (say *a–b* in Figure 2.4), falling by a lump-sum to a reduced constant amount within a lower range (say 0–*a*) and increasing by a lump-sum to a greater constant amount within a higher range (say *b–c*). The steps illustrated in Figure 2.4 are reasonably large and fairly uniform, but this need not necessarily be the case: consider supervision and property costs (e.g. rent and rates). Relative to the volume of output, supervision costs may follow the general pattern shown in Figure 2.4, but what about property costs?

Look at Figure 2.5. Because of the nature of the costs involved, the range of volumes over which property costs remain fixed is very much larger than was the case for supervision, and the size of step, when it occurs, is likewise much larger.

We have one final pattern of cost behaviour to consider.

⇨ Relative to consumption of electricity, what behaviour pattern will be exhibited by the associated cost?

The typical electricity bill consists of two elements: a standing charge (fixed regardless of consumption) plus a charge which depends explicitly on consumption. In other words, the cost is partly fixed and partly variable. Such a cost is referred to as **semi-variable**, **semi-fixed** or **mixed** (*see* Figure 2.6). In this context, 'semi' is slightly misleading, as it does not imply an even division of total cost between fixed and variable elements, merely that both are present in the composition of total cost – the exact proportion of each will differ depending on the cost concerned.

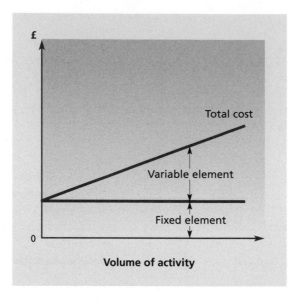

£

Total cost

Variable element

Fixed element

0

Volume of activity

FIGURE **2.6**
Semi-variable cost

In practice, many costs exhibit step or semi-variable behaviour patterns and some costs may be a complex combination of some or all of the patterns we have described.

Exhibit 2.3 presents some further information about NJ Graphic Design.

NJ Graphic Design: further cost data

Additional information about the business's operating costs is given below:

Salaries A fixed annual salary is paid to Naheed, James and to all employees. However, when the volume of business is particularly high, overtime is worked and paid for over and above basic salary.

Paper and stationery Every job worked on requires paper and other stationery, of which a certain quantity is required for general administration of the business, regardless of the volume of work in hand.

Computer diskettes Every job requires at least one diskette.

Rent and rates on premises These are determined in advance on a yearly basis by the landlord and local authority respectively.

Telephone and electricity These services are charged for by their respective providers in the normal manner.

Software licence fee Flat rate of £20 for every job.

EXHIBIT 2.3 **Cost behaviour**

⇨ If the number of jobs undertaken is the cost objective, what is the likely behaviour pattern of each of the costs detailed in Exhibit 2.3?

Relative to the volume of output (i.e. number of jobs), cost behaviour can be summarised as:

■ *Variable* Software licence fee and computer diskettes – the higher the volume of output, the higher will be these costs in total. Since the licence payment is a flat-rate amount per job, the cost function is linear; assuming that different jobs use different numbers of diskettes this cost function will not be linear, since the diskette cost per job is not constant, giving a plot not unlike that in Figure 2.3(a).

■ *Fixed* Rent and rates, depreciation of computer hardware. Within certain fairly wide limits, the amount of these costs is unlikely to be affected by the volume of work.

■ *Semi-variable* Salaries, paper and stationery, computer diskettes, telephone and electricity. The total amount of each of these costs comprises a fixed element (e.g. annual salary) plus an element which varies according to the volume of work (e.g. overtime). Note, however, that a high proportion of telephone and electricity costs may be fixed relative to the volume of *work*, but may be variable relative to consumption of electricity or to number of calls made.

What about step costs? We might say that, looked at over a wide enough range of output volumes, rent and rates will be a step cost. This view is certainly supportable, but we need a classification which is sufficiently clear-cut to be useful, and we can help achieve this by applying the concept of **relevant range** to our classification. The relevant range is the range of output volumes and/or time horizon over which a particular set of assumptions (e.g. about cost behaviour) is a reasonable approximation of reality. For example, if we consider rent and rates over an indefinite range of output volumes and time horizon, we undoubtedly have a step cost. However, if we examine the same cost over a limited output range and time period – say, likely volumes for the forthcoming year – then it is probably reasonable to suggest that the cost is fixed. The concept of relevant range has especial significance in the context of the interrelationship between strategic–tactical–operational information, since a cost which exhibits, say, variable behaviour in operational terms may behave differently in tactical terms, and differently *again* in strategic terms. We shall make particular reference to classification of costs according to their behaviour in Chapter 5 (marginal costing), Chapter 6 (cost/volume/profit analysis), and Chapter 13 (budgetary control).

The usefulness of cost classification on its own is, however, limited; we need to link cost attribution to the inputs, outputs, processes and procedures of the organisation. A number of costing methodologies have been developed in an attempt to achieve this, and we shall now provide a brief overview of these.

'TRADITIONAL' COSTING METHODOLOGIES

The nature of an organisation's output and associated procedures will be reflected in that organisation's method of attributing costs (e.g. by determination of the appropriate cost unit). Figure 2.7 illustrates 'traditional' approaches to this.

Specific order costing applies in situations where output is produced to customer order, whereas, under **continuous operation costing**, products/services result from a repeated procedure or series of procedures.

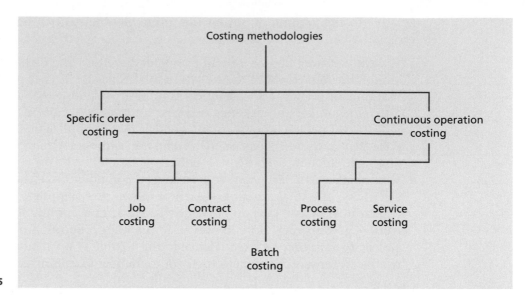

FIGURE 2.7
'Traditional'
costing
methodologies

⇨ Suggest *two* types of output to which each of specific order and continuous operation costing might apply.

Specific order costing would apply to output such as vehicle repairs in a garage, made-to-measure outfitting, or construction of buildings and roads, and would be the method employed by NJ Graphic Design in Exhibit 2.2. Continuous operation costing is relevant to, e.g. provision of health-care, legal and accountancy services, or oil refining and chemical processing. However, some care is necessary in practice when assigning the most appropriate costing methodology to a given type of output, as the distinctions made in Figure 2.7 may be considerably less clear-cut in reality. An organisation's output may be such that more than one approach is necessary; or the method most suitable to the circumstances may be a hybrid of specific order and continuous operation costing. An engineering company, for example, might mass-produce a subassembly (continuous operation costing), which is then customised according to clients' specifications (specific order costing). The output of a legal firm consists of service to its clients, the precise nature of the service provided generally being subject to client instruction – so elements of both continuous operation and specific order costing can be seen here also. The need for a flexible approach to costing methodology is greater in face of factors like the increasingly 'globalised' market within which companies operate, development of advanced manufacturing technologies and emphasis on total quality (which we shall discuss later in the chapter).

Job and contract costing

As subdivisions of specific order costing, each of these approaches is appropriate where work is undertaken to customers' requirements, the essential difference being one of scale: comparatively small-scale customer orders, such as those in NJ Graphic Design, would be subject to job costing, but large-scale orders, like the construction of a road or office-block, would require the use of contract costing. In more precise terms, contract costing is applicable where completion of output substantively, and by design, spans two or more accounting periods (i.e. the time span involved is an inherent feature of the work); job costing is applicable where work is intended to be completed within a single accounting period. Many construction projects require several years to complete; the sort of work being done by NJ Graphics is of much shorter duration and a particular job would probably only span two years due to the 'accident' of commencement towards the end of the earlier year.

The nature of job and contract work is such that each job or contract is separately identifiable as it progresses towards completion; this being the case, individual jobs and contracts will be appropriate cost units under their respective costing methodology.

⇨ Cost units are likely to be much smaller in a job costing than in a contract costing environment. How might this affect cost attribution?

Because contracts are much more sizeable than jobs, a higher proportion of total costs is likely to be direct, which may have the advantage of reducing the need for arbitrary cost apportionments of the type we shall discuss in Chapter 4.

Process costing

Process costing is appropriate to output of identical (or very nearly identical) units, often via a sequence of related processes: oil refining and whisky distilling are typical examples, as are certain types of factory mass-production (e.g. food processing). Because of their mass-produced and identical nature, costs are not generally attributed to individual cost units, but to specific processes, from which point they are averaged over the number of units passing through the process concerned. In some cases, individual cost units may not be separately identifiable until the fairly late stages of production, while in other instances, they may be so small as to render attribution to individual units unattractive in cost/benefit terms; or **joint products** (i.e. two or more main products) may emerge from the same process (**joint process**). This averaging of costs is particularly necessary because the nature of many processes gives rise to losses: that is, output is lower than input, for example due to evaporation. The cost of inputs which are lost as the result of the normal operation of a process cannot simply be ignored and is therefore distributed over the cost of units which finally emerge from the process. Regardless of the specific circumstances, the hallmark of process costing situations is that rather less precision is possible in the attribution of costs to individual units of output than is the case with either contract or job costing.

Batch costing

Here, output of identical items is produced in batches, with costs being traced initially to each batch and then being averaged over the number of units concerned (if a cost per unit is required). As Figure 2.7 suggests, batch costing has some of the characteristics of specific order, and some of continuous operation costing.

As shown in Exhibit 2.4, GNQ Ltd will produce six batches of output in total: that is, three for each style of jacket.

GNQ Ltd

GNQ Ltd, a clothing manufacturer, has just received an order to supply the following to a large chain of retail outlets:

> 500 each, sizes 10,12 and 14, Jacket Style 164/B2
> 300 each, sizes 10,12 and 14, Jacket Style 182/C6

The company's cutting and machining operations are fully automated, and the machinery can be set to produce any number of garments in a given style and size. Once cut and machined, garments are finished manually.

EXHIBIT 2.4 Batch costing

⤷ How will GNQ Ltd's costing methodology reflect aspects of both specific order and continuous operation costing?

GNQ Ltd's output is based on customer requirements, and each batch will be separately identifiable throughout production, with costs being attributed thereto (specific order costing). Garments within each batch will be identical, are produced by a sequence of processes, and a cost per garment within each batch may be obtained by averaging the batch cost over the number of garments in the batch (continuous operation costing).

Service costing

Service costing has certain characteristics which distinguish it from the methodologies outlined above, regardless of whether the service concerned is provided on a commercial basis, by a public sector organisation, by a not-for-profit body, or interdepartmentally within the same organisation.

⤷ What are the essential differences between GNQ Ltd's output in Exhibit 2.4 and that of an investment advisor?

The differences are as follows:

1 *Heterogeneity* Each piece of advice provided by the investment advisor has the potential to be unique, depending on the circumstances and requirements of individual clients. Although GNQ Ltd undertakes six batches for the order referred to in Exhibit 2.4, units within each batch are identical, and the batches themselves consist of reasonably uniform output (i.e. all jackets). Uniformity – even to this limited extent – is unlikely with the investment advisor.

2 *Simultaneity* For GNQ Ltd, there will always be a time-lag between receipt of customers' orders and delivery. In many cases, the investment advisor will be required to respond to an unforeseen query instantaneously (or risk losing the associated business).

3 *Perishability* Once given, advice 'expires', and subsequent amendment or correction may be much less easy than for a fault in one of GNQ Ltd's garments.

4 *Intangibility* The investment advisor's output cannot be seen or touched in the way that GNQ Ltd's can.

Earlier in this chapter, we stressed the need to link subjective with objective cost classifications, and selection of cost units is one area where service costing differs from costing of tangible output.

⇨ What cost unit might we use for the investment advisor's output?

At first glance, we might suggest either clients or even 'pieces of advice' as the cost unit. However, neither of these is entirely satisfactory, as both imply a degree of uniformity which simply does not exist. We might almost treat each piece of advice given as a 'job', but this could afford a misleading impression of the nature of the service being provided. If we want our cost unit adequately to reflect the fact that advice is given to clients and that clients' requirements differ, we really need to use a composite cost unit, such as the client/hour. In this way, costs can be attributed to the work performed on behalf of different clients, and the amount of these costs will reflect its extent/complexity.

Use of composite cost units is a common feature of service organisations: for example, for passenger transport, the passenger/kilometre is often encountered; for a hospital, the patient/bed-day. There is also the possibility of using several cost units: a hospital, for instance, may wish to know both the cost per patient/bed-day and the cost of different categories of surgical procedure.

There is one final set of factors which plays an increasingly important role in the way organisations operate and which as a consequence can have important implications for management accounting. We end our chapter with a brief overview and discussion of these.

MANAGEMENT ACCOUNTING'S DEVELOPING ENVIRONMENT

The increasing dynamism of organisations' environments has been reflected in development of managerial philosophies and of operational methods which may often 'challenge' accepted management accounting wisdoms. For the moment, we will describe those developments which are of most significance to management accounting, providing an indication of which later chapters discuss the potential challenge they may present.

MANAGEMENT ACCOUNTING: FINANCIAL ACCOUNTING 'SUBSET'?

In the last chapter, we highlighted the different information needs of management and external users of accounting information. This suggests that management accounting is (or should be) distinct from financial accounting. However, as Johnson and Kaplan (1987) have observed, management accounting may have become 'subservient' to financial accounting. Every organisation's financial accounting records are subject to some form of external regulation, such as the Companies' Acts in the case of limited companies, or tax requirements in the case of small businesses. Since this is so, it seems reasonable to suggest that such regulation might easily come to dominate the form, content and output of an accounting system, to the possible prejudice of useful information for *internal* use.

The degree of integration which exists in many organisations between management and financial accounting may provide evidence of Johnson and Kaplan's claim. Unfortunately, in many circumstances, information extracted or derived from the financial accounts may provide management with precisely the *wrong* planning, control and decision-making signals. In Chapter 7, for example, we shall see that the sort of historic cost data recorded by the financial accounting system is irrelevant to decision analysis and that there is a very real danger that it might be wrongly included, with the consequent risk of incorrect decisions being made.

Holzer and Norreklit (1991) have suggested that, in the past, provision of separate management accounting information has failed the cost/benefit criterion, but that the reducing cost of information, coupled with the increasing cost of incorrect decisions (e.g. in highly competitive globalised markets), has persuaded organisations of the need to invest in sophisticated management accounting systems. The need for decoupling of management from financial accounting is, hopefully, now a recognised fact.

World-class manufacturing (WCM)

Many organisations operate in markets which are not simply local or national, but global. One instance of this may be seen in the rapid growth of 'on-line' trading via the Internet. WCM attempts to respond to the added competitive pressure of a 'global marketplace'. The term 'world-class manufacturing' does not describe a single philosophy or method, but consists of a number of interrelated views and techniques, each of which addresses specific areas of concern:

- *Quality* Quality of product/service (including after-sales service) is essential in order to maintain or improve market position.
- *Lead time* The length of time between receiving and completing an order – the lead time – may be a critical determinant of market standing.
- *Adaptability* Products/services which are flexible enough to meet different customer requirements are more likely to be successful in a global market.
- *Cost* Delivery of a quality product/service quickly *and* at lower cost than that supplied by competitors can provide a market advantage.

The overall aim of WCM might be summarised as producing output at the lowest possible cost consistent with quality and competitive considerations. WCM therefore advocates holding minimum stocks, training of personnel and their involvement in operational decisions (improving skill levels and possibly commitment to the organisation), effective product/service design, and co-operation with suppliers.

The emergence of WCM suggests the need for a shift of emphasis in management accounting information: away from the predominantly internally-focused and cost-driven towards quality- and market-orientated. It also suggests that greater emphasis be placed on strategic information and on the need for operational and tactical information to conform with the dictates of strategy. The points we have just mentioned are reflected on numerous occasions in later chapters, e.g. the need for qualitative information in Chapters 7, 8, 10 and 15, or the central role of strategy in Chapters 10 and 12.

Value-added and non-value-added activities

One way in which costs may be reduced is to distinguish between **value-added activities** and **non-value-added activities**, attempting to reduce or eliminate the latter, along with their associated costs. Value-added activities are those which increase the perceived worth of a product or service in the hands of its ultimate consumer; non-value-added activities add no such worth and are therefore, arguably, unnecessary. Exhibit 2.5 provides additional information about GNQ Ltd which we shall use to illustrate this distinction.

GNQ Ltd

Some of the activities involved in running the company's clothing factory are as follows:

- cutting of garments;
- machining of garments;
- finishing of garments;
- inspection of raw materials on arrival at factory;
- movement of garments between cutting and machining, machining and finishing, finishing and store;
- inspection of garments after each of cutting, machining and finishing;
- storage of raw materials, partly-finished and complete garments.

EXHIBIT 2.5 Value-added and non-value-added activities

⇨ Which of the activities in Exhibit 2.5 can be classified as value-added and which as non-value-added?

Of the activities listed, only cutting, machining and finishing add worth to the output; all the others are non-value-added and might be the first to be scrutinised in an effort to reduce costs. For example, redesign of factory layout might reduce the need for movement of garments, better training of employees could reduce the degree of inspection required, and negotiation with suppliers may lessen raw materials' stockholding. In each case, it might be possible, by contraction of non-value-added activities, to significantly reduce costs without any adverse effect on the quality of output.

The value-added concept can be extended into a **value chain**: this is essentially an interlinked sequence of value-creating activities starting with product/service development, moving through design, raw materials supply, production and marketing. It is argued that recognition of the relationships between the value chain's different stages will promote cost-efficiency and end-user satisfaction, particularly when each successive stage is treated as its predecessor's 'client'. By adopting this approach, a consumer orientation should be uppermost at all stages of output/ supply, with feedback from internal 'clients' and external end-users providing the basis for improvements.

It can therefore be argued that the management accounting system should centre on the organisation's main activities (rather than on locations or subunits), thereby permitting non-value-added activities to be highlighted and enhancing efforts at cost reduction. We shall discuss **activity-based costing**, **activity-based budgeting** and **activity-based cost management** in Chapters 4, 12 and 13 respectively.

Total quality management (TQM)

One of the principal facets of world-class manufacturing is its emphasis on quality. In this context, 'quality' is all-embracing, covering not only outputs, but also inputs such as materials and labour. The TQM approach can be summarised as 'getting it right first time, all of the time'. The rationale is that, in the long run, the cost of 'getting it right first time, all of the time' will be less than that of rectifying quality failures after they have occurred. The benefits of TQM can be substantial, a fact borne out by Exhibit 2.6.

A LEAP OUT OF THE DARK

Nobody could have associated Mortgage Express, one of TSB's mortgage subsidiaries, with excellence five years ago. The business was losing £1m a week; a third of its customers were in arrears, and the staff, who had all been recruited during the housing boom of the late 1980s, had no experience of dealing with bad debts. Its prospects were so poor that in April 1991, TSB decided to wind it down over the following three years.

But after a remarkable revival, Mortgage Express yesterday became the joint winner of the 1996 UK Quality Award for Business Excellence, a prize organised by the British Quality Foundation . . . Mortgage Express's achievement was 'a real turnaround story', says the Foundation. It transformed a £67m loss into a £38m profit inside three years 'during the deepest recession the market has seen and in the face of unprecedented competition'.

The company attributes much of this success to its adoption in 1992 of total quality management which requires continual improvement of all the main facets of the business, namely leadership, people management, policy and strategy, resources, processes, people satisfaction, customer satisfaction, impact on society and business results. Its enthusiasm is evident as soon as a visitor enters its offices in North London. The building's reception is adorned with a 'quality beacons' pennant, 'employee of the month' photographs, a 'process map', rosettes commemorating Investors in People targets and a huge photograph of the workforce . . .

Source: Vanessa Houlder, *Financial Times*, 4 December 1996

EXHIBIT **2.6 TQM and its benefits**

⇨ What implications does the TQM philosophy have for management accounting?

Perhaps the simplest way to appreciate TQM's implications for management accounting is to consider the prerequisites for effective quality management:

1 training/retraining of staff;
2 good product/service design; and
3 a sound and suitable information system.

The most obvious impact of these three requirements is in terms of cost, and we can classify quality-related costs as follows:

- **Prevention costs** Costs incurred to prevent inferior quality, such as design and training.
- **Appraisal costs** Costs incurred to ensure achievement of the specified quality standard, e.g. inspection of inputs and outputs.
- **Internal failure costs** Costs incurred as a result of quality failure *before* output is delivered to customers (e.g. scrap, reworks).
- **External failure costs** costs incurred as a result of quality failure *after* output is delivered to customers (e.g. replacement of customer returns).

In a TQM environment, it is important that the organisation's information system is capable of tracing and reporting quality-related costs. Similarly, the criteria applied to performance evaluation should recognise quality issues, which suggests the use of qualitative as well as quantitative performance measures – a topic which we shall discuss in Chapter 15.

The importance of an adequate quality assurance system can be seen in the relevant standards set by both the International Organisation for Standardisation (ISO 9000) and the British Standards Institute (BS 5750). In order to obtain accreditation under these standards, an organisation must submit its quality management system to external assessment. Note, however, that accreditation does not guarantee quality of output, it merely approves the quality *system*.

TQM has another, possibly less obvious, implication for management accounting: if the aim is to 'get it right first time, all of the time', then the relevance of the conventional management accounting approach to financial control can be questioned. In the last chapter, we said that, in essence, this consisted of comparison between planned and actual outcomes (or between planned outcomes and objectives); the intention is that significant differences between the two triggers management action. But if we are trying to 'get it right first time', should there be any significant differences to act as a trigger for management action? Arguably not, as their existence suggests failure to 'get it right'. We shall discuss these matters further in Chapters 13 and 14.

Just-in-time (JIT)

One of the quotations in Exhibit 2.1 aptly summarises the goal of **just-in-time purchasing**: 'the ultimate objective would be to have the stock arrive at your back door when you actually want to put it on sale'. As suggested at the end of Exhibit 2.1, this approach can be extended to encompass **just-in-time production**, where output is produced as close to the time of sale as possible. JIT therefore attempts to eliminate unnecessary stockholdings as far as possible, thus reducing the associated cost.

⇨ What sort of costs might be incurred as the result of holding stocks of unsold goods?

Stockholding incurs a variety of costs, some of which may be substantial: storage space may need to be rented which, if not used for storage, may be more profitably used in another way; the store will need heating and lighting; specialised facilities may be required for storing particular types of item (e.g. humidity control); insurance and security will be needed; there is the potential cost of obsolescence, deterioration and damage; staff will be needed to receive items into and issue items from store. Possibly the greatest single cost attaching to stockholdings is *implicit*: holding large quantities of stock 'ties up' an organisation's capital in an unprofitable way – capital which, if invested differently, could earn a return. Decreasing the amount of stock held may therefore have a marked impact on an organisation's costs.

As Exhibit 2.1 states, operation of a JIT system effectively transfers much of the onus of stockholding (and control of the associated costs) from purchaser to provider, and it is in this respect that the WCM notion of co-operation between the two is vital. A breakdown in liaison at any point in the supply chain will very likely more than nullify the benefits of JIT. And, as we shall see in Chapter 5, JIT principles may conflict with the commonly used technique of absorption costing, since the latter may encourage a build-up of stock.

Technological changes

The pace of technological advance – already great – is increasing. At a basic level, we can see its impact in the computerisation of management accounting systems: for example, many of the techniques which we shall describe in subsequent chapters are ideally suited to, and are frequently performed on, computer spreadsheets. The general advantages to management accounting of computerisation can be summarised as follows:

- *Complexity* Techniques such as simulation (*see* Chapter 9), which are extremely unwieldy if performed manually, can be performed with comparative ease on appropriate software.
- *Speed* Response time should be shortened as a result of computers' ability to process large volumes of data quickly and accurately.
- *Job 'enrichment'* Computers can be used to perform tedious and repetitive tasks, thus freeing employees' time for more important and challenging activities.

Management accounting's ability to respond adequately to a complex and dynamic environment may therefore be greatly aided by computers.

⇨ Can you suggest any potential pitfalls in the use of computers?

There are two areas of danger with any computerised system:

1 **Over-reliance** Management may, conceivably, substitute computer output for exercise of their own judgement, wrongly believing the machine to be infallible.
2 **Information overload** There is a possibility that we may provide information merely because a computer is capable of generating it, regardless of whether it is useful in a given situation.

Changes in production technology also have implications for management accounting: the development of **advanced manufacturing technologies (AMTs)** such as computer-aided design and computer-aided manufacture (CAD/CAM), robotics (i.e. adaptable automation), and flexible manufacturing systems, are all having a profound effect on operational practice and on the way in which management accounting reflects this practice.

Automated information?

Although uncommon at present, it is possible to envisage a situation where certain management accounting information is routinely produced as an integral part of the production process. Progress towards this can already be seen in some automated set-ups where material losses are recorded and reported by the production machinery itself. Greater computer integration of manufacturing is likely to lead to automatic production of an increasing amount of management accounting information.

Labour 'free' production?

Improved technology has steadily reduced the significance of labour inputs in many organisations, with a corresponding decrease in the related cost. Conversely, capital costs (e.g. plant and machinery) have tended to assume greater significance. This may, for example, mean a higher proportion of fixed costs than might have previously been the case, coupled with much more substantial overheads. The result is that overheads may receive more managerial attention than in a labour-intensive environment.

'Instant' obsolescence?

The speed of technological advance (e.g. in computers) may require us to amend the way certain management accounting techniques are applied. This is especially true of the capital investment appraisal criteria which we shall describe in Chapter 10. (Hence the significance of our discussion in Chapters 4 and 5).

The sort of changes we have been describing – to both managerial outlook and operational method – do not render management accounting irrelevant or outdated. On the contrary, management's need for useful information has never been greater. However, management accounting must be responsive to the changes taking place: development, flexibility and adaptability are needed. Moreover, there is a particular need for management accounting information to be sensitive to the external environment within which organisations operate.

Summary

In this chapter, we have described the key elements of the management accounting framework – cost classification and costing methodology – describing the potential implications for management accounting of developments in managerial philosophy and operational procedures. We have seen that:

- **Cost attribution** is necessary to permit effective **scorekeeping**, **attention-directing** and **problem-solving**.

- Cost attribution should be dictated by the **cost objective**: that is, the target/purpose of the attribution.

- **Cost classification** groups together costs which share the same attribute(s) *relative to a stated cost objective*.

- The cost classification employed should be appropriate to the purpose for which it is used.

- **Subjective classification** groups individual costs according to specified attributes; **objective classification** links a subjective classification to the stated cost objective.

- **Direct costs** can be unambiguously and quantifiably attributed to a single cost objective, **indirect costs** cannot.

- **Prime cost** is the total of direct labour, direct materials and direct expenses; **overhead** is the total of indirect labour, indirect materials and indirect expenses.

- The total amount of a **variable cost** increases/decreases in line with increases/decreases in the volume of activity; the total amount of a **fixed cost** is unaffected by the volume of activity.

- Cost behaviour is **linear** when variable cost per unit is constant at all volumes of activity and/or where total fixed cost is the same at all volumes.

- **Curvilinear cost functions** occur where the unit cost changes relative to volume of activity.

- A **step cost** is fixed within a given range of volumes, outside which it increases/decreases by a lump-sum amount; a **semi-variable cost** is partly fixed, partly variable.

- The **relevant range** is the range of volumes and/or time horizon over which a particular set of assumptions is a reasonable approximation of reality.

- **Specific order costing** is applicable where output is produced to customer order; **continuous operation costing** is applicable where products/services result from a repeated procedure or series of procedures.

- **Job costing** applies where specific orders are small compared to those to which **contract costing** applies.

- **Process costing** is appropriate to output of identical (or very nearly identical) units, often via a sequence of related processes.

- **Batch costing** applies to output of identical units in batches, possibly to customer specification.

- The output of service organisations has the following characteristics, which distinguish **service costing** from the costing of tangible output: heterogeneity; simultaneity; perishability; and intangibility.

- It is important to recognise the need to separate financial from management accounting information.

- **World-class manufacturing** recognises global competition by stressing quality, lead time and adaptability of output.

- **Value-added activities** add worth to output in the perception of its final consumer; **non-value-added activities** do not.

- **Total quality management** advocates 'getting it right first time, all of the time'.

- Quality-related costs can be categorised as **prevention costs**, **appraisal costs**, **internal failure costs** or **external failure costs**.

- **Just-in-time** aims to purchase/produce as close to the point of sale/use as possible, thereby minimising costly stockholdings.

- Computerised management accounting offers the benefits of complex analysis, speed and job 'enrichment', but may induce overreliance and information overload.

- **Advanced manufacturing technologies** may have possible implications for management accounting: for example, automated information; labour 'free' production; and 'instant' obsolescence.

In the next chapter, we will extend our discussion of the management accounting framework to deal with cost estimation – a particularly important topic given the future's significance to managerial and organisational activity.

FURTHER READING

Bromwich, M. and Bhimani, A., *Management Accounting: Evolution not Revolution*, CIMA Publishing, 1993. This fairly short text discusses management accounting in the context of recent developments in managerial thinking and operational procedures.

Bromwich, M. and Bhimani, A., *Management Accounting Pathways to Progress*, CIMA Publishing, 1994. Chapters 2 and 3 contain further discussion of the impact on management accounting of recent developments.

Chadwick, L. and Magin, M., *Creative Cost and Management Accounting,* Hutchinson Education, 1989. Chapters 2–6 explore the management accounting framework.

Cobb, I., *JIT and the Management Accountant*, CIMA Publishing, 1993. This short text examines current UK practice.

Drury, C., *Management and Cost Accounting*, 4th edn, International Thomson Business Press, 1996. *See* Chapters 6, 7 and 8 for detailed operation of job, contract and process costing.

Gelinas, U., Oram, A. and Wiggins, W., *Accounting Information Systems*, 2nd edn, South-Western Publishing Co., 1993. Part One discusses accounting systems from the information technology viewpoint.

Holzer, H. and Norreklit, H., 'Some thoughts on cost accounting developments in the United States', *Journal of Management Accounting Research*, March 1991.

Johnson, T. and Kaplan, R., *Relevance Lost: The Rise and Fall of Management Accounting*, Harvard University Press, 1987.

SELF-TEST QUESTIONS

2.1   TG Partnership, a recruitment agency, incurred the following costs last year:

Direct labour	£150,000
Direct expenses	£250,000
Indirect labour	£50,000
Indirect materials	£50,000

What was the total prime cost of operating the firm last year?

- **A**   £100,000
- **B**   £150,000
- **C**   £250,000
- **D**   £400,000

2.2   RDC Ltd assembles a car radio under licence from the company which holds the design patent and to which RDC Ltd pays a patent royalty of £10 for each radio assembled. The following statements refer to the patent royalty:

- **I**   relative to the volume of output, the total cost is variable;
- **II**   relative to the volume of output, the total cost is fixed;
- **III**   the patent royalty is a direct cost per unit of output.

Which of the above statements correctly describes the patent royalty?

- **A**   I only;
- **B**   II only;
- **C**   I and III only; or
- **D**   II and III only.

2.3   The costs of operating TGF's Distillation Process last month were:

Direct materials	£60,000
Direct labour	£14,000
Overhead	£6,000

During the month, 10,000 litres were input to the process, of which, 2,000 litres were lost due to evaporation, with the balance being good output. What was the cost per litre of good output for the month?

- **A**   £6.00
- **B**   £7.50
- **C**   £8.00
- **D**   £10.00

2.4   For each of the statements which follow, place a tick in the appropriate box to indicate whether it is true or false.

		True	*False*
(a)	The cost of training employees is an internal failure cost.	☐	☐
(b)	A variable cost function is linear when the cost per unit of activity decreases as volume increases.	☐	☐
(c)	Simultaneity means that the output concerned cannot be produced and stored prior to sale.	☐	☐
(d)	Cost reduction effort should concentrate, first, on value-added activities, and thereafter, on non-value-added activities.	☐	☐
(e)	Just-in-time purchasing and production attempts to eliminate the costs associated with stockholding.	☐	☐
(f)	If a given cost is direct with respect to one stated cost objective, it must be direct with respect to all other cost objectives.	☐	☐

2.5 What would be the most appropriate costing methodology for a firm of painters and decorators specialising in domestic work?

    A   Process costing
    B   Job costing
    C   Batch costing
    D   Contract costing

QUESTIONS WITH ANSWERS

2.6 This question tests whether you can:

- identify, from options provided, the behaviour pattern of given costs;

- prepare sketch diagrams of cost behaviour;

- explain the significance of cost behaviour to planning, control and decision making.

Figure 2.8 illustrates three cost behaviour patterns relative to the volume of activity.

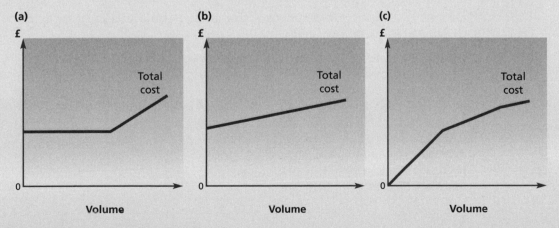

FIGURE 2.8 **Three cost behaviour patterns**

The following costs are some of those incurred by PP Insurance Brokers:

1 *Payment to insurance company* For each of the first 500 of a particular insurance company's policies which PP's agents sell, £5 is payable to that company. For sales of 501–1,000 policies, £4 per policy is payable, and for sales in excess of 1,000, £2 per policy is payable.

2 *Payments to sales staff* All the firm's agents are paid an annual salary of £10,000. Once an agent's sales of insurance policies exceed a stated target number, a commission of £20 per additional policy sold is paid.

3 *Administration costs* £60,000 per annum is payable in respect of PP's offices and of the salaries of the full-time clerical staff employed there. In addition, each policy sold incurs an administration cost of £5 to cover items such as stationery.

Requirements

(a) Match the three costs described above to one of the behaviour patterns illustrated in Figure 2.8, providing a brief explanation of your choice in each case.

(b) Draw a sketch diagram illustrating the behaviour of each cost assuming the following:

   (i)   payment to the insurance company consists of a flat-rate £3 per policy for *all* policies sold;

   (ii) sales staff are paid an annual salary of £8,000 plus commission of £20 per policy for *every* policy sold; and

   (iii) administration costs are £60,000 per annum for all foreseeable sales volumes.

(c) Explain why an awareness of cost behaviour is important to management in their planning, control and decision-making activities.

2.7 This question tests whether you can:

■ group organisations according to the costing methodology applicable in each;

■ classify the costs of a specific organisation into direct and indirect in relation to different cost objectives;

■ explain the concept of just-in-time and its relevance to a specific organisation.

There follows a list of organisations operating in the Northfields area, along with a brief description of the nature of each:

Northfields Passenger Transport Ltd (bus and coach operator)
Dinnie, Kerr & Co (firm of accountants)
NPP plc (paint manufacturer)
Northfields Electrical & Plumbing (small firm of jobbing electricians and plumbers)
NF Engineering Ltd (light engineering company)
CRE Courier Services (motorcycle delivery service)
Window Systems Ltd (manufacturer and installer of double glazing)
Fit Feet (chiropodist)
Maritime Projects Ltd (boatbuilder)

Requirements

(a) Suggest a costing methodology suitable for each of the above organisations, providing a brief explanation of your choice.

(b) Window Systems Ltd's production function is divided into two cost centres – the assembly department and the finishing department – and some of the costs incurred in a typical year are given below:

- depreciation of machinery in the assembly department
- insurance of factory premises
- UPVC for double-glazing units
- supervisory salaries for each of the assembly and finishing departments
- salaries of office staff
- telephone and postage costs
- shatter-proof glass
- royalty payment to designers for each glazing unit produced
- advertising costs
- wages of shop floor operatives
- depreciation of office equipment
- office stationery
- factory rent and rates

Assuming the cost objective to be Window Systems Ltd's cost units (i.e. units of output), classify the costs above into direct and indirect, subdividing each category into materials, labour and expenses.

(c) How (if at all) would the classification in (b) alter assuming the cost objective to be each of the assembly and finishing departments?

(d) Explain the concept of just-in-time and discuss the extent to which Window Systems Ltd may already employ JIT. What benefits and potential problems might stem from use of JIT purchasing (assuming it is not already in use)?

2.8 This question tests whether you can:

- explain the potential conflict between provision of financial information to internal and external users;

- suggest improvements in a system aimed at mitigating the effect of such conflict

(Note: This question also draws on our discussion of financial and management accounting in Chapter 1.)

Management at Seaforth Nursing Home is concerned about the provision of financial information for internal use, as there have been a number of unforeseen budget overspends recently and certain decisions have had a financial impact exactly opposite to that which was expected. The nursing home's accounting system is geared to provision of information to external parties as required by statute and other regulations, and no analysis beyond what is required for this purpose is currently performed on costs and revenues.

Requirement
Draft a report to Seaforth Nursing Home's General Manager which addresses the following issues:

- weakness of the current approach to internal provision of financial information;

- possible actions to improve the situation.

QUESTIONS WITHOUT ANSWERS

2.9 The Copying Centre operates a photocopying service in the centre of a local town. Sally Mullen, the business's owner, is worried about the number of complaints from customers and the cost of rectifying these. The problem is quality of copies, which is often so poor that they must be redone; Sally attributes this to a combination of three factors:

- *Quality of paper used* To date, this has always been purchased in bulk from the cheapest source, requiring storage (often for a lengthy period) at the Copying Centre's premises.

- *Photocopying equipment* This is all leased from the manufacturer and minimisation of lease costs guided selection of the machines leased.

- *Work methods* Although staff and photocopiers are sufficient in number to cope with the heaviest expected demand, particularly busy periods often result in staff using machines which they are not trained to operate.

Requirement
Draft a memorandum to Sally Mullen outlining the principles of total quality management, and explaining how these could be applied to operation of the Copying Centre. Your memorandum should make mention of the relevance of the cost/benefit criterion in this context.

2.10 **(a)** Discuss the contention that the classification of cost should be appropriate to the purpose for which it is to be used, providing relevant illustrations.

(b) In light of your answer to (a), outline the potential advantages and disadvantages of a computerised management accounting system.

(c) Distinguish between subjective and objective classification of cost, stating why one cannot meaningfully exist without the other.

(d) Discuss the implications which developments such as world-class manufacturing and advanced manufacturing technologies may have for cost classification.

CHAPTER 3

Cost estimation

BPI UP 31 PER CENT BUT WARNS ON RAW MATERIAL PRICES

FT

Acquisitions helped British Polythene Industries, Europe's largest polythene film producer, raise pre-tax profits 31 per cent to £25.1m in 1995 . . .

Raw materials prices, high at the beginning of the period, fell throughout the year. However, they were now beginning to rise again. 'We have had increases in January, February and March and all the signs are that there will be one again in April,' said Mr Cameron McLatchie, chairman and chief executive.

Source: Motoko Rich, Financial Times, 5 March 1996.

EXHIBIT 3.1 **Estimates of raw materials' costs**

INTRODUCTION

In the last chapter, we discussed the issue of cost classification and said that the classification used must be appropriate to the purpose for which it is used; we identified the main purpose of classification as the provision of useful information to help management to manage the organisation. However, on its own, classification of costs is of limited value to management. In order to manage effectively, management also needs to be aware of the *amount* of the costs concerned, and this inevitably involves estimation. What is the basis for the prediction in Exhibit 3.1 that raw material prices are likely to rise again in April? Some estimate of future raw materials' costs must have been made by the company concerned. The cost rises referred to will not only affect the company's inputs, but will also (as suggested in the exhibit) affect profit and may raise issues of cost planning and control, sourcing of supplies, and even pricing of finished output. The impact of cost changes is thus potentially wide-ranging – hence the importance of cost estimation.

In this chapter, we will describe and illustrate various methods which may be employed to estimate future costs, and discuss their strengths and weaknesses. Before examining various estimation techniques, we will stress the importance of estimation to management accounting, which, being largely concerned with the future, relies extensively on estimates. We commence our discussion of techniques with a brief overview of what can be termed 'engineering approaches'; this term covers a range of methods which require specialist knowledge beyond the remit of management accounting. Past data form the basis of many estimates, and we proceed to examine what is possibly a rather subjective use of such data (estimation by inspection of accounts), a graphical method (scattergraph), high–low analysis and linear regression analysis. Each of these approaches has its advantages and disadvantages, which we will discuss as we progress.

One particular problem with almost all the methods we shall discuss is the 'single factor' assumption, i.e. the assumption that a single factor (such as volume of output) is the main contributory to cost variability. Similarly, we need to be careful that the estimation technique employed does not produce figures which are questionable within the relevant range.

Labour times (and hence related costs) can be significantly affected by the extent to which employees learn (i.e. become more proficient with practice), and we will illustrate the impact on labour times and cost estimates of this learning effect. Finally, we will examine a factor which has an important influence on all financial estimates – inflation.

OBJECTIVES   When you have completed this chapter, you will be able to:

- appreciate the need for cost estimation and its importance to management accounting;

- describe engineering and inspection of accounts approaches to cost estimation

- use a scattergraph, high–low analysis and simple linear regression analysis to obtain estimates of cost;

- appreciate the significance of the 'single factor' assumption in cost estimation;

- appreciate and calculate the effect of the learning curve on cost estimates;

- discuss the strengths and weaknesses of the different cost estimation techniques and the importance of relevant range in this context;

- adjust past costs for the effect of inflation.

THE NEED FOR COST ESTIMATION

In Chapter 1, we identified *decision making* and *planning and control* as major management activities which management accounting aims to support by the provision of useful information.

⇨ Why is estimation of future costs vital to management accounting's support of both these areas of management activity?

As we observed in Chapter 1, much of the information generated by management accounting must be future-oriented, since decisions and plans can only relate to the future. Financial control (*see* Chapter 13) requires comparison of like with like. If, for example, differences between budgeted and actual volume are partly the cause of differences between budgeted and actual cost, management should be aware of the fact and not wrongly attribute such differences to efficiency or price factors. It would be impossible to prepare next year's budget or properly compare it with the actual outcomes without having some idea about:

1 *Which* costs may increase or decrease as the result of increases/decreases in volume and which may not (i.e. which costs/parts of costs are *variable* and which *fixed*).
2 *How much* variable costs are likely to vary with volume and whether volume changes are likely to have an effect on fixed costs.
3 The impact on all costs (fixed and variable) of *non-volume factors* such as inflation.
4 The appropriate *measure of activity* against which to gauge variable cost behaviour (e.g. the cost unit).

In effect, it is not possible for management accounting to provide useful information in support of decision making and planning/control without a considerable element of estimation being present. Such estimates may be based on past experience, but, as we shall see, only to the extent that the past can be considered a reasonable guide to the future.

Given the crucial role of estimation in management accounting (e.g. in preparing plans or assessing the financial consequences of decisions), how can we obtain the required estimates and how much reliance can we place on the results of the different estimation techniques employed? In the discussion which follows, we shall concentrate on estimation of costs, but you should appreciate that some of the techniques can also be applied to estimation of revenues. In addition, it is important that you appreciate the collaborative aspect of cost estimation. To produce credible estimates, the management accountant needs to liaise closely with other members of the management team, whose specialist knowledge about particular facets of the organisation is a necessary supplement to the estimation techniques themselves.

ENGINEERING APPROACHES TO ESTIMATION

These approaches to estimation typically stem from observation of the processes/procedures giving rise to costs, followed by some sort of engineering or operational research estimate of the input–output relationships involved – which can then be used as the basis for cost estimates. Techniques of this sort are not strictly 'management accounting', but fall within the remit of specialists in operational research or of production engineers. We shall therefore confine ourselves to some general observations about the use of estimation methodologies which fall within the general 'engineering' category.

One major benefit of such techniques is that they will almost certainly provide more accurate cost predictions than anything produced by the techniques which we shall describe shortly. This may be especially true where there is an identifiable relationship between inputs and outputs: for example, in certain chemical processes it is possible to predict with considerable accuracy the outputs which will result from given inputs – and from this it may be a comparatively simple matter to estimate the associated costs.

A further advantage of engineering estimation is that, unlike the other methods which we shall describe below, they can generally be used even where no previous data exist. This may be useful where costs are being estimated for a new product/service or for a new version of an existing one where there are significant differences between the two versions.

⇨ Can you suggest a potential disadvantage associated with use of engineering approaches to cost estimation?

The main disadvantage relating to engineering estimates relates to their very sophistication, which normally requires considerable expertise in operational research or production engineering methodology, and many organisations (especially smaller ones) may not possess such expertise. Although external consultants may be engaged, this could prove costly – so costly, in fact, that the cost/benefit criterion which we described in Chapter 1 may be breached. This may be exacerbated by the need to repeat the estimation exercise regularly (e.g. annually).

The sophisticated nature of engineering techniques may result in another problem: managers could be misled into believing the estimates to be completely accurate. No estimation technique will be totally accurate (except by luck), however, and overreliance on the accuracy of estimates could conceivably result in dangerous overconfidence about the outcome of future events. If you look again at Exhibit 3.1, you will see that the company chairman is quoted as saying that 'all the signs are' that raw material prices will increase again in April – cautious words which allow for potential inaccuracy in the estimates upon which the quotation is presumably based.

Engineering estimates derive from specialised methodology; almost at the opposite extreme in terms of methodical rigour, is estimation by inspection of accounts, which we will now describe.

ESTIMATION BY INSPECTION OF ACCOUNTS

This approach to cost estimation is also referred to as the *account classification* method. The accounts of previous periods are examined for each cost which it is desired to estimate; details of the volume of activity (e.g. output) relating to each of these past costs are also extracted from past records. Based on the pattern of the past costs and related activity levels, a judgement is made about the behaviour of each particular cost: Is it wholly variable with activity? Wholly fixed? A mixture of the two? Once a decision about each cost's behaviour has been made, an estimate of the future amount can be arrived at by adjusting for cumulative inflation, volume and other changes, so that the estimate produced reflects conditions in the future period to which it is to apply.

This sort of methodology, with some variation, is widely used in practice – many organisations base next year's budget on this year's, adjusted for anticipated changes (e.g. inflation and increases/decreases in volume) – and it can result in fairly reasonable estimates. Compared to engineering methods, it is inexpensive to operate as it does not require the same degree of specialised knowledge. In addition, the results of an account inspection may readily be adjusted to allow for all anticipated future changes in conditions, thereby providing some flexibility in response to what may be a volatile environment.

▷ What do you feel might be a major weakness of estimates based on an inspection of accounts?

One significant weakness in this estimation technique lies in its subjectivity: great reliance is placed on the judgement of the person(s) undertaking the inspection. How accurate is the estimate of underlying cost behaviour? Has adequate adjustment been made to allow for future changes in conditions? And, being based on past measures, there may be a danger of assuming that the past is an accurate predictor of the future – in a dynamic environment, this may be a dangerous assumption: for example, production technology may change very rapidly, or may be about to change; the *mix* of products/services being provided may have altered in response to changing market conditions; the type or source of raw materials may be different; and there is the impact of inflation to consider (an exercise we shall undertake later in the chapter). Any anticipated change which has cost implications must be incorporated into the estimation exercise. If it is not, the resulting estimates are likely to be, at best, misleading; at worst, they may have very serious consequences for the organisation.

One way to reduce the subjectivity of our estimates might be to employ past data in a more rigorous manner; estimation using a scattergraph, by high–low analysis and by linear regression analysis all attempt to do this to different degrees.

ESTIMATION USING A SCATTERGRAPH

This is a graphical approach to cost estimation whereby a number of past costs are plotted against their related volumes of activity, from which the plot of an estimated total cost function is derived. We will use the data in Exhibit 3.2 to illustrate the application of a scattergraph to cost estimation.

Northshires Ambulance Service: cost of vehicle maintenance

Northshires Ambulance Service operates a fleet of ambulances over a large geographical area which includes both urban and rural districts; the total maintenance costs of the fleet over the last six years, along with the associated total mileages, have been as follows:

Year	Total maintenance cost (£)	Total mileage
19X2	410,000	3,600,000
19X3	570,000	5,100,000
19X4	360,000	3,100,000
19X5	460,000	3,900,000
19X6	530,000	4,700,000
19X7	610,000	5,600,000

In 19X8, it is anticipated that the total mileage of the fleet of ambulances will be 5,000,000. It is known that some of the maintenance costs vary according to the mileage travelled by ambulances, whilst some costs (e.g. for maintenance of medical equipment within ambulances) are incurred at a fixed amount per annum.

EXHIBIT 3.2 Ambulance service's past maintenance costs

Examination of the previous six years' total maintenance costs relative to total mileages suggests that the cost (in part at least) varies with mileage. The problem we are faced with here is determining to what extent the maintenance cost is variable with mileage and to what extent it is fixed irrespective of mileage. As a first step in our cost estimate for 19X8, we need to plot the past maintenance costs against their related total mileages; this is done in Figure 3.1.

In Chapter 2, we saw that a semi-variable cost has the general outline illustrated in Figure 3.2. The points we have plotted in Figure 3.1 represent different measures of total cost relative to volume. What we must now try to do is to use these points as the basis of an estimate for a total cost 'line' of the pattern shown in Figure 3.2. This is achieved by visual estimate: that is, we 'place' our total cost line by examining the pattern of total costs previously plotted.

⇨ By visual estimate, 'place' a straight line on Figure 3.1 which represents an estimate of total cost. Extend this line to the left until it intersects the vertical axis. At approximately what value (in £s) does this intersection lie?

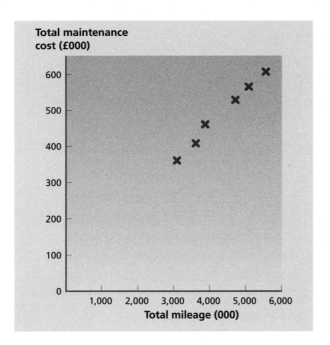

FIGURE **3.1**
**Northshires Ambulance Service
– maintenance costs for the
past six years plotted against
total mileage**

Figure 3.3 shows our estimate of the total cost line based on the six values of total
cost plotted earlier in Figure 3.1. You will see that our estimated total cost line in
Figure 3.3 intersects the vertical axis at a value of £100,000. This may well be different to your own result – but such a difference is to be expected, since we have
used visual estimate to 'place' the total cost line, and visual estimates of where best

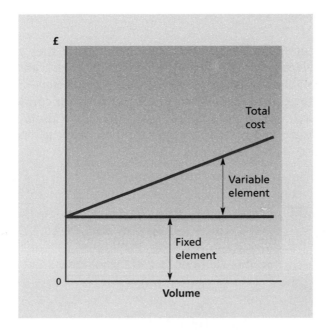

FIGURE **3.2**
General pattern of a mixed cost

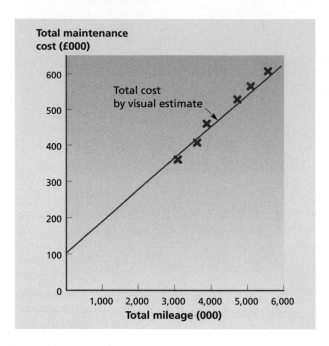

FIGURE 3.3
Estimated total cost line for Northshires Ambulance Service's maintenance cost

to place such a line will almost certainly differ between one individual and another. In our example, the past total costs plotted in Figure 3.1 are fairly close to lying in a straight line, so the extent of differences in visual estimate is likely to be quite small. But this may not be the case, so that the accuracy of the estimated total cost line may be extremely questionable.

▷ What is the significance to our cost estimation exercise of the £100,000 intersection in Figure 3.3?

The point where our estimate of the total cost line intersects the vertical axis represents the fixed element of total maintenance cost; this can be verified by comparing Figures 3.2 and 3.3. The implication of this intersection is that, even if there is zero mileage, £100,000 in maintenance cost will be incurred.

Now that we have a value for the fixed cost, we can substitute this into one of the past costs to derive an estimate of the variable cost per mile:

	£
total maintenance cost in 19X2 (from Exhibit 3.2)	410,000
less fixed element	100,000
variable element	310,000

We can now determine the estimated variable maintenance cost per mile:

$$\frac{\text{variable element of 19X2 total cost}}{\text{19X2 total mileage}}$$

$$= \frac{£310,000}{3,600,000} = £0.086.$$

⇨ Based on the estimates of fixed cost and variable cost per mile which we have just calculated, what is the estimated total maintenance cost for 19X8, when total mileage will be 5,000,000?

The estimated total maintenance cost for 19X8 will be:

	£
fixed element	100,000
variable element (5,000,000 miles @ £0.086)	430,000
total cost	530,000

This is a very straightforward approach to cost estimation, but it does suffer from certain weaknesses. The first is the subjectivity involved in placement of the estimated total cost line which we referred to above. Another problem is that, like the account inspection method (and indeed the other methods which we shall describe below), the scattergraph assumes that the past can be taken as a reasonable guide to the future. Looking again at Figure 3.3, we might argue that one way to help reduce the subjective element in our placement of the estimated total cost line would be to plot a greater number of previous total maintenance costs and related mileages. Suppose we had plotted the total maintenance costs from the last 20 years, would this really have improved the quality of our estimate? That is highly unlikely, as the further into the past we go, the less relevant is the information likely to be for the present or the immediate future, and the harder it will be to make adjustment for changes, both over the time span involved (e.g. the effect of inflation over such a long period) and over that anticipated for the future (e.g. working methods next year relative to those of 20 years ago). In fact, rapid change in organisational environment and methods may render even fairly recent data suspect as a basis for estimation.

In addition, the scattergraph assumes linear cost behaviour – that is, that the fixed element of total cost is unchanged at all volumes and that the variable cost per unit is constant – thereby ignoring the possibility of step fixed costs and curvilinear variable costs of the sort described in the last chapter.

One final weakness of the scattergraph is that the estimate of variable cost may depend on which past cost is selected for the fixed cost substitution procedure.

⇨ Substitute the £100,000 estimated fixed cost into the 19X4 total maintenance cost given in Exhibit 3.2. Then re-calculate the estimated variable cost per mile and the estimated total maintenance cost for 19X8.

Using the 19X4 total maintenance cost for the substitution gives:

	£
19X4 total cost	360,000
less fixed element	100,000
variable element	260,000

So the estimated variable cost per mile is:

$$\frac{£360,000}{3,100,00} = £0.084.$$

Although this is fairly close to our previous estimate (£0.086), the difference is more substantial when a revised total cost estimate for 19X8 is produced:

	£
fixed element	100,000
variable element (5,000,000 @ £0.084)	420,000
estimated total cost	520,000

which is £10,000 less than our first estimate. Which should we accept? If the original £530,000 is used, we may be overstating the cost, whereas the second estimate may understate it. An inaccuracy of this kind exaggerates the inaccuracy inherent to any estimation technique. In some situations, the resulting margin of error could be so great that the credibility of estimates produced is seriously affected. Moreover, if our estimates are inaccurate to this extent, then the value of the information to management may be greatly reduced.

As an alternative to graphing a number of past costs and activity levels to obtain our estimates, we can simplify procedures by using only two past observations – an approach we shall now illustrate.

HIGH–LOW ANALYSIS

The scattergraph used a number of previous costs and activity levels as the basis of an estimate of total cost. High–low analysis uses only two:

- the highest activity level and its associated total cost; along with
- the lowest activity level and its associated total cost.

Assuming that the fixed element of each of these total costs is the same, and that the variable cost per unit is constant, then the difference in total cost between the two activity levels will be attributable to the variable cost of the difference in activity. We can therefore produce an estimated variable cost per unit:

$$\frac{\text{difference in total cost}}{\text{difference in activity}}$$

⇨ From Exhibit 3.2, extract the highest and lowest total mileages along with their related total maintenance costs, and use the formula above to obtain an estimate for the variable cost per mile.

A comparison of the highest and lowest total mileages and related total maintenance costs reveals the following:

	Total mileage	Total cost (£)
highest volume (19X7)	5,600,000	610,000
lowest volume (19X4)	3,100,000	360,000
difference	2,500,000	250,000

The estimated variable cost per mile is:

$$\frac{£250,000}{2,500,000} = £0.10$$

This value can now be substituted into *either* the highest volume total cost *or* the lowest volume total cost to obtain an estimate for the fixed element. Using the highest volume total cost, we get:

	£
total cost	610,000
less variable element (5,600,000 @ £0.10)	560,000
fixed element	50,000

▷ Substitute the £0.10 per mile variable cost estimate into the lowest volume total cost and confirm that the fixed cost estimate is the same.

Using the lowest volume total cost gives:

	£
total cost	360,000
less variable element (3,100,000 @ £0.10)	310,000
fixed element	50,000

Based on our high–low analysis, the estimated total maintenance cost for 19X8 is:

	£
fixed element	50,000
variable element (5,000,000 @ £0.10)	500,000
total cost	550,000

This is another very simple estimation technique but it, too, suffers from certain weaknesses. Like the scattergraph, it assumes linear cost behaviour and that the past is a reasonable guide to the future. A particular weakness of high–low analysis lies in the two activity levels used in the estimation process. If these extreme volumes are significantly different from more 'normal' volumes, then there is every chance that the associated cost behaviour could be significantly different. For example, if the difference between high and low volumes is large, there is a good chance that the fixed element of total cost will contain at least one 'step' at some intermediate volume. Figure 3.4 compares the scattergraph and high–low results.

The reason for the difference in our fixed cost estimate is clear: the scattergraph has attempted to incorporate *all* the past observations, whereas high–low uses only two. Figure 3.4 should also point up our earlier comment about potential distor-

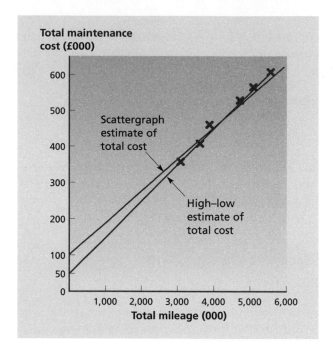

FIGURE 3.4
Scattergraph and high–low
total cost estimates

tion of cost estimates caused by using only two extreme values – and remember, here, the past observations of total cost are very close to exhibiting a linear relationship with volume.

The final technique we will illustrate applies mathematical analysis to past data in order to obtain estimates.

LINEAR REGRESSION ANALYSIS

This technique overcomes the subjectivity inherent in the scattergraph by calculating a precise placement for the estimated total cost line. By using a number of past values, it also addresses the 'two-value' weakness of high–low analysis. Regression analysis operates by obtaining the values for fixed cost and variable cost per unit in a mathematical formula for total cost:

$$y = a + bx$$

where y represents total cost;

a is the fixed element of total cost;
b is the variable cost per unit;
x is the volume of activity.

You should note that '$y = a + bx$' is the standard mathematical equation for a straight line, with a representing the vertical intercept and b the slope of the line.

Based on a number of past total costs (y) and their related volume levels (x), values for the variable cost per unit (b) and fixed cost (a) can be calculated using the following formulae:

$$b = \frac{n\Sigma xy - \Sigma x\Sigma y}{n\Sigma x^2 - (\Sigma x)^2} \text{ and } a = \frac{\Sigma y}{n} - \frac{b\Sigma x}{n}$$

where n represents the number of past observations being used and Σ is the mathematical symbol for 'sum of'.

Northshires Ambulance Service: cost of vehicle maintenance

The total maintenance costs of the ambulance fleet over the last six years, along with the associated total mileages, have been as follows:

Year	Total maintenance cost (£)	Total mileage
19X2	410,000	3,600,000
19X3	570,000	5,100,000
19X4	360,000	3,100,000
19X5	460,000	3,900,000
19X6	530,000	4,700,000
19X7	610,000	5,600,000

In 19X8, it is anticipated that the total mileage of the fleet of ambulances will be 5,000,000.

EXHIBIT 3.3 **Ambulance service's past maintenance costs**

For convenience, Exhibit 3.3 presents again the previous six years' total maintenance costs and associated mileages for Northshires Ambulance Service. There are six past costs and volume levels, so here, $n = 6$. Although the formulae above appear very daunting, a simple tabulation will provide us with the other values we need to enable us to obtain values for a (fixed cost) and b (variable cost per unit). For ease of calculation, all the values for x (total mileage) and y (total maintenance cost) in the table which follows have been stated in millions (£s and miles):

x	y	xy	x^2
3.6	0.41	1.476	12.96
5.1	0.57	2.907	26.01
3.1	0.36	1.116	9.61
3.9	0.46	1.794	15.21
4.7	0.53	2.491	22.09
5.6	0.61	3.416	31.36
Σ 26.0	Σ 2.94	Σ 13.200	Σ 117.24

Inserting the appropriate values into the formula for b gives:

$$b = \frac{n\Sigma xy - \Sigma x\Sigma y}{n\Sigma x^2 - (\Sigma x)^2} = \frac{6(13.2) - (26.0 \times 2.94)}{6(117.24) - 26^2} = \frac{79.2 - 76.44}{703.44 - 676} = \frac{2.76}{27.44} = 0.10$$

In other words, our estimate of the variable cost per mile is £0.10. This value can now be used to obtain a value for *a* (the fixed cost):

$$a = \frac{\Sigma y}{n} - \frac{b\Sigma x}{n} = \frac{2.94}{6} - \frac{(0.1 \times 26)}{6} = 0.49 - 0.43 = 0.06$$

Bearing in mind that the figures are stated in millions, our estimate of the fixed maintenance cost is £0.06 million (i.e. £60,000). The estimated total maintenance cost for 19X8 will be:

	£
fixed element	60,000
variable element (5,000,000 miles @ £0.10)	500,000
total cost	560,000

This approach is undoubtedly more *mathematically* precise than the scattergraph or high–low analysis, but does it provide a more accurate prediction of total cost? Like both of these methods, linear regression analysis assumes linear cost behaviour. (Remember that the mathematical expression for total cost which we gave above ($y = a + bx$) is the general formula for a straight line.) In addition, we are still taking the past to be a reasonable indicator of the future; in mathematical terms, the more past observations which we include in our regression analysis, the more mathematically valid the result. However, as we have already observed, inclusion of a large number of past figures may have exactly the opposite effect on our cost estimation exercise.

One important consideration in cost estimation is what causes variability in costs – is it a single factor (and if so, have we correctly identified it?), or is more than one factor involved (in which case, how do we recognise the fact?) It is to these issues which we now turn.

THE 'SINGLE FACTOR' ASSUMPTION

Thus far, our cost estimation exercise relating to the Northshires Ambulance Service has assumed that the variable element of total maintenance cost varies in relation to increases/decreases in mileage.

⇨ What other factors may affect the variability of total maintenance cost?

Total maintenance cost may vary relative to several factors: for example, the number of ambulances in the fleet; the age of vehicles being maintained; or the number of mechanics' hours required to perform the maintenance. None of these additional factors has been included in our scattergraph, high–low or regression estimates – nor can they be. These techniques assume that cost variability arises because of a single factor (mileage in this case), so we need to be confident that the measure of activity we are using is the main cause of variability in cost.

It is possible to subject the results of an estimation exercise to further mathematical analysis to test whether the 'single factor' used has a significant bearing on cost variability. Although such techniques are beyond the scope of this book, you should be aware that they are, at best, indicative, e.g. they still assume that the past is a reliable guide to the future.

It is also possible to use a **multiple regression model**. This model allows for the impact on cost variability of a range of different factors, so that the total cost formula given above ($y = a + bx$) would appear as follows:

$$y = a + b_1x_1 + b_2x_2 + b_3x_3 + \ldots + b_nx_n$$

where x_1, x_2 and so forth represent the different factors having a bearing on cost behaviour. However, including additional factors in the analysis will not automatically improve the accuracy of the resulting predictions. Although computer software which will perform multiple regression analysis is readily available, identification of all factors affecting cost behaviour may be difficult or impossible; and, even where they can be identified, quantification could be problematic (e.g. making a quantifiable link between vehicle age and variability of maintenance cost in the case of Northshires Ambulance Service).

We also need to be careful that cost estimation does not focus solely or unduly on factors internal to the organisation. Inflation is one important external consideration, but there are others: for example, how do our costs compare with those of our competitors? (We will discuss **benchmarking** in Chapter 15.)

In addition, we must apply the concept of relevant range to the application and results of all estimation techniques; if we do not, then our estimates may be of little value.

THE RELEVANT RANGE AND COST ESTIMATION

We introduced this important concept in the last chapter; the relevant range is the range of activity volumes and/or the time horizon over which a particular set of assumptions can be taken to be reasonable approximations of reality. If we apply this to cost estimation, we can say that our estimates are likely to be reasonable only within a particular volume range and time period. The importance of a limited volume range is particularly evident if we consider high–low analysis. We have said that the main problem with this approach is that the volumes are extremes and so the associated cost behaviour may not be typical of more 'normal' levels of activity. Another way of stating the same problem is to say that these extreme volumes might breach the relevant range.

In more general terms, the assumption of linear cost behaviour – constant variable cost per unit and unchanging total fixed cost – may *only* be reasonable within the relevant range. Consider the scattergraph and regression analysis – is extrapolation of the estimated total cost line as far as the vertical intercept reasonable? or is the range of volumes covered by the cost function thus extrapolated so wide that the relevant range is seriously compromised?

Turning to the issue of time period, we can see the effect of failing to place a limit on this if we look at scattergraphs or regression analysis. These techniques both use a number of past costs and activity levels. It is possible that using a large number of past figures will improve our estimates, but it may also be true that the older the data, the less its relevance to the future: that is, there is a danger that the time aspect of the relevant range may be breached.

If we are to produce acceptable cost estimates, we must recognise the limitations imposed by the relevant range and adapt our calculations accordingly: for example, by limiting the number of past figures used, or by using more measures within the relevant time span (e.g. monthly or quarterly, rather than annual), or by limiting extent of extrapolation.

So far, we have discussed cost estimation in terms of costs in general; we must now consider labour costs in particular and the potential influence on these of the extent to which employees learn.

THE LEARNING CURVE

Even in an age of automation and computerisation, labour costs can be substantial for many organisations: maintenance of Northshires Ambulance Service's vehicles, for example, will be predominantly labour-intensive, so a significant proportion of total maintenance cost is likely to relate to labour. This being so, any major influence on labour time is likely to have implications for labour cost, and needs to be allowed for in estimation. One such influence is the learning curve.

The idea underlying the learning curve is a simple one: the more often a task is performed, the more quickly it can be performed, as the person performing the task becomes more proficient (i.e. learning takes place). If the time required to produce a unit of output, say, is reducing as workers gain experience, it means that the labour cost per unit will likewise be reducing. In general terms, the effect of the learning curve on labour time per unit can be illustrated as in Figure 3.5.

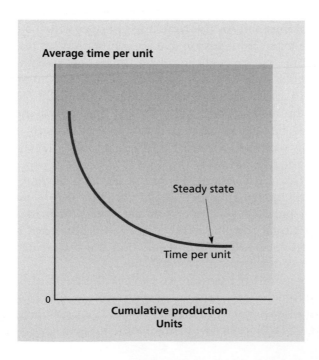

FIGURE 3.5
Effect of the learning curve on labour time per unit

You will see from the gradual 'flattening' of the curve in Figure 3.5 that the greatest reduction in average time per unit occurs at the lower end of the production scale – that is, when cumulative production is low – and that the rate of reduction in the average time per unit declines as cumulative output increases until a *steady state* is achieved. Achievement of the steady state means that learning does not continue indefinitely: that is, there is a limit to how proficiently a particular task can be performed. The fact that the labour time per unit is reducing as output rises means that labour cost per unit is not constant, which results in a *curvilinear* total labour cost function, as illustrated in Figure 3.6.

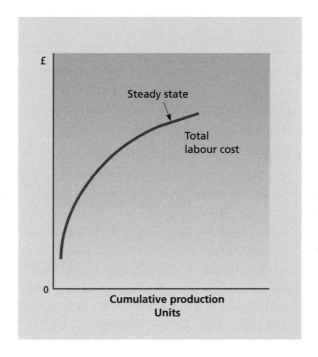

FIGURE **3.6**
Effect of learning curve on total labour cost

The effect of the learning curve on average labour time per unit is mirrored in the total cost function in Figure 3.6: a steeper curve at lower production volumes (corresponding to the higher labour times per unit at these volumes), with the slope becoming less steep as output increases (the reduction in the slope corresponding to the reducing labour time per unit), until the cost function becomes more or less linear (corresponding to the steady state, where the labour time and hence cost per unit will be pretty much constant).

In more precise terms, the effect of the learning curve, derived from the underlying mathematical formulation, can be stated as follows:

for each successive doubling in cumulative output, the average time per unit will reduce to a given percentage of its previous value.

This percentage is referred to as the *learning rate*: for example, if a 90 per cent learning rate (or a '90 per cent learning curve') applies, each successive doubling of cumulative output will result in a reduction in the average time per unit to 90 per cent of its previous value. Exhibit 3.4 contains information about the time required to undertake maintenance work on Northshires Ambulance Service's fleet of vehicles.

Northshires Ambulance Service: maintenance labour times

In an attempt to reduce operating costs, Northshires Ambulance Service has recently employed its own staff of maintenance mechanics – in the past, all maintenance work was subcontracted to local garages. It is estimated that routine servicing of the first ambulance to be dealt with by Northshires' own staff will take 80 hours to perform, due largely to staff inexperience. Information from other ambulance services suggests that this time will be subject to a 90 per cent learning curve.

EXHIBIT 3.4 Impact of learning curve on ambulance service's maintenance costs

The effect of the 90 per cent learning curve on average maintenance time per ambulance and on total maintenance time is assessed as follows:

Cumulative number of ambulances serviced	Average time per ambulance (hours)	Total time (hours)
1	80	80.0
2	$(90\% \times 80) = 72$	144.0
4	$(90\% \times 72) = 64.8$	259.2
8	$(90\% \times 64.8) = 58.32$	466.56
etc.		

▷ Following the pattern established above, determine the average time per ambulance and the total time if the cumulative number of ambulances serviced is: (a) 16; and (b) 32 (answer to two decimal places).

Applying the principle stated earlier that each successive doubling of output causes average labour time per unit to reduce to a given percentage of the previous level of output, we get:

Cumulative number of ambulances serviced	Average time per ambulance (hours)	Total time (hours)
16	$(90\% \times 58.32) = 52.49$	839.84
32	$(90\% \times 52.49) = 47.24$	1,511.68

You will see that the decrease in average hours required per ambulance is becoming smaller and smaller as the cumulative number of ambulances increases. You will also see that the effect of the learning curve on total hours required is significant; had we ignored the learning effect, our estimate of the total hours required to service 32 ambulances would have been:

$$(32 \text{ ambulances} \times 80 \text{ hours per ambulance}) = 2{,}560 \text{ hours}$$

compared to 1,511.68 after taking the learning curve into account. Complete omission of the learning curve from our estimates could have resulted in serious overestimation of the labour and labour-related costs associated with maintenance, and might cause poor decisions to be made by management.

⇨ Assume that an 80 per cent learning curve applies to the ambulance maintenance times. If maintenance of the first ambulance requires 80 hours' work, what will be the average hours and total hours required for cumulative totals of 2, 4, 8, 16 and 32 ambulances? (Work to two decimal places.)

Applying an 80 per cent learning rate to the maintenance times yields the following results:

Cumulative number of ambulances serviced	Average time per ambulance (hours)	Total time (hours)
1	80	80.0
2	$(80\% \times 80) = 64$	128.0
4	$(80\% \times 64) = 51.2$	204.8
8	$(80\% \times 51.2) = 40.96$	327.68
16	$(80\% \times 40.96) = 32.77$	524.32
32	$(80\% \times 32.77) = 26.22$	839.04

Comparison of these times with the ones we calculated for a 90 per cent learning curve reveals that the 80% figures show larger successive reductions in the average time per ambulance maintained. The general effect of different learning rates is that, the lower the percentage learning rate, the larger are the successive reductions in average time per unit required and on total time. Consequently, the lower the percentage learning rate, the greater the impact on labour and labour-related costs. Figures 3.7 and 3.8 illustrate the comparative effect of three different learning rates on average time per unit and on total labour cost respectively.

We have seen that the learning curve can have a major impact on labour times. How can we incorporate this effect in our cost estimation exercise? Exhibit 3.5 provides further details of the Northshires Ambulance Service.

⇨ Following the procedures used above, determine the average hours per ambulance and the total hours required if the cumulative number of ambulances serviced is: (a) 64; and (b) 128 (work to two decimal places).

For 64 and 128 ambulances serviced, the times will be:

Cumulative number of ambulances serviced	Average time per ambulance (hours)	Total time (hours)
64	$(90\% \times 47.24) = 42.52$	2,721.28
128	$(90\% \times 42.52) = 38.27$	4,898.56

Using this information, we can now estimate the number of mechanics who must be employed for the year, along with the associated salary cost.

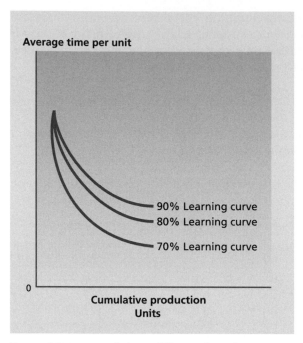

FIGURE **3.7 Impact of three different learning rates on average time per unit**

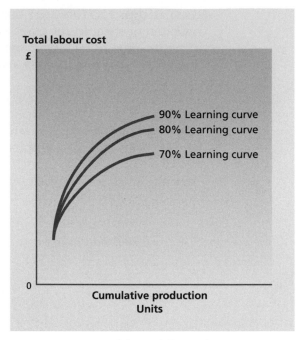

FIGURE **3.8 Impact of three different learning rates on total labour cost**

Northshires Ambulance Service: labour and variable overhead costs

Next year will be the first in which the ambulance service uses its own staff of mechanics to service vehicles. In this first year of operation, it is anticipated that the cumulative number of ambulances which will be serviced will amount to 128, with the first ambulance serviced requiring 80 hours of mechanics' time, this being subject to a 90 per cent learning curve.

Each mechanic employed will have a working year of 48 weeks, each week consisting of 35 hours; of this total annual time, only 70 per cent will be spent actually servicing the ambulances. Each mechanic will be paid a fixed annual salary of £16,000.

Overhead relating to the servicing of vehicles is incurred at the rate of £2 per hour spent by the mechanics on this work.

EXHIBIT **3.5 Incorporating the learning curve into cost estimates**

⇨ Based on the data given in Exhibit 3.5, calculate the number of hours per mechanic per year available for servicing work. Use this in conjunction with the estimated total time required for servicing 128 ambulances (4,898.56 hours) to determine the number of mechanics who must be employed next year (to the nearest whole mechanic), along with the associated salary cost.

Each mechanic can spend (48 weeks × 35 hours per week × 70%) = 1,176 hours per year on servicing work. If 128 ambulances are to be serviced during the year, 4,898.56 hours of work are involved. The number of mechanics required to cover this number of hours is:

$$\frac{4,898.56}{1,176} = 4.165, \text{ say 4 mechanics.}$$

The work represented by 0.165 of a mechanic could be undertaken in overtime, or a fifth mechanic may be employed (which would allow some flexibility in the event of absence). Assuming that five mechanics will be employed, the annual salary cost will be:

$$(5 \times £16,000) = £80,000.$$

Had we ignored the impact of the learning effect, our estimate of the hours required to service 128 ambulances would have been:

$$(128 \times 80 \text{ hours per vehicle}) = 10,240 \text{ hours}$$

which would suggest employing:

$$\frac{10,240}{1,179} = 8.71, \text{ say 9 mechanics,}$$

the estimated annual salary cost of nine mechanics is:

$$(9 \times £16,000) = £144,000.$$

The message is clear. Ignoring the learning effect would result not only in a material overestimate of the mechanics' salary cost, but also in the employment of more mechanics than are really necessary to perform the work. In addition to the salary cost, we need to recognise the learning curve's effect on other labour-related costs (overhead per hour in this example).

⇨ Provide an estimate of the variable overhead cost associated with maintenance: (a) ignoring the learning curve; and (b) taking the learning curve into account.

At a rate of £2 per mechanic hour spent on maintenance, the estimated variable overhead will be:

	£
(a) ignoring learning effect (10,240 hours @ £2)	20,480.00
(b) allowing for learning effect (4,898.56 hours @ £2)	9,797.12

Once again, the result of ignoring the learning effect can be clearly seen.

Our example of the learning curve has thus far been based on cumulative output which falls conveniently at successive 'doubling points'. Suppose, however, that the cumulative number of ambulances to be serviced in the year was not 128 (a doubling point), but, say, 120. To determine the average hours per ambulance for this cumulative total, we need to adopt a formulaic approach. The general formula for a mathematical function of the sort depicted in Figure 3.5 is:

$$y = ax^b$$

where y is the average hours per unit;

a is the number of hours required for the first unit;

x is the cumulative number of units;

b is $\dfrac{\text{logarithm of the learning rate}}{\text{logarithm of 2}}$.

If we apply this formula to a cumulative total of 120 ambulances, values for the different variables in the formula are:

$a = 80$ hours

$x = 120$ units

the learning rate is 90% (i.e. 0.9), so $b = \dfrac{\log 0.9}{\log 2} = \dfrac{-0.0458}{0.301} = -0.152$.

The completed formula is:

$$y = ax^b \;\Rightarrow\; y = 80(120^{-0.152}) \;\Rightarrow\; y = 80(0.483) \;\Rightarrow\; y = 38.64.$$

In other words, the average hours per ambulance serviced will be 38.64 if the cumulative total of ambulances serviced is 120, giving total hours of $(120 \times 38.64) = 4,636.8$.

In addition to its uses in cost estimation and manpower planning, the learning curve may also be important for:

1 production scheduling;
2 determination of productivity bonuses;
3 setting labour efficiency standards (standard costing and the setting of standards will be discussed in Chapter 12).

Problems of practical application

Although the rationale underlying the learning curve is perfectly straightforward – namely, that repetition increases proficiency – there are a number of problems relating to its practical application.

Determining the learning rate

In the Northshires Ambulance Service this was stated to be 90 per cent, but we need to ask how accurate this is. Although it is possible, via techniques such as work study, to obtain an idea about the learning rate, this is unlikely to be a precise quantification of the speed at which workers 'learn'. For example, different individuals will learn at different rates and different tasks may have different learning rates depending on their complexity. If you re-examine our calculation of the number of mechanics required by Northshires Ambulance Service, you will see that we have effectively aggregated five separate (and identical) learning curves to arrive at our answer, i.e. we have assumed that the 90 per cent learning rate is applicable to all employees.

At best, the learning rate will be an 'informed guesstimate'; at worst, it may be so inaccurate as to destroy the credibility of any estimates founded upon it. We need to be aware of a danger that the very precise nature of the mathematical calculations may lend to our estimates an aura of precision which is misleading.

'Output' is continuous

If there are significant breaks in the work being performed, then some or even all of the benefit of the learning curve may be lost. In other words, proficiency requires frequent repetition. The scale and speed of 'unlearning' can often be surprising, so that in situations where breaks in work are likely, the learning curve's predictions should be viewed with a degree of caution.

Tasks are repetitive

In order that workers gain proficiency, the task concerned must be repetitive. If there are significant differences between successive tasks, then learning may be slower or more fragmentary than suggested by the smooth curve in Figure 3.5. Consider maintenance of the Northshires Ambulance Service's fleet of vehicles: although much of the work may be routine, it is highly unlikely that precise maintenance requirements for every vehicle will be identical – and to the extent that these requirements differ, learning is likely to be slower than suggested by the 90 per cent learning curve (e.g. the learning rate may be 95 per cent or 99 per cent).

Output processes are labour-intensive

In order for the learning effect to have any significance, labour must be able to dictate the pace with which work is performed. In many situations, the pace of work will effectively be dictated by machine speeds, to such an extent that the impact of the learning curve is minimal (or even non-existent).

Stable conditions exist

If conditions, methods and personnel change regularly, then there will be little chance of the learning effect having much impact. For instance, if labour turnover is high amongst experienced workers, then we may be faced with a cumulative 'unlearning' effect as the workforce, on average, becomes less experienced.

Other factors may affect labour times

Factors other than the learning effect can have a major bearing on the speed with which work is performed: for example, the motivation of individual employees, or Health and Safety regulations. In the case of the Northshires Ambulance Service, emergency maintenance work which must be carried out more or less instantly may have the effect of reducing the overall average time required to service each vehicle in a way that is not typical of 'average' efficiency.

However, as we have demonstrated, the learning curve can have a material effect on labour and labour-related costs, so ignoring it entirely when making estimates would be unwise. It is almost certainly better to make some allowance for the effect of learning, providing we accept that, like the estimation process generally, assessments of the learning curve will be imprecise to some extent.

Learning effects may also be significant at the organisational level. The **cost experience curve** reflects the tendency for an organisation's costs as a whole to reduce due, for example, to accumulated expertise in particular markets or with particular products/services. This phenomenon can be vitally important in diversification, expansion and takeover decisions, where exploiting or obtaining specialist knowledge is a prime concern.

One final – and vital – consideration in all financial estimates is inflation.

INFLATION AND COST ESTIMATION

Even with comparatively low rates of inflation, the cumulative effect over time can be marked. Therefore, when estimates of future costs are being made, we must incorporate inflation. This raises two potential difficulties:

1 Providing a credible estimate of future inflation;
2 Adjusting past costs for the effect of inflation where these are being used as the basis of our estimate.

We shall discuss each of these issues below.

Assessing future inflation

The problem here lies in producing reasonable estimates of how inflation will affect a particular organisation, and, as Exhibit 3.6 suggests, this may prove difficult. Exhibit 3.6 illustrates the potential volatility of inflation, depending on the

---

STATIC FACTORY GATE PRICES UNDERLINE SLOWDOWN

Official figures published on Thursday are expected to show that the annual rate of retail price inflation fell below 3 per cent last month for the first time in more than a year.

Output prices, including the more volatile components, rose by a non-seasonally adjusted 0.4 per cent between December and January and by 3.8 per cent in the year to January – the lowest annual increase since March last year. Industry was hit by higher oil prices, which rose 5.5 per cent last month, due partly to unusually cold weather, particularly in the US. But this was more than offset by declines in the prices of other raw materials. The price of fuels other than crude oil fell by 1.9 per cent in January.

Manufacturers' overall fuel and raw material costs declined by 0.3 per cent last month, following a rise of 1.8 per cent in December. Input price inflation peaked at about 12 per cent in the first half of last year but it has slowed sharply since. In the year to January input costs rose 4 per cent, the lowest annual increase since July 1994 . . .

Source: Graham Bowley, *Financial Times*, 13 February 1996.

EXHIBIT **3.6 Inflationary pressure is not uniform**

specific resources being considered. For example, 'manufacturers' overall fuel and raw material costs declined by 0.3 per cent last month, following a rise of 1.8 per cent in December' – and these are previous *monthly* figures. Imagine, therefore, how difficult it may be to produce estimated rates of price increase covering, say, a one-year period and relating to the *specific* input resources required by an organisation. In some instances, it may be possible to use published sources for estimates of inflation: for example, the Bank of England's quarterly *Inflation Report*, which contains both historic inflation figures and projections; or figures produced by the Central Statistical Office, such as *Industrial Trends*, showing past and anticipated price movements in various categories of resources. Also, in some economic sectors (e.g. building), organisations can obtain information from specialist trade journals. However, even with these sources, care is necessary.

⇨ Northshires Ambulance Service's management intends to utilise the published Retail Price Index to adjust its past and estimated future maintenance costs for inflation. Is there a possible weakness in this approach?

The weakness in the proposed use of the Retail Price Index is that this index is a general indicator of inflation and is measured with reference to a 'basket' of domestic goods and services as diverse as muesli and mortgage interest. It is thus unlikely that such an index would provide a particularly relevant measure in terms of the price changes affecting the *specific* resources used by the Northshires Ambulance Service. More specific indices such as those contained in the Central Statistical Office's *Industrial Trends* may have greater relevance, though even here some imprecision may exist, as the measures tend to be expressed in terms of categories of goods/services.

Alternatively, an organisation may develop its own measures of inflation based on past experience and expectations about future changes in costs. In situations where costs are particularly volatile, it may be advisable to limit the scope of a detailed estimate to, say, the forthcoming month or quarter, rather than attempting to encompass a full year with a single estimated inflation rate.

Adjusting past costs for inflation

The key fact to bear in mind when adjusting past costs for inflation is that inflation is a *cumulative* phenomenon. Exhibit 3.7 gives some additional information about Northshires Ambulance Service's maintenance costs. However, before we can undertake any estimation exercise based on the data in Exhibit 3.7, we need to adjust the

---

Northshires Ambulance Service: cost of vehicle maintenance

The total maintenance costs of the ambulance fleet over the last six years along with the associated total mileage and annual inflation rates, have been as follows:

Year	Total maintenance cost (£)	Total mileage	Annual inflation rate (%)
19X2	410,000	3,600,000	4.5
19X3	570,000	5,100,000	5.0
19X4	360,000	3,100,000	4.0
19X5	460,000	3,900,000	3.5
19X6	530,000	4,700,000	3.0
19X7	610,000	5,600,000	3.0

From technical journals relating to the vehicles and medical equipment, management has estimated that an annual inflation rate of 2.5 per cent is appropriate for next year.

EXHIBIT 3.7 Impact of inflation on ambulance service's maintenance costs

costs for the effect of inflation, so that they are stated on a common basis. If we fail to do this, our resulting estimate will be distorted by the cumulative effect of inflation over time. In other words, part of the differences between the past costs we used for our earlier estimates is due to inflation, rather than to changes in the volume of activity, and it is the impact of this that we are seeking to neutralise.

It is possible to make such an adjustment in one of two ways: by *removing* the cumulative effect of inflation from all the past costs (known as **deflating**); or by *adding* the cumulative effect of inflation to all the past costs (i.e. **inflating** them). If we deflated the costs in Exhibit 3.7, we would effectively need to state each cost in terms of 19X2 price levels. Since the object of the exercise is to obtain an estimate for 19X8, this approach seems rather cumbersome, as we would then need to inflate the resulting estimate to 19X8 price levels. It is therefore much simpler to inflate all the past costs to 19X8 price levels, although, as we shall see in Chapter 13, deflation may be useful in the context of financial control.

To inflate the 19X2 maintenance cost in Exhibit 3.7 to 19X8 price levels, we need to increase it in line with cumulative inflation in 19X3, 19X4, 19X5, 19X6, 19X7 and also with the estimated inflation rate for 19X8:

$$(£410,000 \times 1.05 \times 1.04 \times 1.035 \times 1.03 \times 1.03 \times 1.025)$$
$$= £503,901 \text{ (rounded to the nearest whole £1)}$$

Note that the 19X2 cost is not adjusted for 19X2 inflation – this will already be included in the stated £410,000.

⇨ Working to the nearest whole £1, inflate the 19X3 maintenance cost from Exhibit 3.7 to 19X8 price levels.

The 19X3 cost will need to be uplifted to reflect cumulative inflation in 19X4, 19X5, 19X6, 19X7, and the estimated rate for 19X8:

$$(£570,000 \times 1.04 \times 1.035 \times 1.03 \times 1.03 \times 1.025)$$
$$= £667,186 \text{ (to the nearest whole £1)}$$

Applying similar adjustments to the other past costs in Exhibit 3.7 gives the full list of inflated past costs:

Year	Cost Inflated to 19X8 price levels (£)	Total mileage
19X2	503,901	3,600,000
19X3	667,186	5,100,000
19X4	405,174	3,100,000
19X5	500,214	3,900,000
19X6	559,548	4,700,000
19X7	625,250	5,600,000

It is worth noting that, despite the comparatively low rates of inflation quoted in Exhibit 3.7, their cumulative effect over a period of seven years is substantial, particularly on the earlier costs.

Now that inflationary discrepancies between past data have been removed, we can apply any of the quantitative estimation techniques described earlier to obtain our cost estimate for 19X8.

⇨ Apply high–low analysis to the inflated past costs given above to obtain an estimate of the variable maintenance cost per mile and the total annual fixed cost. State the variable cost per mile to the nearest £0.01.

The high and low mileages and associated total maintenance costs are:

	Total mileage	Total maintenance cost (£)
High volume	5,600,000	625,250
Low volume	3,100,000	405,174
Difference	2,500,000	220,076

The variable cost per mile is:

$$\frac{\text{Difference in total cost}}{\text{Difference in activity}} = \frac{£220,076}{2,500,000} = £0.09$$

Substituting into the high volume total cost:

	£
total cost	625,250
less variable element (5,600,000 @ £0.09)	504,000
fixed element	121,250

⇨ Use the results of the high–low analysis to provide an estimate of total maintenance cost for 19X8, when total mileage will be 5,000,000.

Using our inflation-adjusted high–low analysis, the 19X8 estimate will be:

	£
fixed element	121,250
variable element (5,000,000 miles @ £0.09)	450,000
total maintenance cost	571,250

Our original high–low estimate for 19X8, which was not adjusted for inflation, was £550,000 – an underestimate of roughly 4 per cent due solely to our failure to adjust the original data for inflation. This difference is an unnecessary inaccuracy, easily corrected, and which, if not remedied, strikes at the credibility of our cost estimate. In addition, had the applicable inflation rates been higher, and/or had the high and low volumes been further in the past, the difference between the adjusted and unadjusted estimates would have been greater.

However, inflating the cost figures in the way we have done poses one problem: the estimated inflation rate given for 19X8 relates to the *year* – so it could be argued that, by applying the full year's inflation of 2.5 per cent, we have overinflated our cost estimate. It will take a full year for all of the 2.5 per cent to feed through into costs and it is unlikely that the costs will all be incurred at the end of the year: that is, at a point in time when the full effect of annual inflation will have occurred. We might combat this by using a mid-year average value for inflation, but even here there may be some distortion in the estimate, depending on when costs are incurred during the year and on the evenness with which inflation occurs. In particularly volatile situations, estimates may be updated, for example on a monthly basis (see Chapter 12 for a description of rolling budgets), but additional accuracy may be gained at the expense of extra cost and effort involved in preparing estimates. However, compared to the potential distortion caused by ignoring inflation altogether, inaccuracy stemming from how we incorporate its effect is probably less significant and need not destroy the credibility of our estimates.

In Exhibit 3.7, the inflation rates were stated as percentages; such information may also be expressed in the form of *index numbers*. If, in Exhibit 3.7, 19X2 is taken as the *base year* (index number 100), and if inflation in 19X3 is 5 per cent, then the 19X3 inflation index is $(100 \times 1.05) = 105$. The 19X4 index will be:

$$100 \times (1.05 \times 1.04) = 109.2$$

indicating that, over the two years from the end of 19X2, cumulative inflation has been 9.2 per cent.

This approach is useful where factors such as inflation need to be expressed relative to a common basis, and could be of especial relevance to financial control and performance evaluation exercises, which we will discuss in Chapters 13, 14 and 15.

Summary

In this chapter, we have discussed techniques which may be used to estimate future costs. Cost estimation is vital to management accounting and its use is central to the subject matter in later chapters dealing with cost/volume/profit analysis, decision making, capital investment appraisal, budgeting, control and performance evaluation. Possibly the most important points that emerge from our discussion are, first, that the figures resulting from a cost estimation exercise are just that – estimates, and second, that these estimates are heavily influenced by the technique used to obtain them. This may be why a study by Drury *et al.* (1993) found that formal analytical techniques such as multiple regression analysis and learning curves were not widely employed, with, respectively, 35 per cent and 64 per cent of respondents 'never' using them; similarly, 59 per cent of respondents classified costs (into fixed/variable) on the basis of managerial judgement.

In this chapter, we have seen that:

■ **Engineering techniques** may be used, and may yield more accurate predictions than the other methods described below. These are, however, very specialised techniques.

■ Estimates may be derived from inspection of past accounting records. Although this is a simple approach, its success is heavily reliant on the judgement of the person inspecting the accounts.

■ A **scattergraph** plots a number of past costs against their related activity levels. The total cost line is placed on the graph by visual estimate, the point where this intersects the vertical axis being the estimated fixed cost. The estimated fixed cost can then be substituted into one of the past costs to obtain an estimate of variable cost. This is another simple method, but placement of the total cost line is subjective.

- **High–low analysis** uses only two past measures: the high and low volume activity levels, and associated total costs. Based on the difference between these two activity levels and total costs, the variable cost can be calculated as:

$$\frac{\text{difference in total cost}}{\text{difference in activity}}$$

the result being substituted into either the high volume or low volume total cost to obtain an estimate of fixed cost. Again, simple to use, but based on two activity levels at which cost behaviour may be different to that at more 'normal' levels.

- **Linear regression analysis** is a mathematical technique used to formulate the equation of the total cost line $y = a + bx$ from a number of past costs and activity levels, where: y is the total cost; a is the fixed cost; b is the variable cost per unit of activity; and x is the volume of activity. The values of a and b are derived from the following formulae:

$$b = \frac{n\Sigma xy - \Sigma x\Sigma y}{n\Sigma x^2 - (\Sigma x)^2} \text{ and } a = \frac{\Sigma y}{n} - \frac{b\Sigma x}{n}$$

- Linear regression analysis is more mathematically precise than account inspection, scattergraph and high–low analysis. Like the two latter methods, however, it assumes linear cost behaviour and its mathematical precision does not necessarily result in more accurate cost predictions.

- Implicit to most estimation techniques is an assumption that a single factor causes variability in cost, but such variability may be the result of several factors. It is possible to recognise this by using multiple regression analysis.

- The implications of the **relevant range** should be borne in mind when estimating costs.

- Where a **learning curve** applies, the average labour time per unit will reduce to a given percentage of its previous value at each successive doubling of cumulative output. This relationship can also be expressed formulaically as:

$$y = ax^b$$

where y is the average time per unit;
     a is the time required for the first unit;
     x is cumulative output;
     b is $\dfrac{\log \text{ learning rate}}{\log 2}$.

The learning rate is the rate of reduction in average time per unit with each successive doubling in output, and tends to fall between 60 per cent and 99 per cent.

- The effect of the learning curve on labour times and cost can be significant and should be allowed for. However, learning curve calculations may not be precise because:

- different individuals learn at different rates;
- output may not be continuous;
- labour may not control the pace of work;
- tasks may not be repetitive; and
- learning may not be the only factor affecting the speed of work.

■ The effect of inflation should be incorporated into cost estimates. The source of inflation statistics may be external (e.g. publications of the Central Statistical Office), or may be generated internally. In either case, care should be taken that the inflation figure to be applied is representative of an organisation's specific input costs.

■ Where past costs are the basis for an estimate of future cost, they should be inflated cumulatively so that they are stated in terms of the price level which will apply in the period to which the estimate relates.

In the next chapter, we shall discuss and illustrate absorption costing and you will note that, before much of the methodology to be described there can be applied, cost estimates must exist.

Further Reading

Daniel, W. and Terrell, J., *Business Statistics for Management and Economics*, 7th edn, Houghton Mifflin Co., 1995. Chapters 10 and 11 deal, respectively, with multiple regression analysis and the learning curve.

Drury, C., Braund, S., Osborne, P. and Tayles, M., *A Survey of Management Accounting Practices in UK Manufacturing Businesses*, ACCA, 1993.

Self-test Questions

3.1 A company's total overhead costs (adjusted for inflation) along with the associated output levels for the last four periods have been:

	Total overhead cost (£)	Output (units)
Period 1	156,000	19,000
Period 2	151,000	17,000
Period 3	140,000	15,000
Period 4	147,000	16,000

Using high–low analysis, what is the estimated variable cost per unit of output?

A £2.00
B £2.50
C £4.00
D £5.50

3.2 For each of the statements which follow, place a tick in the appropriate box to indicate whether it is true or false.

		True	False
(a)	In a linear regression analysis of past costs, the value calculated for *a* represents the variable cost per unit of activity.	☐	☐
(b)	An 80 per cent learning curve will result in larger successive reductions in the average time per unit than a 70 per cent learning curve.	☐	☐
(c)	High–low analysis assumes linear cost behaviour.	☐	☐
(d)	The scattergraph is more mathematically precise than regression analysis.	☐	☐
(e)	The Retail Price Index is a measure of general inflation.	☐	☐
(f)	Learning curve calculations assume that there are no significant breaks in activity.	☐	☐

3.3 LC Ltd is introducing a new product next year, and the first unit produced will require 140 hours of direct labour. It is estimated that an 80 per cent learning curve will apply to output of this product.

Determine the average direct labour hours per unit and the total direct labour hours if cumulative output in the first year will be 64 units (work to two decimal places).

3.4 A local college's total actual costs and applicable inflation rates over the last three years have been:

	Total cost (£)	Inflation rate (%)
19X6	4,000,000	3.5
19X5	3,400,000	4.7
19X4	3,200,000	5.9

The estimated inflation rate for 19X7 is 2.8 per cent.
Working to the nearest whole £1, inflate each of the three costs above to 19X7 price levels.

3.5 Figure 3.9 is a scattergraph prepared from previous periods' total selling costs and unit sales volumes. One of the total costs plotted in this figure is £660,000, with an associated unit sales volume of 200,000. Use this cost and activity information in conjunction with Figure 3.9 to provide an estimate of the variable selling cost per unit.

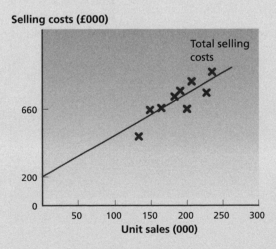

FIGURE 3.9
Scattergraph of total selling costs and unit sales volumes

QUESTIONS WITH ANSWERS

3.6 This question tests whether you can:

- obtain cost estimates using high–low and linear regression analysis;

- comment on the potential weakness of high–low analysis in a particular situation.

MJ Ltd, a light engineering company, is attempting to estimate next year's production costs using the following data from the last six years' operations as the basis:

Year	Total production cost (£) (adjusted for inflation)	Output (units)
19X3	520,000	400,000
19X4	250,000	200,000
19X5	710,000	600,000
19X6	680,000	520,000
19X7	1,850,000	1,800,000
19X8	600,000	440,000

Estimated output for 19X9 is 560,000 units.

Requirements

(a) Use high–low and linear regression analysis to obtain estimates of the fixed production cost per year and the variable production cost per unit of output.

(b) On the basis of each of your answers to (a), provide an estimate of the total production cost for 19X9. Comment on the results.

(c) The company's management accountant has stated that the past data supplied is particularly unsuitable for high–low analysis. Comment briefly on her reasoning and suggest how this problem might be overcome.

3.7 This question tests whether you can:

- inflate a series of past costs to the price level applicable in a future year;

- use high–low analysis to obtain a cost estimate;

- appreciate the impact of factors other than volume and inflation on cost behaviour.

Over the last five years, Weston Council's Computer Services Department has undertaken the following volumes of work and has incurred the following total costs:

Year	Total cost (£) (adjusted for inflation)	Processing time (hours)
19X3	38,146	133,000
19X4	48,170	150,000
19X5	32,000	120,000
19X6	54,138	163,000
19X7	63,680	170,000

The inflation rates which applied to the Computer Services Department's costs each year have been:

Year	Inflation rate (%)
19X3	8
19X4	7
19X5	5
19X6	6
19X7	4

Estimates for 19X8 are that 68,000 hours of processing time will be worked and that the applicable inflation rate will be 5 per cent.

In 19X8, the council intends to charge other departments for use of the Computer Services Department's time and facilities; this charge is to be based on:

- 1/10 of the computer Services Department's estimated annual fixed cost; *plus*

- a charge per hour of each department's usage based on the estimated variable cost per processing hour.

Requirements

(a) Inflate the costs for each of the years 19X3–19X7 to 19X8 price levels, working to the nearest whole £1.

(b) Using your inflation-adjusted costs from (a), perform a high–low analysis to provide an estimate for the Computer Services Department's fixed cost and variable cost per processing hour (to two decimal places) for 19X8.

(c) Based on your estimates in (b), calculate the Computer Services Department's estimated total cost for 19X8 and determine the charge to be made to each user department.

(d) State, and briefly discuss, *two* factors not included in your estimates which could have a bearing on the Computer Services Department's costs in 19X8.

3.8 This question tests whether you can:

- apply learning curve theory to determine average hours per unit and total hours required for a particular volume;

- calculate the total cost of a quotation incorporating the effect of the learning curve;

- appreciate the possible limitation of learning curve theory in a given situation.

De Luxe Caravans Ltd is preparing a quotation for manufacture and supply of 32 six-berth static caravans. These will be assembled from prefabricated parts bought specially and fitted with the company's own interior furnishings. The work will be highly labour intensive. Estimated costs and other data relevant to the quotation are given below:

Prefabricated parts, chassis, wheels, etc.	£1,600 per caravan
Direct labour hours:	
– tradesmen	60 hours for the first caravan
– unskilled	30 hours for the first caravan
Direct labour rate:	
– tradesmen	£8 per hour
– unskilled	£4 per hour
Direct labour-related costs	25% of total direct labour cost
Sundry other costs	£500 per caravan

It is estimated that 75 per cent and 90 per cent learning curves will apply to the work of tradesmen and unskilled workers respectively.

Requirements

(a) Determine the average hours per caravan (correct to two decimal places of one hour) and the total hours required for cumulative output of 32 caravans (correct to the nearest whole hour) for tradesmen and unskilled workers.

(b) Calculate the total cost to De Luxe Caravans Ltd of producing 32 static caravans.

(c) The prospective client on whose behalf the quotation is being prepared has suggested that 16 of the caravans be supplied for the forthcoming holiday season, with the remainder being supplied in the following year. Comment on the possible implication of this suggestion for the learning curve calculations in (a) above, and suggest how any resulting problem could be addressed in the computations.

QUESTIONS WITHOUT ANSWERS

3.9 TL & Co produces an executive laptop computer. As part of next year's budget preparation process, an estimate of production overhead costs is required. Relevant data for the last four years are as follows:

Year	Total production overhead cost (£) (adjusted for inflation)	Output (units)
19X5	1,200,000	38,000
19X6	1,400,000	40,000
19X7	1,100,000	36,000
19X8	1,700,000	60,000

It is estimated that, in 19X9, production will be 50,000 units.

Requirements

(a) Use linear regression analysis to produce an estimate of the firm's fixed production overhead and variable production overhead per unit.

(b) Using your answer to (a), provide an estimate of total production overhead for 19X9.

(c)   TL & Co's General Manager has suggested that the accuracy of the cost estimates would be improved if the past ten years' data were incorporated; the Production Manager has countered this with a claim that the nature of the firm's product, market and production processes renders extensive use of past data for estimation purposes questionable.

Discuss the validity of each of these points of view.

3.10 A council's Housing Department is attempting to determine the number of clerical staff required to process claims from tenants for rent rebates. As the result of a reorganisation of local government, both the council and its Housing Department have been newly created, and, although staff who will process the claims may have some experience of similar work, the paperwork and procedures involved are likewise new.

The first claim processed will require 20 hours of clerical work and, in the forthcoming year, it is anticipated that 2,500 claims will be processed. The council's Technical Services Department believes that a 95 per cent learning curve will apply. Each clerk employed in the Housing Department's rebates section works for 36 hours per week, and there are 48 working weeks in a year.

Requirements

(a)   Apply the learning curve formula to the clerical hours per claim and determine the average time required per claim if the cumulative number of claims processed in the year is 2,500.

(b)   How many clerical workers must be employed in order to process 2,500 claims?

(c)   Because of their newness, claims procedures will be subject to evaluation after six months of the forthcoming year and there is every likelihood that they will be significantly amended as a result. Comment on the possible implication of this with regard to the learning curve.

(d)   State, and explain briefly, any reservations you may have about the application of learning curve theory to this type of work.

CHAPTER 4

Absorption of overheads

GLENMORANGIE CHANGES THE BLEND

Glenmorangie has also simplified production. Catering for multiple export markets had caused a proliferation of materials, peaking at nine whisky blends, 41 bottles, 27 closures, 40 packages, 73 labels and 74 shipping cases. Virtually all have been halved.

Manufacturing overhead has been cut from well over £4 a case to less than £3 and should get close to £2, the industry benchmark, in the new plant . . .

Source: Roderick Oram, *Financial Times*, 15 May 1996.

KWIK SAVE REVIEW FOLLOWS 28 PER CENT FALL

Kwik Save, the UK's biggest discount grocer, announced a strategic review yesterday as interim profits fell 28 per cent . . . Kwik Save's overhead costs rose 19 per cent from £169.5m to £201.6m.

Source: David Blackwell, *Financial Times*, 3 May 1996.

Exhibit **4.1 Overhead costs**

INTRODUCTION

When we discussed cost classification in Chapter 2, we made the distinction between costs which are unambiguously and quantifiably attributable to individual cost objectives (**direct costs**) and costs which are common to two or more cost objectives (**overheads**). However, in some circumstances, it may be necessary or desirable to treat overheads 'as if' they were direct relative to units of output. Procedures for determining costs such as the manufacturing overhead per case of whisky referred to in Exhibit 4.1 – **overhead absorption** (alternatively, overhead *recovery* or *application*) – form the subject-matter of this chapter.

The second quotation in Exhibit 4.1 indicates just how significant an expenditure overhead can be. The proportion of overhead to total cost has been (and is likely to continue) increasing for most organisations. One of the principal causes of this is the ongoing shift from labour-intensive to technology-intensive operations. So treatment of overhead relative to cost units merits careful consideration.

Because overheads are indirect costs, their absorption involves a more complex methodology than that used for attribution of direct costs. Overhead absorption may follow the 'traditional' route or may employ a more recent (arguably more sophisticated) technique – activity-based costing (ABC). Initially, we shall describe these two views of overhead absorption separately before considering the extent to which they may be similar and discussing whether either can be seen as 'superior'.

Regardless of whether a 'traditional' or ABC approach is adopted, we can view the process of overhead absorption as consisting of a series of cost attributions, each moving nearer to the ultimate cost objective – the cost unit. We should also stress that, irrespective of the methodology, overhead absorption will always be subject to a certain element of imprecision – the best we can hope for is that our absorption procedures offer a workable solution which minimises the incidence of such imprecision.

OBJECTIVES When you have completed this chapter, you will be able to:

- explain the rationale underlying absorption of overheads;

- distinguish between allocation and apportionment of overheads;

- develop and apply apportionment and reapportionment bases;

- appreciate the potential subjectivity inherent in the apportionment exercise;

- distinguish between production ('front-line') and service ('support') cost centres and understand the need for secondary distribution of service cost centres' overheads to production cost centres;

- develop overhead absorption rates using different bases and apply them to cost units;

- understand the relative merits of blanket, departmental, actual and predetermined absorption rates;

■ appreciate the significance of normal volume, practical capacity and annual budgeted volume to calculation of absorption rates;

■ explain the meaning of over- and underabsorption and calculate their amount in given circumstances;

■ define the terms activity, overhead cost pool and cost driver;

■ apply the concepts of activity-based costing (ABC) to an overhead absorption scenario; and

■ compare and contrast ABC and 'traditional' systems of overhead absorption.

RATIONALE FOR ABSORPTION OF OVERHEADS

If, as we have said, overheads are not directly attributable to cost units, why is it necessary to undertake the sort of attribution exercise which we will describe below?

Success Direct Ltd

This company operates a correspondence school offering a range of courses in bookkeeping and secretarial skills; included in the company's overheads are lighting, heating and insurance costs.

EXHIBIT **4.2** Correspondence school's overheads

⇨ In Exhibit 4.2, why can it be argued that the cost of each correspondence course provided should include a charge in respect of the overhead costs mentioned?

We can take the view that overhead costs such as those mentioned in Exhibit 4.2 are necessarily incurred because of the company's output (i.e. provision of correspondence courses). If we accept this view, then it is a short step to the conclusion that each unit produced should receive a charge for overheads in addition to its direct costs.

Organisations may absorb overhead to determine a 'full' cost per unit. This could, for example, be important if the selling price is to be based on cost. Omission of some or all overheads from unit costs may result in underpricing and consequent failure to cover *all* costs – a situation which might have serious implications for the organisation if it is allowed to continue for any length of time. Inclusion of overheads in unit costs for purposes such as price setting could be viewed as an attempt to approximate the long-run average cost of output since, in the long run, all costs must be covered to ensure continued profitability and even survival. But you should note that cost is not the only consideration in setting selling prices: as we shall see in Chapter 8, factors like the need for speedy market penetration may relegate cost to a secondary position. In addition, even where cost is highly significant (e.g. for planning and control purposes), overhead absorption may yield unit costs which are inappropriate, and could result in incorrect financial analysis of a particular situation – a potential weakness which we shall examine in later chapters. For the moment, we will confine our discussion of overhead absorption to determination of unit costs.

Another reason for absorbing overheads (at least in the United Kingdom) is given in Statement of Standard Accounting Practice No. 9 (Stocks and Long Term Contracts): '"costs" of stocks should comprise that expenditure which has been incurred in the normal course of business in bringing the product or service to its present location and condition. Such costs will include all related production overheads . . .' In effect, this means that all accounts subject to the provisions of the standard – principally the *published* accounts of limited companies – are required to employ absorption costing for stock valuation, and hence profit-reporting, purposes. We shall examine the precise implications for profit of inclusion or non-inclusion of overheads in stock values in the next chapter.

ABSORPTION COSTING: 'TRADITIONAL' METHODOLOGY

Overview of methodology

Figure 4.1 summarises the procedures which we are about to describe.

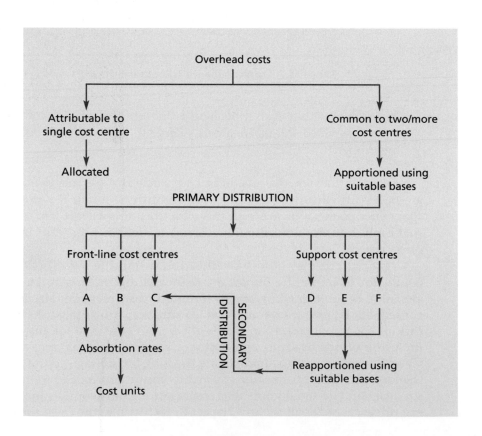

FIGURE **4.1** Overhead absorption: 'traditional' methodology

Primary distribution of overhead

The first step in overhead absorption is to *allocate* and *apportion* overheads to **cost centres**, which are typically (but not invariably)' organisational departments. Exhibit 4.3 provides further cost and other data relating to Success Direct Ltd.

Success Direct Ltd

The company is organised into four departments which are also designated cost centres: Bookkeeping Courses, Secretarial Courses, Reprographic Services and Dispatch. Estimated overhead costs and other data for next year are as follows:

Overhead costs
Supervisory salaries:

Bookkeeping courses	£25,000
Secretarial courses	£28,000
Reprographic services	£30,000
Dispatch	£20,000

Indirect labour costs:

Bookkeeping courses	£40,000	Computer consumables	£14,000
Secretarial courses	£50,000	Insurance	£ 8,000
Reprographic services	£24,000	Stationery	£60,000
Dispatch	£45,000	Property costs	£36,000
Lighting and heating	£ 6,000	Phone/fax/e-mail	£48,000

Other Data	*Bookkeeping*	*Secretarial*	*Reprographic*	*Dispatch*	*Total*
Computer hours	60,000	100,000	10,000	30,000	200,000
Floor area (metres^2)	8,000	9,000	2,000	1,000	20,000
Book value of assets insured	£50,000	£40,000	£100,000	£10,000	£200,000
No. of telephone extensions	20	25	1	4	50
No. of stationery requisitions	40	60	380	20	500

EXHIBIT **4.3 Correspondence school: overhead costs and other data**

⇨ Of the overhead costs listed in Exhibit 4.3, which can be related to a specific cost centre and which relate to two or more?

From Exhibit 4.3, only supervisory salaries and indirect labour costs can be unambiguously associated with a single cost centre; all the other overheads are common to two or more. Overheads which relate to a single cost centre can be **allocated** to that cost centre. Common costs, however, require to be **apportioned** (i.e. shared) between the cost centres concerned. In order to undertake this apportionment, we need to develop an **apportionment basis** suitable to each common overhead cost.

As a general 'rule of thumb', apportionment bases should derive from the underlying cause of the cost concerned, termed the **cost driver**. In addition to reflecting the cost driver, apportionment bases:

1 should be readily quantifiable; and
2 should meet the cost/benefit criterion.

What this may mean in practice is that, even where the true underlying cause of an overhead cost can be identified and precisely quantified, its use as an apportionment basis may be prohibitively expensive. For example, it may be possible to meter calls from individual telephone extensions, which should reduce (or possibly eliminate) the need to apportion phone/fax/e-mail costs. However, the cost of purchasing and installing a sufficiently sophisticated telephone system may be disproportionately high relative to the benefit of a more precise absorption of overheads.

This, of course, assumes that the cost driver is identifiable and quantifiable. Consider the cost of business rates on an organisation's premises: it is a simple matter to identify the underlying cause of this overhead (the premises' rateable value) and to quantify its incidence (£x of rates paid per £1 of rateable value), but how do we use this information to apportion the rates cost to individual cost centres within the premises? In such cases, where it is not practicable, or cost effective, to employ the cost driver as an apportionment basis, we need to use a *proxy* measure, having regard to the nature of the cost and the information which is available or readily obtainable.

⇨ From the information available in Exhibit 4.3, what is the most appropriate apportionment basis to use for Success Direct Ltd's property costs?

Given the nature of the cost (related to occupancy of premises) and the available information, floor area would be the most appropriate apportionment basis. Having selected the apportionment basis, it is now a straightforward matter to split the total property cost according to each department's share of the total floor area:

		%
Bookkeeping	8,000 metres^2	40
Secretarial	9,000 metres^2	45
Reprographic	2,000 metres^2	10
Dispatch	1,000 metres^2	5
	20,000	100

Applying these percentages to the property cost of £36,000 in Exhibit 4.3 provides the required apportionment:

	£
Bookkeeping	14,400
Reprographic	3,600
Secretarial	16,200
Dispatch	1,800

The full allocations and apportionments to cost centres can be shown on an **overhead analysis sheet** (see Table 4.1). Although this sort of tabulation is cumbersome to prepare manually, use of a computer spreadsheet can greatly reduce the time and effort involved.

TABLE 4.1 Partially completed overhead analysis sheet for Success Direct Ltd

Overhead cost	Amount £	Apportionment basis	Percentages	Bookkeeping £	Secretarial £	Reprographic £	Dispatch £
Supervisory salaries	103,000	Allocated	Not applicable	25,000	28,000	30,000	20,000
Indirect labour	159,000	Allocated	Not applicable	40,000	50,000	24,000	45,000
Lighting and heating	6,000	Floor area					
Computer consumables	14,000						
Insurance	8,000	Book value of assets insured					
Stationery	60,000						
Property costs	36,000	Floor area	40%, 45%, 10%, 5%	14,400	16,200	3,600	1,800
Phone/fax/ e-mail	48,000						
Totals	434,000						

⮕ Bearing in mind the nature of each cost involved and the information available in Exhibit 4.3, complete the apportionments in Table 4.1 and determine the total overhead for each department.

Table 4.2 is the completed overhead analysis sheet showing the allocations and apportionments of overhead costs to each of Success Direct Ltd's four departments. The apportionment bases employed in Table 4.2 are all subjective to some extent, so it is important that they are at least defensible in terms of the nature of the cost which is being apportioned and of the cost/benefit criterion. Take Success Direct's phone/fax/e-mail cost: this is linked to usage of the telephone line(s) and, in the absence of more detailed information, it seems reasonable to use the number of extensions as an apportionment basis – the greater the number of a cost centre's telephone extensions, the greater is likely to be that cost centre's usage of phone, fax and e-mail facilities. Heating and lighting relates to occupancy of premises, and, although volume (rather than area) might be more accurate, area is at least an acceptable approximation of the cause of this cost.

TABLE **4.2 Completed overhead analysis sheet for Success Direct Ltd**

Overhead cost	Amount £	Apportionment basis	Percentages	Bookkeeping £	Secretarial £	Reprographic £	Dispatch £
Supervisory salaries	103,000	Allocated	Not applicable	25,000	28,000	30,000	20,000
Indirect labour	159,000	Allocated	Not applicable	40,000	50,000	24,000	45,000
Lighting and heating	6,000	Floor area	40%, 45%, 10%, 5%	2,400	2,700	600	300
Computer consumables	14,000	Computer hours	30%, 50%, 5%, 15%	4,200	7,000	700	2,100
Insurance	8,000	Book value of assets insured	25%, 20%, 50%, 5%	2,000	1,600	4,000	400
Stationery	60,000	No of stationery requisitions	8%, 12%, 76%, 4%	4,800	7,200	45,600	2,400
Property costs	36,000	Floor area	40%, 45%, 10%, 5%	14,400	16,200	3,600	1,800
Phone/fax/ e-mail	48,000	No of telephone extensions	40%, 50%, 2%, 8%	19,200	24,000	960	3,840
Totals	434,000			112,000	136,700	109,460	75,840

Secondary distribution

Table 4.2 completed the first stage in the 'traditional' overhead absorption process, but we are not yet in a position to calculate an overhead cost per unit of output.

⇨ Why would the departmental overhead totals in Table 4.2 provide an unsuitable basis for determination of an overhead cost per unit of output?

Two of the departments in Table 4.2 – Reprographic and Dispatch – provide internal *support services*. A distinction must be made between *front-line cost centres* and *support cost centres*: in a manufacturing organisation, we might term these, respectively, 'production' and 'service' cost centres.

Since it is only front-line cost centres which deal with cost units (i.e. units of output) – the ultimate target of our absorption procedures – we need a mechanism for sharing support cost centres' overhead between front-line cost centres (Bookkeeping and Secretarial in Success Direct Ltd's case). A **secondary distribution** is required, whereby support cost centres' overheads are *re*apportioned to front-line cost centres.

Alternative approaches to secondary distribution for Success Direct Ltd's two support cost centres are illustrated in Appendix A.

The overhead absorption rate

The **overhead absorption rate** (also termed '**recovery**' or '**application**' rate) is the detailed means whereby the departmental overhead for production/front-line cost centres is translated into a cost per unit of output. In general terms, an absorption rate can be defined as:

$$\frac{\text{overhead cost}}{\text{volume measure}}$$

There are three important considerations in developing an absorption rate:

1 choice of volume measure;
2 choice between a plantwide or a departmental absorption rate; and
3 choice between an actual or a predetermined absorption rate.

Choice of volume measure

The most appropriate measure of volume depends on the precise circumstances. In particular, it depends on the nature of the output (e.g. Are all cost units identical?) and on the nature of the processes by which this output is produced (e.g. What mix of labour and machine?). In the same way as we did with apportionment/reapportionment bases, we are trying, in the overhead absorption rate, to reflect the underlying cause of the overheads being absorbed.

Exhibit 4.4 contains some further information about Success Direct Ltd.

At its most basic, 'volume' may be defined in terms of the number of cost units produced:

$$\text{cost unit absorption rate} = \frac{\text{overhead cost}}{\text{number of cost units}}$$

Applying this to Success Direct Ltd's Bookkeeping cost centre gives:

$$\frac{£170,710}{4,000 \text{ courses}} = £42.6775 \text{ per course (say, £42.68)}$$

⇨ Using the data from Exhibit 4.4, calculate a cost unit absorption rate for the Secretarial cost centre.

For the Secretarial cost centre, we get:

$$\frac{£263,290}{5,000 \text{ courses}} = £52.658 \text{ per course (say, £52.66)}$$

Success Direct Ltd

Estimated overhead costs and other information for the company's two front-line cost centres is as follows:

	Bookkeeping	Secretarial	Total
Estimated departmental overhead after primary and secondary distribution	£170,710	£263,290	£434,000
Estimated computer hours	60,000	100,000	160,000
Estimated tutor (direct labour) hours	15,000	19,000	34,000
Estimated tutor salary (direct labour) cost	£178,000	£234,000	£412,000
Number of different courses offered	10	16	26
Estimated total number of courses offered (i.e. cost units)	4,000	5,000	9,000

Estimated data per student for two specific courses are given below:

	Introduction to spreadsheets	Advanced shorthand
Estimated computer hours:		
Bookkeeping	195	nil
Secretarial	5	nil
Estimated tutor (direct labour) hours:		
Bookkeeping	10	nil
Secretarial	1	30
Estimated tutor (direct labour) cost:		
Bookkeeping	£120	nil
Secretarial	£12	£360
Estimated direct material cost	£50	£30

EXHIBIT **4.4** Correspondence school: information for absorption rate calculation

Therefore, every course which involves the Bookkeeping cost centre will receive a charge of £42.68 for departmental overheads *in addition* to its direct costs (£52.66 for every course which involves the Secretarial cost centre):

	Introduction to Spreadsheets	Advanced Shorthand
Direct labour (from Exhibit 4.4):		
Bookkeeping	£120.00	nil
Secretarial	£ 12.00	£360.00
Direct material (from Exhibit 4.4)	£ 50.00	£ 30.00
Prime cost	£182.00	£390.00
Overhead (calculated above):		
Bookkeeping	£ 42.68	£ 42.68
Secretarial	£ 52.66	£ 52.66
Cost per course	£277.34	£485.34

➪ Study the data in Exhibit 4.4 again along with the cost per course shown above. How appropriate is a cost unit absorption rate for Success Direct Ltd?

As we have just seen, a cost unit absorption rate will charge each cost unit the same amount in respect of overhead, so both of the course costs above are charged £52.66 and £42.68 in respect of Secretarial and Bookkeeping overhead. The implication of this is that both courses are identical in terms of resource inputs, since they each receive the same charge for overhead. However, examination of the data in Exhibit 4.4 reveals that this is not the case. Using a unit absorption rate in such circumstances may result in a significant distortion of unit costs, particularly where there are major differences in resource inputs between units. A cost unit absorption rate is therefore only appropriate where the units concerned are identical, or very nearly so.

Alternatively, the activity measure used may be machine hours (computer hours in Success Direct Ltd's case):

$$\text{machine hour absorption rate} = \frac{\text{overhead cost}}{\text{number of machine hours}}$$

Using the data for Success Direct Ltd's Bookkeeping cost centre:

$$\frac{£170,710}{60,000 \text{ computer hours}} = £2.85 \text{ per computer hour}$$

▷ Apply the formula above to the data in Exhibit 4.4 and determine an absorption rate per computer hour for the Secretarial cost centre (work to two decimal places of £1).

For Secretarial, we have:

$$\frac{£263,290}{100,000 \text{ computer hours}} = £2.63 \text{ per computer hour}$$

Thus, every course involving the Secretarial cost centre will receive, in addition to its direct costs, a charge of £2.63 for each computer hour it requires in that department (£2.85 for each computer hour in Bookkeeping):

	Introduction to Spreadsheets	Advanced Shorthand
Direct labour (from Exhibit 4.4):		
Bookkeeping	£120.00	nil
Secretarial	£ 12.00	£360.00
Direct material (from Exhibit 4.4)	£ 50.00	£ 30.00
Prime cost	£182.00	£390.00
Overhead:		
Bookkeeping		
(195/nil computer hours @ £2.85)	£555.75	nil
Secretarial		
(5/nil computer hours @ £2.63	£ 13.15	£ nil
Cost per course	£750.90	£390.00

Use of a machine hour absorption rate overcomes the problem of the unit rate discussed above since it can reflect differences in input resources via the overhead charged to cost units. This is important to organisations such as Success Direct Ltd, where outputs are not uniform.

⇨ Re-examine Exhibit 4.4 along with the cost per course shown above. Why could a machine hour absorption rate be inappropriate for use by Success Direct Ltd?

Use of a machine hour absorption rate assumes that the number of machine hours is the most appropriate measure of activity: that is, that the output process is predominantly machine-intensive (so that the overhead cost being absorbed is principally incurred in relation to machine operations). Whilst this may be true of Success Direct's 'Introduction to spreadsheets' course, it is untrue of the 'Advanced shorthand' course. Examination of Exhibit 4.4 shows that this course requires no computer hours, which means that, using a machine hour absorption rate, it will receive no charge for overhead. But this is unrealistic: some Reprographic and Dispatch work will relate to provision of this course and should be reflected in its cost.

If a front-line cost centre's activity is mostly labour-intensive, the overhead absorption rate may use either direct labour hours or direct labour cost as the measure of activity:

$$\text{direct labour hour absorption rate} = \frac{\text{overhead cost}}{\text{number if direct labour hours}}$$

$$\text{direct labour cost absorption rate} = \frac{\text{overhead cost}}{\text{direct labour cost}} \times 100\%$$

⇨ Use the formulae given above in conjunction with Exhibit 4.4 to determine, for the Secretarial cost centre: (a) an absorption rate per direct labour hour; and (b) a percentage of direct labour cost absorption rate (work to two decimal places).

The two labour-based absorption rates for the Secretarial cost centre are:

$$\text{per direct labour hour: } \frac{£263,290}{19,000 \text{ tutor hours}} = £13.86 \text{ per tutor hour}$$

$$\text{as percentage of direct labour cost: } \frac{£263,290}{£234,000} \times 100\% = 112.52\%$$

⇨ Use the direct labour and direct materials' costs given in Exhibit 4.4, calculate a cost per course for *Advanced Shorthand* using:
(a) the direct labour hour absorption rate above, and
(b) the direct labour cost percentage absorption rate above.

The cost per *Advanced Shorthand* course based on the direct labour hour absorption rate is:

Prime cost (as before)	£390.00
Overhead (30 hours @ £13.86)	£415.80
Cost per course	£805.80

Applying the direct labour cost percentage rate gives a cost per course of:

Prime cost (as before)	£390.00
Overhead (£360 × 112.52%)	£405.07
Cost per course	£795.07

Had we calculated these labour-based absorption rates for the Bookkeeping cost centre, we would also have had two additional versions of the cost per course for *Introduction to Spreadsheets*.

In choosing between the two labour-based absorption rates, we must be guided in the first instance by the nature of the overhead costs which we are trying to absorb. If overhead is predominantly related to the number of labour hours (as supervision may be), then a labour hour absorption is appropriate. If, however, overhead mainly relates to direct labour cost (as in the UK, would employers' National Insurance contributions), then the labour cost percentage rate is suitable. Where such relationships cannot be established with reasonable assurance, then choice of absorption rate may be of less significance in terms of the accuracy with which it reflects resource consumption.

It is also possible to base the overhead absorption rate on direct materials' cost or on prime cost (i.e. the sum of all direct costs):

$$\text{percentage of direct materials' cost} = \frac{\text{overhead cost}}{\text{direct materials' cost}} \times 100\%$$

$$\text{percentage of prime cost} = \frac{\text{overhead cost}}{\text{prime cost}} \times 100\%$$

The problem with using both of these rates is that situations in which direct materials' *cost* or prime *cost* is the underlying cause of overheads being incurred are somewhat hard to imagine. What our discussion and calculations above should highlight is the importance of selecting a volume measure which is appropriate to the particular circumstances. An error in this respect may have serious consequences for unit costs, for stock values and for profit. Consider two possible overhead charges to the 'advanced shorthand' course.

1 £52.66 per course using a cost unit absorption rate; and
2 £415.80 per course using a direct labour hour absorption rate.

The profit reported from this course will be markedly affected by the rate used, as may its selling price (if this is based to any extent on cost).

Departmental v plantwide absorption rate

Our discussion of absorption rates has thus far been based on the use of departmental rates: that is, a separate absorption rate for each production/front-line cost centre. It is, however, possible to use a *plantwide* (or '*blanket*') absorption rate using a single overhead cost and activity measure for the whole organisation (or organisation subunit, such as an individual factory). Exhibit 4.5 summarises certain key data relating to Success Direct Ltd.

Success Direct Ltd: summary of key data	
Estimated total overhead cost	£434,000
Estimated total computer hours	
(Bookkeeping + Secretarial):	160,000
Estimated total direct labour hours	
(Bookkeeping + Secretarial)	34,000

EXHIBIT 4.5 Correspondence school: blanket data

⇨ Use the summary data in Exhibit 4.5 to calculate plantwide absorption rates based on (a) machine hours; and (b) direct labour hours.

The plantwide absorption rates are:

$$\text{machine hour rate: } \frac{£434,000}{160,000} = £2.71 \text{ per computer hour}$$

$$\text{direct labour hour rate: } \frac{£434,000}{34,000} = £12.76 \text{ per tutor hour}$$

The advantage of using plantwide absorption rates lies in their simplicity of calculation. All we need do is determine the total overhead cost and divide by an appropriate volume measure in total for the front-line cost centres. Because we do not need departmental figures, there is no necessity for primary and secondary distributions, which undoubtedly represents a considerable saving in time and effort, and possibly an improvement in the 'objectivity' of the absorption rate, since potentially arbitrary apportionment/reapportionment bases are not involved.

⇨ Can you suggest why a plantwide absorption rate may be unsuitable for a company such as Success Direct Ltd?

The weakness of a plantwide absorption rate is also related to its simplicity. We suggested earlier that Success Direct's outputs are not uniform, and this is true in terms of both the pattern and extent of their resource consumption. Added to this is the possibility that output procedures may differ from cost centre to cost centre: for example, they may be labour-intensive in one and machine-intensive in another. How can we adequately reflect such differences in a single absorption rate?

⇨ Use the plantwide machine hour absorption rate we have just calculated and the information in Exhibit 4.4 to compute the overhead charge to the 'advanced shorthand' course.

Using a plantwide machine hour rate, the 'advanced shorthand' course will receive a zero charge for overhead, since the job does not use any computer hours. Yet is it realistic to suggest that provision of this course incurs no overheads?

A plantwide absorption rate is only really workable where there is considerable uniformity of output method and of output. In any other circumstances, departmental absorption rates are preferable, since these will enable differences between cost centre output procedures and between outputs to be better reflected in the overhead absorbed.

Actual v predetermined absorption rate

All of our absorption rate calculations have used estimates, – of overhead costs and of volume measure: that is, they are **predetermined absorption rates**. Absorption rates which use actual overhead costs and volume measures are also possible, but could suffer from two very serious limitations:

1 actual costs and volume may not be known until the end of the relevant period; and
2 actual costs and volume may fluctuate within a particular period.

The extent to which these limitations render actual absorption rates impractical will depend on specific circumstances. If there are unlikely to be significant differences between estimated and actual costs and volume (e.g. because they are largely fixed by contract) and if costs/output occur reasonably evenly throughout the period, then an actual absorption rate is possible.

Where an organisation's situation is more volatile (involving, say a seasonal pattern of output and cost levels), then use of an actual absorption rate may be inadvisable or impractical. For example, it will not be possible to produce meaningful forecasts of the profit to be reported in published accounts (bearing in mind that absorption costing is required for the published accounts of many organisations); selling prices which use cost as their basis effectively cannot be set in advance, which could cause difficulties for companies such as Success Direct Ltd in preparing tariffs for courses offered; unit costs, stock values, profit and perhaps selling prices may fluctuate from month to month within a year merely because of the time of year at which unit costs are calculated. In practical terms, therefore, use of predetermined absorption rates may be a necessity, but gives rise to problems of its own.

Estimation of overhead costs

We examined the topic of cost estimation at length in the last chapter and you will recall from our discussion that it is far from straightforward. In the case of overhead, the position may be complicated by the fact that 'overhead' is a generic term, describing the sum of a number of different indirect costs. Thus it may be necessary to undertake several estimation exercises for the component elements of a 'global' overhead estimate.

Estimation of volume

The denominator in our overhead absorption rate must also be estimated: that is, we need an estimate of the number of units to be produced, or of machine hours to be worked. The volume measure selected for the absorption rate calculation can have a major effect on the overhead cost per unit of output, and hence on unit costs. This will be particularly true in organisations with predominantly fixed overheads.

➪ Why might the selection of a volume measure be of especial significance to absorption of fixed overheads?

The significance lies in the fact that the cost being absorbed is fixed relative to volume of output: for example, estimated fixed overhead of £500,000 absorbed over a volume of 10,000 units yields £50 per unit, whereas the same amount of fixed overhead absorbed over 15,000 units results in a charge of £33.33 per unit. And if, say, the volume is wrongly set at 10,000 units rather than at 15,000, the result will be a unit cost that is overstated by £16.67, which in turn may mean overstated stock values and possibly selling price (and this latter may have an effect on demand).

Note, however, that this problem does not affect variable overhead, since, by definition, the amount of variable overhead will react to changes in volume.

Three broad views of activity level can be taken.

Normal volume This is a medium-term average volume, allowing for demand over, say, a five-year period and for seasonal and cyclical fluctuations, and is the measure which is recommended for use in Statement of Standard Accounting Practice No. 9, which deals with the question of stock valuation in published accounts. The argument in favour of using normal volume is that fluctuations in absorption rate caused by seasonal and cyclical factors are smoothed out, and that, by attempting to approximate longer-term costs in this way, there may be less danger of overemphasising short-term considerations at the expense of the longer-term view.

➪ Can you see a possible problem with use of normal volume?

The difficulty with using normal volume lies in arriving at a credible estimate spanning the sort of time horizon involved – a problem which may be exacerbated if an organisation's activities are subject to significant cyclical fluctuations.

Practical capacity Practical capacity is effectively maximum operational capacity. It can be argued that, given the drive for optimum efficiency which exists in almost all organisations, practical capacity provides a reasonable measure of volume. It is also suggested that the underabsorption of overhead which will result from use of practical capacity provides management with some measure of the 'cost' of failing to achieve maximum operational capacity. (We shall discuss over- and underabsorption of overhead shortly.) However, because it is based on maximum volume, practical capacity will yield a lower overhead cost per unit than other volume measures and this may result in understatement of unit costs. In addition, assuming maximum capacity may have behavioural implications – may be viewed, for instance, as unachievable and therefore not worth striving for. We shall discuss this sort of behavioural implication in Chapter 16.

Annual budgeted volume This is the expected activity level during the forthcoming year, upon which the organisation's annual budget is based. Unlike normal volume and practical capacity, it reflects current operating conditions and this is the main argument put forward in favour of its use. However, being an annual estimate, it will be subject to cyclical fluctuations from year to year and may fail to reflect the 'cost' of failure to achieve maximum capacity.

Estimation – of both costs and volume – is therefore of crucial importance to determination of an overhead absorption rate, but this leads to the final problem associated with predetermined absorption rates: over- and underabsorption of overhead.

Overabsorption and underabsorption of overhead

It is extremely unlikely that estimates of overhead cost or of volume will be wholly accurate predictions of what actually happens.

⇨ If an organisation uses a predetermined absorption rate to charge overheads to cost units, what will be the result if actual overhead and/or volume differ from the estimates used for the absorption rate?

Where the estimates used in producing an absorption rate differ from actual costs and/or volume, the result will be that the overhead absorbed by cost units will differ from the actual amount of overhead incurred:

- If the overhead absorbed *exceeds* the actual overhead, an **overabsorption** of overhead has occurred.
- If the overhead absorbed is *less than* the actual overhead, an **underabsorption** of overhead has occurred.

In either case, the overhead charged to cost units differs from the actual amount, so a correcting adjustment is required in the accounts.

Exhibit 4.6 provides additional information about Success Direct Ltd. In order to determine whether Success Direct Ltd has overabsorbed or underabsorbed, we need to compute the total amount of overhead absorbed (based on *actual* volume) and compare this to the overhead incurred.

> **Success Direct Ltd**
>
> During the year under consideration, the company has used predetermined departmental absorption rates as follows:
>
> Bookkeeping: £11.38 per tutor hour
> Secretarial: £13.86 per tutor hour
>
> At the end of the year, actual results were discovered to be:
>
> | | |
> |---|---|
> | Total overhead incurred | £440,000 |
> | Bookkeeping: actual tutor hours worked | 14,000 |
> | Secretarial: actual tutor hours worked | 22,000 |

EXHIBIT **4.6** Correspondence school: determination of over/underabsorption of overhead

⇨ From Exhibit 4.6, determine the amount of overhead absorbed by each department and in total for the company; compare this to the actual overhead and state the amount of overabsorbed or underabsorbed overhead.

The amount of overhead absorbed in each department is calculated as (actual tutor hours × departmental absorption rate), giving the following total:

	£
Bookkeeping (14,400 hours × £11.38)	163,872
Secretarial (22,000 hours × £13.86)	304,920
Total	468,792

Actual overhead was £440,000, so we have an overabsorption of (£468,792 − £440,000) = £28,792, which would simply appear in Success Direct Ltd's profit and loss account for the year as a reduction in the cost charged there (an underabsorption would increase the cost charged to the profit and loss account). We shall illustrate this in the next chapter when we examine absorption costing profit statements.

Success Direct Ltd's overabsorption might be interpreted as a measure of the 'benefit' of bettering estimated volume of activity. But use of overabsorptions (or underabsorptions) in this way may be misleading: remember that there are *two* estimates involved in the predetermined absorption rate – activity and cost – so that an over/underabsorption may have as much (or more) to do with differences between estimated and actual cost as with over/underachievement of estimated volume.

ACTIVITY-BASED COSTING (ABC)

ABC developed from a feeling (see Cooper, 1990 and Cooper and Kaplan, 1988) that the 'traditional' approach to absorption of overheads inadequately reflected increasingly complex processes within many organisations. For example, it can be argued that an absorption rate based on direct labour hours (or cost) is inappropriate in an environment characterised by automation. Even the use of a machine hour absorption rate can be seen as too simplistic a representation of the relationship between overheads and their underlying cause. In addition, many overheads are not related to volume of output, so that absorbing them with a volume-based rate may not be the best approach. The overall result of using a 'traditional' absorption methodology may therefore be unit overhead costs which are only a distant cousin of the resources required for output.

The first stage in ABC is to identify the main **activities** within the organisation, since it is these activities which consume resources and thus incur costs. If we examine Exhibit 4.3 again, we might be tempted to say that Success Direct Ltd's main activities are reflected in the four cost centres – Bookkeeping Courses, Secretarial Courses, Reprographic Services and Dispatch. But a closer look might suggest that this is rather imprecise: for example, there are substantial costs for computer consumables and phone/fax/e-mail, so we could take the view that these are, in fact, major activities for which we can develop separate absorption rates. What has to be appreciated is that activities need not be confined to a single cost centre and we may need to cut across traditional departmental lines in order to define major activities. Thus, for example, use of phone/fax/e-mail may be defined as a major activity within Success Direct Ltd, irrespective of which department such usage occurs in.

⇨ Why might additional absorption rates reflecting usage of phone/fax/e-mail and computer resources be an improvement over our 'traditional' rates?

Our 'traditional' absorption rates were based on a single measure of activity – cost units, computer or direct labour hours, direct labour cost – which was measured either departmentally or on a blanket basis. If you look again at the 'Introduction to spreadsheets' course data in Exhibit 4.4, you will appreciate that, regardless of *which* single-measure absorption rate we use, we obtain an overhead cost per unit which is, at best, a rough indication of the resources consumed to provide the course. If, for example, we use a direct labour hour absorption rate for Bookkeeping, we cannot directly reflect, in the course's cost, the estimated computer hours involved.

Having defined the major activities, an **overhead cost pool** is created for each activity, to which the related overheads are allocated and apportioned. The procedures involved are exactly the same as they were in the 'traditional' methodology, the only difference being that here, allocations and apportionments are being made to cost pools, which may have no relationship with departmental structure. Finally, the **cost driver** for each cost pool is identified (i.e. the underlying cause of the costs associated with the activity to which the cost pool relates) and is used as the basis of an absorption rate for that cost pool.

Exhibit 4.7 restates some key figures and gives additional information relevant to the proposed use of ABC by Success Direct Ltd.

Success Direct Ltd

Based on the company's usual absorption methods, departmental absorption rates for next year are:

Bookkeeping: £11.38 per tutor hour
Secretarial: £13.86 per tutor hour

The company is considering the use of ABC to absorb overheads, and investigation has revealed the following:

Activity	Estimated overhead cost pool (£)	Cost driver
Tutoring	168,000	34,000 tutor hours
Computer-related	88,000	160,000 computer hours
Course materials	86,700	9,000 courses offered
Communication	£91,300	100,000 course assignments
	£434,000	

The following estimated information relates to two specific courses:

	Introduction to spreadsheets	Advanced shorthand
Computer hours	200	nil
Tutor hours:		
Bookkeeping	10	nil
Secretarial	1	30
Assignments	6	20

EXHIBIT **4.7** **Correspondence school: cost pools and cost drivers**

⇨ Using the data in Exhibit 4.7, determine, for each activity, the absorption rate per unit of cost driver (work to two decimal places of £1).

On an activity basis, the absorption rates are:

$$\text{Tutoring} = \frac{\text{overhead cost pool}}{\text{tutor hours}} = \frac{£168,000}{34,000} = £4.94 \text{ per tutor hour}$$

$$\text{Computer-related} = \frac{\text{overhead cost pool}}{\text{computer hours}} = \frac{£88,000}{160,000} = £0.55 \text{ per computer hour}$$

$$\text{Course materials} = \frac{\text{overhead cost pool}}{\text{courses offered}} = \frac{£86,700}{9,000} = £9.63 \text{ per course}$$

$$\text{Communication} = \frac{\text{overhead cost pool}}{\text{course assignments}} = \frac{£91,300}{100,000} = £0.91 \text{ per assignment}$$

We can now compare the overhead absorbed by each of the courses in Exhibit 4.7 under each approach. Using the 'traditional' departmental absorption rates, we get:

	Introduction to spreadsheets (£)	Advanced shorthand (£)
Bookkeeping overhead: 10/nil tutor hours @ 11.38	113.80	nil
Secretarial overhead: 1/30 tutor hours @ 13.86	13.86	415.80
Total overhead charged to course	127.66	415.80

⇨ Determine the total overhead charged to each course using the ABC absorption rates calculated above.

Applying the ABC absorption rates to each job gives:

	Introduction to spreadsheets (£)	Advanced shorthand (£)
Tutoring overhead: 11/30 tutor hours @ £4.94	54.34	148.20
Computer-related overhead: 200/nil computer hours @ £0.55	110.00	nil
Course materials	9.63	9.63
Communication: 6/20 assignments @ £0.91	5.46	18.20
Total overhead charged to course	179.43	176.03

As you can see, there is a substantial difference in the total overhead charged to each course under the 'traditional' and ABC methods: an increase of roughly 41 per cent for the 'spreadsheet' course, compared to a decrease of about 58 per cent for 'shorthand'. Differences will likewise occur across Success Direct Ltd's entire range of courses; changing the method of absorbing overhead will alter the comparative cost and profitability of different courses – and may also cause changes in their selling prices. Since choice of absorption method could have a material effect on management perceptions about cost and related issues, we need to consider which approach (if either) is 'superior'.

'TRADITIONAL' ABSORPTION COSTING AND ABC COMPARED

There are several areas where comparison of the two systems is worthwhile, and we shall discuss these below.

Reflection of resource inputs to support outputs

We have already said that absorption rates based on 'simple' activity measures such as direct labour or machine hours may be unrepresentative of complex relationships between support activities and outputs. Closer inspection of the two sets of overhead figures calculated above might suggest why ABC could be superior in this respect. Assuming tolerable accuracy in identification and quantification of activities, cost drivers and overhead costs, the very calculation of a greater range of absorption rates should allow ABC to more accurately reflect consumption of support resources by output. For example, ABC gives overhead charges which explicitly show the two courses' differing requirements for tutor *and* computer hours; under the 'traditional' approach, this difference is not apparent in the overhead charged to each job because computer-related costs (and the reason for their being incurred) are 'hidden' within the single-activity departmental absorption rates. What this means is that:

1 We cannot determine the charge made to each course in respect of computer-related costs.
2 The 'Advanced Shorthand' course has received some charge for computer-related costs, even though no computer hours are actually required to provide the course.

In circumstances such as those we have just described, unit overhead costs derived from ABC will give a more accurate picture of input/output relationships.

The subjectivity 'problem'

We described the potential subjectivity of apportionment bases in the context of the 'traditional' absorption methodology. In most circumstances, ABC is unlikely to improve this aspect of overhead absorption, the effect being, as in Success Direct Ltd's case, to alter which costs need to be apportioned to what cost objectives. For example, under the 'traditional' methodology, supervisory costs were allocated to each of the four cost centres; using ABC, these costs need to be apportioned to the overhead cost pools, bearing in mind that the cost pools cross departmental boundaries. Conversely, under the 'traditional' approach, communication costs required to be apportioned to all four cost centres; whereas under ABC, these costs are allocated to the 'communication' cost pool.

Cost drivers as absorption rates

Where possible, using the cost driver as absorption rate makes sense, given that it is the underlying cause of the cost being absorbed, which is preferable to employing a more general activity measure, such as machine hours. But using cost drivers in this way may pose problems:

1 It may be difficult to identify the cost driver. For example, the cost driver for Success Direct Ltd's communication cost was stated to be the number of assignments, but it could also be the number of students, number of courses, relative complexity of courses, or a combination of all four.
2 It may be difficult to quantify the cost driver once identified: for example, 'relative complexity of courses'.
3 Where there are problems identifying/quantifying cost drivers, any related absorption rate must be open to question.
4 Once identified, quantified and related to output, it will almost certainly be true that the cost driver is, at best, the *main* underlying cause of the costs within a particular pool. For example, each of Success Direct Ltd's overhead cost pools will contain an apportionment of property costs, which are not driven by any of the factors identified in Exhibit 4.7. If a separate 'occupancy' cost pool were to be set up to counter this, problems 2 and 3 above may be very much in evidence.

However, what we have just said does not mean that cost drivers cannot or should not be used as absorption rates, but that complete causal accuracy may need to be traded off against practicality and the cost/benefit criterion (just as it was with the 'traditional' approach).

Identifying activities

Traditional absorption costing systems tend, on the whole, to attribute overheads to departments, which at least has the merit of simplicity, but which may result in a rather inflexible approach in the context of a dynamic environment. But although there is greater potential flexibility in an activity basis, this may itself create a difficulty. Many activities (such as computing at Success Direct Ltd) cross departmental boundaries, and this may make them difficult to define with reasonable precision, especially where there are differences in the exact nature of apparently identical activities being carried on in (or on behalf of) several departments. This could, in turn, affect the cost driver: for instance, in Success Direct Ltd, communication costs for Bookkeeping may be driven by the complexity of courses provided, whereas for Secretarial, the same cost might be driven by the number of assignments. In such circumstances, we may need either to develop a cost driver rate for each department, which raises the problem of apportioning computing costs between departments, or to revert to a 'traditional' departmental absorption rate.

Cost of setting up and operating absorption systems

Whether it be 'traditional' or ABC, there are costs involved in installing and operating an absorption costing system: estimates of costs and activity/volume measure(s) need to be made; actual costs and activity/volume measure(s) must be recorded; and data for apportionment (and possibly reapportionment) bases must be found. Some of this information will be available as a matter of routine (e.g. budgeted and actual costs) and some may be readily obtained. It must nevertheless be recognised that there is a cost involved, and the significance of the cost/benefit criterion should be borne in mind.

It might be that the more complex analysis required by ABC could impose additional costs for information gathering and updating such that the associated benefit is outweighed. In many cases, adoption of ABC necessitates the use of external consultants to identify activities/cost drivers, which could be prohibitively expensive.

ABC as a control aid

One important argument advanced in support of ABC is its use as an aid to cost control: that is, if the major activities and related cost drivers can be identified, then any action to reduce the incidence of either or both should have the effect of reducing the related costs. However, it may also be argued that, where some dubiety attaches to the definition of activities and/or cost drivers, this is a questionable benefit of ABC. We shall discuss the planning and control aspects of ABC in Chapters 12 and 13.

■ 'Traditional' v ABC approaches: a final word

Our discussion of the two broad approaches to absorption costing suggests that each has its strengths and weaknesses – this is not to say, however, that they are mutually exclusive. It is possible to incorporate the 'best' elements of each within a single system: for example, trying to use cost drivers to define apportionment bases; using multiple absorption rates rather than plantwide or 'simple' departmental ones; and avoiding nebulous definitions of activities and cost drivers. In addition, several features of absorption costing are common to both approaches: for example, the need for care in selection of an activity measure is every bit as important in ABC as it was for a volume measure in the 'traditional' method; and predetermined absorption rates are often a practical necessity, whether these are based on 'simple' measures such as machine hours or on the relevant cost driver.

Possibly, as we shall see in the next chapter, the debate should not be about which method of absorption costing is better, but whether absorption costing is itself of limited value in many situations.

Friedman and Lyne (1997) suggest an interesting advantage to adoption of ABC:

'... where activity-based techniques have been implemented [by companies interviewed], management accounting information will be considered more useful, and the bean counter image of management accountants will be dispelled or seriously weakened.'

The authors believe that current interest in activity-based techniques will continue in the short term, but are 'less sanguine' about their long-term effectiveness due to factors such as rapid environmental change.

Perhaps the final word on the matter should rest with two surveys (Innes and Mitchell, 1990 and 1994) of the extent to which ABC has been adopted by UK organisations. In the 1990 study, it was found that 6 per cent of respondents had implemented ABC; the 1994 survey was a follow-up of respondents to the earlier survey and found that 16 per cent were now using some form of ABC. Interestingly, the later survey also found that about 57 per cent of respondents *not* using ABC were considering it. Of the companies which had considered using ABC but had rejected the idea, cost of implementation was commonly cited as the reason. Although the authors of these two studies concede that their direct comparison should be undertaken with care, it would appear to be the case that use of ABC is spreading and is likely to spread further.

ADMINISTRATION, SELLING AND DISTRIBUTION OVERHEADS

For the purposes of certain organisations' published accounts (in the UK), Statement of Standard Accounting Practice No. 9 requires that stock values reflect the cost of bringing goods to their 'present location and condition'. This effectively means that, for the valuation of stocks in the published accounts of organisations subject to the Standard's provisions, selling and distribution overheads along with some or all administration overheads (An element of administration overheads may be included as being required to bring goods 'to their present location and condition') should be excluded. As we explained in Chapter 2, service organisations such as Success Direct Ltd cannot keep stocks of their output, so the problem principally affects manufacturing businesses, where a distinction may need to be drawn between *production overheads* (included in published stock values) and *non-production overheads* (excluded from published stock values).

Organisations subject to the requirements of SSAP No. 9 may choose, for *internal* purposes, to include a charge for non-production overheads in unit costs. This might, for example, be done as part of the price-setting exercise to help ensure coverage of all costs by selling price. The problem with absorbing overheads which are not incurred in direct support of output is that the rate used is likely to be merely indicative of the cost being absorbed and the related cost driver. Thus, for example, selling and distribution costs could be absorbed on the basis of sales revenue (as they are incurred because of sales-related activity):

$$\text{absorption rate} = \frac{\text{estimated overhead cost}}{\text{estimated sales revenue}} \times 100\%$$

▷ Suggest a possible absorption rate for administration overhead.

Sales revenue could be used as the absorption basis, or alternatively, we could use total production cost (i.e. direct cost + production overhead):

$$\text{absorption rate} = \frac{\text{estimated overhead cost}}{\text{estimated total production cost}} \times 100\%$$

Neither sales revenue nor total production cost is entirely satisfactory, since use of the former could suggest that administration is primarily linked to sales, and use of the latter that it is principally production-related. In most cases, administration is likely to be concerned with all organisational activities.

Absorption rates for non-production overheads (where they are used) are unlikely to improve the 'accuracy' of overhead absorption since the link between overhead cost and volume measure is likely to be tenuous.

SUMMARY

Absorption of overheads can be a complex and even contentious affair, but, as the quotations in Exhibit 4.1 make clear, overhead costs are an important item of expenditure in many organisations and their treatment can have significant implications for unit costs, stock values, reported profit and possibly selling prices.

We have seen that:

■ Absorption costing takes the view that overheads are necessarily incurred to support output and should therefore be included in unit costs.

■ Stock values reported in the published accounts of many organisations must include a charge for appropriate overheads.

■ Two broad approaches to absorption costing are possible: 'traditional', and activity-based costing (ABC). The procedures involved in each of these approaches are summarised in Figure 4.2.

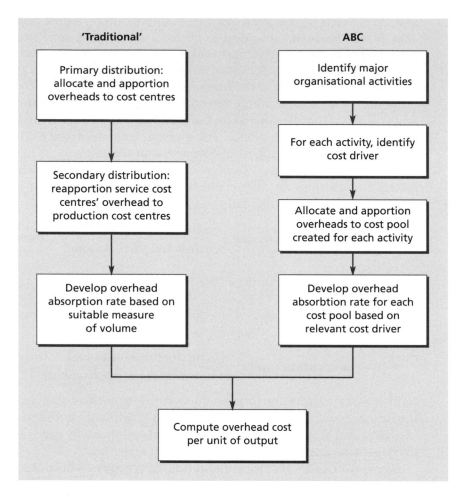

FIGURE 4.2
**'Traditional'
and ABC
approaches to
overhead
absorption**

- Apportionment (and reapportionment) bases should use, wherever practicable, an overhead's **cost driver** (i.e. its underlying cause).

- In general terms, the absorption rate may be calculated as:

$$\frac{\text{overhead cost}}{\text{volume measure}} \quad or \quad \frac{\text{overhead cost pool}}{\text{units of cost driver}}$$

- Predetermined absorption rates are preferable to actual when actual costs and activity fluctuate within a period and will not be known with any certainty until the period end.

- Use of predetermined rates requires both cost and volume/cost driver to be estimated, the latter being based on **normal volume** *or* **practical capacity** *or* **annual budgeted volume.**

- Since the estimates involved in a predetermined absorption rate will differ from actuals, overhead absorbed will not equal overhead incurred:

  – absorbed amount > amount incurred termed **overabsorption;**

  – absorbed amount < amount incurred termed **underabsorption.**

- ABC can produce more accurate unit costs and may enhance cost control, but there may be problems in defining major activities and associated cost drivers.

- Non-production overheads are not absorbed in the published accounts of organisations subject to SSAP 9, but may be for internal purposes such as price-setting.

In the next chapter, we will describe and discuss marginal costing, which takes a different view of the treatment of overheads and calculation of unit costs, examining profit statements based on both marginal and absorption costing principles and making a comparison of the two techniques.

FURTHER READING

Cooper, R., 'Explicating the logic of ABC', in *Management Accounting* (November 1990), CIMA.

Cooper, R. and Kaplan R., 'Measure costs right: make the right decision', in *Harvard Business Review* (Sept.–Oct. 1988).

Elliott, B. and Elliott, J., *Financial Accounting and Reporting*, Prentice Hall, 1993. Chapter 22 provides detailed coverage of SSAP 9 and stock valuation in published accounts.

Friedman, A. and Lyne, S., 'Activity-based techniques and the death of the bean counter' in *The European Accounting Review*, 6:1, 1997.

Innes, J. and Mitchell, F., *Activity Based Costing: A review with case studies*, CIMA, 1990.

Innes, J. and Mitchell, F., 'ABC: a follow-up survey of CIMA members', in *Management Accounting* (July/Aug. 1995), CIMA.

Tanaka, M., Yoshikawa, T., Innes, J. and Mitchell, F., *Contemporary Cost Management*, Chapman & Hall, 1993. Chapter 8 contains an interesting discussion of ABC, along with a useful numerical comparison of ABC and the 'traditional' approach.

Self-test questions

The following information is to be used for Questions 4.1 and 4.2:

TL Ltd absorbs overhead using a predetermined machine hour rate. Relevant information for the year just ended is:

Actual machine hours worked	120,000
Estimated overhead cost	£156,000
Actual overhead cost	£187,200
Estimated machine hours	130,000

4.1 What was the absorption rate per machine hour?

    A £1.20
    B £1.30
    C £1.44
    D £1.56

4.2 What was the amount of over- or underabsorbed overhead for the year?

    A £15,600 overabsorbed
    B £31,200 underabsorbed
    C £33,200 underabsorbed
    D £43,200 underabsorbed

4.3 For each of the following statements, tick the appropriate box to indicate whether it is true or false.

	True	False
(a) Normal volume is the estimated output volume for the forthcoming year.	☐	☐
(b) A cost driver is the main underlying cause of an overhead.	☐	☐
(c) Use of a plantwide absorption rate avoids the need for primary and secondary distribution of overheads.	☐	☐
(d) Overheads which are common to two or more cost centres are allocated to those cost centres.	☐	☐
(e) ABC uses cost drivers as the basis for absorption rates.	☐	☐
(f) Use of activity-based overhead cost pools eliminates the need for apportionment of overheads.	☐	☐
(g) An underabsorption of overhead requires to be charged to the accounts as an additional cost.	☐	☐

4.4 PT Ltd manufactures and installs a range of commercial and domestic satellite decoders. The company is split into two cost centres, Production and Installation, details of which are as follows:

	Production	Installation
Estimated:		
Departmental overhead	£240,000	£330,000
Machine hours	48,000	1,000
Direct labour hours	2,000	15,000
No. of units produced/installed	10,000	7,500

Requirement
Compute an appropriate departmental absorption rate for each of Production and Installation, providing a brief justification of the volume measure you have selected in each case.

4.5 DMF Ltd manufactures smoke detectors and the following information is available for Model DMF/04:

	Per unit
Total direct cost	£5
Selling price	£15
Machine hours: production	0.5
Direct labour hours: inspection and packing	0.1

The following absorption rates are in use by the company:

	Rate
Production:	£4 per machine hour
Inspection and packing:	£10 per direct labour hour
Selling and distribution:	20% of sales value

What will be the cost per unit of Model DMF/04 for stock valuation purposes in the company's published accounts (subject to SSAP 9)?

A £ 7
B £ 8
C £10
D £11

QUESTIONS WITH ANSWERS

4.6 This question tests whether you can:

- calculate a blanket overhead absorption rate;

- allocate and apportion overheads to cost centres, developing appropriate apportionment bases where necessary;

- develop departmental absorption rates; and

- assess the suitability of a blanket rate and departmental rates in given circumstances.

CD & Co, a firm of solicitors, charges its clients on an hourly basis. In order to determine this charge per hour, the firm wishes to absorb its overheads into the cost per client/hour. For the purpose of determining unit costs, the firm is divided into three 'front-line' cost centres: Civil, Criminal, and Property. The following estimates are available for next year:

	Civil	Criminal	Property
No. of junior partners/employees	12	9	4
No. of offices occupied	5	3	2
No. of client/hours	14,000	16,000	10,000

Overhead costs	£
Salary of senior partner in charge:	
Civil	70,000
Criminal	80,000
Property	60,000
Rates and other occupancy costs:	26,000
Employee benefits	50,000
General (e.g. stationery and printing)	20,000

Requirements

(a) Calculate a blanket absorption rate per hour for CD & Co's operations next year.

(b) Using the data given, allocate and apportion the estimated overhead costs to each of the firm's three cost centres, and on the basis of the resulting departmental overhead totals, compute an absorption rate for each cost centre.

(c) Comment on the suitability of each of the approaches taken in (a) and (b) to CD & Co's circumstances.

4.7 This question tests whether you can:

■ calculate an overhead absorption rate based on three different measures of volume;

■ determine the amount of any over- or underabsorption resulting from application of these rates; and

■ evaluate the use of normal volume and practical capacity in absorption rate computation.

HPW Ltd is a printing company which specialises in technical publications and a plantwide machine hour absorption rate is in use. At present, the volume measure incorporated in the absorption rate is annual budgeted volume, but management is considering a change to either practical capacity or normal volume. Next year's production overhead cost (all fixed) is estimated at £600,000. Relevant information about volume levels is as follows:

Budgeted volume: 250,000 machine hours.

Practical capacity: budgeted volume represents 80 per cent of current maximum operational capacity.

Normal volume: the company's strategic plan suggests that the number of machine hours necessary in each of the next six years in order to satisfy demand will be:

	Year 1	Year 2	Year 3	Year 4	Year 5	Year 6
Machine hours (000s)	250	340	370	260	350	380

(The strategic plan also envisages a substantial investment in increased operating capacity at the start of Year 2.)

Requirements

(a) Calculate, to two decimal places of £1, machine hour absorption rates based on:

    (i)   annual budgeted volume;
    (ii) practical capacity; and
    (iii) normal volume.

(b) Assume that, for the year to which the absorption rates in (a) apply, 260,000 machine hours were actually worked and overhead incurred was £595,000. Determine, for each of the absorption rates in (a), the amount of under- or over-absorbed overhead.

(c) Evaluate the proposed use of practical capacity and normal volume by HPW Ltd for next year's absorption rate.

4.8 This question tests whether you can:

■ apply 'traditional' absorption costing methodology to calculation of absorption rates;

■ use an ABC approach to compute absorption rates;

■ use the 'traditional' and ABC absorption rates to determine the amount of overhead absorbed by two jobs; and

■ comment on the suitability of ABC in the given circumstances.

NLS Ltd provides commercial laundry services to local hospitals and nursing homes, two prisons and a variety of other organisations. The company currently absorbs overheads on the basis of a departmental rate for each of its two operational cost centres, Transport and Laundry, but is considering adoption of activity-based costing next year. Because of the bulk nature of the company's work, NLS Ltd's cost unit is 100 individual items of laundry, this being the basis upon which unit costs are calculated.

Estimated data for next year: existing absorption method

Total number of cost units to be processed	48,000
Total transport kilometres for collection/delivery	100,000
Total overhead	£400,000
Allocation and apportionment of total overhead	70% to Laundry
	30% to Transport

Additional data resulting from ABC study

Main activities	Cost driver	Cost pool (% of total overhead)
Collection and delivery of laundry	100,000 transport km	15
Loading/unloading of vans	8,000 transport runs	10
Laundry	300,000 kg dry weight of items cleaned	30
Drying	400,000 kg wet weight of items cleaned	25
Steam pressing	48,000 cost units	20

Data for two sample contracts	Hillsmere Hospital	Goreton Prison
No. of cost units of 100 items	9,000	2,000
No. of transport runs	1,200	300
Transport km	6,000	8,000
Average dry weight per cost unit of 100 items	4 kg	2 kg
Average wet weight per cost unit of 100 items	5.3 kg	3.3 kg

Requirements

(a) Using NLS Ltd's existing method, compute an appropriate absorption rate for each of the Transport and Laundry cost centres.

(b) Determine the absorption rate applicable to each activity assuming an activity-based costing system were in operation.

(c) Calculate the overhead absorbed by each of the Hillsmere and Goreton contracts if:

(i) the absorption rates in (a) are applied; and
(ii) the absorption rates in (b) are applied.

(d) Does your answer to (c) provide any support for the proposed change to activity-based costing? Explain your reasoning.

QUESTIONS WITHOUT ANSWERS

4.9 The Haematology Laboratory within a large local hospital is currently reviewing its costing and charging methodology. Because of the nature of the work undertaken, by far the majority of the laboratory's costs (budgeted at £1.3 million next year) are indirect relative to 'output' and it is the treatment of these costs which is to be reviewed. At present, laboratory overheads are absorbed at a 'flat rate' of 120 per cent of the total direct cost of a specimen or investigation.

For administrative purposes, the laboratory is split into four departments: Blood Transfusion, Routine Investigation, Special Investigation & Coagulation, and Unit Administration. Each department is run by a consultant haematologist, with a senior consultant, based in Unit Administration, having overall charge of the laboratory.

With the exception of Unit Administration, each department is divided into a number of work stations. Some of these work stations are capable only of highly specialised work associated with the specific department within which they are located, while the remainder can undertake work of a more general nature which is common to all departments.

Although medical staff and technicians are assigned to a particular department, they are not assigned to a particular work station and it is frequently necessary for staff to perform work in departments other than that to which they are assigned. Similarly, roughly 30 per cent of the laboratory's work requires the use of facilities in two or more departments and, at times of peak demand for the laboratory's services, all suitable facilities and staff are utilised, irrespective of the department within which they are located.

Requirement
Draft a report to the hospital's Board of Management explaining why overheads may need to be included in unit costs and why the existing system of charging the Haematology Laboratory's overheads to cost units is unsatisfactory. Suggest *two* alternative systems which might be adopted, detail the strengths and weaknesses of each in relation to the laboratory's circumstances, and, on this basis, recommend the most suitable approach.

4.10 TMM Ltd operates a large vehicle testing, service and repair centre at Holborough and is revising its costing procedures. Overheads are presently absorbed using a plantwide rate based on direct labour cost, but management feels that this results in inaccurate unit costs.

The following estimates are available for next year:

	Departments			
	Servicing and repairs	*MoT testing*	*Tyres and exhausts*	*Office*
Floor area (metres^2)	4,000	3,500	2,000	500
Number of employees	20	15	10	5
Direct wages costs	£300,000	£240,000	£180,000	£80,000
Number of equipment hours	2,000	6,000	4,000	nil
Number of tests	nil	7,000	nil	nil
Number of parts orders	1,500	nil	2,500	nil
Vehicle recoveries	600	nil	nil	nil

Overhead costs

	£
Wage-related overheads	20% of total wages costs
Rent, rates and insurance on premises:	30,000
Departmental supervision:	
Repairs	20,000
MoT testing	24,000
Tyres/exhausts	22,000
Office	30,000
MoT stationery and related costs	2,000
Vehicle recovery costs	10,000
Parts ordering costs	14,000
Equipment maintenance and running costs	60,000
Lighting and heating	12,000
Sundry office administration costs	30,000

Requirements

(a) Calculate, to the nearest whole 1 per cent, TMM Ltd's plantwide direct labour cost absorption rate for next year.

(b) Primary and secondary distribution of overheads yields the following departmental totals:

Servicing and repairs	£142,567
MoT testing	£153,250
Tyres and exhausts	£118,183

Compute (to the nearest whole 1 per cent) departmental direct labour cost absorption rates for each of Servicing and repairs, MoT testing and Tyres and exhausts.

(c) An investigation of TMM Ltd's operations reveals that the main activities and related share of total company overhead are:

	%
Labour-related work	40
Machine operation	35
Ordering and receipt of parts	15
MoT administration	10

From the information available, develop a suitable cost driver absorption rate for each of these activities.

(d) Data for two jobs currently in hand are:

	Job 1014	*Job 1022*
Parts' cost	£200	nil
Direct labour costs:		
Servicing and repairs	£40	£10
MoT testing	£20	£20
Tyres and exhausts	£40	£50
	£100	£80
Parts' orders	1	nil
Equipment usage	0.5 hour	4 hours

Determine the full cost of each job using:

(i)   the plantwide absorption rate in (a);
(ii) the departmental absorption rates in (b); and
(iii) the cost driver absorption rates in (c).

Explain whether the different job costs resulting from application of these absorption rates confirms or refutes management's feeling that the existing rate may lead to inaccurate job costs.

CHAPTER 5

Absorption costing and marginal costing

CATALYTIC SLIDE DENTS
JOHNSON MATTHEY

Shares in Johnson Matthey fell 41p to 530p yesterday after it announced lower than expected first-half profits and warned that problems in its catalytic systems business would dent full-year figures . . .

Mr David Davles, chairman, said the figures were disappointing but claimed the group was at a watershed following September's $170m (£107m) acquisition of Advanced Circuits (ACI), the US maker of semiconductor products and multi-layered printed circuit boards . . .

Although ACI made a negligible contribution to first-half profits, Mr Davies predicted it could make electronic materials the largest profit centre in the medium term . . . Contribution from Cookson Matthey Ceramics, its joint venture with Cookson Group, rose to £10.6m . . .

Source: Tim Burt, *Financial Times*, 1 December 1995.

EXHIBIT 5.1 'Contribution': a key concept in marginal costing

INTRODUCTION

When we examined absorption costing in the last chapter, we saw that all output-related costs (direct and indirect) were included in unit costs and said that this approach was necessary for the published accounts of many organisations. By classifying costs in this way, absorption costing effectively ignores cost *behaviour* in relation to volume. In this chapter we shall describe and illustrate an alternative view – marginal (or variable) costing, which attributes only variable costs to cost units, and which may be more useful for *internal* purposes, although not permissible for published accounts (in the United Kingdom). We shall compare and contrast profit statements prepared under both approaches and show how the different profit figures may be reconciled. In addition, we shall see how marginal costing principles may be useful to management: for example, we shall demonstrate a marginal costing approach to determining the contribution of different business segments and illustrate how this might be used to aid decision making. Finally, we shall compare absorption and marginal costing, discussing their relative strengths and weaknesses.

What we should also point out is that, irrespective of how costs are classified and attributed to cost units, they require to be matched with revenue in order to arrive at a profit figure.

OBJECTIVES   When you have completed this chapter, you will be able to:

- appreciate the difference in rationale and cost classification underlying absorption and marginal costing;

- prepare simple profit statements using both marginal and absorption costing;

- explain the reason for differences in profit resulting from application of each of the two systems and reconcile such differences;

- adjust an absorption costing profit statement for over-/underabsorbed overhead;

- apply marginal costing principles to decision-making scenarios; and

- assess the relative strengths and weaknesses of marginal costing and absorption costing.

MARGINAL AND ABSORPTION COSTING: DIFFERENT RATIONALES

Absorption costing stems from the view that certain overheads are necessarily incurred to allow output to occur and should therefore be included in unit costs. In effect, absorption costing is based on a *functional* classification of costs: that is, all output-related (or production) costs are attributed to cost units, with non-production costs being excluded from unit costs (at least for stock valuation and profit measurement purposes). Marginal costing, however, is based on a distinction between variable and fixed costs (*see* Chapter 2), with the former being attributed to cost units and the latter being dealt with in total for a particular period. The justification for this treatment of fixed costs is that, in general, costs such as rent, rates and insurance relate to a *period of time*, rather than to volume of output and their accounting treatment should reflect this fact.

Not only can absorption of fixed costs be viewed as illogical in light of their predominantly time-based nature, but it may also cause confusion about their behaviour and even amount. Under absorption costing, increases/decreases in the volume of output will result in increases/decreases in the amount of fixed overhead absorbed, which might give the misleading impression that the amount of the underlying costs *incurred* is increasing/decreasing in line with output: that is, that we are dealing with variable costs. Consider Figure 5.1 which compares fixed overhead absorbed with fixed overhead incurred over the relevant range.

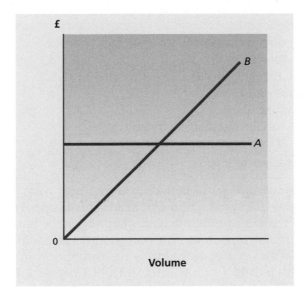

FIGURE 5.1
Fixed overhead incurred versus absorbed over relevant range

⇨ Which line on Figure 5.1 represents fixed overhead incurred and which the absorbed amount?

Line *A* represents fixed overhead incurred while Line *B* represents the absorbed amount and it is possible that use of absorption costing could result in a misunderstanding of cost behaviour: for example, if the 'absorbed' line in Figure 5.1 were erroneously thought to depict the behaviour of the costs concerned, then zero fixed overhead would be predicted at the lowest volume within the relevant range, which is very unlikely to be the case. Potential misconceptions of this sort may, as we shall see, suggest adoption of courses of action which are financially inadvisable. (You should note that this difficulty does not arise in the case of *variable* overheads: by definition, total variable overhead increases/decreases in line with increases/decreases in output.)

A final problem with absorption of fixed costs is that it may give rise to some anomalies in reported profit relative to sales and production volume; we will illustrate this shortly. Marginal costing seeks to remove any potential difficulty which might be caused by treating fixed costs 'as if' they were variable, attributing only variable costs to units of output and treating *all* fixed costs on a total basis for the period to which they relate. The unit output cost as calculated for each of marginal and absorption costing is as follows:

Marginal costing: unit output cost	£
Variable costs:	
direct materials	x
direct labour	x
direct expenses	x
variable production overhead	x
Cost per unit	x

Absorption costing: unit output cost	£
Direct costs:	
direct materials	x
direct labour	x
direct expenses	x
Prime cost	x
Indirect costs:	
variable production overhead	x
fixed production overhead	x
Cost per unit	x

You will see that the only difference between the two unit costs lies in the treatment of fixed output-related production overhead. This is important to our later discussion of how to reconcile profit differences and should be borne in mind. You will see that the marginal version of unit output cost treats direct costs as also being variable. Whilst this is a useful simplifying assumption for the illustrative profit statements which follow, you will recall from Chapter 2 that direct costs (and in particular labour) are not necessarily variable in nature.

ABSORPTION AND MARGINAL COSTING: PROFIT STATEMENTS

The different treatment of fixed output-related overhead, and the difference in the underlying cost classification are reflected in the profit statement produced by each system. In absorption costing, all costs incurred in generating sales (direct and indirect, fixed and variable) are included in the cost of sales calculation, hence in determination of **gross profit**. In a marginal costing system, all variable costs are included in the cost of sales calculation, hence in determination of **contribution**. In the first instance (sales *less* all variable costs) provides contribution towards covering fixed costs, thereafter providing contribution to profit. The concept of contribution is central to marginal costing; we shall use it later in the chapter, and also extensively in Chapter 6, so it is important to distinguish it clearly from absorption costing's gross profit:

contribution = sales *less* all variable costs incurred to generate sales
gross profit = sales *less* all output-related costs incurred to generate sales.

We shall use the data in Exhibit 5.2 to illustrate the basic construction of profit statements using absorption and marginal costing. Unlike Success Direct Ltd in the last chapter, we will use a manufacturing business so that we can demonstrate the impact on profit of stock movements; but marginal costing is equally applicable to service organisations (as shown by Questions 5.4, 5.5 and 5.7).

OSN Ltd

OSN Ltd manufactures a single type of lawnmower at one of its factories and estimated figures for next year are:

	Per unit (£)
Selling price	120
Variable costs:	
direct materials	40
direct labour	20
production overhead	10
selling overhead	5

Production/sales will be 18,000 units and there were no stocks at the start or end of the year.

Fixed costs for the year:	£
production overhead	288,000
selling and distribution overhead	120,000
administration overhead	155,000

OSN Ltd absorbs fixed production overhead using a cost unit rate derived from annual budgeted volume.

EXHIBIT 5.2 Lawnmower manufacturer: bugeted cost, output and sales data

⇨ From Exhibit 5.2, determine the production cost per unit using: (a) absorption costing; and (b) marginal costing.

Before we can calculate the absorption costing unit cost, we must obtain an absorption rate for fixed production overhead:

$$\frac{\text{fixed production overhead cost}}{\text{units of output}} = \frac{£288,000}{18,000} = £16 \text{ per unit}$$

The cost per unit is thus:

	£	£
Direct materials		40
Direct labour		20
Prime cost		60
Variable production overhead	10	
Fixed production overhead	16	26
Production cost per unit		86

Applying marginal costing principles gives:

	£
Direct materials	40
Direct labour	20
Variable production overhead	10
Production cost per unit	70

Note that the variable selling overhead is not included in *production* cost. Bearing in mind the definition we gave above, contribution per unit is:

	£	£
Selling price per unit		120
less Marginal production cost	70	
Variable selling overhead	5	75
Contribution per unit		45

You will see that *all* variable costs – production and non-production – have been deducted from selling price in order to determine contribution. Total contribution is therefore:

$$\text{(units sales} \times \text{contribution per unit)}$$
$$= (18,000 \times £45) = £810,000$$

If £810,000 is sufficient to cover all of OSN Ltd's fixed costs, the company will earn a profit equal to the excess of total contribution over total fixed costs; to the extent that £810,000 does not cover total fixed costs, a loss will be incurred. We can confirm the total contribution and the company's profit/loss position from the following marginal costing profit statement:

OSN Ltd: marginal costing profit statement for the year

	£	£
Sales (18,000 @ £120)		£2,160,000
Cost of sales:		
Opening stock	nil	
add Marginal cost of production (18,000 @ £70)	1,260,000	
	1,260,000	
less Closing stock	nil	
	1,260,000	
Variable selling overhead (18,000 @ £5)	90,000	1,350,000
Contribution (18,000 @ £45: see above)		810,000
Fixed costs:		
Production overhead	288,000	
Selling and distribution overhead	120,000	
Administration overhead	155,000	563,000
Net profit		247,000

From the profit statement, you will once again note that *all* variable costs are deducted from sales to determine contribution.

You will also see from the profit statement that we have shown a *stock adjustment* even although there was no stock brought forward from last year nor carried forward to next year. Its inclusion here (and in the absorption costing profit statement which follows) is merely to allow consistency of presentation with later statements, where stocks are present.

If you are unfamiliar with this adjustment, its purpose is to permit revenues earned in a period to be matched with the costs incurred in earning them. The cost of stock not sold in the previous period must be brought forward ('opening stock') and added to the current period's production costs, whilst the cost of stock unsold at the end of the current period ('closing stock') must be deducted for carry-forward to next period. In this way the cost of sales charged against revenue reflects only the goods sold during the current period.

OSN Ltd's profit statement based on absorption costing is as follows:

OSN Ltd: absorption costing profit statement for the year

	£	£
Sales (18,000 @ £120)		2,160,000
Cost of sales:		
Opening stock	nil	
add Cost of production (18,000 @ £86)	1,548,000	
	1,548,000	
less Closing stock	nil	1,548,000
Gross profit		612,000
Selling and distribution overhead:		
fixed	120,000	
variable (18,000 @ £5)	90,000	
Administration overhead	155,000	365,000
Net profit		247,000

Since both of our profit statements reveal the same net profit, does it really make any difference which approach we use? To answer this, let us examine the impact on the two systems' relative profit of stock changes.

Impact on relative profit of stock increase

Our first pair of profit statements was based on production equalling sales. Suppose now that the year's production is estimated at 24,000 units, rather than the 18,000 in Exhibit 5.2. If sales and opening stock remain, respectively, at 18,000 units and nil, stock increases by 6,000 units during the year. How will this affect our profit calculations?

For ease of illustration, we will assume that the increased production volume will have no effect on OSN Ltd's costs: that is, that the amount of fixed costs is unaffected and that the variable costs per unit are as stated in Exhibit 5.2. Given this assumption, a change in estimated production volume will alter the absorption rate for fixed production overhead, this being derived from annual budgeted volume:

$$\frac{\text{fixed production overhead cost}}{\text{units of output}} = \frac{£288{,}000}{24{,}000} = £12 \text{ per unit}$$

Production cost per unit is now:

	£	£
Direct materials		40
Direct labour		20
Prime cost		60
Variable production overhead	10	
Fixed production overhead	12	22
Production cost per unit		82

⇨ Insert the missing figures in the profit statement below to determine the absorption costing profit under the revised circumstances.

OSN Ltd: absorption costing profit statement for the year

Sales (.............@ £120)   £.................

Cost of sales:

    Opening stock (.............@ £82)   £.................

    add Cost of production (.............@ £82)   £.................

                                                    £.................

    less Closing stock (..............@ £82)   £.................   £.................

Gross profit   £.................

Selling and distribution overhead:

    fixed   £.................

    variable (............ @ £5)   £.................

Administration overhead   £.................   £.................

Net profit   £.................

The completed absorption costing profit statement is:

OSN Ltd: absorption costing profit statement for the year

	£	£
Sales (18,000 @ £120)		2,160,000
Cost of sales		
Opening stock (0 @ £82)	nil	
add Cost of production (24,000 @ £82)	1,968,000	
	1,968,000	
less Closing stock (6,000 @ £82)	492,000	£1,476,000
Gross profit		684,000
Selling and distribution overhead:		
fixed	120,000	
variable (18,000 @ £5)	90,000	
Administration overhead	155,000	£ 365,000
Net profit		319,000

Note that the variable selling and distribution overhead varies with the volume of *sales*, not production. Simply by increasing stocks, OSN Ltd has improved net profit by (£319,000 – £247,000) = £72,000. We shall return to this point later.

⮞ Look again at the original marginal costing profit statement. Will the stock increase of 6,000 units have any effect on the profit of £247,000?

The short answer is 'no': although the volume of production has increased, *sales* volume is unchanged, which means that revenue, cost of sales and fixed costs are also unchanged, so that net profit remains at the £247,000 originally calculated. For sceptics, a revised marginal costing profit statement is given below.

OSN Ltd: marginal costing profit statement for the year

	£	£
Sales (18,000 @ £120)		2,160,000
Cost of sales:		
Opening stock (0 @ £70)	nil	
add Marginal cost of production (24,000 @ £70)	1,680,000	
	1,680,000	
less Closing stock (6,000 @ £70)	420,000	
	1,260,000	
Variable selling and distribution overhead (18,000 @ £5)	90,000	1,350,000
Contribution		810,000
Fixed costs:		
Production overhead	288,000	
Selling and distribution overhead	120,000	
Administration overhead	155,000	563,000
Net profit		247,000

We could argue that this unchanged profit figure is a better reflection of what has actually happened (i.e. no change in sales volume, or in any factors other than production volume/stock) than the £72,000 increase in net profit recorded in the absorption costing statement.

Impact on relative profit of stock reduction

Assume now that OSN Ltd will have opening stock of 4,000 units and that estimated production during the year is 16,000 units – all other factors being the same as those set out in Exhibit 5.2. How will this change in circumstances affect the net profit reported under each system? We will deal with absorption costing first.

⇨ Compute the cost unit absorption rate for fixed overheads based on output of 16,000 units and use this to determine the production cost per unit using absorption costing principles.

Using a denominator of 16,000 units, the fixed overhead absorption rate is:

$$\frac{£288,000}{16,000 \text{ units}} = £18 \text{ per unit}$$

which gives a production cost per unit of:

	£
Prime cost (as before)	60
Variable production overhead (as before)	10
Fixed production overhead	18
	88

For simplicity, we will assume that a production cost of £88 per unit is applicable to the opening stock. In practice, however, opening stock would very likely have a different unit cost (being produced in the previous period). Our absorption costing profit statement is now:

OSN Ltd: absorption costing profit statement for the year

	£	£
Sales (18,000 @ £120)		2,160,000
Cost of sales:		
Opening stock (4,000 @ £88)	352,000	
add Cost of production (16,000 @ £88)	1,408,000	
	1,760,000	
less Closing stock (2,000 @ £88)	176,000	1,584,000
Gross profit		576,000
Selling and distribution overhead:		
fixed	120,000	
variable (18,000 @ £5)	90,000	
Administration overhead	155,000	365,000
Net profit		211,000

Units of closing stock are calculated as:

	Units
Opening stock	4,000
add Production	16,000
	20,000
less Sales	18,000
Closing stock	2,000

The effect of the stock reduction has therefore been a reduction of £36,000 in net profit initially calculated (£247,000).

⇨ What will be the effect on marginal costing net profit of the reduction by 2,000 units in stock?

Once again, the answer is 'none': marginal costing will report a net profit of £247,000 irrespective of changes in volume of *stock*. Only if sales volume were to change from the original 18,000 units would marginal costing net profit react, increasing if sales volume increases, decreasing if it decreases.

Summary of relative net profit reported

We can summarise the relative net profit reported under each of absorption and marginal costing for OSN Ltd as follows:

Sales volume *(units)*	*18,000*	*18,000*	*18,000*
Stock change *(units)*	*none*	*+6,000*	*–2,000*
Absorption costing net profit (£)	247,000	319,000	211,000
Marginal costing net profit (£)	247,000	247,000	247,000

In other words, assuming other factors to be unchanged – and, in particular, that none of the production volumes lies out with the relevant range – absorption costing net profit reacts to changes in both sales *and* stock volumes, whereas marginal costing net profit reacts to changes in sales *only*. A set of general relationships between relative net profit, production and sales volumes can be derived, as follows:

1 Where production = sales (i.e. no stock increase), both systems yield the same net profit.
2 Where production > sales (i.e. stock increases), absorption costing yields the higher net profit.
3 Where production < sales (i.e. stock decreases), marginal costing yields the higher net profit.

However, in the long term (i.e. over the life of the organisation) both systems will report the same total profit, as the same total costs will be incurred over that life span, irrespective of how we attribute them to cost units.

Reason for profit differences and their reconciliation

If you review our earlier description of unit production costs for each of absorption and marginal costing, you will see that the only cost which is treated differently under the two systems is *fixed production overhead*. Since this is the only difference in unit production cost under the two approaches, it follows that this is the reason for profit differences between the two systems. Looking at the statement of comparative profit above, we can also see that the situations in which profit differs are those where there are stock movements during the period.

The link between these two factors is stock valuation: because of the different unit costs, stock values will differ between absorption costing and marginal costing. Absorption costing stocks will include fixed production overhead, marginal costing stocks will not. We can therefore effect a reconciliation between the different profit figures by examining the increase or decrease in stocks and determining the amount of fixed production overhead absorbed by that increase or decrease.

OSN Ltd: summary of key figures for 'stock change' situations

	Scenario 1	Scenario 2
Opening stock (units)	nil	4,000
Closing stock (units)	6,000	2,000
Production (units)	24,000	16,000
Sales (units)	18,000	18,000
Fixed overhead absorption rate per unit (£)	12	18
Absorption costing net profit (£)	319,000	211,000
Marginal costing net profit (£)	247,000	247,000

EXHIBIT 5.3 Reconciliation of absorption and marginal costing profit

Using the data for Scenario 1 in Exhibit 5.3, the profit reconciliation is:

	£
Absorption costing net profit	319,000
Marginal costing net profit	247,000
Difference	72,000
Fixed production overhead absorbed in stock increase: (6,000 units @ £12)	72,000

▷ Using the Scenario 2 data from Exhibit 5.3, reconcile absorption and marginal costing profit.

The Scenario 2 reconciliation is:

	£
Absorption costing net profit	211,000
Marginal costing net profit	247,000
Difference	(36,000)
Fixed production overhead absorbed in stock decrease (2,000 units @ £18)	(36,000)

We are now in a position to see why absorption costing net profit reacts the way it does to stock increases/decreases. Because the absorption unit cost is higher than the marginal, absorption stock values will be higher for the same volume of stock. This means that when there is a stock increase, absorption costing will carry forward for charging as a future cost (when the stock is sold) a higher amount of the current period's cost than marginal costing. Conversely, when there is a stock decrease, absorption costing will charge in the current period a higher amount of previous period's cost than marginal costing. This is why OSN Ltd's absorption costing net profit increased by £72,000 when production exceeded an unchanged sales volume: that is, under absorption costing £72,000 more of the current period's cost was deferred than under marginal costing, and when sales exceeded production, £36,000 more of a previous period's cost was charged in the current period.

Absorption costing: treatment of over- and underabsorption

In the last chapter, we saw that one of the problems associated with using a predetermined overhead absorption rate is that the estimates of volume and overhead cost employed in its calculation can differ from actual volume and/or cost, giving rise to overabsorption and underabsorption. Exhibit 5.4 presents OSN Ltd's actual results for the year under consideration. For simplicity, we have assumed that the only differences between estimate and actual have arisen in respect of production volume and fixed production overhead cost.

OSN Ltd: actual information for the year

The company's predetermined absorption rate for fixed production overhead (£16) during the year in question was based on production volume of 18,000 units and overhead cost of £288,000. At the end of the year, it is known that actual production was 19,000 units and fixed production overhead incurred £290,000. In all other respects, actual results were in line with estimates, as follows:

- Sales: 18,000 units @ £120 each
- Opening stock: nil
- Prime cost per unit: £60
- Variable production overhead per unit: £10
- Variable selling overhead: £5 per unit
- Fixed selling and distribution overhead for the year: £120,000
- Fixed administration overhead for the year: £155,000

Exhibit **5.4 Lawnmower manufacturer: over-/underabsorption of overhead**

⇨ From Exhibit 5.4, determine the amount of over- or underabsorbed fixed production overhead for the year.

In Chapter 4, we saw that determination of over- or underabsorption involves comparison of the amount absorbed using a predetermined rate with the amount incurred; remembering that the amount absorbed is based on actual *production* (not sales), we get:

	£
Fixed production overhead absorbed (19,000 @ £16)	304,000
Fixed production overhead incurred	290,000
Overabsorption	14,000

Because overhead absorbed exceeds that incurred, we have an overabsorption: in other words, use of the predetermined rate of £16 per unit has resulted in £14,000 too much overhead being charged, and we need to adjust the absorption costing profit statement accordingly:

OSN Ltd: absorption costing profit statement for the year

	£	£
Sales (18,000 @ £120)		2,160,000
Cost of sales:		
Opening stock	nil	
add Cost of production (19,000 @ £86)	1,634,000	
	1,634,000	
less Closing stock (1,000 @ £86)	86,000	
	1,548,000	
less Overabsorbed overhead	14,000	1,534,000
Gross profit		626,000
Selling and distribution costs:		
variable (18,000 @ £5)	90,000	
fixed	120,000	
Administration overhead	155,000	365,000
Net profit		261,000

You will see that the overabsorption does not affect *unit* production cost, which is calculated as before:

	£
Prime cost	60
Variable production overhead	10
Fixed production overhead	16
	86

➪ Suppose OSN Ltd had had an *underabsorption* of £14,000 for the year, how would the absorption costing profit statement be adjusted to reflect this?

If an underabsorption had arisen, the overhead absorbed would be less than that incurred and it would be necessary to *add* £14,000 to the cost of sales (as opposed to deducting in the case of the overabsorption illustrated above). Adjusting for over-

and underabsorption means that the profit statement reflects actual overhead incurred. Such an adjustment is not necessary in the marginal costing profit statement, nor does it have any impact on the difference in profit reported (which, as we have seen, is a function of fixed production overhead absorbed in stock changes).

MARGINAL AND ABSORPTION COSTING: DECISION MAKING

Having examined the profit implications of the two systems, we will now look at their use in decision-making situations. Exhibit 5.5 provides some information about a special order which OSN Ltd has the opportunity to undertake.

OSN Ltd: special order

A large wholesale customer has asked OSN Ltd to supply, as a 'special' order, 1,500 of its standard model of lawnmower at a reduced price of £78. The unit production cost and normal selling price of this model are as follows:

	Per unit	
	£	£
Selling price		120
Production costs:		
variable	70	
fixed	16	86

(No variable selling cost would be incurred if the order were accepted.)

The company has sufficient idle capacity to undertake the order and other sales will be unaffected. Management is keen to accept the order, as there is a good chance of substantial repeat business in future, but at the same time does not wish to incur a loss on the 1,500 units involved.

EXHIBIT **5.5 Lawnmower manufacturer: special order**

⇨ Should the special order be accepted on financial grounds?

Superficial examination of the figures in Exhibit 5.5 suggests rejection of the order:

	£
Revenue from accepting (1,500 units @ £78)	117,000
Production costs of order (1,500 units @ £86)	129,000
Loss from accepting	(12,000)

This, however, is exactly the sort of incorrect analysis we referred to earlier when discussing Figure 5.1 and the danger inherent in treating fixed costs (via the overhead absorption rate) 'as if' they were variable. The £129,000 production 'cost' above consists of additional variable production costs (which will presumably only be incurred if the extra units are produced) *plus* fixed production overhead *absorbed* at £16 per unit. Inclusion of £16 per unit for fixed production overhead suggests that the overhead *incurred* will increase as a result of accepting the order, but there is nothing to suggest any such increase. Assuming that the amount of fixed production overhead *incurred* will be unaffected by the order, we can restate our financial analysis:

	£
Revenue from accepting	117,000
Additional costs *incurred* (variable production costs) (1,500 @ £70)	105,000
Contribution from accepting	12,000

It now appears that acceptance, even at the heavily discounted selling price, is financially worthwhile.

If we are reasonably confident that fixed costs will not be affected, we can take a short-cut approach to determination of the profit resulting from acceptance of the order. You will recall that contribution is (sales – all variable costs); given this, an increase/decrease in sales will cause a corresponding increase/decrease in contribution and, assuming no change in fixed costs, this increase/decrease in contribution will be the same as the increase/decrease in net profit.

⇨ Determine the contribution *per unit* for OSN Ltd's special order and confirm the total contribution from acceptance calculated above.

The unit contribution for the special order is:

	£
Selling price	78
Variable costs	70
Contribution	8

If the order is undertaken, total contribution will be (1,500 units @ £8) = £12,000, which is the same as the figure we calculated above.

Although marginal costing contribution can provide a useful 'ready reckoner' for the profit impact of certain decisions, its use in this way depends on the assumption that fixed costs incurred will be unaffected by the decision in question. As we shall see below (and also in Chapters 6 and 7), this is not always true. It is particularly important that you appreciate the *short-term* and *ad hoc* nature of the financial analysis we have just performed: in the short term, OSN Ltd's fixed costs are unaffected by the decision and can be safely ignored, but in the *long term*, and for *routine* decisions, this would be foolhardy – a point we shall return to shortly.

Contribution analysis

In our 'special' order scenario above, OSN Ltd's fixed costs were assumed to be unaffected by acceptance. Is it possible to employ marginal costing in situations where fixed costs *are* affected by a decision? Consider Exhibit 5.6, which gives details of both product lines produced by OSN Ltd.

OSN Ltd: two product lines

In addition to a lawnmower, the company produces an electric hedge-trimmer. Separate statements are prepared in order to assess the profitability of each product. Next year's estimated profit statement for each product and for the company as a whole is as follows:

	Lawnmower	Hedge trimmer	Total
Production/sales (units)	20,000	12,000	
	£	£	£
Sales revenue	2,400,000	480,000	2,880,000
Cost of sales	1,688,000	384,000	2,072,000
Gross profit	712,000	96,000	808,000
Selling and distribution costs	140,000	70,000	210,000
Administration costs	160,000	50,000	210,000
Net profit/(loss)	412,000	(24,000)	388,000

Management is concerned at the loss being incurred by production/sale of the hedge trimmer and it has been suggested that this product line be discontinued next year in order to improve overall profitability. The following additional information is available:

- *Cost of sales* 80 per cent of this is variable and the balance fixed. Of the fixed element, 60 per cent is an apportionment of general production overheads which will not be avoided should a product line be discontinued; the remaining 40 per cent, being product-specific, will be avoided on discontinuance.
- *Selling & distribution costs* 30 per cent of these costs are product-specific and will be avoided should a product line be discontinued, the remainder being an apportionment of companywide cost.
- *Administration costs* These are general company costs.

EXHIBIT 5.6 Lawnmower manufacturer: 2-product output/sales

At first glance, it might seem that discontinuation of the hedge trimmer product line is financially advisable, since production/sale appears to incur an estimated loss of £24,000 next year. But, as with the 'special' order scenario above, we need to remember that the £24,000 'loss' is based on absorption costing principles. If we claim that discontinuing the product line will avoid the £24,000 loss, what we are also claiming is that *all* the costs associated with hedge trimmers in Exhibit 5.6 will be avoided – and the additional information makes clear that this will not happen. We therefore need to restructure the product and company profit statements in such a way that we are able to distinguish between avoidable and unavoidable (or product-specific and general) costs; only by doing this can we properly assess the profit impact of the proposed discontinuance.

OSN Ltd: revised profit statement

	Lawnmower £	Hedge trimmer £	Total £
Sales revenue	2,400,000	480,000	2,880,000
Marginal cost of sales (80% of Exhibit 5.6)	1,350,400	307,200	1,657,600
Contribution	1,049,600	172,800	1,222,400
Other product-specific costs:			
Cost of sales (40% × 20% of Exhibit 5.6)	135,040	30,720	165,760
Selling and distribution costs (30% of Exhibit 5.6)	42,000	21,000	63,000
Product contribution to general costs	872,560	121,080	993,640
General costs:			
Cost of sales (60% × 20% of Exhibit 5.6)			248,640
Selling and distribution costs (70% of Exhibit 5.6)			147,000
Administration costs			210,000
Net profit			388,000

⇨ Based on OSN Ltd's revised profit statement above, will discontinuing production/sale of hedge trimmers improve overall profit next year?

The revised profit statement indicates that discontinuing production/sale of hedge trimmers next year will worsen overall profitability: company net profit will fall by £121,080 (i.e. the hedge trimmers' contribution to general costs). General costs are *assumed* (in the absence of information to the contrary) to be unaffected by the discontinuance and will still require to be covered, but by the product contribution from lawnmowers only.

Revisions to profit statements to produce product (or department/division) contributions to general costs are termed **contribution analysis**, although it might be more accurate to place 'contribution' in inverted commas in this context, since, to arrive at the product contributions above, we have deducted from sales revenue *all* product-specific costs, fixed and variable, whereas contribution in a strict definition is sales *less* variable costs only. However, what we have demonstrated is that the concept of contribution can be adapted to suit different circumstances. We shall extend our discussion of marginal costing's application to decision analysis in the next chapter.

ABSORPTION AND MARGINAL COSTING: A COMPARISON

Now that we have described the principles and operation of absorption and marginal costing systems, it is necessary to evaluate their relative strengths and weaknesses.

External v internal reporting

In the last chapter, we said that Statement of Standard Accounting Practice No. 9 requires many organisations (in the United Kingdom) to use absorption costing to value stocks in their published accounts. For such organisations and for this purpose, marginal costing cannot be used. However, for *internal* purposes – that is, decision making, planning and control – marginal costing may be more appropriate.

Decision making

Our analysis of the 'special' order and product discontinuation decisions faced by OSN Ltd provides a good illustration of the applicability of marginal costing to decision making. Since marginal costing distinguishes between variable and fixed costs and since many (but not necessarily all) fixed costs will be unaffected by decisions, the resulting cost classification may be roughly analogous to the relevant/irrelevant classification which should underpin the financial analysis of all decisions (and which we shall discuss in Chapter 7). If absorption costing is applied to financial analysis of a decision, there is a danger (as we have seen) that incorrect decisions may result because:

1 the fixed overhead absorption rate treats fixed costs 'as if' they were variable; and
2 some, or even all, of the underlying amount of the fixed costs being absorbed will be unaffected by a decision and is therefore irrelevant.

However, marginal costing should be used with care in decision analysis. We have already mentioned the possibility of making a simplistic assumption about the reaction of all fixed costs to a decision and there are other potential difficulties.

We used marginal costing as an aid in two different decisions: accept/reject a special order, and discontinue/retain a product line. For the special order, which is likely to be a 'one-off' decision with short-term implications, our financial analysis may be adequate (although non-financial considerations will also have a bearing). The product-line decision, however, is different, having longer-term and strategic implications; our contribution analysis of this situation is inadequate, as it is based solely on a single year's figures and therefore imposes a short-term outlook on a decision which has more than a short-term impact. For example, general costs may not be affected in the short term, but, over a period of, say, five years, may well reduce if the product line is discontinued. Next year's healthy product contribution from hedge trimmers may be totally unrepresentative of the longer-term position to such an extent that immediate discontinuation could save substantial future costs arising as a consequence of continuing production/sale for another year. If marginal costing is to be used in the financial analysis of decisions which have significant effect beyond the short term, then it must be used in a way which recognises this effect: that is, by incorporating estimates for a number of years and in conjunction with the sort of techniques which we will encounter in Chapter 10.

In addition, marginal costing is based on a fixed/variable cost classification which may itself pose problems, as follows:

1 Making a reasonably accurate split between fixed and variable costs may not be possible for many organisations.
2 Marginal costing may have little relevance in situations where only a small proportion of total cost is variable. This might, for example, be the case with advanced manufacturing technologies.

Planning and control

When budgets are being prepared, or when they are being compared with actual results, an appreciation of cost behaviour is necessary. For example, if budgeted and actual volumes are different, which costs will react to this difference and which will not? As we shall see in Chapter 13, failure to allow for the impact of volume changes on budgeted and actual costs may undermine the value of a budget/actual comparison because like is not being compared with like. If a budget based on one estimated volume is compared to actual results based on a different volume, then the differences between the two will result partly from the volume difference and partly from efficiency and price differences. For effective control, it is desirable to separate these influences on budget/actual variation as far as possible. Marginal costing should help clarify these issues by segregating fixed and variable costs. Absorption costing, however, may make differentiation between volume, price and efficiency factors less clear because of the 'unitisation' of fixed costs via the absorption rate.

Absorption costing may suffer from another weakness. In Chapter 4 we saw that an element of subjectivity is inevitable for apportionment and reapportionment bases. To the extent that such apportionments and reapportionments exist, control may be hampered. If, for example, a cost centre's budgeted and actual costs contain significant apportionments/reapportionments, we can ask to what extent these are genuinely controllable by the cost centre concerned; and the fact that there are apportionments/reapportionments may not be obvious from absorption costing profit or cost statements. Marginal costing, for example by using a contribution analysis format, may help to highlight those costs which are specific to a cost centre (and therefore presumably controllable by it) and apportionments of general costs (which are unlikely to be directly controllable by the cost centre).

What we have, then, is a situation where many organisations must use absorption costing for external purposes, but where marginal costing may be superior for internal purposes. It might be possible to use marginal costing for internal reporting and absorption costing for external reporting, either by running the two systems in parallel or by employing marginal costing and making year-end adjustments in order to comply with the requirements of published accounts.

⮑ Can you see any problems in operating a 'dual' absorption/marginal system either in whole or in part?

The drawbacks to use of any form of 'dual' system are the cost of operation and the potential for confusion and error, which may be so great that the cost/benefit criterion is not met.

Variability of profit

Earlier in the chapter, we used OSN Ltd's data to demonstrate that, under absorption costing, net profit varies with both sales and stock changes, whereas marginal costing net profit varies with sales volume only. This facet of absorption costing may cause serious confusion. For example, does the higher absorption costing net profit in the 'stock increase' situation indicate better performance than the lower corresponding marginal costing net profit? A rather cynical view of this would suggest that absorption costing profit could be manipulated up or down as circumstances dictate merely by increasing/decreasing the volume of output (regardless of the sales volume).

But marginal costing may also be problematic with respect to variability of profit. In highly seasonal businesses (e.g. toy manufacturing), stocks may be deliberately built up during the 'off-peak' season in order to cope with peak demand. In this sort of situation, marginal costing profit is likely to fluctuate widely. By reacting to stock changes as well as to sales, absorption costing profit will somewhat smooth (but not eliminate) these fluctuations, giving, perhaps, a more balanced picture of the business over the entire period.

Marginal costing and price-setting

In Chapter 4, we suggested that inclusion of fixed overheads in unit costs could be seen as an attempt to approximate longer-term cost. Extending this argument, it might be said that, by using only variable costs, marginal costing takes a particularly short-term view of cost, and that this may cause problems where selling price is based to any extent on cost. To ensure long-term profitability, revenue must cover *all* costs, whether direct, indirect, fixed or variable. Marginal costing, by excluding fixed costs from the cost per unit, may run the risk of understating unit costs, with an associated risk of failure to set a price high enough to cover all costs. We saw, for example, that OSN Ltd would earn a profit of £12,000 on its special order at a selling price of £78; if this selling price were set for the company's *regular* sales, contribution would be insufficient to cover fixed costs and a loss would result:

	£
Unit selling price	78
Unit variable cost (including variable selling cost)	75
Unit contribution	3

Regular sales (from Exhibit 5.2)	18,000 units
	£
Total contribution	54,000
Total fixed costs (from Exhibit 5.2)	555,000
Loss	(501,000)

However, this assumes that prices are mainly cost-driven which, as we shall see in Chapter 8, may be a rather narrow view.

'Marginal' v 'variable' cost

So far in this chapter, we have implied that the terms 'marginal' and 'variable' are synonymous, but this is not strictly true. A marginal cost is the additional cost incurred to provide one extra unit. Within the relevant range of output volumes and time horizon, this may be the same as a unit's variable cost, but outside the relevant range this correlation becomes suspect. Consider, for example, the impact of step costs: as output increases, a volume will eventually be reached where the 'true' marginal cost of the next unit will consist of that unit's variable cost *plus* the amount of increase in step cost resulting. Although this may appear to be largely a problem of terminology, it does have a more practical aspect, as evidenced in OSN Ltd's decision about discontinuation of a product line: namely, that it is danger-ously unrealistic to assume that general fixed costs remain unchangeably fixed. In addition, it is unlikely that variable/marginal cost per unit is constant at all vol-umes (due, for example, to the presence of a learning curve).

Even if marginal and variable cost are roughly equivalent, marginal costing is dependent on our ability to separate costs into their fixed and variable elements with tolerable precision. Although problems of cost estimation and behaviour also affect absorption costing, it is possible to claim that, because of the different emphasis of the underlying cost classification (i.e. direct/indirect), simplistic assumptions such as 'marginal = variable' or 'fixed costs stay fixed' are less likely with absorption costing. On the other hand, a direct/indirect classification may divert attention from important issues of cost behaviour.

The overall picture is distinctly fuzzy. Neither absorption nor marginal costing is clearly superior in all circumstances. In practice, absorption costing is the most common approach. For many organisations, its use is dictated by the requirements of published accounts, and for the rest, a desire to be aware of the 'full' unit cost of products/services provided is the governing consideration. However, this does not preclude the use of marginal costing on an *ad hoc* basis. For instance, recent National Health Service guidelines on costing and pricing of contracts within the NHS 'inter-nal market' recommended that full (i.e. absorption) costing should normally be used, as marginal costing would result in underrecovery of costs, but goes on to say that marginal costing might be appropriate for costing the use of any spare capacity.

A similar type of approach can be seen in the sale of deep-discounted airline tick-ets by 'bucket shops' and of reduced cost 'off-peak' rail travel. In both cases, the fixed costs are irrelevant to the pricing decision (as the flight/train will presumably run regardless of the number of passengers), meaning that any price in excess of variable cost per passenger will generate additional profit – just as it did in the case of OSN Ltd's special order.

Summary

In this chapter, we have described and illustrated marginal costing, comparing and contrasting this approach with the absorption costing methodology discussed in the last chapter. We have seen that:

■ Marginal costing is based on the principle that, since many fixed overheads are time-related rather than volume-related, they should be treated as costs in their entirety within the period to which they relate.

■ Under marginal costing, the production cost per unit will exclude fixed production overhead, but this is the only difference between marginal and absorption unit costs.

■ In an absorption costing profit statement, all output-related costs incurred in generating revenue (direct and indirect, fixed and variable) are deducted from sales to determine gross profit. In a marginal costing profit statement all variable costs incurred in generating sales are deducted from sales to determine **contribution** – in the first instance to meeting fixed costs, and thereafter to profit.

■ Marginal costing net profit reacts to changes in sales volume only. Absorption costing net profit reacts to changes both in sales and in stock volumes.

■ The pattern of relative net profit reported by the two systems is:

production = sales: same under both approaches

production > sales: absorption costing higher

production < sales: marginal costing higher.

■ Where the two systems report a different profit, this difference is solely attributable to the fixed production overhead absorbed in the stock increase/decrease during the period.

■ Because many fixed costs are unaffected by decisions (and are therefore irrelevant), marginal costing may provide a useful aid to the financial analysis of decisions.

■ Contribution analysis extends marginal costing to encompass situations where fixed costs are affected by a decision.

■ Marginal and absorption costing may be compared in a number of ways, with the results being summarised as:

– absorption costing is necessary for many organisations' published accounts;

– marginal costing may be more appropriate for many internal purposes;

– absorption costing may be seen as an attempt to approximate longer-term unit costs, whereas marginal costing concentrates on short-term costs;

– the variability of absorption costing net profit with both sales and production volume may cause confusion;

– marginal and variable costs are not synonymous and the impact of non-linear costs should not be ignored.

In the next chapter, we will extend our discussion of marginal costing to illustrate its use in determination of such key indicators as breakeven point and margin of safety, along with its use in further decision scenarios.

FURTHER READING

Bromwich, M. and Bhimani, A., *Management Accounting Pathways to Progress*, CIMA, 1994. Chapter 4 contains an interesting discussion of the problem of fixed overheads and a suggested accounting report format based on the characteristics of cost.

Chadwick, L., *The Essence of Management Accounting*, Prentice Hall, 1991. *See* Chapter 6 for a concise summary of the 'absorption v marginal' costing debate.

Sᴇʟғ-ᴛᴇsᴛ ǫᴜᴇsᴛɪᴏɴs

5.1 A garden nursery specialises in growing and selling flowering cherry trees; last year, the following data applied:

Trees grown: 8,000
Trees sold: 6,000 @ £40 each
Cost per tree:
variable £6
fixed £12

What was the total contribution from sales of cherry trees during the year?

A £132,000
B £168,000
C £204,000
D £320,000

5.2 KX Ltd manufactures and sells children's car seats. Each car seat is sold for £80, and during the quarter just ended, the company's absorption costing system reported a net profit of £70,000. The marginal costing profit for the same quarter was £67,000. The following statements relate to the quarter just ended:

I production exceeded sales;
II sales exceeded production;
III absorption costing stock values exceeded marginal costing.

Which of the statements above is correct?

A I only
B II only
C I and III
D II and III

5.3 For each of the statements below, tick the appropriate box to indicate whether that statement is true or false:

	True	False
(a) Absorption of fixed overhead into unit costs may give the impression that the underlying cost is variable.	☐	☐
(b) Marginal costing net profit varies with both sales and production volumes.	☐	☐
(c) Unit costs as calculated using marginal principles are approximations of long-term unit costs.	☐	☐
(d) Marginal costing cannot be used for the published accounts of organisations subject to the requirements of Statement of Standard Accounting Practice No. 9.	☐	☐

(e) Variable selling, distribution and administration costs are excluded in calculation of marginal costing contribution. ☐ ☐

(f) Changes in the amount of fixed costs can readily be accommodated in a marginal costing analysis of a decision. ☐ ☐

5.4 RTQ Ltd, a passenger transport company, is considering increasing the frequency with which it runs buses on one of its routes. Information about this route is given below:

	£	£
Average fare revenue per passenger/kilometre		0.30
Variable cost per passenger/kilometre	0.08	
Fixed cost per passenger/kilometre	0.10	0.18
Profit per passenger/kilometre		0.12

Each additional journey run along the route under consideration should yield an average of 500 passenger/kilometres.

Assuming no increase in the amount of fixed cost incurred, by how much will RTQ Ltd's profit increase if 10 additional journeys are run on this particular route?

A £500
B £600
C £1,100
D £1,500

5.5 A summary profit statement for the sportswear department within a retail store for last year is given below:

	£	£
Sales		30,000
Cost of sale		14,000
Gross profit		16,000
Staff wages	20,000	
Apportionment of general store running costs	5,000	25,000
Net loss		(9,000)

It has been suggested that, due to the net loss reported, the sportswear department be closed, in which case the staff concerned would be redeployed to other departments within the store and the general costs would be reapportioned amongst the remaining departments.

If the proposal is proceeded with, what will be the effect on the store's overall profit?

A Increase of £4,000
B Increase of £9,000
C Decrease of £11,000
D Decrease of £16,000

QUESTIONS WITH ANSWERS

5.6 This question tests whether you can:

- prepare profit statements based on marginal and absorption costing principles;

- explain the reason for, and effect a reconciliation of, any profit difference between the two statements; and

- explain the relationship between marginal costing profit, production volume and sales volume.

FDS Ltd manufactures and sells computer monitors. Data for last year in respect of this company's 14-inch SVGA model were:

Sales:	24,000 units
Production:	26,000 units
Opening stock:	2,000 units
Closing stock:	4,000 units
Selling price per unit:	£90

Variable costs per unit:	£
Direct materials	20
Direct labour	10
Direct expenses	6
Selling overhead	4

Fixed costs for the year:	£
Production overhead – incurred	324,000
Production overhead – estimated	300,000
Selling overhead	110,000
Administration overhead	80,000

The company absorbs fixed production overhead on the basis of the annual budgeted volume of cost units, which was 25,000 for the year just ended.

Requirements

(a) Prepare FDS Ltd's profit statement for the year just ended based on: (i) absorption costing principles; and (ii) marginal costing principles.

(b) Explain the reason for any difference in net profit reported in the two statements in (a) and reconcile any such difference.

(c) Comment on a claim by FDS Ltd's Operations Manager that, when production fluctuates but sales remain constant, marginal costing net profit will likewise fluctuate.

5.7 This question tests whether you can:

- apply marginal costing principles to determine the contribution to general costs and to profit of different segments of a business; and

■ analyse the effect of a proposed decision on one particular segment's contribution and advise on the proposal's financial viability.

MP & Co, an insurance agent, sells three broad categories of insurance: house, car, and commercial. The following estimates are available for next year:

	Revenue £	Variable costs £	Wages £	Selling costs £	Admin. costs £
House insurance	80,000	16,000	28,000	12,000	6,000
Car insurance	220,000	90,000	50,000	30,000	10,000
Commercial insurance	105,000	40,000	34,000	14,000	8,000
Totals	405,000	146,000	112,000	56,000	24,000

Additional information

1 Of the total wages cost, 40 per cent is a fixed general company cost, representing the salaries of sales and office staff, and is apportioned to each of the three areas of operation. The balance represents sales commission which, being variable with revenue, is specifically attributable to the different types of insurance.

2 Selling costs are wholly fixed, with 30 per cent being specific to the particular type of insurance and the remainder being an apportionment of general costs.

3 Admin. costs are general costs which are apportioned to each category of insurance.

Requirements

(a) Prepare a marginal costing statement showing the contribution of each type of insurance to the firm's general costs, the firm's total contribution and profit.

(b) It has been suggested that a sales campaign be undertaken next year in order to improve the profitability of house insurance. It is estimated that this campaign would result in the following increases in next year's estimates:

Revenue:	30%
Variable costs:	15%
Specific selling costs:	£10,000

On the basis of house insurance's contribution to the firm's general costs, advise whether the sales campaign is financially worthwhile.

5.8 This question tests whether you can:

■ prepare a marginal costing profit statement which shows individual products' contribution to general costs and to profit;

■ provide advice about maximising profit based on product contributions to general costs; and

■ explain two assumptions which underlie your advice.

PM Ltd sells three models of mobile phone. On the basis of last year's results, which are given below, management feels that all three products are equally profitable and should continue to be sold.

Results for last year	Model XX/3l	Model YY/7k	Model ZZ/4t
	£	£	£
Sales	180,000	360,000	228,000
Cost of sales	100,000	170,000	104,000
Gross profit	80,000	190,000	124,000
Selling and distribution overhead	30,000	96,000	48,000
Administration overhead	30,000	30,000	30,000
Net profit	20,000	64,000	46,000

In the profit statement above, selling and distribution and administration overheads, being wholly fixed, have both been apportioned fairly arbitrarily to the three products, but further investigation reveals the following:

1 *Cost of sales* 80 per cent is variable, the balance being an apportionment of general costs.

2 *Selling and distribution overhead* Of the total incurred, 20 per cent is an apportionment of general costs, 40 per cent is specific to Model XX/3l, and 20 per cent is specific to each of Models YY/7k and ZZ/4t.

3 *Administration overhead* Of the total incurred, 40 per cent is specific to Model XX/3l, 10 per cent is specific to each of the other models, and the remainder is a general cost.

Requirements

(a) Prepare a profit statement based on marginal costing which shows, for each product, the contribution to general costs; your statement should also show aggregated figures for the company overall.

(b) Using your answer to (a), advise on the possibility of changing the sales mix in order to maximise profit, and quantify the effect that making such a change would have had on the company's profit last year.

(c) Explain *two* assumptions which underlie your analysis in (b).

QUESTIONS WITHOUT ANSWERS

5.9 CC Ceramics Ltd has provided the following information about production/sales of one of its tiles for the last two quarters:

	Quarter II	Quarter III
Sales (square metres)	41,000	53,000
Production (square metres)	44,000	47,000
Opening stock (square metres)	6,000	9,000
Closing stock (square metres)	9,000	3,000
Selling price per square metre	£18	£18
Total production costs incurred	£320,000	£335,000
Selling overhead:		
variable per square metre	£1	£1
fixed for quarter	£70,000	£70,000
Fixed administration overhead for quarter	£110,000	£110,000

Notes

1 Total production cost is semi-variable, the fixed element being production overhead.

2 Fixed production overhead is absorbed at the rate of £3 per square metre.

Requirements

(a) For *each* of Quarters II and III, prepare profit statements using: (i) absorption costing; and (ii) marginal costing.

(b) Assuming that CC Ltd employs marginal costing, determine the amount of adjustment necessary to both the opening and closing stock in Quarter III in order to bring the stock values into line with the absorption costing principles required for the company's published accounts. Explain whether this adjustment will represent an increase or a decrease in stock values compared to those reported under marginal costing.

(c) CC Ltd's volume of output and sales is subject to some fluctuation and uncertainty from one year to another and the company generally prepares several budgets based on different volume levels. Why would marginal costing be preferable to absorption costing in this context?

5.10 Management of SL & Co, which manufactures beds and related accessories, is dissatisfied with the profits earned by its 'Posturite' Orthopaedic Mattress. The following estimated data relate to next year's production/sale of this product:

Production/sales (units)	12,000
	£m
Sales revenue	1.26
Variable cost of sales	0.60
Specific fixed costs	0.30
Apportionment of general fixed costs	0.25
Net profit	0.11

In an attempt to improve the situation, various members of the management team have suggested four mutually exclusive options, details of which are given below.

Option 1
Increase the unit selling price by 20 per cent. This could be achieved if a promotional campaign costing £75,000 were mounted and if product quality were slightly improved, thereby increasing unit variable cost by £10. Production/sales volume would remain at its originally estimated level of 12,000 units.

Option 2
Maintain the unit selling price at its originally estimated amount, but markedly improve product design. This would increase unit variable cost by 25 per cent and specific fixed costs by £40,000. Production/sales volume under this option would increase to 18,000 units.

Option 3
Introduce, in addition to the existing 'Posturite' mattress, a cheaper version which would be sold as a substitute. Estimated unit sales of this new product are 1,000 at a

price of £70; variable cost per unit would be £30; and specific fixed costs of £10,000 would be incurred. It is reckoned that sales of 300 units of the original 'Posturite' mattress would be lost as a result of the introduction of this cheaper alternative.

Option 4
Improve the quality of customer service offered. This would increase the specific fixed costs by £200,000, but would also increase sales volume by 1,000 units.

Management is aware that, for every 'Posturite' mattress sold, £20 of additional contribution from sale of other company products is earned. This extra contribution would not, however, be earned on sale of the cheaper substitute, should that be introduced.

Requirements

(a) Using marginal costing principles, determine which (if any) of the four options offers the biggest improvement in estimated profit next year.

(b) Indicate any factors not included in your analysis in (a) which may be relevant to the final decision.

5.11 PPF Ltd is a publishing house whose output falls into three broad categories: Children's, Fiction, and Non-fiction. The company aims, over the next five years, to increase its share of the market for both Children's and Non-fiction publications. At a recent board meeting to discuss the projected expansion, the following figures were produced:

	Children's £000	Fiction £000	Non-fiction £000	Total £000
Sales revenue	8,900	11,400	5,800	26,100
Cost of sales	3,700	6,200	2,100	12,000
Gross profit	5,200	5,200	3,700	14,100
Administration costs				6,300
Selling and distribution costs				5,100
Net profit				2,700

In the course of the board meeting, a heated dispute arose between PPF Ltd's Managing Director and Sales Director, details of which are summarised as follows:

1 *Managing Director's contention* On the basis of the figures above, the Managing Director has claimed that doubling sales of Children's and Non-fiction titles over the next five years will double the gross profit associated with each of these lines of business (i.e. to £10.4 and £7.4 million respectively). He further claimed that the effect of this would be to increase PPF Ltd's net profit to £11.6 million.

2 *Sales Director's contention* The Sales Director's view is that the figures used by the Managing Director, along with the related conclusion, are questionable, and she has urged that further analysis be undertaken before any firm decision is reached.

PPF Ltd's Chairman, concerned at the dispute, adjourned the meeting and requested that you, as Development Director, prepare an urgent report on the situation.

Requirement

Prepare a report for the Chairman which addresses the following issues:

1 The suitability or otherwise of the figures provided as a basis for the board's decision and the possible impact of this on the Managing Director's conclusion.

2 An explanation of how (if at all) the figures could be made more useful, with supporting rationale for, and reservations about, your suggestions.

3 A statement of any additional information or improvements to available information which would aid the board's deliberations.

PART 2

Decision analysis

In this section, we explore management accounting's role as an aid to decision making, illustrating the different techniques applicable in a range of different situations. What we will also emphasise is that, whilst it is important, financial analysis can provide only part of the picture. Part 2 comprises the following chapters:

6 Cost/volume/profit analysis

7 Relevant costs and benefits for decision making

8 More decisions: price setting and limiting factors

9 Decision making under conditions of risk and uncertainty

10 Capital investment appraisal

11 Capital investment appraisal: further issues

In Chapters 6 and 7, we develop topics introduced in Part 1; specifically, cost classification and attribution and financial analysis of short-run decisions. Chapter 8 deals with two 'special-case' decisions – pricing and product/service prioritisation where resources are limited, while Chapter 9 covers the incorporation of risk and uncertainty into decision analysis. Chapter 10 extends the discussion of decision analysis to encompass long-term decisions (where the relevance of strategic considerations is especially evident); related issues, such as sources of finance for decisions and derivation of the cost of capital central to so many evaluative criteria, are considered in Chapter 11.

CHAPTER 6

Cost/volume/profit analysis

BACK FROM THE BRINK

In the 1960s, Leyland's truck manufacturing business was the largest outside the eastern bloc. The Albion factory in Scotstoun, Glasgow, made all the group's truck and van axles. Set up for high-volume manufacture, its plant had become increasingly inflexible as the number of trucks built fell. According to a plan revealed after Leyland Daf collapsed – Leyland's trucks and vans business had been taken over in the mid-1980s – the Dutch parent Daf had been intending to close the Albion plant in 1994 as part of a rescue plan . . .

With the prospect of job losses on the Clyde looming large, Glasgow Development Agency called in Dan Wright, a former Ford and Leyland automotive design engineer turned consultant who wanted to move back into a hands-on engineering business. Wright's medium-term goal was to expand the company to a size where it would be taken seriously in the motor industry and to put it in a position where it could invest . . .

While the marketing, sales, finance and purchasing functions were being strengthened – adding about 40 people to the payroll over the next year – Albion struck lucky. The market in trucks started recovering in a way it had not planned for, says Wright. 'By the end of the first full financial year, in March 1995, instead of planned losses of £1.5m we reached breakeven – three years ahead of plan.'

Source: Richard Gourlay, *Financial Times*, 12 December 1995

EXHIBIT **6.1 Breakeven: an important indicator in cost/volume/profit analysis**

167

INTRODUCTION

A vital set of relationships for management to be aware of is that which exists between cost, volume and profit. For example, it may be of great importance for management to be aware of the volume of sales which must be achieved in order to cover costs and avoid a loss being made – as it was with Albion in Exhibit 6.1; or it may be important to have an idea of the vulnerability of a business's profit to reductions in demand, or to know what volume of sales will yield a particular target profit.

In this chapter, we will discuss and illustrate the use of cost/volume/profit analysis – which attempts to address these issues – along with its underlying assumptions and the extent to which these can be reconciled with reality.

OBJECTIVES   When you have completed this chapter, you will be able to:

- explain the concepts of breakeven point, margin of safety and sensitivity analysis;

- use a formulaic approach to calculate breakeven point, margin of safety and sales required to earn a target profit;

- present cost/volume/profit relationships graphically in the form of breakeven charts, contribution charts and profit/volume charts;

- use sensitivity analysis to assess the impact of changes to one or more variables within the cost/volume/profit model; and

- appreciate the assumptions on which the model rests and the importance of relevant range in this context.

BREAKEVEN POINT

Central to cost/volume/profit analysis is the concept of **breakeven point**. This is the sales volume – expressed either in units or in revenue – at which costs are exactly covered by revenue: that is, at breakeven point, profit is zero. Cost/volume/profit analysis is a marginal costing technique and all the calculations which we are about to describe derive from the principles introduced in the last chapter. Exhibit 6.2 contains the basic data which we shall use to illustrate the cost/volume/profit model.

Key-cutting franchise

A locksmith has acquired the franchise to provide a key-cutting service within the ironmongery department of a large local store. He estimates that he will be able to charge £2.50 per key cut and that the variable cost per key cut (covering the key blank and power costs) will be £0.60. Fixed costs for the first year's operations will consist of a £2,000 payment to the store under the terms of the franchise agreement plus £2,750 for hire of fittings and equipment.

EXHIBIT 6.2 **Information for breakeven calculation**

⤷ Complete the abbreviated marginal costing profit statement below to determine the total contribution which must be earned if the franchise is to break even (i.e. if profit is to be zero)?

	£
Total contribution	....
less Total fixed costs	....
Profit	0

Working backwards from profit, the completed statement reads:

	£
Total contribution	4,750
less Total fixed costs (£2,000 + £2,750)	4,750
Profit	0

Thus, at breakeven point:

total contribution = total fixed costs

⤷ From Exhibit 6.2, determine the contribution per key cut. How many keys need to be cut at this unit contribution in order to earn total contribution of £4,750 (i.e. in order to attain breakeven point)?

The contribution per key cut is:

(unit selling price – unit variable cost) = (£2.50 – £0.60) = £1.90

The issue of determining breakeven point now resolves itself into: 'How many keys at a unit contribution of £1.90 must be cut in order to earn total contribution of £4,750?' The required number is:

$$\frac{\text{total fixed costs}}{\text{contribution per unit}} = \frac{£4,750}{£1.90} = 2,500 \text{ keys}$$

We now have a formula for obtaining breakeven point in terms of unit sales:

$$\frac{\text{total fixed costs}}{\text{contribution per unit}}$$

We can check that a volume of 2,500 keys cut does result in profit of zero if we insert the data from Exhibit 6.2 into a marginal costing profit statement:

	£
Sales revenue (2,500 @ £2.50)	6,250
less Marginal cost of sales (2,500 @ £0.60)	1,500
Total contribution	4,750
less Total fixed costs	4,750
Profit	0

If we want breakeven point in terms of revenue rather than unit sales, we can simply multiply the breakeven volume by the selling price per unit:

$$(2,500 \times £2.50) = £6,250$$

Suppose, however, that no unit data are available. Here we need to amend the breakeven formula by using the contribution/sales (CS) ratio as the denominator. The CS ratio is simply contribution expressed as a proportion of sales – either unit contribution and unit selling price or total contribution and total sales revenue.

⇨   What is the key-cutting franchise's contribution/sales ratio?

Based on the unit data in Exhibit 6.2, the CS ratio is:

$$\frac{\text{contribution}}{\text{selling price per unit}} = \frac{£1.90}{£2.50} = 0.76$$

The same ratio results from use of total contribution and total sales revenue (both figures are taken from the marginal costing profit statement above):

$$\frac{\text{total contribution}}{\text{total sales revenue}} = \frac{£4,750}{£6,250} = 0.76$$

Rearranging the CS ratio calculation, we can say that:

$$\textbf{contribution} = (\textbf{CS ratio} \times \textbf{sales})$$

At breakeven point,

$$\textbf{total contribution} = \textbf{total fixed costs}$$

so

$$(\textbf{CS ratio} \times \textbf{sales}) = \textbf{total fixed costs}$$

⇨ The data for the franchise has been inserted into the last formula to give the following:

$$(0.76 \times \text{sales}) = £4,750$$

What is the breakeven point in sales revenue?

To determine the value of sales we need one final rearrangement to the formula:

$$\text{sales} = \frac{£4,750}{0.76} = £6,250$$

This is the same revenue figure we obtained in our marginal costing profit statement for the breakeven unit volume of 2,500 keys cut: (2,500 @ £2.50). In general terms, breakeven point in revenue is:

$$\frac{\textbf{total fixed costs}}{\textbf{CS ratio}}$$

Sales required to earn a target profit

Achieving a breakeven position is unquestionably better than incurring a loss, but a positive profit would be even better (see Exhibit 6.3).

Key-cutting franchise: target profit

For the first year's operations, the franchise's owner aims to earn a target profit of £9,500. All other information is as set out in Exhibit 6.2.

Exhibit 6.3 Sales required to earn a target profit

⇨ Complete the statement below to determine the total contribution required to yield target profit of £9,500.

	£
Total contribution	....
less Total fixed costs	....
Profit	9,500

The completed statement reads:

	£
Total contribution	14,250
less Total fixed costs	4,750
Profit	9,500

⇨ How many keys must be cut in order to earn total contribution of £14,250?

At a contribution per unit of £1.90:

$$\frac{£14,250}{£1.90} = 7,500 \text{ keys}$$

need to be cut to earn the desired target profit. From this, we can derive a formula for sales volume in units required to earn a specified target profit:

$$\text{sales units to earn target profit} = \frac{\text{total fixed costs} + \text{target profit}}{\text{contribution per unit}}$$

This is really just an extension of the breakeven formula, the difference here being that there is a positive target profit (whereas the target profit was zero in the breakeven formula).

⇨ What sales revenue is required to provide the target profit of £9,500?

All that is needed is to change the denominator to the CS ratio:

$$\frac{\text{total fixed costs} + \text{target profit}}{\text{CS ratio}}$$

$$= \frac{£14,250}{0.76} = £18,750$$

⇨ Confirm that a volume of 7,500 keys cut yields a profit of £9,500.

We can use a marginal costing profit statement to confirm our result:

	£
Sales revenue (7,500 @ £2.50)	18,750
less Total variable costs (7,500 @ £0.60)	4,500
Total contribution	14,250
less Total fixed costs	4,750
Profit	9,500

At volumes in excess of breakeven point, total contribution exceeds total fixed costs, so contribution and profit *per unit* are the same. Similarly, above breakeven point, increased/decreased total contribution will correspond with increased/decreased profit. This provides an alternative route to the required sales:

$$\frac{\text{profit/contribution required } \textit{above} \text{ breakeven point}}{\text{contribution per unit}} = \text{units required } \textit{above} \text{ breakeven point}$$

$$= \frac{£9,500}{£1.90} = 5,000$$

Since we know the breakeven point to be 2,500 units, sales of 7,500 units will give the desired profit.

THE MARGIN OF SAFETY

Cost/volume/profit analysis can help management assess the vulnerability of profit to reductions in demand.

> **Key-cutting franchise: estimated volume of keys cut**
>
> In the first year's operations, the franchise's owner estimates that the volume of sales will be 8,000 keys cut. Breakeven volume is 2,500 keys cut and 7,500 keys must be cut to earn the owner's target profit of £9,500 for the first year of operations.

EXHIBIT 6.4 Margin of safety

⇨ In Exhibit 6.4, by how much will target profit be exceeded if sales volume is 8,000 keys cut?

We could prepare a marginal costing profit statement based on sales of 8,000 units:

	£
Sales revenue (8,000 @ £2.50)	20,000
less Total variable costs (8,000 @ £0.60)	4,800
Total contribution	15,200
less Total fixed costs	4,750
Profit	10,450

The estimated volume thus provides extra profit of (£10,450 – £9,500) = £950.

Alternatively, we can take a short-cut approach, derived from the fact that, above breakeven point, contribution and profit per unit are the same:

Units in excess of sales required (8,000 – 7,500)	500
Contribution per unit	£1.90
Additional contribution/profit	£950

⇨ By how many units must estimated volume fall before losses are incurred?

At any volume lower than breakeven point, losses will be incurred, so estimated sales will need to fall by more than (8,000 – 2,500) = 5,500 units or (£20,000 – £6,250) = £13,750 in revenue terms.

To facilitate comparisons (e.g. between different years' operations), this volume difference can be expressed as a percentage of estimated sales (occasionally, actual sales are used instead of estimated):

$$\frac{(\text{estimated or actual sales} - \text{breakeven sales})}{\text{estimated or actual sales}} \times 100\%$$

⇨ What is this percentage figure for the franchise and what does it indicate?

The relevant percentage is:

$$\frac{(8,000 - 2,500)}{8,000} \times 100\% = 68.75\%$$

This tells us that the franchise's sales must fall by an amount in excess of 68.75 per cent of their estimated volume before losses are incurred. Using revenue in the formula yields the same result:

$$\frac{(£20,000 - £6,250)}{£20,000} \times 100\% = 68.75\%$$

The difference between estimated (or actual) sales volume and breakeven sales volume is termed the **margin of safety**. This provides management with a measure of the vulnerability of profit to reductions in sales volume – profit will be less vulnerable to demand drops with a higher than with a lower margin of safety.

However, in the case of the franchise, we cannot definitely say whether 68.75 per cent is 'good' or 'bad'. It appears to be quite healthy, especially for a first year of operation, but we need to have some sort of yardstick (e.g. data from comparable businesses, or from previous years' trading) before we can be more certain. We also need to have reasonable confidence in the accuracy of the estimated sales volume before too much significance can be attached to the margin of safety. *If* the estimate is reasonable, then the margin of safety may be more than adequate. Another way of looking at the same thing is to ask: 'How likely is it that estimated sales volume is overstated by more than 68.75 per cent?'

GRAPHICAL PRESENTATIONS

The advantage possessed by graphical representations of cost/volume/profit relationships over a formulaic approach lies in their immediacy and impact on the reader. For example, the bald statement that a business has a margin of safety of 68.75 per cent may have considerably less effect and meaning than a graphical illustration of the same fact; a well-designed chart can highlight the significance of a large or small margin of safety without using a complex-looking formula. However, graphical presentations may suffer the drawback of being somewhat inaccurate, as figures may be difficult to plot with absolute precision. But this need not be a major deterrent to their use. In most cases, the data being plotted will relate to estimates, which will themselves be subject to error, and use of computers can greatly reduce inaccuracy of plots.

Graphical presentations: scaling the axes

Selection of an appropriate scale for the axes of a graphical presentation may sometimes be problematic. You may find the following general guidelines useful:

1 *What is the breakeven point?* It may be worthwhile determining this by formula before preparing your chart.
2 *What is the maximum volume?* If none is specified, select one which is high enough to accommodate both the breakeven and estimated sales volumes. This will permit the margin of safety to be illustrated if required.
3 *What is the maximum monetary amount involved?* This can be determined by reference to the maximum volume in item 2 above.

In the graphical presentations of the key-cutting franchise which follow, a maximum volume of 10,000 keys has been used. This is sufficiently high to cover both the breakeven and the estimated sales volumes for the period under consideration.

The breakeven chart

To construct a breakeven chart, we need to plot the following against volume: *total fixed cost; total cost*; and *sales revenue*.

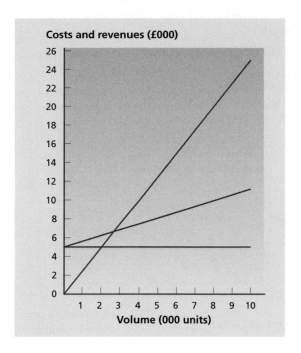

FIGURE 6.1
Incomplete breakeven chart for key-cutting franchise

⇨ Figure 6.1 is a breakeven chart for the franchise, but with labels missing from all of its lines. Indicate the *total fixed cost, total cost* and *sales revenue* lines on Figure 6.1, along with the breakeven point. (The two cost lines should be familiar to you from Chapter 3, and we have already calculated the breakeven point.)

Figure 6.2 is the franchise's completed breakeven chart. The total fixed cost line will run parallel to the horizontal axis at a height of £4,750. Total cost at any volume will comprise (total variable cost + total fixed cost). Bearing in mind that we need total costs for only two volumes to enable us to plot this line, we select two volumes:

	£
Zero volume	
Total variable costs	nil
Total fixed costs	4,750
Total cost	4,750
10,000 keys	
Total variable costs (10,000 @ £0.60)	6,000
Total fixed costs	4,750
Total cost	10,750

Joining the total cost plots for these two volumes provides the total cost line on our breakeven chart. We have taken the assumed maximum volume in addition to zero; any volume in excess of zero will serve, although it helps if the associated total cost is easy to plot.

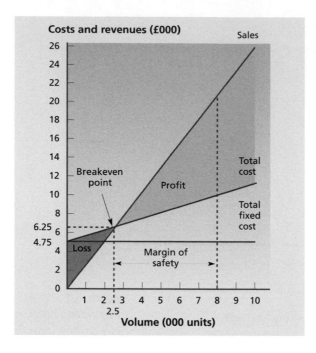

FIGURE 6.2
Completed breakeven chart for key-cutting franchise

The sales revenue line can be plotted in a similar manner by selecting revenue at two volumes (zero and any volume greater than zero):

Volume	Revenue
Zero	nil
10,000 keys	(10,000 @ £2.50) = £25,000

Joining these plots in a straight line gives the sales revenue function.

The breakeven point in Figure 6.2 occurs where the sales revenue and total cost lines intersect: that is, where revenue = total cost. Profit will be zero at this point. We can then read down to the horizontal axis to obtain the breakeven point in units or across to the vertical axis to obtain the revenue equivalent. At all volumes to the left of the breakeven point, the total cost line lies above the revenue line (i.e. total cost exceeds revenue), so losses are incurred. At all volumes to the right of breakeven point, however, sales revenue exceeds total cost, so profits are earned.

The breakeven chart is a clear representation of the key variables in the cost/volume/profit model. However, it does not show total variable cost, total contribution or profit at different volumes; these can certainly be determined from the breakeven chart, but not *directly*. For example, profit at different volumes can be determined by calculating the vertical distance between the revenue and total cost lines, or total variable cost as the vertical distance between the total cost and total fixed cost lines. An alternative presentation may therefore be desirable in order to highlight elements of the model not directly revealed by this approach. The contribution chart is one such alternative.

The contribution chart

Figure 6.3 is an incomplete contribution chart for the franchise.

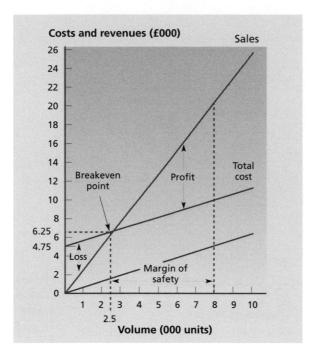

FIGURE **6.3**
Incomplete contribution chart for key-cutting franchise

⇨ Only two of the lines in Figure 6.3 are labelled. What does the third line represent? Are total fixed costs shown on this chart? If so, where? What about total contribution?

This type of presentation differs from the breakeven chart in that total variable costs are plotted against volume – this is what the third line in Figure 6.3 represents. This line is plotted in the same manner used for the sales line in Figure 6.2, using zero and some volume greater than zero:

Volume	Total variable cost
Zero	Zero
Maximum	(10,000 @ £0.60) = £6,000

Plotting and joining these two values gives the required cost function. Total fixed cost is not shown separately, but is the vertical distance between the total variable cost and the total cost lines. Since total fixed cost is the same at all volumes, these lines are parallel, and we can read the fixed cost value from the vertical axis (£4,750). The sales revenue and total cost plots are exactly the same as they were in Figures 6.1 and 6.2. The franchise's completed contribution chart is shown in Figure 6.4.

Despite its name, this sort of chart does not show total contribution directly. Instead, total contribution can be determined by calculating the vertical distance between the sales revenue and total variable cost lines. As it did in the breakeven chart, breakeven point occurs where the sales revenue and total cost lines intersect,

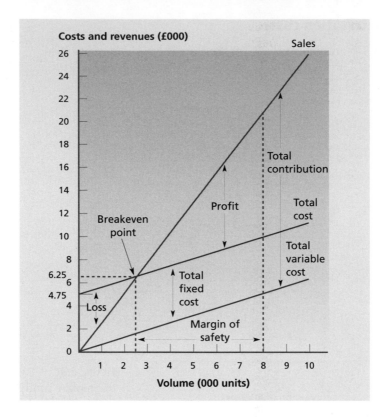

FIGURE **6.4**
Completed contribution chart for key-cutting franchise

and we can read the corresponding unit volume from the horizontal axis and revenue amount from the vertical axis.

We have just said that the contribution chart in Figures 6.3 and 6.4 does not permit total contribution to be assessed directly. But, since changes in total contribution can provide a useful 'ready reckoner' for management when examining the increase/decrease in profit caused by changes in volume, it may be more useful to present an 'abbreviated' contribution chart which plots total contribution directly against total fixed cost. With this sort of chart, the impact on total contribution (and hence on profit)of volume changes may be more readily appreciated. Figure 6.5 is an 'abbreviated' contribution chart for the franchise.

The total fixed cost line in Figure 6.5 has been plotted in the same way as before: for the total contribution line we again need two values (for zero and a volume greater than zero) joined in a straight line:

Volume	Total contribution
Zero	Zero
Maximum	(10,000 @ £1.90) = £19,000

Breakeven point occurs where the total contribution and total fixed cost lines intersect. Note that in this presentation, it is only possible to read the breakeven volume from the horizontal axis.

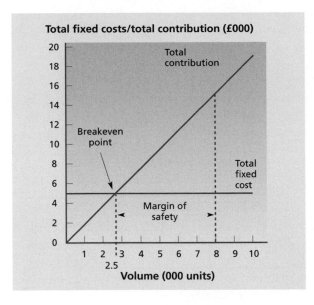

FIGURE 6.5
'Abbreviated' contribution chart
for franchise

As well as permitting quick assessment of profit changes relative to volume changes, our 'abbreviated' contribution chart has two further advantages:

1 Only two lines need be plotted, which makes the chart easier to construct and read.
2 It is consistent with the formulaic approach to breakeven calculation: that is, it highlights the fact that breakeven point occurs where total contribution equals total fixed cost.

The profit/volume chart

This approach aims to remedy a weakness of all the previous presentations: namely, that none directly shows profit/loss against volume. Figure 6.6 is a profit/volume chart for the key-cutting franchise.

Of all presentations, this is probably the easiest to prepare, since only a single line need be plotted. We need two values for profit/loss to enable us to do this. At maximum volume, profit is as follows:

	£
Sales (10,000 @ £2.50)	25,000
less Total variable costs (10,000 @ £0.60)	6,000
Total contribution	19,000
less Total fixed costs	4,750
Profit	14,250

▷ What is the amount of the loss which is incurred at zero volume?

At zero volume, revenue will be zero, as will total variable cost and hence total contribution. However, total fixed cost will still be incurred, so the amount of the loss will be equal to total fixed cost. Joining this point to the profit calculated above provides the profit/loss plot, breakeven point occurring where the profit/loss line intersects the horizontal axis.

179

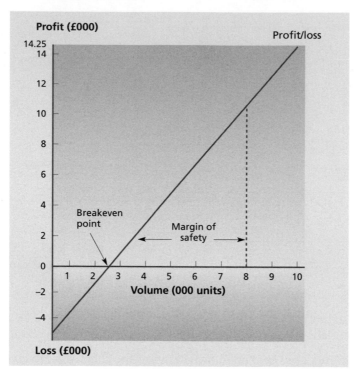

**FIGURE 6.6
Profit/volume chart for
franchise**

So far, we have assumed that the situation we are analysing is static; how can we analyse a changing or uncertain situation?

SENSITIVITY ANALYSIS

Sensitivity analysis is a 'what-if' technique which allows management to gauge the effect of changing one or more of the variables within the cost/volume/profit model. It permits uncertainty about the value of different variables such as unit variable cost or selling price to be allowed for and can also aid in assessing the financial desirability of different courses of action.

Key-cutting franchise: alternative source of supply for key blanks

An alternative supplier has been found who offers to supply suitable key blanks at a lower price, which will reduce the variable cost per key cut from £0.60 to £0.50. However, in order to cut these cheaper blanks properly, different cutting equipment will need to be hired, which will increase the hire cost per annum from £2,750 to £3,800 (the £2,000 payment under the franchise agreement being unaffected). Estimated sales for the year are 8,000 keys cut at a selling price of £2.50 per key and target profit is £9,500.

EXHIBIT 6.5 **Assessing an alternative source of supply**

Applying sensitivity analysis to the situation in Exhibit 6.5 means asking the question: 'What will happen to the original cost/volume/profit model for the franchise if unit variable cost and total fixed cost change?' The answer involves recalculation of the model's indicative values: breakeven point, margin of safety and sales required to earn £9,500 profit. Once we have these revised values, we can make a comparison of the financial viability of each source of supply.

▷ Based on the alternative data in Exhibit 6.5, what is the franchise's breakeven point (in units), its margin of safety (as a percentage of estimated sales) and the volume of sales required to earn £9,500 profit?

The contribution per key based on the alternative source of supply is (£2.50 – £0.50) = £2.00, giving a breakeven point of:

$$\frac{\text{total fixed cost}}{\text{contribution per unit}} = \frac{(£2,000 + £3,800)}{£2.00} = 2,900 \text{ units}$$

The margin of safety is:

$$\frac{(\text{estimated sales} - \text{breakeven sales})}{\text{estimated sales}} \times 100\%$$

$$= \frac{(8,000 - 2,900)}{8,000} \times 100\% = 63.75\%$$

And the revised sales volume necessary for £9,500 profit is:

$$\frac{(\text{total fixed cost} + \text{target profit})}{\text{contribution per unit}}$$

$$= \frac{(£2,000 + £3,800) + £9,500}{£2} = 7,650 \text{ units}$$

Table 6.1 compares these three indicative values with the ones we obtained earlier based on the original source of supply.

TABLE 6.1 **Key outcomes from each option**

Indicator	Original source	Alternative source
Breakeven point (units)	2,500	2,900
Margin of safety	68.75%	63.75%
Sales required for target profit (units)	7,500	7,650

▷ Using the comparative data in Table 6.1, which source of supply is more attractive in financial terms and why?

Financially, the original source of supply is better: breakeven volume and sales required to earn the target profit are both lower (which means that they should be easier to achieve), and the margin of safety is higher (meaning that profit is a little less vulnerable to drops in demand).

Suppose the franchise owner wished to know at what volume of sales the two sources of supply yield the same profit (the 'indifference' volume: that is, the volume at which he will be indifferent as to the source of supply). This can be determined using some simple algebra. If we convert the summary marginal costing profit statement at the start of this chapter into equation form, we get:

$$\text{sales} - \text{total variable cost} - \text{total fixed cost} = \text{profit}$$

which can be 'tidied up' to read:

$$\text{total contribution} - \text{total fixed cost} = \text{profit}$$

If each source of supply is to yield the same profit, we can say that:

$$\begin{array}{cc}\text{total contribution} - \text{total fixed cost} = \text{total contribution} - \text{total fixed cost} \\ \text{[original source]} \qquad\qquad\qquad \text{[alternative source]}\end{array}$$

Bearing in mind that total contribution is (unit contribution × sales volume), we will call the unknown factor (i.e. sales volume) X and insert the figures which we already know:

$$\begin{array}{cc}(£1.90 \times X) - £4,750 \;=\; (£2.00 \times X) - £5,800 \\ \text{[original]} \qquad\qquad\qquad \text{[alternative]}\end{array}$$

⇨ Remembering that X has the same value for both sources of supply, determine the sales volume at which each yields the same profit.

Rearranging the equation above gives

$$£0.1X = £1,050$$
$$\therefore X = 10,500 \text{ units.}$$

In other words, at a sales volume of 10,500 units, each source of supply will earn the same profit. We can confirm that this is correct and obtain a value for that profit by preparing a marginal costing profit statement for each option:

	Original source £	Alternative source £
Sales:		
(10,500 @ £2.50)	26,250	26,250
less Total variable costs:		
(10,500 @ £0.60)	6,300	
(10,500 @ £0.50)		5,250
Total contribution	19,950	21,000
less Total fixed costs	4,750	5,800
Profit	15,200	15,200

Alternatively, we could obtain the indifference volume by graphical means: Figure 6.7 is a profit/volume chart showing a profit/loss line for each option across a range of volumes from zero to 12,000 keys cut. (Note that it has been necessary to increase the assumed maximum volume from the original 10,000 in order to accommodate the 'indifference' volume.) Reading down from the point where the two profit/loss lines intersect gives the desired volume.

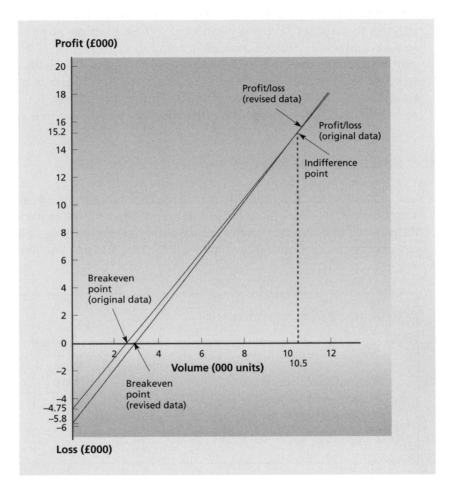

FIGURE 6.7
Profit/volume chart for alternative sources of supply

⇨ Which source of supply is financially better at a volume of: (a) 11,000 keys; and (b) 8,000 keys?

At a volume of 11,000 keys, the alternative source of supply is better. We can see from Figure 6.7 that, at volumes in excess of 10,500 keys, this is the more profitable option, as the related profit/loss line lies above that associated with the original source of supply. Conversely, at volumes lower than 10,500, the original source is better. So if it were confidently expected that sales volume might exceed 10,500 keys, the franchise owner may consider changing the source of supply.

For this sort of presentation – that is where two or more options are being graphed on the same chart – the profit/volume chart is the best method to use. The cost, contribution and revenue lines variously required by the other charts will make them difficult to plot and interpret.

Application of sensitivity analysis thus requires a complete reworking of the cost/volume/profit model to reflect possible changes in its variables. Thus, although sensitivity analysis can be a valuable aid to planning and decision making and can provide considerable flexibility in use, it can also be rather cumbersome and time-consuming – especially if several different possible sets of changes to variables are being considered. Where multiple or particularly complex sets of changes are being examined, a computer spreadsheet is of great help, permitting complex combinations of changes to be analysed speedily and without the need for lengthy calculation. Once the relationships between a cost/volume/profit model's variables have been specified within the spreadsheet, it is a simple matter to 'interrogate' the computer about the effect of changes to input values.

MULTIPLE PRODUCTS/SERVICES

Our analysis of the key-cutting franchise has thus far been based on the cutting of a single type of key. This might happen in practice, but it is more likely that a range of different types of product/service are offered. For example, several different types of key may be cut, each with its own unit selling price and unit variable cost.

Key-cutting franchise: sales mix

During the first year's operations, three types of key will be cut as follows:

	House	Cylinder	Car
Estimated number of keys cut	4,000	2,400	1,600
Selling price per key cut	£2.50	£3.70	£2.00
Variable cost per key cut	£0.60	£1.00	£0.80

The franchise's total fixed cost for the year will be £4,750.

EXHIBIT 6.6 Franchise's sales mix

Our calculations must reflect the **sales mix** in Exhibit 6.6: that is, the proportion of total sales represented by each type of key cut:

Key Type	%
House	50
Cylinder	30
Car	20

We can use these percentages to 'weight' the contribution per key:

(50% × house key unit contribution) + (30% × cylinder key unit contribution)
+ (20% × car key unit contribution)

= (50% × {£2.50 − £0.60}) + (30% × {£3.70 − £1.00}) + (20% × {£2.00 − £0.80}) = £2.00

⇨ What is the franchise's breakeven point in unit sales based on the weighted average contribution?

Using the weighted average unit contribution in our breakeven formula, we get

$$\frac{\text{total fixed cost}}{\text{weighted average unit contribution}} = \frac{£4,750}{£2.00} = 2,375 \text{ units}$$

Of this breakeven volume, 50 per cent will be house keys, 30 per cent cylinder keys and 20 per cent car keys.

⇨ Use the data in Exhibit 6.6 to determine the franchise's CS ratio based on total contribution and total sales revenue.

By calculating the CS ratio on the basis of total contribution and total sales revenue, we automatically reflect the sales mix: that is, the resulting ratio is the **weighted average contribution/sales ratio**:

Total sales revenue

	£
House keys (4,000 @ £2.50)	10,000
Cylinder keys (2,400 @ £3.70)	8,880
Car keys (1,600 @ £2.00)	3,200
	22,080

Total contribution

	£
House keys (4,000 @ {£2.50 − £0.60})	7,600
Cylinder keys (2,400 @ {£3.70 − £1.00})	6,480
Car keys (1,600 @ {£2.00 − £0.80})	1,920
	16,000

The weighted average CS ratio is thus:

$$\frac{\text{total contribution}}{\text{total sales revenue}} = \frac{£16,000}{£22,080} = 0.725$$

We can now use this as the denominator in our breakeven formula:

$$\frac{\text{total fixed cost}}{\text{weighted average CS ratio}} = \frac{£4,750}{0.725} = £6,552$$

⇨ What volume of sales (in revenue) must the franchise achieve in order to earn the target profit of £9,500?

Again, we can use the weighted average CS ratio as the denominator in our formula:

$$\frac{\text{(total fixed cost + target profit)}}{\text{weighted average CS ratio}} = \frac{(\pounds4,750 + \pounds9,500)}{0.725} = \pounds19,655$$

Note that the values for breakeven point and sales to earn £9,500 profit *only* apply if the sales mix specified in Exhibit 6.6 remains constant. If the sales mix changes (see Exhibit 6.7), the weighted average contribution per unit and CS ratio will change to reflect the new relative weightings for each type of key.

Key-cutting franchise: revised sales mix

During the first year's operations, three types of key will be cut as follows:

	House	Cylinder	Car
Estimated number of keys cut	1,600	1,600	4,800
Selling price per key cut	£2.50	£3.70	£2.00
Variable cost per key cut	£0.60	£1.00	£0.80

The franchise's total fixed cost for the year will be £4,750.

EXHIBIT **6.7** **Franchise: change in sales mix**

The sales mix in Exhibit 6.7 has a weighted average CS ratio of :

$$\frac{\text{total contribution}}{\text{total sales revenue}} = \frac{\pounds13,120}{\pounds19,520} = 0.67$$

giving a breakeven point in revenue of:

$$\frac{\text{total fixed cost}}{\text{weighted average CS ratio}} = \frac{\pounds4,750}{0.67} = \pounds7,090$$

To earn profit of £9,500 from the sales mix from Exhibit 6.7, the franchise now needs revenue of:

$$\frac{\text{(total fixed cost + target profit)}}{\text{weighted average CS ratio}} = \frac{(\pounds4,750 + \pounds9,500)}{0.67} = \pounds21,269$$

We can also obtain the margin of safety for each sales mix, here based on sales revenue:

$$\frac{\text{(estimated sales revenue – breakeven sales revenue)}}{\text{estimated sales revenue}} \times 100\%$$

$$\text{mix in Exhibit 6.6} = \frac{(\pounds22,080 - \pounds6552)}{\pounds22,080} \times 100\% = 70.33\%$$

$$\text{mix in Exhibit 6.7} = \frac{(\pounds19,520 - \pounds7,090)}{(\pounds19,520} \times 100\% = 63.68\%$$

⇨ Why are breakeven point and sales required to earn profit of £9,500 higher and the margin of safety lower for the sales mix in Exhibit 6.7 than they were for that in Exhibit 6.6?

TABLE 6.2 Analysis of relative profitability of sales mixes

Key type	Unit contribution (£)	Sales mix (%)	
		Exhibit 6.6	Exhibit 6.7
House	1.90	50	20
Cylinder	2.70	30	20
Car	1.20	20	60

Comparison of data in Exhibits 6.6 and 6.7 is shown in Table 6.2. The least profitable type of key dominates the revised sales mix, reducing the weighted average CS ratio to 0.67 (from 0.725), and thus causing an increase in breakeven point and sales required for target profit. The margin of safety has reduced because of the higher breakeven point *and* because estimated revenue from the revised mix is lower.

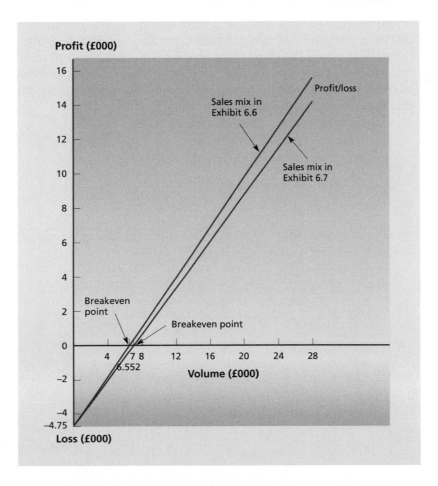

FIGURE 6.8
Profit/volume
chart for 3-key
sales mixes

If we wish to graph a multiproduct/service situation, all we need do is to amend the horizontal axis to reflect sales revenue rather than units. Figure 6.8 is a profit/volume chart for the franchise, showing profit/loss from both sales mixes specified above.

The assumed maximum volume in Figure 6.8 is 10,000 keys in mixes of 50/20 per cent house, 30/20 per cent cylinder and 20/60 per cent car. We have obviated the need to calculate profit at a volume greater than zero by using the predetermined breakeven point (in revenue) as our second plot on the profit/loss line.

ASSUMPTIONS OF COST/VOLUME/PROFIT ANALYSIS

As we have progressed through our franchise example, you will have realised that several assumptions have been made in order to permit analysis. An understanding of these assumptions is vital to correct interpretation and use of the cost/volume/profit model. We discuss these assumptions below before considering whether they can be reconciled with the reality that our model is attempting to reflect.

Linear sales revenue function

When we plotted sales revenue against volume in our graphical presentations, we plotted a straight line: in other words, we assumed that the unit selling price was constant at all volumes from zero upward. This is unlikely to be the case in reality. It is far more likely that, as sales volume increases, selling price per unit must fall in order to attract additional sales. The revenue function may therefore be **curvilinear**, as illustrated in Figure 6.9.

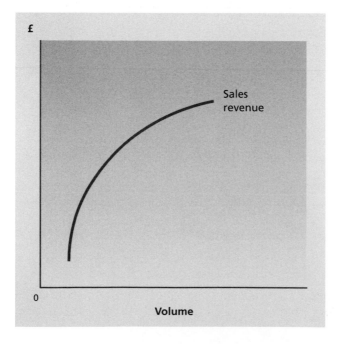

FIGURE **6.9**
Curvilinear sales revenue function

This type of revenue function reflects what is known as **price elasticity of demand:** that is, the idea that, if unit selling price increases, quantity demanded decreases and vice versa. We will have more to say on this topic in Chapter 8 when we discuss management accounting inputs to pricing decisions.

Linear cost functions

A linear cost assumption means total fixed cost is constant in amount at all volumes from zero upward and that the unit variable cost is likewise constant. This assumption ignores the possibility of economies and diseconomies of scale and of step costs. Adjusting our cost function to allow for these factors means that we are more likely to have the kind of curvilinear cost function described in Chapter 2, an illustration of which is reproduced in Figure 6.10.

If we combine the curvilinear revenue and total cost functions from Figures 6.9 and 6.10 into a breakeven chart, the result is markedly different to Figures 6.1 and 6.2. Figure 6.11 shows two breakeven points. In fact, though, this may still be a simplistic view of reality, where cost and revenue behaviour may be extremely complex, resulting in multiple breakeven points.

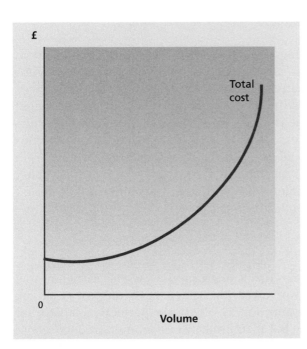

FIGURE **6.10**
Curvilinear total cost function

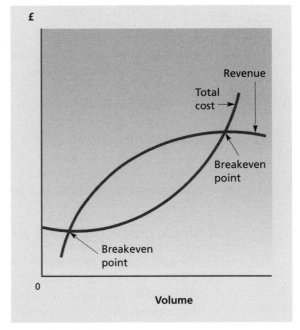

FIGURE **6.11**
Breakeven chart based on curvilinear revenue and total cost functions

Single period model

The cost/volume/profit model treats the period under review as being independent of either the following or previous periods. The implication of this assumption is that (production = sales), or at least that there is no significant change in stocks during the period covered by the model. If, however, a significant part of the current period's sales is being made from stock produced last period, and if the unit variable cost of this stock is markedly different to that of the current period's output, then the results of the model may be seriously distorted if allowance is not made for that fact (e.g. by taking a 'weighted average' approach not unlike that adopted for multiproduct situations).

Lack of significant stock changes also suggests that the volume of production/ sales is the *only* factor which causes variation in costs. But, if stockholding is important, this could have as great a bearing on cost structure as volume of activity. Fixed costs may be greatly affected by the amount of stock held – storage costs can be high. Unit variable cost may be influenced not only by the volume of activity, but also by the volume of *purchases*: for example, the owner of the key-cutting franchise may decide to make a bulk purchase of key blanks in order to take advantage of quantity discounts being offered by suppliers. It may often be the case that *environmental* factors, such as relationships with suppliers, inflation or exchange rates play a big part in cost structure.

Deterministic model

The model which we have been using assumes certainty (is **deterministic**): about unit selling price, unit variable cost, and fixed costs. Such certainty is something of a luxury in practical terms. Sensitivity analysis can help to incorporate uncertainty into the model, but requires the model to be reworked for each different set of component variables that are thought to be possible. And although computer spreadsheets can greatly ease the burden of numerous or complex calculations, sensitivity analysis does nothing to *quantify* uncertainty. For instance, if we are unsure about unit variable cost, it may be helpful to have some idea of how likely the occurrence of a particular possibility might be. We shall return to this topic in Chapter 9.

Single product/constant mix

The cost/volume/profit model assumes that a single product/service is sold, or that if more than one product/service is involved, the sales mix is constant at all volumes from zero upward. This assumption is obviously perfectly realistic for single-product/service organisations, but is an unlikely one in multiproduct/service situations. In much the same way that it may be necessary to reduce unit selling price in order to increase quantity demanded, it may be necessary to alter sales mix at different volumes of sales so as to increase overall demand. For example, if the total sales volume of 8,000 keys cut envisaged in Exhibit 6.6 were to increase to 10,000, this increase may be due solely to an increase in the number of car keys cut, in which case the sales mix of 50/30/20 per cent will alter, necessitating recalculation of the model's indicative values.

Static model

Our model assumes a static environment: for example, it assumes constant technology at all volumes. But as volume increases, the technology involved may well become more sophisticated, with a resultant effect on cost structure.

Cost structure may also be dependent on the *mix* of products/services being produced/sold. Looking again at Exhibit 6.6, we can see that any change to the relative weightings of each type of key cut will cause cost structure to change – if only because a different mix of unit variable costs will apply. But it may also be the case that a change in mix will affect fixed costs: for example, different cutting equipment may be required to deal with a higher proportion of car keys.

Only quantitative, financial variables included

The cost/volume/profit model cannot deal with qualitative or non-financial variables. Imagine the operational difficulties faced by our franchise owner if relations with the supplier of key blanks suddenly soured, resulting in late deliveries of blanks and frequent (temporary) inability to meet customer requirements. This would be a serious situation as regards the franchise's supplier and customer goodwill – but it would be impossible to incorporate directly into a cost/volume/profit analysis, since the effect of reduced goodwill is hard to quantify.

RECONCILING ASSUMPTIONS WITH REALITY

In the foregoing discussion of the model's assumptions, the phrase 'at all volumes from zero upward' was repeated several times. Is it reasonable, however, to suppose that management is concerned with *all* possible volumes? Management will be much more concerned with the volume range within which operations are likely to occur in the period under review. Similarly, the time horizon of concern to management will be finite (possibly a year). Given these limitations, what we can say is that management will be principally interested in the **relevant range**: that is, that range of volumes and time horizon which encompass operational possibilities. We met this concept in Chapter 2 in our discussion about cost behaviour. Figure 6.12 superimposes the relevant range on the curvilinear revenue and cost functions presented in Figures 6.9 and 6.10.

Within the relevant range in Figure 6.12, the revenue and total cost lines are similar to those we drew in our breakeven and contribution charts earlier. What we are suggesting is that, *within the relevant range*, the assumptions which underpin the cost/volume/profit model may be acceptable approximations of reality. Outside the relevant range, they are much less realistic and their application may seriously distort the true position. For example, it may be reasonable to assume that, within a volume range of, say, 60–80per cent of maximum and within a one-year time frame, unit variable cost and selling price are more or less constant, that total fixed cost is unaffected by volume changes, and that sales mix is constant. You should appreciate that restricting the cost/volume/profit model in this way is

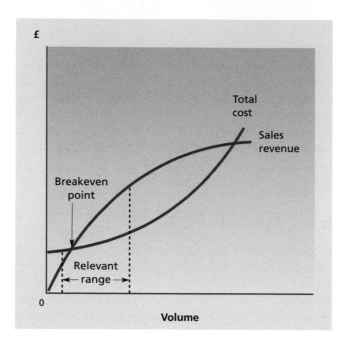

FIGURE **6.12**
The relevant rage and curvilinear revenue and costs

perfectly consistent with the *short-term* information needs of management: short-term planning and decision making will be confined to a short time horizon (typically one year) and to the likely range of operational volumes.

However, a warning note needs to be sounded here. From our discussion in Chapter 1, you will recall that a distinction must be drawn between *operational, tactical* and *strategic* considerations, and that assumptions which may hold true in operational and/or tactical terms are unlikely to be reasonable in strategic. For example, the range of possible volumes within a five-year strategic plan may be considerably wider than that within a one-year tactical planning period, with consequent effect on the complexity of cost and revenue functions – step fixed costs, changing unit variable cost, and price elasticity of demand may be very much in evidence, meaning that the applicable cost/volume/profit model will be much more like that presented in Figure 6.11.

You should also realise from our discussion in Chapter 3 that accurate separation of fixed and variable costs may be problematic in practice. Since the cost/volume/profit model relies on such separation, any significant inaccuracy may have an adverse impact on the model's usefulness. However, we are not claiming that restricting cost/volume/profit analyses to the relevant range results in a model which is 100 per cent accurate. Since the model is primarily future-oriented, some predictive inaccuracy is inevitable, and, if the importance of the relevant range is borne in mind when constructing and using the model, valuable results may be obtained.

SUMMARY

In this chapter, we have seen that

■ **Breakeven point** is the sales volume in units or revenue where profit is zero and can be calculated as follows:

$$\text{in units:} \quad \frac{\text{total fixed cost}}{\text{contribution per unit}}$$

$$\text{in revenue:} \quad \frac{\text{total fixed cost}}{\text{CS ratio}}$$

■ The **contribution/sales (CS) ratio** is:

$$\frac{\text{contribution}}{\text{sales}}$$

and can be calculated using either total contribution and total sales revenue, or unit contribution and unit selling price.

■ Sales required to earn a target profit may be calculated as:

$$\frac{(\text{total fixed cost} + \text{target profit})}{\text{contribution per unit [CS ratio]}}$$

■ **Margin of safety** is the difference between estimated (or actual) sales and breakeven sales, and gives an indication of the vulnerability of profit to reductions in demand. For comparative purposes, it can be expressed as a percentage of estimated (or actual) sales:

$$\frac{(\text{estimated or actual sales} - \text{breakeven sales})}{\text{estimated or actual sales}} \times 100\%$$

■ Cost/volume/profit relationships can be presented graphically, which may have greater impact, but may sacrifice accuracy.

■ A **breakeven chart** plots total fixed cost, total cost and sales revenue against volume, breakeven point occurring where total cost and revenue lines intersect.

■ A **contribution chart** can take one of two forms:
  – it can plot total variable cost, total cost and revenue against volume, breakeven point occurring where total cost and revenue lines intersect; *or*
  – it can plot total fixed cost and total contribution against volume, breakeven point occurring where these two lines intersect.

■ A **profit/volume chart** plots profit/loss against volume, breakeven point occurring where the profit/loss line intersects the horizontal axis.

■ In situations which involve multiple products/services, breakeven calculations should be based on the **weighted average unit contribution** or on the **weighted average CS ratio.**

■ **Sensitivity analysis** is a 'what-if' technique which can be used to analyse the impact of changing one or more of the variables within the cost/volume/profit model.

■ The cost/volume/profit model rests on a number of assumptions:
   – linear revenue function;
   – linear cost functions;
   – single period model;
   – deterministic model;
   – single product/constant mix;
   – static environment; and
   – only includes quantitative, financial variables.

■ In addition to the above assumptions, the model's accuracy depends on our ability to separate costs into their fixed and variable elements with reasonable accuracy.

■ Within the **relevant range**, the above assumptions can be taken as reasonable approximations of reality.

The financial analysis of decisions introduced in this and in the last chapter will be further developed in Chapter 7, where we will discuss the important concept of relevant costs and benefits in relation to decision making.

FURTHER READING

Hirsch, M., *Advanced Management Accounting*, South-Western Publishing, 1994. Chapter 7 explores extensions to the basic cost/volume/profit model.

Warner, A., *The Bottom Line*, Gower, 1988. Chapter 11 contains an interesting scenario-based explanation of cost/volume/profit analysis.

SELF-TEST QUESTIONS

6.1 For each of the statements which follow, place a tick in the appropriate box to indicate whether that statement is true or false.

	True	False
(a) Other factors being unchanged, an increase in total fixed cost will increase breakeven point.	☐	☐
(b) Taken in relation to the same volume of estimated sales, a higher breakeven point will mean a higher margin of safety than a lower breakeven point.	☐	☐
(c) For a business selling four services in different proportions, the weighted average contribution per unit will be the sum of the four services' individual unit contributions divided by four.	☐	☐
(d) Other factors remaining unchanged, an increase in sales required to earn a target profit will result from a reduction in unit contribution.	☐	☐
(e) Total contribution at different volumes is most easily displayed on a breakeven chart.	☐	☐

6.2 A joiner charges £15 per hour to customers for work performed. The estimated variable cost per hour's work for next year is £6 and fixed costs are £6,000 for clerical support plus £3,000 for premises. What is the joiner's breakeven point in revenue?

A £5,000
B £10,000
C £15,000
D £22,500

6.3 A bakery has a margin of safety of 40 per cent and estimated sales revenue of £70,000 for next year. What is the breakeven revenue?

A £28,000
B £42,000
C £58,800
D £64,000

6.4 Figure 6.13 is the profit/volume chart showing profit/loss at various volumes and breakeven point for each of two alternative courses of action.

The following statements relate to the options shown in Figure 6.13. Tick the box for the option to which a particular statement correctly applies.

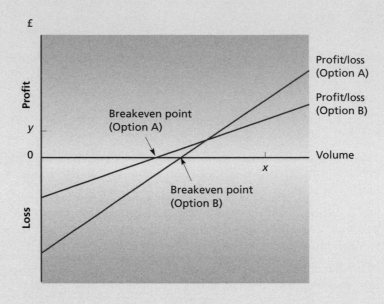

FIGURE 6.13
Two-option
profit/volume
chart

(a) The higher level of fixed costs is incurred by:

Option A ☐   Option B ☐

(b) The more profitable option at volume 'x' is:

Option A ☐   Option B ☐

(c) Each option has the same estimated sales volume. The option with the higher margin of safety is therefore:

Option A ☐   Option B ☐

(d) The target profit applicable to each option is 'y'. Which option will require the lower sales volume to achieve this target?

Option A ☐   Option B ☐

(e) Based on Figure 6.13 and assuming that both options have the same estimated sales volume, which is preferable on financial grounds?

Option A ☐   Option B ☐

6.5 The following paragraph relates to certain assumptions underlying cost/volume/profit analysis. From the list given, supply the missing word(s).

The assumption of linear costs means that unit variable cost is...............at all..............and that total fixed cost is not............. In reality, the impact of................................means that costs will more likely be.............. This discrepancy can be overcome by application of the concept of.........................which limits...........................to operational possibilities. This approach is consistent with the............... information requirements of management.

stepped	*time and volume*
short term	*curvilinear*
volumes	*constant*
economies/diseconomies of scale	*relevant range*

6.6 A business requires to sell 22,000 units in order to earn a target profit of £150,000. The contribution per unit is £15. What is this business's breakeven point in units?

    A 10,000

    B 12,000

    C 14,000

    D 15,000

QUESTIONS WITH ANSWERS

6.7 This question tests whether you can:

- use a formulaic approach to calculation of breakeven point in units, sales required to earn a target profit, and margin of safety as a percentage of estimated sales;

- prepare a breakeven chart from given information; and

- appreciate the impact on the model's assumptions of a change in circumstances.

BX Ltd produces and sells a single type of specialised computer graphics program. Estimated unit data for next year are:

	£
Selling price	600
Variable costs:	
Labour	200
Materials	40
Selling	10
	250

Anticipated fixed costs for the year are £80,000 for administration and £60,000 for selling and distribution. Estimated sales for the year are 640 programs.

Requirements

(a) Determine the following for BX Ltd:

    (i) breakeven point in terms of number of programs sold; and

    (ii) the margin of safety as a percentage of estimated sales.

(b) The company's target profit for the year is £56,000. Will the estimated sales volume be sufficient to achieve this? By how much will profit from the estimated sales volume exceed or fall short of the target profit?

(c) Prepare a breakeven chart for BX Ltd, showing clearly the breakeven point and margin of safety.

(d) The company is currently negotiating with an overseas client. If the negotiations are successful, a five-year contract will be signed for purchase by this client of 3,000 programs per year in each year of the contract. Discuss the possible implications for the cost/volume/profit model employed above if BX Ltd wins the overseas contract and expands accordingly.

(*Note:* Calculations are not required.)

6.8 This question tests whether you can:

■ determine breakeven point in units by formula;

■ determine margin of safety as a percentage of estimated sales volume; and

■ appreciate the impact on the model of a change in circumstances.

A local stable charges £30 per horse per day to look after clients' animals, the variable cost per horse per day being £5 and total fixed cost £46,000. The stable has 20 stalls suitable for this purpose, which are available 365 days per annum, and it is anticipated that the occupancy rate next year will be 80 per cent. At present, no reduction to the £30 per day charge is made in respect of any days when clients feed, groom and exercise their own horses, which is likely to occur on about 40 per cent of the days during which stalls are occupied.

Requirements

(a) Determine:

(i) the stable's breakeven point in terms of the number of occupied stall-days per annum; and

(ii) the margin of safety as a percentage of estimated occupied stall-days.

(b) Following representations by some of the clients concerned, the stable's owner has offered a flat-rate discount of 30 per cent per day for all days on which clients look after their own horses. On all other days, the £30 charge will remain in force. Assuming that all other factors remain the same, how will the cost/volume/profit model used in (a) need to be adapted to accommodate this new charging structure?

(*Note*: No calculations are required.)

6.9 This question tests whether you can:

■ use the weighted average contribution/sales ratio to determine breakeven point for a business selling three services; and

■ present a profit/volume chart to illustrate the business's cost/volume/profit relationships.

Speedi Ltd is a car- and van-hire company which offers three categories of vehicle hire. Next year's hire details are as follows:

	Car	Minibus	Van
Number of full days' hire	10,000	4,000	8,000
Charge per full day's hire	£30	£50	£37.50
Variable cost per full day's hire	£4	£25	£12.50

Total fixed costs for the year are estimated at £420,000.

Requirements

(a) Determine the company's breakeven point in revenue for next year.

(b) Prepare a profit/volume chart for Speedi Ltd, clearly showing the breakeven point.

6.10 This question tests whether you can

■ calculate breakeven point and margin of safety from a marginal costing profit statement;

■ apply sensitivity analysis in order to assess the impact of changes to the original data; and

■ appreciate the importance of non-financial factors to a decision.

CM Ltd specialises in the installation of suspended ceilings. The following is the company's estimated profit statement for next year, prepared using marginal costing principles:

	£	£
Sales		440,000
less Variable costs:		
Materials	102,000	
Labour	140,000	242,000
Contribution		198,000
less Fixed costs:		
Administration	40,000	
Other	50,000	90,000
Profit		108,000

Two suggestions have been made in an attempt to improve profit next year:

1 *Managing director's suggestion* The managing director has suggested that cheaper materials could be used, which will reduce the total material cost to £80,000. However, this will mean additional fixed costs of £24,000 to cover inspection of the cheaper materials.

2 *Sales director's suggestion* The sales director has suggested an intensive advertising campaign. She estimates that this will increase sales volume by 20 per cent over the estimated amount above. Variable costs as a percentage of revenue will be unaffected by this option, but extra fixed costs of £45,000 will be incurred in order to cover the advertising campaign.

Requirements

(a) For *each* of the original estimates, the managing director's suggestion and sales director's suggestion, calculate:

(i) the company's breakeven point; and

(ii) the margin of safety as a percentage of estimated sales.

(b) On purely financial grounds, explain whether CM Ltd should adopt the original plan, or amend it in line with either the managing director's or sales director's suggestion.

(c) What factors (not included in your analysis above) should CM Ltd's management consider before committing the company to a course of action?

QUESTIONS WITHOUT ANSWERS

6.11 Q owns two newsagents' shops and expects total sales revenue next year to be £200,000, with variable costs amounting to 40 per cent of revenue, and total fixed costs of £61,200. In order to achieve the owner's target profit of £82,800, it has been suggested that a limited line of toys should be sold. If this suggestion is implemented, total sales will rise to £230,000 and the higher profit margin on toys will mean that variable cost will fall to 35 per cent of sales. Total fixed cost will rise by £2,250 to cover some extra administrative work if the toys are sold.

Requirement
Determine which, if either, of the two sales patterns (i.e. with or without toys) will achieve the owner's target profit of £82,800.

6.12 Figure 6.14 shows two breakeven charts. One of these has been prepared on the basis of the assumptions employed in the management accounting cost/volume/profit model, whilst the other bears a closer relationship to economic theory.

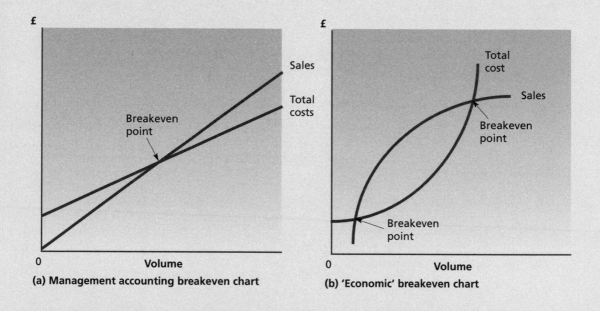

FIGURE 6.14 Alternative breakeven charts

Requirement
Compare and contrast the two breakeven charts shown in Figure 6.14, explaining the reasons for the differences and commenting on the extent to which the two models are incompatible or otherwise.

6.13 SKD Ltd is a courier service which undertakes express delivery of small packages. The charge per delivery is based on a combination of the weight of package and the delivery distance. Next year, the charge per kilogramme per kilometre will be £0.50, with an associated variable cost of £0.10. Estimated fixed costs next year will be £400,000.

Requirements

(a) Prepare an 'abbreviated' contribution chart for SKD Ltd, clearly indicating the company's breakeven point in revenue.

(b) On the *same* contribution chart, indicate the effect of an increase in fixed costs of £100,000.

6.14 A driving school charges £16 per hour for tuition. The associated variable cost is £6 and estimated total fixed cost for next year is £86,000. The school employs 10 instructors, each of whom can provide tuition for a maximum of 40 hours per week, 46 weeks per year. It is anticipated that each instructor will work for 75 per cent of the maximum hours next year. At present, the driving school does not offer evening or weekend tuition, and a proposal to do so is under consideration. Such tuition would be charged at £18 per hour, the variable cost per hour being £6. Additional fixed costs of £8,500 would be incurred if such tuition were offered. It is estimated that total demand for evening and weekend tuition will amount to 4,000 hours, of which 1,380 hours will represent transfers from existing tuition times, which will continue to be charged at £16 per hour (variable cost £6 per hour).

Requirements

(a) For *each* of the existing and proposed schemes of tuition, calculate:

　(i) breakeven point in hours' tuition; and

　(ii) margin of safety as a percentage of estimated hours' tuition.

(b) Determine the number of hours' tuition at which the driving school will be indifferent between the two patterns of work.

(c) Prepare a single profit/volume chart showing a profit/loss line for *each* pattern of tuition.

(d) Comment on the financial viability of the proposal to change the pattern of tuition as revealed by your answers above.

6.15 SC Ltd manufactures a single type of fax machine and it is expected that, next year, 8,000 machines will be sold at a price of £500 each. Total costs (adjusted for inflation), along with their associated output levels for the last five years are:

Total cost (£)	Unit output
2,145,000	8,500
2,640,000	11,100
1,890,000	7,400
1,690,000	6,350
2,300,000	9,280

Some construction work presently under way at the company's factory offers the opportunity to rearrange production facilities, should this prove financially beneficial; two alternative schemes of rearrangement are possible:

■ *Scheme 1* This will incur additional fixed costs of £157,500, but a reduction of £30 in the unit variable cost will result.

■ *Scheme 2* Estimated fixed costs will fall to £382,500 under this scheme, but the variable cost per unit will increase by £45.

Requirements

(a) For *each* of the existing estimates, Scheme 1 and Scheme 2, calculate

  (i) breakeven point in units; and

  (ii) margin of safety as a percentage of estimated sales.

(b) Advise the company as to its best course of action on financial grounds, based on your calculations above.

(c) Discuss the practical implications of *three* assumptions utilised in your analysis in (a) above.

6.16 The outdoor swimming pool at Summerston, a seaside resort on the West Coast, has been closed to the public for the last five years. As a means of helping reduce next year's anticipated budget deficit, the Town Council, which owns the pool, is to investigate the possibility of its reopening. The following information is available:

Refurbishment
Because of its lengthy closure, extensive renovation and refurbishment will be necessary prior to reopening, the cost of this being £22,500. If the work is commenced within the next few weeks, the pool should be ready for the start of the forthcoming holiday season.

Admission charges and demand
There are no comparable pools in the locality, but investigations have revealed that an outdoor pool on the South Coast charges as follows:

Adults	£1.60 per session of two hours
Senior citizens & children	£0.70 per session of two hours

Based on these prices being charged at the Summerston pool, average demand per session is estimated to be 30 adults and 60 senior citizens/children. For safety reasons, the pool has a maximum capacity of 150 bathers in any session.

Cost structure
Estimated operating costs are:

Variable per bather	£0.10
Fixed per month	£4,500

Fixed costs will only be incurred when the pool is open.

Opening hours/season
During the five-month holiday season (1 May–30 September), it is proposed that the pool should be open Monday–Saturday inclusive, with three two-hour sessions per day. It is thought unlikely that demand outside these five months would be sufficiently high to justify opening, although a local swimming club has expressed some interest in the possibility of using the pool during the off-season.

Uncertainty over estimates

All the figures given above (with the exception of admission charges, which will be set at the levels stated) are 'most likely estimates', but it is thought that these may be subject to the following margins of error:

		Adult	Senior citizen/child
All costs	± 20%		
Bather mix/volume:			
best		60	80
worst		10	30

Requirement

As the town's Director of Tourism and Leisure, prepare a report for the council's Chief Executive, dealing with the following aspects of the proposed reopening:

(a) cost/volume/profit indicators based on 'most likely' estimates for all variables.

(b) A sensitivity analysis of the results in (a), using, first, 'best estimates' for all variables, and second, 'worst estimates' for all variables.

(c) A statement of any assumptions relevant to (a) and (b).

(d) An explanation of factors not considered in (a), (b) or (c) which may have a bearing on the decision.

CHAPTER 7

Relevant costs and benefits for decisions

WOOLWORTHS SNIFFS A SEASONAL OPPORTUNITY TO INCREASE SALES

Shoppers from London to Lancashire should notice a hint of mulled wine in the air when they next step through the doors of their local Woolworths.

But Woolworths does not sell alcohol. The smell is the result of the company's decision to fill 20 of its stores with 'a seasonal aroma to enhance the festive season' . . . For Woolworths, the mulled wine smells are the olefactory equivalent of tinsel and holly – part of the drive to be more imaginative in point-of-sales marketing . . .

Woolworths festive smell was picked by a panel of the company's staff. They rejected cloves and Christmas pudding in favour of the winner.

Source: Daniel Green, *Financial Times*, 15 December 1995.

EXHIBIT 7.1 How would the financial implications of this decision be assessed?

INTRODUCTION

In Chapter 1, we described the alternative choice decision process and stressed that management accounting information plays a vital decision-support role. If management perceives that a decision about a particular aspect of the organisation is necessary, then the financial implications of that decision – its costs and benefits – must be analysed. The decision faced by Woolworths in Exhibit 7.1 would have undergone financial analysis: the costs (e.g. of installing and running the system) would need to be weighed against the benefits (in terms of a potential increase in sales) and, if the latter exceeded the former, the decision would be financially worthwhile. The financial implications of decisions can be substantial and it is essential that the manager or managers who have ultimate responsibility for reaching the decision are fully aware of them. Flawed or incomplete understanding of financial data in the context of decision making can result in incorrect decisions being taken, with possibly disastrous results for the organisation concerned. In this chapter, we shall examine the basic management accounting technique for analysing decision-related costs and benefits, illustrate its application, and discuss possible pitfalls in its use. In Chapters 8, 9, 10 and 11, we will extend our discussion to encompass 'special' decision situations, such as limiting factor and capital investment decisions. The principles described in this chapter are a necessary foundation for the more complex analyses dealt with in the later chapters.

OBJECTIVES   When you have completed this chapter, you will be able to:

- explain the concepts of relevance, sunk cost, incremental cost, directly attributed fixed cost and opportunity cost;

- use these concepts to analyse the costs/benefits relating to simple decision scenarios; and

- discuss the potential problems of a relevant costing approach.

THE CONCEPT OF RELEVANCE

Exhibit 7.2 contains a basic decision situation which we shall develop in order to establish a definition of relevance. Analysis of the costs and benefits relating to the decision in Exhibit 7.2 is essentially a matter of classification:

> **Costs and benefits used in the financial analysis of a decision should be relevant to the decision to which they relate.**

If you are to grasp the meaning of 'relevance' as it is applied to decision-related costs and benefits, you must appreciate two fundamental features of all decisions. As we saw in Chapter 1, these features are:

- decisions involve choice between alternative courses of action; and

- decisions relate to the future.

DS & Co

DS & Co, a firm of management consultants, is considering whether or not to undertake a special one-month project on behalf of a new client. The firm would use its permanent staff of consultants to complete part of the project, the remainder of the work being performed by a freelance consultant who would be hired specially for this purpose. The monthly wages cost of DS & Co's permanent staff is £15,000; this is expected to remain the same whether or not the project is undertaken. Employing a freelance consultant for the duration of the project will cost £10,000 in extra wages. The prospective client has offered to pay DS & Co £30,000; the firm's revenue from other work during this particular month will be £250,000, and will be unaffected by the project under consideration.

Exhibit 7.2 Relevance: basic scenario

If we examine Exhibit 7.2 in light of the first of these features, we can see that there are two alternatives: 'undertake the project', and 'do not undertake the project'.

▷ List all the costs and benefits (i.e. revenue) of each alternative in Exhibit 7.2, so that you obtain a total cost and a total benefit for each course of action.

The total costs and benefits of each course of action are:

	Undertake £	Do not undertake £
Costs		
Wages:		
Permanent staff	15,000	15,000
Freelance consultant	10,000	nil
Total cost	25,000	15,000
Benefits		
Revenue:		
Other work	250,000	250,000
Project	30,000	nil
Total benefit	280,000	250,000

▷ Of the total cost and total benefit listed above for each course of action, how much relates *specifically to the alternatives under consideration*?

The difference in total cost is £10,000 and this is the relevant cost of undertaking the project: that is, this course of action costs £10,000 *more* than the alternative. You will notice that the wages cost of the firm's permanent staff is the same under each alternative: that is, it is unaffected by the decision made, will be paid irrespective of whether the project is undertaken or not, and is therefore irrelevant. The £10,000 additional wages cost is relevant, as the cost of the freelance consultant arises (or does not arise) solely as a result of the decision reached.

Applying the same type of reasoning to the benefits of each alternative, the relevant benefit of undertaking is £30,000 (i.e. the *additional* revenue resulting).

⇨ Is undertaking the project financially desirable?

To assess the financial desirability of undertaking the project, we can easily determine the net relevant cost or net relevant benefit of this course of action:

	£
Relevant benefit of undertaking	30,000
less Relevant cost of undertaking	10,000
Net relevant benefit of undertaking	20,000

As this course of action yields a net relevant benefit, it is financially desirable. We could have chosen to analyse the relevant costs and benefits of *not* undertaking the project:

	£
Relevant benefit of not undertaking (freelance's salary avoided)	10,000
less Relevant cost of not undertaking (sales revenue lost)	30,000
Net relevant cost of not undertaking	20,000

Since only two options are being considered, saying that one is financially undesirable ('do not undertake') is exactly the same as saying that the other is financially desirable ('undertake'). Where the choice is between two options, we need only evaluate one in order to determine which is financially preferable.

Our analysis of the data in Exhibit 7.2 provides us with the first part of a definition of relevance:

Relevant costs and benefits must differ between alternatives.

Another way to think about this aspect of relevance is that relevant costs and benefits are **incremental costs and benefits**: that is, they are the *extra* costs and benefits associated with alternative courses of action. We could therefore say that the **incremental cost** of undertaking the project is £10,000, and that the **incremental benefit** of undertaking is £30,000, yielding a net incremental benefit of £20,000.

The other feature of decisions is that they relate to the future; how does this affect our definition of relevance? Exhibit 7.3 contains some additional information about DS & Co's proposed project.

⇨ What is the relevant cost to DS & Co of using the computer equipment on the proposed project?

There is no relevant cost to the firm if the computer equipment is used on the proposed work. This is because the hardware and software have already been bought.

> ### DS & Co: project computing requirements
>
> If the project is undertaken, DS & Co will need to use computer facilities. The required hardware and software are presently available within the firm and sufficient spare capacity exists to cope with the extra work without affecting other work for which the computer is required. This computer installation was bought two years ago at a cost of £40,000, annual depreciation being £10,000.

EXHIBIT 7.3 Relevance: further information about proposal

A decision about whether or not to undertake this project cannot affect this cost.

It is simply not possible to take a decision which alters the past. This being the case, all past costs and benefits are irrelevant:

Relevant costs and benefits are future costs and benefits.

The irrelevance of past ('historic') costs and benefits can occasionally be hard to come to terms with – especially where the amount involved is large. This difficulty can be compounded by the fact that *financial accounting* is largely based on historic transactions.

Items such as the £40,000 acquisition cost of the computer facilities in Exhibit 7.3 are termed **sunk costs**. A sunk cost is defined as:

A past ('historic') cost
or
A future cost whose payment is committed as the result of a different decision to the one under consideration.

Sunk costs are always irrelevant because they will never be affected by the particular decision being analysed.

⇨ Suppose DS & Co is purchasing the computer facilities by means of a hire purchase agreement and, at the time the project is being considered, two years' payments still require to be made. Will this alter the irrelevant status of the computer cost?

The answer is 'no'. Although the remaining payments for the computer are future costs, they are future costs which the firm is committed to incurring because of another decision: that is, how to finance purchase of the computer equipment.

Everything we have just said about the irrelevance of sunk costs is equally true of benefits: all past benefits and any future benefits the receipt of which is unrelated to the decision under consideration are irrelevant. Thus the £250,000 revenue from other work during the month in which the proposed project will occur is irrelevant. Although it is a future benefit, this revenue does not arise as a consequence of the decision about this project, but as the result of another decision (or decisions): that is, whether the other work should be undertaken.

⇨ Is the £10,000 per annum depreciation on DS & Co's computer equipment, referred to in Exhibit 7.3, relevant to the decision about the project?

As for the original cost, the answer is 'no'. Relevant costs and benefits must be *cash flows*, and depreciation is not a cash flow. Depreciation, an accounting measure aimed at spreading the cost of a long-life asset over the periods during which it is in use, is essentially apportionment under another guise. You should be careful to exclude all non-cash items from the financial analysis of decisions. This is particularly important as management accounting abounds in non-cash terminology such as depreciation, absorption and apportionment. The rule is that:

> Cost apportionments, overhead absorbed and depreciation are always irrelevant as they are non-cash items.

We provided an overview of cost apportionment and overhead absorption procedures in Chapter 4. If you review our earlier discussion of these topics, you will see that even the most logically defensible basis for apportioning or absorbing overhead costs is open to question, and for this reason is unsuitable for use in a decision analysis, which should be based on the most objective figures available.
You should never allow yourself to be misled into treating non-cash items as relevant merely because a decision scenario contains a great deal of information about, for example, the bases used to apportion common costs, or the method used to calculate depreciation. Such information may be readily available, but availability is no guarantee of relevance.

Confusion can sometimes arise in situations where a decision affects the amount of overhead *absorbed*. From our discussion in Chapter 4, you will recall that overhead absorption is essentially a series of cost apportionments with progressively smaller cost objectives, culminating with the cost unit (via the overhead absorption rate). You will also recall that overhead is generally absorbed on a predetermined basis, so the amount of overhead absorbed is unlikely to equate with overhead *incurred* (except by chance). In other words, any increase/decrease in overhead absorbed which may result from a decision cannot automatically be taken to imply an increase in the overhead incurred. If an overhead cost is to be relevant, it must be a future cash flow, as must any other relevant cost or benefit.

DS & Co: overhead implications of project

For the month during which work on the proposed project will take place, it is estimated that fixed overhead incurred will be £48,000 and that variable overhead incurred will be £4 per chargeable client hour. Fixed overhead is absorbed at a rate of £28 per chargeable client hour. Of the 2,000 hours required to complete the proposed project, 1,500 will be worked by DS & Co's permanent staff, the remainder being worked by a freelance consultant specially employed for the purpose. Other work during the month will require 2,200 hours of work from DS & Co's permanent staff; if the freelance consultant is employed, £2,000 of additional fixed overhead will be incurred, along with variable overhead at the normal rate of £4 per chargeable client hour.

EXHIBIT **7.4 Relevance/irrelevance of overheads**

⇨ In Exhibit 7.4, what is the total overhead *incurred* for each of the 'undertake' and 'do not undertake' options?

The total overhead incurred under each option is as follows:

	Undertake	Do not undertake
	£	£
Estimated fixed overhead	48,000	48,000
Additional fixed overhead for freelance	2,000	nil
Variable overhead:		
Proposed project (2,000 hours @ £4)	8,000	nil
Other work (2,200 hours @ £4)	8,800	8,800
Total overhead incurred	66,800	56,800

⇨ What is the relevant (or incremental) overhead cost of a decision to undertake the proposed project?

The relevant overhead cost of undertaking the proposed project will consist only of those items which differ between the two alternatives: that is, the additional fixed overhead for the freelance (£2,000) plus the variable overhead relating to the proposed project (£8,000), giving a total relevant cost of £10,000: that is, the difference in total overhead incurred between the two options. The £28 per chargeable client hour for fixed overhead absorbed has been totally omitted from the calculation, as it is not a cash flow. Although undertaking the project will increase the fixed overhead absorbed by (2,000 hours @ £28), this will not affect the estimated future cash flow of £48,000: that is, the estimate of fixed overhead to be *incurred* for the month.

Inclusion of the variable overhead of £4 per chargeable hour may seem odd in light of what we have just said about overhead absorbed, but you should remember that this is a variable cost – if the number of chargeable client hours increases, so will the amount of variable overhead *incurred*. Assuming that the rate of £4 per chargeable client hour is an accurate reflection of the future cash flow, then the extra variable overhead incurred will be the same as the extra variable overhead absorbed. This is merely a feature of variable overhead; it does not invalidate our rule that only future cash flows are relevant.

However, you should be careful not to fall into the trap of treating variable costs as relevant and fixed costs as irrelevant: that is, you should not confuse cost behaviour with relevance. It is quite possible for a fixed cost to be relevant, always providing it is a future cash flow which differs between alternatives. For example, the additional £2,000 fixed overhead that will be incurred as a result of employing the freelance consultant is relevant (even although it is a fixed cost). Fixed costs of this type are termed **directly attributable fixed costs**: that is, they are fixed costs which are incurred as a direct consequence of the decision under consideration. Another example of such a cost relating to DS & Co is the £10,000 additional wages cost relating to employment of the freelance consultant (referred to in Exhibit 7.2).

A FULL DEFINITION OF RELEVANCE

From the foregoing discussion, we can obtain a full definition of relevance:

Relevant costs and benefits are future cash flows which differ between alternatives.

In order to qualify as relevant, all three criteria in this definition must be met: that is, the item being examined must be a future item *and* a cash flow *and* must differ between alternatives. An item which meets only one (or two) of these criteria is irrelevant. For example, the extra fixed overhead absorbed by DS & Co if the project is undertaken undoubtedly differs between alternatives, and is also a future item, but it fails the cash flow test and hence is irrelevant.

APPLYING THE DEFINITION IN ANALYSIS

As with so many other aspects of management accounting, there is no 'set' format for presenting analyses of relevant costs and benefits. What *is* required is rigorous application to all financial data of the three criteria contained in the definition above. When we analysed the data from Exhibit 7.4, we extracted the relevant overhead cost by comparing the total overhead cost of each course of action, the difference being the relevant amount. This is perfectly acceptable, providing we list *all* the costs and benefits for *each* alternative.

However, this approach may become cumbersome to operate: irrelevant items (such as the £48,000 fixed overhead cost in Exhibit 7.4) will be listed under each alternative. This could cause confusion and may lead to errors where a great many irrelevant items are concerned, or where more than two options are being considered. In addition, we can argue that this 'total' approach is illogical, since the aim of the exercise is to isolate the relevant items.

It is possible to adopt a much more direct approach to analysis by employing the criteria contained in our definition of relevance to include every item which satisfies all three criteria and to exclude every item which fails one or more. Exhibit 7.5 presents all the data from Exhibits 7.2, 7.3 and 7.4 relating to DS & Co's decision. At first glance, you may find Exhibit 7.5 rather off-putting. Remember, however, that it is just a 'welding together' of the fragmentary information we have already encountered.

⇨ Apply the three criteria contained in the definition of relevance in order to determine which financial items in Exhibit 7.5 are relevant. You may find it helpful to draw up a table with the following headings:

Item   Future?   Cash?   Differs?   Amount

For every item listed, place a tick in the column for each criterion which that item meets. Only items with a tick in all three columns are relevant.

DS & Co: the full scenario

DS & Co is a firm of management consultants and is considering whether or not to undertake a one-month project on behalf of a client. The firm will use its staff of permanent consultants to complete part of the project, the remainder of the work being performed by a freelance consultant who will be hired specially for this purpose at a wages cost of £10,000. The wages cost of DS & Co's permanent staff will be £15,000 for the month under consideration, and will be unaffected by any decision about the project.

The prospective client has offered to pay DS & Co £30,000 for the completed project. This amount will be received in addition to the firm's monthly revenue of £250,000 from other work, which will be received irrespective of whether the project is undertaken.

Undertaking the project will require the use of computer facilities. The necessary hardware and software is presently available within the firm and sufficient spare capacity exists to undertake the project work without affecting any other work being performed on the computer. The computer installation cost £40,000 two years ago, and annual depreciation is £10,000.

Fixed overhead costs for the month in question are estimated at £48,000, and variable overhead is incurred at £4 per chargeable client hour. Fixed overhead is absorbed at £28 per chargeable client hour. Of the 2,000 chargeable hours required to complete the project, 1,500 will be worked by DS & Co's permanent staff, the remainder being worked by the freelance consultant. Employing the freelance consultant will incur additional fixed overhead of £2,000 and variable overhead at £4 per chargeable client hour. Other work by the firm's permanent staff during the month will amount to 2,200 chargeable client hours.

EXHIBIT 7.5 Relevance: the full scenario thus far

Table 7.1 tests each financial item from Exhibit 7.5 against the three criteria contained in the definition of relevance. It is not absolutely necessary to prepare a

TABLE 7.1 Criteria for relevance applied

Item	Future?	Cash?	Differs?	Amount (£)
Wages cost:				
Permanent staff	✔	✔		15,000
Freelance	✔	✔	✔	10,000
Revenue:				
Other work	✔	✔		250,000
Project	✔	✔	✔	30.000
Computer:				
Cost to buy		✔		40,000
Depreciation	✔			10,000
Fixed overhead:				
Month's estimate	✔	✔		48,000
Additional	✔	✔	✔	2,000
Absorbed	✔		✔	56,000
Variable overhead:				
Other work	✔	✔		8,800
Project	✔	✔	✔	8,000

table such as 7.1 in order to perform a relevant/irrelevant analysis. However, such an approach should encourage you to apply all three criteria to every item of financial data in a decision scenario.

⇨ Of the financial data identified in Table 7.1, which items are relevant *costs* and which are relevant *benefits* of the 'undertake' option?

There is only one relevant benefit of undertaking the project, namely, the £30,000 receivable from the client. The relevant costs are: wages cost of freelance consultant; extra fixed overhead relating to employment of the freelance; and the variable overhead relating to the project.

⇨ Using the information above, and referring to earlier workings if necessary, determine the net relevant cost or net relevant benefit of undertaking the project.

The net relevant benefit of undertaking is:

	£	£
Relevant benefit		
Payment by client		30,000
Relevant costs		
Wages cost of freelance consultant	10,000	
Additional fixed overhead	2,000	
Additional variable overhead (2,000 hours @ £4)	8,000	20,000
Net relevant benefit		10,000

As this course of action has a net relevant benefit, it is the better on financial grounds.

Had we chosen to analyse the net relevant cost/net relevant benefit of *not* undertaking the project, we would have:

	£
Relevant benefits (costs avoided)	
Wages cost of freelance consultant	10,000
Additional fixed overhead	2,000
Additional variable overhead	8,000
	20,000
Relevant cost (revenue lost)	
Payment by client	30,000
Net relevant cost	10,000

As we said earlier, where two courses of action are possible, we need consider the financial implications of only one in order to determine the preferred option.

What does the £10,000 net relevant benefit of undertaking represent? It indicates the *extra* profit which DS & Co will earn if the project is undertaken. This should make sense, since the £10,000 net relevant benefit is calculated as the extra benefit (i.e. revenue) *less* the extra costs involved in this course of action. Similarly, the net relevant cost of £10,000 associated with not undertaking the project represents the loss of profit or reduction in potential profit resulting from pursuing this course of action.

We can confirm that our definition-based approach provides the correct answer if we use the 'total' approach adopted earlier:

	Undertake £	Do not undertake £
Benefits		
Revenue:		
Other work	250,000	250,000
Project	30,000	nil
Total benefits [A]	280,000	250,000
Costs		
Wages:		
Permanent staff	15,000	15,000
Freelance	10,000	nil
Computer purchase	40,000	40,000
Fixed overheads for month	48,000	48,000
Fixed overheads for freelance	2,000	nil
Variable overheads:		
Other work	8,800	8,800
Project	8,000	nil
Total costs [B]	131,800	111,800
Total net benefit [A–B]	148,200	138,200

The net relevant benefit of undertaking is the difference in total net benefit between the two courses of action: that is, £10,000, which is the same answer we obtained using the shorter definition-based approach.

Before proceeding to the next section, you may wish to attempt questions 7.2 and 7.6, which deal with the topics covered so far.

OPPORTUNITY COST

Before we consider a comprehensive example, we must introduce a final concept: that of **opportunity cost**. So far, all the relevant costs we have encountered have been 'out-of-pocket costs': that is, additional costs which require to be paid if a particular course of action is pursued. Opportunity costs are different: they are *implicit* in most decision-making situations. What this means is that, if we pursue one course of action, we may be unable to pursue another course of action and this inability may involve a loss of benefit.

⇨ In Exhibit 7.6, what is the relevant cost to DS & Co of using the questionnaire forms for the proposed project?

DS & Co: questionnaire forms

If the firm undertakes the project, a large quantity of pre-printed questionnaire forms will be needed. A sufficient quantity of suitable forms was purchased by DS & Co some time ago for £2,000; if not used on this project, they can be sold to another firm of consultants for £800, but have no other foreseeable use by DS & Co.

EXHIBIT 7.6 Opportunity cost

The £2,000 purchase cost of the forms is a sunk cost (because it is a past cost) and is thus irrelevant. The potential sale proceeds of the stock of forms is a future cash flow and will differ between alternatives (£800 if the project is not undertaken, zero if it is), and is therefore a relevant cost of undertaking the proposed project. The sale value of the forms will be lost to DS & Co if the project is undertaken: that is, a loss of benefit results from this course of action, so £800 is an **opportunity cost** of undertaking the project.

Opportunity cost is defined as:

The benefit foregone as a result of pursuing one course of action rather than pursuing the best alternative course of action.

Since decisions involve choice between alternatives and since opportunity costs specifically reflect this aspect of decisions, opportunity costs are always relevant.

It may be necessary to determine the 'best alternative course of action' in order to obtain the amount of an opportunity cost (*see* Exhibit 7.7).

DS & Co: questionnaire forms – additional information

The stock of questionnaire forms, which cost £2,000 to buy some time ago, can be used on the proposed project, sold for £800 to another firm of consultants, or used on other work by DS & Co. If used on other work by DS & Co, purchase of additional forms costing £1,000 would be avoided.

EXHIBIT 7.7 Opportunity cost: determining the 'best alternative'

⇨ What is the 'best alternative use' of the questionnaire forms as opposed to use on the project?

In this case, both £800 and £1,000 are *potentially* relevant. The best alternative use of the forms is on other work as this will save DS & Co additional purchase costs of £1,000 (compared to £800 gained from sale to another firm of consultants). The opportunity cost of using the forms in the project is thus £1,000. You may have been tempted to suggest an opportunity cost of (£1,000 – £800) = £200: this is incorrect because inclusion of £1,000 and £800 implies that there are two 'best alternative' courses of action. There is, of course, only one 'best alternative', as it is not possible to sell the forms *and* use them on other work.

It can also happen that an opportunity 'benefit' results from a course of action. Suppose the questionnaire forms could be used on the prospective project, failing which they would need to be shredded at a cost of £50 to DS & Co. In these circumstances, using the forms on the project will save DS & Co £50 – a benefit of undertaking.

A common opportunity cost is loss of sales resulting from a decision, which is the situation described in Exhibit 7.8 in relation to DS & Co.

DS & Co: potential loss of sales

Some of the work involved in the prospective project is highly specialised and can only be done by a particular member of DS & Co's permanent staff. However, this staff member is currently extremely busy and if she worked on the proposed new project, would need to abandon work on another project which is presently under way. Such abandonment would cost DS & Co £4,000 in lost sales revenue. The costs associated with this revenue are the staff member's salary of £1,000 plus sundry materials costing £500 (not yet ordered).

EXHIBIT 7.8 **A common opportunity cost**

⇨ Of the three financial items mentioned in Exhibit 7.8, which qualify as relevant?

The sales revenue of £4,000 is a future cash flow which differs between alternatives (zero if the project is undertaken, £4,000 if it is not), and so qualifies as relevant. The staff member's salary is a future cash flow, but it will be incurred irrespective of whether the project is undertaken (i.e. it does not differ between alternatives): this is irrelevant. The sundry materials have still to be ordered, and thus constitute a future cash flow which does differ between alternatives (zero if the proposed project is undertaken, £500 if it is not – these materials will presumably not be ordered if the work to which they relate is not carried out), so this item is relevant.

⇨ What is the amount of the opportunity cost if the new project is undertaken and sales are lost as detailed above?

We have said that, of the three financial items relating to the potential loss of sales, only the revenue and sundry materials' cost are relevant. So, if the new project is undertaken, £4,000 in revenue is lost, but *some* of the associated costs are saved (i.e. the materials' cost of £500), giving an opportunity cost of:

	£
Revenue lost	4,000
less Associated costs saved	500
Opportunity cost	3,500

In situations such as the one just examined, it is essential that the concept of relevance be applied consistently. The wages cost of DS & Co's permanent staff is irrelevant to the decision about undertaking the proposed project, and must be *totally excluded* from the analysis. The opportunity cost of lost sales arises as a consequence of this decision and it would be illogical to say that a particular cost is irrelevant to the decision in general terms but is nevertheless relevant in assessing the detail of one of that decision's consequences.

A COMPREHENSIVE EXAMPLE

You will realise that the variety of different decisions which an organisation may need to take is potentially extremely wide. For this reason, we have adopted what might be termed a *contingency approach* to the financial analysis of decisions: that is, the development of a 'general rule' for identification of relevant costs and benefits which can be applied to any decision:

Future cash flows which differ between alternatives.

It will therefore be useful at this stage to apply our 'general rule' to a quite different scenario to underline the fact that this approach works regardless of the specifics of a particular decision. The example in Exhibit 7.9 combines all the individual facets of relevance which we have discussed in relation to DS & Co.

VK Ltd: dust extraction system

VK Ltd operates a timber sawmill in a local town. Following a recent visit by the Health & Safety Inspectorate, the company has been required to install a dust extraction system. This could either be done by VK Ltd's own staff, or by subcontracting the work to BPM Ltd. The following information is available:

1 *Consultants' report* VK Ltd has employed consultants to advise on the most suitable extraction system. Their report, which has already been received, will form the basis of installation, whether undertaken by VK Ltd's own staff or by the subcontractor. The cost of this report is £4,500 and the related invoice will be paid in the near future.
2 *Subcontractor quotation* BPM Ltd has quoted a firm price of £70,000 which covers supply of the extraction equipment, installation and all associated work.
3 *Cost of extraction equipment* If VK Ltd's own staff undertake installation, the extraction equipment and sundry materials needed for installation will need to be purchased at a total cost of £42,000.
4 *VK Ltd staff requirement* VK Ltd presently employs staff with the necessary skills to undertake installation. All of the staff concerned are employed on long-term contracts and are paid an average rate of £6 per hour. It is estimated that 800 hours' work will be needed by these employees to install the extraction equipment. Of the 800 hours, 200 will be worked in overtime which would not otherwise be necessary; overtime working is paid at an hourly rate of time and one half.

EXHIBIT **7.9 Relevance: a comprehensive example**

5 *Interruption to output* Installation of the extraction equipment by VK Ltd's own staff will cause an interruption to normal operation of the sawmill which will result in lost sales of 4,000 square metres of timber. The average selling price and unit cost per square metre of timber is:

	£	£
Selling price		10.50
Direct materials	0.90	
Direct labour	0.70	
Fixed overhead	6.20	7.80
Profit		2.70

The direct labour cost per square metre refers to the cost of permanent employees on long-term contracts and the direct materials have still to be bought.

6 *Supervision* VK Ltd can use one of its own supervisors on the installation work. This individual is presently extremely busy and is paid £8 per hour. If he supervises installation work, VK Ltd will need to employ another supervisor on a temporary basis at a cost of £3,000.

EXHIBIT 7.9 continued.

⇨ Which items of financial data in Exhibit 7.9 are relevant? Adopt the same approach as for Exhibit 7.5: that is, using Table 7.2, place a tick in the appropriate column to indicate whether or not a particular item satisfies that criterion. Items with a tick in all three columns are relevant.

TABLE 7.2 Testing the data for relevance

Item	Future?	Cash?	Differs?	Amount (£)
Consultants' report				4,500
Subcontractor quotation				70,000
Cost of extraction equipment				42,000
Labour cost of own staff:				
600 hours (normal time)				3,600
200 hours (overtime)				1,800
Interruption to output:				
Lost revenue				42,000
Direct material costs				3,600
Direct labour costs				2,800
Fixed overhead costs				24,800
Supervision:				
Existing supervisor				6,400
Temporary supervisor				3,000

Table 7.3 is the full analysis of VK Ltd's data into relevant/irrelevant.

TABLE 7.3 Results of test for relevance

Item	Future?	Cash?	Differs?	Amount (£)
Consultants' report	✓	✓		4,500
Subcontractor quotation	✓	✓	✓	70,000
Cost of extraction equipment	✓	✓	✓	42,000
Labour cost of own staff:				
600 hours (normal time)	✓	✓		3,600
200 hours (overtime)	✓	✓	✓	1,800
Interruption to output:				
lost revenue	✓	✓	✓	42,000
direct material costs	✓	✓	✓	3,600
direct labour costs	✓	✓		2,800
fixed overhead costs	✓		✓	24,800
Supervision:				
existing supervisor	✓	✓		6,400
temporary supervisor	✓	✓	✓	3,000

▷ Of the items identified in Table 7.3 as being relevant, which are relevant costs and which are relevant benefits of using VK Ltd's own staff to undertake the installation work?

If VK Ltd uses its own staff for installation, there will be two relevant benefits: the subcontractor's quotation (a cost avoided), and the direct materials associated with the lost sales (a cost avoided). The relevant costs are: cost of extraction equipment, overtime working, lost sales due to interruption, and the temporary supervisor.

▷ What is the total opportunity cost associated with the lost sales (i.e. of losing the sales of 4,000 square metres)?

Per metre, the opportunity cost of the lost sales is:

Revenue lost	£10.50
less Associated costs saved – direct materials	£ 0.90
Opportunity cost	£ 9.60

giving a total opportunity cost of (4,000 @ £9.60) = £38,400.

▷ Remembering that the direct materials' cost saving associated with the lost sales is included in the total opportunity cost above, what is the net relevant cost or net relevant benefit to VK Ltd of using its own staff to install the extraction equipment? Advise the company on this basis.

The net relevant cost of the identified course of action is:

	£	£
Relevant benefit		
Payment to subcontractor avoided		70,000
Relevant costs		
Extraction equipment	42,000	
Overtime (200 hours × £6 × 1.5)	1,800	
Opportunity cost of lost sales	38,400	
Temporary supervisor	3,000	85,200
Net relevant cost		15,200

On a financial basis, it would therefore be better to subcontract installation work, as using the company's own staff yields a net relevant cost. Had we analysed the relevant costs and benefits of subcontracting, the result would have been a net relevant benefit of £15,200. You may wish to check that this is so.

There is one vital point to make about analyses such as that which we have just completed: as a preliminary, it is wise to assure ourselves that we are isolating costs and benefits which are relevant to the *correct decision*. Items which are relevant to one decision will not necessarily be relevant to another: that is *relevance is decision-specific*. In the last example, the decision was 'who should undertake installation' *not* 'should installation occur'. If we had incorrectly identified the decision as the latter rather than the former, we would almost certainly have misclassified some costs and benefits, which may have resulted in the wrong decision being taken.

RELEVANT COSTING: POTENTIAL PROBLEMS

We have discussed and illustrated application of the relevance concept at some length and you should appreciate its logic in light of the essential features of decisions which it mirrors. However, a cautionary note must be sounded: relevant costing is not a 'cure-all' device and possible pitfalls in its application must be appreciated if the technique is to be used to good effect; we discuss these below.

Short-term 'one-off' decisions

If you examine the decision faced by DS & Co, you will see that it is a 'one-off' decision of a short-term nature and that its financial implications are relatively small. In our analysis, we ignored as irrelevant some substantial costs (e.g. the wages cost of the firm's permanent staff and the £48,000 fixed overhead).

⇨ Can you see a potential danger in this approach?

Suppose the firm's decision related to 'normal' business: that is, the business which provides £250,000 of revenue during the month covered by the proposed project. The danger is that we may be tempted to continue treating items such as the fixed overhead cost as irrelevant, which could result in understatement of costs. Think of the impact of a major understatement of costs on breakeven calculations of the sort we performed in Chapter 6: other things being equal, the breakeven volume will be understated and the margin of safety overstated. Such a situation may induce a false sense of security about the profitability of the estimated sales volume and may even (in an extreme case) result in sales effort being concentrated on achieving a loss-making volume. In addition, as we shall see in Chapter 8, an underestimation of costs may mean artificially low selling prices. This may be desirable in certain specific circumstances, but is not consistent with long-term profitability, which requires that all costs be covered.

You may feel that the danger we have just described is so serious as to render our relevant cost/benefit analyses worthless. However, this danger is not an inherent feature of the management accounting technique; it stems from a lack of appreciation of the different decisions involved. Decisions like the one about DS & Co's special project are non-routine and short term, and this is reflected in the associated relevant costs/benefits. A decision about 'normal' business is rather different in nature: it is routine and is likely to have longer-term implications, and this difference should be reflected in the associated relevant costs/benefits. For example, the £48,000 fixed overhead which we treated as irrelevant in our earlier analysis of DS & Co's decision would certainly be relevant to a decision about, say, the sales volume required in order to earn a target profit during the month under consideration. This is simply another manifestation of our earlier statement that it is necessary to identify the correct decision before undertaking a classification of costs/benefits into relevant/irrelevant. As we shall see in Chapter 10, the concept of relevance is equally important to evaluation of decisions with long-term implications.

Obtaining financial data

In practice, it may be difficult to obtain financial data about alternative courses of action. It may even be difficult to identify the alternatives available. Identifying and quantifying opportunity costs can be particularly problematic. Can we identify the 'best alternative course of action'? Can we quantify the 'benefit lost' because we may not pursue this best alternative? The danger here is that financial data may degenerate into subjective guesswork by managers – and no analytical technique (relevant costing or any other) is superior to the quality of input data. However, we must accept that, since decisions are future-oriented, related financial data can only be estimated, and an analysis based on such estimates can never be 100 per cent accurate (except by merest chance). This need not prove an insurmountable problem, providing the estimates are as objective and reasonable as possible. If assumptions need to be made, these should be explicit and reasonable and, as we shall see in Chapter 9, uncertainty about estimates can readily be incorporated into the analysis.

Qualitative factors

The management accounting technique we have described in this chapter deals only with a decision's financial implications. These are undoubtedly very important, but it would be rash to base decisions on financial considerations alone. Other, non-financial factors may be equally important as, or more important than, the net relevant cost/benefit of a decision. For example, qualitative factors such as the timing of a decision, the reaction of competitors or the skills of the workforce may have a major bearing on the final decision. There may be a conflict between qualitative and financial considerations for the decision-making manager. Managerial performance evaluation, for instance, based on keeping actual costs within budget, may pressurise a manager into placing too much emphasis on financial factors and too little on qualitative.

⇨ Suggest some qualitative factors which DS & Co may need to consider before reaching a final decision about undertaking the proposed project.

Possible non-financial factors which the firm may wish to consider include:

■ Will the quality of the freelance's work be consistent with that of work undertaken by DS & Co's own staff? Will it be completed on time? Will conflicts arise between the freelance and the firm's permanent staff?
■ Will the proposed project lead to further work from the same client?
■ How will existing clients react if undertaking the proposed project has an adverse impact on their work?

You may have suggested different or additional qualitative factors to those above. The important point, however, is that factors of this sort are highly significant to the ultimate decision. For example, if undertaking the project would lead to a large volume of future work for the same client, it might be worthwhile undertaking the project even if it has a net relevant cost, the aim being to gain the additional future work.

The 'Acceptance' Problem

Persuading some managers to accept the business rationale of the relevance concept can cause problems. The 'acceptance' problem for the manager may be due to a combination of two reasons:

1 Accounting records are conventionally based on historic (i.e. past) data. This stems from a need for objective evidence of the figures recorded in the form of verifiable transactions. The concept of relevance, with its emphasis on the future, could be viewed as too subjective compared to the accounting status quo and as a concept to be resisted for that reason.
2 If, in the past, resources have been committed to a course of action which is currently under review, there may be a feeling among managers that the original course of action must be pursued. This could manifest itself in expression of opinions such as, 'We've already spent £2 million on this project, therefore we *must* proceed with it'. Such opinions could arise partly from a misunderstanding about the future orientation of decisions (along with their financial evaluation), and partly from a fear that the concept of relevance represents an attempt to use hindsight to 'fix blame' for wrong decisions taken in the past.

Overcoming the 'acceptance' problem (where it exists) is basically a matter of understanding the purpose of management accounting: that is, to provide useful information to help managers to manage – in this instance, to provide information which will help managers to reach sound decisions.

Financing of Decisions

A distinction needs to be drawn between the financial implications of *pursuing* a particular course of action and the method of *financing* that course of action. In Exhibit 7.9, VK Ltd was faced with a decision which involved some quite large cash outlays. Although our analysis demonstrated that, on financial grounds, the company should subcontract installation, it did not indicate where the necessary £70,000 payment to the subcontractor was to be found. How a course of action is to be financed is a different decision with different relevant costs/benefits. You should therefore not assume that the net relevant benefit arising from a course of action also means that financial resources to pursue that course are available. (We shall discuss possible sources of finance in Chapter 11).

SUMMARY

In this chapter, we have discussed management accounting's basic approach to the financial analysis of decisions and have seen that:

- Relevant costs and benefits are *future cash flows which differ between alternatives.*

- Relevant costs and benefits are **incremental costs and benefits.**

- Apportioned costs, overhead absorbed and depreciation are all irrelevant, as they are not cash flows.

- **Sunk costs** are always irrelevant, and are defined as: *past costs or future costs which must be incurred as a result of different decisions to the one under consideration.*

- **Directly attributable fixed costs** are always relevant and are defined as: *fixed costs which arise as a specific consequence of the decision under consideration.*

- **Opportunity costs** are always relevant and are defined as: *the benefit foregone as a result of pursuing one course of action rather than pursuing the best alternative course of action.*

- Using the concept of relevance may involve certain problems, which can be summarised as:
  - short-term/'one-off' decisions;
  - obtaining financial data;
  - qualitative factors;
  - the 'acceptance' problem; and
  - financing of decisions.

In Chapter 8, we shall extend the principles discussed here to deal with two 'special' categories of decision: price-setting and limiting factor.

FURTHER READING

Amey, L., 'On opportunity costs and decision making', in *Accountancy*, July 1980.

Dillon, R. and Nash, J., 'The true relevance of relevant costs', in *Accounting Review*, January 1978.

Ezzamel, M. and Hart, H., *Advanced Management Accounting: an organisational emphasis*, Cassell, 1987. See Chapter 7 for an interesting discussion of relevant costs and benefits.

SELF-TEST QUESTIONS

7.1 A restaurant is considering running several *gourmet* nights next month. Special cutlery, napery, crockery and serving equipment which will be required for these *gourmet* nights was purchased six months ago by means of a bank loan. Next month's repayment on this loan will be £400.

Relative to a decision about running the *gourmet* nights, what is the status of next month's loan repayment?

    A Directly attributable fixed cost
    B Sunk cost
    C Incremental cost
    D Opportunity cost

7.2 A computer retailer has the opportunity to sell for £600 some obsolete hardware which originally cost £900. In order to make this sale, the retailer's full-time engineer will need to spend 20 hours modifying the hardware, thereby using some idle time which he presently has. The engineer's hourly rate of pay is £10. What is the net relevant cost or net relevant benefit of a decision to sell the hardware for £600?

    A Net relevant loss of £500
    B Net relevant loss of £300
    C Net relevant benefit of £400
    D Net relevant benefit of £600

7.3 A manufacturing business, which has no spare capacity, can accept a special customer order only by forfeiting existing work with sales value of £10,000. The special order has a sales value of £15,000 and the cost of using the business's permanent workforce on either the special order or existing work is £7,000. What is the opportunity cost of a decision to accept the special order?

    A £3,000
    B £5,000
    C £8,000
    D £10,000

7.4 A landscape gardening firm has the chance to undertake some work at a local sports centre, which will require the firm's entire stock of topsoil to be used. This was purchased some time ago for £250 and if not used on the sports centre job, it can either be used on another job which is currently under way (saving a purchase of £300), or it can be sold to a client at its retail value of £450 (which will cost the firm a £100 delivery charge). What is the opportunity cost of using the topsoil on the sports centre job?

    A £50
    B £100
    C £350
    D £450

7.5 Due to the imminent absence, on maternity leave, of a key employee, a firm of solicitors is trying to decide how best to distribute her workload. Two options are available:

1 appoint a temporary employee to undertake all the work of the staff member on leave; or

2 re-distribute her work amongst other, existing, members of staff.

For each of the following statements relating to this decision, place a tick in the appropriate box to indicate whether it is true or false.

	True	*False*
(a) The maternity pay of the staff member on leave is relevant.	☐	☐
(b) The wages cost of existing members of staff to whom some work may be redistributed is a sunk cost.	☐	☐
(c) Potential loss of goodwill from clients whose work will be temporarily switched to another staff member is a qualitative factor.	☐	☐
(d) Prior to her departure on leave, the staff member concerned will brief whoever is to undertake her work and this would be done outside normal office hours. The extra cost involved in keeping the office open for these additional hours is relevant.	☐	☐
(e) If a temporary replacement is employed, the firm's wages clerk will need to process an additional monthly salary during the period of this person's employment. The wages clerk's salary for the period amounts to £8,000 and he estimates that 5 per cent of his normal working time will be devoted to dealing with the temporary employee's salary, this being time during which he would otherwise have little to do. The clerk's wages cost of (5 per cent of £8,000) is a directly attributable fixed cost.	☐	☐

QUESTIONS WITH ANSWERS

7.6 This question tests whether you can:

■ identify relevant financial data for a decision;

■ state any assumptions made in identifying relevant data; and

■ obtain the net relevant cost/net relevant benefit of a course of action and provide advice on that basis.

A charitable organisation is trying to decide on the venue for a special fund-raising event. The Fund-raising Manager favours Venue A whereas some of the Management Committee have proposed Venue B as better. The following information is available.

Venue A
It is estimated that the total funds raised will amount to £300,000. However, the Fund-raising Manager will need to travel to this venue and stay there before and during the fund-raising event, at a cost of £1,600 to the charity.

Various materials and volunteer staff will require transport to this venue, and the charity will use its own vehicles for this. These vehicles were originally purchased for £60,000 and depreciation is £10,000 per annum. Use of the charity's vehicles in this way will mean that other vehicles will need to be hired to provide transport for some of the charity's beneficiaries, which will cost £4,000.

The Fund-raising Manager has been unable to obtain free use of suitable premises at Venue A and will need to rent them temporarily at a cost of £10,000.

Because most of the volunteers who will run the fund-raising event do not live at or near Venue A, the charity has undertaken to provide refreshments at an estimated cost of £2,000.

Venue B

If the event were to be held at this venue, anticipated total funds raised are £280,000 and none of the extra costs associated with Venue A will be incurred.

Other information

The purchase cost of certain materials necessary for the fund-raising event will be £30,000 and the Fund-raising Manager's salary for the period of the event will be £1,500. Printing of promotional posters will cost £6,000.

Requirements

(a) List the financial data relevant to a decision about where to hold the fund-raising event, stating any assumptions you make.

(b) Determine the net relevant cost or net relevant benefit of holding the fund-raising event at Venue A, and on that basis advise the charity.

7.7 This question tests whether you can:

- apply the criteria for relevance to identify the financial data relevant to a decision;

- determine which relevant items are costs and which are benefits of a stated course of action;

- use the data above to obtain the net relevant cost/benefit of a stated course of action and provide advice on this basis; and

- appreciate the significance of qualitative data in the decision-making process.

LP Ltd is a light engineering company which specialises in manufacture of padlocks. The company has received an enquiry from a building firm which wishes to make a bulk purchase of 100 high-security padlocks of type HSP 101. The following information is available:

Purchase price

LP Ltd normally sells each HSP 101 for £80 but, because of the size of order, is considering offering a discount of £10 per unit.

Materials

Most of the materials required to complete the order are already in stock. These were bought last month for £1,200 and, if not used on this order, have no immediately foreseeable alternative use. Additional materials costing £2,200 would need to be purchased if the order is accepted.

Labour

Accepting the order will require 200 hours of skilled and 50 hours of semi-skilled labour. LP Ltd's skilled workers are not particularly busy at the moment and there are sufficient idle skilled hours to cover the order's requirements. A casual semi-skilled worker would, however, need to be employed for work on the order. Hourly rates of pay are:

Skilled	£5.50
Semi-skilled	£3.50

Supervision

If the order is accepted, no additional supervision costs are anticipated. However, the Production Manager has already spent 20 hours' overtime estimating production requirements for the order at a cost to LP Ltd of £300.

Plant and equipment

If the order is accepted, a special machine will need to be hired for two months at a cost of £500 per month. All other plant and equipment is already owned by LP Ltd and there is sufficient spare capacity to produce the order. The original cost of LP Ltd's plant and equipment was £60,000 and depreciation of £2,000 relates to the two months during which the order will be in progress.

Overhead

Fixed overhead (excluding supervision and depreciation) is absorbed at a rate of £12 per labour hour and variable overhead is £6 per labour hour.

Requirements

(a) Identify the relevant financial data relating to the decision faced by LP Ltd.

(b) Determine the net relevant cost or net relevant benefit of a decision to accept the order and on that basis advise the company.

(c) State, and briefly explain the significance of, *three* qualitative factors which LP Ltd's management should consider before arriving at a final decision.

7.8 This question tests whether you can:

■ determine the net relevant cost or net relevant benefit of a stated course of action and on that basis provide advice; and

■ appreciate the practical difficulties involved in determining opportunity costs.

GP Ltd, a wholesale chemical supplier, currently operates its own secure storage unit for dangerous substances. However, due to an increasing risk of contamination and theft, it has been decided to close this unit – either now or in one year's time when the lease-hold expires. On expiry of the leasehold, GP Ltd will enter into a long-term contract with a manufacturer for supply on an 'as required' basis. The following additional information may be relevant:

Chemicals purchased/stored

72,000 kg of chemicals are purchased and stored in the secure storage unit per annum. Turnover of these chemicals is such that no stocks are envisaged at either the start or the end of the year under consideration. If the store is closed now, CF Ltd, a chemical manufacturer, has offered a one-year contract to supply the chemicals which would otherwise need to be stored in the secure store in the quantities required and at the time required by GP Ltd. This will eliminate the need for the secure store. The average

229

price per kg quoted by CF Ltd for this service is £6 compared to £5 per kg if GP Ltd stores the chemicals itself.

Maintenance costs
If the store is retained for the year, maintenance costs will be £2,000, of which 40 per cent represents an apportionment of the full-time maintenance operative's salary to reflect the time he spends working in the secure store, and the balance is the cost of materials which would be bought specifically for this maintenance work.

Equipment
Temperature and humidity control equipment within the store is extremely old and will be sold as scrap for £1,800 either now or in one year's time. There is presently a stock of £400 worth of fuel for the store's heating system and this is sufficient for one year's running. If the store is closed now, this fuel could either be sold for £350 or used elsewhere within GP Ltd to save fuel purchases of £500.

Storekeeper
The storekeeper has agreed to transfer to a vacancy elsewhere within GP Ltd on closure of the store; his present salary of £15,000 per annum will be conserved. If the store is operated for the year, this vacancy will be covered by casual labour at a cost of £8,000.

Leasehold payment
Under the terms of the leasehold on the secure store, GP Ltd will pay £4,000 during the year under consideration. Insurance premiums will be £2,000 if the store operates for the year and £800 if it closes now.

Overheads
Overheads charged to the store for the year will be £60,000. This represents a variable element of £0.80 per kg of material stored, the balance being an apportionment of general company fixed costs.

Requirements

(a) Calculate the net relevant cost or net relevant benefit to GP Ltd of a decision to close the secure store now, and on that basis advise the company.

(b) State, and briefly explain, any practical difficulties which may be encountered when incorporating opportunity costs into an analysis such as that in (a).

7.9 This question tests whether you can:

■ apply the three criteria for relevance in order to identify relevant financial data;

■ use the relevant financial data to obtain the net relevant cost/benefit of a stated course of action; and

■ provide advice on the basis of your analysis of the financial data.

MCM & Co., a firm of marketing consultants, has been undertaking extensive market research (not yet completed) on behalf of a client company which has now been liquidated, and there is no chance of any future payment from that source. Another possible client has expressed interest in the results of the completed research and has offered to pay £35,000 for completion.

Costs incurred to date on the research are £50,000 and the original client made a non-returnable payment of £15,000 at the commencement of the work. In addition,

MCM & Co.'s senior partner has spent 50 hours (at a total cost of £1,300) attempting to attract a new client for the incomplete work.

The following information relates to completion of the research.

Materials and consumables

Total cost to complete is £5,000. Of this amount, £3,000 worth has already been purchased and has no alternative use, whilst the remainder will need to be specially purchased.

Labour

The cost of completing the research will be £8,000, but MCM & Co.'s employees are extremely busy, so that completion of this research will lose the firm sales as follows:

	£	£
Sales revenue		26,000
Labour cost	8,000	
Expenses cost	6,000	
Fixed overhead absorbed	4,000	18,000
Profit		12,000

The expenses cost associated with the sales above will be avoided if the sales are lost.

Fixed overheads

Completion of the market research will incur £5,000 of additional fixed overheads. MCM & Co. absorbs fixed overheads at 50 per cent of labour cost.

Requirements

(a) Identify the financial data which is relevant to a decision about whether to complete the research.

(b) Use your figures from (a) to obtain the net relevant cost or net relevant benefit of completing the research and, on that basis, advise MCM & Co.

7.10 This question tests whether you can:

■ determine the net relevant cost or net relevant benefit of a course of action and provide advice on that basis;

■ state and explain any assumptions made in arriving at the net relevant cost/benefit above; and

■ explain the difference in analytical approach between a non-routine decision and a decision affecting 'normal' business.

In an attempt to improve profitability, the Boomtown Hotel is considering whether or not to offer 'reduced rate' two-night holidays during the next off-peak season (November–February inclusive). These two-night holidays would be additional to the hotel's normal (but very small) volume of business during this period. The following information is available:

Room lettings

For the November–February period, total revenue from room lettings is estimated at £12,500 from 'normal' business. The two-night holidays will provide an estimated £24,000 of additional revenue during the same period. Associated variable costs will be £625 ('normal' business) and £1,200 (two-night holidays).

Bar and restaurant

Revenue from 'normal' business from the bar and restaurant will total £72,000 for the four-month period and will increase to £88,000 if the two-night holidays are offered. The variable cost will be £43,000 ('normal' business only), rising to £52,000 if the two-night holidays are offered.

Staff wages and salaries

Total wages payable to the hotel's complement of permanent staff for November–February inclusive will be £14,000, rising to £22,000 if the two-night holidays are offered.

Adminstration costs

The total administration cost of running the hotel over the relevant period will be £16,000 under normal circumstances, rising to £19,000 if the two-night holidays are offered.

Rates and insurance

These will amount to £5,000 in total for the four months.

Absorption of fixed overheads

Fixed overheads which have been allocated and apportioned to room lettings are absorbed at a rate of £14 per occupied room–night for single and £20 per occupied room–night for double rooms. These absorption rates are predetermined estimates based on a full year's fixed overhead cost and room occupancy.

Other costs

New equipment for the hotel's kitchen has already been ordered at a cost of £20,000. It was originally scheduled for delivery/installation in January, but, if the two-night holidays are offered, this would need to be brought forward to October, at an additional cost of £1,500. When the new equipment is installed, existing equipment (which cost £4,000 to buy eight years ago) can be sold as scrap for £800.

Requirements

(a) Determine the net relevant cost/benefit of offering the two-night holidays, and on that basis advise the Boomtown Hotel.

(b) State any assumptions made in arriving at your answer to (a), providing a brief explanation of the significance of each assumption to the analysis.

(c) Assume that the decision being made by the hotel related to discontinuation of room-letting during next off-peak season. Give *two* examples of financial items whose analytical treatment would differ to that accorded them in (a), explaining the reason for such difference.

QUESTIONS WITHOUT ANSWERS

7.11 The Roads Department of a local authority is experiencing a temporary difficulty obtaining replacement bulbs for streetlamps. The usual supplier has problems with supplies of raw materials and will be unable to supply replacements for the next six months. Two alternative sources of supply for this period are under consideration, details of which follow.

LS Ltd

This company has offered to supply the Roads Department with replacement bulbs at a cost of £2 per bulb, subject to a minimum order of 20,000 bulbs. The department's estimated maximum requirement over the six-month period is 16,000 bulbs and, if 20,000 were ordered from LS Ltd, the surplus could be sold back to LS Ltd for £1 per bulb. This resale would cost the roads Department £1,200 in delivery costs.

Because the bulbs supplied by LS Ltd do not exactly match the fittings in the streetlamps, some minor modifications will be needed. Although the Roads Department employs some staff with the necessary skills to make these modifications, they will be too busy with other work during the relevant period to make the modifications. It is therefore proposed that, for the six-month period, two additional members of staff be employed at a cost of £15,000.

CRM Ltd

Any quantity of suitable bulbs can be purchased from this source at a cost of £2.30 per bulb. However, it is reckoned that roughly 10 per cent of the bulbs purchased will prove defective, and although the supplier will replace these free of charge, it is thought advisable to set up a testing facility at the Roads Department's main depot at a cost of £16,000. It was the department's intention to set up such a facility next year, but at a more favourable price of £9,000.

Requirement

Advise the Roads Department as to its best course of action on financial grounds.

7.12 AFA Ltd, a paint manufacturer, has a short-term problem with disposal of the toxic waste caused by one of its processes. Normally, this waste is removed under contract by WNS Ltd, but this will prove impossible next year due to major restructuring of that company. After next year, it is confidently expected that WNS Ltd will be able to resume its contractual obligations.

Two options for overcoming this disposal problem are under consideration by AFA Ltd:

1 employ Scaffie Ltd, an external contractor, to remove the waste for a one-year period; or

2 reprocess the waste on-site, after which it can be sold.

In the year under consideration, it is estimated that 46,000 litres of toxic waste will require to be dealt with. Scaffie Ltd has quoted a price of £5.50 per litre to remove the waste and has also offered to purchase, for £20,000, some scrap materials which are presently at AFA Ltd's premises. These scrap materials have no other use and Scaffie Ltd will only make the purchase if awarded the toxic waste removal contract.

Under the terms of its contract, WNS Ltd will be required to make a penalty payment of £75,000 to AFA Ltd in respect of non-performance of contractually specified duties.

The following information relates to possible reprocessing of the waste by AFA Ltd:

233

Consultant

AFA Ltd has employed a consultant to advise on reprocessing. Fees paid to date amount to £15,000. If reprocessing is decided on, the consultant will be retained for the year at an additional fee of £45,000.

Adaptation of equipment

Reprocessing will involve the adaptation of equipment presently owned by AFA Ltd. This was purchased some time ago for £200,000 and, if not adapted for the reprocessing work, will need to be disposed of at a cost of £10,000. Materials required for adaptation cost £14,000 in total and these would need to be bought specially. To prevent disruption of normal plant operation, adaptation would take place at weekends, thereby incurring additional wages costs of £6,000.

Sale of reprocessed waste

Each litre of waste reprocessed can be sold for £30 and the associated unit costs are:

	£
Direct materials	6.00
Direct labour (1 hour @ £8)	8.00
Fixed overhead	12.00
	26.00

The direct materials involved will need to be specially purchased. Fixed overhead is absorbed into the cost of each litre of waste reprocessed at a rate of 150 per cent of direct labour cost.

AFA Ltd's direct labour force is extremely busy and, if reprocessing occurs, use of direct labour hours on this work will result in loss of other sales. For each direct labour hour spent on reprocessing work, it is anticipated that other sales will be lost as follows:

	£	£
Sales revenue		28.00
Direct labour (1 hour @ £8)	8.00	
Direct materials	2.00	
Fixed overhead	12.00	22.00
Profit		6.00

Advertising

AFA Ltd's Sales Director has just received reimbursement of £400 of travelling expenses incurred as a result of discussions with the company's advertising agents about the best method of promoting sales of the reprocessed waste.

Requirement

Prepare a report for AFA Ltd's board of directors containing a financial analysis of a decision to reprocess the waste, stating any assumptions made and drawing attention to any non-financial factors which may have a bearing on the ultimate decision.

7.13 The Parks Department of a local authority is assessing the frequency with which the grassed areas for which it is responsible should be cut: weekly, fortnightly, three-weekly or monthly. The following information is available:

1 1,300 acres of grass require to be cut during the cutting season, which lasts for 24 weeks between April and September.

2 The Parks Department owns four tractors, each with its own cutting equipment. These will be sufficient to undertake the monthly, three-weekly and fortnightly cuts, but, if the grass is cut weekly, one additional tractor and equipment will need to be hired at a cost of £600 per month for each of the six months of the cutting season. The Department's own tractors cost £80,000 to buy three years ago and are depreciated on a reducing balance basis, each having an estimated remaining life of five years.

3 The basic cost per month of maintaining one tractor and its cutting equipment during the cutting season is £300. Cutting on a monthly basis will increase this to £500, on a three-weekly or fortnightly basis to £600, and on a weekly basis to £650.

4 The variable cost per acre cut depends on the frequency with which cuts are made:

	£
Weekly	0.02
Fortnightly	0.30
Three-weekly	0.45
Monthly	0.70

5 The basic wages of staff involved in the grass-cutting operation will be £2,000 per month during the April–September season. If the grass is cut weekly or fortnightly, this will rise to £3,000 or £2,500 respectively, due to the need for overtime working; no such overtime will be necessary for three-weekly or monthly cuts. However, if cutting is undertaken monthly, the workers concerned will have a significant amount of idle time and it is felt that this will lead to an absenteeism problem which will cost an additional £100 per month during April–September.

6 During the cutting season, the Parks Department will receive an apportionment of central costs from the local authority to cover administration and accounting functions. This will amount to £1,000 per month irrespective of the frequency with which the grass is cut.

Requirement
Prepare a memorandum for the Director of the Parks Department which provides an analysis of the grass-cutting options available. Full supporting calculations should be shown, along with any relevant non-financial or qualitative factors which may have a bearing on the decision.

7.14 A council-owned sign factory presently makes signs solely for the council's own use. Because of spending limits which have been imposed on the council, the sign factory's budget for next year will almost certainly be cut. Faced with this prospect, the factory manager is considering undertaking outside work on a commercial basis, her hope being that the profit earned on this work will at least equal the proposed cut in council funding.

Three other councils have expressed an interest in having work undertaken on their behalf at the sign factory. If undertaken, these jobs are *not* mutually exclusive and, apart from any extra costs detailed below, the sign factory will have more than adequate spare capacity for them all. Information currently available about these three jobs is given below.

Easthill Borough Council
This involves preparation of a large batch of road repair signs and has a sales value of £40,000. Materials worth £8,000 will be needed. Of this amount, £2,000 is already in stock at the sign factory and has no other use, while the balance requires to be specially

purchased. Using the materials which are in stock will save £500 in storage costs. Additional labour costs amounting to £3,000 will be incurred if this work is undertaken, along with extra fixed overhead of £2,000.

Midhampton Municipal Council

The sign factory has been asked about the urgent supply of room numbers, corridor signs, etc. for the council's new municipal building, the sales value of the contract being £27,000. Materials costing £6,000 will need to be specially purchased; £3,000 in overtime payments will need to be made to the sign factory's workforce; and delivery costs of £2,000 will be incurred.

Dunfield Town Council

This order for assorted signs would have a sales value of £12,000. Materials required are already in the sign factory's store and originally cost £3,500 to purchase; if used on this order, they will need to be replaced at a cost of £5,800. In addition, use of these materials for the Dunfield work will delay work for the sign factory's 'parent' council, thereby incurring additional costs of £1,600. Extra overhead of £5,200 will be incurred if this work is undertaken.

In addition to the information specific to each of the orders above, £6,000 of extra overheads will be incurred by the sign factory if any one of the orders is undertaken, rising to £8,000 if any two are undertaken, and to £10,000 if all three are undertaken.

Requirements

(a) What amount of reduction in council cash funding to the sign factory (if any) would be compensated by acceptance of the Easthill Borough Council job *only*?

(b) State the extra (or reduced) cash benefit to the sign factory if, in addition to the Easthill Borough Council job:

(i) the Midhampton Municipal Council work *only* were undertaken; and

(ii) *both* the Midhampton Municipal Council *and* Dunfield Town Council jobs were undertaken.

(c) On the basis of your answers to (a) and (b), advise the sign factory manager as to which external job(s) should be undertaken in order to provide the greatest 'cushion' against potential budget cuts. State any non-financial and qualitative factors which may be relevant to the final decision.

CHAPTER 8

More decisions: price-setting and limiting factors

WHY APPLE IS BOXED IN

Price. An innovative product can usually command a premium price. But a would-be standard-setter cannot afford to exploit that potential premium too ruthlessly. To ensure that the product becomes widely accepted – becomes the mainstream standard – it is essential to hold the price down. This is what Microsoft did with its MS-Dos operating system; in an extreme form, it is what Netscape is doing by giving away its 'browser' software for the World Wide Web. Of course, this is easy if you are in the software business, where each individual copy costs little or nothing to produce. It is harder if you manufacture computer hardware, where your cost structure may make it hard to sell units cheaply . . .

Source: Peter Martin, Financial Times, 8 February 1996.

EXHIBIT 8.1 **Price-setting conflicts**

INTRODUCTION

In the last chapter, we introduced the concept of relevant costs and benefits, illustrating their use in the financial analysis of decisions. We will now extend this type of analysis to encompass certain 'special' situations. We made the point in Chapter 7 that one of the potential drawbacks to relevant costing is the assumption that finance is available to enable decisions to be implemented. In fact, we can go further than this and say that the analysis employed in Chapter 7 ignored the possibility of *any* potential limitations on what an organisation may do. Finance is one resource which may impose limitations, but there are other possibilities such as the potential lack of suitably skilled workers, and we need to consider the impact of such limitations on our short-term decision analyses. (In the long term, the problem becomes, not one of analysing constraints, but of overcoming them.)

We shall start by examining a particularly important decision: the setting of selling price. As Exhibit 8.1 suggests, cost is an important consideration in price-setting, so we shall examine its use for this purpose, paying special attention to the potential dangers in adopting an exclusively cost-based approach to pricing.

OBJECTIVES

When you have completed this chapter, you will be able to:

- understand the operation of cost-plus pricing, along with its strengths and weaknesses;

- distinguish between different definitions of 'cost' in a cost-plus pricing formula and appreciate their implications;

- illustrate the product life cycle and discuss its implications for the relationship between cost/price/product/market;

- explain the meaning of price elasticity of demand, price elastic and price inelastic, along with their significance to the price-setting process;

- use a schedular approach to determine the profit-maximising price/demand combination;

- explain the term 'limiting factor' along with its relevance to decision-making situations;

- analyse limiting factor decisions using
  - contribution per unit of limiting factor
  - minimum extra cost to subcontract per unit of limiting factor

- appreciate the use of graphical and simplex methods of linear programming, and interpret output from a computerised linear programming exercise.

PRICE-SETTING

One of the most important decisions faced by many organisations is that of setting a selling price for the goods/services which they produce. Selling price is a major determinant of the quantity demanded, although, as we shall see later, it is not the only determinant.

⇨ Why is cost likely to be a major factor in pricing decisions?

Cost is a major factor in the pricing decision because, for commercial organisations, profit will only be earned if revenue exceeds cost. For non-profit organisations, the aim of any sales which they make will be slightly different: to breakeven, to minimise the operating deficit or to accumulate a 'revenue surplus' (as universities seek to do). In both cases, knowledge about the cost of the goods/services being offered is necessary.

Our discussion of the management accounting input to pricing decisions will start from a basic 'cost-plus' approach. We shall then illustrate the potential dangers in such a restricted view of the pricing decision.

'Cost-plus' pricing

At its simplest, the pricing decision can be reduced to determination of unit cost and addition of a profit **mark up** (if profit is expressed in terms of unit cost) or a **profit margin** (if profit is expressed in terms of selling price). Exhibit 8.2 provides the data for an illustrative example.

LC Computers Ltd

LC Ltd produces a range of computer hardware and software. Next year's anticipated direct costs per unit of a particular type of hard disc drive are as follows:

	£
Direct materials	50
Direct labour (12 hours @ £6)	72
Direct expenses	18
Prime cost	140

Production overheads for next year are estimated at £360,000 and these are absorbed into output on the basis of direct labour hours, which are estimated at 90,000 for the year.

To determine unit selling price, the company increases full production cost by a mark-up of 25 per cent of that cost, this being deemed sufficient to cover non-production costs and to provide a satisfactory profit.

EXHIBIT **8.2 Cost-plus price-setting**

⇨ Use the data in Exhibit 8.2 to obtain LC Ltd's overhead absorption rate for next year.

The overhead absorption rate is:

$$\frac{\text{estimated overhead cost}}{\text{estimated direct labour hours}} = \frac{£360,000}{90,000} = £4 \text{ per direct labour hour}$$

⇨ Bearing in mind that full production cost is (prime cost + production overhead), what is the full production cost per unit of the hard disc drive?

The full cost per hard disc drive is:

	£
Direct materials	50
Direct labour (12 hours @ £6)	72
Direct expenses	18
Prime cost	140
Production overhead (12 hours @ £4)	48
Full production cost per unit	188

⇨ Based on the addition to full production cost of a mark-up equal to 25 per cent of that amount, what is the selling price per unit of the hard disc drive?

Using the given pricing formula, selling price per unit is:

	£
Full production cost per unit	188
add mark-up (25% × £188)	47
Unit selling price	235

We can term the £47 per unit mark-up gross profit per unit: 'gross' because the mark-up is intended to cover non-production costs as well as provide a satisfactory *net* profit (i.e. gross profit *less* non-production costs = net profit).

Note that the profit per unit could also be expressed as a profit *margin*: that is, in terms of selling price:

$$\frac{\text{gross profit per unit}}{\text{selling price per unit}} = \frac{£47}{£235} = 20\%$$

Setting selling prices in this way is certainly simple enough and management has the reassurance of knowing that, providing actual costs are not significantly different from estimated, unit selling price more than adequately covers cost – so profits should be earned if breakeven volume is exceeded. However, there are a number of difficulties and dangers in adopting an exclusively 'cost driven' approach to pricing.

Which cost?

The price calculations above were based on full production cost, but other definitions of 'cost' are possible. A problem with use of full production cost is that the profit mark-up or margin must be sufficiently large to cover non-production costs as well as to provide a satisfactory level of profit. In LC Ltd's case, 25 per cent of full production cost was deemed sufficient for this, but there may be some doubt about how much of this 25 per cent represents profit, and how much is required to cover the non-production costs. It may therefore be preferable to use 'total' cost per unit:

	£
Prime cost	X
add Production overhead	X
Full production cost	X
add Non-production cost	X
Total cost per unit	X
add Profit	X
Selling price per unit	X

This sort of calculation will clarify the amount of profit earned per unit, rather than giving a 'profit' per unit which includes an element of non-production costs. Moreover, because non-production costs are dealt with separately, the risk of failing to fully cover them via a 'catch-all' profit percentage may be reduced.

Alternatively, variable cost per unit may be used as the basis of selling price, in which case the profit percentage will need to be large enough to cover all fixed costs. The danger in this approach is that, because such a large proportion of costs is being dealt with by a lump-sum addition to unit variable cost, some fixed costs may 'slip the net', resulting in losses being incurred. A 1993 survey by Drury *et al.* found that 27 per cent of respondents always used total manufacturing cost, 27 per cent always used total cost, and 26 per cent always used variable product cost, as the basis for cost plus pricing.

There may, however, be circumstances where selling at a price which barely covers unit cost, or even selling at a loss, may be desirable.

LC Computers Ltd: special order

The company has received an enquiry from a prospective customer for supply of 400 hard disc drives. Costs and selling price per unit are:

	£	£
Selling price		235
less Costs:		
Direct materials	50	
Direct labour	72	
Direct expenses	18	
Production overhead	48	188

LC Ltd has sufficient spare capacity to undertake the special order without affecting other work or incurring additional labour costs. The amount of production overhead and non-production costs incurred would be unaffected by acceptance of the order.

The customer has offered to pay £185 per unit for each of the 400 hard disc drives.

EXHIBIT **8.3 Pricing a special order**

▷ Is acceptance of the special order in Exhibit 8.3 financially worthwhile?

Financial evaluation of the special order resolves itself into a relevant costing exercise. Per unit, the net relevant benefit of accepting the order is:

	£	£
Relevant benefit		
Selling price		185
Relevant costs		
Direct labour	72	
Direct materials	50	
Direct expenses	18	140
Net relevant benefit		45

The calculation of net relevant benefit assumes that the direct labour cost will only be incurred if the special order is accepted. Alternatively, we could have assumed that direct workers will be paid regardless of whether the order is undertaken, in which case the cost is irrelevant and the net relevant benefit would be (£45 + £72) = £117. Production overhead and non-production costs are unaffected by acceptance of the special order, and are irrelevant. Likewise, production overhead per unit (i.e. absorbed) is not a cash flow and is also irrelevant. Therefore, on a purely financial basis, acceptance of the special order is worthwhile at a price per unit of £185 – even though this price is lower than *both* the 'normal' selling price of £235 and the full production cost of £188.

In the circumstances, LC Ltd may be quite willing to sell at a price which is apparently loss making, particularly if there is a chance of repeat orders from the same customer in future (on which higher prices may be charged), or if the company is especially concerned to utilise the spare capacity which exists. In fact, the company may consider accepting the special order at any price greater than the relevant cost per unit of £140, as a price in excess of this amount will yield a net relevant benefit: that is, will increase profit. Note, however, that this is only likely to be true within the relevant range. Outside this range the relevant costs will be different (e.g. additional overhead may be incurred because of a need to increase capacity to meet the order). Knowing the relevant cost per unit may thus be useful to the company in price negotiations for the special order, providing the minimum acceptable price per unit from LC Ltd's viewpoint – although the company will clearly wish to obtain the highest price possible consistent with winning the order.

▷ Should LC Ltd set *all* of its selling prices on the basis of a relevant cost per unit of £140?

Unless the company were prepared to incur losses, £140 per unit should not be used as the basis of selling price for all units. This cost excludes production overheads and non-production costs – costs which must be covered by selling prices overall in order to earn a profit.

One problem with offering a deep-discounted price on LC Ltd's special order could be that existing customers may become dissatisfied if they hear of it, either taking their business elsewhere or pressing for similar treatment. In addition, the special order customer, having once obtained a low price, may strive for further reduction or at least insist on no increase.

⇨ Can you envisage any circumstances in which a 'loss-making' price might be acceptable?

A 'loss-making' price may be acceptable in the following circumstances::

1 The market for the company's product is suffering a temporary recession and low prices are necessary to maintain market share. Once market conditions improve, price can be increased to a 'profitable' level.
2 The product has just been introduced, or the company is attempting to gain a foothold in a new market. A low selling price may be one way of achieving *market penetration*. Again, the hope is that, once the desired market share has been achieved, price can be increased.
3 A new competitor may be attempting to enter LC Ltd's market, in which case a large reduction in LC Ltd's price may render such entry uneconomic to the potential competitor due to the high cost of entering a new market (e.g. advertising) coupled with depressed revenue prospects.
4 LC Ltd may use a *loss leader* approach to pricing. If the company sells more than one product, it may be worthwhile selling the hard disc drive at a loss by way of 'inducement' to customers: that is, in the hope that customers who purchase the hard disc drive will also purchase some other product(s) which are profitable.
5 The company is anxious to use spare capacity (which can be costly) and/or to obtain an order.
6 A product/service is at a stage of its life cycle (see below) that requires a low price. This factor is important in its own right and also has a bearing on points 2 and 3 above.

In addition to defining 'cost' with care, it will be necessary, in most cases, to use estimated, rather than actual costs. Actual costs will not be known until 'after the event' and so are useless if price lists or customer quotations are needed before sales are made. Another drawback is that actual costs tend to fluctuate (e.g. from month to month) and it is not desirable from a marketing standpoint to have selling prices which fluctuate in a similar, possibly random, manner. Another important influence on cost is the stage reached by a product/service in its life cycle.

The product life cycle

With some exceptions (e.g. basic foodstuffs), every product/service has a finite life span, within which are several identifiable phases, as illustrated in Figure 8.1. Each stage of the life cycle shown in the figure has implications for both cost and price-setting.

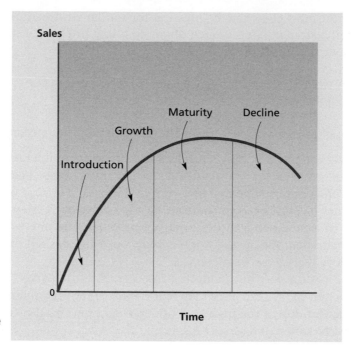

FIGURE 8.1
The product life
cycle

Introduction

Costs of introducing a new product maybe high: for example, cost of investment in assets like plant and machinery, and promotional and advertising costs. The business may therefore be torn between two approaches to pricing. First, penetration pricing may be adopted in an attempt to capture market share quickly, with the likelihood that a low price will encourage high sales volume which will help recover these high initial costs quickly.

Penetration pricing is well exemplified by organisations introducing new credit cards: in most cases, the initial interest rate (i.e. the 'price') is lower than the 'going rate', with prospective clients being actively encouraged to transfer balances from existing cards to the new one. In many cases, once a new credit card becomes established in the market, the interest rate which it charges will begin to rise towards the 'going rate'.

Alternatively, *market skimming* may be used: this is the approach mentioned in Exhibit 8.1 when 'charging premium prices for innovative products' is referred to. Market skimming charges a high initial price (supported by the novelty of the product/service), which is gradually reduced as the life cycle progresses. In this way, it is hoped that highly profitable early sales (albeit at a lower volume than with a penetration price) will quickly cover introduction costs. Examples of market skimming *may* be compact discs, digital watches and digital cameras, where introductory price, supported by the products' novelty value, started high and subsequently reduced. The problem here is that we cannot be positive (without 'inside knowledge') that the initially high prices were a matter of conscious skimming policy on the part of the sellers, or whether the downward movement in prices reflects cost reductions stemming from improved production technology.

Growth

At the growth stage, volume of output/sales will be increasing and, given the likelihood of fixed costs predominating the business's cost structure, unit costs may be falling.

Maturity

This is the most profitable stage of the life cycle, where market share is established and possibly fairly stable, as are production methods, distribution channels, marketing methods, and so forth. However, competitors may begin to appear, with price and/or non-price differentiation becoming evident within the market. Prices may therefore start to fall at this point in the life cycle to meet price competition. Costs, on the other hand, may begin to rise, as changes are made to product/service specifications in pursuit of competitive advantage through differentiation.

Decline

Not only is this stage of the life cycle characterised by falling sales, but possibly also by falling selling prices and rising unit costs. In addition to this, major expenditure will be needed to research, develop and test market a replacement product/service.

Our exposition of the product life cycle has been brief, but it serves to illustrate the potential for different marketing and financial pressures over the life of a product/service. The importance of the product life cycle is becoming more pronounced, with the trend towards increasingly short product lives – so much so that it can be argued that 'traditional' management accounting, based principally on an annual outlook, is becoming irrelevant. This has been recognised with the development of **life cycle costing** which attempts to trace budgeted and actual product costs and revenues through each stage of the life cycle. This, it is argued, provides a more market- and strategic-oriented view which should help focus attention on the cost/price/product/market interrelationship, rather than adopting the predominantly cost-driven perspective implied by 'traditional' accounting methodology.

Impact of changes in unit costs

We have seen that the definition of 'cost' can have an impact on selling price; for any definition of cost, so also can changes in the amount of that cost. This is particularly true where cost includes a significant element of apportioned overhead. Consider Exhibit 8.4.

> ## LC Computers Ltd
>
> LC Ltd produces a range of computer hardware and software. Next year's anticipated direct costs per unit of a particular type of hard disc drive are as follows:
>
> | | £ |
> |---|---|
> | Direct materials | 50 |
> | Direct labour (12 hours @ £6) | 72 |
> | Direct expenses | 18 |
> | Prime cost | 140 |
>
> Production overheads for next year are estimated at £360,000 and these are absorbed into output on the basis of direct labour hours. Because of a reduction in demand for this product, estimated direct labour hours for next year will be 72,000 as opposed to the 90,000 originally anticipated.
>
> To determine unit selling price, the company increases full production cost by a mark-up of 25 per cent of that cost, this being deemed sufficient to cover non-production costs and to provide a satisfactory profit.

Exhibit 8.4 **The effect on price of cost changes**

➩ Re-calculate the company's production overhead absorption rate based on the revised estimate of next year's direct labour hours.

The absorption rate is

$$\frac{\text{estimated overhead cost}}{\text{estimated direct labour hours}} = \frac{£360{,}000}{72{,}000} = £5 \text{ per direct labour hour}$$

➩ Use this absorption rate to determine the full production cost and selling price per unit.

The full production cost and selling price per unit are:

	£
Prime cost (as before)	140
add Production overhead (12 hours @ £5)	60
Full production cost	200
add Mark-up (25% of full production cost)	50
Selling price per unit	250

Compare this to the £235 selling price per unit we calculated earlier. A change in the absorption rate has had the effect of causing a substantial increase in selling price. In fact, if a 'cost plus' approach is rigidly applied to pricing calculations, *any* change in cost will have an effect on selling price.

⇨ Faced with the reduction in demand mentioned in Exhibit 8.4, would an increase in unit selling price from £235 to £250 make commercial sense?

Increasing selling price in the face of falling demand is almost certainly the wrong decision to make as it may result in a further fall in demand. If demand falls so that estimated direct labour hours next year will be reduced to, say, 65,000, does this mean that full production cost per unit and hence selling price per unit should be increased even more?

⇨ Assume that LC Ltd's circumstances have changed such that the full production cost per unit falls to £160. Should the company reduce the unit selling price from the original £235 to £200 as a result?

As we said earlier, selling at a reduced price may be a useful method of increasing or obtaining market share, but price reductions should not be based solely on unit costs. Market share may increase, but market considerations such as the actions of competitors and the relationship between selling price and quantity demanded should be explicitly considered before a firm decision to cut price is reached. Suppose LC Ltd does cut selling price on the basis of its reduced unit cost – a price cut which is not followed by competitor firms. This could increase LC Ltd's market share but the benefit of such an increase could well be lost due to the setting of a price which is *unnecessarily* low in terms of prevailing market conditions, thereby losing profit which could otherwise be earned.

A further problem is that the reduction in unit cost may only be temporary. Suppose LC Ltd does decide to reduce unit selling price to £200 to reflect reduced unit costs and that these subsequently increase. Increasing selling price as a result is likely to be a tricky marketing exercise if it occurs relatively soon after a substantial price cut. Likely future trends in unit costs must therefore also be considered before a decision about selling price is reached and should be allowed for in the setting of estimated unit costs. Finally, different methods of apportioning and absorbing overheads can affect unit cost not just within a single firm, but also across an entire industrial sector. Thus price differences between suppliers of essentially the same goods/services may be as much due to differences in internal accounting methodology as to what is being sold and to whom.

Inflexible linking of price with cost may therefore lead to dangerous circular reasoning, especially where a high proportion of fixed costs is involved (e.g. in organisations with a heavy investment in advanced manufacturing technology):

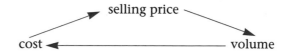

Target costing

One possible remedy for the internal focus of cost-driven price-setting is the use of **target costing**. Here, management will start by determining desired market share and the selling price which is necessary to achieve it. Suppose that LC Ltd's management wishes to sell 10,000 hard disc drives in the forthcoming year and knows that, in order to do so, selling price needs to be set at £200 per unit. The next stage is to deduct the desired profit from selling price, the residual amount representing target cost per unit:

	£
Unit selling price	200
less Desired profit (25% of cost = 20% of selling price)	40
Target cost per unit	160

You will see that the target cost of £160 is less than the full production cost per unit (£188) which we calculated earlier. The implication is that, in order to capture the desired market share *and* earn profit of 20 per cent of sales, the company must somehow reduce unit cost to £160, ideally without compromising product quality. In this context, product deisgn is crucial: cost reductions to meet target cost may be effected by examining the product's functions, for example, and asking 'are they all necessary?' or 'how could the product perform the same functions but at lower cost?' (We shall discuss cost reduction further in Chapter 13). Target costing has two advantages compared to the more 'traditional' cost-based method described earlier:

1 It is explicitly market driven, thereby recognising the crucial importance of market factors to price-setting. As we have demonstrated, a rigid cost-based pricing formula may ignore such factors.
2 It can provide a vehicle for cost control by providing target costs which are determined by both profit and market considerations. If, for example, LC Ltd's unit costs are likely to exceed £160 next year, efforts at reduction can be made so as to earn the desired profit and capture the required market share.

And as a corollary to 1 above:

3 The need for firms to determine 'what the market will bear' requires the gathering and evaluation of strategic information (e.g. about competitor action/reaction, consumer preferences, etc.).

Target costing is a technique widely used (and to good effect) in Japan. For a succinct overview of this *see* Bromwich and Bhimani (1994).

Price elasticity of demand

We said above that cost considerations alone do not allow for market factors such as competitive reaction to a change in price. Equally important is the relationship between changes in the selling price of goods and services and changes in the quantity demanded. This relationship is known as **price elasticity of demand**. A rigidly cost-based pricing formula does not allow for this relationship, thereby ignoring the fact that a profit-maximising combination of price and demand will exist.

Exhibit 8.5 gives information about the price/demand relationship faced by LC Ltd for its hard disc drive.

LC Ltd: price/demand relationship

The company's market research indicates the following price/demand relationships for next year:

Unit selling price (£)	200	210	220	235	250	260	275	285
Demand (000 units)	10	9	8.5	7.5	6.5	6	5	4.5

Variable cost per unit will be £140 and fixed costs for the year will amount to £360,000.

EXHIBIT **8.5 Price elasticity of demand**

Our earlier calculations based solely on full production cost plus a 25 per cent mark-up yielded a unit selling price of £235. From Exhibit 8.5 we now know that, at this price, the quantity demanded will be 7,500 units. Does this combination of price and quantity optimise the company's profit from sale of the hard disc drive? If not, what is the optimum combination?

In order to answer this, we need to determine profit for each price/demand combination; if we assume that the fixed cost remains £360,000 and that the unit variable cost is constant at £140 for all volumes under consideration, then the price/demand combination yielding maximum total contribution will also yield maximum profit.

⇨ Complete Table 8.1 to determine which selling price maximises profit from sale of the hard disc drive, bearing in mind that the *unit* contribution will alter when the selling price changes.

TABLE **8.1 Partly completed price–demand–contribution schedule**

Unit selling price (£)	Quantity demanded (units)	Unit contribution (£)	Total contribution (£)
200	10,000		600,000
210	9,000		
220	8,500		
235	7,500	95	712,500
250	6,500		
260	6,000	120	
275	5,000		
285	4,500		

Table 8.2 shows the complete calculations of total contribution at the specified price/demand combinations.

TABLE 8.2 Completed price–demand–contribution schedule

Unit selling price (£)	Quantity demanded (units)	Unit contribution (£)	Total contribution (£)
200	10,000	60	600,000
210	9,000	70	630,000
220	8,500	80	680,000
235	7,500	95	712,500
250	6,500	110	715,000
260	6,000	120	720,000
275	5,000	135	675,000
285	4,500	145	652,500

Total contribution (and hence profit) is maximised at a price of £260 per unit. Our original cost-based price of £235 therefore fails to optimise profit. Useful as the analysis of total contribution has been, it does suffer from certain weaknesses:

1 It assumes linear cost behaviour: that is, fixed cost is unchanged in amount and unit variable cost is constant. The relevant range is clearly important here and, if you look at the range of volumes spanned in Table 8.2, it is not hard to imagine that some may fall outside it, with consequent implications for cost behaviour at those volumes. However, changes in either or both fixed and variable costs can easily be incorporated into the calculations. Changes to unit variable cost can be allowed for in the unit contribution calculation and changes in the amount of fixed cost would mean that *profit* for each price/demand combination would need to be determined (by deducting fixed costs from total contribution).

2 It examines only a limited number of possible price/demand combinations (eight in this case). Such a simplification may be desirable for ease of calculation, but it does mean that the *true* profit-maximising price/demand combination may be missed. For example, further analysis of LC Ltd's market may reveal that a unit selling price of, say, £264.75 yields the highest profit. This problem may be overcome by a more sophisticated analysis involving the use of calculus.

3 It assumes certainty about price/demand relationships. In practice, these can be extremely difficult to predict. Price is unlikely to be the *sole* determinant of demand. Other factors, such as the disposable income of consumers, consumer taste, product 'image' and quality, have a major bearing on demand that may be difficult to assess quantifiably. In the next chapter, we will discuss how the effect of uncertainty can be incorporated into the analysis of decisions.

Although it may be difficult to measure price elasticity of demand precisely, to ignore its existence when setting selling prices would be foolhardy. An awareness of the sensitivity of demand to changes in selling price is a vital element in a successful pricing policy.

Figure 8.2 illustrates two demand functions, each with a different price elasticity. Demand function D_1 is said to be **price elastic** (or simply 'elastic'): a change in sell-

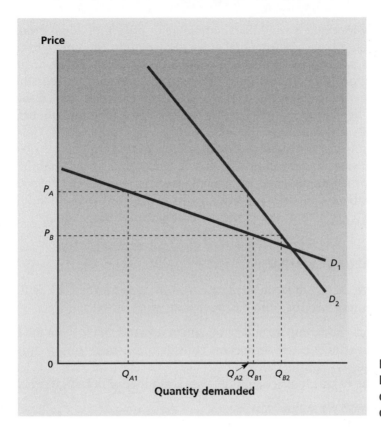

FIGURE 8.2
Demand functions with differing elasticity of demand

ing price from P_A to P_B causes a disproportionately large change in quantity demanded (from Q_{A1} to Q_{A2}). For products/services which have elastic demand, great care will be needed in setting selling price, as a small change in price could have major consequences in terms of quantity demanded. Demand function D_2 is **price inelastic** ('inelastic'): here, a change in price from P_A to P_B results in a proportionately smaller change in quantity demanded (from Q_{A2} to Q_{B2}). This relative insensitivity to changes in selling price means that non-price factors such as product/service quality or after-sales service may have a major bearing on demand.

The significance of price elasticity of demand may be seen if we consider tickets for air travel: a 10 per cent change in the price of economy tickets could have a major effect on demand, whereas a similar change in the price of first class tickets might have comparatively little effect on demand (the key selling points of first class travel being quality of in-flight service).

Product line pricing and cross-elasticity of demand

A further consideration in the pricing decision is the extent to which complementary or substitute products/services are available – **cross-elasticity of demand**. Many organisations produce a range of products/services which complement each other: for example, a manufacturer of photographic equipment may produce several different types of camera, along with accessories such as film, flashbulbs and so on; sales of all the separate items within the product range may be interrelated in such a way that it would be inadvisable to price individual products in isolation as this could have a detrimental effect elsewhere in the range. In this sort of situation, the pricing decision should encompass the full range of products/services offered – **product line pricing**. However, recognising the possible interrelationships between different products within a range may be very difficult – a problem likely to be further complicated by the existence of complements/substitutes *outside* the firm's own range (i.e. being offered by competitors). Cost considerations alone cannot reflect marketing relationships of this kind.

In addition, as we saw in Chapter 5, the apparent 'profitability' of individual products may be distorted by apportionments of overhead costs, and care should be taken to exclude such apportionments in any decision which hinges on product profitability (e.g. to drop a particular product from the range).

Price-setting summary

Before we discuss decisions involving source resources, we will summarise the main points emerging from our discussion of price-setting:

1 Price may be an important determinant of demand, but it is not the *only* determinant.
2 Unit cost may be an important consideration in setting selling price, but it is not the *only* consideration.
3 The use of cost in price-setting raises a number of potential problems:

 ■ how do we define 'cost'?;

 ■ the relationship between cost and the product life cycle;

 ■ the impact of changes in unit cost;

 ■ the difference between 'traditional' and target costing definition of cost.

One means by which non-cost factors may be allowed for in price-setting is by adopting a flexible approach to the amount of profit which is added to cost to arrive at selling price. Rather than simply adding a 'flat rate' 25 per cent to unit costs (as we did earlier with the data in Exhibit 8.5), management can assess 'what the market will bear' in terms of selling price, with the profit mark-up being tailored accordingly, or target costing may be used.

The need for a flexible approach to price-setting is, perhaps, reflected in the results of a 1993 study by Drury *et al.* in the United Kingdom: whilst cost-based pricing predominated (84 per cent of respondents), 16 per cent of respondents did not use it at all and, of the 84 per cent who did, some 59 per cent used it for 50 per cent or less of their sales.

LIMITING FACTOR DECISIONS

SHORTAGE OF SKILLS 'POSES THREAT TO WELSH EXPANSION'

Skills shortages in Wales could threaten future expansion there by international companies, according to Coopers & Lybrand, the accountants . . . Thirty companies said they had already experienced skills shortages, the majority in engineering and associated disciplines.

Concern was expressed that the supply of professional, qualified and skilled workers was not increasing, and that competition for staff could lead to higher labour costs.

In addition to the fears of shortages of qualified engineers and technicians, there were worries about the recruitment of apprentices and 'high-quality' school leavers. There was disappointment that the apprentice workforce in Wales might be diminishing, due to parental and school pressure to continue full-time education . . .

Source: Roland Adburgham, *Financial Times*, 19 January 1996.

EXHIBIT **8.6 Shortage of skilled employees: a potential limiting factor**

A *limiting factor* – such as the potential shortage of skilled workers referred to in Exhibit 8.6 – is a constraint. Constraints vary from legal and social constraints to financial and resource constraints. We are concerned here with the two latter types of constraint, but legal and social constraints should never be ignored in decision making: for example, there is no benefit in undertaking a possibly complex and time-consuming financial analysis if there is only one possible course of action which must be followed in order to comply with legal requirements such as those contained in Health and Safety legislation. For a commercial organisation, sales demand will almost invariably impose a limit on activity. The situation would be simple enough if limiting factors were restricted to sales demand: sales effort would be channelled into maximising sales of the most profitable product(s)/service(s). As we saw in Chapter 5, contribution analysis can be a useful aid in assessing the relative profitability of different products/services. The problem, however, is that demand is often not the only limiting factor, and it may not even enter into consideration for non-profit organisations.

⇨ Can you suggest *three* financial or resource-related limiting factors other than sales demand which may be faced by an organisation?

There are many possibilities. You may have thought of some of the following:

1 shortage of suitably skilled staff;
2 shortage of appropriate materials;
3 lack of available funding; and
4 insufficient space within premises.

If constraints of the type described above can be overcome, a financial analysis of the options available for overcoming them will be needed, involving assessment of the related relevant costs and benefits. However, it may not be possible – at least, in the short term – to recruit more staff, or to raise additional funding. In fact, constraints may be linked so that, for example, additional staff cannot be recruited partly because extra funding cannot be raised. In some cases, the problem may be more than short term: for example, increasingly strict cash limits are a major concern for public sector and non-profit organisations.

Where limiting factors other than demand exist, the implication is that demand will exceed the ability to supply. And if resource constraints cannot be overcome, we must have a technique which allows us to 'make the best of a bad situation' – at least, in financial terms. This means using the limited resources available so that demand is satisfied as far as possible and in such a way that profit is maximised (or cost minimised). We shall now consider a typical limiting factor situation and illustrate a method of financial analysis which attempts to achieve this twofold aim. Exhibit 8.7 contains the basic data, initially involving a single constraint and no option for subcontracting.

Single Limiting Factor

GL (Paints) Ltd

GL Ltd produces four basic types of paint in bulk, details of which are as follows for next period:

	Emulsion (matt)	Emulsion (silk)	Gloss	Gloss (non-drip)
Maximum demand (100 litre drums)	3,000	5,900	4,500	4,000
Selling price per 100 litre drum (£)	185	200	205	275
Costs per 100 litre drum:				
	£	£	£	£
Direct labour	21	30	21	42
Direct materials	28	51	29	60
Processing cost	21	30	21	30
Production overhead	35	50	35	50
Administration overhead	20	20	30	30
Selling overhead	20	15	30	37

Notes:

1 Direct labour and direct materials are wholly variable with the volume of output.
2 Processing cost varies with the number of processing hours at a rate of £6 per hour.
3 Production overhead is charged to each 100 litre drum at a composite rate of £10 per processing hour – £8.00 per hour being in respect of fixed overheads, £2.00 in respect of variable.
4 Selling overhead is fully variable with the number of drums sold.
5 Administration costs are 80 per cent fixed and 20 per cent variable with the number of drums sold.
6 Due to a reorganisation of production methods, processing hours will be limited to 40,000 in total next period.

EXHIBIT 8.7 A limiting factor problem

The problem faced by GL Ltd is that the limitation on the number of processing hours next period may mean that potential demand cannot be fully satisfied.

➪ Determine the number of processing hours required to produce a 100 litre drum of each kind of paint and confirm or refute the suggestion that 40,000 processing hours is insufficient to fully satisfy next period's demand.

Processing hours per drum are:

$$\frac{\text{Processing cost per drum}}{\text{£6 per processing hour}}$$

This gives 3.5, 5, 3.5 and 5 hours per 100 litre drum of matt emulsion, silk emulsion, gloss and non-drip gloss respectively. In order to fully satisfy next period's demand, the total processing hours required are:

Emulsion (matt)	3,000 drums × 3.5 hours	10,500
Emulsion (silk)	5,900 drums × 5.0 hours	29,500
Gloss	4,500 drums × 3.5 hours	15,750
Gloss (non-drip)	4,000 drums × 5.0 hours	20,000
		75,750

No subcontract option

Our calculations confirm that there will be insufficient processing hours to fully satisfy next period's demand. If demand cannot be fully satisfied, we need to decide which products should be concentrated on so that the greatest profit can be earned in the circumstances. In other words, we need a criterion to rank the products in order of preference, given the limitation in processing hours.

➪ Based on the information in Exhibit 8.7, are the fixed overheads relevant to this decision?

The fixed overheads are irrelevant. Although they may be future cash flows, in amount they will be unaffected by this decision: that is, they will not differ between alternatives, thus failing one of the criteria for relevance described in the last chapter. Since the fixed overheads are irrelevant (the same amount is incurred irrespective of the decision), the higher the amount of total contribution earned, the higher the resultant profit.

➪ What is the contribution per 100 litre drum of each of the four products?

Bearing in mind that contribution is (selling price – *all* variable costs), unit contributions for each type of product are:

	Emulsion (matt) (£)	Emulsion (silk) (£)	Gloss (£)	Gloss (non-drip) (£)
Selling price per 100 litre drum	185	200	205	275
less Variable costs per drum:				
Direct labour	21	30	21	42
Direct materials	28	51	29	60
Processing cost	21	30	21	30
Production overhead	7	10	7	10
Administration overhead	4	4	6	6
Selling overhead	20	15	30	37
	101	140	114	185
Contribution per drum	84	60	91	90

We are now faced with a problem of *ranking:* that is, which products should be produced and in what quantities in order to obtain the best possible total contribution? It is at this stage that we must make allowance for the limiting factor: we want to obtain maximum total contribution *given the limitation in processing hours*. We should therefore concentrate scarce processing hours on those products having the highest *contribution per processing hour*. Once we have determined each product's contribution per processing hour, we can produce a ranking in terms of financial desirability. Contribution per hour is easily calculated:

$$\frac{\text{contribution per unit}}{\text{processing hours per unit}}$$

▷ Determine each product's contribution per processing hour. Rank the four products on this basis in descending order.

The contributions per processing hour and product rankings are:

	Emulsion (matt)	Emulsion (silk)	Gloss	Gloss (non-drip)
Contribution per drum (£)	84	60	91	90
Processing hours per drum	3.5	5.0	3.5	5.0
Contribution per hour (£)	24	12	26	18
Ranking	II	IV	I	III

Now that we have ranked the four products in order of financial desirability, we can prepare a production plan, remembering that there is no point in producing more of a product than we are able to sell. So the sales maxima in Exhibit 8.7 will place an upper limit on output of each product. The production plan is as follows:

Maximum processing hours	40,000
Produce 4,500 drums of gloss – uses (4,500 × 3.5) hours	15,750
Hours remaining for other products	24,250
Produce 3,000 drums of matt emulsion – uses (3,000 × 3.5) hours	10,500
Hours remaining for other products	13,750

Non-drip gloss is the next best-ranked product, with maximum demand next period estimated at 4,000 drums, each of which requires 5 processing hours. We cannot produce 4,000, which requires 20,000 processing hours, and must restrict output of this product to utilise the remaining 13,750 processing hours. We will therefore be able to produce

$$\frac{13,750 \text{ hours}}{5 \text{ hours per drum}} = 2,750 \text{ drums of non-drip gloss.}$$

The limited availability of processing hours means that some demand for non-drip gloss will be unsatisfied next period, and no silk emulsion will be sold. Given the constraint on processing hours, maximum contribution will be:

	£
4,500 drums of gloss @ £91	409,500
3,000 drums of matt emulsion @ £84	252,000
2,750 drums of non-drip gloss @ £90	247,500
Total contribution	909,000

This will fully utilise the available processing hours.

▷ Would it be possible to improve the £909,000 contribution above by increasing sales of non-drip gloss and reducing sales of, say, matt emulsion, assuming no change to the processing hour constraint or to any other factor?

At first glance, increasing sales of non-drip gloss (limited in the contribution calculation) might appear worthwhile, since the contribution *per drum* is higher than that earned for matt emulsion. But this ignores the fact that, in order to sell one additional drum of non-drip gloss, we will lose sales of matt emulsion:

	£
Extra contribution on one drum of non-drip gloss	90
Contribution lost on sales of matt emulsion:	
$\left(\frac{5}{3.5} \times £84\right)$	120
Net loss of contribution	30

Each additional drum of non-drip gloss requires five processing hours to be removed from production/sale of matt emulsion, each drum of which uses only 3.5 hours (i.e. sales of roughly 1.43 drums of matt emulsion will be lost).

You should note, however, that our analysis is based solely on optimising contribution/profit: that is, it ignores qualitative factors.

➪ State *two* qualitative factors which will have a critical bearing on the ultimate decision by GL Ltd.

The company would be extremely ill-advised to implement the production plan indicated above without careful consideration of the reaction of both customers and competitors. Sales of non-drip gloss will be severely reduced next period, and no silk emulsion will be produced/sold. This could result in lost custom which may not be recovered, not only for the two products just mentioned, but also for the other products – especially if GL Ltd's competitors take advantage of the situation by actively trying to expand their own sales.

➪ Our financial analysis is based on certain assumptions which we have already encountered in Chapters 6 and 7. What are they?

Our analysis rests on five key assumptions:

1 *Certainty exists* For example, certainty about sales maxima for products and constraint identification/quantification.
2 *Revenue is linear* The selling price per drum is the same at all volumes under consideration.
3 *Costs are linear* Variable cost per drum is constant and total fixed costs are unchanged in amount;
4 *Production = sales* If significant stocks exist at the start of the period under review, it would be possible to reduce (or even eliminate) any shortfall in supply relative to demand. Such a situation would require our basic technique to be amended slightly to allow for the reduction in sales maxima that would result from sales being made from stock.
5 *Sales of different products/services are independent* Restricting output/sales of one or more product(s)/service(s) will not have a 'knock-on' effect on demand elsewhere within the sales mix.

Providing we are working within the *relevant range*, these assumptions may be reasonably acceptable approximations of reality and need not invalidate the analysis. If, however, a limiting factor is likely to have a major effect on volume, possibly over a lengthy time horizon – that is, if the analysis falls outside the relevant range – then these assumptions may be misleadingly simplistic.

The analysis further assumes that the organisation aims either to maximise profit or to minimise cost. There may, however, be other, non-financial objectives which render this assumption questionable. For example, maintaining customer goodwill may militate strongly against limiting supply of particular product(s)/service(s). In such circumstances, it may be desirable to make strenuous efforts to overcome a limiting factor – even if this means a reduction in short-term profit. Subcontracting may be one solution and it is to this aspect of limiting factor situations that we now turn.

The subcontract option

Suppose GL Ltd is able to subcontract production of any products which the constraint on processing hours prevents the company from manufacturing itself. Will this change the optimal production plan arrived at above? Exhibit 8.8 provides details of subcontracting options open to GL Ltd:

GL Ltd: subcontracting

Any shortfall in GL Ltd's production can be made up by subcontracting. An external supplier has quoted the following firm prices to supply any quantity of 100 litre drums of identical paint to that produced by GL Ltd:

	£
Emulsion (matt)	107
Emulsion (silk)	141
Gloss	114
Gloss (non-drip)	157

EXHIBIT **8.8 Overcoming a limiting factor by subcontracting**

From our earlier calculations, we know that GL Ltd requires 75,750 processing hours to produce a volume of output sufficient to fully meet demand for all four products; since only 40,000 hours are available in the period under review, there is a shortage of 35,750, which can be made up by subcontracting. Assuming that the company will wish to subcontract (e.g. to protect their market from competitors, or to retain customer goodwill), the problem resolves itself into one of *cost minimisation*: that is, the company will subcontract sufficient production to cover the shortage of processing hours at the least additional cost, since it will almost certainly be more expensive to subcontract than produce in-house.

⇨ What is the relevant cost to GL Ltd of producing a 100 litre drum of each type of paint in-house?

The relevant cost of producing a 100 litre drum of each type of paint is:

	Emulsion (matt) (£)	Emulsion (silk) (£)	Gloss (£)	Gloss (non-drip) (£)
Direct labour	21	30	21	42
Direct materials	28	51	29	60
Processing cost	21	30	21	30
Production overhead	7	10	7	10
Relevant cost per drum	77	121	78	142

Note that the selling overhead and variable element of administration overhead vary with units *sold*, not produced. These costs will therefore be incurred irrespective of who *manufactures* the paint and are irrelevant to this decision.

⇨ What is the additional cost per 100 litre drum to subcontract production of each type of paint?

The additional cost per drum of subcontracting is:

	Emulsion (matt) (£)	Emulsion (silk) (£)	Gloss (£)	Gloss (non-drip) (£)
Relevant cost to make	77	121	78	142
Cost to subcontract	107	141	114	157
Additional cost	30	20	36	15

We now need to recognise the impact of the limiting factor. GL Ltd wishes to subcontract sufficient production to cover the shortfall of 35,750 processing hours. There is no need to subcontract more, since 40,000 hours are available internally and a total of 75,750 hours will fully meet expected demand for the period. The company needs to rank the four products in terms of their additional cost to subcontract *per hour of processing time*. In this case, the ranking will be in ascending order, with the lowest-cost option ranking first.

⇨ Determine the extra cost per processing hour of subcontracting one drum of each product and rank the products on this basis.

We determined the processing hours per drum earlier; the additional cost of subcontracting per processing hour is simply:

$$\frac{\text{additional cost per drum}}{\text{processing hours per drum}}$$

Applying this to GL Ltd's data, we get:

	Emulsion (matt)	Emulsion (silk)	Gloss	Gloss (non-drip)
Additional cost per drum (£)	30	20	36	15
Processing hours per drum	3.5	5	3.5	5
Additional cost per hour (£)	8.57	4	10.29	3
Ranking	III	II	IV	I

A subcontracting schedule can now be prepared based on these rankings:

Subcontract 4,000 drums of non-drip gloss: releases (4,000 × 5) processing hours	20,000
Shortfall in hours	35,750
Hours still to be covered by subcontracting	15,750

Silk emulsion is the second-ranked product. Subcontracting 5,900 drums of this product will cover (5,900 × 5) = 29,500 processing hours. This is more than is required. Sufficient silk emulsion should therefore be subcontracted to cover the remaining shortfall after non-drip gloss has been subcontracted (i.e. 15,750 hours):

$$\frac{15{,}750 \text{ hours}}{5 \text{ hours per drum}} = 3{,}150 \text{ drums}$$

The optimum production/subcontracting plan can now be summarised:

      Sub-contract:
          4,000 drums of non-drip gloss
          3,150 drums of silk emulsion
      Produce:
          3,000 drums of matt emulsion
          (5,900 − 3,150) = 2,750 drums of silk emulsion
          4,500 drums of gloss.

Given the constraint on processing hours and the subcontracting possibilities available, this plan will minimise GL Ltd's cost, thereby maximising contribution.

As always in decision situations, qualitative factors should be carefully considered.

⇨ State *one* qualitative factor which will be particularly important in a decision which involves a subcontracting option.

The quality of goods/services being subcontracted is probably the single most important non-financial factor to bear in mind. If quality is questionable, there may be additional costs involved in a decision to subcontract (e.g. inspection of subcontracted items), along with the possibility of dissatisfied customers. There may also be a problem with consistency between goods/services produced in-house and subcontracted: in GL Ltd's case, there may, for example, be minor differences in the colour of paint.

MULTIPLE LIMITING FACTORS

Where an organisation is faced with several constraints, it is not possible to use the approach based on contribution or additional cost per unit of limiting factor which we have just described. Say, for example, that GL Ltd had limited availability of processing hours *and* limitations on direct materials and direct labour. Clearly, it would not be feasible to calculate a contribution per unit of limiting factor, as there are now two of these in addition to sales demand, and we must use a technique known as **linear programming**. This is a mathematical approach to maximising or minimising a particular outcome, given the existence of constraints.

Graphical linear programming

Certain constraint problems can be solved graphically. For the purpose of our graphical exercise, we will assume that GL Ltd produces only two products. Further details are given in Exhibit 8.9.

GL Ltd: two products, multiple constraints

Details of the company's two products are as follows:

	Silk emulsion	Gloss
Contribution per drum (£)	60	91
Processing hours per drum	5.0	3.5
Direct labour hours per drum	1.0	2.0
Maximum demand (drums)	5,900	4,500

During the period under review, processing hours are limited to 35,000 and direct labour hours to 12,000.

EXHIBIT **8.9 Problem for solution by graphical linear programming**

The first stage in our linear programming exercise is to formulate the constraints algebraically; designating the number of drums of silk emulsion as 'X' and of gloss as 'Y', we get:

Processing hours	$5.0X + 3.5Y \le 35,000$
Direct labour hours	$X + 2Y \le 12,000$
Demand	$X \le 5,900$
	$Y \le 4,500$
	$X, Y \ge 0$

The last 'non-negativity' constraint is added to indicate that X and Y cannot have negative values (i.e. the axes on our graph do not extend below the origin). Since it is not possible to plot inequalities, we must substitute '=' for '≤' in each of the above expressions and plot the resultant equations. In order to plot the processing hour constraint, we have to determine the points at which it intersects the vertical and horizontal axes by setting, first X, then Y to zero and solving for the other variable:

$$\text{processing constraint } 5.0X + 3.5Y = 35,000$$
$$\text{if } X = 0, Y = 10,000 \text{ and if } Y = 0, X = 7,000$$

⇨ Using the same approach, determine the points at which the direct labour constraint intersects the vertical and horizontal axes.

The direct labour constraint in equation form is:

$$X + 2Y = 12,000$$
$$\text{if } X = 0, Y = 6,000 \text{ and if } Y = 0, X = 12,000$$

Figure 8.3 plots processing and labour hour constraints along with maximum demand for each product.

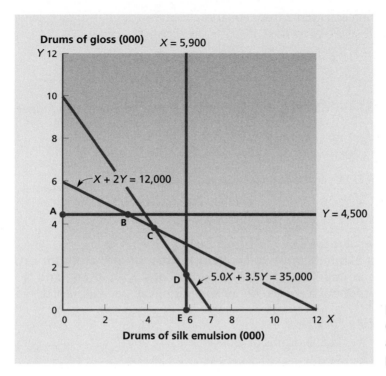

FIGURE 8.3
Graphical solution to
a linear programming
problem

☞ Looking at Figure 8.3, what does the area bounded by 0, A, B, C, D, E represent?

This area is known as the *feasible region*: that is, the area of the graph containing output solutions for X and Y which are within the given constraints. Because this problem involves '≤' constraints, the feasible region will lie to the left of the constraint functions, such that it lies within *all* constraints simultaneously. Within the feasible region, one combination of X and Y will be optimal: that is, it will provide maximum total contribution. This will lie at the outermost limit of the feasible region: in other words, will be at one of points A, B, C, D or E. We therefore need to evaluate total contribution earned from the combinations of X and Y at each of these points, meaning that we must first obtain values for X and Y.

Points A and E present no problem, having respective values which can be read directly from Figure 8.3: ($X = 0$, $Y = 4,500$) and ($X = 5,900$, $Y = 0$) respectively. B lies at the intersection of lines with the following equations:

$$X + 2Y = 12,000$$
$$Y = 4,500$$

Solving these simultaneous equations for X gives a value of 3,000.

Point C lies at the intersection of:

$$X + 2Y = 12,000............................equation\ 1$$
$$5X + 3.5Y = 35,000.........................equation\ 2$$

Multiplying equation 1 by 5, we get:

$$5X + 10Y = 60,000.........................equation\ 3$$

Deducting equation 2 from equation 3:

$$5X + 10Y = 60,000$$
$$5X + 3.5Y = 35,000$$
$$6.5Y = 25,000$$

so $Y = 3,846$ (rounded). Substituting this value of Y into equation 1, we get:

$$X + 2(3,846) = 12,000$$

So X is 4,308.

Point D lies at the intersection of:

$$5X + 3.5Y = 35,000$$
$$X = 5,900$$

giving a value for Y of 1,571 (rounded).

From Exhibit 8.9, we know the contribution per drum for each product, and, bearing in mind that 'X' signifies drums of silk emulsion, and 'Y' drums of gloss, total contribution at each of our five points can be determined:

Point	Produce/sell	£
A	4,500 drums of gloss @ £91	405,900
B	4,500 drums of gloss @ £91	405,900
	3,000 drums of silk emulsion @ £60	180,000
		585,900
C	3,846 drums of gloss @ £91	349,986
	4,308 drums of silk emulsion @ £60	258,480
		608,466
D	1,571 drums of gloss @ £91	142,961
	5,900 drums of silk emulsion @ £60	354,000
		496,961
E	5,900 drums of silk emulsion @ £60	354,000

Optimum contribution therefore occurs at Point C: produce/sell 3,846 drums of gloss and 4,308 drums of silk emulsion.

Graphical linear programming can be used to solve problems involving any number of constraints (unlike the contribution per unit of limiting factor approach taken earlier). However, the technique is limited to two-product/service situations, as each product/service requires its own graphical axis.

Simplex

Simplex is a computer-based approach to solution of limiting factor problems (Simplex can be performed manually, but is time-consuming, even for a fairly simple problem); subject to computer-based restriction (imposed, for example, by a particular software package or availability of memory), Simplex can tackle problems with large numbers of products/services and constraints. For illustrative purposes, we will apply Simplex to the two-product problem given in Exhibit 8.9.

Inputting a linear programming problem to the computer requires formulation of one additional expression – the **objective function**. This is what we are attempting to maximise. For GL Ltd, the objective function is total contribution – remember that fixed costs are assumed to be unaffected by the decision, so that maximising total contribution will also maximise profit. Using the two-product problem in Exhibit 8.9, 'X' to represent drums of silk emulsion, and 'Y' drums of gloss, the objective function is

$$60X + 91Y$$

The complete problem for input is thus:

maximise	$60X + 91Y$	[row 1]
subject to	$5X + 3.5Y \leq 35,000$	[row 2]
	$X + 2Y \leq 12,000$	[row 3]
	$X \leq 5,900$	[row 4]
	$Y \leq 4,500$	[row 5]
	$X, Y \geq 0$	

(Note that the row numbers are not part of the input data, but are shown here to allow us to identify each expression in the problem with the corresponding parts of the solution; nor is the non-negativity constraint input, as this is incorporated within the software.) The precise format for inputting the objective function plus constraints depends on the specific software package. Many, such as LINDO© (which we shall use to generate our solution), allow input in 'natural' form: that is, as it is set out above.

In order to solve the problem, the computer adopts an *iterative* approach: that is, starting from a 'do nothing' position, a mathematical operation is repetitively performed – the effect of each repetition (*iteration*) being steadily to improve the solution – until optimal values are arrived at. Exhibit 8.10 shows the result of computer analysis of the problem in Exhibit 8.9.

Objective function value, variable, and value

▷ In Exhibit 8.10, what do 'objective function value', 'variable' and 'value' indicate?

The objective function value is the total contribution generated by the optimal solution (£608,461.60), whilst the variables and their respective values indicate that 4,307.692 drums of silk emulsion and 3,846.154 of gloss should be produced/sold. Allowing for rounding differences, these are the same results we obtained from our graphical analysis. The computer output provides additional information – this can be obtained from a graphical approach, but not directly – which may be of considerable significance to the decision-making process.

Slack or surplus, and dual prices

The next section of output refers to row, slack or surplus and 'dual values'. From our initial formulation, we know that Row 2 refers to the processing hours constraint,

```
OBJECTIVE FUNCTION VALUE

1) 608461.600

VARIABLE              VALUE

   X                4307.692
   Y                3846.154

ROW          SLACK OR SURPLUS        DUAL PRICES

 2)               .000000             4.461538
 3)               .000000            37.692310
 4)           1592.308000              .000000
 5)            653.846000              .000000

No ITERATIONS = 3

DO RANGE (SENSITIVITY) ANALYSIS?

? yes

RANGES IN WHICH THE BASIS IS UNCHANGED

                  OBJ COEFFICIENT RANGES

VARIABLE  CURRENT COEFFICIENT  ALLOWABLE INCREASE  ALLOWABLE DECREASE

   X           60.000000          70.000000          14.500000
   Y           91.000000          28.999990          49.000000

                  RIGHTHAND SIDE RANGES

ROW       CURRENT RHS      ALLOWABLE INCREASE   ALLOWABLE DECREASE

 2)      35000.000000        5175.000000          4250.000000
 3)      12000.000000         849.999900          2957.143000
 4)       5900.000000          INFINITY           1592.308000
 5)       4500.000000          INFINITY            653.846100
```

EXHIBIT **8.10** LINDO©-generated solution to linear programming problem

Row 3 to that for direct labour hours, Row 4 to demand for drums of silk emulsion and Row 5 to demand for gloss.

⇨ What do the values in the 'slack or surplus' column represent?

These values indicate unused resources (in the case of Rows 2 and 3) and unsatisfied demand (Rows 4 and 5). Available processing and direct labour hours are thus fully utilised by the optimal solution (slack/surplus of 0), whereas there is unsatisfied demand of 1,592.308 drums of silk emulsion and 653.846 of gloss. Unsatisfied demand is simply the difference between the quantity produced/sold in the optimal solution and maximum demand:

silk emulsion	(5,900 − 4,307.692)	= 1,592.308
gloss	(4,500 − 3,846.154)	= 653.846

The **dual prices** (also referred to as **shadow prices** or **shadow values**) may be of particular interest to management. A dual price is:

> The change in objective function value resulting from obtaining/losing one unit of scarce resource.

Therefore, if GL Ltd were able to obtain one more processing or direct labour hour, total contribution would increase by £4.461538 and £37.692310 respectively.

⇨ GL Ltd's management can obtain additional direct labour hours by means of overtime working at a cost of £16 per hour. Is working overtime financially worthwhile?

Since one additional direct labour hour will increase total contribution by £37.692310, it is financially worthwhile to pay £16 to obtain it. However, you should note that, in this instance, an additional labour hour will only be of value if the constraint on processing hours can *also* be overcome, as these are already fully utilised by the optimal solution.

⇨ Why is there no dual price attaching to unsatisfied demand?

At first glance this might seem odd, but, if GL Ltd succeeded in increasing demand for either product, what would the benefit be? Given no change in production constraints, there will be no benefit, since it will be *unsatisfied* demand which increases. This leads to an important conclusion:

> Dual prices only attach to constraints which are fully met by the optimal solution.

Having provided slack/surplus quantities and dual prices for each constraint, the software then indicates the number of iterations required to solve the problem: that is, the number of improvements to the initial 'do nothing' scenario necessary to discover the optimum. The user now has the option of instructing the software to undertake some further analysis.

Objective coefficient ranges

The objective function in our example is an expression for total contribution:

$$60X + 91Y$$

'60' and '91' are the current coefficients referred to in the computer output: that is, the contribution per drum of silk emulsion and gloss. The coefficient ranges show the range of unit contributions within which the optimal solution will be unchanged: for silk emulsion, this is:

maximum (£60 + £70) = £130   minimum (£60 − £14.50) = £44.50

Outside the range of unit contributions £44.50–£130 for silk emulsion and £42–£119.99999 (gloss), the optimal solution will change. This information may be useful if there is uncertainty about unit selling price and/or variable cost.

Righthand side ranges

These indicate the range of constraint values within which dual values remain as stated, 'current RHS' being the value specified in formulation of the problem. For processing hours (Row 2), total contribution will increase by £4.461538 as long as the available number of hours falls between:

maximum (35,000 + 5,175) = 40,175   minimum (35,000 − 4,250) = 30,750

Such information will be of interest to management in assessing acquisition of additional resources, as the quantity acquired may affect the financial viability of acquisition: that is, if more than 5,175 additional processing hours were to be acquired, then the associated contribution increase will change from £4.461538 per hour. For the demand constraints (Rows 4 and 5), you will see that the allowable increase is infinity. This reflects the zero dual price attaching to additional demand so long as unsatisfied demand exists. The 'allowable decrease' figures indicate that, were demand to drop to a level below optimal/output sales, a dual price will arise.

Linear programming: assumptions

Although linear programming can provide sophisticated analysis of a problem, it still relies on the same five assumptions we set out earlier when discussing the contribution per unit of limiting factor approach: namely, certainty exists; costs are linear; revenues are linear; production = sales; and products are independent. In addition, we have assumed that products are *divisible*: that is, that part-units can be produced/sold, which may not always be realistic. (This assumption was also *implicit* in the contribution/relevant cost per unit of limiting factor approach.) More complex analytical techniques – for example, non-linear programming and integer programming – can be used to overcome these weaknesses. But such complex techniques do not necessarily guarantee more accurate results, and their very complexity may prove a barrier to effective understanding and use.

SUMMARY

In this chapter, we considered price-setting and the impact of constraints on decision making, and have seen that:

- Cost is an important factor in setting selling price, as the difference between selling price and cost, coupled with quantity demanded, will determine whether profit is being earned, whether breakeven is being achieved, or whether an operating deficit is being minimised (in the case of non-profit organisations).

■ Profit can be expressed as a **mark-up** or as a **margin**: a mark-up states profit relative to cost whereas a **margin** states profit relative to sales value.

■ Taking a rigid 'cost plus' approach to pricing has certain dangers, which can be summarised under the following headings:
   - Which cost to use?
   - Impact of changes to unit cost
   - Price elasticity of demand
   - Cost elasticity of demand

■ The product life cycle consists of introduction, growth, maturity and decline, each stage having implications for the interrelationship between cost/price/product/market.

■ **Price elasticity of demand** refers to the relationship between changes in price and changes in the quantity demanded; a product/service is price elastic if demand is sensitive to changes in selling price and is price inelastic if demand is relatively insensitive to changes in selling price.

■ **Cross elasticity of demand** refers to the extent to which complementary or substitute products/services are available – either within a firm's own range or offered in the market by competitor firms.

■ Non-cost factors can be allowed for in price-setting by using a flexible approach to setting the required profit or by using **target costing**, whereby target unit costs are the residual after first determining selling price necessary to obtain desired market share and deducting required profit.

■ A **limiting factor** is a constraint placed on the activity of an organisation.

■ When an organisation is faced with a sales constraint plus shortage of some other resource, profit will be maximised if products/services are ranked in descending order according to their contribution per unit of *limiting factor*; production/sales should be based on this ranking up to a maximum imposed by demand for each product and this will maximise contribution and hence profit.

■ Contribution per unit of limiting factor is calculated as:

$$\frac{\text{contribution per unit pf product service}}{\text{units of limiting factor per unit of product/service}}$$

The 'contribution per unit of limiting factor' approach rests on certain key assumptions: certainty; linear cost and revenue behaviour; production = sales; and independence of products/services.

■ If a subcontract option is available to an organisation faced with a limiting factor, products/services should be ranked in ascending order according to each product/service's *extra cost to buy per unit of limiting factor*. Subcontracting/ producing according to this ranking will minimise cost.

- Extra cost to buy per unit of limiting factor is calculated as:

$$\frac{\text{extra cost to buy per unit of product/service}}{\text{units of limiting factor per unit of product/service}}$$

- Decisions involving multiple products/services and constraints require to be solved by **linear programming.**

- A graphical approach to linear programming is appropriate to two product/service scenarios.

- **Simplex** is a computer-aided technique for solving multiproduct/service constraint problems.

- **Dual price** is the increase/decrease in objective function caused by acquisition/loss of one unit of scarce resource.

- **Objective coefficient ranging** indicates the range of objective function coefficients for each product/service within which the optimal solution is unchanged.

- **Righthand side ranging** indicates the range of constraint values within which a given dual price is unchanged.

- **Linear programming** rests on the same assumptions as the 'cost per unit of limiting factor' approach.

In the next chapter, we will discuss the incorporation of uncertainty into decision analyses – an important issue, as decisions relate to the future and are thus inherently uncertain.

FURTHER READING

Anderson, D., Sweeney, D. and Williams, T., *An Introduction to Management Science*, 7th edn, West Publishing Co., 1994. See chapters 5 and 6 for description of the mathematical procedures underlying simplex.

Bromwich, M. and Bhimani, A., *Management Accounting Pathways to Progress*, CIMA, 1994. Chapter 6 includes a concise account of the use of target costing by Japanese organisations.

Drury, C., Braund, S., Osborne, P. and Tayles, M., *Survey of Management Accounting Practices in UK Manufacturing Companies*, ACCA, 1993.

Hanna, N. and Dodge, R., *Pricing Policies and Procedures*, Macmillan, 1995.

Rosser, M., *Basic Mathematics for Economists*, Routledge, 1996. Chapter 8 describes the application of calculus to determination of profit-maximising prices.

LINDO copyright (1989) Lindo Systems Inc, portions copyright (1981) Microsoft Corporation.

Sɛʟғ-ᴛᴇsᴛ ǫᴜᴇsᴛɪᴏɴs

8.1 B Ltd manufactures bricks. Unit cost and selling price for one particular type of brick are as follows:

	£	£
Selling price		0.40
Direct materials	0.05	
Direct labour	0.10	
Fixed production overhead	0.04	
Variable selling costs	0.03	0.22

The direct materials required for production of this brick are in short supply, and cost per kg is £0.20. What is the contribution per kg of scarce material for this type of brick?

A £0.045
B £0.055
C £0.720
D £0.880

8.2 B Ltd can subcontract production of the type of brick referred to in Question 8.1 at a cost per unit of £0.25. Using this price per unit to subcontract, along with the data in Question 8.1, what is the extra cost per kg of direct material of subcontracting production of one brick?

A £0.12
B £0.16
C £0.28
D £0.40

8.3 Figure 8.4 is the graphical solution to a linear programming problem. Given that all the constraints plotted in Figure 8.4 are '≤', what is the feasible region?

A The area bounded by A, B, C
B The area bounded by B, C, D, 0
C The area bounded by C, E, D
D The area bounded by A, E, 0

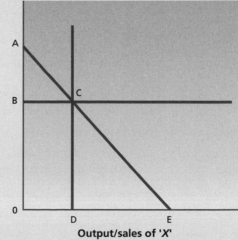

FɪɢᴜʀE 8.4
Graphical solution to a linear programming problem

8.4 MF Ltd, a manufacturer and distributor of mobile phones, knows that, in order to achieve a 20 per cent share of the domestic market next year, the selling price per unit for its standard product should be set at £120. The company wishes to earn profit equal to 10 per cent of sales. Unit cost is anticipated to be £110 next year. What is the target cost per unit for MF Ltd's standard product?

    A £84
    B £96
    C £108
    D £110

8.5 For each of the following statements, place a tick in the appropriate box to indicate whether that statement is true or false.

	True	False
(a) Demand that is *price elastic* will be relatively insensitive to changes in selling price.	☐	☐
(b) It may sometimes be advantageous to set selling price lower than cost per unit.	☐	☐
(c) Cost + pricing is unlikely to result in maximum profit.	☐	☐
(d) Profit expressed relative to unit cost is termed a *profit margin*.	☐	☐
(e) Use of predetermined costs in price setting is preferable to use of actual costs.	☐	☐

QUESTIONS WITH ANSWERS

8.6 This question tests whether you can:

- use contribution per unit of limiting factor to determine the optimum production plan;
- explain the use of linear programming; and
- suggest how a resource shortage might be overcome.

CBG Ltd is a wholesale manufacturer of menswear. Because of a series of machine-related accidents at one of its factories, working practices have been revised and altered. This has resulted in a reduction in the number of machine hours available next period to 100,000. Four styles of suit are produced in this particular factory and estimated data for next period are as follows:

	Style 1	Style 2	Style 3	Style 4
Maximum demand (units)	8,000	6,500	4,800	3,200
Per unit	£	£	£	£
Selling price	80	110	145	170
Direct materials	12	30	35	40
Direct labour	16	20	15	20
Production overhead	20	25	35	40
Selling overhead	10	12	16	18

Notes

1 Production overhead is charged to units at a composite absorption rate of £5 per machine hour, comprising £3 per hour for fixed overhead and the balance for variable overhead.

2 Selling overhead is likewise charged to units at a composite rate of £4 per unit for variable overhead and the balance for fixed overhead.

Requirements

(a) Determine which products should be produced/sold, and in what quantities, in order to maximise profit next period.

(b) Explain how the profit maximising output/sales plan would be determined if, in addition to machine hours, direct labour hours were *also* a constraint (calculations are not required).

(c) Suggest *two* courses of action which may be open to CBG Ltd in order to overcome the shortage of machine hours, stating any advantages and problems which might apply in each case.

8.7 This question tests whether you can:

- determine the extent of a resource shortage;
- rank options on the basis of minimum extra cost per unit of limiting factor; and
- appreciate the impact of qualitative factors on the ranking produced.

Northbridge General Hospital is faced with a potential shortage of operating theatre hours next year. The hospital has four operating suites, each of which is capable of undertaking all types of surgical procedure and has a maximum workload of 16 hours per day, 365 days per year. Estimates relating to each main category of surgical procedure for next year are as follows:

	General	Orthopaedic	Renal	Coronary
Anticipated number of procedures	3,500	2,400	1,800	1,200
Per procedure	£	£	£	£
Direct labour	180	200	220	360
Surgical and medical supplies	102	120	160	180
Variable theatre costs	60	75	120	170
Apportioned general overhead	200	140	120	200
Totals	542	535	620	910

Notes

1 Direct labour costs relate to the hospital's permanent medical and auxiliary staff.
2 Surgical and medical supplies' costs are only incurred if a procedure takes place.
3 Variable theatre costs are incurred at a rate of £25 per theatre hour.
4 Theatre hours for the four categories of surgery are based on average procedure times under each heading.
5 Surgical procedures for which Northbridge General Hospital has insufficient theatre hours can be undertaken at the nearby Southford Royal Infirmary, which will charge Northbridge General the following rates:

Category	Per procedure (£)
General	558
Orthopaedic	600
Renal	760
Coronary	1,302

Management of Northbridge General Hospital wishes to prioritise the transfer of surgical cases to Southford Royal Infirmary so as to minimise the additional cost involved.

Requirements

(a) Determine the shortfall in theatre hours faced by Northbridge General Hospital next year.

(b) Produce a ranking of the four surgical categories based on minimum extra cost per theatre hour.

(c) State, and explain briefly, *three* problems which may be faced by management of Northbridge General Hospital in implementing the priority ranking in (b) above.

8.8 Discuss the circumstances under which it may be appropriate to set a selling price which is lower than cost.

8.9 This question tests whether you can:

■ use a 'cost plus' pricing formula and assess the implications of this for sales volume;

■ determine target cost from given sales and required return data;

■ recalculate overhead absorption rates on the basis of a new volume level; and

■ restate unit cost incorporating new overhead absorption rates, and comment on the difference between this unit cost and the target cost.

PGC Ltd manufactures a standard prefabricated concrete garage. For next year, the following are the estimated direct costs per unit:

	£
Direct materials	140
Direct labour (14 hours @ £5.50)	77
Direct expenses	13
	230

Production overheads are absorbed at £7.50 per direct labour hour and non-production costs at £67 per unit. Both of these absorption rates are based on an anticipated production/sales volume of 5,000 units next year. The company adds a profit margin of 25 per cent of sales value to the total cost per unit in order to arrive at selling price.

Management wishes to increase next year's sales volume by 20 per cent (i.e. to 6,000 units) and believes that this could be achieved if selling price per unit were £492.

Requirements

(a) Determine whether unit selling price as calculated using the company's 'total cost + 25 per cent margin' formula is likely to yield the increased sales volume desired by management. Show supporting calculations.

(b) What target cost is necessary if the company is to achieve profit of 25 per cent of sales value on a unit selling price of £492?

(c) Assuming that a volume increase from 5,000 to 6,000 units will not incur any additional overhead costs, re-calculate the cost per unit for

    (i) production overhead; and
    (ii) non-production overhead

on the basis of production volume of 6,000 units (work to the nearest whole £1).

(d) Using the new overhead costs from (c), confirm whether or not the target cost necessary in order to obtain the desired market share and earn the required profit will be achieved.

8.10 This question tests whether you can:

■ apply relevant costing principles to determine a minimum quotation price; and

■ appreciate other considerations which may have a bearing on the quotation.

The DSC Partnership operates a deer farm, selling high-quality venison for both domestic and export markets. Due to a temporary recession in the market for venison, the farm has surplus capacity, which the partnership is anxious to utilise for short-term profit, if at all possible. The Ministry of Agriculture and Fisheries has asked the partnership to provide a quotation for use of the farm's facilities and livestock in order to undertake a one-year experiment into the effect of different feeding methods. DSC Partnership's management is keen to obtain this work, as it appears to be an ideal way of profitably using the existing spare capacity.

The following information is available:

Alternative feed
This will be supplied as required by the Ministry of Agriculture and Fisheries, resulting in a saving in feed purchase costs to the farm of £4,000. However, the farm's existing stock of feed will need to be disposed of at a cost of £1,600, since it cannot be used during the period of the experiment, nor can it be stored until this is complete. Special feeding equipment will be supplied by the Ministry and the farm will need to remove and store its own equipment during the experiment. This will cost £750 in total, but, whilst in storage, the equipment can be refurbished, thereby saving future costs of £200.

Labour costs
The farm will not need to employ any additional workers in order to undertake the experiment. However, the more intensive feeding methods required by the experiment will mean that work which the employees concerned could otherwise do must be subcontracted. If not used on the experiment, the workers concerned could either:

1 clear some scrubland and make it suitable for grazing, saving subcontracting costs of £2,000; or

2 undertake repairs to some of the farm's outbuildings, which would save subcontracting costs of £3,400 but would incur material costs of £600.

Irrespective of whether their time is spent on the experiment or on one of the other projects above, 300 hours' work is involved. The farmhands concerned are paid £4 per hour.

Other costs

The Ministry of Agriculture and Fisheries will supply a desktop computer and necessary software on which to record the results of the experiment. The farm manager will need to attend a training course in London before he can use this recording system; travel and subsistence costs incurred by DSC Partnership as a result will be £2,200. While the farm manager is absent on this training course, it will be necessary to recall the charge-hand from holiday, for which he will receive a special payment of £400. The deer farm's fixed costs for the period of the experiment are estimated at £28,000 and will increase by £2,700 due to extra administration if the experiment is undertaken.

Quotation

DSC Partnership's management reckons that a quotation of less than £7,000 is likely to be successful in obtaining the work.

Requirement

Draft a report to DSC Partnership's management determining the lowest quotation price which is financially viable and setting out any other relevant considerations which management should bear in mind when making their decision.

QUESTIONS WITHOUT ANSWERS

8.11 Hilldown Community Centre hires its hall to various sporting and social organisations. The objective of such hiring is to obtain the maximum possible contribution towards the community centre's running costs. Next year, the hall is available for hire for a maximum of 400 hours. Details of prospective hirers and associated financial data are as follows:

User	Aerobics Class	Amateur Dramatic Society	Floral Art Class	Gilbert & Sullivan Society	Judo Club
Maximum number of hires in year	100	50	30	50	40
	£	£	£	£	£
Charge per hire	20	60	40	70	30
Costs per hire:					
Labour	3	8	4	10	4
Light and heat	8	12	6	12	8
Fixed overhead	4	14	10	16	8

Notes

1 The lighting and heating cost varies at the rate of £4 for each hour the hall is in use.
2 The community centre is obliged, under an agreement with the local council which partly funds its operation, to guarantee a minimum of 10 hires to *each* of the five user groups above. Once this commitment has been met, the community centre is free to hire the hall to whichever user(s) it wishes.

Requirements

(a) Determine the mix of hiring which will maximise contribution towards the running costs of Hilldown Community Centre and state the amount of that contribution.

(b) State any assumptions you have employed in arriving at your answer to (a).

8.12 MF Ltd provides business training courses on a commercial basis. The company wishes to run an intensive two-day course on cash forecasting and management and is considering the price which should be charged. Estimated direct costs per student per course are:

	£
Direct labour	100
Direct material	16
Direct expenses	4
	120

The fixed element of these costs – and direct labour in particular – has been calculated on the basis of:

$$\frac{\text{budgeted annual cost}}{\text{budgeted number of students}}$$

Course-specific overheads are absorbed at a rate of 25 per cent of prime cost and it is company policy to charge a profit mark-up of 2/3 of full cost on all courses to cover general overheads and to provide a satisfactory profit.

MF Ltd's Director of Courses is concerned that adopting the company's normal policy will result in a charge which fails to maximise profit from provision of the course, and she has undertaken some market research in support of her view. This research suggests the following possible combinations of price and demand:

Demand (students)	120	160	210	230	270	290	310	320	350
Charge per student per course (£)	300	280	260	250	240	230	210	200	180

The variable cost per student per course will be £24 for all volumes up to and including 270 courses. Above this level, the variable cost per student per course will reduce to £20. Fixed costs specific to running the course will be £3,000 for all volumes up to and including 270 courses, above which volume the amount will be £5,000.

Requirements

(a) Determine the price per student per course based on the company's normal pricing procedure of 'full cost + 2/3'. Comment on the unit cost which has been used to set this price.

(b) From the schedule of price/demand combinations revealed by the Director of Courses' market research, calculate the price per student per course which should be set in order to maximise profit.

(c) Explain any reservations you may have about adoption of the price arrived at in (b).

8.13 Ecclefechan Thistle FC will be upgrading its stadium during the football close season. Plans for three new all-seater stands have already been prepared and approved by the club's board of directors. The problem now being considered is allocation of different types of seating within each of these new stands, subject to capacity, cost and demand constraints. Three types of seating will be installed, each with a different degree of comfort, and for which different prices can be charged. As a matter of policy, the club wishes to have the same number of seats of each type in each stand. Therefore, once the total optimum number of seats in each category has been determined, it can be equally divided between the three new stands. For the purpose of analysing the problem, the seat types have been designated as A, B and C. Unit variable costs of installing the seats are:

Type A: £14 Type B: £8 Type C: £5

Once installed, there will be no variable costs associated with use/sale of seats, so that the unit contribution from each type will be its selling price:

Type A: £10 Type B: £7 Type C: £6

Ecclefechan Thistle FC's technical advisor has formulated the seat allocation problem for solution by computerised simplex as follows:

maximise $10A + 7B + 6C$ [row 1: total contribution per home game]
subject to $14A + 8B + 5C \leq £250,000$ [row 2: cost maximum]
$A + B + C \leq 24,000$ [row 3: capacity]
$A \leq 3,000$ [row 4: demand per home game]
$B \leq 10,000$ [row 5: demand per home game]
$C \leq 15,000$ [row 6: demand per home game]
$A, B, C \geq 0$

Exhibit 8.11 on page 279 shows the solution generated by the computer.

Requirements
Prepare a report to the board of Ecclefechan Thistle FC explaining the meaning of the output in Exhibit 8.11 and discussing any relevant issues not explicitly addressed there.

OBJECTIVE FUNCTION VALUE

1) 166000.000

VARIABLE	VALUE
A	3000.000000
B	10000.000000
C	11000.000000

ROW	SLACK OR SURPLUS	DUAL PRICES
2)	73000.000000	.000000
3)	.000000	6.000000
4)	.000000	4.000000
5)	.000000	1.000000
6)	4000.000000	.000000

No ITERATIONS = 4

DO RANGE (SENSITIVITY) ANALYSIS?

? yes

RANGES IN WHICH THE BASIS IS UNCHANGED

OBJ COEFFICIENT RANGES

VARIABLE	CURRENT COEFFICIENT	ALLOWABLE INCREASE	ALLOWABLE DECREASE
A	10.000000	INFINITY	4.000000
B	7.000000	INFINITY	1.000000
C	6.000000	1.000000	6.000000

RIGHTHAND SIDE RANGES

ROW	CURRENT RHS	ALLOWABLE INCREASE	ALLOWABLE DECREASE
2)	250000.000000	INFINITY	73000.000000
3)	24000.000000	4000.000000	1100.000000
4)	3000.000000	8111.111000	3000.000000
5)	10000.000000	11000.000000	4000.000000
6)	15000.000000	INFINITY	4000.000000

EXHIBIT **8.11** LINDO©-generated solution to linear programming problem

CHAPTER 9

Decision making under conditions of risk and uncertainty

INFLATION ANALYSIS: THE BANK COULD DO EVEN BETTER

I wonder if you were aware that Rorschach tests had suddenly become *de rigeur* among British policy-makers. Rorschach, you will recall, was the Swiss psychiatrist who discovered the diagnostic value of inkblots. He would invite unsuspecting patients to describe his inky creations in the hope of revealing their subjective fantasies. The response 'it looks like a serial killer' risked 10 years incarceration in the sanatorium. Patients soon learnt the advantages of replying in terms of butterflies and birds.

Rorschach tests may have fallen out of favour in some psychiatric circles but clearly not at the Bank of England. In its latest Inflation Report you will find several examples disguised as graphs depicting the Bank's latest inflation projections and the range of uncertainty surrounding them. The charts fan out as time passes and the uncertainty deepens. By 1998, they encompass inflation forecasts as high as 4.5 per cent and as low as 0.5 per cent, all in shades of vermilion and violet. What does this image remind you of, old boy? Beware the response 'a hand-waving economist'. It guarantees 10 years incarceration in the UK forecasting industry. It is therefore preferable to reply that the chart represents a probability distribution of projected inflation outcomes – an attempt by the Bank to convey a sense of forecasters' uncertainty. But this does not get us very far. We know that forecasts are inherently uncertain and that the crystal ball gets ever-cloudier the further we peer into it. The problem is that the Bank's approach blends together various sources of uncertainty and is insufficiently precise about the circumstances in which inflation could head north or drop south . . .

Presenting uncertainty is not easy but the Bank could do better . . . It could present several forecasts, clearly conditional on different states of the world and on different assumptions about the way the economy behaves. This would clarify the nature of the uncertainty and quantify those aspects which pose the greatest threat to the Chancellor's inflation goals. Had this been done, the Chancellor might have had a better idea of the risks he was running by cutting interest rates in the face of strong monetary growth . . .

Source: Bill Martin, *Independent*, 11 March 1996.

EXHIBIT 9.1 The difficulty of incorporating uncertainty into an analysis

INTRODUCTION

On several occasions during the last three chapters, we have remarked on the fact that the management accounting technique under discussion does not allow for the impact of uncertainty. Because management accounting is so much concerned with the future – planning and decision making are entirely future-oriented – a substantial element of estimation is involved, and it is unrealistic to expect that such estimates will provide totally accurate predictions of the future. This is precisely the difficulty experienced by the Bank of England in Exhibit 9.1, and although the Bank is attempting to make economy-wide estimates, the same difficulty faces individual organisations. In this chapter, we shall demonstrate how uncertainty and risk can be incorporated into a decision analysis: by employing sensitivity analysis, three-level analysis and by attaching probabilities to uncertain events. We shall also discuss the strengths and weaknesses of the different approaches illustrated.

OBJECTIVES   When you have completed this chapter you will be able to:

- distinguish between uncertainty and risk;

- apply sensitivity analysis to uncertain situations;

- use three level analysis to deal with uncertainty;

- calculate expected values based on simple probability distributions;

- prepare decision trees for basic decision scenarios;

- appreciate the value of information, calculate the value of perfect information and explain its significance; and

- appreciate the strengths and weaknesses of the different techniques for incorporating risk and uncertainty which have been described and illustrated.

UNCERTAINTY VERSUS RISK

Although these terms tend to be used somewhat interchangeably in practice, we need to make a distinction between them for the purpose of the discussion which follows. Exhibit 9.2 contains the basic data which we shall use to illustrate how uncertainty and risk may be allowed for in financial analyses.

> ## Charity fund-raising: proposed sale of soft toy
>
> As part of its fund-raising activities next year, a charity proposes to sell a soft toy. This will be manufactured in one of the charity's own workshops and the proposed unit selling price and variable cost are £10 and £4 respectively. Market research suggests potential demand for the soft toy will fall somewhere between 70,000 and 110,000 units. Fixed costs associated with production of the soft toy will amount to £480,000.

EXHIBIT **9.2 Uncertainty and risk**

▷ What volume of unit sales is necessary in order for the soft toy venture to break even?

In Chapter 6 we saw that breakeven point in unit sales is:

$$\frac{\text{total fixed costs}}{\text{contribution per unit}}$$

The contribution per unit is:

$$(\text{unit selling price} - \text{unit variable cost}) = (£10 - £4) = £6$$

which gives a breakeven point of:

$$\frac{£480,000}{£6} = 80,000 \text{ units}$$

We can use our simple calculation to draw a distinction between *uncertainty* and *risk*: because the volume of sales is *uncertain* (it may be anywhere between 70,000 and 110,000 units), there is a *risk* that the venture will fail to break even (because breakeven volume is 80,000 units). A more formal definition of the two terms can be derived from this example:

> **Uncertainty is the recognition that different outcomes may occur**
> (a range of possible sales volumes here).

and

> **Risk is the possibility that undesirable outcomes might occur**
> (failure to achieve breakeven volume in this example).

You may feel that the distinction we are drawing is somewhat artificial, but it can be an important one in the context of financial analysis. Incorporating the effect of uncertainty into a decision analysis is not the same as assessing the risk attaching to that decision; and it would be dangerous to assume that a decision carries little or no risk simply because its outcome can be assessed with reasonable certainty. It would also be misleading if we were to treat risk as a 'downside' phenomenon only. There are risks attendant on *over*achievement: e.g. demand for the charity's soft toy may exceed breakeven point by so much that problems of undercapacity arise, such as lost sales and extra costs arising from overintensive use of production resources.

SENSITIVITY ANALYSIS

We described this technique in Chapter 6 as a 'what-if' approach to dealing with uncertainty, whereby the effect of changing the value(s) of one or more variable(s) within an analysis is examined. Exhibit 9.3 contains some further data relating to the charity's proposed soft toy sales.

Charity fund-raising: proposed sale of soft toy

Further market research suggests that demand could be 70,000, 80,000, 95,000, 100,000, 105,000 or 110,000 units, depending on the selling price set:

Sales volume	Unit selling price set:
70,000	£14 or £15
80,000	£13 or £14
95,000	£12 or £13
100,000	£11
105,000	£10
110,000	£9 or £8

EXHIBIT 9.3 Uncertain demand and selling price

▷ How might sensitivity analysis be applied to the data in Exhibit 9.3?

Application of sensitivity analysis to Exhibit 9.3 could involve listing the different total sales revenues resulting from each given combination of unit price and demand, as illustrated in Table 9.1.

TABLE 9.1 Different possible levels of sales revenue from soft toy sale

Possible unit sales	Possible unit selling price(s) (£)	Possible sales revenue (£)
70,000	14	980,000
	15	1,050,000
80,000	13	1,040,000
	14	1,120,000
95,000	12	1,140,000
	13	1,235,000
100,000	11	1,100,000
105,000	10	1,050,000
110,000	9	990,000
	8	880,000

This is similar to the contribution analysis which we undertook in the last chapter when examining the impact on profit of different price/demand combinations. By recognising a range of possible revenue figures, our analysis in Table 9.1 goes some way towards allowing for uncertainty about the outcome of the decision faced by the charity. This simple analysis can easily be extended to incorporate variable and fixed costs, contribution and profit, allowing some assessment to be made of the volume necessary in order to break even. Sensitivity analysis is probably most useful when combined with a computer spreadsheet, which allows examination of complex combinations of change to variables.

This sort of analysis has great value in the decision-making process, and is widely used in practice. The major weakness with sensitivity analysis is that it does not attempt to *quantify* uncertainty. In other words, how likely is the occurrence of a particular combination of unit demand and unit selling price in Table 9.1? Without such quantification, it is difficult to decide on the likelihood of the venture breaking even. Since this likelihood will have a major bearing on the ultimate decision, some attempt at its quantification can only improve the decision-making process.

A further problem is the potential complexity of sensitivity analysis, at least if undertaken manually. Listing the possible outcomes is cumbersome enough; imagine how much more unwieldy Table 9.1 would become if it reflected several values for unit sales, unit selling price, unit variable cost and total fixed cost. A computer spreadsheet may ease the burden of calculation, but this in no way addresses the problem of quantifying our uncertainty.

THREE-LEVEL ANALYSIS

One way of reducing the potential complexity referred to above is to use *three-level analysis*. Under this approach, each uncertain element is assigned three values:

1 a best possible value;
2 a worst possible value; and
3 a most likely value.

Exhibit 9.4 illustrates how this method could be applied to the earlier data in Exhibit 9.3.

⇨ Use the data in Exhibit 9.4 to determine the following:

1 worst possible total contribution;
2 best possible total contribution; and
3 most likely total contribution.

The *worst possible* total contribution will occur where unit variable cost and unit demand are both at their worst outcomes (£5.45 and 60,000 units respectively); total contribution will be: $60,000 \times (£12 - £5.45) = £393,500$. The *best possible* total contribution will occur at maximum demand (110,000 units) in conjunction with minimum unit variable cost (£4): $110,000 \times (£12 - £4) = £880,000$. The *most likely* total

285

Charity fund-raising: sale of soft toy

Market research and previous experience in similar sorts of venture suggest that, at a selling price of £12 per toy, the range of possible demand levels is likely to be as follows:

	Units
worst possible demand	60,000
best possible demand	110,000
most likely demand	95,000

The purchase cost of raw materials for the toy is somewhat volatile, with the result that unit variable costs are likely to be:

	£
worst possible estimate	5.45
best possible estimate	4.00
most likely estimate	4.75

EXHIBIT **9.4 Three-level analysis**

contribution will arise from a combination of the most likely values for demand (95,000 units) and unit variable cost (£4.75): $95,000 \times (£12 - £4.75) = £688,750$.

Thus, we have a range of possible total contribution figures:

	£
Worst possible	393,500
Best possible	880,000
Most likely	688,750

By 'bracketing' the possible outcomes in this way, we have a rather more structured and manageable view of the problem than that provided by our analysis in Table 9.1. If desired, the analysis of total contribution can be broadened to combine, say, best possible demand with, say, worst possible unit variable cost. However, the extent of uncertainty is still not quantified, so that it is not possible to answer the key question 'What is the likelihood of the venture breaking even or better?'

USE OF PROBABILITIES AND EXPECTED VALUES

Assigning probabilities to uncertain events lets us reflect on the extent of our uncertainty about the occurrence of different outcomes and allows an assessment of risk. Exhibit 9.5 assigns probabilities to the uncertain events surrounding the charity's soft toy venture.

Note that the probabilities have been combined with the earlier three-level analysis. While this is convenient, there may be as many different outcomes and associated probabilities as are necessary to provide a thorough analysis of the situation. You will also see that the total probability attaching to each of the uncertain events in Exhibit 9.5 is 1. What this means is that, although we are unsure about

> ### Charity fund-raising: sale of soft toy
>
> Market research and previous experience of similar ventures suggests that unit demand at a selling price of £12 is likely to be as follows:
>
> | | | |
> |---|---|---|
> | worst possible | 60,000 units | probability 0.2 |
> | best possible | 110,000 units | probability 0.3 |
> | most likely | 95,000 units | probability 0.5 |
>
> Potential volatility of raw material cost results in unit variable cost estimates as follows:
>
> | | | |
> |---|---|---|
> | worst possible | £5.45 | probability 0.1 |
> | best possible | £4.00 | probability 0.2 |
> | most likely | £4.75 | probability 0.7 |
>
> Total fixed costs are confidently expected to amount to £620,000.

EXHIBIT 9.5 **Probabilities attached to possible outcomes**

the precise volume of sales and the precise unit variable cost, we are 100 per cent certain that each will have *some* value if the venture is proceeded with.

Having assigned probabilities to the uncertain elements of the problem, we can now determine a single **expected value (EV)** for sales demand and unit variable cost. Expected value is simply a weighted average outcome. Using the data from Exhibit 9.5, the expected value of unit demand is:

	Units
(60,000 units × 0.2 probability)	12,000
(110,000 units × 0.3 probability)	33,000
(95,000 units × 0.5 probability)	47,500
Expected unit demand	92,500

Note carefully that, for each uncertain event, there is only *one* expected value: that is, for a given set of predicted outcomes and associated probabilities, only one weighted average outcome can exist. (You should also appreciate that, because it is a weighted average outcome, it is unlikely to actually occur).

⇨ Using the same approach as we took above for the calculation of expected unit demand, determine the expected unit variable cost.

Expected unit variable cost will be:

	£
(£5.45 × probability 0.1)	0.545
(£4.00 × probability 0.2)	0.800
(£4.75 × probability 0.7)	3.325
Expected unit variable cost	4.670

Expected unit contribution will therefore be

(unit selling price – expected unit variable cost) = (£12 – £4.67) = £7.33

and expected total contribution will be:

(expected unit sales × expected unit contribution) = (92,500 × £7.33) = £678,025.

As this exceeds expected total fixed costs (£620,000), it appears that the soft toy venture is likely to break even, assuming that the estimates of demand, unit variable cost and associated probabilities are accurate.

Calculation of expected value (EV) can be summarised in a simple mathematical formula:

$$EV = \sum \left[x\{p(x)\} \right]$$

where: x denotes each possible outcome for an uncertain event

$p(x)$ denotes the probability attached to each possible outcome

$\sum$ is the mathematical symbol representing "sum of".

Extending the analysis

We can take our analysis further by constructing a probability distribution which will allow us to answer questions such as: 'What is the probability of the soft toy venture at least breaking even?' or 'What is the probability of the venture earning profit in excess of £10,000?' Before we can do this, it is necessary to make an assumption about the relationship between unit variable cost and demand volume in Exhibit 9.5. For the purpose of the calculations which follow, we will assume that these two uncertain variables are *independent*: that is, that there is no link between the two. If we adopt this assumption, we can determine the **joint** (or **combined**) **probability** attaching to each possible combination of sales demand and unit variable cost. A joint probability is defined as:

the probability that two or more independent events will occur together.

If sales demand and unit variable cost are independent events, then the probability of demand being, say, 60,000 units *and* of unit variable cost being, say, £4 is simply the product of the probabilities attaching to these two events:

$p(60,000 \text{ unit demand}) = 0.2$
$p(£4 \text{ unit variable cost}) = 0.2$

so the probability of demand being 60,000 units and unit variable cost being £4 is:

(0.2 × 0.2) = 0.04.

We can therefore say that, for two independent events, A and B, their joint probability is:

$$p(A) \times p(B)$$

where: p represents the probability of each event occurring.

⇨ Use the data in Exhibit 9.5 to determine the following joint probabilities:

 – demand of 110,000 units *and* unit variable cost of £4.00;
 – demand of 95,000 units *and* unit variable cost of £4.75.

The joint probabilities are:

p(110,000 unit demand) = 0.3 p(£4 unit variable cost) = 0.2
so p(110,000 unit demand *and* £4 unit variable cost) = (0.3 × 0.2) = 0.06

and:

p(95,000 unit demand) = 0.5 p(£4.75 unit variable cost) = 0.7
so p(95,000 unit demand *and* £4.75 unit variable cost) = (0.5 × 0.7) = 0.35.

If we know that the joint probability of demand being 95,000 units *and* of unit variable cost being £4.75 is 0.35, then we can also say that there is a 0.35 probability of total contribution of:

$$95,000 \text{ units} \times (£12 - £4.75) = £688,750$$

▷ If demand is 60,000 units, variable cost is £5.45 per unit and selling price £12 per unit, what is the total contribution and its associated joint probability?

Total contribution is: 60,000 units × (£12 – £5.45) = £393,000; the joint probability of this level of total contribution is the joint probability of demand being 60,000 units *and* of unit variable cost being £5.45: (0.2 × 0.1) = 0.02.

We can undertake the same type of calculation for each potential combination of unit demand and variable cost. Since there are three possible demand levels and three possible unit variable costs, and since these variables are independent of each other, there will be (3 × 3) = 9 combinations of demand and variable cost – and therefore 9 possible total contribution figures. A tabulation of the possible outcomes can now be prepared (*see* Table 9.2).

TABLE 9.2 Possible outcomes and associated probabilities

Unit demand	Unit variable cost (£)	Unit contribution (£)	Total contribution (£)	Probability (demand)	Probability (unit variable cost)	Joint Probability
60,000	5.45	6.55	393,000		0.1	0.02
	4.00	8.00	480,000	0.2	0.2	0.04
	4.75	7.25	435,000		0.7	0.14
110,000	5.45	6.55	720,500		0.1	0.03
	4.00	8.00	880,000	0.3	0.2	0.06
	4.75	7.25	797,500		0.7	0.21
95,000	5.45	6.55	622,250		0.1	0.05
	4.00	8.00	760,000	0.5	0.2	0.10
	4.75	7.25	688,750		0.7	0.35

The joint probabilities shown in column 7 of Table 9.2 represent the probabilities attaching to the various different amounts of total contribution: that is, to the simultaneous occurrence of a particular level of demand *and* a particular unit variable cost. You will see that these sum to 1: that is, we are 100 per cent certain that some combination of demand and unit variable cost will result if the venture is proceeded with.

We can use the information in Table 9.2 to obtain various probabilities which may be of interest: for example, the probability of the soft toy venture at least breaking even, or of its earning profit in excess of a particular amount.

▷ Bearing in mind (from Chapter 6) that, at breakeven point, total contribution = total fixed cost, use Table 9.2 to list the joint probabilities attaching to all total contributions which equal or exceed the total fixed cost of £620,000.

Table 9.2 shows six levels of total contribution greater than or equal to £620,000; along with their joint probability, these are:

Total contribution (£)	Joint probability
720,500	0.03
880,000	0.06
797,500	0.21
622,250	0.05
760,000	0.10
688,750	0.35

The probability of the venture at least breaking even is the sum of the six joint probabilities listed above:

$$(0.03 + 0.06 + 0.21 + 0.05 + 0.10 + 0.35) = 0.80$$

Alternatively, we can say that there is a 0.20 probability of the venture failing to break even.

▷ Using the same approach as we have just done for the probability of at least breaking even, determine from Table 9.2, the probability that the venture will:

    – earn a profit of at least £50,000 (i.e. total contribution $\geq$ £670,000)
    – incur a loss of at least £50,000 (i.e. total contribution $\leq$ £570,000).

There are five total contribution figures which equal or exceed £670,000:

Total contribution (£)	Probability
720,500	0.03
880,000	0.06
797,500	0.21
760,000	0.10
688,750	0.35

The probability of earning profit of at least £50,000 is thus:

$$(0.03 + 0.06 + 0.21 + 0.10 + 0.35) = 0.75$$

Table 9.2 shows three total contributions which are less than or equal to £570,000:

Total contribution (£)	Probability
458,500	0.02
560,000	0.04
507,500	0.14

The probability of incurring a loss of at least £50,000 is therefore:

$$(0.02 + 0.04 + 0.14) = 0.20.$$

DECISION TREES

A decision tree is a diagrammatic representation of a decision, along with its various outcomes. Such a representation can be extremely helpful in clarifying a potentially complex series of alternatives plus related outcomes. We will use the data in Exhibit 9.5 to construct a simple decision tree, assuming for simplicity that £12 per unit is the only possible selling price. Thus, only a single *decision* is involved: proceed with the soft toy venture or do not proceed. If we use the symbol ☐ to denote this decision, we can start our decision tree as shown in Figure 9.1.

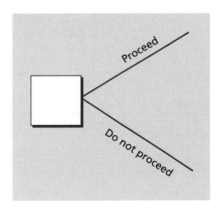

FIGURE 9.1
The soft toy venture decision

We must now consider the outcome(s) of each course of action shown in Figure 9.1. If the 'proceed' option is chosen, Exhibit 9.5 indicates three possible levels of unit demand. Adopting the symbol O to indicate a point in the decision process where more than one outcome is possible, the decision tree can be extended as shown in Figure 9.2.

You will see that the probability attaching to each demand level is shown in Figure 9.2. Not only will this help our subsequent calculations, but it also helps make a critically important point – decisions are within our control, outcomes are *not*. Since demand and unit variable cost are assumed to be independent, each possible demand level will have three potential unit contributions associated with it (as calculated in Table 9.2), allowing a further extension of the decision tree.

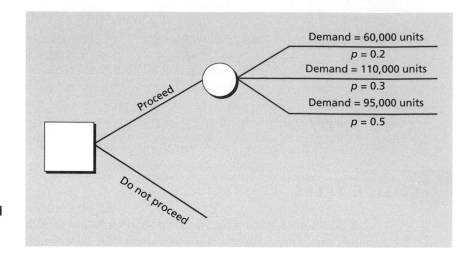

FIGURE 9.2 Decision tree for soft toy venture showing possible demand levels resulting from 'proceed' option

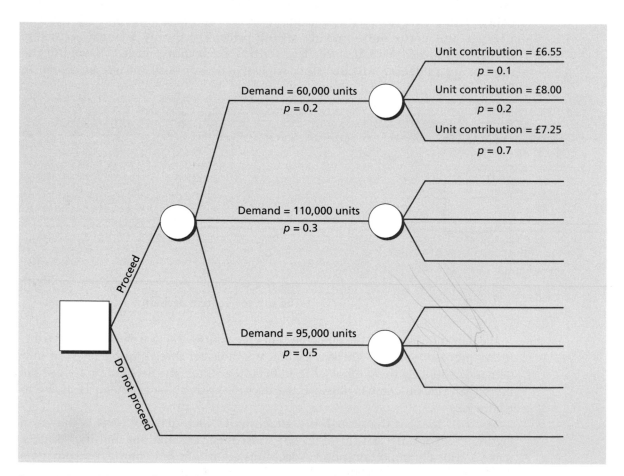

FIGURE 9.3 Decision tree for soft toy venture showing partial information about predicted demand/unit contribution combinations

⇨ Referring to Table 9.2 for your data, complete Figure 9.3 to show all predicted combinations of demand and unit contribution resulting from the 'proceed' option, along with the probability attaching to each unit contribution you have shown. Show also the outcome and associated probability relating to the 'do not proceed' option.

Figure 9.4 is the completed decision tree for the soft toy venture. You will see that the 'do not proceed' option yields a contribution of zero with an associated probability of 1: that is, if we choose not to proceed with the venture, then we are absolutely certain that no contribution will be earned from it.

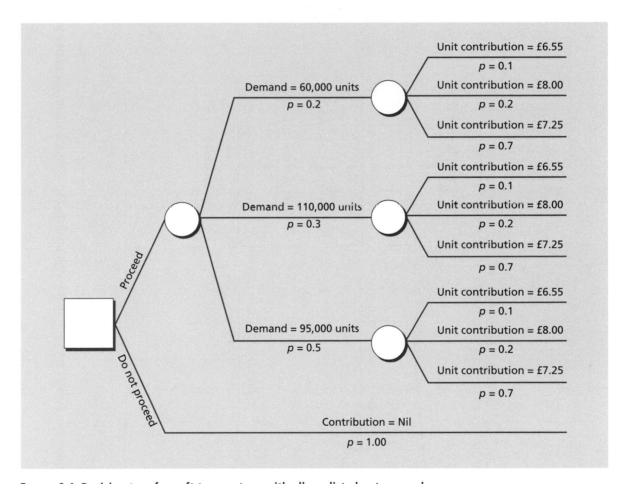

FIGURE 9.4 Decision tree for soft toy venture with all predicted outcomes shown

The decision tree can now be extended to show total contribution from each predicted combination of demand and unit contribution, the associated joint probability and the expected value of each decision option.

⇨ Using Table 9.2 to provide your data, insert the missing total contributions and joint probabilities in Figure 9.5. Calculate the missing figures in the 'expected value' column.

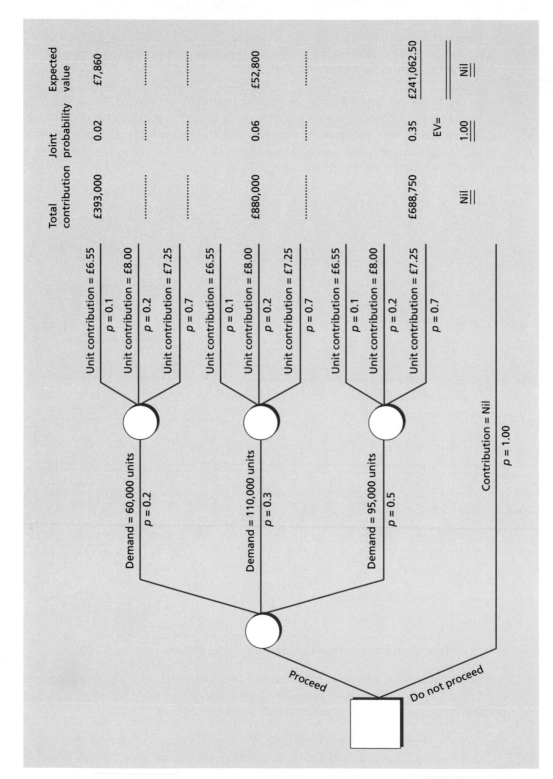

FIGURE 9.5 Incomplete decision tree for soft toy venture showing predicted total contributions, associated joint probabilities and expected value of each course of action

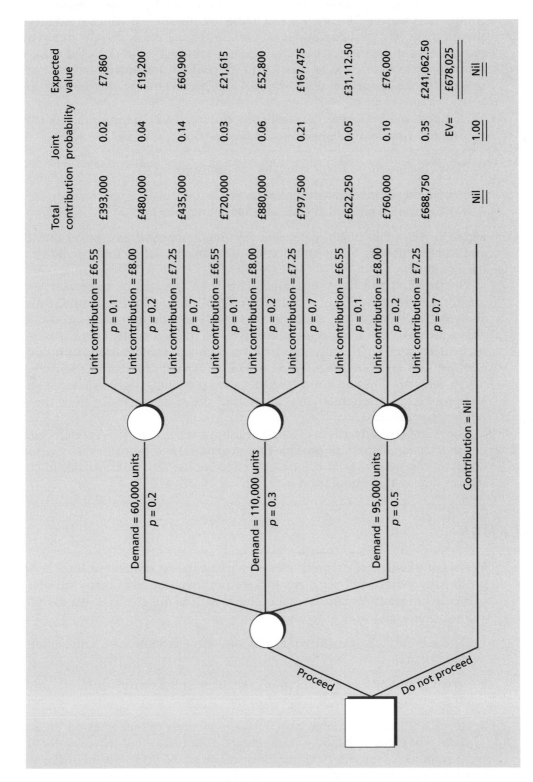

	Total contribution	Joint probability	Expected value
Unit contribution = £6.55, p = 0.1	£393,000	0.02	£7,860
Unit contribution = £8.00, p = 0.2	£480,000	0.04	£19,200
Unit contribution = £7.25, p = 0.7	£435,000	0.14	£60,900
Unit contribution = £6.55, p = 0.1	£720,000	0.03	£21,615
Unit contribution = £8.00, p = 0.2	£880,000	0.06	£52,800
Unit contribution = £7.25, p = 0.7	£797,500	0.21	£167,475
Unit contribution = £6.55, p = 0.1	£622,250	0.05	£31,112.50
Unit contribution = £8.00, p = 0.2	£760,000	0.10	£76,000
Unit contribution = £7.25, p = 0.7	£688,750	0.35	£241,062.50
		EV=	£678,025
Contribution = Nil	Nil	1.00	Nil

FIGURE 9.6 Completed decision tree for soft toy venture

Figure 9.6 is the completed decision tree showing all pertinent information. A comparison between Figure 9.6 and Table 9.2 reveals a distinct similarity. This should make sense, since the decision tree in Figure 9.6 is merely an alternative presentation of the information contained in Table 9.2, with expected value being additionally calculated. Note that Figure 9.6 could be extended further to encompass more than one selling price, with associated outcomes and expected values.

⇨ Suppose the charity were considering three possible selling prices for the soft toy. How many *decisions* would our decision tree show?

In these circumstances, there would be *two* decisions:

1 Proceed/do not proceed with the venture.
2 If the venture is proceeded with, at what selling price?

Figure 9.7 illustrates how the decision tree might appear if, say, prices of £12, £10 and £8 per unit were being considered. For simplicity, values for demand etc. have been omitted.

The decision tree has more immediacy than the tabular approach. As with graphical representations of a cost/volume/profit model, a diagrammatic decision analysis can highlight the alternatives available and their possible outcomes in a way which may be much more meaningful to management. This is likely to be particularly true where a decision involves complex combinations of interdependent options and outcomes. Also, unlike breakeven charts and their relatives, which can sometimes be difficult to plot with precision, decision trees are no less accurate than a purely numerical analysis of the same situation, since they need not be drawn to scale.

One possible disadvantage of using decision trees is that, for especially complex decisions, mapping out all possible options and related outcomes may result in a diagram so unwieldy as to preclude its effective use as a decision aid. In circumstances such as this, **simulation** may provide the answer.

SIMULATION

In essence, simulation attempts to *model* a particular set of relationships. Because it is normally performed on a computer, we can incorporate as many variables as a particular situation demands. For a problem such as the charity's soft toy venture, a simulation would work as follows:

1 Define the variables involved: in this case, unit variable cost, unit selling price and demand.

2 Attach probabilities to all uncertain variables: in the charity example, unit variable cost and demand.

3 For each uncertain variable, assign *random numbers* to outcomes on the basis of their probabilities. Random numbers are a statistical tool whereby, for any set of numbers – say, the 100 numbers in the range 00 to 99 inclusive – every number has the same chance of occurring.

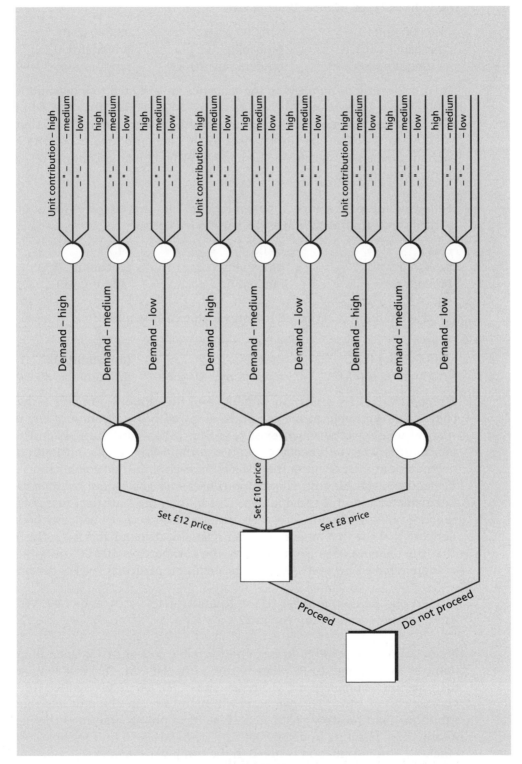

FIGURE 9.7 Outline decision tree for three selling prices

Using the demand data for a £12 price from Exhibit 9.5, random numbers would be assigned in the following way:

60,000 units	110,000 units	95,000 units
probability 0.2	probability 0.3	probability 0.5
random nos: 00–19	random nos: 20–49	random nos: 50–99

The first 20 random numbers in the sequence are assigned to a demand level of 60,000 units, as there are 20 chances out of 100 (i.e. 0.2) that this will be the level of demand; the *next* 30 random numbers are assigned to demand of 110,000 units (30 out of 100 chances of this demand level); and the *last* 50 random numbers are assigned to demand of 95,000 units (50 out of 100 chances of this demand level).

⇨ Following the same approach, assign random numbers to the different unit variable costs from Exhibit 9.5 which are listed below:

£5.45	£4.00	£4.75
probability 0.1	probability 0.2	probability 0.7
random nos: ………	random nos: …………	random nos: …………

The random numbers assigned to unit variable costs would be:

£5.45	£4.00	£4.75
probability 0.1	probability 0.2	probability 0.7
random nos: 00–09	random nos: 10–29	random nos: 30–99

4 Different values for uncertain variables and the random numbers assigned to these values are input to the computer, along with specification of any mathematical relationships which exist (e.g. that (£12 – unit variable cost) = unit contribution and (unit demand × unit contribution) = total contribution). The computer can then calculate these values for each simulated combination of unit demand and variable cost. The computer uses a *random number generator* to simulate demand and unit variable cost. This follows the statistical rule governing random numbers: that is, that each number has the same chance of occurring. Suppose that the first random number relates to demand and is 17: this means that the demand level 'simulated' by the computer is 60,000 units, since all random numbers between 00 and 19 relate to this particular level of demand.

⇨ The second random number relates to unit variable cost, and is 49. What unit variable cost does this indicate?

A random number of 49 indicates a unit variable cost of £4.75, since all random numbers in the range 30–99 relate to this particular cost. Our first simulation of the situation is complete and yields demand of 60,000 units coupled with a unit variable cost of £4.75. The computer will then calculate the unit and total contributions (and possibly profit/loss, if we have pre-programmed the requisite information) resulting from a 60,000 unit demand/£4.75 unit variable cost combination. This information is stored in the computer's memory.

5 The simulation process just described is repeated a great many times, the result of each repetition being stored in the computer's memory. Once the specified number of simulation runs is complete, the results can be output in a variety of manners, depending on the requirements of the user and on how the computer program operates. One particularly useful format which can be produced by most simulation software is a probability distribution of the results, which can be used by management as part of the risk assessment and decision-making process.

Our description of the operation of computerised simulation has necessarily been limited to a very simple scenario. However, given the processing power available in most computers, extending the analysis to encompass complex situations is comparatively straightforward. Even our simple scenario could readily be expanded to consider, say, ten levels of demand and five levels of unit variable cost. Different amounts for total fixed cost could also be incorporated, and profit/loss (rather than total contribution) simulated.

THE VALUE OF INFORMATION

It is possible that an organisation may attempt to reduce uncertainty by obtaining additional information. You should remember (from Chapter 1) that information is costly and the cost of obtaining additional information may exceed the benefit derived from its possession.

Suppose the position faced by the charity in respect of the soft toy venture were as set out in Exhibit 9.6.

Charity fund-raising: sale of soft toy

Market research and previous experience of similar venture suggests that unit demand relative to the three selling prices under consideration is likely to be as follows:

	£8 per unit (units)	£10 per unit (units)	£12 per unit (units)
Worst possible (probability 0.2)	150,000	70,000	60,000
Best possible (probability 0.3)	200,000	130,000	110,000
Most likely (probability 0.5)	170,000	105,000	95,000

The expected value of unit variable cost is £4.67.

EXHIBIT 9.6 **Demand levels at different selling prices**

From our earlier calculations, we know that the expected total contribution from a £12 per unit selling price is £678,025 and that this was determined as:

$$\text{expected unit sales} \times \text{expected unit contribution}$$

⇨ From Exhibit 9.6, obtain the expected unit contribution, expected unit sales and expected total contribution for the £8 *and* £10 selling prices. On the basis of expected total contribution, advise the charity as to the best selling price to set.

At a price of £8, expected unit contribution is (£8 – £4.67) = £3.33 and expected unit demand is (150,000 × 0.2) + (200,000 × 0.3) + (170,000 × 0.5) = 175,000. Expected total contribution is thus:

$$(175,000 \times £3.33) = £582,750.$$

A £10 price yields an expected unit contribution of (£10 – £4.67) = £5.33 with expected unit demand of (70,000 × 0.2) + (130,000 × 0.3) + (105,000 × 0.5) = 105,500. Expected total contribution is therefore:

$$(105,500 \times £5.33) = £562,315.$$

As maximum expected contribution is earned from a £12 selling price, this is the price which should be set, assuming maximisation of expected value to be the charity's objective, and given the limitations of the information available.

Suppose an external firm of market researchers undertakes to supply the charity with 100 per cent accurate advance information (**perfect information**) about whether demand will be at the best possible, the worst possible or the most likely level. If the cost of this information is £5,000, is its acquisition financially worthwhile for the charity? In other words, if the charity has the additional information, will this improve the expected total contribution? As a starting-point, we need to list the possible total contributions which may result from proceeding with the venture. Table 9.3, sometimes described as a 'payoff matrix', does this.

TABLE **9.3 Different possible total contributions at a range of selling prices**

	£8 per unit price (unit contribution £3.33)	£10 per unit price (unit contribution £5.33)	£12 per unit price (unit contribution £7.33)
Worst possible demand (probability 0.2)	(150,000 × £3.33) = £499,500	(70,000 × £5.33) = £373,100	(60,000 × £7.33) = £439,800
Best possible demand (probability 0.3)	(200,000 × £3.33) = £666,000	(130,000 × £5.33) = £692,900	(110,000 × £7.33) = £806,300
Most likely demand (probability 0.5)	(170,000 (£3.33) = £566,100	(105,000 × £5.33) = £559,650	(95,000 × £7.33) = £696,350

We must now decide what selling price the charity will set, given that the objective is to obtain the maximum expected total contribution from the venture and given also that the 100 per cent accurate advance information is being used to guide the decision. From Table 9.3 we can see that, if the information predicts the 'most likely' demand level, price should be set at £12, as this yields the greatest total contribution.

▷ What selling price should be set if the perfect advance information predicts:

- 'worst possible' demand;
- 'best possible' demand?

If the perfect advance information predicts 'worst possible' and 'best possible' demand, selling price should be set at £8 per unit and £12 per unit respectively, as this maximises total contribution. So we now have:

Predicted demand	Selling price(£)	Total contribution(£)	Probability
Worst possible	8	499,500	0.2
Best possible	12	806,300	0.3
Most likely	12	696,350	0.5

Note that the probabilities above refer, not only to the possible occurrence of each outcome, but also to the perfect information predicting each outcome (*because* the information is perfect).

▷ What is the expected value of total contribution based on use of the perfect advance information? Is it financially worthwhile for the charity to pay £5,000 for its acquisition?

The expected total contribution resulting from use of the perfect advance information is:

$$(£499,500 \times 0.2) + (£806,300 \times 0.3) + (£696,350 \times 0.5) = £689,965$$

Comparing this revised value with the original 'best' expected total contribution calculated from Exhibit 9.6, we get:

	£
Original 'best' expected value of total contribution	678,025
Expected value of total contribution with perfect information	689,965
Increase	11,940

Since it will cost £5,000 to obtain the information necessary to gain the £11,940 increase, we can conclude that obtaining this information is financially worthwhile. We could also say that the £11,940 difference represents the *maximum* amount which the charity should be prepared to pay in order to obtain perfect information. It is thus the **value of perfect information**.

However, perfect information is unlikely to be available in practice, so is there any point in attempting to place a value on its acquisition? The clue lies in the word 'maximum' above. If we have an idea of the value of *perfect* information, then we also have an upper limit to the amount which we should be prepared to pay for information which will almost certainly be *imperfect*.

Our calculation of the value of perfect information can be summarised as follows:

1 Determine the optimum expected value obtainable without perfect information.
2 Decide which courses of action would be followed for each perfect prediction of the future.
3 Recalculate expected value based on item 2 above.
4 The difference between the expected values in items 1 and 3 above will provide the value of perfect information. If its value exceeds its cost, acquisition of the information is financially worthwhile.

ASSESSING RISK

In Exhibit 9.6, our charity example was faced with a choice between three possible unit selling prices, and we demonstrated above that, if the aim is to maximise the expected contribution, a price of £12 should be set. However, this ignores the question of how much risk attaches to each of the proposed selling prices. In this example, 'risk' can be thought of as the likelihood that the venture will fail to break even or to earn a desired profit.

We could assess risk by using the approach applied earlier to the data in Table 9.2, when we determined that, at a £12 selling price, there is a 0.80 probability of the venture at least breaking even. This can be extended to produce a **probability distribution** for the £12 selling price. Using the total contributions and joint probabilities from Table 9.2 in conjunction with the predicted fixed costs of £620,000, we can produce a distribution such as the following:

Outcome	Probability
loss ≥ £100,000	0.02
loss ≥ £ 50,000	0.20
profit ≥ 0	0.80
profit ≥ £ 50,000	0.75
profit ≥ £100,000	0.40

The probability relating to each of the specified outcomes above has been calculated in the same cumulative manner that we used to determine the probability of at least breaking even. A similar distribution can be prepared for each selling price under consideration and management may then assess each option's risk by comparing the probabilities of certain key outcomes (such as at least breaking even or achieving a particular level of profit). You should note that the profit/loss levels in our distribution above are arbitrary – there is no compelling reason for the selection of £100,000 and £50,000 – and the precise amounts used may be tailored to meet the requirements of a specific situation. Similarly, the distribution can contain as many or as few outcomes plus associated probabilities as is necessary to permit an informed judgement to be made about the riskiness of competing options.

Alternatively (or additionally), we can provide a single risk measure for each option which encompasses all of an option's predicted outcomes, rather than listing the probabilities of certain specified outcomes in a probability distribution. The potential advantage of a single risk indicator for each option is that comparison of options may be eased – especially where there are several options with widely diverse ranges of possible outcomes. For a detailed discussion of such measures, refer to Drury (1996) and Waters (1994) in Further Reading at the end of this chapter.

Risk and the decision maker

When we provided financial advice based on Exhibit 9.6, you will recall that the £12 price yielded the highest expected total contribution, and, on that basis, a £12 price should be set. This advice assumes the decision maker(s) to be **risk neutral**: that is, when faced with a choice between options with uncertain outcomes, the decision maker(s) will choose whichever outcome maximises the desired result (expected total contribution in this case), irrespective of the chance of undesirable results (failure to break even here). However, it is highly unlikely that a decision maker will be truly risk neutral. Attitude to risk will lie somewhere between **risk-averse** at one extreme and **risk seeking** at the other. As the term suggests, a risk-averse decision maker, faced with uncertainty in a decision, will seek to adopt the course of action with the least chance of failure or with the best possible 'worst outcome'. Consider Exhibit 9.7, which presents a summary of some of our previous calculations relating to the charity's soft toy venture.

Charity fund-raising: sale of soft toy – summary of analysis

Analysis of each of the proposed selling prices and associated outcomes is given below:

	Unit selling price		
	£8	£10	£12
Expected value of total contribution (£)	582,750	562,315	678,025
Worst possible total contribution (prob. 0.2) (£)	499,500	373,100	439,800
Best possible total contribution (prob. 0.3) (£)	666,000	692,900	806,300
Most likely total contribution (prob. 0.5) (£)	566,100	559,650	696,350

EXHIBIT 9.7 **Results of decision analysis**

⇨ Which of the three selling prices in Exhibit 9.7 would a risk-averse decision maker be likely to choose and why?

A risk-averse decision maker would select the £8 selling price because this option has the best of the 'worst possible' outcomes: the lowest total contribution associated with this price is £499,500, which is higher than the lowest total contribution associated with either of the other prices. This ultra-cautious approach is termed **maximin**: the decision maker seeks the course of action which will *max*imise the *min*imum outcome. Whilst it may minimise the risk of adverse outcomes, maximin can be criticised for its extreme caution, which may possibly result in the avoidance of highly profitable (but more risky) alternatives.

At the opposite end of the scale, a decision maker may be **risk seeking**. The justification for ostensibly risky decisions such as the one referred to in Exhibit 9.8 is the possibility that the resultant return will be considerably higher than that obtainable from a less risky option. In other words, there is a 'trade-off' between risk and return: the higher the perceived risk, the greater the return required to justify taking that risk.

RISK-TAKING IN BERKELEY SQUARE

It is not every day that a privately owned company in Berkeley Square decides to invest nearly $1bn (£600m) in a run-down steelworks with 38,000 staff in the former Soviet Union.

But Ispat International, the steel group which recently announced plans to invest $950m in Karmet, Kazakhstan, thrives on taking risks that other steelmakers might have avoided . . .

Source: Stefan Wagstyl, *Financial Times*, 14 March 1996.

EXHIBIT 9.8 A risk-seeking attitude?

⇨ Look again at the data relating to the soft toy venture given in Exhibit 9.7. Which price would a risk-seeking decision maker choose?

A risk-seeking decision maker would set the selling price at £12, as the best possible return from this option (total contribution of £806,300) is better than that from either of the other two selling prices. (The fact that £12 would also be the risk-neutral choice is purely coincidental.) A risk-seeking decision maker will adopt what is termed a **maximax** approach: that is, will choose the course of action which *max*imises the *max*imum outcome.

In reality, it is unlikely that a decision maker's attitude to risk will lie at either extreme (risk seeking/risk averse); nor is it likely that a decision maker will be indifferent to risk (risk neutral). Exactly where on the averse–neutral–seeking continuum a decision maker's attitude to risk lies is likely to be influenced by a number of factors, such as the following:

- *The personality of the individual(s) concerned.* How inherently cautious is a person?
- *The decision-making process.* For example, will the decision be made by an individual in virtual isolation or will it be made by a group? Research tends to suggest that decisions taken by groups may, on the whole, be more risky than those taken by individuals in isolation (the 'risky shift' phenomenon).
- *The organisational culture within which the decision is taken.* For example, does the organisation allow managers some freedom to take risks or is decision making inhibited by a fear of 'blame-fixing' if things go wrong? (See Chapter 16 for further discussion of this issue.)
- *The interrelationship between the risk of a decision currently under consideration with other risks faced by the organisation.* For example, a decision to diversify into a new market is an extremely high-risk course of action in its own right. But the effect of taking this high-risk decision may be to reduce the organisation's *overall* risk, since the addition of a new market may cushion the business from the impact of

adverse conditions in an existing market. This is known as the *portfolio effect* and is the reason why ownership of a range of stocks and shares is preferable to ownership of only one. (*See* Chapter 11 for more on the portfolio effect.)

Attitude to risk is, therefore, a complex matter. However, even if we cannot accurately predict what that attitude may be in a given decision situation, we must recognise its influence, which may be so great in some circumstances as to completely override purely financial considerations.

STRENGTHS AND WEAKNESSES OF PROBABILISTIC DECISION ANALYSIS

Strengths

1 Management is required both to recognise that different outcomes may result from a decision and to quantify expectations about what these different outcomes may be. Although it may be difficult to quantify these outcomes with absolute precision, the very fact of their recognition will do much to enhance the decision-making process.
2 The degree of uncertainty attaching to different outcomes needs to be quantified; this will allow some assessment of risk to be made which should, again, improve the decision-making process.

Weaknesses

1 The probabilities used will, to some extent, be *subjective* in nature. For example, probabilities relating to sales may be based on extensive market research or on past experience – but some element of informed guesswork will be present (even if a comparatively small one). It is hard to envisage a business situation where *objective* probabilities, such as the one-in-six chance of obtaining a particular number on throwing a die, could be obtained. To the extent that the probabilities employed in our decision analyses are subjective, the analysis will be weakened and its results open to question.
2 The predicted outcomes and related probabilities which we used are 'point' estimates: in other words, there are a limited number of specified outcomes and probabilities. In the soft toy example, only three possible selling prices were examined and, for each of these selling prices, only three possible levels of demand. We can justify this sort of approach on the basis of ease of analysis, but it clearly represents a simplification.
Statistically, the point estimates of demand which we have employed lie at the mid-point of a range of possible values and some doubt may exist as to whether such statistical mid-points are sufficiently accurate reflections of the underlying reality. If simplifications made for analytical simplicity turn out to be *over*simplifications, then our results may have limited value to decision makers.
3 Expected value is a weighted average outcome. We stated earlier that the expected value of total contribution associated with setting a £12 selling price was £678,025, but this figure may bear little relationship to the actual total contribution which would result from this selling price. What the £678,025

indicates is that, if a number of decisions (say, 30 or more) were taken to set selling price at £12, and if these decisions were taken under identical conditions (i.e. same expected demand levels and associated probabilities, same expected unit variable costs), then the average total contribution resulting from all these decisions would be £678,025. It can thus be argued that expected value is an inappropriate criterion to apply to 'one-off' decisions. Moreover, even if a particular decision is repeated a number of times – as the pricing decision might if the charity decides to proceed with the soft toy venture – it would be quite unrealistic to assume that conditions will be unchanged.

4 Our analysis has dealt only with *independent* outcomes, but in reality, outcomes may be linked with each other. If, for example, unit cost is an important determinant of selling price, then that price (and very probably its consequent demand) will be linked to unit cost.

Use of a more rigorous statistical approach may help overcome some of the weaknesses mentioned above: for example, conditional probabilities and Bayesian analysis to deal with situations where uncertain events are linked, or the normal distribution and its related analytical tools to deal with the problem of point estimates. Detailed consideration of such techniques is outwith the scope of this text, but two general points about their use may be worth making:

1 There may be more sophistication and statistical validity to these approaches, but this, in itself, does not guarantee better decision-support information. For example, the underlying probabilities will still be as subjective as they were in our more basic analysis, so results may be equally open to question.

2 In Chapter 1, we said that, in order for information to be useful, it must be understood. The very sophistication of some of the methods used could present a barrier to such understanding.

Use of probabilistic decision analysis appears to be rather limited in practice, as revealed by Drury *et al.* in a 1993 study:

	Use of statistical analysis			
	Frequent	*Sometimes*	*Rarely*	*Never*
% of respondents	6	20	25	49

Such lack of widespread use may be partly attributable to the difficulty of assigning probabilities to outcomes and partly to the perception that analytical 'sophistication' presents a barrier to understanding.

SUMMARY

In this chapter, we have discussed and illustrated how the effects of risk and uncertainty may be incorporated in the financial analysis of decisions. We have placed particular emphasis on the use of a probability-based approach and the calculation of expected values, which, like so many other aspects of management accounting, have their strengths and weaknesses; and these must be appreciated if the techniques are to be employed to good effect.

We have seen that:

- **Sensitivity analysis** may be used to deal with risk and uncertainty and that this is basically a 'what-if' technique which examines the effect of changing one or more of the variables involved in a decision situation.

- **Three-level analysis** may also be employed. This involves estimating three possible outcomes of a decision: the best possible, the worst possible and the most likely outcomes.

- Neither sensitivity analysis nor three-level analysis quantifies the degree of uncertainty associated with the different outcomes involved.

- Probabilities can be attached to uncertain outcomes and an **expected value** calculated for those outcomes.

- **Expected value** is a weighted average outcome, calculated as:

$$\Sigma[x\{p(x)\}]$$

where: x is each possible outcome; and
$p(x)$ is the probability attaching to each possible outcome.

- The probability of two independent events occurring simultaneously is known as the **joint probability** (or **combined probability**) and is the product of the probabilities of each of the independent events concerned.

- A probability distribution of possible outcomes can be constructed, based on the *cumulative probabilities* of different outcomes.

- In order to reduce uncertainty, additional information may be obtained. The **value of perfect information** is the difference between the best expected outcome which can be obtained without the information and the expected value which will result if the information is obtained. This value sets an upper limit to the amount which should be paid to obtain imperfect information.

- A **decision tree** is a schematic representation of the possible outcomes of a decision and may be a useful way of clarifying decision options and any interrelationships between outcomes.

- The attitude to risk of the decision maker is vital. A **risk-neutral** attitude implies indifference to risk and pursuit of the optimum expected value irrespective of any associated risks. In practice, the decision maker's attitude will fall somewhere between **risk averse** and **risk seeking**.

- **Maximin** is an ultra-cautious decision criterion which accepts the option with the best possible 'worst outcome' and is consistent with a risk-averse attitude.

- **Maximax** is a decision criterion consistent with a risk-seeking attitude, accepting the option with the optimum 'best possible' outcome.

- Probabilistic decision analysis has two strengths:
  - it recognises the possibility of different outcomes resulting from a decision; and
  - it requires quantification of expectations about the likelihood of these different outcomes occurring.

- The weaknesses of probabilistic analysis can be summarised as:
  - subjective nature of the probabilities involved;
  - the use of point estimates;
  - the fact that expected values are average values; and
  - the assumed independence of possible outcomes.

- **Simulation** is a computer-based technique based on use of *random numbers* which permits inclusion of multiple outcomes in the analysis.

In the next chapter, we shall extend our decision analysis to encompass decisions with a strategic orientation – 'capital investment' decisions – and describe how their long-term nature may be incorporated in a financial appraisal.

FURTHER READING

Drury, C., *Management and Cost Accounting*, 4th edn, International Thomson Business Press, 1996. See chapter 14 for discussion of risk measures and of the workings of the portfolio effect.

Drury, C., Braund, S. and Tayles, M., *A Survey of Management Accounting Practices in UK Manufacturing Companies*, ACCA, 1993.

Waters, D., *Quantitative Methods for Business*, Addison-Wesley, 1994. Chapter 13 outlines the basic rules of probability and chapter 17 discusses the application of probability theory to business decision making. More advanced aspects of probabilistic analysis are covered in chapters 14, 15 and 16.

SELF-TEST QUESTIONS

9.1 A business is faced with a choice between four mutually exclusive courses of action, details of which are as follows:

	Option A £	Option B £	Option C £	Option D £
Expected value of total contribution	420,000	715,000	560,000	630,000
Best outcome (total contribution)	630,000	910,000	710,000	990,000
Worst outcome (total contribution)	195,000	60,000	100,000	115,000

Which of the options above would each of a *risk-neutral*, *risk-averse* and *risk-seeking* decision maker be likely to choose and why?

9.2 A council's Housing Department has produced the following estimates of the number of repairs to its housing stock next year:

Repairs	Probability
8,000	0.15
10,000	0.25
14,000	0.30
17,000	0.20
20,000	0.10

What is the expected value of the number of repairs next year?

Note: *The information which follows is to be used for Questions 9.3, 9.4 and 9.5.*

UC Ltd plans to sell one of its products at a price of £35 per unit next year. At this price, demand is estimated at:

Units	Probability
16,000	0.4
22,000	0.6

It is anticipated that unit variable cost will be:

£	Probability
10	0.3
12	0.4
14	0.3

9.3 Determine:

(a) the expected value of UC Ltd's demand; and

(b) the expected unit variable cost for the next year.

9.4 Using your answer to Question 9.3, what is the expected value of:

(a) the product's unit contribution; and

(b) the product's total contribution?

9.5 What is the *joint probability* of the following events occurring:

(a) demand of 16,000 units *and* unit variable cost of £12;

(b) demand of 22,000 units *and* unit variable cost of £14?

9.6 For each of the statements which follows, indicate whether it is true or false by placing a tick in the appropriate box.

	True	*False*
(a) Applying the maximin criterion means selecting the option with the worst possible outcome.	☐	☐
(b) Expected value may be more appropriate to repetitive than to one-off decisions.	☐	☐
(c) Probabilities relating to business decisions will always be objective.	☐	☐
(d) Sensitivity analysis does not allow for the quantification of uncertainty.	☐	☐
(e) The maximax criterion is consistent with a risk-seeking attitude on the part of the decision maker.	☐	☐

QUESTIONS WITH ANSWERS

9.7 This question tests whether you can:

- employ three-level analysis to calculate a range of possible outcomes;

- calculate breakeven points based on three-level data; and

- appreciate the shortcomings of three-level analysis and their possible solution.

MM Ltd produces multimedia educational software and is about to launch a new management accounting program. The following estimates of unit variable cost have been made:

	£
Low estimate	80
High estimate	140
Most likely estimate	100

Management believes that, at the proposed selling price of £220 per program, demand will be somewhere in the range:

	Units
Low demand	4,000
High demand	10,000

Total fixed cost associated with the new program will be £210,000.

Requirements

(a) Prepare a schedule of potential total contribution figures which will result from the different combinations of unit variable cost and demand given above.

(b) Calculate the new program's breakeven points based on:

   (i) lowest unit contribution;

   (ii) highest unit contribution:

   (iii) most likely unit contribution.

(c) Discuss the usefulness (or otherwise) to management of your analysis in (a) and (b) above and suggest any improvements which might be made.

9.8 This question tests whether you can:

- calculate expected values, including use of joint probabilities; and

- use cumulative joint probability to determine the probability of a given outcome.

The Duncaster Water Company is concerned about the level of leakage from its pipes, which has had an increasing impact on costs and quality of service over the last few years. The company's engineers have prepared the following estimates of water leakage for next year:

	Leakage (% of throughout)
Best outcome (probability 0.1):	10
Most likely outcome (probability 0.6):	20
Worst outcome (probability 0.3):	30

Anticipated throughput of water next year is:

	Litres (m.)
Highest throughput (probability 0.2):	800
Most likely throughput (probability 0.5):	600
Lowest throughput (probability 0.3):	350

For each litre of water lost as the result of leakage next year, the water company will incur a variable cost of £0.02. Total fixed costs associated with leakage will be £3 million for all leakages in the range 5–35 per cent of throughput inclusive. The company's management has proposed a budget allowance of £5 million next year to cover the total cost (fixed plus variable) arising from leakages. You should assume statistical independence of all variables.

Requirements

(a) Determine the following:

   (i) expected value of leakage as a percentage of throughput;

   (ii) expected value of litres throughput;

   (iii) expected value of leakage in litres.

(b) Based on the expected value of leakage in litres calculated in (a) above, provide the Duncaster Water Company with an expected value for the total cost (fixed plus variable) likely to be incurred as the result of leakages next year.

(c) Complete Table 9.4 and, from the completed table, determine the probability that the total cost of water leakages next year will not exceed the water company's budget allowance of £5 million.

TABLE 9.4 Possible outcomes, related costs and probabilities

Throughput (million litres)	Leakage as % of throughput	Leakage (million litres)	Total variable cost (£m)	Total fixed cost (£m)	Total cost (£m)	Probability (throughput)	Probability (leakage %)	Joint probability
800	10 20 30							
600	10 20 30							
350	10 20 30							

9.9 This question tests whether you can:

- calculate expected values for two options;

- provide decision advice based on expected values;

- appreciate the importance of managerial attitude to risk; and

- describe the operation of simulation.

TWR & Co is a firm of financial advisers and is trying to determine what charge to make to clients in respect of a special advice service about the implications of major tax changes made in the last budget. Two rates per hour are under consideration and details are as follows:

Charge per hour: £30

Revenue:	£
High estimate (probability 0.15)	800,000
Low estimate (probability 0.30)	420,000
Most likely estimate (probability 0.55)	570,000

Charge per hour: £40

Revenue:	£
High estimate (probability 0.10)	660,000
Low estimate (probability 0.35)	360,000
Most likely estimate (probability 0.55)	500,000

Fixed costs specifically associated with this new venture will not be affected by the volume of work, but there is some uncertainty as to the amount involved:

	£
High estimate (probability 0.2)	280,000
Low estimate (probability 0.2)	200,000
Most likely estimate (probability 0.6)	230,000

TWR incurs very few variable costs, and contribution is confidently expected to be 90 per cent of sales revenue. Revenue and fixed costs may be assumed to be statistically independent.

Requirements

(a) Determine, for *each* proposed charge per hour, the expected value of profit or loss. Assuming that management's objective is to maximise the expected value of profit, which charge rate should be set?

(b) State what managerial attitude to risk is implicit in the advice provided in (a).

(c) Describe how *simulation* might be employed by TWR & Co in analysing its decision. Explain how such an approach might improve the analysis.

9.10 This question tests whether you can:

- draw a decision tree;

- calculate expected values incorporating joint probabilities;

- provide decision advice based on expected value;

■ calculate the value of perfect information and advise whether it should be obtained; and

■ appreciate the relevance of qualitative factors to a decision.

Caledonian Hospital Trust is preparing its business plan for next year. The trust subcontracts its laundry work to an outside supplier and the Board of Management is examining the potential cost of placing this contract next year. There is some uncertainty about the level of demand for laundry services, but the following estimates have been prepared:

	Probability
High demand	0.25
Low demand	0.30
Medium demand	0.45

The problem faced by the Board of Management is that the contract must be placed in advance and must specify the anticipated volume of demand. The total cost of the contract at each demand level will be:

	£
High demand contract	1,000,000
Low demand contract	400,000
Medium demand contract	700,000

Should the Board of Management place an initial contract based on low or medium demand and actual demand turns out to be medium or high, arrangements will be made to upgrade the size of the contract. This, however, will incur additional costs as follows:

	Extra cost (£)
Upgrade low demand contract to medium demand:	350,000
Upgrade low demand contract to high demand:	700,000
Upgrade medium demand contract to high demand:	400,000

There is no facility for downgrading the volume of an initial contract.

Requirements

(a) Draw a decision tree of the problem faced by the trust's Board of Management, showing the probability and estimated total cost associated with each combination of outcomes. Show also the expected value of cost for each size of initial contract.

(b) Advise the Board of Management as to the optimum size of initial contract, based on minimum expected value of total cost.

(c) An independent adviser has offered to provide totally accurate information about the level of demand for laundry services at a cost of £60,000. Should the Board of Management accept this offer? Provide calculations to support your view.

(d) Enumerate and discuss briefly *three* factors not included in your analysis above which the Board of Management should consider before reaching a final decision about the laundry contract.

QUESTIONS WITHOUT ANSWERS

9.11 Rubble Ltd is a demolition contractor. Faced with a potential increase in demand for its services next period, the company is proposing to expand its workforce temporarily by employing casual labour for the period. The following estimated information is available:

Increase workforce by 2.5 per cent
The additional total contribution which could result has been assessed as:

£	Probability
400,000	0.3
470,000	0.4
510,000	0.3

Increase workforce by 5 per cent
The additional total contribution resulting from this increase has been estimated as:

£	Probability
440,000	0.3
530,000	0.5
800,000	0.2

Increase workforce by 7.5 per cent
Possible additional total contribution figures are:

£	Probability
770,000	0.2
930,000	0.4
1,100,000	0.4

The additional total contribution figures quoted above have been calculated *before* deduction of the additional cost of increasing the workforce by the specified percentages. There is some uncertainty about the exact amount of this cost due to possible recruitment difficulties, but the following estimates have been prepared:

Additional cost	2.5% increase	5% increase	7.5% increase
	£	£	£
Low estimate (probability 0.2)	180,000	390,000	510,000
High estimate (probability 0.3)	290,000	560,000	780,000
Most likely estimate (probability 0.5)	220,000	470,000	650,000

Variables may be assumed to be statistically independent.

Requirements

(a) Draw a decision tree of the problem faced by Rubble Ltd. Your decision tree should show, for each possible combination of outcomes, the joint probability and the resulting additional total contribution *after* deduction of the appropriate extra labour cost.

(b) Determine the expected value of net contribution (i.e. total additional contribution *less* the extra cost of increasing the workforce) for each proposed percentage increase in workforce and, on the basis of maximum expected value, advise management as to its best course of action.

(c) Assuming that Rubble Ltd's management is *risk averse*, apply the **maximin** criterion to the decision data and reformulate your advice to management on that basis (if necessary). Briefly discuss the extent to which the caution inherent in this approach might conflict with good business management.

9.12 Brougham Ltd is a road transport company and management is considering placing a tender for the franchise to operate a passenger rail service on a prestigious main-line route. Research suggests that, over the two-year period of the franchise, income from fares is likely to be:

£	Probability
15,000,000	0.10
20,000,000	0.20
30,000,000	0.40
35,000,000	0.20
40,000,000	0.10

Anticipated costs over the two-year period are:

Total variable cost		Total fixed cost	
£	Probability	£	Probability
6,000,000	0.20	8,000,000	0.10
10,000,000	0.50	12,000,000	0.50
14,000,000	0.30	16,000,000	0.40

The total fixed costs above are inclusive of payment to obtain the franchise.

Requirements

(a) Using the expected values of revenue, total contribution and total fixed cost as the basis, determine:

(i)   the franchise's breakeven point in revenue;

(ii) the franchise's margin of safety as a percentage of expected revenue; and

(iii) the revenue required in order to earn a target profit of £4,000,000 from the franchise over the two-year period.

(b) Prepare a schedule showing all the possible total contributions which might result from winning the franchise, along with the joint probability attaching to each.

(c) Use your schedule in (b) to determine the cumulative probability of the franchise:

(i)   at least breaking even; and

(ii) earning a profit of at least £4,000,000 over the two-year period.

(d) The company's Marketing Director has suggested that, since Brougham Ltd's existing road transport business is under severe threat from aggressive competitors, the risk attendant on the proposed diversification into rail transport is not warranted and that, consequently, the franchise should not be sought. Comment on the Marketing Director's suggestion.

CHAPTER **10**

Capital investment appraisal

RAILTRACK PLANS £10BN UPGRADE

Leaks during the weekend prompted Railtrack to issue its 10-year, £1 billion-a-year plan 'to deliver a railway network for the 21st century' . . .

Railtrack intends to replace 2,900 miles of sleepers and 1,400 miles of rails by 2004, renew dozens of bridges, and upgrade stations and depots. Further improvements will be made to signalling and control equipment, some of which is 40 years old.

Source: Keith Harper, *Guardian*, 18 December 1995.

EXHIBIT **10.1 A capital investment programme is unveiled**

INTRODUCTION

In the last three chapters, we have discussed and illustrated various management accounting techniques for analysing the financial implications of *short-term* decisions. These decisions stem from operational and tactical considerations. We must now turn our attention to decisions which stem more directly from strategic requirements – capital investment decisions. Examples of such decisions are: acquisition of major operating assets; introduction of new products/services; divestment and shutdown; and improvement programmes of the sort announced by Railtrack in Exhibit 10.1. Every decision has a strategic aspect: for example, short-term decisions, taken cumulatively, are strategic. But with capital investment decisions the strategic aspect predominates. These decisions have certain common characteristics:

1 they involve substantial costs and benefits;
2 they have cost/benefit implications which span a number of years; and
3 they are of significance to the entire organisation.

The criteria which we use for financial evaluation of such decisions must therefore be capable of reflecting these characteristics. In particular, they must be able to reflect relevant costs and benefits over a capital investment proposal's entire life (which will span a number of years). Not only this, but our evaluative criteria must reflect the significance to the organisation of the decision under consideration – e.g. by incorporating the organisation's cost of capital into the appraisal.

This is especially important in helping counter 'short-termism': that is, emphasising short-term benefits to the exclusion or detriment of long-term. The extent to which short-termism is a problem in the United Kingdom is suggested by responses to a questionnaire (Collison, Grinyer and Russell, 1993) in which 66 per cent of the finance directors who responded believed that stock market valuation of companies was based principally on their expected earnings for the *current* year. Although there is some debate about the source of pressure towards short-termism, the existence of such pressure in many organisations is clear.

OBJECTIVES When you have completed this chapter, you will be able to:

- place capital investment decisions in their strategic perspective;
- evaluate capital investment proposals using:
  - accounting rate of return;
  - payback;
  - net present value; and
  - internal rate of return;
- explain the strengths and weaknesses of each of the above criteria;
- appreciate the significance of the time value of money in capital investment appraisal;
- use tables of discount factors for single sums and annuities;
- understand the importance of 'relevance' to DCF calculations;

- identify and employ differential cash flows in net present value calculations;

- compare net present value and internal rate of return as capital investment criteria;

- appreciate the drawbacks common to all financial criteria for evaluating capital investment proposals; and

- explain the meaning of project post-audit, along with its advantages and problems.

CAPITAL INVESTMENT APPRAISAL AND ORGANISATIONAL STRATEGY

Given the common characteristics mentioned in the Introduction, it is important that capital investment decisions are consistent with an organisation's overall strategy. Exhibit 10.1 makes quite explicit reference to what may be Railtrack's mission statement from which strategy will derive: 'to deliver a railway network for the 21st century'. A major capital investment should not be made merely because it offers a healthy financial return in the short run. In pursuance of an organisation's strategic aims, it may be necessary to accept a decision which yields net costs in the short run, but which will prove valuable when a long-term perspective is applied. Capital investment decisions should therefore be viewed not only in light of financial criteria, but also in terms of how well they will help in achieving strategic objectives and the extent to which they 'mesh' with other proposed (or existing) capital investment proposals. This is not to suggest that financial considerations should be ignored – quite the contrary. What we are suggesting is that, before a financial evaluation is made, the need for major investment should be assessed in light of the organisation's strategic aims. As we said in Chapter 1, these aims may be varied, so the reason for capital investments will likewise vary: for example, achieving or improving competitive advantage; improvement in products/services offered; increasing profit; enhancing efficiency; effectiveness and economy; or complying with legal requirements.

Suppose a retailing group is considering acquisition of a new store in a location where the group has never previously operated; suppose also that the group's main strategic aim is to capture a 10 per cent share of its particular market. Financial evaluation of a proposal to acquire the new store should only occur if such acquisition will help to capture the desired market share. It may – but equally it may not. For instance, the store may be located in an area of declining demand, in which case proceeding with the acquisition will have the effect of committing substantial amounts of finance for no strategic gain.

Assessing the extent to which capital investment decisions, once taken, achieve their desired objective(s) is a matter of rigorous post-implementation review (project post-audit), which we shall discuss later in the chapter. Such review is important for all decisions, but is particularly so for strategic decisions. We therefore need to have a clear objective (or objectives) in mind before prospective courses of action are considered, and to use evaluation techniques which adequately reflect the strategic time frame involved. But note that these techniques have a narrow financial focus, and do not, in themselves, assess the *strategy* from which capital investment decisions stem.

ACCOUNTING RATE OF RETURN

This criterion links the key accounting measures of profit and the amount of capital which must be invested in order to earn that profit. You may also see **accounting rate of return** referred to as **return on capital employed** or **return on investment**. Accounting rate of return can be calculated as:

$$\frac{\text{average annual profit}}{\text{initial capital cost}} \times 100\%$$

The numerator in the formula is the total profit generated by the specific proposal during its estimated life divided by the number of years comprising that life. Once a proposal's accounting rate of return has been obtained, it is compared with a **target return** (also termed the **hurdle rate** or **cutoff rate**). The target return may be based on an organisation's **cost of capital** (*see* next chapter), or it may be derived from other sources: for example, for many public sector bodies, target return is stipulated in regulations governing that body's accounting procedures. If a proposal's return exceeds the target, it is financially viable; if it is lower than the target, the proposal should be rejected.

Exhibit 10.2 contains a scenario involving a capital investment decision; although the amounts involved are small in *absolute* terms (for ease of illustration), they may be substantial from the point of view of the firm concerned.

R & Co Interior Designers

As part of its long-term aim of enhancing its competitive position, R & Co is considering purchase of new computer hardware and software. This will allow speedier preparation of drawings and quotations to customers' specification and should result in additional profit due to increased customer orders. The following estimates apply:

Initial cost of hardware and software	£40,000
Useful life	4 years
Profit increase if bought:	
Year 1	£2,000
Year 2	£6,000
Year 3	£6,000
Year 4	£8,000
Resale value at the end of Year 4	£4,000

The profit increases above are stated after deducting £9,000 per annum depreciation from the proposal's annual net cash inflows. R & Co's required return is 15 per cent.

EXHIBIT 10.2 A capital investment decision

⇨ What is the average annual profit which will result from purchase of the computer installation?

The average annual profit will be:

$$\frac{\text{total profit over proposal's life}}{\text{number of years of proposal's life}}$$

$$= \frac{(£2,000 + £6,000 + £6,000 + £8,000)}{4 \text{ years}} = £5,500$$

▷ Using the average annual profit just calculated, determine the proposal's accounting rate of return, compare this with the firm's target return, and advise whether the proposal is acceptable.

The proposal's accounting rate of return is:

$$\frac{\text{average annual profit}}{\text{initial capital cost}} \times 100\%$$

$$= \frac{£5,500}{£40,000} \times 100\% = 13.75\%$$

As this is lower than the target return of 15 per cent, the proposal is unacceptable.

You may feel that basing the numerator on an average profit figure and the denominator on initial capital cost is inconsistent. In order to overcome this, we can amend the denominator and calculate accounting rate of return as:

$$\frac{\text{average annual profit}}{\text{average capital cost}} \times 100\%$$

A little care is needed when determining average capital cost. You may be tempted to *deduct* the estimated resale value of £4,000 from the initial cost, but this is incorrect. We are trying to obtain the average capital cost of the proposal over its life: at the start, the capital cost is £40,000 and at the end it is £4,000. In other words, we are looking at the accounting *book values* of the asset concerned at the start and end of its useful life. The average capital cost is a simple arithmetic average of these two values:

$$\frac{\text{initial capital cost + final capital cost}}{2}$$

Since this figure derives from only two measures of cost, we could argue that it is not a true average value, and in this sense is inconsistent with average annual profit as the accounting return's numerator.

Note that there is no change to the numerator in our revised definition of accounting rate of return – it is still average annual profit.

▷ Recalculate the computer proposal's accounting rate of return using average capital cost as the denominator.

First, we need to determine the proposal's average capital cost:

$$\frac{(\text{initial capital cost} + \text{final capital cost})}{2}$$

$$= \frac{(£40{,}000 + £4{,}000)}{2} = £22{,}000$$

This gives a revised accounting rate of return of:

$$\frac{\text{average annual profit}}{\text{average capital cost}} \times 100\%$$

$$= \frac{£5{,}500}{£22{,}000} \times 100\% = 25\%$$

As this is higher than the target return of 15 per cent, the proposal is acceptable. This assumes that the target return of 15 per cent is applicable to the revised method of calculating accounting rate of return; it may well be that the target return will be revised upwards to take account of the fact that accounting rate of return from individual proposals will be higher under the new method of calculation.

Advantages of accounting rate of return

This criterion has two distinct advantages:

1 It is straightforward to calculate.
2 It is readily understood, since it relates two key accounting benchmarks: profit and capital. It is easy to appreciate the significance of a decision criterion which expresses the profit earned by a proposal in terms of the amount of capital which must be invested in order to earn that amount of profit.

Disadvantages of accounting rate of return

These advantages are offset by a number of disadvantages:

1 At the beginning of this chapter, we said that the various evaluative criteria should be able to reflect the strategic orientation of the decisions being evaluated. Accounting rate of return is only partially successful in this respect: by using average profit (and possibly average capital cost), some recognition is given to the time aspect of proposals. However, this has two drawbacks:
   (a) The averaging process may hide the *pattern* of returns each year of a proposal's life and some knowledge of this may be important (e.g. for projecting cash flows or reported profit).
   (b) The calculation *implies* that all costs/benefits occur at the same point in time (i.e. now), otherwise we could not validly add and average profit and/or capital cost. In other words, we are implying that £1 spent/received now has the same 'value' as £1 spent/received four years from now. What we can say is that accounting rate of return disregards the **time value of money**. We shall discuss this concept later in the chapter.
   In terms of strategic orientation, accounting rate of return can therefore be argued to be very weak.

2 Accounting rate of return has no generally accepted definition. We have illustrated two possible versions – other variations exist. Even without these additional versions, we can see from our example just how major can be the effect of changing the basis of calculation:

(a) using initial capital cost: 13.75 per cent;

(b) using average capital cost: 25.00 per cent.

A substantial difference! In fact, so substantial as to indicate quite different decisions if the target return remains constant. This is an unsatisfactory situation – a capital expenditure proposal's acceptability or otherwise should not depend on the definition used in calculation of the appraisal criterion. Consistency of definition may remove anomalies such as this, but it will not remove the potential worry that a viable proposal has been rejected on the basis of how accounting rate of return happens to have been defined.

3 As we have seen, accounting rate of return is based on *profit* – in fact, of all the criteria we shall discuss, it is the *only* profit-based approach. As we observed in Chapter 7, profit is not the best basis for measuring the financial impact of decisions. For example, profit can be affected by the method of depreciation chosen, which is likely to be somewhat subjective. So it is better to use cash flows, which do not contain the same amount of 'informed guesswork'.

4 Accounting rate of return is expressed as a percentage. This gives no indication of the *size* of a proposal, nor does it indicate how much better (or worse) off the organisation will be if a particular proposal is undertaken. This makes the use of accounting rate of return difficult in situations where a choice must be made between two or more mutually exclusive proposals. Imagine we were faced with the following:

> Proposal A: accounting rate of return 15 per cent
> Proposal B: accounting rate of return 20 per cent
> Target rate of return: 10 per cent

If only one of these proposals can be undertaken, Proposal B would seem to be better at first glance. But how much do we need to invest in order to obtain these returns? And what is the *amount* of return from each proposal? These may be critically important questions, answers to which could determine the ultimate decision.

In general, use of percentages is likely to cause difficulty where choice between different proposals exists, and, at the least, some supplementary information should be provided (in the example above, knowing the amount of the initial investment for each of Proposals A and B would have been helpful).

PAYBACK

The **payback period** is the time (usually expressed in years: *see* Exhibit 10.3) which is required for a proposal's *cash inflows* to equal its initial cost. A target payback period will be set and proposals which recover their initial cost within this time will be acceptable. When comparing two or more mutually exclusive proposals, shorter paybacks within the target period are preferred to longer.

HANSON INCREASES INVESTMENT PAYBACK TIME

Hanson, the Anglo-US conglomerate, has lengthened its payback period for new investments by up to two years, in a move to take advantage of low interest rates and inflation.

Mr Derek Bonham, Hanson's chief executive, confirmed that the company had lowered its payback criteria for capital investments. They will be authorised if they pay for themselves within five or six years instead of the previous target of three to four . . .

Hanson's change of strategy is partly based on the company's outlook for interest rates and inflation, which Mr Bonham expects to remain under control. But Hanson is keen to allay fears of short-termism often levelled at conglomerates . . .

Hanson believes the falling cost of capital will enable it to take the longer-term view of capital investment which has been urged by the Bank of England and the Confederation of British Industry . . .

Source: Roland Rudd, *Financial Times*, 16 May 1994.

EXHIBIT **10.3 Payback: a common capital investment criterion**

R & Co Interior Designers

As part of its long-term aim of enhancing its competitive position, R & Co is considering purchase of new computer hardware and software. This will allow speedier preparation of drawings and quotations to customers' specification and should result in additional profit due to increased customer orders. The following estimates apply:

Initial cost of hardware and software	£40,000
Useful life	4 years
Profit increase if bought:	
Year 1	£2,000
Year 2	£6,000
Year 3	£6,000
Year 4	£8,000
Resale value at the end of Year 4	£4,000

The profit increases above are stated after deducting £9,000 per annum depreciation from the proposal's net cash inflows. R & Co's required return is 15 per cent and an acceptable payback period is two years.

EXHIBIT **10.4 Basic data for payback calculation**

⇨ In Exhibit 10.4, what are the annual net cash inflows for each of Years 1–4?

Annual net cash inflows will be (profit increase *plus* depreciation). You should bear in mind that depreciation is not a cash item and it is essential that you distinguish between profit and cash flow – the two are very unlikely to be the same. The net cash inflow each year is:

	£
Year 1 (£ 2,000 + £9,000)	11,000
Year 2 (£ 6,000 + £9,000)	15,000
Year 3 (£ 6,000 + £9,000)	15,000
Year 4 (£8,000 + £9,000 + £4,000)	21,000

Assuming that the estimated resale value of £4,000 is what the computer will actually be sold for at the end of Year 4, this amount represents an additional *cash inflow* in that year. The cash inflows for each of Years 1–4 are 'net' because relevant *cash* costs (e.g. cost of operating the new computer) have been deducted in their computation.

⇨ Will the proposal pay back its initial cost within the target period of two years?

By the end of Year 2, the proposed computer system will have generated cumulative cash inflows of £11,000 (Year 1) plus £15,000 (Year 2) = £26,000. It will therefore not recover its initial cost within the target period of two years and is unacceptable using payback as the criterion.

We may wish to ascertain the payback period with more precision. If we assume that the proposal's cash inflows arise evenly during each year, we can say that, by the end of Year 2, the proposal has recovered £26,000 of its initial cost and must recover a further (£40,000 − £26,000) = £14,000 in Year 3. Given the assumption about cash flows arising evenly during each year, the proportion of Year 3 needed to gain a further £14,000 will be:

$$\frac{\text{cash flow required}}{\text{total cash flow for year}} = \frac{£14,000}{£15,000} = 0.93 \text{ of Year 3}$$

so the payback period is 2.93 years.

Advantages of payback

1 Like accounting rate of return, payback is simple to calculate and understand.
2 Compared to accounting rate of return, it has the advantage of concentrating on cash flows, which are more objective than profit.
3 Because it is such a quick, simple method to employ, it may be useful in situations where a great number of competing proposals need to be compared or ranked, with shorter-than-target payback being one criterion for a proposal being further investigated.
4 Payback may be significant where an organisation has cash flow problems (*liquidity* problems). In these circumstances, it may be important that capital investment proposals cover their initial cost quickly so that proposal cash flows which arise after the (short) payback period will help alleviate the cash flow problem.
5 If a proposal is considered to be particularly risky, management may prefer that the initial cost be recovered sooner rather than later, feeling that, for an inherently risky proposal, the longer it takes for initial cost to be recovered, the greater is the chance of the related risks adversely affecting the outcome.

Disadvantages of payback

1 Payback (in the form in which we have just calculated it) ignores the **time value of money**. Like accounting rate of return, the implication of this approach is that all proposal cash flows arise at the same point in time. We shall discuss the time value of money shortly.

2 Even if the payback criterion is modified to allow for the time value of money (as it can be), it may still have a serious shortcoming. If you look again at the net cash inflows associated with R & Co's computer installation, you will see that, once the payback period has been determined, cash flows which arise *after* that time are effectively removed from the analysis. In R & Co's case, this amounts to:

$$(£1,000 \text{ [in Year 3]} + £21,000 \text{ [in Year 4]}) = £22,000$$

that is, we have excluded cash flows equivalent to 55 per cent of the proposal's initial cost – a substantial omission. What this could mean is that we will accept proposals simply because they have heavy cash inflows in their earlier years (giving a short payback period), but which may not be particularly worthwhile *over their full lives*, while at the same time rejecting proposals that are extremely financially desirable *over their full lives*, but which happen to have heavier cash inflows in later, rather than in earlier years (giving a long payback period).

3 Like accounting rate of return, payback gives no indication of the amount of capital investment required, nor of the overall cost/benefit resulting from acceptance or rejection of a proposal. This, together with the last point regarding omission of some cash flows from the analysis, means that comparison of competing projects on the basis of payback may be dangerously flawed.

Based on the disadvantages above, we can therefore suggest that payback is weak as an evaluative criterion relating to the strategic orientation of capital investment proposals.

THE TIME VALUE OF MONEY

We are all aware of the existence of the time value of money, although we may not use this term for it. Phrases such as '£1 today is worth more than £1 in the future' tend to crop up quite often.

⇨ Why is it true that £1 today is worth more than £1 in the future?

There are two reasons why £1 today is worth more than £1 in future:

1 Money which is received now can be invested to earn a return. If receipt is deferred, we will lose this return. For example, if we receive £50 now, we may be able to invest at, say, 8 per cent per annum interest, so that, one year from now, our £50 is worth (£50 × 1.08) = £54. If we had to wait one year to receive the £50, we would lose that year's interest at 8 per cent, so the value to us today of £50 receivable in one year, given the lost interest of 8 per cent per annum, is *less* than £50. (Or alternatively, we would need to receive *more* than £50 in one year to compensate for this loss of interest.)

2 Individuals and organisations have a *liquidity preference*: that is, they prefer to have cash available to spend on goods/services now, rather than the chance of having cash to spend in future.

> ### Time value of money
>
> We receive £1,000 which we can immediately invest for four years at 8 per cent per annum interest, the annual interest being reinvested.

EXHIBIT **10.5 Investment over time**

⇨ In Exhibit 10.5, what will be the value of our £1,000 investment at the end of:

■ one year from now;
■ two years from now;
■ three years from now;
■ four years from now?

(Work to the nearest whole £1.)

Remembering that annual interest is reinvested ('compounded'), the original £1,000 will be worth:

$$(£1,000 \times 1.08) = £1,080 \text{ one year from now}$$
$$(£1,080 \times 1.08) = £1,166 \text{ two years from now}$$
$$(£1,166 \times 1.08) = £1,259 \text{ three years from now}$$
$$(£1,259 \times 1.08) = £1,360 \text{ four years from now}$$

Arithmetically, this is the same as saying that the value of our £1,000 is:

$$(£1,000 \times 1.08) = £1,080 \text{ one year from now}$$
$$(£1,000 \times 1.08^2) = £1,166 \text{ two years from now}$$
$$(£1,000 \times 1.08^3) = £1,259 \text{ three years from now}$$
$$(£1,000 \times 1.08^4) = £1,360 \text{ four years from now}$$

These calculations provide us with a general expression for compounding:

$$\text{future value} = \text{present value} \times (1 + r)^n$$

where: r is the applicable rate of interest or other return;
n is the number of years concerned.

⇨ What is the value in today's terms (the present value) of £1,259 receivable three years from now if the applicable interest rate is 8 per cent compound?

From the workings above, we know that £1,259 is the future value of £1,000 invested at 8 per cent per annum compound interest for three years: that is, the present value of £1,259 at 8 per cent is £1,000. Expressing future values in present-day terms is known as *discounting*. Rearrangement of the general formula for compounding yields one for discounting:

$$\text{future value} = \text{present value} \times (1 + r)^n$$

so:

$$\text{future value} \times \frac{1}{(1 + r)^n} = \text{present value}$$

In discounting calculations, 'r' is referred to as the 'discount rate'.

▷ Use the discounting formula to confirm that the present value of £1,360 received four years from now is £1,000 at a discount rate of 8 per cent.

$$\text{future value} \times \frac{1}{(1 + r)^n} = \text{present value}$$

so:

$$£1,360 \times \frac{1}{(1 + 0.08)^4} = \text{present value}$$

that is:

$$£1,360 \times 0.735 = £1,000 \text{ (rounded to nearest whole £1)}$$

You may feel that these calculations are rather daunting. However, a short-cut is available. Fractions such as the 0.735 above are known as *discount factors* and Appendix B lists such factors for a variety of different discount rates and time horizons. A listing of this sort is available in any book of mathematical tables, so calculation is not usually necessary. We need only refer to tables such as Appendix B and apply the relevant factor to the cash flow which we wish to discount. Examination of the 8 per cent column in Table B1 of Appendix B shows 0.735 in the '4 years' row.

▷ Use the discount factors in Table B1 of Appendix B to obtain discount factors where:

$n = 7$ years	$r = 12\%$
$n = 10$ years	$r = 6\%$
$n = 15$ years	$r = 4\%$

The relevant discount factors are 0.452, 0.558 and 0.555. Looking at the pattern of discount factors in Table B1 of Appendix B you will notice that, as the time horizon lengthens, the factors for each discount rate decrease. This is a reflection of the time value of money: that is, the greater the time involved, the greater the impact of 'lost' interest and liquidity preference and so the lower is the present value of the cash flow.

Where a proposal has equal annual cash flows – an **annuity** – we can take another short cut. Table B2 in Appendix B lists *cumulative* discount factors (also known as **annuity** factors). We can use these to discount equal annual cash flows. If you compare the factors in Table B2 to those in Table B1, you will see that Table B2 contains the cumulative totals of those in Table B1.

⇨ Use Table B2 in Appendix B to obtain the cumulative discount factors where:

$n = 8$ years $r = 16\%$
$n = 12$ years $r = 5\%$
$n = 6$ years $r = 10\%$

The relevant factors are 4.344, 8.863 and 4.355

⇨ Both Table B1 and Table B2 begin with factors which relate to cash flows which arise one year from now. What is the discount factor for cash flows which arise now?

Cash flows which arise now have a discount factor of 1: the present value of £1 spent/received today is £1. In discounting calculations, 'now' is conventionally referred to as 'Year 0' (or 'Time 0').

DISCOUNTED CASH FLOW (DCF) TECHNIQUES

The appraisal methods we are about to describe are both based on the principle that a proposal's cash flows should all be stated in today's terms before its acceptability is assessed: that is, they make use of the discounting procedures illustrated above. For this reason, they are known collectively as **discounted cash flow (DCF)** techniques.

Net present value (NPV)

To obtain **net present value** (NPV), we discount a capital investment proposal's cash flows at the organisation's cost of capital (*see* next chapter). NPV is the sum of these discounted cash flows: that is, outflows (i.e. cash payments) plus inflows (i.e. cash receipts or savings). Where the discounted cash inflows exceed the discounted cash outflows, NPV is *positive*; where the discounted cash outflows exceed the discounted cash inflows, NPV is *negative*.

A proposal is acceptable if it has a positive NPV, but should be rejected if it has a negative NPV. When evaluating two or more mutually exclusive proposals, that with the highest positive NPV should be accepted. In certain circumstances, a proposal having a negative NPV may be accepted: for example, where we are evaluating mutually exclusive proposals both of which have a negative NPV, but where we *must* nevertheless choose one or the other. Here, we will accept the proposal having the negative NPV closest to zero. This kind of situation may arise, for example, where an organisation is obliged by Health & Safety legislation to install a sprinkler system in its premises: since the associated cash inflows will be either non-existent or minimal relative to cash outflows, NPV will be negative.

Exhibit 10.6 restates the *undiscounted* cash flows associated with the capital investment decision faced by R & Co.

R & Co: proposal net cash flows

The annual net cash flows resulting from acquisition of the new computer installation are:

	£
Paid now (initial cost – cash outflow)	40,000
Year 1 (net cash inflow)	11,000
Year 2 (net cash inflow)	15,000
Year 3 (net cash inflow)	15,000
Year 4 (net cash inflow)	21,000

The firm's cost of capital is 15 per cent.

Exhibit 10.6 Undiscounted proposal cash flows

▷ Use the discount factors from Table B1 of Appendix B and the firm's cost of capital of 15 per cent to obtain the present value of each year's cash flow. Include the Year 0 cash flow in your answer.

The discounted cash flows are shown in Table 10.1. The Year 0 cash flow has been placed in brackets to make clear that it is a cash outflow (i.e. a payment), whereas all the other cash flows in this example are inflows (i.e. receipts). Now that we have stated all the proposal's cash flows on a common basis – that is, in to-day's terms – we can validly add them up. Such addition is arguably invalid using undiscounted figures, because they arise at different points in time over the proposal's life and are thus all affected to a different degree by the time value of money.

Table 10.1 Discounted cash flows for R & Co's new computer

Year	Cash flow	Amount (£)	Discount factor	Present value (£)
0	Initial cost	(40,000)	1.000	(40,000)
1	Net cash inflow	11,000	0.870	9,570
2	Net cash inflow	15,000	0.756	11,340
3	Net cash inflow	15,000	0.658	9,870
4	Net cash inflow	21,000	0.572	12,012

▷ Use the discounted cash flows from Table 10.1 to obtain the proposal's net present value (i.e. the sum of its discounted cash flows). Is the proposal acceptable?

The NPV is:

$$(£40,000) + £9,570 + £11,340 + £9,870 + £12,012 = £2,792$$

(Remember that the Year 0 cash flow is a payment, so it is treated as a negative figure in the NPV calculation.) Since its NPV is positive, the proposal is acceptable.

What does a positive NPV of £2,792 represent? It is the increase in absolute wealth which R & Co will obtain if it acquires the new computer system. In other words, even after allowing for 'lost' interest and liquidity preference, the firm will still be £2,792 'better off' as a result of acquisition.

Internal rate of return (IRR)

Internal rate of return is another discounted cash flow technique and is defined as:

> The discount rate yielding a zero NPV.

This is the return implicit to a proposal and if it exceeds the organisation's cost of capital, the proposal is acceptable; if it is less than the cost of capital, the proposal should be rejected.

The relationship between NPV and discount rates is as shown in Figure 10.1 – the greater the discount rate, the lower the associated NPV. Note that the relationship is not linear. The point where the NPV plot intersects the horizontal axis is the internal rate of return: that is, the discount rate yielding a zero NPV. We could use such a graph ('present value profile') to determine a project's IRR, but this is cumbersome if done manually, as a number of NPVs must be calculated using different discount rates sufficient to permit reasonably accurate plotting of the NPV function.

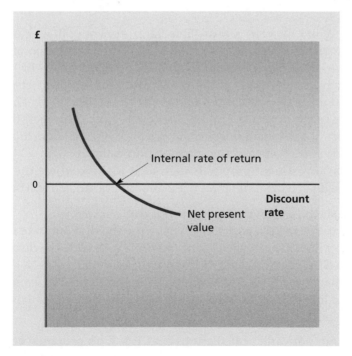

FIGURE **10.1**
NPV and discount rates

Where a project's cash inflows consist of equal annual amounts, IRR can be obtained as follows:

1 Discounting project proposals at the IRR gives NPV of zero:

(annual cash inflow × appropriate cumulative discount factor)
less
initial cost of proposal
equals
zero

Rearranging this, we get:

$$\frac{\text{initial cost}}{\text{annual cash inflow}} = \text{appropriate cumulative discount factor}$$

2 Since we know the number of years involved, we can use a table of cumulative factors (Table B2 in Appendix B) to obtain the IRR.

▷ A capital investment proposal has an initial cost of £84,750, with an annual cash inflow of £15,000 in each of its ten years of life. What is the proposal's IRR?

The appropriate cumulative discount factor is:

$$\frac{\text{initial cost}}{\text{annual cash inflow}} = \frac{£84,750}{£15,000} = 5.65$$

Reading along the '10-year' row of Table B2 in Appendix B, we can see that 5.65 is the cumulative factor for a 12 per cent discount rate. The proposal thus has an IRR of 12 per cent. If necessary, we can interpolate between factors in Table B2: had our calculation given an answer of, say, 5.538, then the IRR lies between 12 per cent and 13 per cent. Since 5.538 is the mid-point of the factors for 12 per cent and 13 per cent, we can estimate IRR as 12.5 per cent. Note, however, that IRRs derived from this sort of interpolation are estimates only. The relationship we are approximating is curvilinear, whereas the interpolation is linear.

For capital investment proposals such as R & Co's, where the pattern of cash inflows is irregular, determining IRR is a matter of trial and error. The procedures are:

1 Discount the proposal's cash flows at the cost of capital.
2 If item 1 above yields a positive NPV, *increase* the discount rate to obtain a negative NPV; if item 1 above yields a negative NPV, *decrease* the discount rate to give a positive NPV.
3 Interpolate between the discount rates in items 1 and 2 to estimate the value at which the line joining their NPVs intersects the horizontal axis. This value will be the proposal's approximate IRR.

We know from our earlier calculations that R & Co's proposed computer acquisition has a positive NPV of £2,792 when discounted at the firm's cost of capital of 15 per cent. To obtain a negative NPV, we must therefore *increase* the discount rate.

▷ What is the NPV of R & Co's computer acquisition proposal at a discount rate of 25 per cent?

TABLE **10.2 NPV of R & Co's new computer at 25 per cent**

Year	Cash flow	Amount (£)	Discount factor	Present value (£)
0	Initial cost	(40,000)	1.000	(40,000)
1	Net cash inflow	11,000	0.800	8,800
2	Net cash inflow	15,000	0.640	9,600
3	Net cash inflow	15,000	0.512	7,680
4	Net cash inflow	21,000	0.410	8,610

NPV   (5,310)

To obtain the NPV at a 25 per cent discount rate, all we need do is rediscount the proposal's cash flows using the 25 per cent discount factors from Table B1 of Appendix B (as illustrated in Table 10.2). The proposal's IRR will therefore lie somewhere between 15 per cent and 25 per cent. We can approximate the IRR by interpolating between 15 per cent and 25 per cent:

$$\text{IRR} = 15\% + \left[\frac{£2,792}{(£2,792 + £5,310)} \times (25\% - 15\%) \right] = 18.45\% \text{ (rounded)}$$

Or alternatively:

$$\text{IRR} = 25\% - \left[\frac{£5,310}{(£2,792 + £5,310)} \times (25\% - 15\%) \right] = 18.45\% \text{ (rounded)}$$

Since the proposal's IRR exceeds the 15 per cent cost of capital, it is acceptable using this criterion.

You should note that, for all their seeming complexity, the IRR calculations above are nevertheless approximations; this is because the fraction within the square brackets assume a linear (i.e. straight-line) relationship between NPV and discount rate, whereas, in fact, the relationship is curvilinear, as illustrated in Figure 10.1. Not only this, but the degree of inaccuracy of the approximation resulting from calculations of this sort will be affected by the difference between the two discount rates used: the greater this difference, the greater will be the inaccuracy in our estimate of IRR. Figure 10.2 illustrates this point: the line *AB* represents the linear approximation of the NPV/discount rate relationship based on the R & Co proposal's NPVs at rates of 15 per cent and 25 per cent and line *AC* approximates the same relationship at discount rates of 15 per cent and 50 per cent. You will see from Figure 10.2 that, as the difference between the two discount rates widens, so the estimate of IRR moves to the right (i.e. increases).

Although this trial and error approach to determination of IRR can be cumbersome if performed manually, computer spreadsheets can greatly reduce the burden of calculation. In fact, many spreadsheet packages contain a pre-programmed facility for calculating IRR.

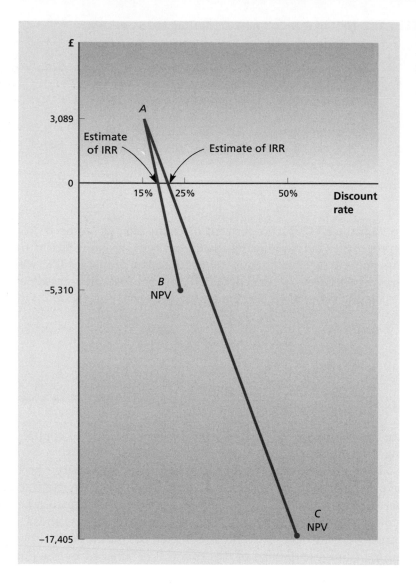

£

3,089 ─── *A*

Estimate of IRR

Estimate of IRR

0 ───

15%   25%   50%   **Discount rate**

B
NPV

−5,310 ───

C
NPV

−17,405 ───

FIGURE **10.2**
Inaccuracy
in estimation
of IRR

▨ DCF techniques and the concept of relevance

In Chapter 7, we defined relevant costs and benefits as:

> **future cash flows which differ between alternatives.**

We must apply this definition so as to ascertain *which* cash flows are to be discounted in appraisal of a capital investment proposal.

Suppose R & Co's capital investment appraisal involved a *choice* of new computer system as detailed in Exhibit 10.7. We have already calculated System A's net present value (at the 15 per cent cost of capital) as £2,792.

R & Co Interior designers: choice of new computer system

The firm has a choice of specification for its new system: System A will meet all the firm's basic requirements while System B, although more costly to acquire, is reckoned to have greater profit-earning potential because of its greater sophistication. Details are as follows:

	System A	System B
Initial cost of hardware and software	£40,000	£60,000
Useful life	4 years	4 years
Net cash inflow if bought:		
Year 1	£11,000	£16,000
Year 2	£15,000	£20,000
Year 3	£15,000	£22,000
Year 4	£17,000	£24,000
Resale value at the end of Year 4	£4,000	£8,000

The firm's existing computer system was bought five years ago for £10,000 and will be sold for £2,000 irrespective of which new system is acquired. The firm's cost of capital is 15 per cent.

EXHIBIT **10.7 Mutually exclusive options**

⇨ Using the discount factors from Appendix A and the 15 per cent cost of capital, determine System B's net present value. Is System B financially preferable to System A?

System B's NPV is shown in Table 10.3. The original cost of the existing computer system is a sunk cost, and the sale proceeds of £2,000 will be received irrespective of which new system is bought. Both are therefore irrelevant to the decision. The total cash inflow from System B in Year 4 includes the resale value of £8,000. As System B's NPV is lower than System A's (£2,792), System A is preferable on financial grounds.

TABLE **10.3 NPV of alternative new computer system**

Year	Cash flow	Amount (£)	Discount factor	Present value (£)
0	Initial cost	(60,000)	1.000	(60,000)
1	Net cash inflow	16,000	0.870	13,920
2	Net cash inflow	20,000	0.756	15,120
3	Net cash inflow	22,000	0.658	14,476
4	Net cash inflow	32,000	0.572	18,304
			NPV	£ 1,820

By discounting *all* the relevant cash flows of each system, we have arrived at the correct financial evaluation. However, we can shorten the discounting procedures by using **differential cash flows**: that is, the difference between the relevant cash flows relating to each option.

335

⇨ What are the differential cash flows associated with purchase of System B?

The differential cash flows are:

		£
Year 0:	additional purchase cost	(20,000)
Year 1:	additional cash inflow	5,000
Year 2:	additional cash inflow	5,000
Year 3:	additional cash inflow	7,000
Year 4:	additional cash inflow	11,000

⇨ What is the NPV of the differential cash flows at a cost of capital of 15 per cent?

TABLE 10.4 Systems A & B – NPV of differential cash flows

Year	Cash flow	Amount (£)	Discount factor	Present value (£)
0	Initial cost	(20,000)	1.000	(20,000)
1	Net cash inflow	5,000	0.870	4,350
2	Net cash inflow	5,000	0.756	3,780
3	Net cash inflow	7,000	0.658	4,606
4	Net cash inflow	11,000	0.572	6,292
			NPV	(972)

The differential cash flows' NPV is shown in Table 10.4. The differential cash flows have a negative NPV, so acquisition of System B is less financially attractive than System A. Alternatively, we could have discounted the differential cash flows associated with purchase of System A, in which case the differential NPV would be £972 (positive); you may wish to check that this is so. Our differential NPV is simply the difference between the NPVs we obtained when we discounted all the relevant cash flows for each system:

	£
NPV System B	1,820
NPV System A	2,792
Difference in NPV	(972)

Either approach is acceptable, and differential costing can reduce the volume of calculations necessary for the financial appraisal. But caution must be exercised when interpreting the results of differential analysis. A positive *differential* NPV in favour of System A is not the same as saying that System A has a positive NPV. Assume the proposals' NPVs are:

	£
Proposal A	(5,000)
Proposal B	(5,972)
Difference in NPV	(972)

Here, use of differential NPV unsupported by other information could result in acceptance of a proposal which should, prima facie, be rejected.

DCF techniques v accounting rate of return and payback

Since NPV and IRR not only incorporate all cash flows over a proposal's life, but also make explicit allowance for the time value of money, both appraisal criteria seen strong in their ability to reflect capital investment proposals' strategic orientation. However, there may be some difficulty in determining the most appropriate cost of capital to employ, a point we shall examine in more detail in the next chapter.

It is also worth noting that the mechanics of calculating the present value factors contained in Appendices A and B imply that cash flows arise *at the end* of each year, and that this is likely to be a simplification of reality. But the effect is, in most cases, unlikely to be sufficiently material to alter the acceptability of a proposal (and it is possible to amend discounting calculations to allow for more complex patterns of cash flows).

We can also argue that the discounting process, by giving greater 'weight' to earlier than later cash flows, could introduce the same kind of short-term bias that we suggested earlier might occur with payback.

A comparative study of appraisal techniques used by the same 100 large UK companies over a period of time (Pike and Wolfe, 1988) seems to suggest that usage of DCF techniques is increasing:

	1975	*1981*	*1986*
	%	%	%
Internal rate of return	44	57	75
Net present value	32	39	68
Average accounting rate of return	51	49	56
Payback	73	81	92

These results are echoed by Drury *et al.* (1993), with payback and IRR being the most frequently used techniques. The popularity of payback is interesting – and perhaps worrying – in light of our earlier comments about short-termism; but it is worth noting that payback is also the dominant approach in Japan and in UK-based Japanese subsidiaries, where a long-term orientation in business operations is common (*see* Bromwich and Inoue, 1994). Problems may therefore lie in the way payback is applied, rather in the technique itself – a suggestion perhaps borne out by careful reading of Exhibit 10.3.

NPV VERSUS IRR

We have examined two DCF criteria for evaluation of capital investment decisions, and we must now ask if either approach is better and why.

Of the two criteria, NPV is technically superior for the reasons we shall discuss below. Where any conflict exists between the two DCF approaches as to the acceptability of a particular proposal, or the ranking of competing proposals, then 'acceptability' as indicated by NPV should be preferred to that indicated by IRR. If

NPV conflicts with accounting rate of return and/or payback, then the situation may be less clear; as the only 'wealth maximisation' model, NPV is probably superior.

1 As we have seen, determination of IRR is often a matter of trial and error, and the result can thus be much less precise than net present value. Depending on the extent of this imprecision, the acceptability of proposals may be affected.

2 IRR, like accounting rate of return, considers neither the size of the investment required, nor the gain/loss which will result from undertaking or not undertaking a particular proposal. It will therefore be difficult to use IRR to make comparisons between competing proposals, and it may happen that the two DCF appraisal criteria – IRR and NPV – will give conflicting indications about the acceptability of a particular proposal.

3 IRR is unable to cope with a change in the cost of capital (i.e. the discount rate) during the life of a proposal. If the cost of capital does change during a proposal's life, it means that there is more than one target return against which to compare IRR. For example:

Proposal's estimated life	10 years
Proposal's IRR	12%
Cost of capital applicable to:	
Years 1–5 of proposal's life	10%
Years 6–10 of proposal's life	14%

Using IRR as the criterion, the proposal seems to be acceptable for Years 1–5, but unacceptable for Years 6–10. Is the proposal acceptable over its entire life? IRR does not provide the answer. But NPV can easily accommodate such a change. If the cost of capital changes, all we need do is use the present value factors appropriate to the changed cost of capital in our calculations. It is perfectly possible for the cost of capital to change over time where changes are expected in the factors which underlie the derivation of cost of capital (*see* next chapter).

4 Where a proposal has annual cash flows which are a mixture of net inflow and net outflow, that proposal may have a single IRR (as did R & Co's proposal), it may have no IRR, or it may have more than one. Consider the following pattern of cash flows relating to a capital investment proposal:

		£
Year 0	net cash outflow	100,000
Year 2	net cash outflow	50,000

The pattern of cash flows above will have a negative IRR. Since a discount rate of less than zero is virtually meaningless, implying a reversal of the time value of money, we can effectively say that this proposal has no IRR. You may think that this is rather contrived, but you must remember that a capital investment proposal need not have cash inflows associated with it: for example, the sprinkler system we mentioned earlier. You may also feel that, since the pattern of cash flows above will yield a negative NPV at all discount rates, NPV offers no advantage over IRR. This is true if only one sprinkler system can be installed, but, if there are alternatives, we can use NPV to select the least cost option: that is, we should install the system with the negative NPV which is closest to zero.

Such a comparison is impossible using IRR, as there will be no IRRs to compare. In fact, it can be proved mathematically that a proposal will have as many IRRs as there are changes in the sign attaching to the annual cash flows (i.e. from net outflow to net inflow or vice versa). In R & Co's case, there is an initial outflow followed by a series of inflows – one change of sign – so this proposal has one IRR. Had we been faced with an initial net outflow, followed, say, by net inflows in each of Years 1, 2, and 3, followed by another net outflow in Year 4 – that is, *two* changes in the sign attaching to proposal cash flows – then there would be two IRRs, thus rendering IRR almost meaningless as an evaluative criterion. NPV, on the other hand, can deal with any pattern of cash flows and so does not suffer from this shortcoming.

5 Implicit to the NPV approach is the assumption that project cash inflows are reinvested to earn a return equal to the cost of capital; you may wish to review our earlier description of compounding and discounting to see that this is so. IRR, on the other hand, assumes reinvestment at the project's IRR. The logical flaw in this is not hard to see:

	Proposal	
	A	*B*
Estimated life	10 years	10 years
IRR	15%	25%

Assuming both proposals to be acceptable and to start at the same point in time, how can it happen that the rate of return on reinvestment of the cash flows from each differs so markedly?

Despite its theoretical shortcomings, surveys of practice, such as those cited earlier, indicate widespread use of IRR. It may be that management finds percentages easier to work with than absolute amounts such as NPV.

GENERAL DIFFICULTIES WITH CAPITAL INVESTMENT CRITERIA

All the criteria we have described in this chapter have some common difficulties:

1 They are all financial measures. For decisions of the type we are considering, non-financial factors may be of major significance, especially for proposals with no associated cash inflows, such as the sprinkler system mentioned earlier, or for many public sector projects where there are large intangible costs and benefits.

2 None of the measures indicates how a proposal is to be funded. Given that the cost of many capital projects is substantial, their funding must be a major consideration in assessing financial viability. (We will discuss possible sources of finance for capital investment decisions in the next chapter.)

3 Since the lifespan of many capital investment projects is long, there may be a problem in producing credible estimates – particularly for the later years. And even if reasonable estimates can be produced, it may be the case – particularly with 'high-tech' assets such as computers – that the proposal's life needs to be artificially shortened to allow for obsolescence. This might be a somewhat arbitrary process which could distort the apparent financial viability of a proposal.

Estimation difficulties may somewhat erode the 'simplicity' benefit claimed for accounting rate of return and payback, and could be one reason for the predominance of short target payback periods in practice.

4 Over-reliance on financial criteria for evaluating capital investment decisions may obscure the strategic context. In particular, these criteria may be too internally focused, where strategic assessment requires a much wider perspective. It is also possible that imposition of relatively inflexible financial targets, coupled with their short-term bias, might stifle innovation. For example, adoption of a particular proposal may ultimately pave the way for further developments – a factor unlikely to be shown by financial analysis.

CAPITAL INVESTMENT DECISIONS AND TAXATION

Tax has important implications for capital investment proposals; although detailed consideration of these is beyond the scope of this book, we can make some general points.

- Capital expenditure (e.g. the initial cost of R & Co's new computer system) usually qualifies for some form of tax allowance. In the UK, this takes the form of an annual 'writing down allowance' equal to 25 per cent of the tax book value of the asset(s) concerned, which is calculated on a reducing balance basis:

    Initial cost: £40,000   Writing down allowance: (25% × £40,000) = £10,000
    New tax book value: (£40,000 – £10,000) = £30,000
        Writing down allowance: (25% × £30,000) = £7,500
    New tax book value: (£30,000 – £7,500) = £22,500
        Writing down allowance: (25% × £22,500) = £5,625
    – and so on.

- Operational cash inflows and outflows associated with the capital investment proposal will, with certain exceptions, be taxable and tax-deductible respectively.

- The tax effects of capital investment expenditures will occur some time after the related cash inflows and outflows.

- Tax benefits and penalties attaching to a particular proposal are treated as 'cash inflows' and ' cash outflows' respectively.

Since capital investment expenditures are often substantial in amount, the tax implications are also potentially substantial, and an organisation's ability to derive full benefit from tax allowances, while minimising tax liabilities, can be a major influence in assessing the desirability of a proposal. For example, does the organisation have sufficient taxable profit to make full use of all allowances relating to a prospective capital investment? How will the timing of tax liabilities affect the organisation's cash position?

PROJECT POST-AUDIT

Also termed **post-completion audit**, project post-audit reviews the financial impact of a capital expenditure decision on one or more occasions during its life and/or at the end of its life. The main thrust of post-audit is a comparison of a project's actual cash flows with the estimates which were used in its original appraisal. In addition, the 'fit' between a proposal and the strategy which it was adopted in order to support may be assessed.

Benefits and problems of post-audit

Post-auditing capital investment decisions offers a number of benefits:

1 Knowledge that a proposal will be post-audited, if implemented, may result in more rigorous estimation of related costs and benefits at the appraisal stage.
2 Post-audit during a project's life may reveal problems (both with the project itself and on a wider front) which can be corrected, or may indicate problems of such magnitude that project abandonment is required.
3 The post-audit process could suggest hitherto unforeseen opportunities for worthwhile capital investments or strategic improvement.
4 Post-audit results may be incorporated in evaluations of managerial performance.

▷ Can you suggest any potential problems with post-audit?

Arguably the major danger inherent in post-audit arises from overemphasising its financial control aspect: that is, the comparison of estimated and actual costs/benefits, which might inhibit managers. Such inhibition could be reflected in a managerial risk aversion which reinforces pressures towards short-termism. Post-audit can also be a costly, time-consuming exercise, and, given the strategic implications of the audit's subject-matter, we may be committing scarce resources to little or no good effect unless the post-audit can adequately reflect these. Once a capital investment project is under way, its ramifications might be so wide that it is virtually impossible to identify related costs and benefits (let alone quantify them). Similarly, post-audit must recognise the possibility of a lengthy time lapse between project inception and proper appreciation of its consequences.

SUMMARY

In this chapter, we have discussed techniques for financial evaluation of capital investment proposals and have seen that:

■ Appraisal of capital investment proposals should be linked to overall organisational strategy.

■ **Accounting rate of return** is measured as:

SELF-TEST QUESTIONS

10.1 For each of the following statements, tick the appropriate box to indicate whether it is true or false:

		True	False
(a)	The higher the cost of capital used to discount a proposal's cash flows, the higher will be that proposal's net present value.	☐	☐
(b)	A short payback period indicates quick recovery of a proposal's initial cost.	☐	☐
(c)	Use of initial capital cost to determine a proposal's accounting rate of return will yield a lower return than use of average capital cost for the same proposal.	☐	☐
(d)	Annual profit arising from a proposal can be determined by adding depreciation to the proposal's cash flows.	☐	☐

(e) Average capital cost can be defined as

$$\frac{(\text{initial capital cost} - \text{resale value})}{2}$$

☐ ☐

(f) £1 received three years from now has a higher present value than £1 received five years from now. ☐ ☐

(g) The same cash sum received each year for 15 years is termed an annuity. ☐ ☐

(h) A proposal which has several changes from annual cash inflow to cash outflow over its life will have a single internal rate of return. ☐ ☐

10.2 Using Appendix B, calculate the present value of:

(a) £750,000 receivable at the end of 7 years from now at a cost of capital of 6 per cent;

(b) £20,000 payable each year for 15 years at a cost of capital of 14 per cent;

(c) £250,000 payable immediately;

(d) £8,000 receivable at the end of each year for 8 years at a cost of capital of 20 per cent;

(e) £12,000 receivable at the end of 10 years from now at a cost of capital of 18 per cent.

10.3 EP Ltd is considering the purchase of a new press for its printing business. This will have an initial cost of £110,000, an estimated life of 12 years and a resale value of £6,000 at the end of its life. The additional annual profit which will be earned if the new press is bought is as follows:

	Per year (£)
Years 1–4	12,000
Years 5–8	16,000
Years 9–12	20,000

The company's cost of capital is 20 per cent.

Requirement
Determine the new printing press's accounting rate of return based on:

(a) initial capital cost; and

(b) average capital cost.

For each accounting rate of return calculated, advise the company as to the acceptability of the proposal, commenting on the results.

10.4 CH & Co, a coach hire firm, is expanding its fleet of vehicles. The firm has a target payback period of three years and each new coach purchased has a five-year lifespan, with the following associated cash flows:

	£
Initial cost	60,000
Net cash inflows:	
Year 1	15,000
Year 2	20,000
Year 3	20,000
Year 4	24,000
Year 5	26,000

Requirement
Determine the payback period for a new coach and advise CH & Co on its acceptability.

10.5 AB Ltd specialises in installation of burglar alarms at clients' premises and wishes to acquire new installation equipment. Relevant details are as follows:

Initial cost of equipment	£80,000
Estimated useful life	5 years
Estimated annual net cash inflow in each of Years 1–5	£20,000
Estimated resale value at end of Year 5	£3,000

The company's cost of capital is 10 per cent.

Requirement
Determine the new equipment's net present value and on that basis advise the company on the financial desirability of its acquisition.

QUESTIONS WITH ANSWERS

10.6 This question tests whether you can:

- calculate a proposal's net present value;
- approximate its internal rate of return; and
- provide appropriate financial advice, explaining which criterion is preferable and why.

  A local college wishes to purchase its own minibus, as it is felt that this will be cheaper than hiring vehicles as and when required. The following information is available:

Estimated life	4 years
	£
Purchase cost	22,000
Annual saving in vehicle hire costs:	
Year 1	6,000
Year 2	10,000
Year 3	15,000
Year 4	15,000
Estimated resale value at end of Year 4	2,000

Purchase of the minibus will, however, incur annual running costs amounting to £3,000 in each of Years 1 and 2, £3,800 in Year 3 and £4,400 in Year 4. The college's cost of capital is 8 per cent.

Requirements

(a) What is the net present value of the cash flows associated with purchase of a new minibus?

(b) Provide an approximation of the proposal's internal rate of return.

(c) Advise the college on the acceptability of the proposal.

(d) The college's Principal advocates use of internal rate of return to evaluate capital investment proposals. The Finance Officer disagrees, claiming that net present value is superior. Draft a brief report to the Principal explaining which criterion is preferable and why.

10.7 This question tests whether you can:

■ calculate a capital investment proposal's payback, net present value and internal rate of return;

■ convert proposal cash flows into profit to determine accounting rate of return;

■ provide financial advice based on these calculations; and

■ explain the concept of the time value of money.

A firm of dry cleaners is assessing the acquisition of new cleaning equipment, details of which are given below.

Estimated useful life	6 years
	£
Initial cost	260,000
Net cash inflows:	
Year 1	40,000
Year 2	50,000
Year 3	70,000
Year 4	90,000
Year 5	60,000
Year 6	10,000
Estimated resale value at the end of Year 6	20,000
Annual depreciation	40,000

In addition to the net cash inflows listed above, purchase of the new equipment will allow sale of existing equipment. This will occur at the end of Year 1, the cash proceeds being £2,000.

The dry cleaning firm has a 15% cost of capital and a maximum acceptable payback period of five years.

Requirements

(a) Determine the new equipment's payback, net present value and internal rate of return.

(b) Convert the proposal's annual net cash inflows to profit and determine the accounting rate of return. (Include the sale proceeds of the existing equipment in your Year 1 calculation.)

(c) Based on your calculations in (a) and (b), advise the firm as to its best course of action on financial grounds, explaining the reasoning behind your advice.

(d) Explain why it could be argued that the calculation of payback and accounting rate of return is based on an invalid assumption about the value of associated monetary amounts.

10.8 This question tests whether you can:

■ assess the net present value and payback of two mutually exclusive capital investments; and

■ explain any conflict between the two criteria, basing your financial advice on this explanation.

PTK Ltd is a manufacturer of power tools and has decided to renew outdated production machinery at one of its plants. This machinery cost £200,000 eight years ago and has no current scrap value, but will cost £10,000 to remove, payable now.

Two mutually exclusive replacement options are possible:

	Option A	Option B
Estimated life	6 years	6 years
	£	£
Initial cost (payable immediately).	400,000	640,000
Net cash inflows:		
Year 1	180,000	50,000
Year 2	140,000	50,000
Year 3	120,000	150,000
Year 4	80,000	200,000
Year 5	80,000	320,000
Year 6	40,000	430,000

The company's cost of capital is 12 per cent.

Requirements

(a) For *each* option, calculate:
   (i) its net present value; and
   (ii) its payback period.

(b) Explain why the two criteria calculated in (a) give different indications about the acceptability of the two options and advise PTK Ltd as to its best course of action.

10.9 This question tests whether you can:

■ determine the differential cash flows for a proposed capital investment proposal;

■ obtain the NPV of these differential cash flows;

■ provide advice as to the best course of action based on NPV; and

■ state examples of qualitative information which may be relevant to the decision in question.

A local authority's Fire Service is considering replacement of a turntable ladder which, although still serviceable, has steeply rising maintenance costs, and it is thought that a replacement will prove less expensive in the long term. The purchase cost of a new turntable ladder will be £360,000 – half payable immediately and half one year from now. The following information is available:

	Existing	Replacement
Estimated useful life	8 years	8 years
Estimated maintenance costs:		
	£	£
Year 1	40,000	10,000
Year 2	45,000	10,000
Year 3	50,000	14,000
Year 4	60,000	15,000
Year 5	72,000	18,000
Year 6	80,000	18,000
Year 7	90,000	20,000
Year 8	98,000	22,000
Full overhauls:		
Year 2	5,000	
Year 4	10,000	4,000
Year 6	14,000	
Estimated resale value:		
Now	10,000	
Year 8	1,000	8,000

The local authority applies a cost of capital of 5 per cent in evaluating capital investment proposals.

Requirements

(a) Calculate the net present value of the differential cash flows attaching to purchase of the new turntable ladder and, on that basis, advise the local authority as to the best course of action.

(b) State *three* qualitative factors which may be relevant to the final decision, providing a brief explanation of the significance of each.

10.10 This question tests whether you can:

■ apply the concept of relevance in determination of a capital investment project's cash flows and calculation of its net present value; and

- provide financial advice about the best course of action, along with an assessment of relevant qualitative factors.

A large supermarket presently operates a subsidised canteen for the benefit of its staff, but, due to its continual failure to break even, management is considering subcontracting canteen provision to an external caterer. The subsidised canteen's annual operating statement for the year just ended is as follows:

	£	£
Income		20,000
less:		
Cost of food purchases	19,200	
Power for equipment	3,000	
Depreciation of equipment	8,800	
Apportionment of general overheads	12,000	43,000
Net loss		23,000

Projections for the next four years indicate that the above figures will increase as follows:

Income	£2,000 per year
Food and power costs	£800 per year *each*
Apportionments of general overhead	£1,500 per year
Depreciation of equipment	no change

If canteen provision is subcontracted, two full-time members of the supermarket's staff will be made redundant at a cost of £12,000, payable immediately.

An outside caterer has offered to provide canteen facilities within the supermarket for the next four years. The caterer would receive all the income from operation of the canteen, would meet all the related operating costs, and would pay the supermarket £6,000 per annum rent for use of the existing canteen facilities within the supermarket's premises (which have no foreseeable alternative use). The supermarket's cost of capital is 12 per cent.

Requirements

(a) Assess the acceptability of the proposal to subcontract canteen provision, using net present value as the criterion.

(b) What areas of non-financial concern should be brought to management's attention before a final decision is reached?

QUESTIONS WITHOUT ANSWERS

10.11 In a bid to increase its market share, BFG Ltd, a retail supplier of domestic appliances, is assessing the desirability of opening a prestigious new showroom in a locale where the company has not previously operated. The following information is available:

Appraisal criteria
The appropriate cost of capital for this proposal is 22 per cent and the maximum acceptable payback period is four years. Although the proposed new showroom has a useful life which is estimated to be in excess of 20 years, BFG Ltd has placed a maxi-

mum time horizon of 10 years on the appraisal, as the directors believe that estimates relating to periods beyond this limit will be too uncertain for meaningful incorporation into the evaluation.

Initial cost of premises and annual depreciation
The new showroom will cost £1,300,000 to purchase, 50 per cent of which is payable immediately, with the balance being payable in five equal instalments at the end of each of Years 1–5 inclusive. Following the company's normal accounting procedures, depreciation on the showroom will be provided at an annual rate of 2 per cent of its purchase cost.

Estimated financial results
If the new showroom is acquired, estimated summary profit statements are as follows:

	Years			
	1–3	*4 and 5*	*6 and 7*	*8–10*
	(£000)	*(£000)*	*(£000)*	*(£000)*
Sales	600	1,000	1,250	1,400
less Operating costs	480	725	914	1,010
Depreciation	26	26	26	26
Profit	94	249	310	364

Requirements

(a) In respect of the proposal to open the new showroom, calculate the following:
   (i) accounting rate of return based on initial capital cost;
   (ii) payback;
   (iii) net present value; and
   (iv) internal rate of return.

(b) Critically compare the use of discounting and non-discounting techniques in appraisal of capital investment projects.

(c) Advise BFG Ltd as to its best course of action on financial grounds.

10.12 KG (Construction) plc is considering tendering for a major road construction project. The main portion of the work will last five years, but, due to the nature of the job, certain associated costs and revenues will arise after this period. Details of the project are given below.

Tender price and progress payments
Company management believes that a tender of £38 million is likely to prove successful in obtaining the work. The client – a consortium of local authorities and central government – will make progress payments of £7 million at the end of each of Years 1–5 inclusive, the balance being paid at the end of Year 6.

Capital costs
KG plc will require to purchase £5m of new plant and equipment – £3.6m to be paid immediately, the balance after one year.

Materials' costs
Estimated materials' costs each year are:

	£m
Year 1:	2.4
Year 2:	2.9
Year 3:	4.2
Year 4:	2.7
Year 5:	1.8

Of the estimated materials' requirement in Year 1, £0.6 million is already owned by KG plc, having been purchased some time ago for another job which was not completed. If not used on the road project under consideration, these materials could be used on another job, thereby saving the company purchases of £0.9 million. All other materials for the road project will need to be specially purchased.

Labour requirements
A total direct labour cost of £1 million is anticipated in Year 1, rising by £0.2 million in each of Years 2–5 inclusive. Of these labour costs, 10 per cent relates to 'core' workers who are permanently employed by KG Ltd and, if not used on this road project, would be carrying out minor rectification work on other completed jobs. Use of the core workers on the road project will necessitate subcontracting the rectification work at a cost of £50,000 per annum to KG Ltd in each of Years 1–5. Labour requirements other than the core workers will be met by short-term or casual employment as required.

Apportionment of general company costs
If the tender is successful, the road project will receive an apportionment of £2 million per year to cover Head Office and general administrative costs.

Sundry costs
These include plant hire, engineers' and surveyors' fees, fixed costs specifically attributable to the road project, depreciation, and rectification work, and are estimated at the following amounts:

	£m
Year 1:	3.0
Year 2:	2.0
Year 3:	2.5
Year 4:	1.3
Year 5:	1.1
Year 6:	0.8
Year 7:	0.7
Year 8:	0.2

The sums quoted above for each of Years 1–5 include £0.4 million for depreciation.

KG plc's cost of capital is 18 per cent and the company uses net present value to assess capital investment proposals.

Requirement
Draft a report to the directors of KG plc advising on the financial desirability of submitting the tender. Include supporting calculations, state any assumptions made, and indicate any qualitative factors which you feel may be relevant to the directors' assessment of the situation.

10.13 The Education Department of Holmforth City Council operates six careers offices at various locations across the city. These offices are widely dispersed geographically and are controlled from Education Department offices in the centre of town. At present, the system of providing information to schools and individuals is as follows:

■ Careers Officers from the appropriate local office make twice-yearly visits to each Secondary School within the council's authority, each visit consisting of a presentation to senior pupils followed by individual interviews. On average, each of these visits requires the equivalent of three full days of a Careers Officer's time. Further interviews at the careers office are arranged at the request of pupils wishing additional information.

■ Careers offices must also deal with ad hoc enquiries from school-leavers, their parents and prospective employers. When relevant information is not available at the specific office handling the enquiry, a telephone request is made to Careers Service central office, which will then either supply the requisite information itself or will phone round the other local offices to obtain it. All requests for information made to external organisations must be handled by central office.

At the last meeting of the council's Education Committee, councillors were concerned about the antiquated approach being taken by the Careers Service. In particular, worry was expressed about frequent delays in providing information which was quite often

---

Holmforth Education Department: Careers Service

Three viable options for improving the quality of response have been identified. Each involves computer networking and, regardless of which option (if any) is implemented, it is proposed that it be run in parallel with the present system. The options and the results of their appraisal are as follows:

	Option 1	Option 2	Option 3
Initial cost of hardware and software	£120,000	£100,000	£150,000
Theoretical life	10 years	8 years	15 years
Estimated operational life	5 years	5 years	5 years
Net present value (initial cost against annual cost savings over estimated operational life)	£16,000	£20,000	£24,000
Internal rate of return over estimated operational life	12%	16%	10%
Recommended period of parallel running	1 year	6 months	3 months
Staffing implications over 5 years	+ 2	neutral	– 3
Staff training required:			
in-house?	Yes	Yes	Yes
external?	No	No	Yes
Internet site?	Yes	No	Yes
Post-implementation review after	1 year	6 months	3 months

All discounting calculations have been based on Holmforth City Council's required rate of return of 6 per cent.

EXHIBIT **10.8 Appraisal of Careers Service options**

out of date, an increasing volume of complaints about the quality of service being provided, and the increasingly widely held view that the careers service was 'a farce'. Against this background, the Director of Education commissioned a report from external consultants (at a cost of £10,000) about options for improving the situation, and the related financial implications. This report has now been received and a summary of its key points is given in Exhibit 10.8.

Having read the consultants' report, the Director of Education is uncertain about which option (if any) she should recommend to the next meeting of the Education Committee, and has asked you, as Assistant Director, for your advice.

Requirement
Prepare a report for the Director of Education which discusses what you consider to be the main financial and non-financial issues arising from the situation.

11

Capital investment appraisal: further issues

EXHIBIT **11.1 Some sources of funds for capital investment projects**

INTRODUCTION

In the last chapter, we discussed the financial mechanics of capital investment appraisal and of net present value in particular. We must now extend our discussion to cover some very important associated issues. First, where might an organisation obtain the often substantial funds necessary to undertake a capital investment proposal? Some possible sources are mentioned in Exhibit 11.1, but there are others, each with its potential advantages and disadvantages. Second, the cost of capital (discount rate) is central to discounted cash flow calculations: for example, a proposal may have a positive net present value at a 15 per cent discount rate but a negative net present value at 20 per cent. Since the cost of capital can have a major bearing on the acceptability of proposals, its derivation and associated problems must be appreciated

OBJECTIVES

When you have completed this chapter, you will be able to:

- describe the main sources of finance available for capital investment projects along with the attractions and drawbacks of each;

- appreciate the meaning of gearing, the possible benefit and risk to ordinary shareholders which could result, and calculate the gearing ratio;

- calculate the cost of ordinary shares based on constant future dividends and on a constant expected future growth rate in dividends;

- discuss the arguments in favour of and against use of dividend-based approaches to the cost of ordinary shares;

- appreciate the broad workings of portfolio theory and distinguish between systematic and unsystematic risk;

- apply the capital asset pricing model to determine the cost of a company's ordinary shares and discuss the strengths and weaknesses of this approach;

- use regression analysis to estimate beta for a company's ordinary shares;

- determine the cost of preference shares assuming these to be irredeemable and the cost of redeemable and irredeemable debentures;

- derive a company's weighted average cost of capital based on both balance sheet and market values of capital;

- explain the arguments for and against use of the weighted average cost of capital as a discount rate in capital investment appraisal; and

- understand the application and problems of cost/benefit and cost-effectiveness analysis relative to public sector and non-profit capital investment projects.

SOURCES OF FINANCE

As we saw in the last chapter, the amount of finance necessary for capital investment projects can frequently be considerable. We therefore need to examine the main sources from which an organisation might obtain such finance. Table 11.1, an extract from the Central Statistical Office's *Financial Statistics* (1994), shows the sources of funds for industrial and commercial companies.

TABLE **11.1 Sources of company finance**

Sources	1988 (£bn)	1989 (£bn)	1990 (£bn)	1991 (£bn)	1992 (£bn)	1993 (£bn)
Retained profit	44	29	36	36	34	51
Bank borrowing	31	33	19	(3)	(2)	(12)
Issue of ordinary shares	4	2	3	10	5	14
Debentures and preference shares	4	6	3	5	2	3
Other	6	16	12	12	16	23
	89	86	73	60	55	79

The basic principle which should guide decisions about the source of funding is that the term of the funding should match the term of the asset(s) being funded that is, a source of short-term finance such as a bank overdraft should not be used to finance acquisition of fixed assets, since the operational life of these will almost certainly exceed the time span of the overdraft and they will therefore require to be refinanced (possibly at increased cost). We shall therefore confine our discussion to sources of long-term finance, since our concern is with funding capital investment proposals.

Retained profit

Virtually every profit-making organisation will distribute (e.g. by way of dividend) only a part of annual profit. The remainder will be retained within the business for purposes such as financing expansion or the purchase of new fixed assets. The predominance of retained profit as a source of finance is evident from Table 11.1. The major attraction of retained profit is its controllability by the organisation: that is, a lack of external restriction of the sort which might be attached to a loan, or a potential shift in the balance of shareholder voting power which could accompany an issue of ordinary shares. In addition, there are no issue costs associated with use of retained profit (as there would be in the case of an issue of shares or debentures), nor is there the necessity to pay dividends or interest – but, as we shall see, this is not to say that no cost is involved. There may, however, be some problems.

Retained profit does not necessarily equate with cash availability

The availability of large reserves of retained profit does not necessarily guarantee the availability of sufficient cash to undertake a capital investment project.

⇨ Why are retained profit and cash balances unlikely to be the same?

Accounting profit is not determined on a cash basis, but on an *accruals* basis: that is, sales and expenses are included in the accounts when cash is *due* to be received/paid, rather than when it actually *is*. Some non-cash items are also involved in calculation of accounting profit: depreciation, for example (which may be a large amount in many organisations' accounts) or a provision for doubtful debts. So although sufficient retained profit (as reflected on a company's balance sheet) may exist for a particular project, raising cash could still be necessary before the project can proceed: for example, by realising (selling) surplus assets, or by some other means.

Misconception that retained profit is a 'free' source of funding

Because use of retained profit involves no issue costs, and already exists within the company, management might be tempted to believe that this is a 'free' source of finance.

⇨ What is the danger of believing that retained profit is a 'free' source of finance?

If management believes that retained profit is somehow 'free', there may be a danger that such funds will be used in projects offering suboptimal returns, or that normally stringent appraisal criteria might be relaxed. However, retained profit is not 'free'. At the very least, there will be an opportunity cost attached to its use: that is, we need to recognise the fact that by using retained profit to fund a particular proposal, we cannot use it to fund the best alternative, and the 'lost' return on this best alternative must be allowed for in appraisal. The expectations of the business's owners must be considered. In a limited company, for example, retained profit is the 'property' of the shareholders (i.e. owners), who will either expect it to fund dividend payments or to be reinvested to yield a minimum return. If one or other does not occur, there is every likelihood of shareholdings being sold, which may severely depress a company's market value and might, in extreme circumstances, cause a crisis of confidence in that company.

Bank borrowing

The kind of borrowing principally involved here is **term loans**: that is, loans made for a fixed period of time ('term'), sometimes at a fixed rate of interest, sometimes at a rate which fluctuates in line with changes in the market rate of interest. Banks are a readily accessible source of finance and, although interest must be paid, issue costs are minimal (although an 'arrangement fee' is often charged) and interest payments (unlike dividends) qualify as a tax-deductible expense. And, for many organisations (e.g. businesses which are not limited companies), little or no practical alternative to bank finance may be available. Despite these advantages, Table 11.1 indicates a marked decline in the popularity of bank borrowing as a source of finance between 1988 and 1993. This may have been due to a combination of factors: a tightening of banks' lending criteria; imposition of greater restrictions on the use of borrowed funds; interest rate movements; and a decline in the general economic situation.

Despite its importance as a potential source of funding, bank borrowing by UK companies has largely been confined to short and medium-term loans. In contrast, bank borrowing is predominantly long-term in countries such as Germany and Japan, with bank representation at board level being common. It is possible that banks' more proactive and long-term involvement in these countries has had a positive effect on capital investment decisions.

Issue of shares and debentures: some general points

Before we consider issue of shares and debentures as a possible source of finance, it is worth noting that the Companies' Act 1985 permits only a *public* limited company (plc) to offer its shares and debentures for sale to the general public in the United Kingdom. A plc must have minimum authorised share capital of £50,000 and must state (in the documentation associated with its formation, constitution and registration) that it is a public limited company. In addition, public companies which have, or wish to apply for, a 'full' listing on the London Stock Exchange must be of sufficient size to ensure the marketability of their securities. What all this means is that the majority of businesses – smaller plcs, private limited companies, partnerships and sole traders – have fewer options as to the sources of capital funding.

Where a company's securities (shares and debentures) are available for purchase/sale, we need to distinguish between their **nominal** (or *par*) **value**, their issue price and their market value.

1 *Nominal value* This is the face value of shares/debentures (e.g. ordinary shares of £1 each).
2 *Issue price* This is the price at which a company issues (i.e. 'sells') securities to investors, and is often in excess of their nominal value. Where shares/debentures are issued at a price in excess of their nominal value, they are said to be issued 'at a premium'. Issue of shares at less than nominal value (at a discount) is illegal in the United Kingdom; debentures may be issued at a discount.
3 *Market value* When a company's securities are available for purchase/sale (e.g. via the Stock Exchange), their value is essentially determined by the supply/demand relationship for the securities concerned, and, in the case of debentures, by their interest rate relative to the current market rate. Strength of supply/demand in a particular company's shares/debentures is largely a reflection of investors' expectations about future company performance, interest rates and general market conditions.

Issue of ordinary shares

Ordinary shareholders are effectively the 'owners' of a limited company, being entitled to vote at company meetings and to share in the distribution of assets should the company be wound up. The normal procedure for an existing company (like Shaftesbury in Exhibit 11.1) wishing to raise funds in this way is to make a **rights issue**, whereby existing shareholders have a 'right' to buy the new shares being issued. The new shares will be offered to existing shareholders in proportion to their present shareholding: for instance, a company making a 'one-for-five' rights issue will issue one new share for each five existing shares. If current shareholders do not wish to take up their new shares, then the 'rights' may be sold, either to other current shareholders, or to new purchasers. Compared to an issue of debentures or preference shares on the open market, a rights issue could have lower issue costs and may raise funds rather more quickly, without imposing undue restrictions on the operational use of these funds. Moreover, in extreme situations, dividend payments may be reduced (or withheld entirely) – something not normally possible with debenture interest or preference dividends.

However, a significant time lag will exist between the decision to make a rights issue and receipt of the associated cash. In addition, the balance of voting power may shift in the event that a significant number of existing shareholders decline to exercise their rights, and, where the number doing so is especially high, confidence in the company may be damaged. The success of a rights issue will depend on investors' views about the company's future performance, and this could result in the paradoxical situation that those companies most in need of a successful rights issue (i.e. whose performance is, or is perceived to be, poor) are those least able to obtain the required funds by this method.

Debentures and preference shares

A **debenture** is the term applied to a loan made to a limited company under the company's seal and would normally be raised from investors other than banks. For convenience, debentures are often subdivided into 'stock' units: for example, 15 per cent debentures with a total face value of £500,000 could be subdivided into 5,000 units of 15 per cent debenture stock, each with a face value of £100. From the company's point of view, debentures could be attractive because the balance of voting power is not affected by their issue (debenture holders do not normally have a vote at company meetings), the interest rate is generally fixed for the life of the loan, and interest payments qualify as tax-deductible expenses. Interest payable on debentures is based on their nominal value: for example, 10% debenture stock with a nominal value of £100 and a market value of £102 would pay annual interest of (10% × £100) = £10 (known as the **coupon rate**). In addition, issue costs associated with debentures can be fairly low, since a large part of debenture issues is often 'taken up' by a pre-arranged consortium of institutional investors.

However, although debenture holders do not usually exercise a vote at company meetings, they may nevertheless exert some influence over operations. Debentures are generally *secured* against some/all of the company's assets and this security will restrict the company's use of the relevant assets: for example, they may not be sold without the prior consent of the debenture holders. And, unlike dividends on ordinary shares (a matter of company policy), debenture interest must be paid as a matter of contractual obligation.

⤷ What problem might the obligation to pay debenture interest pose for a company?

If the company has insufficient cash to meet interest payments, then these must be 'financed' in some other way: for example, by reducing dividends to ordinary shareholders, or by further borrowing. It may even be necessary to negotiate a suspension of interest payments, which might, if repeated, prompt the debenture holders to *foreclose*: that is, to require repayment of the entire debt before its due term – with dire consequences for the company concerned. This aspect of debentures will be examined in more detail shortly.

Preference shares – as the name suggests – carry the right to preferential payment of dividends compared to ordinary shares: that is, preference dividends will be paid first out of available profit. From the company's standpoint, preference shares have the advantages of paying a fixed dividend (compared to fluctuating ordinary dividends) and of conferring no voting rights on their holders. Preference dividends, like debenture interest, are based on the share's nominal value, so a 15 per cent preference share with a £1 nominal value will pay a fixed annual dividend of £0.15.

But although a company may be able to defer payment of preference dividends more readily than debenture interest, preference shares are usually *cumulative*: that is, any unpaid dividends accumulate until the company is in a position to pay them, which may have serious implications for cash resources. And, unlike debenture interest, preference dividends are not a tax-deductible expense for the company.

Debentures and preference shares are often *convertible*: that is, may be converted into ordinary shares, subject to conditions specified at the time of issue. This may be attractive to investors because, if they believe that the company will perform well, dividends on ordinary shares may turn out to be higher than debenture interest or preference dividend. This may offer the company slightly more flexibility in negotiation of the terms of a debenture or preference share issue and, in the case of a debenture issue, might substantially reduce the final amount which has to be repaid to lenders.

We need to appreciate one final point, that the time and cost associated with issues of shares and debentures can be significant. The former should be borne in mind in deciding the timing of capital investments and the latter when assessing the amount of funds required for a particular proposal.

Other sources of finance

As Table 11.1 suggests, the significance of 'other sources' has, in recent years, increased to the point where these are second only to retained profit. The problem is that 'other sources' describes a wide range of different sources, so we shall deal here only with the more commonly encountered.

Divestment/disposal

In Exhibit 11.1, Shaftesbury plans to raise £20.7m from divestments and disposals. The attraction of this approach, like use of retained profit, is that management can control events to a much greater degree than would be possible if funds were raised by borrowing, or issue of shares/debentures, and compared to these methods, the costs involved are likely to be less. However, the organisation will lose ownership of potentially valuable assets, and there is a possibility that strategic interests could be harmed if disposals/divestments are misjudged. This may be particularly true where planned disposals fail to raise the desired level of funds (perhaps necessitating further disposals), or where circumstances are volatile.

Mortgages, and sale and leaseback arrangements

When an organisation owns premises, or is considering their purchase, a mortgage may be arranged, typically over 25 years and secured on the property concerned. A sale and leaseback arrangement involves the sale by an organisation of property which it owns and on which the seller then takes a long term lease from the purchaser (e.g. for 99 years). Both of these sources have the advantage of making funds available relatively quickly and at low cost, but mortgage instalments and lease payments (like loan interest) must be paid as a matter of contractual obligation, which might lead to cash flow problems. In addition, the terms of a mortgage will restrict disposal and possibly use of the property secured, whilst sale and leaseback effectively means that the organisation forfeits ownership of a valuable asset.

Leasing and hire purchase

The two principal forms of lease are the *operating lease* and the *finance lease*. In both cases, the lessor, in return for the lease payment, permits the lessee to use an asset (or assets) which are legally the lessor's property.

Under an operating lease, the lessor is usually the supplier or manufacturer of the asset, with the lease running for a period shorter than the asset's economic life and maintenance being provided by the lessor. Operating leases may be attractive in respect of assets with a short technological life span (e.g. computing equipment). This would help avoid the danger of organisations making large capital outlays on assets which may become obsolete well before the end of their theoretical working lives.

A finance lease, on the other hand, will normally involve a specialist finance house providing the funding necessary to allow the lessor to acquire the desired asset, the lease more or less spanning the asset's estimated life and the lessee providing any necessary maintenance. At the end of the lease, the lessee will normally have the option either to buy the asset for a reduced price, to continue the lease at a greatly reduced ('peppercorn') payment, or to sell the asset on the lessor's behalf with the proceeds being split between lessor and lessee.

Hire purchase (HP) agreements differ from leases in that, at the end of the hire period (i.e. when all the instalments have been paid), the asset becomes the legal property of the purchaser. Leases and HP agreements offer speed and convenience as methods of funding capital projects. In addition, organisations are saved the need to obtain sizeable 'one-off' amounts of capital funding since cost will be spread via the instalment scheme. But serious default in lease or HP payments could result in the lessor/hirer repossessing the asset(s) concerned, and lease/HP agreements may place unacceptable limitations on operational use of the relevant asset(s).

Venture capital providers

A number of institutional investors, or investment syndicates backed by institutions, aim to provide 'venture capital' (i.e. capital funding) to new and existing businesses. Investment trusts such as Electra Risk Capital, the 3i Group and Equity Capital for Industry specialise in venture capital provision. In most cases, the provider of capital will become a shareholder in the business and/or obtain management representation (e.g. at board level). Smaller companies may also use the Alternative Investment Market (AIM) to raise funds; AIM is a public market operated by the London Stock Exchange with the objectives of providing newer, smaller and expanding businesses with a source of extra capital and with a forum for wider trading of their shares.

In addition to the general sources of finance which we have been describing, certain types or classes of capital investment may be eligible for subsidy or grant aid.

Grants and subsidies

A range of financial assistance is available from local and central government, and from the European Community, of which the following are some examples applicable in the UK:

- *The Enterprise Initiative* Operated by the Department of Trade and Industry, this offers various financial and other assistance to small businesses.
- *Loan Guarantee Scheme* Provides a Government guarantee against default on loans of up to £100,000 made to small businesses.
- *Inner cities* Various forms of assistance are available in inner cities: for example, help for small firms may be obtained from Urban Development Corporations.
- *Enterprise Allowance Scheme* Provides aid to unemployed persons wishing to set up their own businesses by making a weekly allowance during the first year's operation.
- *Enterprise Zones* To facilitate investment, these zones (currently 19) are free from non-domestic rates and subject to greatly simplified planning controls.
- *Regional Selective Assistance* This most commonly takes the form of *project grants*: that is, grants which are based on the cost of a specific project and the number of jobs it is expected to create. It is also possible to obtain, from the European Investment Bank, loans of up to half the cost of specific projects to create/safeguard jobs within designated 'assisted areas'.

In addition to the sort of 'active' assistance of which we give examples above, government may also provide more 'passive' assistance, particularly in the form of tax incentives for capital investment. For instance, exemption from non-domestic rates within Enterprise Zones is a tax concession on the part of local government; and central government may provide an incentive by allowing automatic tax-deductibility of certain expenditures (e.g. health and safety), or by making tax allowance for capital expenditure at the start of the asset's life (rather than spreading such allowance over the asset's life).

Advantageous though such sources undoubtedly are, they will generally only cover a limited proportion of the capital investment necessary: for example, under the Enterprise Allowance Scheme, unemployed persons must invest at least £1,000 of their own in the business before qualifying for the weekly allowance. In addition, the procedures necessary to obtain certain forms of assistance may be so cumbersome, and the conditions attached to its receipt so stringent, as to discourage some businesses from applying. There have also been instances where organisations have undertaken capital investment programmes simply as a means of obtaining some additional benefit from the assistance offered: for example, purchase of new assets to obtain tax allowances and reduce corporate tax liability. Decisions made on this basis are unlikely to be consistent with strategic organisational interests or the intention of government economic policy.

Public sector and non-profit capital sources

Public sector organisations may raise funds for capital investment projects in a number of ways: for example, by using reserves, by borrowing, by imposing taxes such as corporation and council taxes (central and local government respectively), or by receiving grant aid from central government and the European Community. However, the fund-raising powers of public sector organisations are strictly controlled: the use of reserves by local authorities, for example, is subject to central government regulation, as are their tax-raising and borrowing powers. Two fairly recent UK developments in this general area are worth mentioning: the impact of the National Lottery and the Private Finance Initiative (PFI). Both of these developments have stemmed partly from a growing awareness of the fact that the more 'traditional' sources of finance for public sector and non-profit organisations are finite in amount but are nevertheless subject to increasing demands, and partly from a political desire to limit state involvement. This last factor can be seen in the progressive removal from the state-funded sector of various organisations (e.g. the rail network) and the introduction of compulsory competitive tendering of services previously solely in the public domain.

As well as providing a profit for its operators (and tempting cash prizes for participants), the National Lottery also provides funds for 'good causes'. Many public sector and non-profit organisations have successfully applied for funding from National Lottery sources: for example, some £30 million has been earmarked from the 'millennium fund' to help in the development of a new University of the Highlands. Despite the usefulness of such grants, their receipt is not guaranteed – organisations must make a case for lottery funding – and, because of the high publicity profile of the National Lottery, some awards have (and could) attract criticism, which can only be undesirable from the recipient's point of view. Lottery funding also leaves unanswered the question of ongoing operating costs – a one-off grant is unlikely to provide for these to any significant extent (if at all).

The Private Finance Initiative (PFI) was introduced with the objective of involving private organisations in the funding of public projects such as road-building. This kind of public/private partnership, it is hoped, will reduce the call on scarce government funding, whilst at the same time providing a return on the private finance injected. To date, the PFI has been less successful than anticipated – partly because many public projects cannot offer an acceptable commercial return and partly because commercial firms view the PFI as administratively unwieldy.

GEARING

Bearing in mind that the ordinary shareholders are the company's 'owners', their interests should have a major influence on any decision about sources of finance. We mentioned earlier that debenture (and other loan) interest is a tax-deductible expense as far as the borrowing company is concerned. Compared to financing in some other ways, this may provide a benefit to ordinary shareholders in terms of the amount of profit available to them. We will use the information from Exhibit 11.2 to illustrate.

JKM plc

The company, which operates a nationwide chain of DIY retail superstores, is deciding how to finance a proposed capital expenditure project. Details are as follows:

■ capital funds to be raised: £10 million
■ alternative funding sources:
  – issue, at nominal value, of 10 million 10 per cent £1 preference shares; or
  – issue of £10 million of 10 per cent debenture stock.

Over the life of the proposed project, additional annual profit could be as high as £2 million, but might fall as low as £500,000. It is expected that, over the project's life, JKM plc's profit will be liable to corporation tax at a rate of 40 per cent.

EXHIBIT **11.2 Alternative sources of funds and company gearing**

Assuming that the best estimate for additional annual profit eventuates, we can calculate the amount of this available to ordinary shareholders under each financing option:

Finance by issue of preference shares

	£
Additional profit before taxation	2,000,000
less Corporation tax @ 40%	800,000
Additional profit after taxation	1,200,000
less Preference dividend (10% × £10 million)	1,000,000
Additional profit available for ordinary shareholders	200,000

Finance by issue of debentures

	£
Additional profit before taxation	2,000,000
less Debenture interest (10% × £10 million)	1,000,000
Additional profit subject to taxation	1,000,000
less Corporation tax @ 40%	400,000
Additional profit available for ordinary shareholders	600,000

From the ordinary shareholders' standpoint, financing the proposal by means of debentures is clearly very advantageous – *if* the additional profit is high.

⇨ How much additional profit would be available for ordinary shareholders if the additional annual profit earned were only £500,000, assuming the project to have been financed by £10 million of 10 per cent debentures?

Inserting the revised additional profit figure into our calculation gives:

	£
Additional profit before taxation	500,000
less Debenture interest (10% × £10 million)	1,000,000
Additional loss subject to taxation	(500,000)
add Corporation tax allowance on loss @ 40%	200,000
Reduction in profit available for ordinary shareholders	(300,000)

365

Because additional profit generated by the proposed capital investment is insufficient to cover interest on the debentures, the ordinary shareholders are now worse off than they would have been had the project not been invested in. If allowed to continue for any length of time, such a situation could have serious repercussions for JKM plc, possibly even culminating in the company's liquidation – in which event, the chance of ordinary shareholders receiving any residual payment will be considerably lessened by the need to first repay the debenture holders in addition to other creditors of the company.

The existence in a company's capital structure of **prior charge capital** – that is, capital such as debentures and preference shares which take precedence over ordinary shares for payment/repayment – is referred to as **gearing** (or **leverage**) and can be measured using the **gearing ratio**:

$$\frac{\text{prior charge capital}}{\text{all long term capital} + \text{reserves}}$$

Suppose JKM plc's capital without the proposed new investment is £75 million, of which £30 million is prior charge capital. The company's gearing ratio is

$$\frac{\text{£30 million}}{\text{£75 million}} = 0.4.$$

In other words, 40 per cent of JKM plc's current capital consists of prior charge items.

⇨ What will be the company's gearing ratio if the proposed capital investment project proceeds, the necessary £10 million being funded by an issue of debentures?

In the revised gearing ratio, both numerator and denominator are increased to reflect the additional £10 million of debentures:

$$\frac{\text{£30} + \text{£10 million}}{\text{£75} + \text{£10 million}} = 0.47.$$

Since the gearing ratio has increased, the company is said to have 'geared up'. Whether or not this increase is viewed as more of a threat than a benefit by ordinary shareholders will depend on a number of factors: for example, the expected volatility of future profits, given the extra interest payments which must be made, or the gearing level of other, comparable companies. Although ordinary shareholders may increase their required return in order to compensate for any increase in perceived risk resulting from a company's gearing up, there will nevertheless be a gearing level beyond which a company will be unable to proceed without jeopardising its future welfare and even existence.

THE COST OF CAPITAL

As we said at the start of the chapter, the cost of capital is central to discounted cash flow calculations. The sources of finance we have discussed can be divided into two general categories for cost of capital calculations:

1 ordinary shares; and
2 preference shares and debentures.

We shall examine the cost of each of these sources in turn, before illustrating how they may be combined to provide a cost of capital for the company as a whole. Note that, for simplicity, tax considerations have been omitted from the following discussion.

Cost of ordinary shares

Dividend-based approach

We can identify two broad approaches to calculating the cost of ordinary shares: a dividend-based approach and the Capital Asset Pricing Model. Investors purchase a company's shares in the expectation of earning a return, comprising dividends plus capital growth (i.e. increase in the market value of their shares). It is therefore possible to argue that the current market value of shares is based on investors' expectations about future returns and that, in order to render its shares attractive to investors, companies must offer returns which are at least equal to these expectations. Investors' minimum return thus represents the cost of this source of capital to the company.

In order to determine the cost of ordinary shares, we need to make the following two key assumptions:

1 Investors discount expected future returns at a personal discount rate.
2 Shares are not redeemed by the company, so that future returns are effectively received in perpetuity.

In general, the present value of a perpetual future cash flow is

$$\frac{\text{annual cash flow}}{\text{discount rate}}$$

Amending this so that it relates to the current market value of a share and its anticipated future dividend stream, we get:

$$P_0 = \frac{d}{r}$$

where: P_0 is the share's current market price;
d is the expected future annual dividend; and
r is shareholders' required rate of return.

The above formula assumes a constant rate of future dividend. Where dividends are expected to grow at a fixed rate per annum, we can adjust the price formula accordingly:

$$P_0 = \frac{d(1 + g)}{r - g}$$

where: d is the *most recent* dividend; and
g is the anticipated rate of growth in annual dividends.

If P_0, d and g are known, we can rearrange these formulae to derive r – the shareholders' required return:

$$r = \frac{d}{P_0}\text{(future dividends constant at the current rate)}$$

and:

$$r = \frac{d(1 + g)}{P_0} + g\text{(future dividends grow at a constant rate)}$$

P_0 in the formulae is the *ex-div* market price: when a dividend is about to be paid, shares' market values rise temporarily in anticipation of the fact (*cum-div* price), falling after the dividend has been paid (ex-div price). The ex-div price is thus a better indication of long-term expectations, since it excludes the short-term distortion caused by impending dividend payments.

JKM plc

JKM plc has just paid an annual dividend of 33p on each of its ordinary shares, for which the most recently quoted market price is 220p (ex-div). The company also has in issue 12 per cent irredeemable debenture stock with a current market price of £96 per £100 nominal and some 20 per cent preference shares with a current market value of 125p per £1 nominal.

Exhibit **11.3 Data for calculation of cost of ordinary shares**

▷ Based on Exhibit 11.3, use the formulae above to determine the ordinary shareholders' required rate of return assuming:

1 that future dividends continue to be paid at an annual rate of 33p per share; and
2 that future dividend payments are expected to grow at a constant rate of 5 per cent per annum.

Assuming a constant future dividend stream of 33p per share per annum, the rate of return is:

$$\frac{d}{P_0} = \frac{33\text{p}}{220\text{p}} = 0.15$$

If dividends are expected to increase at a constant annual rate of 5 per cent, this becomes:

$$\frac{d(1 + g)}{P_0} + g = \frac{33\text{p}(1 + 0.05)}{220\text{p}} + 0.05 = 0.2075. \text{ (i.e. 20.75\%)}$$

▷ What is the significance of the 20.75 per cent cost of ordinary shares to the company in its appraisal of specific capital expenditure proposals?

Assuming that it has no significant effect on a company's risk, ordinary shareholders will view any specific capital investment proposal as being merely an extension of their investment in the company and, to the extent that it is funded by ordinary shares, it must earn at least the same return as the company overall (i.e. 20.75 per cent) if the market value of shares is to be maintained. The ordinary shareholders' required rate of return therefore has a bearing on the discount rate which the company will use in its appraisal of capital expenditure projects.

For all its attractive simplicity, our 'dividend valuation' approach to the cost of ordinary shares is based on certain key assumptions. We have assumed, first, that the dividend stream (or the rate of growth therein) is constant in perpetuity. In reality, however, companies' dividend patterns are likely to be uneven, so a more sophisticated approach to calculation may be necessary. Second, we have assumed that all shareholders have the same expectations about the future, which is questionable. Different shareholder expectations about the future suggests that required returns may differ between shareholders. Third, we have assumed that dividends are paid at annual intervals (so that normal discounting techniques can be applied). This would be unusual in practice, with twice-yearly dividend payments being much more common. There may also be a problem with both P_0 and g. The current market value of the share may be temporarily affected by factors such as a rumoured takeover, and defensible estimation of the rate of dividend growth may be difficult. For example, to what extent should g be based on past growth rates? How is g affected by a company's retained profits? Finally, our simple valuation model equates dividends with 'earnings'. For some shareholders this may well be true, but for others, 'earnings' in terms of capital growth (i.e. increase in market value) may be more relevant – a view not adequately reflected via the discounted value of expected future dividends.

The capital asset pricing model (CAPM)

The CAPM is founded on explicit recognition of the risk–return relationship: that is, the higher the perceived risk of an investment, the higher will be the investor's required return (and the lower the perceived risk, the lower the required return). As a general proposition, this is eminently sensible, whether viewed in the context of stock market investments or of individual capital investment proposals. The difficulty lies in quantifying the relationship, and it is just such a quantification which the CAPM sets out to provide. However, before we can consider the model's operation, we need to give an overview of its backdrop – portfolio theory.

Portfolio theory

The fundamental principle of portfolio theory is simply stated: 'Don't put all your eggs in one basket.' More formally, an investment which consists of a diverse range (portfolio) of securities has less overall risk than an equivalent investment consisting of a single security.

⇨ Why will £10,000 invested in a portfolio of securities have less risk than the same amount invested in a single security?

A portfolio of securities is less risky than a single-security investment because, within a portfolio, some of the risk attaching to individual constituents of the portfolio can be neutralised because of their diversity. This portfolio 'effect' can be illustrated if we imagine two securities whose performance over time presents a mirror image, as shown in Figure 11.1.

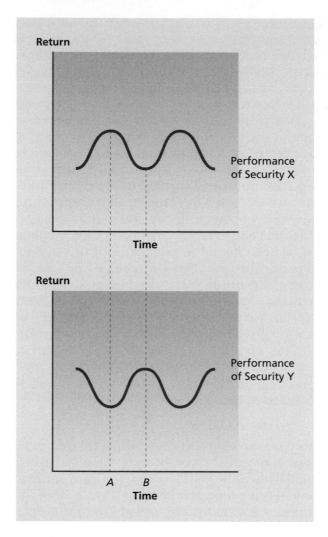

FIGURE 11.1
Two securities with mirror-image performance

If we look at Figure 11.1, we can see that, at time 'A', the trough in Security Y's performance is counterbalanced by the peak in Security X's performance. Conversely, at time B, the trough in Security X's performance is counterbalanced by the peak in Security Y's. What we can therefore say is that an investment consisting entirely of Security X or of Security Y will have more variable performance than a portfolio of *both* securities. Further, a portfolio of both Security X and Security Y will have a greater average return over time than an investment in one of these securities only. Our example is clearly a simple one, but it serves to illustrate the principle that holding a diversified portfolio of securities is less risky than investing in a single security only; and our example may readily be extended to show a similar risk reduction effect operating with a more complex portfolio.

The CAPM

The CAPM develops portfolio theory by distinguishing between different types of risk.

⇨ Does the portfolio effect we have just described mean that *all* risk can be eliminated from investments?

The simple answer is 'no' – but we need to be rather more precise about the definition of 'risk'. In general, the risk attaching to an investment (or portfolio of investments) can be divided into **systematic risk** and **unsystematic risk**. Systematic risk (also referred to as **market risk**) affects all securities and stems from economic factors which affect the continued survival of every organisation (e.g. the rate of inflation, conditions of economic depression or boom). This kind of risk cannot be diversified away, regardless of the number of securities in a portfolio. Unsystematic (or **unique**) risk stems from factors peculiar to an individual company, such as the degree of competition within its market or the danger of its being subject to a hostile takeover; because of its specific nature, unsystematic risk can be reduced in the manner suggested in Figure 11.1: that is, by holding a diversified portfolio of securities.

⇨ Is there such a thing as an investment which is 'risk-free'?

Strictly speaking, 'no' – every investment carries some element of risk. However, if we define risk as variability of return (and ignore the effect of inflation), we could take the view that any security offering a fixed rate of return, such as Government loan stock, is effectively risk-free and can be incorporated with risky securities in a portfolio.

If, as we have suggested, unsystematic risk can be diversified away, investors will expect to be 'rewarded' for that risk which cannot be diversified away: that is, for systematic risk. It is investments' systematic risk which the CAPM attempts to measure. This is done by measuring an investment's **beta** (β) – its systematic risk – relative to the **market portfolio**, which represents the theoretical optimum in diversified portfolios: that is, one from which unsystematic risk has been completely removed by diversification – an 'average' market portfolio. If we assign a β value of zero to a risk-free security and a β value of 1 to the market portfolio, we can plot the **security market line**, which shows the relationship between different degrees of systematic risk (different values of β) and the associated returns required (*see* Figure 11.2).

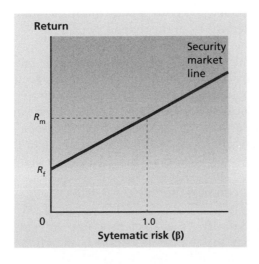

FIGURE 11.2
Relationship between systematic risk and return

In Figure 11.2, R_m represents the return on the market portfolio, R_f the return on a risk-free security and the security market line indicates that the greater the level of systematic risk, the higher is the required return. We can express the security market line as the equation

$$R_x = R_f + \{\beta_x(R_m - R_f)\}$$

where: R_x and β_x are, respectively, the required return and beta of security 'x'.

The problem is, how can we assess β_x? We can use regression analysis to examine the relationship between past returns from a specific company's securities and those from the market portfolio. Consider Figure 11.3 which shows historic comparisons between returns on Security A and Security B and returns on the market portfolio.

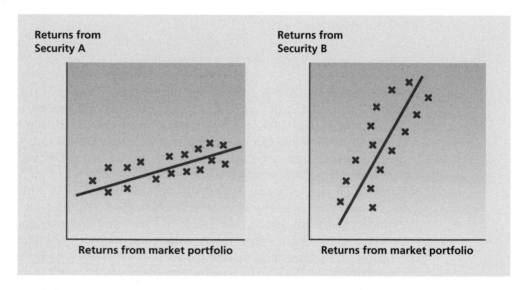

FIGURE 11.3 Returns on Securities A and B compared with returns from the market portfolio

▷ Of the two securities depicted in Figure 11.3, which has returns that are more volatile relative to returns from the market portfolio?

Examination of the slope of the lines in Figure 11.3 indicates the relative volatility of each security. Security B's line has a much steeper slope than Security A's: that is, changes in the rate of market return are matched by more-than-proportionate changes in that security's return. So Security B is the more volatile of the two relative to the market portfolio, and the steepness of its 'characteristic line's' slope is such that this security will have systematic risk in excess of 1: that is, greater than that possessed by the market portfolio. In other words, Security B's β will be greater than 1.

▷ Will Security A's β be greater or less than 1?

Examination of the slope of Security A's 'characteristic line' in Figure 11.3 indicates that a change in return from the market portfolio is matched by a less-than-proportionate change in return from this specific security: that is the security is less volatile than the market portfolio, and so will have a β of less than 1.

Exhibit 11.4 contains some additional information about JKM plc which we shall use to illustrate how regression analysis can be used to obtain an estimate of a particular security's β.

JKM plc: comparison between market returns and returns on company's ordinary shares

Over the last six months, management has gathered the following information about percentage returns on the company's own ordinary shares and on an average market investment:

Month	Return on market portfolio (R_m)	Return on JKM plc ordinary shares (R_x)
1	2.0	2.4
2	2.5	3.0
3	0.0	0.5
4	– 1.5	– 2.5
5	– 0.5	– 1.0
6	1.4	2.1

For the forthcoming year, the market portfolio is expected to have a return of 16 per cent and the risk-free return is expected to be 5 per cent.

EXHIBIT **11.4 Data for estimating a security's beta**

You will recall from Chapter 3 that the general formula for a straight line is:

$$y = a + bx$$

where b represents the slope of the line. In that chapter, we also saw that regression analysis provides the following formula for determination of b:

$$b = \frac{n\Sigma xy - \Sigma x \, \Sigma y}{n\Sigma x^2 - (\Sigma x)^2}$$

where n is the number of observations of x and y being used.

Treating returns from the market portfolio as x and from JKM plc's ordinary shares as y, we can calculate b from Exhibit 11.4 as follows:

x	y	xy	x^2
2.0	2.4	4.8	4.0
2.5	3.0	7.5	6.25
0.0	0.5	0.0	0.0
–1.5	–2.5	3.75	2.25
–0.5	–1.0	0.5	0.25
1.4	2.1	2.94	1.96
$\Sigma 3.9$	$\Sigma 4.5$	$\Sigma 19.49$	$\Sigma 14.71$

$$b = \frac{n\Sigma xy - \Sigma\, x \,\Sigma\, y}{n\Sigma x^2 - (\Sigma x)^2} = \frac{6(19.49) - (3.9 \times 4.5)}{6(14.71) - 3.9^2} = \frac{116.94 - 17.55}{88.26 - 15.21} = 1.36$$

JKM plc's ordinary shares are therefore 1.36 times as volatile as the average market return: that is, they have a β of 1.36. This value is the slope of the 'characteristic line' associated with JKM plc's ordinary shares.

Now that we have a β for JKM plc's ordinary shares, we can use the CAPM formula, along with the information from Exhibit 11.4, to determine their cost.

▷ Use the CAPM formula, $R_x = R_f + \{\beta_x(R_m\text{-}R_f)\}$, inserting 1.36 as the value of β_x and appropriate values from Exhibit 11.4 for R_f and R_m, to determine a cost of capital appropriate to JKM plc's ordinary shares.

From Exhibit 11.4, we know that R_m is 16 per cent and R_f 5 per cent. Combined with βx of 1.36, this gives a cost of capital of:

$$5\% + \{1.36(16\% - 5\%)\} = 19.96\% \text{ (say, 20\%)}$$

We can therefore say that a **risk premium** of (20% – 5%) = 15% – that is, the return over and above the risk-free rate – is required in order to compensate investors for the systematic risk associated with JKM plc's ordinary shares.

Beta factors for most large UK companies are published quarterly by the London Business School in their *Risk Management Service*, calculation being based on the method we have just illustrated. For each security, a regression analysis of the last 60 monthly returns against market return (taken as the *Financial Times* actuaries all-shares index) is performed.

Using the CAPM

Our 20 per cent CAPM-based cost of ordinary shares has the advantage of highlighting the risk–return relationship. However, its use poses problems, some of which may be addressed by using a more sophisticated approach, some of which are rather more intractable.

Problems which may be overcome by using a more sophisticated model

Use of the 20 per cent cost of capital assumes that a project's β is the same as that for the company as a whole – which may not necessarily be the case. Although we might estimate a project-specific β, tolerable accuracy in such an estimate is likely to be extremely hard (if not impossible) to achieve. In addition, by incorporating a risk-related cost of ordinary shares in the discount rate applied to capital investment projects, we are assuming that risk increases over time (due to the compounding effect of the discount rate as time progresses) – which is not necessarily the case. Although it is possible to adjust project cash flows to compensate for this, such adjustment could be argued to add complication to what is already a sufficiently complex evaluative process.

General problems

Estimation of R_m and R_f may be problematic. For example, there are a number of different rates which might validly be taken as the proxy for 'risk-free'. Which is relevant and should be used? Estimating beta may also be difficult. Use of regression analysis assumes that the past is a reliable guide to the future, so we may be reduced to estimation based to a marked extent on judgement.

Of more fundamental importance is the exclusion of unsystematic risk from the CAPM. By including only systematic risk, we assume that all investors hold well-diversified portfolios approximating the market portfolio. This may not be the case, however, and the unsystematic risk associated with a particular project is likely to be of especial significance to management (who must ultimately make the decision, and who may not even be investors in the company). The CAPM also fails to distinguish between *types* of return from investments (i.e. between dividends and capital growth) – a distinction which could be of particular importance to individual investors. Finally, the CAPM is essentially a single-period model. You will recall that Exhibit 11.4 gives R_m and R_f relative to a particular future period. In practice, these will not be constant over time, and care is therefore needed if the CAPM's results are incorporated into a discount rate that will be applied to a project which spans a number of years.

The cost of debentures and preference shares

Since debentures are loans, and since the rate of interest on debentures is generally fixed for the duration of the loan, derivation of the cost of debentures is less open to question than that of ordinary shares. For **irredeemable debentures** (i.e. where the loan is made in perpetuity), the calculation is straightforward:

$$\text{cost of debentures} = \frac{i}{P_0}$$

where: i represents the interest payable; and
P_0 is the current market price of the debenture.

Although irredeemable debentures are very unlikely in practice, the formula above may be adapted to deal with the cost of preference shares, as these carry a fixed rate of dividend and may effectively be irredeemable:

$$\text{cost of preference shares} = \frac{d}{P_0}$$

where: d is the annual dividend payment; and
P_0 is the current market price of the preference share.

You will notice that both of these formulae are similar to that which we used above to determine the cost of ordinary shares where the dividend stream was expected to be constant. The principle being applied here is the same: that is, that the market value of irredeemable debentures and preference shares can be thought of as the future interest payments/preference dividends discounted at the debenture holders'/preference shareholders' required rate of return.

⇨ Apply the two formulae above to the data in Exhibit 11.3 to determine the cost of JKM plc's irredeemable debentures and preference shares.

The cost of JKM plc's debentures is:

$$\frac{i}{P_0} = \frac{(12\% \times £100)}{£96} = 0.125 \text{ (i.e. 12.5\%)}$$

whilst the company's preference shares will have a cost of:

$$\frac{d}{P_0} = \frac{(20\% \times £1)}{125\text{p}} = 0.16 \text{ (i.e. 16\%)}$$

As we have said, irredeemable debentures are somewhat unlikely in reality, so we will now consider the cost of redeemable debentures. Because the principal will be repaid at some specified point in the future, the market value of a redeemable debenture will consist of future interest payments plus final repayment of the loan, discounted at debenture holders' required rate of return. We therefore need to find the discount rate at which (future interest payments + loan repayment) equate with the current market value: this rate of return (ignoring tax implications) is referred to as the **gross redemption yield** (or **yield to maturity**). It might be a useful analogy to think of the current market price as being the 'initial cost' of a 'capital investment' with interest and ultimate repayment being the associated cash inflows. Equating the discounted cash inflows with the 'initial cost' means that the net present value is zero, and to obtain the discount rate which provides this result, what we need to obtain is the 'capital investment's' internal rate of return (IRR).

Let us assume that JKM plc's 12 per cent debenture stock is redeemable at nominal value (i.e. redeemable at £100 per £100 of stock held) at the end of 10 years from now, and that annual interest is payable at the end of each year, the final interest payment coinciding with the loan repayment. Using the trial and error approach to IRR calculation (described in the last chapter) and treating the debentures as a 'capital investment proposal', with current market value representing 'initial cost', discounting at 12 per cent gives the NPV set out in Table 11.2. Since 12 per cent yields a positive NPV, we must increase the discount rate for our second trial. Using 14 per cent, we achieve the NPV set out in Table 11.3.

TABLE **11.2 NPV of redeemable debenture at 12 per cent**

Year	Cash flow	Amount (£)	Discount factor	Present value (£)
0	Initial cost	(96.00)	1.000	(96.00)
1–10	Annual interest	12.00	5.650	67.80
10	Loan repayment	100.00	0.322	32.20
			NPV	4.00

TABLE **11.3 NPV of redeemable debenture at 14 per cent**

Year	Cash flow	Amount (£)	Discount factor	Present value (£)
0	Initial cost	(96.00)	1.000	(96.00)
1–10	Annual interest	12.00	5.216	62.59
10	Loan repayment	100.00	0.270	27.00
			NPV	(6.41)

Interpolating, we get an IRR of:

$$12\% + \left[\frac{£4}{(£4 + £6.41)} \times (14\% - 12\%) \right] = 12.77\% \text{ (rounded)}$$

JKM plc's redeemable debentures therefore have a cost of approximately 12.77 per cent. In practice, cumbersome IRR-type calculations are unnecessary, with bond yield tables being used to determine figures such as the 12.77 per cent above.

Determining a cost of capital for bank lending is rather more problematic, as bank loans do not have a market value in the way that debentures do; in this case, our best approximation of market value will probably be loan amount as recorded in the company's accounts.

The cost of capital and small companies

Many small companies may be faced with a particular difficulty in assessing their cost of capital. If their securities are not traded on the Stock Exchange, or otherwise bought and sold, obtaining investors' required returns in any objectively defensible way could be virtually impossible. As a general guide, all we are able to say is that investments in small companies and companies whose securities are not publicly traded tend to be viewed as more risky than those in large companies whose securities are publicly traded. Because of this, raising finance is often more difficult for smaller companies, and its associated cost higher. A partial solution might be to obtain the cost of capital for a similar (but larger, publicly traded) company, applying an increase to allow for higher perceived risk.

WEIGHTED AVERAGE COST OF CAPITAL (WACC)

Our cost of capital calculations have so far applied only to a single type of capital (i.e. ordinary shares, debentures or preference shares). In reality, capital structure will comprise a mix of different types of capital: for example, a 'simple' capital structure for a limited company may consist partly of ordinary shares and partly of debentures. By weighting the cost of each element relative to total capital employed, it is possible to derive the overall cost of capital.

Calculating the WACC

We will use the information from Exhibit 11.5 to demonstrate how JKM plc's WACC may be calculated.

JKM plc

An extract from the company's most recent balance sheet reveals the following:

	£
Issued £1 ordinary shares	40,000,000
Retained profit	5,000,000
20% preference shares of £1	7,000,000
Irredeemable 12% debenture stock of £100	23,000,000
	75,000,000

The cost of each individual element of the company's capital, along with its current market value, is:

	Cost (%)	Current market value
Ordinary shares	20.00	220p per share
20% preference shares	16.00	125p per share
Irredeemable 12% debenture stock	12.50	£96 per £100

EXHIBIT **11.5** Data for WACC calculation

The cost of ordinary shares in Exhibit 11.5 is that which we obtained by using the CAPM. It could alternatively have been stated as 20.75 per cent (i.e. the result of our dividend based calculations.)

⇨ Two sets of values for capital are shown in Exhibit 11.5 – balance sheet and market values. Which should be used to weight the cost of each individual element of JKM plc's capital?

As we have seen, the cost of capital derives from investors' required returns: that is, from the market. Thus, where they are available (as they are for a plc such as JKM, whose securities are traded on the Stock Exchange), market values for capital should always be used. From Exhibit 11.5, the total market value of JKM plc's capital is:

	£
Ordinary shares (40 million shares × 220p)	88,000,000
Preference shares (7 million shares × 125p)	8,750,000
Debentures (£21 million × £96/100)	20,160,000
	116,910,000

You will see that retained profit has been excluded from the calculation. This is because it is effectively included in the market value of the ordinary shares.

Ordinary shareholders, to whom retained profit 'belongs', will have incorporated its future use in their expectations about company prospects (upon which the market value of shares largely depends). Applying the market-based weightings to each type of capital, we get:

	%
Ordinary shares (88/116.91 × 20.00%)	15.05
Preference shares (8.75/116.91 × 16.00%)	1.20
Debentures (20.16/116.91 × 12.5%)	2.16
WACC	18.41

If – and only if – market values for a company's securities cannot be obtained, balance sheet figures may be used. For JKM plc, this would give a WACC of:

	%
Ordinary shares plus retained profit (45/75 × 20.00%)	12.00
Preference shares (7/75 × 16.00%)	1.49
Debentures (23/75 × 12.5%)	3.83
	17.32

(For convenience of discounting calculation, we might round this to 17 per cent.)

Note that, using the balance sheet values, retained profit is included in the weighting accorded to ordinary shares, since it effectively 'belongs' to ordinary shareholders (the company's owners).

Use of WACC as the discount rate for proposal evaluation

Use of the WACC to discount the cash flows associated with specific capital investment proposals may be supported or questioned, depending on the specific circumstances. If a project is to be funded from sources already existing within the organisation, then it may be reasonable to use the WACC on the basis that the exact origin of these funds is no longer traceable, thereby precluding determination of a more precise cost of capital. We can also justify the WACC on the grounds that a company's capital structure will change fairly slowly over time (and possibly not at all during the lifespan of a particular proposal) and that any capital investment project must meet the minimum expected returns of all investors in the company (rather than satisfying one narrow sectional interest at the possible expense of others).

But there are arguments against use of the WACC. If a proposal is to be funded from an identifiable source (particularly a new one, such as by a share issue), then it could be said that the proposal's first priority should be to satisfy the required return of the investors who are funding it. Taking this sort of 'marginal' approach to the cost of capital may create difficulties of its own if the particular types of funding fluctuates over time, i.e. a proposal which is unacceptable this year may become acceptable next year, merely because the cost of a particular type of finance has fallen. The danger in this is that the varying cost of finance may overshadow the organisational desirability of capital investment proposals (e.g. in terms of their strategic 'fit'). A further problem with the WACC is that it does not make explicit allowance for the risk of a project relative to the risk of existing operations. This weakness might be addressed by basing the cost of ordinary shares on the CAPM in conjunction with a project-specific β (rather than a company β), as suggested earlier.

What all of this means is that, if we use an unadjusted WACC to discount project cash flows, we are assuming that:

1 the project is funded in a manner consistent with the organisation's overall funding; and
2 the project has the same risk as existing operations.

Only the specific circumstances of a particular capital investment proposal can determine if these assumptions are reasonable.

CAPITAL INVESTMENT APPRAISAL IN PUBLIC SECTOR AND NON-PROFIT ORGANISATIONS

Our discussion of capital investment appraisal has, thus far, been largely confined to commercial scenarios. We must now consider how public and non-profit expenditure projects can be appraised, describing the techniques of cost/benefit and cost-effectiveness analysis and examining how an appropriate cost of capital might be determined.

Cost/benefit analysis

The abiding problems for public sector and non-profit capital investment projects are the intangible nature of many of the costs and benefits involved allied to difficulty in defining a yardstick against which to measure them. If these cannot be meaningfully quantified and defined, then evaluation will, at best, be incomplete. **Cost/benefit analysis** attempts to quantify both the monetary and non-monetary consequences of a capital project so as to allow both to be incorporated in the appraisal exercise. Subject to the caveat of obtaining credible figures, the direct monetary costs and benefits of a public expenditure programme can be readily estimated.

⇨ What direct monetary consequences could be associated with the decision by a local authority to build a library in a locale which has not previously possessed one?

The direct monetary consequences would include the following:

■ Cost of building, stocking and staffing the library.
■ Sundry costs of operating the library (e.g. lighting and heating).
■ Cost of finance (e.g. interest payments on a loan raised to finance building).

Items of the kind listed above are relatively easy to identify, quantify and include in a financial appraisal of the costs and benefits of building the library.

⇨ What non-monetary consequences might arise as the result of a decision to build the library?

Non-monetary aspects of the decision are, however, much less easy to pin down. We might suggest factors such as:

■ An increase in local 'amenity' resulting from existence of the library.
■ An improvement in literacy.

Furthermore, existence of the library could possibly have implications for less obvious areas (e.g. reduction in local crime rate). The problem with these non-monetary factors is twofold: first, we need to be able to identify all that have a significant bearing on the decision (which may not be easy); and second, we need to be able to quantify their financial impact.

Two broad approaches to quantification can be identified:

1 Establish 'surrogate' figures – either by survey of public opinion or by inference from present behaviour.
2 Trace the effects of a particular project to their ultimate practical limit and then place values on each of these effects.

Whichever approach is adopted, the results are likely to be open to question. How, for example, could we quantify an improvement in local 'amenity' resulting from building the library? We might make projections about the library's impact on statistics – such as the speed with which vacant council houses in the neighbourhood are relet – to which financial values could then be attached; but it might equally be true that changes in 'proxy' statistics of this sort may be due to factors other than building the library. Benefit could also be measured in terms of how willing the public is to fund them (e.g. by tax increases).

Despite the difficulties involved in such quantification exercises, cost/benefit analysis has been applied in practice to public expenditure programmes, perhaps most notably in assessing the siting of a third airport for London, of the M1 motorway and of the London Underground Victoria Line. In the last case, the financial implications (costs and benefits) of factors such as the line's effect on traffic congestion and on travel times were incorporated into the appraisal, along with the more 'obvious' cash flows, prior to discounting.

Cost-effectiveness analysis

Because of the extreme difficulty in quantifying the kind of social impact we have just been describing, **cost-effectiveness analysis** adopts a more limited view, concentrating on quantifying only those aspects of a proposal which are readily quantifiable: that is, its direct financial consequences. Indirect or non-quantifiable consequences are merely listed as costs or benefits and are used to inform the final decision about a project's desirability. Two approaches to cost-effectiveness analysis are possible, as follows:

1 *Point-scoring system* Key criteria for capital projects are identified and are 'scored' (e.g. out of five) according to how well a particular proposal achieves each crite-

rion. This can be especially useful where mutually exclusive options are being considered. Suppose, for example, that there is more than one possible location for the proposed library discussed above. A table such as Table 11.4 (which is a greatly simplified version of reality) can be prepared to score each against desirable criteria. Assuming a score of five to be optimal for each criterion, Location C in the table starts to emerge as potential front-runner; but before a final decision is reached capital and revenue implications will require to be quantified for all options. A degree of subjectivity is involved in the scoring process – and, in particular, for intangible criteria such as amenity and accessibility. However, by giving explicit recognition and weighting to a range of criteria, a point-scoring system should improve decision making.

TABLE **11.4 Point-scoring assessment of different locations for proposed library**

	Location			
Criterion	A	B	C	D
		Score out of 5		
Capital implications	2	3	2	1
Revenue implications	3	1	2	2
Amenity improvement	1	2	3	2
Accessibility	1	3	3	2
Land requirement	1	2	2	1

2 *Option appraisal* This is a more general approach to cost-effectiveness analysis, and does not necessarily preclude use of point scoring. Options which will potentially meet objectives are identified, along with their costs and benefits (quantified as far as possible). Management then subjects these options to review and/or refinement, a process which may have the effect of reducing their number. Finally, the most suitable option is selected (e.g. on the basis of discounted cash flow evaluation).

Difficult though capital investment appraisal may be in public sector organisations, Ferguson and Lapsley (1988) present evidence which suggests that recognition of this difficulty has resulted in well-developed option identification procedures. Rigorous attempts to identify the best options prior to appraisal may go some way towards offsetting the problems involved in their subsequent appraisal.

The cost of capital

Public sector and non-profit organisations do not possess investors in the way that commercial organisations do, and this renders our WACC/CAPM approach to the cost of capital irrelevant. As an additional complication, many of the costs and benefits associated with a particular public sector or non-profit capital investment project will be intangible, which will render assessment of 'required return' difficult. For public sector bodies in the United Kingdom, central government guidance suggests a *test discount rate* (8 per cent in 1996) which is intended to reflect economic and social factors relevant to discounting public expenditure proposals.

This test rate is quite widely used, especially in the UK National Health Service. Non-profit organisations may consider the cost of financing specific projects. For example, if funds require to be borrowed for a particular project, then the loan's interest rate could be used as the cost of capital. Alternatively, it would be possible to take an opportunity cost approach, using as the discount rate the return obtainable from the funds if these were used in the best alternative way to that currently under consideration (e.g. interest on deposit lost).

Another possible approach – adopted in the Victoria Underground Line cost/benefit analysis mentioned above – is to discount proposal cash flows at more than one rate. For example, the 8 per cent test rate could be used as the 'norm', with an additional discounting exercise being undertaken at a higher rate for proposals having potentially wide-ranging ramifications (or at a lower rate for more narrowly focused projects) – positive net present value at both rates being then taken as indicative of desirability.

Summary

In this chapter, we have provided an overview of: the sources of finance from which capital expenditure projects may be funded; the possible derivation of the cost of capital appropriate for discounting proposal cash flows; and appraising public sector and non-profit capital expenditures. In particular, we have seen that:

- The main potential sources of capital funding for companies (in descending order of significance) are: retained profit, other sources, issue of ordinary shares, issue of preference shares and debentures, bank borrowing.

- Care should be exercised in the use of retained profit, as this will not necessarily equate with cash availability, nor is it a 'free' source of finance.

- Public sector finance sources include use of reserves, borrowing, taxation and grant aid from various sources.

- **Gearing** refers to the existence of **prior charge capital** in a company's capital structure, and its extent is measured by the **gearing ratio**:

$$\frac{\textbf{prior charge capital}}{\textbf{all long-term capital + reserves}}$$

- Gearing up may benefit ordinary shareholders, but may also threaten their interests.

- The cost of ordinary shares can be obtained from the expressions:

$$r = \frac{d}{P_0} \text{ (constant future dividend)}$$

or: $$r = \frac{d(1 + g)}{P_0} + g \text{ (constant future growth in dividends)}$$

where: r is the required rate of return
d is the most recent dividend;

P_0 is the market price of the share (ex-div); and

g is the anticipated future growth rate in dividends.

- **Systematic risk** is the unavoidable risk of holding any security and cannot be diversified away; unsystematic risk is the risk specific to a particular security and portfolio theory suggests that holding a range of securities permits this to be diversified away.

- The **capital asset pricing model (CAPM)** measures the systematic risk of a security by determining its **beta (β)** relative to the return from risk-free securities and from the **market portfolio** (from which all unsystematic risk is assumed to be diversified away).

- A specific security's β can be obtained from a regression analysis of that security's returns relative to returns from the average market investment in the past, by applying the following formula:

$$\frac{n\Sigma xy - \Sigma x \, \Sigma y}{n \, \Sigma x^2 - (\Sigma x)^2}$$

where: n is the number of past observations being used;

x is each return from the average market investment; and

y is each return from the security under consideration.

- The CAPM derives the cost of capital from the following expression:

$$R_x = R_f + \{\beta_x(R_m - R_f)\}$$

where: R_x is the required rate of return;

R_f is the return from risk-free securities;

R_m is the return from the market portfolio; and

β_x is the security's beta.

- The CAPM expressly allows for risk in its determination of the cost of capital, but the result
  - may require adjustment to reflect the risk of a specific project and to remove the effect of compounding risk over time;
  - may pose problems in estimation of R_m, R_f and β;
  - excludes unsystematic risk, which may be important to management;
  - does not distinguish between types of return from an investment; and
  - is strictly a single-period result.

- The cost of irredeemable debentures and preference shares can, respectively, be calculated as:

$$r = \frac{i}{P_0} \qquad \text{and} \qquad \frac{d}{P_0}$$

with: i representing the interest payment on debentures;

d being the preference dividend; and

P_0 being the current market price of the security concerned.

- Determination of the **gross redemption yield** on redeemable debentures requires estimation of the internal rate of return at which the present value of the debenture's future interest payments plus capital repayment equate with its current market price.

- The **weighted average cost of capital (WACC)** uses each individual element of capital's proportion of total capital (either in balance sheet or in market values) to obtain a cost of capital for the organisation as a whole.

- Use of the WACC as a discount rate may be justifiable where a project:
    - is funded in a manner consistent with the company's overall funding; and
    - is of the same risk class as the company's other business.

- **Cost/benefit analysis** attempts to quantify monetary and non-monetary consequences arising from a public or non-profit capital expenditure project, but the latter may be difficult to identify and quantify.

- **Cost-effectiveness analysis** quantifies only those outcomes of public sector/non-profit capital expenditures which are readily quantifiable, stating the non-monetary costs and benefits to better inform the final decision.

In the next chapter, we will commence our discussion of management accounting's input to the key managerial activities of planning and control with an examination of budgetary planning.

FURTHER READING

AIM – A guide for companies, London Stock Exchange, 1995. This is a concise guide aimed at companies wishing to obtain a listing on AIM.

Brealey, R. and Myers, S., *Principles of Corporate Finance*, 5th edn, McGraw-Hill, 1996. Chapters 7, 8 and 9 contain detailed discussion of portfolio theory and cost of capital calculations.

Chadwick, L. and Pike, R., *Management and Control of Capital in Industry*, CIMA, 1985.

Coggan, P, *The Money Machine*, Penguin, 1996. This fairly short text provides a readable overview of the workings of the 'City'.

Ferguson, K. and Lapsley, I., 'Investment Appraisal in the National Health Service', in *Financial Accountability and Management*, 4(4), 1988.

Jones, R. and Pendlebury, M., *Public Sector Accounting*, 4th edn, Pitman Publishing, 1996. Chapter 6 deals with public sector capital investment appraisal, along with detail of the Victoria Line cost/benefit analysis.

Layard, R. and Glaister, S. (eds), *Cost-Benefit Analysis,* 2nd edn, Cambridge University Press, 1994. Part III contains some interesting case studies.

Samuels, J., Wilkes, F. and Brayshaw, R., *Management of Company Finance*, 6th edn, Chapman & Hall, 1995. *See* Chapter 10 for discussion of obtaining and using values for beta.

Sᴇʟꜰ-ᴛᴇsᴛ QUESTIONS

11.1 HJM plc's ordinary shares have a nominal value of £1 each and current market price of 79.8p (ex-div). The most recent annual dividend paid was 19p per share and this is expected to grow at a constant rate of 5 per cent per annum. What is HJM plc's cost of ordinary shares?

> A 19%
> B 20%
> C 25%
> D 30%

11.2 A company's balance sheet reveals the following capital structure:

	£
Ordinary shares of £1 each	50,000,000
Retained profits	4,000,000
10% debentures	21,000,000
	75,000,000

The company's cost of ordinary shares is 24 per cent and the debentures have a cost of 12 per cent. What is the company's weighted average cost of capital?

> A 18.00%
> B 19.36%
> C 20.00%
> D 20.64%

11.3 FDK plc's β is 1.5, the return on an average market portfolio is 14 per cent, and the risk-free return 8 per cent. According to the capital asset pricing model, what is FDK plc's cost of capital?

> A 12%
> B 15%
> C 17%
> D 21%

11.4 For each of the following statements, place a tick in the appropriate box to indicate whether it is true or false.

	True	False
(a) Systematic risk is that risk which is specific to a particular investment.	☐	☐
(b) Use of the weighted average cost of capital to discount the cash flows associated with a project assumes that project to have the same risk as the company's other business.	☐	☐
(c) For the duration of a lease, the lessee has legal ownership of the asset leased.	☐	☐
(d) Adequacy of retained profit for a capital investment proposal guarantees adequacy of cash for the same purpose.	☐	☐

(e) Returns from a security which has β in excess of 1 are more volatile than returns from the average market portfolio. ☐ ☐

(f) Unsystematic risk will be irrelevant to those who must decide whether or not to proceed with a particular capital investment proposal. ☐ ☐

(g) Debenture interest is a tax-deductible expense, preference dividend is not. ☐ ☐

11.5 TRA plc's balance sheet shows the following:

	£
Ordinary shares of 50p each	22,000,000
Retained profits	6,000,000
15% preference shares of £1 each	5,000,000
10% debentures	7,000,000
	40,000,000

What is TRA plc's gearing ratio?

A 12.5%
B 15.0%
C 17.5%
D 30.0%

Questions with Answers

11.6 This question tests whether you can:

- use regression analysis to determine β for a specific security, commenting on the weaknesses of this method of estimation;
- use this β to determine the cost of capital according to the CAPM; and
- explain how the cost of capital could be adjusted to reflect the risk of a specific capital investment proposal.

Over the last eight quarters, percentage returns on GM plc's ordinary shares and on an average market investment have been as follows:

Return on average market investment	Return on GM plc's ordinary shares
2.2	1.6
2.8	2.1
2.0	1.5
1.8	1.0
1.2	0.6
0.7	0.0
0.3	–0.8
0.8	0.1

For the life of a proposed capital investment, the annual return from a risk-free investment is expected to be 8 per cent and from the market portfolio to be 14 per cent.

Requirements

(a) Using regression analysis, obtain an estimate of β for GM plc's ordinary shares.

(b) Briefly explain any weaknesses in the use of regression analysis as an estimation technique.

(c) Use the capital asset pricing model (CAPM) to derive the cost of GM plc's ordinary shares.

(d) Suggest how your answer to (c) could be adjusted to allow for the fact that the specific capital investment project under consideration is estimated to be twice as risky as GM plc's normal operations. Comment on the suitability of the adjustment you are suggesting.

(*Note*: work to two decimal places.)

11.7 This question tests whether you can:

■ use a dividend growth approach to determination of the cost of ordinary shares;

■ estimate the cost of redeemable debentures;

■ obtain a company's weighted average cost of capital (WACC) based on both balance sheet and market values; and

■ comment on the potential problem with the WACC as a discount rate in given circumstances.

An extract from NBV plc's most recent balance sheet is given below:

	£
Ordinary shares of £1 each	25,000,000
Retained profit	5,000,000
15% £100 debenture stock	10,000,000
	40,000,000

The current ex-div market value of the company's ordinary shares is 415p, on which the last annual dividend paid was 30p, this being expected to grow at a constant annual rate of 2.5 per cent. Each £100 nominal of debenture stock presently has a market value of £130. Debenture interest is paid annually at the end of each year, the final interest payment being timed to coincide with repayment of the £10 million at the end of 15 years from now.

Requirements

(a) Using the dividend growth approach, obtain NBV plc's cost of ordinary shares.

(b) Provide an estimate of the cost of NBV plc's redeemable debentures.

(c) Calculate the company's weighted average cost of capital (WACC) based on:

 (i) balance sheet values; and

 (ii) market values.

(d) Comment on the suitability of the WACC in (c) as the discount rate for a capital investment proposal that the company intends to finance by means of a term loan from the bank at an average annual rate of interest of 8 per cent.

(*Note*: work to two decimal places.)

11.8 This question tests whether you can:

- calculate the effect of different gearing levels on profit available to ordinary shareholders along with the relevant gearing ratios;

- determine a company's weighted average cost of capital based on different capital structures and comment on the implications for capital investment appraisal; and

- explain the attractions and weaknesses of different funding sources.

AFG plc's existing capital structure is as follows:

	£
Ordinary shares of £1 each	50,000,000
Retained profit	8,000,000
8% debenture stock	22,000,000
	80,000,000

In order to undertake a programme of expansion, the company requires to raise additional capital of £20 million, and three alternative financing schemes are under consideration:

1 a rights issue, at nominal value, of an additional 20 million £1 ordinary shares; or

2 issue, at nominal value, 20 million 10 per cent preference shares of £1; or

3 issue an additional £20 million of 8 per cent debenture stock.

Without the expansion programme, AFG plc's estimated annual profit before interest and taxation for the foreseeable future is £10 million. If the programme proceeds, this will rise to £14 million.

At present, the market values of the company's securities are:

Ordinary shares	540p (ex-div)
Debenture stock	£110 per £100 nominal

and the last ordinary dividend was 20p per share. If expansion does not take place, ordinary dividends are expected to grow at a constant rate of 2.5 per cent per annum. After some initial fluctuations, the anticipated effect of expansion on dividends and market values is expected to stabilise as follows:

	Expansion financed by:		
	Rights issue	Preference shares	Debentures
Market value of ordinary shares	560p	580p	600p
Market value of debentures per £100 nominal	£110	£110	£108
Market value of preference shares	n/a	114p	n/a
Annual growth rate in ordinary dividends	3.5%	4%	5%

The company's profit is subject to Corporation Tax at 35 per cent, and this rate is unlikely to change in the foreseeable future.

(*Note*: for ease of calculation, you may assume that all the company's debentures (those currently in issue and the proposed issue) along with the preference shares (if issued) are irredeemable.)

Requirements

(a) For the existing and each of the proposed capital structures, determine (correct to two decimal places):

   (i) the gearing ratio;

   (ii) the profit available per ordinary share; and

   (iii) AFG plc's weighted average cost of capital based on market values.

(b) AFG plc's management assessed the desirability of the proposed expansion scheme using the company's existing weighted average cost of capital as the discount rate. Briefly discuss the suitability of this rate and suggest the possible implications for the proposal's appraisal of using the alternative rates obtained in (a).

(c) Outline the strengths and weaknesses of each of the sources of finance proposed for the expansion programme.

QUESTIONS WITHOUT ANSWERS

11.9 BMM plc, a company financed entirely by ordinary shares, is appraising a capital investment opportunity with the following characteristics:

- initial cost: £5 million;

- estimated life: 6 years;

- estimated residual value: £0.2 million; and

- anticipated increase in annual profit (after depreciation of £0.8 million): £0.6 million.

Returns from BMM plc's securities (based on existing operations) are approximately 1.2 times as volatile as those from the average market portfolio, which has a return of 15 per cent compared to a risk-free return of 10 per cent. However, the particular proposal detailed above is reckoned to have a beta of 2.8.

Requirements

(a) Apply the capital asset pricing model to obtain BMM plc's cost of capital based on:
   (i) beta for existing operations; and
   (ii) the project-specific beta.

(b) Use each of your answers to (a) to determine the proposal's net present value. Comment on your results.

11.10 Middleford Municipal Council, faced with an ongoing problem regarding disposal of commercial and domestic refuse, is considering three proposals to alleviate the situation, details of which are given below.

Build new high-volume incinerator
Following closure of a steelmaking plant within the council's boundaries, a tract of derelict land (already owned by the council) is available which could be used for the purpose. This land is very close to a large council housing estate, which has a high rate of unemployment. It is estimated that the incinerator would cost £50m to build, have

an operational life of 20 years and annual running costs of £8m. There is a possibility that central government and/or the European Community might provide assistance with the building cost, but council officials reckon that, at most, this will amount to some 40 per cent of the £50m required. Annual running costs and the remainder of the initial cost would require to be funded from the council's own budget. If this option is proceeded with, it is believed that, in addition to the building work, which it is hoped will employ local labour, about 100 permanent jobs would be created once the incinerator is fully operational.

Acquire one/more landfill sites

Within Middleford's boundaries are several disused quarries (in predominantly rural locations), which could be purchased, in-filled with suitable refuse, and, once full, landscaped. Purchase costs would amount to approximately £10-£15m with annual operating costs of £8–£12m, and final landscaping costs of £2–£4m. The exact amount of these costs will depend on the number of sites acquired, but should be within the range given. At the present rate of refuse disposal, this option should have a useful life of 3–8 years, again dependent on the number of sites acquired. The only use to which the quarries are currently put is to provide practice ascents for a local climbing club.

Recycling

The council presently has a small recycling operation, dealing mainly with newspapers. This facility could be extended to deal with other suitable refuse like aluminium cans, but would not, on its own, be sufficient to deal with all disposals. Adequate extension to the recycling plant would cost approximately £100m to build and would have an operational life of about 15 years. Annual operating costs are estimated at £6m, but it is anticipated that a large proportion of this would be offset by sale of recycled refuse.

The council's budget is under severe pressure, and substantial increases in the council tax and business rates charged to local domestic and commercial residents are proposed for next financial year.

Requirements

Prepare a report for Middleford Municipal Council's Chief Executive dealing with the following aspects of appraising the refuse disposal options:

1 The distinction between cost/benefit and cost-effectiveness analysis, explaining which is likely to be most appropriate here.

2 Financial considerations, including potential sources of necessary finance.

3 Non-financial costs and benefits which may have a bearing on the appraisal exercise.

PART 3

Planning, control and performance evaluation

In this section we discuss management accounting's input to planning, control and evaluation – standard costs, budgetary planning and control, analysis of budget variances, and financial performance measures – and finish by considering some behavioural aspects of management accounting. This section comprises the following chapters:

In Chapter 12, we examine budget preparation, making the important link between this and the strategic-tactical-operational classification of information introduced in Chapter 1. On its own, planning has little value, and must be accompanied by control, which we deal with in Chapters 13 and 14. Chapter 15 considers a particularly important (and potentially problematic) aspect of planning and control – performance evaluation, and we reiterate the point we have made on several earlier occasions that financial criteria can present only part of the picture. If, as we suggested in Chapter 1, management accounting is principally concerned with communication, then it is essentially a *people* process, and Chapter 16 concludes with a discussion of some of the behavioural aspects of the subject.

CHAPTER 12

Budgetary planning

> ## VODAPHONE ADVERTISING BUDGET TO RISE TO £20M
>
> Vodaphone, the UK's biggest mobile telephone group, is to more than treble its advertising budget over the next year to £20m in response to the growing threat of competition, particularly from Orange, the newest entrant to the £4.5bn UK cellular telecoms market.
>
> Vodaphone considers the competitive 'war' has now moved away from issues of price and coverage to marketing. Orange spends around £30m a year on advertising, and the size of its expenditure has helped the group, which floated earlier this year, to a 7 per cent market share in its three years of operation . . .
>
> *Source*: Christopher Price, *Financial Times*, 13 May 1996.

> ## TRIBUNALS COULD FACE CUTS TO MEET BUDGET TARGETS
>
> Industrial tribunals could face sweeping cuts in funding under Department of Trade and Industry plans to reduce the size of its overall spending to meet last November's Budget targets.
>
> A possible reduction of £4m in the tribunals' budget of £37m for the financial year beginning in April has led to fears that the service will deteriorate just as the number of workers with employment grievances is rising rapidly . . .
>
> *Source*: Robert Taylor, *Financial Times*, 17 January 1996.

EXHIBIT **12.1 Two different aspects of budgets**

INTRODUCTION

Budgets are a pervasive fact of life and affect us all - directly and indirectly – in both our working and personal environments. Large organisations, such as Vodaphone and the Government in Exhibit 12.1, will have well-developed formal budget systems. Small organisations and individuals, although possibly more informal in their approach, must likewise possess some kind of planning mechanism. In Chapter 1, we identified planning as one of management's primary functions – and, simply put, budgets represent a statement of managerial plans for the organisation as a whole and for various subsections of the organisation. Since effective planning is so vital to the success of an organisation, an understanding of budgets – a major planning mechanism – is essential not only for those tasked with the responsibility of preparing, implementing and achieving budgets (i.e. management), but also for those whose operations are governed and influenced by management actions (i.e. the workforce, customers, shareholders, suppliers and possibly society in general). Consider the potential ramifications of the two differing budget decisions in Exhibit 12.1: Vodaphone will need to find a substantial amount of additional funding to finance the extra advertising budget and the company's consumer profile and sales will almost certainly alter; the proposed budget reduction for industrial tribunals may have implications for staffing levels and possibly for the quality of service provided.

OBJECTIVES   When you have completed this chapter, you will be able to:

- provide a definition of the term 'budget' and explain the major purposes of budgets, along with their potential shortcomings;

- distinguish between operational, tactical and strategic budgets and appreciate their relationship;

- describe the role of the budget committee, budget officer and budget manual;

- understand the meaning of standard costing, its significance in the budgeting process, and its objectives and problems;

- prepare functional and cash budgets for a manufacturing organisation and appreciate how these are summarised in the master budget;

- outline the particular budgeting problems faced by service and public sector organisations; and

- describe the operation, advantages and problems of line item, programme, incremental, zero base, rolling and activity-based budgets.

'BUDGET': A DEFINITION

Our definition is so straightforward as to seem, perhaps, self-evident: a budget is *a quantified plan* targetted at achievement of an objective (or objectives). Simple as it may seem, this definition encompasses the three essential elements of a budget. A budget is a plan: that is, it is *future-oriented* – the past is only relevant in so far as it provides a reasonable indicator of the future. We must also be clear that a plan is not an end in itself, but a means to an end – achieveing a particular objective (or objectives). In effect, our definition of 'budget' also encompasses control: we prepare budgets to achieve objectives and then assess how far performance, budgets and objectves are in line with each other. Of course, we are assuming here that objectives are clearly defined, which may not always be the case (as we observed in Chapter 1).

⇨ Why is it important that plans be quantified?

If they lack quantification, plans can lose much of their value. Suppose a business plans to earn 'some profit' in the forthcoming year. Without knowing how much profit, it is difficult to assess the amount of 'effort' which should be expended in pursuit of the plan: that is, the required sales and related costs. At the end of the year, how can the business gauge how successful it has been in achieving its plan (and hence its objectives)? In short, the 'plan', having provided neither a meaningful target for future effort nor a benchmark for associated performance, is almost as bad as no plan at all. Quantifying the plan – for example, 'Earn £500,000 profit next year' – helps to remedy these problems.

OBJECTIVES OF BUDGETS

Our definition of 'budget' provides an indication of the major objectives of a system of budgeting. The extent to which budgets succeed in achieving these objectives is, however, questionable.

Compel planning

The existence of a budget forces managers to think ahead, trying to anticipate possible problems and their solution. Although budgets cannot prevent the unforeseen from occurring or remove future difficulties, their formulation can allow some degree of preparedness. For example, awareness of a potential future problem with material suppliers would allow contingency arrangements to be made (e.g. finding alternative suppliers) in advance. All of which presupposes that budgets are reasonable estimates of the future; but producing credible estimates, especially in rapidly changing environments, can be extremely difficult. The budget process therefore places great reliance on managerial knowledge and judgement. On the one hand, it might be said that the need to exercise such knowledge and judgement within a formalised budgeting framework will reduce the effect of any overly subjective elements. On the other hand, a formal system might inhibit freedom of management action, thereby adding undue weight to risk-averse courses of action. A further difficulty is that, whilst budgets may indicate what we should do, they do not necessarily tell us *how* to do it.

Provide a performance benchmark and financial control mechanism

A typical budget system will identify managerial responsibility with particular areas of the budget (**responsibility accounting**), financial control and performance evaluation being frequently based on comparison of budgeted and actual outcomes (**feedback control**) and of budgeted outcomes with objectives (**feedforward control**). It is quite common for managerial salary bonuses to be linked to performance defined in feedback/feedforward terms. We will discuss these topics in Chapters 13, 14 and 15 where we will also see that financial measures of control have limitations, possibly even dangers.

Provide motivational impetus

Setting targets may have motivational benefits. If we have a clearly stated and quantified target, it is possible that we will make more effort to achieve it than we might otherwise do. However, as we shall see in Chapter 16, the motivational effect of budgetary target-setting is far from clear. Budgeting, and participation in budget-setting, *may* be motivationally beneficial, but may also have exactly the opposite effect – especially where budgets are viewed by management as a constraint or as a 'big stick' to punish underachievement.

Provide a medium of communication

There is no point in having targets, benchmarks and control mechanisms if they are kept secret: people need to know what is expected of them. Budgets provide one means of disseminating such awareness through the organisation. In addition, communication should be enhanced by the budget-setting process where this is undertaken by a combination of 'top-down' and 'bottom-up' procedures: that is, where budgets are the result of consultation, participation and flow of information from top management downwards (e.g. strategic targets) and from operational management upwards (e.g. detailed estimates – **standard costs** – for individual cost units). However, the success of budgets as a medium of communication relies on the extent to which the principles and information involved are understood. Thus the criteria governing useful information which we set out in Chapter 1 are especially important. Effective budgetary communication is also predicated on the clarity and openness of formal transmission channels. The extent to which informal channels do/do not predominate over formal could give some indication of the effectiveness of budgetary communication. (You should also bear in mind the barriers to communication which we discussed in Chapter 1.)

It is also possible that the administrative burden associated with budgets could overshadow the purpose of budget preparation, causing the exercise to flounder in bureaucratic 'overkill'.

Enhance co-ordination

In larger organisations particularly, co-ordination between different divisions, departments and managers is of vital importance, especially where these enjoy any significant degree of independence from central control.

⇨ In a manufacturing business, why is it important that the activities of the sales and production departments are co-ordinated?

If there were no co-ordination between these two departments, chaos would almost certainly result. For example, the sales department might promise delivery to customers within unrealistic time limits, or quantities produced might be far in excess of what can be sold, causing an unnecessary build-up in stocks. Formalised budget preparation, by explicitly recognising interrelationships between different organisational segments, should help reduce the chance of such undesirable situations. One of the objectives of budgets is thus to promote **goal congruence**: that is, to encourage actions by individual employees, managers, sections, departments or divisions which are consistent with overall organisational aims (or at least which do not directly conflict with them). Where conflicts of this kind do arise, the results are suboptimal (or **dysfunctional**): for instance, promises of impossibly unrealistic delivery dates could well result in lost custom, which is scarcely in the organisation's best interest.

This is a very laudable objective, but it requires that organisational objectives be clearly and unambiguously stated. Not only do we have the problem of diffuse and potentially conflicting organisational objectives (see Chapter 1), but we are also faced with the fact that, as Cyert and March (1963) observe, organisations do not have objectives, *people* do (an issue which we shall explore in greater depth in Chapter 16). Problems in objective-setting can only hamper proper co-ordination of diverse activities, and this may be exacerbated by unduly dominant informal communication channels.

Instil financial awareness

Without the existence of budgets, managers may be quite unaware of the financial implications of their actions, or of the need to look for alternatives which are more financially effective. Such a lack of awareness would be detrimental to the organisation as a whole, since there is the danger of scarce resources being carelessly used, as if they were somehow 'free'. But it is also possible to argue that this sort of awareness can (and does) exist independently of any formal budget system – in which case, is the formal system redundant? Formalising managerial expectations within a budget system might result in a situation where there is conflict between managerial expectations as expressed in the budget and their *true* expectations.

Budgets may instil cost consciousness but, if used in a 'carrot and stick' manner, may also inspire feelings almost of fear and loathing amongst managers. In addition, it is rare for a budget system explicitly to reflect its own cost: that is, the cost of set-up, maintenance and operation. Not only can these financial costs be substantial, but there is also the question of management time involved in budget-related activities, time which could be more profitably spent in other ways.

So perhaps the sort of cost consciousness instilled by budgets could be organisationally undesirable, focusing managers' attention on annual, financial and internal considerations at the expense of longer-term, non-financial and environmental factors.

STRATEGIC, TACTICAL AND OPERATIONAL BUDGETS

Whilst achieving budgets can be viewed as a target, budgets themselves must tend towards the achievement of some aim. In Chapter 1, we made the distinction between strategic, tactical and operational planning, control and decision making, contrasting their respective span, scope and level of detail. Thus, the **budget period** (i.e. the length of time to which the budget relates) applicable to strategic budgets will be considerably longer than that applicable to tactical and operational budgets – say, somewhere between 3 and 10 years for the former, one year for the latter. The scope of strategic budgets will likewise be broader, dealing with major issues of organisational development over the specified time horizon, whereas tactical and operational budgets will be much more limited, dealing, perhaps, with specific aspects of strategic issues.

⇨ Would you expect strategic budgets to be more or less detailed than tactical and operational?

Strategic budgets will be considerably less detailed than tactical and operational budgets, being confined to quantifications of strategic aims, such as 'achieving a 25 per cent market share within seven years', 'doubling return on capital over the next five years' or 'achieving world-class status'. Tactical and operational budgets, as we shall see, must contain sufficient detail to guide short-term operations towards attainment of strategic goals and also to provide meaningful information about how to run these operations efficiently, effectively and economically. The key point here is that not only should budgets encourage goal congruence between individual subunits and the organisational whole, but also between strategic, tactical and operational considerations: that is, tactical and operational budgets should, over a given strategic time frame, be consistent with achievement of strategic goals, as illustrated in Figure 12.1.

What Figure 12.1 illustrates is the close integration which should exist between strategic, tactical and operational levels of budgeting, although in practice, the relationships may be less well-defined, e.g. 'operational' is often used to describe everything which is not strategic. An example of why such integration is important can be seen in the impact of capital investment decisions. Strategic objectives will dictate the need for a particular capital expenditure project which will be evaluated using the kind of criteria we discussed in Chapter 10; if acceptable, this project will be incorporated within the strategic budget. This will 'feed through' to tactical level in the form of costs and benefits associated with the project for each year of its life; in the first year, for example, we might expect to see the initial acquisition cost (likely to be a substantial sum) plus current costs and benefits (e.g. annual running costs and increased revenue resulting from acquisition of new plant). At the operational level, the capital expenditure decision could affect work methods, material type and quantity, labour requirements and speed of throughput.

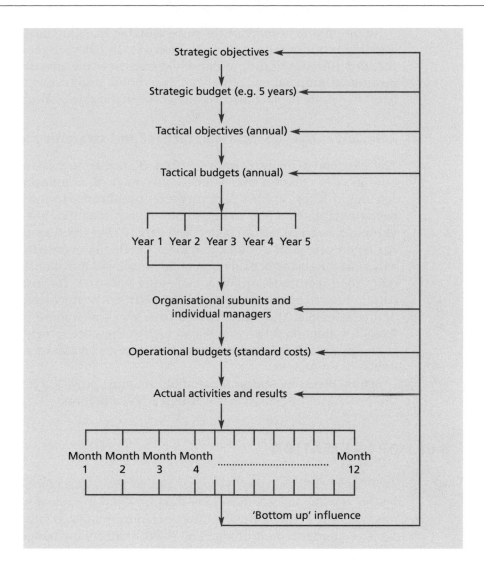

FIGURE 12.1
Top-down and
bottom-up
linkages in the
budget process

⇨ What dangers might result from a failure to recognise the sort of stategic/
tactical/operational relationships we have just described?

There are three potential dangers here:

1 The implications of strategic and tactical budgets may not be appreciated at
operational level, e.g. installation of new plant may require re-training of operatives or re-specification of material inputs.

2 The implications of strategic and operational budgets may not be appreciated at
tactical level, e.g. re-training of operatives may be costly and may temporarily
depress the rate of output.

3 The implications of tactical and operational budgets may not be appreciated at
strategic level, e.g. strategic objectives may need to be revised in light of tactical
and operational constraints.

Failure in one or more of the three areas we have just mentioned, will almost certainly result in failure to meet objectives. In Chapter 15, we will encounter a common instance of this, when we illustrate how the adverse impact of a capital investment proposal on tactical and operational results might tempt managers to reject it, despite the fact that acceptance is beneficial in strategic terms.

Relevant range, operational, tactical and strategic budgets

The concept of relevant range – that is, the time horizon and/or range of output/sales volumes over which a given set of assumptions (e.g. about cost behaviour) is reasonable – is of particular significance to the distinction between operational, tactical and strategic budgets. For example, costs which are fixed in terms of an annual tactical budget will very likely exhibit marked step characteristics when placed in a strategic framework. Or the organisation's cost structure, which will probably be fairly immobile in tactical/operational terms, may change quite significantly for strategic budgeting purposes: for instance, strategy may require heavy capital investments/disinvestments, which could alter the balance of direct/indirect and variable/fixed costs very much more towards indirect and fixed. It is important that differences such as these are recognised within the budgeting process. If they are not, then the value of organisational planning – at all levels – is prejudiced.

Before discussing budget preparation, we must provide a brief overview of how this process may be co-ordinated within an organisation.

BUDGET ORGANISATION

At the start of this chapter, we suggested that the degree of formality attaching to a budget system may well be greater in larger than in smaller organisations. Where the system is highly formalised, its operation frequently hinges on the deliberations of a **budget committee** and on the contents of the **budget manual**.

Ideally, each **budget centre** should be represented (i.e. each organisational sub-unit for which a budget is separately prepared). We shall have more to say about the precise definition of budget centres in the next chapter. In practice, however, membership of the budget committee is often limited – both for managebility and to reflect the extent to which budget authority is delegated.

▷ What major functions might a budget committee perform?

The budget committee's precise remit will differ from organisation to organisation, but the following types of activity are fairly common:

1 *Conversion of strategic to operational budgets* Although the budget committee may be consulted as part of the strategy formulation process, this is ultimately the responsibility of the very top management level (e.g. the board of directors, who could well be represented on the budget committee). What the budget committee needs to decide is how best to translate the strategic budget into a series of tactical (i.e.

annual) budgets. In addition, the budget committee will filter, collate and pass on to senior management operational and tactical data relevant to strategic planning.

2 *Negotiation of functional budgets* The budget committee will provide a forum in which managers can negotiate the amount of their budgets (e.g. making a case for substantial increase compared to previous years).

3 *Approval of functional budgets and consolidation into the master budget* Because budget centres often correspond to organisational functions such as sales or production, these individual budgets are referred to as **functional budgets**. Once they have been approved, functional budgets are consolidated and summarised into a **master** (or **summary**) **budget**, typically consisting of a budgeted profit and loss account, cash budget and probably a budgeted balance sheet. (We will look at the mechanics of budget preparation shortly.)

4 *Investigation of significant variances* Since managerial, as well as organisational, performance may be assessed on the basis of comparison between budget and actual, any possibility of personal bias in the investigation process would be highly undesirable. The budget committee may therefore decide what represents a significant difference (**variance**) between budget and actual, which manager should have the responsibility for investigation, and what action can be taken as a result of such investigation.

5 *Resolution of disputes* Perhaps one of the most important functions which the budget committee can perform is to resolve any disputes which may arise as a consequence of the budgetary system. For example, there may be areas of budget responsibility which are common to several managers and the budget committee may need to determine the most equitable method of dealing with the cost of these shared areas.

In general, the budget committee will be responsible for budget administration. Liaison between the different functions represented on the committee is often provided by a budget officer (typically a management accountant), who can also supply technical advice relating to budgetary matters.

One important role of the budget committee which we have not mentioned is that of preparing and updating the **budget manual**. In essence, this document is a user manual, setting out key aspects of budgetary procedure (e.g. the budget-setting timetable, areas of personal responsibility and details of specific budgets). In large and/or complex organisations, the budget manual can be especially significant, so it is important that the procedures which it documents are described as clearly and comprehensibly as possible.

We will commence our discussion of budget preparation with an explanation of the operational end of the spectrum before we illustrate how tactical budgets are prepared.

STANDARD COSTS: BUDGETARY BUILDING BLOCKS

Tactical budgets are expressed at a comparatively aggregated level (e.g. functional or organisational) and therefore require to be based on detailed unit-level estimates. **Standard costs** are just such estimates.

⇨ In order to prepare an annual (i.e. tactical) budget for the cost of direct materials used in production, what information would a manufacturing firm require to have?

We would need to know:

1 the volume of production in units;
2 the material requirement per unit of output; and
3 the cost per unit of material.

Production volume will be obtained from the production budget (a tactical budget), but we need to estimate the material requirement per unit of output and the cost per unit of material. Suppose we know that budgeted production volume is 10,000 units and have estimated that each unit of output requires 6 kg of direct material at a cost of £0.40 per kg. The **standard direct materials' cost** per unit of output will be (6 kg @ £0.40) = £2.40. The budgeted cost of direct materials used in production will thus be (10,000 units produced × £2.40) = £24,000. The standard quantity (i.e. 6 kg per unit of output) and standard price (£0.40 per kg) of direct materials will also be used in construction of the budget for direct materials' purchases.

Similar estimates will be prepared for direct labour – of **standard hours** (labour hours per unit of output) and standard rate (labour rate per hour). Predetermined overhead absorption rates will be developed (*see* Chapter 4) allowing a standard overhead cost per unit to be calculated. In addition to estimating the input resources necessary per unit of output, a standard selling price will be set and standard profit (or standard contribution) per unit determined.

The detailed estimates which support standard costs (e.g. of materials' usage or labour time per unit) often require considerable experitse to produce. Direct materials' requirements, for example, may result from engineering analysis of inputs and outputs.

Exhibit 12.2 contains some data which we will use to assemble a standard cost card per unit of output.

DPA Ltd

One of the company's products is an organic fertiliser which is sold in 5kg bags. Standard data for next year per 5kg bag are:

Direct materials	6 kg @ £0.40 per kg
Direct labour	0.2 hours @ £10 per hour
Packing	£0.50
Production overhead	£1.50 per direct labour hour
Selling price	£5.75

Of the 6 kg direct materials' input, 1kg is expected to be lost under normal operating conditions.

EXHIBIT **12.2 Data for standard product specification**

▷ From Exhibit 12.2, what is the standard direct labour cost per 5 kg bag?

The standard direct labour cost per bag is (0.2 hours @ £10) = £1. A standard cost card detailing the physical and financial specifications of each 5 kg bag might be as follows:

5 kg bag of fertiliser: standard specification	£
Direct materials (6 kg @ £0.40)	2.40
Direct labour (0.2 hours @ £10)	2.00
Packing	0.50
Standard prime cost	4.90
Production overhead (0.2 hours @ £1.50)	0.30
Standard production cost	5.20
Standard selling price	5.75
Standard gross profit	0.55

Note that the expected direct material loss of 1 kg per bag is incorporated within the standard cost per bag, since it is a consequence of 'normal operating conditions' and should be allowed for in the same way as any other production cost.

The standard profit is 'gross' because non-production costs must still be deducted.

Types of standard

When standards are being set, one question which inevitably arises is: 'How tight a standard?' In other words, what level of operational efficiency does the standard assume? Two broad categories of standard may be identified: **ideal** (or **potential**) and **currently attainable**. An ideal standard assumes optimum efficiency, whereas a currently attainable standard is based on efficient operation under current conditions. An ideal standard would thus make no allowance for items such as the 'normal' materials' loss suffered by DPA Ltd, machine downtime or labour idle time; a currently attainable standard, on the other hand, would make allowance for such factors. This is not to say, however, that currently attainable standards are 'slack' – a high level of efficiency is still assumed.

⇨ Suggest one major drawback which might be associated with the use of ideal standards.

Because they assume optimum efficiency, ideal standards may lack credibility, as it is possible to take the view that optimum efficiency is simply not attainable in reality. And, if the standards lack credibility, then so will any budget which is constructed from them. A 1993 survey by Drury *et al.* indicated that only 4 per cent of the respondent UK manufacturing companies used standards based on maximum efficiency, the remainder employing either currently attainable standards or standards derived from past performance. However, the impact of total quality management, with its 'get it right first time all of the time' approach, coupled with organisations' desire to achieve world-class status, may mean that ideal standards will be more widely used in future. If, for example, current expectation is that performance will be, say, 75 per cent of ideal, then an actual which betters this could indicate a move towards improved quality (although quality might also suffer in a 'push' to exceed standard). Conversely, standards with an inbuilt allowance for waste – such as the 1 kg material loss in the standard specification of a 5 kg bag of fertiliser above – imply that such waste is acceptable and improvement is not necessary, which could possibly become a self-perpetuating misconception.

The standard hour

Rather confusingly, the **standard hour** is a measure of work, not of time: it is the amount of work which should be performed at standard efficiency in one hour.

DPA Ltd: range of organic fertilisers

The company produces its organic fertiliser in four different sizes of bag; details are:

	Size of bag			
	2 kg	5 kg	10kg	20 kg
Standard labour hours per bag	0.10	0.20	0.40	0.50
Budgeted output (number of bags)	12,000	10,000	8,000	5,000
Actual output (number of bags)	14,000	9,000	6,000	7,000

EXHIBIT **12.3 Data for calculation of standard hours**

As a statement of budgeted and actual output, the information in Exhibit 12.3 is useful, but rather unwieldy: for instance, it is not readily apparent whether actual output *overall* exceeded budget or not. In order to assess this, we need to express output on a common basis, and this common basis is provided by the standard hour. Budgeted output in standard hours is:

	Standard hours
2 kg bags (12,000 × 0.10 hours per bag)	1,200
5 kg bags (10,000 × 0.20 hours per bag)	2,000
10 kg bags (8,000 × 0.40 hours per bag)	3,200
20 kg bags (5,000 × 0.50 hours per bag)	2,500
	8,900

We can therefore say that budgeted output, *in total*, represents 8,900 standard hours' worth of work.

⇨ Convert DPA Ltd's actual output in Exhibit 12.3 to standard hours and compare this with the budgeted output.

In standard hours, actual output is:

	Standard hours
2 kg bags (14,000 × 0.10 hours per bag)	1,400
5 kg bags (9,000 × 0.20 hours per bag)	1,800
10 kg bags (6,000 × 0.40 hours per bag)	2,400
20 kg bags (7,000 × 0.50 hours per bag)	3,500
	9,100

Compared to budget, this represents an increase in total output of (9,100 − 8,900) = 200 standard hours, or approximately 2 per cent of budget. Ability to express output of diverse products/services in a unitary measure may be important for resource planning (e.g. manpower required to achieve budgeted output) and for financial control (as we shall see in the next chapter).

Advantages of standard costing

Like budgets in general, the formality of a standard costing system will vary from organisation to organisation, and differences in specifics may be particularly marked when we compare manufacturing and service organisations. For tactical budgets to be effective, some degree of estimation at cost unit (i.e. operational) level is necessary, and can offer a number of advantages:

Accuracy of budgets is improved

Building a tactical budget from cost unit estimates should yield a more accurate result than is likely from attempts to estimate on a 'total' basis, especially where a range of different resource inputs and product/service outputs is involved. Consider the problems which would face DPA Ltd in Exhibit 12.3 were the company to attempt to produce a manpower budget based purely on estimated unit output of each product, without the availability of standard unit labour times.

Cost consciousness is instilled

The existence of standard unit specifications, of the type we prepared above for DPA Ltd's 5 kg bag of fertiliser, should help raise awareness of cost-related issues amongst employees – especially if employees are involved in setting standards, and if standard resource and cost information is disseminated by management to those employees principally involved in output of products/services. In addition, the fact that standards comprise not only financial information, but also resource quantities (e.g. standard materials' usage quantities), may help reinforce the role of budgets as targets and performance benchmarks. Employees who might feel 'intimidated' by purely financial information may be more comfortable if this is supported by non-financial data. Standards per unit may also provide a target of greater immediacy to employees 'at the sharp end'. As we have already said, the existence of a target may have beneficial motivational effects.

Methods may be improved

Setting standards for resource inputs such as labour times and material quantities could encourage a search for improved work methods or better materials.

Permits detailed control analysis

As we shall see in Chapter 14, standard costing allows 'global' budget variances to be subdivided into their constituent elements, thereby allowing potential problem areas to be more accurately pinpointed.

Provides a better costing and pricing basis than actual costs

Actual costs and resource inputs per unit are likely to fluctuate: for example, over a one-year period and between different cost units. Such fluctuations would mean that unit costs would also fluctuate, as would stock values and profit – and also selling prices, if these are based to any significant extent on cost.

⇨ If selling prices are based on cost, what problem (in addition to fluctuation) would arise from use of actual costs?

As we saw in Chapter 4 (in the context of overhead absorption rates), actuals will not be known until after the event. Producing quotations for work, or price lists, would therefore be difficult – or even impossible – with obvious implications for the organisation's sales effort.

Problems of standard costing

Despite the advantages offered, standard costing may also present some difficulties in operation:

Incorporating inflation into standards

Even where inflation rates are low, this may still be troublesome. Not only is there the difficulty of estimating future rates with tolerable accuracy, but there may also be a problem in comparing budget and actual where the rate of inflation affecting each is materially different (a point we shall return to in the next chapter). Even where future rates of inflation can be estimated with reasonable confidence and where these estimates are fairly close to reality, the very fact of their inclusion in standards can cause distortions, as we will illustrate using the information in Exhibit 12.4.

DPA Ltd: effect of inflation on standard and actual material costs

For a particular year, the standard material usage quantity and cost per kg of material for each of the company's 5 kg bags of fertiliser is: 6 kg @ £0.40 per kg. The standard cost of £0.40 per kg makes allowance for estimated inflation of 3.5 per cent for the year to which the standard applies. In Month 1 of that year, the actual cost per kg of material was £0.39.

EXHIBIT **12.4 Standard/actual costs and inflation**

On the face of it, the actual material cost per kg in Month 1 was lower than standard, which might be taken to suggest better-than-standard performance in purchasing.

⇨ Why is comparison of the £0.40 per kg standard cost with the Month 1 actual of £0.39 potentially misleading?

The problem is that the £0.40 standard cost incorporates a full year's inflation. Even assuming that the 3.5 per cent inflation estimate for the year is accurate, Month 1 actual costs will not have been affected by a full year's inflation: that is, the standard is effectively overstated as far as Month 1 is concerned. The apparently 'better-than-standard' purchasing performance may therefore be illusory. We might try to redress this by using, in the standard, an average inflation rate for the year, but even this does not solve the problem. Assuming inflation arises evenly throughout the year and that actual inflation is in line with estimate, then standards for the first half of the year will be overstated, whereas those for the second half will be understated. A more sophisticated form of weighting could be employed, but this might complicate the standard setting and budget/actual comparison process so much that its benefits are lost. Alternatively, we might ignore the effect of inflation entirely, in which case any comparison of budget and actual will be distorted by the existence of inflation in the latter figures and its absence from the former. In the next chapter, we will demonstrate how the potential distortion caused by inflation may be removed from a budget/actual comparison by **deflating** the figures concerned.

Setting an acceptable labour efficiency standard

Where direct labour is a significant element in the output process – as it is in many service industries – setting an appropriate standard for efficiency is important. Adoption of a standard which is too 'tight' could adversely affect labour relations, or be viewed by employees as an impossible target (and thus one which it is pointless to try and achieve). On the other hand, an efficiency standard which is too 'slack' may not motivate employees to improve performance. In either case, the standard, consequent budget and comparison of actual with budget are all likely to be suspect. (*See* Chapter 16 for further consideration of these issues.)

Inapplicability to heterogeneous output

Standard costing is well suited to situations where output procedures consist of repetitive processes and where the output itself is fairly standardised. But in job costing and many service industries, where cost units are markedly different to each other, standard costing may work less well. What, for example, should be the standard labour time allowed for settling an insurance claim? It really depends on the specific claim. Attempting to arrive at some kind of 'average' standard based on all estimated output could well result in standards which bear little relationship to the resources and costs involved in particular jobs, thereby cancelling much of the benefit of standard costing.

This is not to suggest that standard costing cannot be applied to output other than mass produced homogeneous items. The technique is becoming increasingly prevalent in service organisations. For example, within the UK health service, considerable work is currently under way aimed at producing standard costs for surgical procedures.

Cost of introducing and maintaining system

Standard costing systems can be costly to introduce and maintain. For example, estimates need to be obtained for resource inputs and their costs, and previously set standards will require to be updated periodically – all of which may involve considerable time, effort and cost. The need to review and update standards may incur a less obvious cost. The frequency of this event needs to be handled sensibly, as review which is too frequent or too infrequent may reduce standards' credibility. As a minimum, standards should really be reviewed as part of the annual budget-setting exercise.

May overemphasise operational considerations

Because of their necessarily detailed and precise nature compared to strategy's less-defined approach, there may be a danger that development of workable standards (e.g. on an annual basis) may overshadow the link between operational, tactical and strategic factors, or even entirely mask the need for strategic planning.

Now we have discussed the operational aspect of budgets, we can demonstrate how the more aggregate tactical budgets are obtained.

PREPARATION OF FUNCTIONAL BUDGETS

Tactical budgets are generally prepared for individual **budget centres**; these can be individual organisational functions like sales or production (hence the term **functional budgets**), or subunits (e.g. departments). Although the precise definition of budget centres will depend on the structure of specific organisations, they will almost always correspond to areas of managerial responibility: in a manufacturing business, for example, the Production Manager would normally be responsible for achieving (and very likely helping to set) the production budget, which might itself be subdivided into budgets covering narrower areas of managerial responsibility within the production function. Where budget centres reflect managerial responsibility in this way, they are more commonly referred to as **responsibility centres** – a topic which we shall discuss in detail in the next chapter. You should note that, for ease of presentation, the functional budgets which we will prepare are based on a fairly simple organisational structure.

For the same reason, our functional budgets with employ annual figures. While this may provide a useful tactical overview of the period, effective planning and control require these budgets to be *profiled*. For example, the production budget could show budgeted output and stocks of each product on a month-by-month basis during the year and in total for the year, thus reflecting factors such as seasonal fluctuations and allowing better scheduling of dependent activities such as materials' purchasing. Strategic budgets may also be profiled (e.g. by year within the strategic time-frame). (Question 12.9 addresses the issue of preparing a profiled purchases budget, and you will see that the computational approach is identical to that adopted below.) A further reason for profiling the budget is to allow preparation of the cash budget. Within any budget period, it is essential to be able to identify variations in cash flows, so that the timing of possible shortages and surpluses may be assessed. Profiling budgets in this way can be seen as another illustration of the close link between tactical and operational issues, with the latter having a major bearing on how profiling occurs.

The budgetary 'cycle'

We said earlier that one of the main objectives of budgets is to enhance co-ordination between different organisational functions. This may be seen in the order in which budgets are prepared. Figure 12.2 illustrates how this might occur in DPA Ltd.

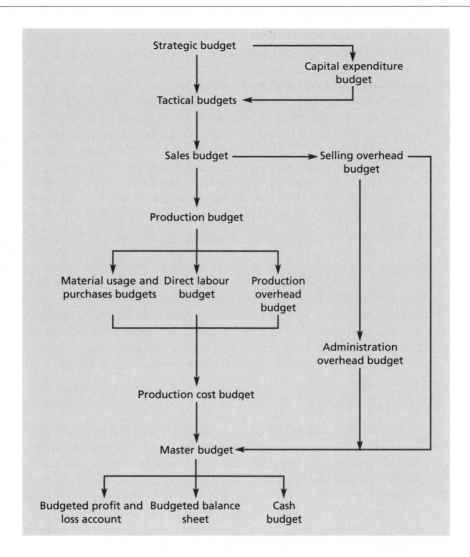

FIGURE 12.2
DPA Ltd:
illustrative
budgetary
'cycle'

⇨ Why does the budget preparation sequence in Figure 12.2 start with the sales budget?

The sales budget for is first in sequence because, without an estimate of sales, a meaningful production budget cannot be prepared – and without a meaningful production budget, budgets for material usage, material purchases, manpower and so on will have equally little meaning. The pattern of budgetary interrelationships illustrated in Figure 12.2 appears to be fairly complex, but it is almost certainly an oversimplification of reality. If reality is even more complicated, this simply emphasises the need for effective budget co-ordination. Although the precise budget 'cycle' may vary from one organisation to the next, the broad principle of a co-ordinated approach applies equally to all, and we can say that, in general, the starting-point needs to be an estimate of activity volume. In practice, it is unlikely that budgets will be prepared in strict sequence from start to finish. In particular, the preparation of budgets may be affected by the existence of one or more **principal budget factors** (i.e. limiting factors of the type we described in Chapter 8).

⇨ How would the fact that direct materials is a principal budget factor affect DPA Ltd's budget preparation?

Assuming that this limitation cannot be overcome (e.g. by subcontracting), then its existence will determine the mix and quantity of products produced, and may mean that the company cannot fully satisfy expected demand in the forthcoming period. In effect, the principal budget factor becomes the starting-point for budget preparation. It could also happen that an unforeseen limitation may emerge during budget preparation; in this case, budgets would need to be revised accordingly. Failure to reflect such a resource limitation – for example, by undertaking a ranking exercise of the type we described in Chapter 8 – will render budgets pointless at best, and seriously misleading at worst. What all of this means is that budget preparation may be a protracted affair, requiring proper scheduling. Preparation timetables are one area for which the budget committee may have ultimate responsibility, arranging for these to be detailed in the budget manual. Although the administrative effort (and possibly cost) may be significant, it can be justified by the need to have budgets in place prior to the start of the period to which they relate. In some organisations (e.g. local and central government), operations simply cannot proceed without advance preparation and approval of a budget for the relevant period.

We will now consider the budgets shown in Figure 12.2 in more detail.

The sales budget

In preparing the sales budget, management will consider any known internal constraints in conjunction with estimates about conditions within the business's specific market (e.g. possible actions by competitors, or the price sensitivity of the product/service being sold), coupled with an assessment of the wider economic prospects for the period under review (e.g. projected inflation rate or changes in taxation policy). Included in management's assessment will be qualitative factors, such as potential shifts in consumer taste, and the impact of proposed changes in product/service specification or in the sales mix. Only after a thorough appraisal of all factors (internal and external to the organisation) which might have an effect on sales should the sales budget be prepared.

The sales budget for DPA Ltd is, effectively, contained within Exhibit 12.5: that is, the unit selling prices and sales volumes for each product. The only additional information we need to show is the sales revenue for each product and in total:

	Sales revenue (£)
2 kg bags (15,000 × £4.25)	63,750
5 kg bags (12,000 × £7.10)	85,200
10 kg bags (8,200 × £13.50)	110,700
20 kg bags (5,400 × £24.75)	133,650
	393,300

Only once the sales budget has been prepared is it possible to give detailed consideration to production and its related budgets. (Had our example involved a principal budget factor, we would have required to employ our limiting factor

DPA Ltd: sales and stock data

After careful consideration of the market for its products and related factors next year, management has produced the following estimates of sales volumes, standard unit selling prices and desired levels of closing stock, along with anticipated stock levels at the end of the current year:

Size of bag	2 kg	5 kg	10 kg	20 kg
Selling price per bag	£4.25	£7.10	£13.50	£24.75
Sales volume (number of bags)	15,000	12,000	8,200	5,400
Stock (number of bags):				
Anticipated at end of current year	4,000	2,500	400	600
Desired at end of next year	1,000	500	200	200

EXHIBIT **12.5 data for sales and production budget preparation**

techniques from Chapter 8 to determine the optimum mix of products; i.e. the production budget would be prepared first).

The production budget

The company will aim to produce each product in sufficient quantity to meet the level of demand anticipated in the sales budget *and* to give the desired amount of stock at the end of the year, but after adjusting for the current year's closing stock (which will also be next year's opening stock):

	Units
Sales budget	X
add Closing stock desired at end of budget period	X
	X
less Opening stock at beginning of budget period	X
Production required	X

Exhibit 12.6 is DPA Ltd's production budget, completed for 2 kg bags only.

DPA LTD: PRODUCTION BUDGET

	Size of bag			
	2 kg	5 kg	10 kg	20 kg
Sales budget (bags)	15,000			
add Closing stock desired	1,000			
	16,000			
less Opening stock	4,000			
Production required	12,000			

EXHIBIT **12.6 Partly complete production budget**

⇨ Use the data from Exhibit 12.5 to complete the production budget in Exhibit 12.6.

DPA Ltd's completed production budget is given in Exhibit 12.7.

DPA Ltd: production budget

	Size of bag			
	2 kg	5 kg	10 kg	20 kg
Sales budget (bags)	15,000	12,000	8,200	5,400
add Closing stock desired	1,000	500	200	200
	16,000	12,500	8,400	5,600
less Opening stock	4,000	2,500	400	600
Production required	12,000	10,000	8,000	5,000

EXHIBIT **12.7 Completed production budget**

Following our suggested budgetary 'cycle', it is only now that production-related budgets, such as direct labour, materials' usage and materials' purchases can be prepared – a process which could reveal unforeseen limiting factors.

Direct materials' usage and purchases budgets

DPA Ltd: direct materials' standards
The same direct material is used in all the company's products, standard input quantities being as follows for each size of bag produced:

	Size of bag			
	2 kg	5 kg	10 kg	20 kg
Kg of material input	2.4	6.0	12.0	24.0

The standard cost per kg of materials is £0.40, and the following amounts of stock are anticipated and desired:

Anticipated stock at the end of the current period	60,000 kg
Desired stock at the end of the budget period	80,000 kg

EXHIBIT **12.8 Data for preparation of materials' usage and purchases budgets**

You will see that the material usage per 5kg bag, along with the standard cost per kg of materials are these which we gave in Exhibit 12.2 when we built up the standard specification of this product. The materials' usage budget will be determined by output quantities specified in the production budget and by the standard materials' input for each size of bag given in Exhibit 12.8:

DPA Ltd: direct materials' usage budget

	kg
2 kg bags (12,000 × 2.4 kg per bag)	28,800
5 kg bags (10,000 × 6.0 kg per bag)	60,000
10 kg bags (8,000 × 12 kg per bag)	96,000
20 kg bags (5,000 × 24 kg per bag)	120,000
Direct materials' usage	304,800

You will notice that, as with the standard cost card for 5 kg bags which we prepared earlier, the expected material losses have been incorporated into the usage budget.

Management may wish to show the extent of expected material losses within the usage budget:

	Material losses (kg)
On 2 kg bags {12,000 × (2.4 – 2.0)}	4,800 kg
On 5 kg bags {10,000 × (6 – 5)}	10,000 kg
On 10 kg bags {8,000 × (12 – 10)}	16,000 kg
On 20 kg bags {5,000 × (24 – 20)}	20,000 kg
Total	50,800 kg

Total losses as percentage of total input are therefore:

$$(50,800 \div 304,800) \quad \underline{16.67\%}$$

Inclusion of anticipated material losses will allow management to monitor actual losses and, where these exceed the expected level, to take action to remedy the problem. The usage budget now forms the starting-point for the materials' purchases budget. We want to purchase sufficient materials to cover the estimated usage in production *and* to leave us with the stock desired at the end of the budget period, but adjusted for anticipated stocks at the start of the budget period (i.e. at the end of the current period):

DPA Ltd: direct materials' purchases budget

	kg
Budgeted direct materials' usage	304,800
add Closing stock desired	_____
less Opening stock	_____
Purchases required	_____
Standard cost per kg of material	£0.40
Total direct materials' purchases cost	£ ___

⇨ Complete the materials' purchases budget above, using appropriate figures from Exhibit 12.8.

The completed purchases budget is as follows:

DPA Ltd: direct materials' purchases budget

	kg
	kg
Budgeted direct materials' usage	304,800
add Closing stock desired	80,000
	384,800
less Opening stock	60,000
Purchases required	324,800
Standard cost per kg of material	£0.40
Total direct materials' purchases cost	£129,920

It is possible to amalgamate the usage and purchases budgets, but this might give an unwieldy statement, especially in situations involving several different direct materials. In addition, purchasing and usage may well occur in different budget centres, so that a combined usage/purchases budget (although offering the benefit of a materials' overview) could create a misleading impression about exactly who, within the management team, is responsible for specific aspects of the budget.

Direct labour budget

Like the materials' budgets which we have just prepared, direct labour requirements will stem from the production budget.

DPA Ltd: standard direct labour requirements

For each of the company's products, standard labour times are:

	Size of bag			
	2 kg	5 kg	10 kg	20 kg
Standard direct labour hours per bag	0.1	0.2	0.4	0.5

After making allowance for idle time, absences through sickness and holidays, management has estimated that 35.6 *productive* hours per worker per week will be available, compared to 44.5 *total* hours per worker per week. The standard weekly wage for direct workers will be £356 during the budget period under consideration and 50 weeks in the year are considered to be working weeks.

EXHIBIT 12.9 Data for preparation of direct labour budget

Before we prepare the company's direct labour budget, we need to make an adjustment to the standard labour cost to reflect non-productive time:

$$\frac{\text{standard weekly wage}}{\text{estimated productive hours per week}}$$

$$= \frac{£356}{35.6} = £10 \text{ per hour}$$

Again, you will see that the standard labour specification per 5 kg bag is the same as that given in Exhibit 12.2. The £10 per direct labour hour could therefore more accurately be termed the standard labour charge per productive hour (to distinguish it from the standard hourly rate of pay, which is (£356 ÷ 44.5) = £8 in this instance).

Based on Exhibit 12.9, DPA Ltd's direct labour budget is as follows:

DPA Ltd: direct labour budget
Productive hours required for budgeted output of:

	Hours
2 kg bags (12,000 × 0.1 hours per bag)	1,200
5 kg bags (10,000 × 0.2 hours per bag)	2,000
10 kg bags (8,000 × 0.4 hours per bag)	3,200
20 kg bags (5,000 × 0.5 hours per bag)	2,500
	8,900
Standard charge per productive hour	£10.00
Total direct wages cost	£89,000
Productive hours per direct worker per week	35.6
Productive direct worker weeks required (8,900 ÷ 35.6)	250
Working weeks per worker per year	50
Number of direct operatives required (250 ÷ 50)	5

▷ What is the implication for the direct labour budget of a significant inaccuracy in the production budget?

If the production budget is materially understated, then the company will find itself understaffed (overstaffed if the production budget is markedly overstated). In either case, additional costs will be incurred (e.g. cost of overtime working), which could have repercussions elsewhere (e.g. the need to pay for unforeseen overtime could reduce the amount of cash available for other purposes). Once again, we can see the need for proper co-ordination of budget preparation.

An alternative presentation of the direct labour budget could 'gross-up' productive hours to total hours, using the proportion of productive to total hours from Exhibit 12.9:

$$\frac{35.6 \text{ productive hours/worker/week}}{44.5 \text{ total hours/worker/week}} = 0.8$$

	Hours
Productive hours required for budgeted output (as before)	8,900
Equivalent total hours (8,900 ÷ 0.8)	11,125
Standard rate of pay per hour	£8.00
Budgeted direct labour cost	£89,000
Total hours per direct worker per week	44.5
Total direct worker weeks required (11,125 ÷ 44.5)	250
Working weeks per worker per year	50
Direct operatives required	5

For monitoring of actual, the direct labour budget may also show the expected number of non-productive hours:

Non-productive hours (11,125 – 8,900)	2,225
Non-productive hours as % of total hours (2,225 ÷ 11,125)	20%

Production overhead budget

The key point to bear in mind about overhead (whether production, selling, distribution or administration overhead) is the fact that the word 'overhead' is generic: that is, it represents the aggregate of different individual costs. For this reason, the factors which influence the amount of overhead will almost certainly be more wide-ranging than those affecting direct production costs. If, for example, the capital expenditure budget indicates the purchase of new production plant, then the related depreciation will be production overhead.

If possible, the overhead budget should distinguish between fixed and variable costs. As we will see in the next chapter, this could be important in the context of financial control. DPA Ltd's production overhead budget is as follows:

DPA Ltd: production overhead budget (all fixed relative to output)

	£
Apportionment of supervisory costs	4,000
Apportionment of occupancy costs	3,000
Direct-wage related costs	3,400
Indirect materials	2,000
Depreciation of equipment	950
	13,350

⇨ Using the direct labour and production overhead budgets, obtain DPA Ltd's overhead absorption rate, assuming this is based on direct labour hours.

As we saw in Chapter 4, a direct labour hour absorption rate is calculated as:

$$\frac{\textbf{budgeted overhead cost}}{\textbf{budgeted direct labour hours}}$$

$$= \frac{£13,350}{8,900} = £1.50 \text{ per direct labour hour}$$

Note that productive hours have been used as the denominator and that the company employs a **blanket absorption rate** (*see* Chapter 4).

You will see that the production overhead budget contains apportionments (as do the selling and administration overhead budgets which we shall illustrate shortly). In Chapter 5, we suggested that such apportionments may be inappropriate for planning and control because of their potentially arbitrary nature. In the next chapter, we shall explore this question further.

Production cost budget

Existence of a production budget also permits preparation of the production cost budget. Applying absorption costing principles and using the standard specifications given in Exhibit 12.10, the production cost budget is as follows:

DPA Ltd: production cost budget

	2 kg	5 kg	10 kg	20 kg	Total
Budgeted output (number of bags)	12,000	10,000	8,000	5,000	
	£	£	£	£	£
Direct material cost	11,520	24,000	38,400	48,000	121,920
Direct labour cost	12,000	20,000	32,000	25,000	89,000
Packing	5,400	5,000	4,160	2,750	17,310
Prime cost	28,920	49,000	74,560	75,750	228,230
Production overhead	1,800	3,000	4,800	3,750	13,350
Production cost	30,720	52,000	79,360	79,500	241,580

The budgeted figures for the separate elements of production cost for each product are calculated as:

budgeted output × standard cost per unit.

⇨ In what respect might the production cost budget above be misleading?

The production cost budget we have just prepared was based on a standard cost per unit (see Exhibit 12.10), which included a charge in respect of direct labour and production overhead. Within the relevant range, these costs will be either fixed or will exhibit step behaviour. By 'unitising' direct labour and production overhead, we may give the misleading impression that they are variable in nature. If management were considering total production cost over a range of output volumes, or were comparing actual production costs with budget, then inaccurate cost estimates and budget/actual comparisons could result. It may therefore be better to distinguish between variable costs and fixed costs: that is, to apply marginal costing principles. This would give the following revised production cost budget:

DPA Ltd: summary of standard cost data

Standard data per unit for each of the company's products is given below:

	2 kg	*5 kg*	*10 kg*	*20 kg*
			Size of bag	
Direct materials (2.4/6/12/24 kg @ £0.40)	0.96	2.40	4.80	9.60
Direct labour (0.1/0.2/0.4/0.5 hours @ £10)	1.00	2.00	4.00	5.00
Packing	0.45	0.50	0.52	0.55
Standard prime cost	2.41	4.90	9.32	15.15
Production overhead (0.1/0.2/0.4/0.5 hours @ £1.50)	0.15	0.30	0.60	0.75
Production cost	2.56	5.20	9.92	15.90
Selling price	4.25	7.10	13.50	24.75

EXHIBIT **12.10 Data for preparation of production cost budget**

DPA Ltd: production cost budget (marginal costing version)

	2 kg	5 kg	10 kg	20 kg	Total
Budgeted output (number of bags)	12,000	10,000	8,000	5,000	
	£	£	£	£	£
Direct material cost	11,520	24,000	38,400	48,000	121,920
Packing	5,400	5,000	4,160	2,750	17,310
Variable production cost	16,920	29,000	42,560	50,750	139,230
Fixed production costs:					
Direct labour (from direct labour budget)					89,000
Production overhead (from production overhead budget)					13,350
Production cost					241,580

Using the marginal costing format above should help clarify the relationship between volume of output and production cost, which will almost certainly enhance planning and control. We will explore these issues more fully in the next chapter.

Selling overhead and administration overhead budgets

Budgets for selling and administration overhead, like that for production overhead, will comprise several individual costs. Selling overhead will reflect not only the anticipated volume of sales for the budget period, but also the marketing effort involved (e.g. advertising and promotion). You should also note that activities such as advertising and promotion are especially strongly linked to the business's strategic aims, since costs will often be incurred within the time frame of a tactical budget with the objective of improving or maintaining market standing in the longer term. (If you look again at the first extract in Exhibit 12.1, this is very evident.) The budget for administration overhead will stem from management expectations about the effort and cost of supporting all of the organisation's activities. For DPA Ltd these two budgets are as follows:

DPA Ltd: selling overhead budget

	£
Wages and salaries allocated and apportioned	27,000
Depreciation of delivery vans	4,000
Van running and maintenance costs	3,000
Advertising	5,000
Apportionment of occupancy costs	1,000
Sales commission (1% of budgeted revenue)	3,933
	43,933

DPA Ltd: administration overhead budget

	£
Wages and salaries allocated and apportioned	22,000
Depreciation of office equipment	2,000
Insurance, stationery, increased provision for doubtful debts	3,000
Apportionment of occupancy costs	1,000
	28,000

The increased provision for doubtful debts reflects management expectations that the value of credit sales for which customers fail to pay will be greater next year than this.

⮞ Of the costs listed in the two budgets immediately above, which are likely to vary and which are likely to be fixed relative to the volume of output/sales, given that the budgets are tactical?

Within the relevant range dictated by tactical budgets, only sales commission, and the anticipated change in the provision for doubtful debts are variable relative to the volume of sales, rather than of production (although the change in provision for doubtful debts may depend on other factors besides sales volume). Van running and maintenance costs may be semi-variable within the relevant range. The other costs are likely to be fixed.

THE MASTER BUDGET

Now that we have prepared a series of functional budgets for DPA Ltd, we can illustrate how these will be summarised in the **master budget**. Before we do so, however, we should point out that the functional budgets we have prepared are not intended to represent an exhaustive classification, but are indicative of the major types of such budget that may be encountered in a manufacturing organisation. The precise budgets which an organisation prepares are determined by that organisation's structure and by the nature of its output – a point we shall return to shortly.

The cash budget

Cash is such an important resource that the cash budget can almost be considered as a functional budget in its own right, having the following purposes:

■ to ensure that sufficient cash is available when required to meet the organisation's commitments; and

■ to ensure effective use of surplus cash.

Budgeting the organisation's cash flows allows periods of potential cash shortage and surplus to be anticipated. This permits advance arrangements to be made to overcome the former (e.g. by negotiating an overdraft facility or by attempting to reduce costs) and to take advantage of the latter (e.g. by making short-term investments).

⇨ Unexpectedly running out of cash is obviously not in an organisation's interest, but why might the holding of unnecessarily large cash balances be equally detrimental?

Holding large cash balances in an organisation's bank account is not the best use of this resource. Any interest payable on the bank balance will almost invariably be lower than the return which could be earned from short-term investment of the surplus elsewhere. In addition, a large cash surplus may prompt an unwelcome takeover bid. The somewhat inelegant sobriquet 'cash cow', sometimes attached to the target of such a bid, amply explains the bidder's motivation. Moreover, defending against a hostile takeover may be extremely costly and possibly damaging to the target.

Exhibit 12.11 contains information about DPA Ltd's budget profiling, along with some additional data relevant to preparation of the company's cash budget. You will see that, for ease of presentation, profiling has occurred on a quarterly basis. In practice, a shorter time frame would be used – monthly, weekly or even daily – such is the importance of cash.

Examination of the detail contained in Exhibit 12.11 provides another illustration of the importance of budget co-ordination. In addition to estimates about the time taken by debtors to pay DPA Ltd and for the company to pay its own creditors, a meaningful cash budget could not be prepared without the prior existence of the functional budgets prepared earlier in the chapter.

⇨ Why do the annual cash flows for administration overhead in Exhibit 12.11 total only £26,000 when the functional budget for this item amounts to £28,000?

Reference to the administration overhead budget shows that, of the £28,000 total, £2,000 is for depreciation. Since this is not a cash flow, it should not appear in the cash budget. Other non-cash items, such as the estimated bad debts (i.e. the value of credit sales for which customers are expected not to pay) or discounts given/received should similarly be omitted from the cash budget.

When preparing a cash budget, it is important to make a distinction between timing of the right to receive (or obligation to pay) cash and of receipt (or payment) itself. The profit and loss account and balance sheet are based on rights and obligations, whereas the cash budget is based on receipts and payments. You should also note that cash budgets, unlike the profit and loss account and balance sheet, make no distinction between *revenue* (profit and loss) and *capital* (balance sheet) items: all

DPA Ltd: budget profiling and cash-flow data

Management has obtained the following estimated cash flows from the company's pro-filed functional budgets for next year:

	Quarter I £	Quarter II £	Quarter III £	Quarter IV £
Sales revenue	140,000	105,000	85,000	63,300
Purchases of direct materials	68,920	27,000	20,000	14,000
Direct wages	26,000	23,000	20,000	20,000
Production overhead	3,100	3,100	3,100	3,100
Selling overhead:				
fixed	8,000	5,000	10,000	13,000
variable	1,400	1,050	850	633
Administration overhead	6,500	6,500	6,500	6,500

Additional information

1 Examination of the capital expenditure budget reveals cash payments of £83,000 and £60,000 in Quarters II and III respectively. In Quarter I, sale of a capital asset will realise £2,000 in cash.

2 Corporation tax of £21,000 in respect of last year's profit will be payable in Quarter III.

3 10 per cent of sales are made on a cash basis, the remainder being credit sales. Of the credit customers, 80 per cent pay in the quarter after sale, 18 per cent pay two quarters after sale, and the balance is irrecoverable bad debts. At the end of the current year, it is estimated that debtors will amount to £142,000, of whom 70 per cent will pay in Quarter I, and 26 per cent in Quarter II, the balance being bad debts.

4 Purchases of materials are paid for 50 per cent in the quarter of purchase, and the remainder in the quarter after purchase. At the end of the current year, it is estimated that creditors for purchases will amount to £4,000, all of which will be paid in Quarter 1.

5 Direct wages, selling overheads and administration overheads are paid in the quarter in which they are incurred.

6 At the end of the current year, it is expected that the cash balance at the bank will be £3,000.

EXHIBIT **12.11 Data for cash budget preparation**

cash flows, regardless of their nature, are reflected in the cash budget. We may therefore see cash receipts arising from issue of shares and debentures, or from the sale of fixed assets. Cash payments may be made in respect of loan redemptions, purchase of the company's own shares or of fixed assets.

Exhibit 12.12 shows DPA Ltd's cash budget by quarter and for the year as a whole and involves calculating, for each quarter in sequence:

opening cash balance + cash receipts – cash payments

which will yield the closing cash balance.

⇨ Why is it necessary to calculate the quarterly closing cash balances in sequence?

DPA Ltd: cash budget

	Quarter I £	Quarter II £	Quarter III £	Quarter IV £	Year £
Opening balance	3,000	34,940	13,550	(24,620)	3,000
add Cash receipts:					
Sale of capital asset	2,000				2,000
Sales:					
cash	14,000	10,500	8,500	6,330	39,330
credit:					
70% /26% of debtors at start	99,400	36,920			136,320
80% of credit sales		100,800	75,600	61,200	237,600
18% of credit sales			22,680	17,010	39,690
	118,400	183,160	120,330	59,920	457,940
less Cash payments:					
Capital expenditure		83,000	60,000		143,000
Corporation tax			21,000		21,000
Purchases:					
creditors at start of year	4,000				4,000
50% in quarter of purchase	34,460	13,500	10,000	7,000	64,960
50% in quarter after purchase		34,460	13,500	10,000	57,960
Direct wages	26,000	23,000	20,000	20,000	89,000
Production overhead	3,100	3,100	3,100	3,100	12,400
Selling overhead	9,400	6,050	10,850	3,633	39,933
Administration overhead	6,500	6,500	6,500	6,500	26,000
	83,460	169,610	144,950	60,233	458,253
Closing balance	34,940	13,550	(24,620)	(313)	(313)

Exhibit **12.12 Cash budget**

A sequential approach to calculation of closing cash balances is necessary because each quarter's closing cash balance will provide the following quarter's opening balance. The opening and closing balances for the year as a whole are, respectively, the anticipated balance at the end of the current year (which will be next year's opening balance) and the estimated closing balance for Quarter IV. Cash receipts and payments for the year are simply cross-additions of the quarterly figures.

The bracketed figures in Exhibit 12.12 reflect the fact that, in Quarters III and IV, cash payments exceed cash receipts: that is, the company's bank account will potentially be overdrawn in those quarters. If expectations come to pass in reality, then the company will suffer a 'liquidity crisis' (i.e. will be unable to meet all of its financial commitments as they fall due) in the quarters concerned, unless management takes action to address the cash-flow problem.

⇨ What steps might DPA Ltd's management take in order to meet the cash shortfall anticipated in Quarters III and IV?

Management might try to arrange overdraft facilities with the company's bank, or might try to improve cash flows from sales, or reduce costs. In this latter respect, management may wish to consider the capital expenditures in Quarters II and III, which are largely responsible for the cash deficit. Could these payments be deferred? Or could the assets concerned be financed in a way which does not require such large 'one-off' payments (e.g. by leasing)? An issue of shares or debentures would be no use, since it is unlikely that the cash from such an issue would be received sufficiently early to assist in the periods of predicted cash shortage. It is exactly this sort of vital information about an organisation's liquidity which the cash budget is intended to provide.

In certain situations, the cash budget will not show opening and closing cash balances and it will thus be necessary to amend its format. Where cash inflows and outflows are involved, the latter may be subtracted from the former to give the net cash inflow (or outflow). It is also possible to prepare cash budgets showing simply cash inflows or cash outflows. For example, an organisation with a number of branches in different locations may operate a single central bank account, but may nevertheless wish to prepare cash budgets for each individual branch. Here, a 'net cash flow' approach would be used for each branch's cash budget, with these separate budgets being amalgamated by head office to give a companywide cash budget of the type illustrated in Exhibit 12.12.

The budgeted profit and loss account

The second element of a master budget is the budgeted profit and loss account, and it is important to appreciate that profit and cash flows are unlikely to be the same.

⇨ Why will profit and cash flows be different?

As we have just seen, the cash budget is based on the timing of cash receipts and payments. Profit, however, is based on the legal right to receive, or obligation to pay, cash – which may well arise at a different point in time to that at which cash is actually received/paid. In addition, the profit and loss account contains certain non-cash items, of which depreciation and a provision for doubtful debts are typical examples. In addition to information from the functional budgets already prepared, some data required to permit completion of the budgeted profit and loss account are set out in Exhibit 12.13.

DPA Ltd: additional information for budgeted profit and loss account

The capital asset which is to be sold in Quarter I for £2,000 will have a book value of £1,000 at the time of sale. Corporation tax on next year's profit is estimated to be £14,000.

EXHIBIT **12.13 Sale of fixed asset and corporation tax**

Unlike the cash budget, which shows the *proceeds* of sale, the profit and loss account reflects the *profit/loss* arising from sale of the capital asset:

	£
Proceeds of sale	2,000
Book value of asset sold	1,000
Profit on sale	1,000

This will have the effect of increasing budgeted profit for the year. Exhibit 12.14 shows DPA Ltd's budgeted profit and loss account – in this case, for the year as a whole, but it is perfectly possible to profile this statement in the same way as we did the cash budget.

DPA Ltd: budgeted profit and loss account for the year

	£	£
Sales revenue		393,300
less Standard production cost of sales:		
2 kg bags (15,000 bags @ £2.56)	38,400	
5 kg bags (12,000 bags @ £5.20)	62,400	
10 kg bags (8,200 bags @ £9.92)	81,344	
20 kg bags (5,400 bags @ £15.90)	85,860	268,004
Gross profit		125,296
Selling overhead	43,933	
Administration overhead	28,000	
Profit on sale of capital asset	(1,000)	70,933
Net profit before taxation		54,363
Estimated corporation tax		14,000
Net profit after taxation		40,363

EXHIBIT **12.14 Budgeted profit and loss account**

Stocks of finished goods and materials, along with purchases of materials, are not shown on the budgeted profit and loss account in Exhibit 12.14. However, this is simply for clarity of presentation, and these values could be included if desired (although already available in units in the production and materials' purchases budgets). The cost of sales is therefore calculated as sales volume for each product multiplied by that product's standard production cost from Exhibit 12.10.

⇨ Why does Exhibit 12.14 show no adjustment to the profit and loss account for over-/underabsorbed overhead?

You will recall from Chapter 4 that over- or underabsorbed overhead is the difference between the amount of overhead absorbed using a predetermined absorption rate and the amount of overhead incurred. Because the statement in Exhibit 12.14 is a *budgeted* profit and loss account (i.e. based on budgeted production overhead cost and budgeted production), no such difference will exist.

As with the production cost budget, it is possible to argue that a marginal costing approach to the profit and loss account might be preferable, as it better shows the relationship between volume of sales and profit. Such an approach is presented in Exhibit 12.15.

DPA Ltd: budgeted profit and loss account (marginal costing basis)

	£	£
Sales revenue (same as Exhibit 12.14)		393,300
less Variable production cost of sales:		
2 kg bags (15,000 bags @ £1.41)	21,150	
5 kg bags (12,000 bags @ £2.90)	34,800	
10 kg bags (8,200 bags @ £5.32)	43,624	
20 kg bags (5,400 bags @ £10.15)	54,810	
	154,384	
Variable selling overhead (1% of budgeted sales revenue)[1]	3,933	158,317
Contribution		234,983
less Fixed costs:		
Direct labour	89,000	
Production overhead	13,350	
Selling overhead (£43,933 – £3,933 variable)	40,000	
Administration overhead[2]	28,000	
Profit on sale of capital asset	(1,000)	169,350
Net profit before taxation		65,633
Estimated corporation tax		14,000
Net profit after taxation		51,633

Notes: [1] Based on the assumption that only sales commission is variable.
[2] All costs assumed to be fixed.

EXHIBIT 12.15 Budgeted profit and loss account based on marginal costing principles

---

The standard variable production cost per unit consists of direct materials plus packing, and is extracted from Exhibit 12.10. The variable selling overhead is obtained from the relevant budget, as are the figures for direct labour, production overhead and administration overhead. Because sales exceed production, marginal costing yields the higher profit. You may wish to revise Chapter 5 to remind yourself about why this is the case.

⇨ Assume that sales volume increases by 20 per cent and that there is no change to the sales/production mix, to the unit selling prices and variable costs or to the total fixed costs. What will be the effect of such a volume increase on net profit before taxation in Exhibit 12.15?

Given our assumptions about sales mix, unit selling price and unit variable cost, a 20 per cent increase in sales volume will result in a 20 per cent increase in contribution:

$$\text{increase in contribution: } (20\% \times £234{,}983) = £46{,}996.60$$

If fixed costs are unaffected by the change in volume, then the increase in contribution is also the increase in net profit before taxation. Use of a marginal costing format may therefore aid management in assessing the impact on profit of different output/sales volumes – a topic we shall return to in the next chapter.

One point to note is that, regardless of whether absorption or marginal costing is employed, the company earns a budgeted profit for the year. Contrast this with the £313 overdraft at the end of the year that the cash budget revealed. Profit and cash do *not* equate. If management were to suffer any confusion about this, believing, say, that profit reflected cash availability, then decisions might be taken which could deepen the potential liquidity crisis in the last two quarters of next year.

The budgeted balance sheet

A budgeted balance sheet is the final element of the master budget and requires prior preparation not only of functional budgets, but also of the cash budget and profit and loss account. The capital expenditure budget will be explicitly reflected in the balance sheet (via changes to the fixed asset section), as will certain other strategic budgets (e.g. relating to share or debenture issues). Exhibit 12.16 shows DPA Ltd's budgeted balance sheet for next year.

Details of existing fixed assets will be obtained from accounting records, with the capital expenditure budget providing information about acquisitions/disposals. The tax liability is that which is shown in the budgeted profit and loss account, whilst existing share capital will be extracted from the company's records, any proposed issues and/or redemptions being specified in the strategic budget. Anticipated retained profit at the end of the current year will consist of last year's actual retained profit plus an estimate of retained profit for the current year. Since the master budget will be finalised fairly late in the current accounting year, this estimate is likely to be reasonably accurate.

⇨ State the source from which the following figures in Exhibit 12.16 have been derived:

- stock of finished goods;
- stock of raw materials;
- debtors;
- bank overdraft; and
- creditors.

(You do not need to verify the amounts involved.)

DPA Ltd: budgeted balance sheet

Fixed assets	Cost	Accumulated depreciation	Net book value
	£	£	£
Premises	80,000	10,000	70,000
Production equipment	46,000	9,000	37,000
Office equipment	72,000	12,000	60,000
Delivery vans	64,000	14,000	50,000
	262,000	45,000	217,000
Current assets			
Stocks:			
Finished goods	10,324		
Raw materials	32,000		
Debtors	69,601	111,925	
Current liabilities			
Bank overdraft	313		
Creditors for purchases	7,000		
Taxation	14,000	21,313	90,612
			307,612
Share capital and reserves			
Ordinary shares of £1			220,000
Retained profit:			
Anticipated at end of the current year		47,249	
add Budgeted net profit after taxation		40,363	87,612
			307,612

EXHIBIT **12.16 Budgeted balance sheet**

The *quantity* of finished goods and raw materials' stocks will be taken, respectively, from the production and the raw materials' purchases budgets. Assuming absorption costing to be in operation, the finished goods stocks will be valued at the standard unit production costs set out in Exhibit 12.10:

	£
2 kg bags: 1,000 @ £2.56	2,560
5 kg bags: 500 @ £5.20	2,600
10 kg bags: 200 @ £9.92	1,984
20 kg bags: 200 @ £15.90	3,180
	10,324

The desired closing stock of raw materials is shown in the purchases budget to be 80,000 kg, which, valued at the standard cost of £0.40 per kg, gives £32,000.

The bank overdraft can be obtained directly from the cash budget, where it is the closing bank balance for the year. Debtors and creditors must be determined from the information about payment timings which was used to prepare the cash budget (see Exhibit 12.11):

Debtors	£
18% of Quarter III's sales	13,770
90% of Quarter IV's sales	56,970
less Bad debts (2% × £56,970)	1,139
Total outstanding at year end	69,601
Creditors	
50% of Quarter IV's purchases	7,000

It would be unusual for a budgeted balance sheet to be profiled, since it is essentially of a static nature: that is, it is intended to present a 'picture' of the organisation's financial position at a given point in time. Functional budgets, the cash budget and budgeted profit and loss account, however, are all *dynamic*: that is, reflect flows of resources over time – and so will benefit from profiling.

BUDGETING FOR SERVICE INDUSTRIES

The budget preparation example we have just completed is set in an organisation which is producing a tangible output. In other words, DPA Ltd is essentially a manufacturing business.

⇨ Bearing in mind the heterogeneity, simultaneity and intangibility of its output (described in Chapter 2), how would a service business's budgets differ from those we have just prepared for DPA Ltd?

The nature of an organisation's input/output processes has major implications for its budget system. The main differences between service and manufacturing organisations are: that the former cannot store either their output or the majority of their inputs (simultaneity); that output, along with its relationship to input, may be difficult to quantify (intangibility); and that cost units could well be markedly different to each other (heterogeneity). The most visible sign of these differences will be the absence, in service organisations' budgets, of a 'production' budget and of budgeted stock levels for finished goods. Depending on the precise nature of the service being offered, there may or may not be budgets for materials' usage/purchases. A bank, for example, will incur substantial expenditure on materials such as stationery, cheque books, cheque guarantee cards, credit cards and so forth. Some of these (e.g. stationery) may be held in stock by the bank, other items (e.g. cheque books) ordered as required. There are two important points which we can make here:

1 Substantial though such expenditures may be, they are unlikely to form the major input to the service provided. In the bank's case, the main input will probably be staff time and expertise.

2 The link between inputs (whether materials, labour or overhead) and outputs can be more difficult to quantify than for many manufacturing businesses. For example, what labour time is required to service each personal current account?

Unlike manufacturing organisations, detailed standard costing will therefore not aways be possible at the cost unit level. A bank could not meaningfully prepare a standard cost card for each personal current account to the same degree of detail as used by DPA Ltd in Exhibit 12.10. At best, standard costing can be only partially implemented. We may, for example, have a standard salary scale for employees at the bank's branches and, based on our expectations about the future volume of business, estimate the number of employees of each grade required during the budget period (along with the related cost). What we cannot readily do, however, is say that each current account in operation during the year requires a given number of staff hours to service. In addition to this, definition of the cost unit may be problematic – a composite cost unit, such as passenger/kilometre, may be necessary, or there may be some dubiety about the most appropriate cost unit to use (e.g. number of personal bank clients versus number of personal accounts of each different category). We should stress, however, that it is the nature of the service provided, along with our understanding of its inputs, outputs and processes which governs the extent to which we can employ standard costing. A landscape gardener may be well aware of the standard input times, quantities and costs for a particular job, but a firm of solicitors might find this less easy.

What we are describing are really areas of *difference* between service and manufacturing sectors. Yet there is much common ground between the two in budget preparation: for instance, strategic aims and budgets should govern tactical; an estimate of sales (or other volume of activity in a non-profit situation) will often be the necessary starting-point for the budget preparation process; functional budgets should stem from this initial volume estimate; principal budget factors must be recognised; and functional budgets will require to be summarised in a master budget. (Questions 12.6, 12.8 and 12.9 deal with preparation of service organisation budgets.) Moreover, budget preparation is every bit as problematic for manufacturing as for service businesses – it is the nature, rather than the scale of such problems which differs.

PUBLIC SECTOR BUDGETING

Although the general principles of budget preparation apply equally to public sector as to other types of organisation, the influences and constraints operative in the public sector are rather different, and we shall now outline these. At the outset, it must be said that, for many public sector bodies, the budgeting process may be considerably more complex and time-consuming than for many others and well-defined procedures are essential. Not only will the budget, once set, represent authority to spend, but, in all probability, it will also represent a maximum amount which can be spent. Such is the significance of budgeting that Jones and Pendlebury (1996) have stated that: 'as far as local and central government are concerned, it is probably the single most important financial exercise that they undertake.'

In areas of the public sector which are relatively 'commercialised' – for example, the quasi-autonomous Direct Service Organisations which provide road maintenance or refuse collection services to many local authorities – budgetary procedures are very similar to those employed in such organisations' commercial equivalents. However, despite their apparent independence from the parent body, and their more commercial outlook, they are subject to the same influences and constraints as more overtly 'public' bodies, although possibly in a more indirect way.

Revenue budgets and capital budgets

Almost every public sector organisation distinguishes between *revenue* budgets and *capital* budgets. Revenue budgets are analogous to tactical budgets in the private sector, with capital budgets having the same strategic orientation in both sectors. Not only is it necessary to recognise the impact of capital on revenue budgets (particularly where capital projects are to be funded from revenue sources such as taxation), but it is also important to recognise that the sources of funding for each category of budget are essentially, but not exclusively, different. Revenue budgets are funded from a combination of taxation and other charges levied (along with central government support in the case of local authorities), whereas capital budgets are funded by other means (e.g. borrowing, again possibly supplemented by grant aid). These different sources of finance are subject to different regulations and, statutory requirements aside, this must largely determine the budgetary framework.

Political influences

As well as the 'budget politics' which will exist in every system (and which we shall discuss in Chapter 16), public sector budgets are subject to party political influence. For example, a local authority budget which is financially acceptable may fail to gain ultimate approval by elected councillors because its priorities are at odds with those of the majority party, or party political disagreement may disturb the relationship between local and central government. It may therefore be necessary to revise public sector budgets more often than private, in order not only to reflect unforeseen principal budget factors, but also to allow for such political considerations. Scheduling of budget preparation and the need for co-ordination may thus assume even greater significance in public sector than in other organisations.

High public profile

Public sector budgets are subject to considerable public scrutiny and comment, whereas for private sector organisations, budgeting is primarily an internal affair, with little or no information being made public. This means that in the public sector any shift in spending priority or need for additional finance (e.g. via additional taxation) requires to be justified not only in financial, but also in political and social terms. Failure to justify budget changes in social terms may render a budget politically unacceptable; rejection of proposed changes for such reasons may conceivably result in a budgetary 'philosophy' which is too rigid in a dynamic environment. Some local authorities, for example, might argue that strict limits on their spending and finance-raising powers are inconsistent with the need to provide local services to a desired standard. Although such disagreement may stem from opposing political viewpoints, it might also be seen as evidence of unnecessary rigidity within the budget-setting process. One possible indicator of the extent of such rigidity could be the frequency with which 'virement' is exercised within public sector budgets: that is, transfer of funds from underspent to overspent budgets.

In the public sector, budgetory difficulties may be compounded by the absence of a charge for the services provided, which will remove one output measure common to all commercial organisations – profit. There is a danger that budgets may stress what is readily measurable ('inputs' – i.e. costs) at the expense of proper consideration of the outputs which result.

APPROACHES TO BUDGET FORMULATION

We defined budgets as 'quantified plans' – but *how* are plans quantified? Do we perhaps use current events as a guide, or should we 'wipe the slate clean' before each budget is prepared? How should costs and revenues be categorised within budgets? These issues are discussed below.

Line-item and programme budgets

A **line-item budget** classifies costs according to their nature. A summarised budgeted profit statement prepared using line-item principles might look like the following:

	£	£
Sales revenue		X
less:		
Materials' costs	X	
Labour costs	X	
Overhead costs	X	X
Profit		X

⟳ Why would a statement such as that above be inadequate for budgetary planning purposes?

The weakness of line-item budgets is that they do not reflect the purpose of expenditure, and if we do not know why costs are being incurred, it is impossible either to plan or to control them in any effective way. **Programme budgets** classify costs according to the reason for their being incurred (e.g. production, selling, administration, and so on), which allows much more accurate planning of expenditures. If you examine the budgets which we prepared for DPA Ltd, you will be able to see elements of both approaches: the company's production cost budget is a programme budget (the expenditures relate to production) and, within the budget, individual costs are stated on a line-item basis (materials, packing, direct labour and production overhead). This kind of combination approach is predominant in public and private, commercial and non-profit sectors.

Incremental budgets

One possible starting-point for budget formulation is recent experience. **Incremental budgets** start with the current budget, which is then revised to reflect factors such as:

■ anticipated events occurring before the end of the current budget period; and
■ anticipated data for the next budget period, such as the estimated inflation rate, volume of activity, and changes in mix of activity.

Such an approach is undoubtedly straightforward (assuming tolerably accurate estimates) and may be justified on the basis that the focus of budgetary attention should be on *changes* from one budget period to the next, thereby reducing budgetary complexities and narrowing the areas of possible dispute.

▷ What is the potential weakness inherent to incremental budgeting?

The danger of incremental budgets is that, if they are applied in a mechanistic manner – that is, 'next year's budget is this year's budget + *x* per cent' – then the past will come to dominate the future, with past inefficiencies being carried forward to future periods. Use of incremental budgeting may tempt management to believe that previous levels of expenditure were justified and that the reasons for such expenditure will remain. Such views are not consistent with effective planning. Past experience may *influence* planning, but not to the exclusion of expectations about the future. Carrying forward past inefficiencies to future periods within the budget is one reason for the existence of **budgetary slack**, which is the difference between minimum necessary expenditure and actual/budgeted expenditure. In Chapter 16, we shall have more to say about budgetary slack.

Zero base budgeting (ZBB)

One solution to the problem of budgetary slack is **zero base budgeting (ZBB)**. Unlike incremental budgeting, ZBB starts from the position of zero previous expenditure and requires justification of budgeted amounts. Figure 12.3 illustrates how a system of ZBB would operate.

Although the terminology may appear rather daunting, the basic principles being illustrated in Figure 12.3 are quite straightforward:

1 The budget is based on consideration (in mutually exclusive decision packages) of alternative ways of achieving objectives.
2 For the best method of achieving their objectives, different levels of expenditure by organisational subunits (decision units) are 'justified' with reference to each unit's activities (in incremental decision packages): that is, if a particular functional budget is set at, say, 90 per cent of its current level, how will that function's performance be affected?
3 Ranking of competing subunit decision packages occurs in the context both of scarce budget resources and of achieving organisational objectives: for example, if increasing market share is an objective, then decision packages submitted by the sales department may receive higher ranking than those from some other

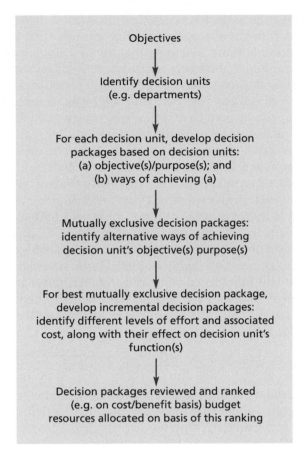

FIGURE 12.3
A system of zero base budgeting

functions – at least until the specified objective is achievable with the budget resources allocated to sales, at which point other functions may take priority.

As a method of combating budgetary slack, of encouraging managers to examine alternative ways of achieving objectives, and in its explicit linking of allocations of scarce budgetary resources to achievement of objectives, ZBB is hard to fault. In addition, ZBB's rationale is (or should be) that which is applied to proposed expenditure in new areas, which should support or encourage systematic use of appraisal techniques like net present value. ZBB may therefore be valuable where organisations are faced with particularly volatile environments.

⇨ What difficulty would you foresee if an organisation were to adopt ZBB for preparation of its tactical budgets?

If the procedures outlined in Figure 12.3 were to be used for tactical budgeting (i.e. on an annual basis), then the system would be extremely cumbersome administratively. Much management time and effort would be required in preparation of mutually exclusive and incremental decision packages, for example. In addition, it may not be possible to define organisational and subunit objectives with sufficient precision to permit their use as the basis of budget allocations, thereby increasing the possibility of dispute. It might also be said that adopting a strict interpretation of 'zero base' is of questionable value. Assuming that the organisation is to continue in existence, some expenditure is absolutely necessary, so it makes more sense to concentrate on what is likely to change between one budget period and the next.

One answer to the administration difficulty might be to subject tactical (and strategic) budgets to periodic zero base review (say, every five years). In this way, the chance of carrying forward past inefficiencies might be reduced. Where it is proposed to undertake expenditure in new areas, ZBB *must* be used, as there will be no previous data on which to base the budget. In such cases, the correlation between planning and decision appraisal is particularly evident, with the results of the latter serving as explicit justification for budget inclusion/exclusion.

A variant on ZBB is the planning, programming and budget system (PPBS), under which the programmes and programme elements (i.e. subdivisions of programmes) that best meet objectives are selected from the available alternatives on a cost/benefit basis. Unlike zero base budgets, PPBS is not predicated on zero previous expenditure, but still requires consideration of alternative courses of action and allocation of budget resources according to cost/benefit ranking. PPBS is similar to activity-based budgeting in the sense that programmes, like activities, often span traditional departmental boundaries.

Rolling budgets

The problem of uncertainty about the future is one which affects all budgets to a greater or lesser degree – greater for strategic than for tactical budgets and for volatile than stable environments. One way in which the impact of such uncertainty may be reduced is to use **rolling** (or **continuous**) **budgets**. Within a particular strategic or tactical budget period, functional and master budgets will be prepared in the normal manner, but the budget period concerned will be subdivided into a number of shorter periods, for which extremely detailed operational budgets will be prepared on an ongoing basis. Figure 12.4 illustrates how such a system could be applied to annual budgets.

As you will see from Figure 12.4, the rolling nature of budget preparation applies, not only within a particular budget period, but also from one budget period to the next.

▷ How would the time effort and expense involved in operation of a rolling budget be justified?

The time, effort and expense involved in continually updating the budget as suggested in Figure 12.4 is justifiable if the associated cost is exceeded by the benefit derived from additional budget accuracy. This may be particularly true when conditions are volatile and subject to considerable uncertainty.

Activity-based budgeting (ABB)

We discussed the principles of **activity-based costing (ABC)** in Chapter 4, where the main emphasis was on calculation of unit costs. This approach can be

436

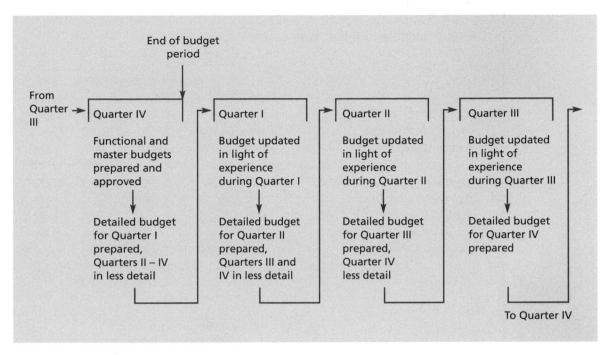

FIGURE 12.4 Operation of a rolling budget

extended to produce a system of **activity-based budgeting (ABB)**, which in outline is very similar, but with the main aim being planning and control. Once the organisation's major activities have been identified, and a budgeted cost pool assigned to each activity, then the cost driver(s) relating to that cost pool are determined, the budget being constructed on the basis of total budgeted cost for each cost driver and budgeted cost per unit of each cost driver. Morrow and Connolly (1991) have suggested the use of an activity matrix for this purpose. Based on their approach, Exhibit 12.17 illustrates how such a matrix may be constructed for an administration budget.

Four cost drivers have been identified in Exhibit 12.17 as being the main underlying cause of the budgeted administration costs. 'Sustaining costs' are those which cannot meaningfully be related to any specific cost driver, and might be thought of as general administration necessary to support the organisation as a whole. Once a system of ABB is in place, management will plan future expenditure by estimating the volume of activity for each cost driver, and then work back to determine the cost necessary to support that volume. It is argued that budgeting in this way highlights the cost of activities – for example, the fact that each employee incurs a £256 administration cost – and knowledge of such figures may encourage management to seek more cost-effective methods of administration. However, the validity of such figures depends on the accuracy with which cost drivers have been identified and on the objectivity with which costs can be related to particular cost drivers.

DPA Ltd: administration activity cost matrix

| | Cost drivers | | | | | |
	No. of employees	No. of customers	Volume of output	Value of sales	Sustaining costs	Total
Administration costs:	£	£	£	£	£	£
Management salaries	12,000	16,000	14,000	8,000	20,000	70,000
Clerical salaries	10,000	20,000	6,000	4,000	12,000	52,000
Occupancy costs					15,000	15,000
Computer costs	3,000	2,000	4,000	2,000	6,000	17,000
Bad debts				5,000		5,000
Stationery etc.	5,000	7,000	1,000		2,000	15,000
Insurance					9,000	9,000
Sundry costs	2,000	1,000	2,000	1,000	5,000	11,000
Total	32,000	46,000	27,000	20,000	69,000	194,000
Cost driver volume (number)	125	1,150	90,000	£1m		
Cost per unit of cost driver	£256	£40	£0.30	£0.20	£69,000	

EXHIBIT **12.17 Activity-based budgeting**

SUMMARY

In this chapter, we have examined budgetary planning – an activity of funda-mental importance to all concerned with an organisation, regardless of its nature, function or size. We have seen that:

■ A budget is a quantified plan targetted at achievement of an objective (or objectives).

■ The objectives of budgets are to:
  – compel planning;
  – provide a performance benchmark and financial control mechanism;
  – provide a motivational impetus;
  – provide a medium of communication;
  – promote **goal congruence** (i.e. consistency between the actions of individual managers/organisational sub-units and overall organisational objectives); and
  – instil financial awareness.

■ Budgets may suffer from the following problems:
  – producing credible estimates of the future;
  – bureaucratic 'overkill';

- encouraging an ultra-cautious approach by management; and
- behavioural implications.

■ Strategic objectives and budgets should dictate tactical objectives and budgets which in turn should determine operational aspects.

■ Budget preparation and monitoring may be overseen and co-ordinated by a **budget committee**, with interfunctional liaison being provided by the **budget officer.**

■ The **budget manual** is a user guide to the detailed working of the organisation's budget system.

■ Budgets are constructed using **standard costs**, which are predetermined costs (or selling prices) expressed at the cost-unit level and require estimation of the resource inputs per unit of output along with the associated costs.

■ **Ideal standards** are based on maximum efficiency; **currently attainable standards** are based on optimum operations under current conditions.

■ The **standard hour** measures the amount of work which should be performed in one hour at standard efficiency and is a useful measure of global output in multiproduct/service organisations.

■ The aims of standard costing are to:
  – improve budgetary accuracy;
  – instil cost consciousness;
  – encourage the search for improved methods;
  – permit detailed control analysis; and
  – provide a superior costing/pricing basis than actual figures.

■ standard costing may suffer from problems of:
  – incorporating inflation;
  – setting an acceptable labour efficiency standard;
  – inapplicability to heterogeneous output;
  – cost of introduction and maintenance of system; and
  – danger of overemphasising operational considerations.

■ Tactical budget preparation is sequential, often beginning with the sales budget, or with some estimate of activity volume for the forthcoming budget period, and culminating with the **master budget**.

■ Budgets must reflect the impact of any **principal budget factor**.

■ Production (and purchases) budgets should be adjusted to allow for stocks:

	Units
Production (purchases) required to meet sales (production) budget	X
add Desired closing stock	X
	X
less Stock at end of current period	X
Production (purchases) required	X

439

- Labour and material usage budgets should be adjusted to allow for expected non-productive time and losses respectively.

- The cash budget is prepared to help predict periods of possible cash shortage and surplus so that advance measures may be taken to mitigate the effect of the former and to take advantage of the opportunity offered by the latter.

- Cash flow and profit will not be the same because profit is calculated on the basis of rights to receive/obligations to pay cash and after inclusion of certain non-cash items, whereas cash flows are based on cash receipts and payments.

- Because of the importance of cash, the cash budget will be profiled (e.g. on a monthly basis) within the budget period.

- Non-cash items such as depreciation and provision for bad debts are omitted from the cash budget, which makes no distinction between capital and revenue items, calculating the periodic closing balance as (opening balance + cash receipts – cash payments), with the opening balance being the previous period's closing balance.

- The budgeted profit and loss account and balance sheet will summarise key information contained in separate functional budgets and in the cash budget.

- Depending on the nature of their input, processes and output, service organisations may have difficulty implementing a full system of standard costing because of imprecise input/ output relationships and composite cost units.

- Public sector organisations tend to distinguish between revenue budgets and capital budgets, budgets which are subject to political influences and have a high public profile.

- **Line-item budgets** classify costs according to their nature; **programme budgets** classify costs according to the reason for their being incurred. Effective planning requires the use of a combination of both approaches.

- **Incremental budgets** take the current year's adjusted budget as their starting-point, but, whilst simple to operate, they may have the effect of perpetuating current inefficiencies into the future.

- **Budget slack** is the difference between minimum necessary expenditure and budgeted/actual expenditure, and may arise as a result of incremental budgeting.

- **Zero base budgeting (ZBB)** attempts to address the problem of budgetary slack by requiring justification of all expenditures, assuming zero prior expenditure, and may be administratively cumbersome.

- **Rolling (continuous) budgets** are produced in detail on an ongoing basis within the budget period and may be a useful device for dealing with uncertainty.

- **Activity-based budgeting (ABB)** extends the principles of activity-based costing (ABC) to deal with budgetary planning, and may produce more useful budgetary information depending on the accuracy of the cost drivers and objectivity of costs assigned to each activity and cost driver.

In the next chapter, we shall extend our discussion of budgeting to cover the corollary to planning – control. That is, how do we set about assessing the extent to which we have managed to achieve the plans quantified in our budgets?

FURTHER READING

Cyert, R. and March, J. *Behavioural Theory of the Firm*, Prentice-Hall, 1963.

Drury, C., *Standard Costing*, Academic Press/CIMA, 1992. Chapter 1 provides an overview of the nature and scope of standard costing.

Drury, C., Braund, S., Osborne, P. and Tayles, M., *A Survey of Management Accounting Practices in UK Manufacturing Companies*, CACA, 1993.

Greenall, A., *Finance and Budgeting for Line Managers*, The Industrial Society, 1996. Chapter 5 is a readable management perspective on the budgetary process.

Jones, R. and Pendlebury, M., *Public Sector Accounting*, 4th edn, Pitman Publishing, 1996. Chapters 3, 4 and 5 deal with public sector budgeting.

Morrow, M. and Connolly, T., 'The emergence of activity-based budgeting', in *Management Accounting*, February 1991, CIMA.

SELF-TEST QUESTIONS

12.1 DFG Ltd produces four products, details of which are given below:

	Product A	Product B	Product C	Product D
Output (units):				
Budgeted	10,000	14,000	17,000	15,000
Actual	9,000	16,000	12,000	18,000
Hours per unit:				
Standard	1.0	1.5	2.0	2.2
Average actual	1.4	1.2	2.1	2.0

Which of the following expresses the relationship between actual total output and budgeted total output for the period?

A Actual total output was 5,000 standard hours lower than budgeted.
B Actual total output was 3,500 standard hours lower than budgeted.
C Actual total output was 1,400 standard hours lower than budgeted.
D Actual total output was 100 standard hours lower than budgeted.

12.2 Bushton Housing Association collects rent from the tenants of its properties on a monthly basis. An extract from the association's budget schedules for next year shows the following:

	January	February	March	April	May
Rent due from tenants	£60,000	£64,000	£58,000	£56,000	£60,000

Experience indicates that, of the amounts listed above, 10 per cent will be received in the month before payment is due, 60 per cent in the month payment is due, 20 per cent in the month after payment is due, and 5 per cent two months after payment is due. The balance represents rent which the association will be unable to collect. What will be the amount of April's cash receipts from rent payments?

A £54,200

B £54,400

C £54,800

D £55,200

Note: The following data is to be used to answer Questions 12.3 and 12.4.

One of AMI Ltd's products is a well-known brand of wood glue, which the company packages and sells in two different sizes of container: 250 ml and 500 ml. The standard specification for bonding agent, the main raw material used in production, is:

250 ml container	100 ml
500 ml container	200 ml

Budgeted sales of each product next year are 60,000 and 25,000 containers of 250 ml and 500 ml respectively. At the end of the current year, it is anticipated that closing stocks will be 6,000 × 250ml and 2,500 × 500 ml containers and management wishes to effect a stock reduction for each product of 1,000 containers by the end of next year. Stocks of bonding agent will be 200,000 ml at the end of both the current and next year.

12.3 What will AMI Ltd's budgeted production quantities for next year be?

A 49,000 × 250 ml and 21,000 × 500 ml containers

B 59,000 × 250 ml and 24,000 × 500 ml containers

C 60,000 × 250 ml and 25,000 × 500 ml containers

D 61,000 × 250 ml and 26,000 × 500 ml containers

12.4 What will be AMI Ltd's budgeted usage of bonding agent next year?

A 6,300,000 ml

B 8,300,000 ml

C 8,500,000 ml

D 10,700,000 ml

12.5 Place a tick in the appropriate box to indicate whether each of the following statements is true or false:

	True	False
(a) Depreciation should be excluded from the payments recorded in a cash budget.	☐	☐
(b) Strategic budgets will show less detail than tactical.	☐	☐
(c) Budgetary slack is the difference between budgeted expenditure and actual expenditure.	☐	☐
(d) A line-item budget classifies expenditure according to its nature.	☐	☐
(e) An ideal standard for direct labour will make allowance for idle time.	☐	☐
(f) Incremental budgeting explicitly requires that all future expenditure be justified.	☐	☐

(g) Profit is calculated on the basis that transactions be recorded when cash is due for receipt or payment. ☐ ☐

(h) Where selling price is based on cost, actual cost is superior to standard. ☐ ☐

QUESTIONS WITH ANSWERS

12.6 This question tests whether you can:

■ prepare a cash budget for four months' operation of a service business;

■ comment on a suggestion for improving the liquidity position revealed by this budget and suggest alternative approaches; and

■ explain the use of a computer spreadsheet for cash budgeting, and the benefits this offers.

The Alexandra Nursery, which provides facilities for pre-school children on a commercial basis, is preparing its cash budget for next year. A profile of the estimated revenues and expenses for the first four months of the year is as follows:

	January £	February £	March £	April £
Revenue:				
Fees due for payment	58,000	60,000	66,000	59,000
Costs:				
Wages and salaries	11,000	11,000	12,000	12,000
Purchase of equipment		28,000	22,000	
Payment of taxation	8,000			
Purchases of consumables	2,000	2,500	2,200	1,400
Rent and rates	3,000			3,000
Sundry overheads	7,000	8,000	8,000	8,000
Telephone	1,200			1,400
Insurance		2,800		
Building renovations	12,000	16,000	20,000	25,000

The following additional information is available:

1 At the end of the current year, it is estimated that the nursery's bank account will be overdrawn by £4,000.

2 In addition to receipts from fees, the nursery will receive a loan of £5,000 from one of its owners in April, and sale of unwanted toys and equipment will raise £500 in February.

3 At the end of the current year, it is anticipated that £48,000 in unpaid fees will be outstanding: 40 per cent of this will be received in January, 40 per cent in February, and 18 per cent in March, with the balance being bad debts. The pattern of fee receipts next year is expected to be: 20 per cent received in the month due, 50 per cent received in the month after they are due, 28 per cent received two months after they are due, with the balance being bad debts.

4 The nursery's creditors at the end of this year are estimated at £12,000, all of which amount will be paid during January next year.

5 Purchases of consumables and of equipment will be paid for in the month following purchase. Building renovations will be paid for 70 per cent in the month due, and 30 per cent in the month following.

6 With the exception of item 5 above, all costs will be paid in the month incurred. Sundry overheads includes £1,000 per month depreciation.

Requirements

(a) Prepare the Alexandra Nursery's cash budget for each of the first four months of next year.

(b) In response to the cash flow position revealed by the budget in (a), one of the nursery's owners has proposed that fees should be increased by 10 per cent effective from 1 January next year.

   (i) Assuming that all other factors remain as stated, calculate the effect on the nursery's cash balances in each month of the proposed fee increase.

   (ii) Assess the likely effectiveness of the owner's proposal and suggest other means by which the budgeted cash-flow position may be improved.

(c) Explain in general terms how a computer spreadsheet could be used in the preparation of cash budgets and what benefits this could offer.

12.7 This question tests whether you can:

- prepare functional budgets for a manufacturing business;

- state the principal budget factor affecting these functional budgets; and

- demonstrate whether budgeted machine capacity will be sufficient to meet production targets, and suggest how any capacity shortfall might be overcome.

LGP Ltd manufactures and sells three sizes of extending ladder: 3 metre, 5 metre and 10 metre. Information relating to each of these is given below.

Standard data per unit

	3 metre £	5 metre £	10 metre £
Selling price	30.00	58.00	95.00
Raw materials costs:			
Aluminium: 3.5/6/12 metres @ £2	7.00	12.00	24.00
Fixings: 100/200/400 @ £0.01	1.00	2.00	4.00
Direct labour: 0.1/0.5/1.0 hours @ £8	0.80	4.00	8.00
Machine costs: 4/6/10 hours @ £1	4.00	6.00	10.00
Anticipated sales volume in current year (units)	20,000	15,000	10,000
Anticipated stock levels at end of current year:			
Finished goods (units)	4,000	2,000	800
Raw materials:			
aluminium (total)		16,000 metres	
fixings (total)		60,000 units	

At the end of next year, management wishes stocks of both finished goods and raw materials to be 25 per cent lower than their anticipated levels at the end of the current year. It is expected that sales volumes next year will be 20 per cent higher than the current year for both 3 metre and 5 metre ladders, and 10 per cent lower than the current year for 10 metre ladders.

Each of LGP Ltd's direct workers has a 35-hour working week for 48 weeks of the year. However, of these total hours, only 75 per cent will be productive, the remainder being lost due to sickness, machine breakdown and a variety of other reasons. The company currently has 30 machines which are used to shape and fix the ladders, each being capable of producing any length of ladder. To allow for maintenance and set-up time, each machine has an effective operational year of 8,000 machine hours. LGP Ltd's capital budget stipulates that two additional such machines will be in place as from the first day of next year.

Requirements

(a) Prepare the following functional budgets for LGP Ltd for next year:

(i)   sales in units and revenue for each product and showing total budgeted sales revenue;

(ii) production in units for each product;

(iii) material usage in metres and units for aluminium and fixings respectively;

(iv) material purchases in metres and units for aluminium and fixings, along with the purchase cost for each type of material and in total; and

(v)   direct labour hours for budgeted output of each product and in total, plus the number of direct workers required for overall production.

(b) Identify the assumed principal budget factor underlying the budgets prepared in (a).

(c) Based on the production budget in (a), prepare a statement of budgeted machine utilisation for next year and demonstrate the extent to which next year's machine capacity will/will not be sufficient to deal with next year's budgeted output. In the event that next year's machine capacity proves insufficient to meet projected output, suggest ways in which LGP Ltd might overcome the shortfall, explaining any associated advantages and disadvantages.

12.8 This question tests whether you can:

■ adjust the current year's budget for inflation and to reflect different possible levels of service provision;

■ profile budgeted expenditure by quarter; and

■ distinguish between incremental and zero-base budgeting.

The Home Help Section of Boroughmere Council's Social Work Department has been requested to submit a profiled budget proposal for next year. As a starting-point, the Senior Administration Officer (Home Help) refers to the current year's cost budget for the section, as follows:

Boroughmere Council Social Work Department
Home Help Section Cost Budget 19X7/X8

	£000
Employee costs:	
Wages & salaries	614
Wage-related costs	128
Employee benefits	10
Transportation:	
Vehicle running costs	86
Vehicle depreciation	27
Vehicle maintenance	34
IT costs:	
Depreciation of equipment	8
Running and maintenance costs	12
Consumables	15
Other costs:	
Sundry administration	50
Property-related	30
Insurances	6
Gross expenditure	1,020
Expenditure recovered through grants and from other sources (5%)	51
Net expenditure	969

Inflation for next year is expected to increase this year's costs as follows: employee costs – 2 per cent; transportation – 5 per cent; IT – 6 per cent; other – 10 per cent. Depreciation charges are unaffected by inflation.

In light of experience during the current year and expectations about next year's operations, the Senior Administration Officer believes that the Home Help Section's minimum expenditure next year in order to meet statutory and other obligations must be 80 per cent of the current year's budget (after adjusting for inflation). Provision of the same level of service next year as this year would require the same budgeted expenditure (after adjustment for inflation). Proposed improvement and expansion of the service over this year's levels would require next year's budget to be 120 per cent of this year's (after adjusting for inflation). For all levels of service, 6 per cent of total expenditure will be recoverable next year.

Expenditure by quarter next year is estimated to be: Quarter I – 35 per cent; Quarter II – 30 per cent, Quarter III – 20 per cent, Quarter IV – 15 per cent . You may assume that these percentages apply to every individual cost and to the 6 per cent recovery factor.

Requirements

(a) Adjust the current year's budget for inflation and apply the revised recovery percentage to determine next year's budget based on *each* of the following scenarios:
   (i) next year's level of service being the same as this year's;
   (ii) next year's level of service being the minimum possible; and
   (iii) next year's service being at the improved and expanded level.

   Your budgets should follow the format of that presented in the question.

(b) For (a)(i) *only*, profile the annual budget by quarter, again using the format from the question.

(c) Explain how elements of both incremental and zero-base budgeting can be seen in the Home Help Section's budgeting exercise.

QUESTIONS WITHOUT ANSWERS

12.9 Sampson Ltd operates a chain of retail clothing stores throughout the country, each individual store being treated as a separate budget centre. Estimates relating to operation of the company's Kingsmere Superstore for the first six months of next year are given below.

	Jan. (£000)	Feb. (£000)	Mar. (£000)	Apr. (£000)	May (£000)	June (£000)
Sales revenue	600	400	350	320	300	260
Costs:						
Wages and salaries	70	68	65	62	60	60
Rent and rates				120		
Insurance			50			
Overheads	130	130	130	130	130	130

The following additional information is available:

1 *Purchases* The average cost of purchases is 60 per cent of sales revenue. Purchases in any month are sufficient to cover that month's sales, and to provide closing stock equivalent to 20 per cent of the following month's sales. Purchases are paid for 80 per cent in the month following purchase and 20 per cent two months after purchase.

2 *Sales* 70 per cent of sales are made on a cash basis, the remainder being on credit. Of the credit customers, 50 per cent are expected to pay in the month following sale, 45 per cent two months after sale, with the balance being bad debts.

3 *Wages and salaries* These are paid in full on the fifth day of the month following that in which they are incurred.

4 *Other costs* Rent and rates, insurance and overheads are paid in the month in which they are incurred. Of the monthly overhead, £15,000 is for depreciation.

Requirements

(a) Prepare the Kingsmere Superstore's purchases budget (in £s) for each of the months of March, April and May.

(b) Individual stores operated by Sampson Ltd do not have separate bank accounts, but a cash budget is prepared for each store showing cash inflows and outflows, along with the net inflow/outflow. Prepare such a cash budget for the Kingsmere Superstore for each of the months of March, April and May.

(c) Prepare the Superstore's budgeted profit statement for each of March, April and May. Explain why the budgeted profit/loss and budgeted net cash inflow/outflow are different.

12.10 KB Ltd is a coffee-blender, producing two blends, AM and PM, which are sold in bulk packs to manufacturers of instant coffee. The company's budget estimates for next year contain the following information.

	AM	PM
Standard selling price per pack (£)	57	48
Estimated sales revenue (£m)	2.736	3.072
Standard direct materials per pack:		
Ugandan coffee beans @ £1 per kg	5 kg	4 kg
Kenyan coffee beans @ £0.50 per kg	22 kg	10 kg
Brazilian coffee beans @ £1.50 per kg	6 kg	4 kg
Standard direct labour per pack:		
Skilled @ £8 per hour	0.5 hours	0.25 hours
Unskilled @ £4 per hour	2.0 hours	3.00 hours

Production overhead

This is estimated at £1,228,000 for next year, and is absorbed into unit costs on the basis of direct labour hours. Budgeted direct labour hours for next year are 307,000.

Stock values

	Anticipated at end of current year (£)	Desired at end of next year (£)
Ugandan coffee beans	24,000	20,000
Kenyan coffee beans	17,000	22,000
Brazilian coffee beans	21,000	15,000
Packs of AM	376,000	470,000
Packs of PM	840,000	504,000

Stocks of coffee beans are valued at the appropriate standard cost per kg. Packs of AM and PM are valued at the standard production cost per pack.

Requirements

(a) Prepare a standard cost card showing the standard production cost per pack of each of AM and PM.

(b) In respect of next year, prepare KB Ltd's budgets for:

(i) production quantities;

(ii) material usage quantities for each type of coffee bean;

(iii) material purchase quantities and cost for each type of coffee bean; and

(iv) direct labour hours and cost for each grade of labour.

12.11 Outline the main objectives of a budget system and discuss the extent to which these may or may not be achievable in an environment characterised by global competition, total quality management and advanced manufacturing technology.

Budgetary control

EXHIBIT **13.1 Expenditure control**

INTRODUCTION

In the last chapter, we discussed the role of budgets as a planning mechanism. However, planning on its own is of limited value. It is necessary also to assess the extent to which plans have been achieved (or otherwise) and to take some form of action where it seems that they will not be achieved. In other words, we need to exercise *control,* of the sort referred to in Exhibit 13.1. The chief executives and chairmen concerned presumably involve themselves in setting the budgets for these costs – but how do they exert (and tighten) control? Comparison of budgeted and actual costs (and revenues) is the most common starting-point for financial control. It is important to appreciate that control cannot be exercised without the existence of some form of plan or objective; similarly that failure to assess the extent to which plans have been achieved severely curtails the benefit to be derived from the planning process.

In this chapter, we shall examine the use of budgets as an aid to financial control, consider managerial responsibility in this context, and discuss the potential problems of using budgets in this way.

OBJECTIVES When you have completed this chapter, you will be able to:

- appreciate the existence of different types of control;

- understand the principles of exceptions reporting;

- distinguish between feedback control and feedforward control;

- appreciate the difference between fixed and flexible budgets and the use of flexible budgets for control purposes;

- prepare flexible budgets and budget control reports, identifying volume and flexible budget variances;

- describe the different approaches which may be adopted in determining the significance of variances;

- describe the features and objectives of a system of responsibility accounting and control reporting;

- explain the use of activity-based management, activity-based costing and activity-based budgeting in a control context;

- discuss the potential problem areas of financial control in general, and also with particular reference to the philosophy of total quality management; and

- distinguish between cost control and cost reduction, and describe the main approaches to cost reduction and the possible problems of cost reduction schemes.

FORMS OF CONTROL

Before we examine financial control mechanisms and procedures, we need to be aware of the different types of control which can exist. Hopwood (1974) identifies three types of control:

1 social controls;
2 self controls; and
3 administrative controls.

Financial control may be classified under the general heading of 'administrative controls', i.e. procedures which are consciously designed and implemented with the intention of affecting how people act within an organisation. However, as we shall see in Chapter 16, social and self control issues (i.e. behavioural issues) should not be viewed as separate matters. For the moment, we will confine ourselves to the comment that the design and operation of administrative control within an organisation may be greatly affected by, and may even derive from, social and self controls.

In broad terms, administrative controls can be divided into:

- rules and regulations (i.e. statements of desired patterns of organisational behaviour on the part of individuals); and
- output controls (i.e. controls which focus on the results of actions, leaving individuals with some discretion about how tasks are to be performed).

Although an element of the 'rules and regulations' category will be present in virtually every budget system (e.g. the budget manual), financial control essentially concentrates on the outcomes of actions, e.g. in the forms of costs incurred or revenue earned. Otley and Berry (1980) suggest four conditions which must exist in order for output controls to operate. These are:

1 The activity subject to control must have an objective or objectives. In the last chapter, we saw that budgets stem from objectives. Once set, the budgets will effectively form an objective to be attained.
2 The activity subject to control must have measurable outputs so that success in achieving the objective(s) can be assessed, e.g. costs, revenues, volume of output.
3 A 'predictive model' of the activity subject to control must exist, so that the reason for any failure to meet objectives, along with appropriate corrective action, can be determined. Where we understand the processes and procedures being subjected to control reasonably well – as we may do in the case of material input costs relative to volume of ouptut, for instance – this 'predictive model' can be relatively straightforward. If, say, material costs are unacceptably high relative to volume of output, appropriate remedial action may be relatively easy to determine. But consider a cost such as that associated with training – here, the processes and procedures are probably less clearly understood, so that action to correct a failure to meet objectives may be the subject of considerable judgement.
4 There must be an ability to take action so that failure to meet an activity's objective(s) can be addressed.

Otley and Berry's four conditions provide an outline for the operation of a system of financial control, and we must now add some specifics to these general propositions. As a starting-point, we need to consider how a financial control system assesses the extent to which objectives have been achieved.

EXCEPTIONS REPORTING

Exceptions reporting (also termed **management by exception**) forms the basis of financial control and assesses achievement of objectives by comparing budgeted costs and revenues with actual (**feedback control**) or of budgeted costs and revenues with some predetermined objective(s) (**feedforward control**). The two sets of outcomes being compared are most unlikely to be the same (except by chance) and the idea of exceptions reporting is that managerial action should be triggered by any significant differences revealed by this comparison.

⇨ Why should managerial action be triggered only by *significant* differences in outcome, rather than by *all* differences?

Managerial time is an extremely scarce resource. If all differences in outcome were to result in management action – that is, investigation of cause and/or taking corrective action once cause has been established – then a great deal of valuable time and effort would inevitably be lost in pursuit of trivia, distracting managers from more important concerns. This raises the question of what constitutes a 'significant' difference, an issue which we shall discuss later in the chapter.

Differences in outcome of the kind we have been describing are referred to as **variances** and you should not confuse management accounting variances with the statistical measure of the same name. A *favourable* variance indicates a better-than-expected outcome, whereas an *adverse* (or *unfavourable*) variance reflects a worse-than-expected outcome. When deciding whether a particular variance is favourable or adverse, a distinction needs to be made between costs, on the one hand, and revenue/profit, on the other: for example, higher-than-expected costs represent an adverse variance, whilst higher-than-expected revenues constitute a favourable variance. It is also important to realise that *all* significant variances should be investigated. There may be a danger of concentrating attention on significant adverse variances, which could result in failure to pursue any potential opportunity offered by significant favourable variances. In addition we need to realise that some variances may arise for reasons which are beyond management's immediate control, so that little or no action may be possible in the short term. We shall explore this issue later in the chapter.

Before we provide a detailed discussion and illustration of budget control reporting, we must consider the basic principles of feedback and feedforward control.

FEEDBACK AND FEEDFORWARD CONTROL

We have said that exceptions reporting is based on a comparison of outcomes. The terms 'feedback' and 'feedforward', in essence, describe *which* outcomes are being compared.

Feedback control compares budgeted and actual results, feedforward control compares desired results (i.e. objectives) and budgeted results. You will see from Figure 13.1 that actual processes and procedures are central to control. Objectives and plans aim to govern actual performance while actual performance governs achievement of objectives and plans. The key to effective control is therefore provision of information to allow managers to ensure not only that actual conforms with plans/objectives, but also that plans/objectives remain consistent with actual circumstances.

Because feedback control involves actual results – which will not be known until after the event – it is retrospective. Feedforward control, on the other hand, is forward-looking. This does not mean that the two operate in isolation, as Figure 13.1 shows.

⇨ As one of its short-term objectives, a company wishes to reduce its over-draft by 10 per cent during the forthcoming accounting year. Bearing Figure 13.1 in mind, how might feedforward *and* feedback control be applied to this situation?

Having determined the objective, the company will prepare functional budgets of the type we described in the last chapter (e.g. sales, production, material purchases) and a cash budget will be drawn up based on these functional budgets. If the cash budget suggests that the 10 per cent reduction can be achieved, or will fail to be achieved by an acceptably small margin, then the functional budgets will be implemented. Should the cash budget suggest a significant failure to achieve the desired reduction, then management may do either or both of the following:

■ *Amend the objective* Perhaps a 10 per cent reduction in the overdraft next year is too optimistic, and should be revised downward.
■ *Amend the budgets* Management may examine the various functional budgets to see if cash flows can be improved by reducing expenditure or increasing revenue.

When budgets which achieve the desired objective have been agreed and implemented, feedback control will be applied on a regular basis (e.g. monthly) within the budget period to determine the extent to which actual costs and revenues are in line with budget. After the reason for any significant variances has been investigated, control action may consist of one or more of the following:

■ *Amend the objective* Actual operating conditions may be such that the objective requires further amendment.

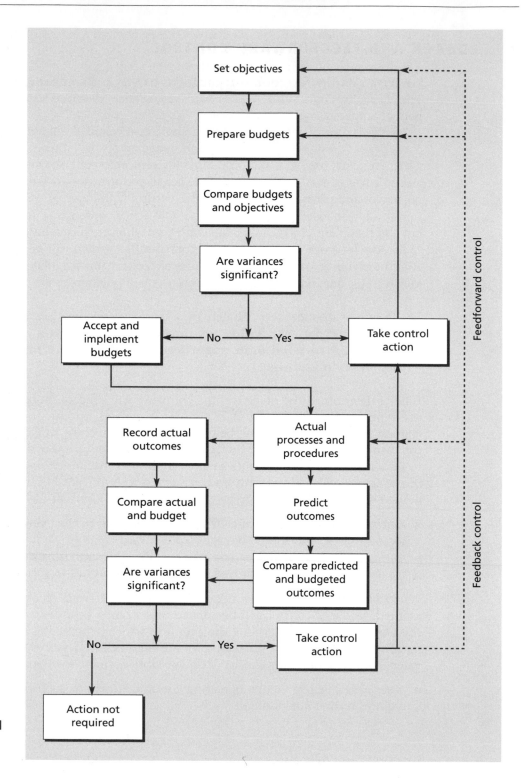

FIGURE 13.1
Feedback and
feedforward
control

- *Amend the budgets* Budgets prepared prior to commencement of the accounting year may need to be revised in light of experiences during the year (e.g. rolling budgets, as described in Chapter 12, may be used).
- *Improve future performance* Management may act to take advantage of any significant favourable variances (positive feedback) or to reduce the impact of any significant adverse variances (negative feedback).

A look at Figure 13.1 indicates that feedforward control will also occur within the feedback cycle, as management predicts the actual outcomes of ongoing activities, and, where necessary, takes steps to bring these into line with budget.

But we need to be careful: feedback and feedforward control neither indicate the reason for any variances, nor do they suggest what corrective action ought to be taken. The extent to which we are able to identify the reason for variances, the appropriate corrective action and its efficancy, depend on the accuracy of our 'predictive model', i.e. on how well we understand the processes and procedures we are attempting to control.

There is another aspect of the interrelationship between feedback and feedforward control.

⇨ How might the results of feedback control during the current budget period be used in a feedforward context?

Results of the feedback control exercise during the current period will almost invariably have a bearing on future planning. For example, amendments made to objectives, budgets and actual performance will inform the setting of short-term objectives and budgets for next year, and may also (if they are of sufficient significance) result in revision of strategic objectives and budgets.

In practice, the feedback and feedforward aspects of control may be so closely related as to be indistinguishable. For example, local authorities will apply feedback/feedforward principles as a matter of routine within their budgetary procedures. Not only is it important to keep actual expenditure within budget, but budgets must also be set such that various restrictions are met (e.g. council tax capping levels). Feedback control will monitor budget/actual expenditure; feedforward control will be applied in advance to ensure the proposed budget is within any restrictions and will be applied after the budget has been implemented to ensure that restrictions *continue* to be met.

Now that we have described the general principles of financial control, we can illustrate the budgetary mechanics involved – in particular, the nature and use of flexible budgets.

FLEXIBLE BUDGETS

The basis of a **flexible budget** is the fact that certain financial (and non-financial) items will react to changes in the volume of activity and the budget can be 'flexed' to reflect this.

PTB Ltd: flexible budget for planning

PTB Ltd, a long-established company which until recently manufactured cash registers, has moved to production of a single type of electronic point-of-sale (EPOS) equipment. The following estimates apply for next year:

Standard per unit produced

	£	£
Selling price		300
Variable costs:		
Direct materials	100	
Direct expenses	40	
Selling and distribution	20	160

Fixed costs for the year

	£
Direct labour	280,000
Production overhead	300,000
Administration overhead	200,000
Selling and distribution overhead	150,000

Volume

Maximum volume for the company's only factory is 12,000 units in the year under review. Some uncertainty attaches to next year's level of output/sales and PTB Ltd wishes to prepare budgeted profit statements based on 60, 65 and 70 per cent of maximum volume.

EXHIBIT **13.2 Data for flexible budget preparation**

⇨ What budgeted financial items will react to changes in the volume of activity?

Revenue, wholly variable costs, the variable element of semi-variable costs and step costs will all react to changes in the volume of activity, and we can incorporate this reaction into budgets as an aid to planning (by preparing a series of budgets based on different volumes of activity) and as part of the control process (to ensure like is being compared to like). These applications of flexible budgets are illustrated below.

Flexible budgets as a planning aid

Consider the data in Exhibit 13.2, which we shall use to demonstrate how flexible budgets may be used as part of the planning process. (For examples set in public sector and service organisations, see Questions 13.2, 13.3, 13.6, 13.8 and 13.9.)

Since flexible budgets are intended to reflect the reaction of revenue and certain costs to volume changes (i.e. to reflect cost behaviour relative to volume), it seems reasonable that we adopt a marginal costing format for PTB Ltd's budgeted profit statements, since this format is likewise based on cost behaviour

⇨ Complete the budgeted profit statements in Exhibit 13.3.

PTB Ltd: flexible budget

| | Output/sales volume | | |
	60%	65%	70%
Output/sales volume (units)	7,200	7,800	8,400
	£	£	£
Revenue			2,520,000
Variable costs:			
Direct material			840,000
Direct expenses			336,000
Selling and distribution			168,000
			1,344,000
Contribution			1,176,000
Fixed costs:			
Direct labour			280,000
Production overhead			300,000
Administration			200,000
Selling and distribution			150,000
			930,000
Net Profit			246,000

EXHIBIT **13.3 Partly completed flexible budget**

Exhibit 13.4 presents PTB Ltd's completed flexible budget for the year. You will see that the basis upon which the profit statements have been flexed is the number of cost units, but there are circumstances where an alternative basis is more appropriate (*see* later). For each budgeted level of activity, totals for those items which react to changes in volume (revenue and variable costs in this case) have been calculated by multiplying the standard unit data in Exhibit 13.2 by the budgeted number of units for each level of output/sales. Note that the fixed costs are unaffected by the volume changes.

⇨ What assumption regarding the behaviour of costs and revenue underlies the flexible budget in Exhibit 13.4?

Cost behaviour and revenue are both assumed to have a linear relationship with volume: that is, the unit selling price and unit variable costs are the same at all volumes and the fixed costs are unaffected by changes in volume. Although this may be rather simplistic in practice, budgets such as that in Exhibit 13.4 can easily accommodate non-linear price and cost functions: for example, the impact of step costs or of the need to reduce selling price at higher volumes.

A further assumption underlying Exhibit 13.4 is that the variable elements of the budget all vary according to the same measure of activity – units of

PTB Ltd: flexible budget

	Output/sales volume		
	60%	65%	70%
Output/sales volume (units)	7,200	7,800	8,400
	£	£	£
Revenue	2,160,000	2,340,000	2,520,000
Variable costs:			
Direct material	720,000	780,000	840,000
Direct expenses	288,000	312,000	336,000
Selling and distribution	144,000	156,000	168,000
	1,152,000	1,248,000	1,344,000
Contribution	1,008,000	1,092,000	1,176,000
Fixed costs:			
Direct labour	280,000	280,000	280,000
Production overhead	300,000	300,000	300,000
Administration	200,000	200,000	200,000
Selling and distribution	150,000	150,000	150,000
	930,000	930,000	930,000
Net profit	78,000	162,000	246,000

EXHIBIT **13.4 Completed flexible budget**

output/sales in this case – and (as we shall see later) there may be situations where we need to use more than one basis for flexing a budget. The exhibit also assumes that *volume* is the cause of cost variability, but this is not necessarily the case. Changes in factors such as technology or batch size can also cause costs to vary.

The approach taken in Exhibit 13.4 may also be applied to budgets other than the profit statement. For example, budgeted production cost may be assessed at different volume levels and the same general principle of distinguishing between variable and fixed items should be applied, the difference here being that revenue, contribution and profit will not be shown. Similarly, budgets such as production, material usage and material purchases may be prepared for different levels of activity.

Flexible budgets provide a useful form of sensitivity analysis in the planning process and will exist to some extent in virtually every budget system, as management will generally consider a range of possible outcomes before finalising the budget. However, a single budget must ultimately be set: that is, PTB Ltd must decide which volume of activity represents the most likely expectation for next year's operations (and which is most consistent with achieving strategic objectives), as it is not possible to implement more than one budget simultaneously. Otherwise, how would managers know which budget to aim to achieve and how could the extent to which the budget has been achieved be measured? The budget which the company finally adopts is known as a **fixed** (or **static**) **budget**, since it is based on a single volume of activity.

Flexible budgets and control

Exhibit 13.5 contains further information about PTB Ltd which we shall use to illustrate the use of flexible budgets as control indicators.

PTB Ltd: fixed budget and actuals for the year

After consideration of next year's likely operating conditions, PTB Ltd's management had set the budgeted volume at 65 per cent of maximum. At the end of the year, the fixed budget (based on this volume) and actual results were compared, as shown below.

	Fixed budget	Actual
Volume as % of maximum	65%	72%
Volume (units)	7,800	8,640
	£	£
Revenue	2,340,000	2,548,800
Variable costs:		
Direct material	780,000	812,160
Direct expenses	312,000	371,520
Selling and distribution	156,000	181,440
	1,248,000	1,365,120
Contribution	1,092,000	1,183,680
Fixed costs:		
Direct labour	280,000	302,000
Production overhead	300,000	291,000
Administration	200,000	216,000
Selling and distribution	150,000	177,000
	930,000	986,000
Net profit	162,000	197,680

Although satisfied by sales and profit in excess of budget, management is very concerned about the substantial amounts by which all three variable costs exceed budget.

EXHIBIT **13.5** Fixed budget and actual

⇨ Look at the budgeted and actual variable costs in Exhibit 13.5. Why might management concern about the higher actual costs be misplaced?

Management concern may be misplaced because the budget/actual comparison which is being made is not altogether valid. A budget based on 7,800 units is being compared with actuals based on 8,640 units, and this increased volume will be part of the reason for the differences in variable costs. A more valid budget/actual comparison would use a budget based on actual volume, so that like is being compared to like: that is, we should prepare a flexible budget based on actual volume.

Exhibit 13.6 shows the fixed budget (65 per cent volume), flexible budget based on actual volume (72 per cent) and actual. The revenue and variable cost figures in the flexible budget have been arrived at by multiplying the standard unit selling price and variable costs in Exhibit 13.2 by the actual output/sales volume. As in Exhibit 13.4, fixed costs are assumed to be unaffected by the volume difference between the two budgets.

PTB Ltd: fixed budget, flexible budget and actuals for the year

	Fixed budget	Flexible budget	Actual
Volume as % of maximum	65%	72%	72%
Volume (units)	7,800	8,640	8,640
	£	£	£
Revenue	2,340,000	2,592,000	2,548,800
Variable costs:			
Direct material	780,000	864,000	812,160
Direct expenses	312,000	345,600	371,520
Selling and distribution	156,000	172,800	181,440
	1,248,000	1,382,400	1,365,120
Contribution	1,092,000	1,209,600	1,183,680
Fixed costs:			
Direct labour	280,000	280,000	302,000
Production overhead	300,000	300,000	291,000
Administration	200,000	200,000	216,000
Selling and distribution	150,000	150,000	177,000
	930,000	930,000	986,000
Net profit	162,000	279,600	197,680

EXHIBIT **13.6** **Fixed budget, flexible budget and actual**

Comparison of the flexible budget and actuals in Exhibit 13.6 sheds a rather different light on the apparent adverse variable cost variances suggested by Exhibit 13.5. When the effect of the volume difference between actual and fixed budget is removed, the adverse variances for direct expenses and for selling and distribution costs are markedly reduced, whilst the direct materials variance is now favourable, indicating a lower expenditure than would have been expected for the actual volume of output/sales. However, revenue and profit do not emerge so well from such a comparison – both are lower than would be expected from the actual volume of output/sales.

We are now in a position to extract two sets of variances from our comparison of budgeted and actual data, as follows:

1 *Volume variances* These are the differences between the fixed and flexible budgets and show the revenue, variable cost, contribution and profit impact of the difference between fixed budget volume and actual volume (there will be no volume variances for fixed costs, since these are assumed not to react to changes in volume and are therefore the same in both fixed and flexible budgets).

2 *Flexible budget variances* These are the differences between flexible budget and actual, reflecting the impact on revenue, variable cost, contribution, fixed cost and profit of budget/actual differences in factors other than volume (e.g. cost, rate, usage and efficiency).

Exhibit 13.7 shows the full statement of fixed budget, flexible budget and actual, with volume and flexible budget variances identified. At first sight, Exhibit 13.7 appears extremely complex; in fact, it is merely Exhibit 13.6 with two additional columns inserted. Adverse variances are designated '*A*' and favourable variances '*F*'. Remember that a distinction must be made between revenue, contribution and profit elements and cost elements for the purpose of deciding whether a particular variance is adverse or favourable.

PTB Ltd: fixed budget, flexible budget and actuals for the year, with volume and flexible budget variances identified

	Fixed Budget	Volume Variances	Flexible Budget	Flexible Budget Variances	Actual
Volume as % of maximum	65%	7% F	72%	nil	72%
Volume (units)	7,800	840F	8,640	nil	8,640
	£	£	£	£	£
Revenue	2,340,000	252,000F	2,592,000	43,200A	2,548,800
Variable costs:					
Direct material	780,000	84,000A	864,000	51,840F	812,160
Direct expenses	312,000	33,600A	345,600	25,920A	371,520
Selling and distribution	156,000	16,800A	172,800	8,640A	181,440
	1,248,000	134,400A	1,382,400	17,280F	1,365,120
Contribution	1,092,000	117,600F	1,209,600	25,920A	1,183,680
Fixed costs:					
Direct labour	280,000	nil	280,000	22,000A	302,000
Production overhead	300,000	nil	300,000	9,000F	291,000
Administration	200,000	nil	200,000	16,000A	216,000
Selling and distribution	150,000	nil	150,000	27,000A	177,000
	930,000	nil	930,000	56,000A	986,000
Net profit	162,000	117,600F	279,600	81,920A	197,680

EXHIBIT **13.7** Fixed and flexible budgets, actual and variances

A presentation such as that in Exhibit 13.7 may convey additional information. For example, sales volume has been higher than originally budgeted (favourable volume variance for revenue), but selling price has been lower (adverse flexible budget variance for revenue) – possibly, the lower selling price has been the cause of the higher sales volume, although investigation of the circumstances behind the figures would be necessary.

⇨ What conclusions might be drawn from Exhibit 13.7 about budgeted and actual direct materials?

A higher direct materials cost has been incurred than that originally budgeted as the result of a higher-than-budgeted output/sales volume (adverse volume variance). The adverse flexible budget variance suggests that either or both of the following may have occurred:

1 A difference may have arisen between the standard price of materials and the actual price paid.
2 A difference may have arisen between the standard quantity of materials required per unit of output and the actual quantity used.

Once again, further investigation would be required, and, in the next chapter, we will illustrate how flexible budget variances may be subdivided to show the effect of such price and usage differences.

The flexing basis

We said earlier that the basis for flexing the budget will normally be the organisation's cost unit. However, this is only practicable where all cost units are identical. If a budget centre or organisation produces several different types of cost unit, then the budget will require to be flexed in a slightly different way.

Flexing on the basis of standard hours

You will recall from the last chapter that the **standard hour** is a measure of the work which should be performed in one hour at the specified standard efficiency level, and that use of this concept allows output of diverse types of cost unit to be expressed as a single figure. Where different cost units are produced by an organisation or budget centre, a single flexible budget (and fixed budget) can be produced by expressing output in terms of standard hours and flexing variable costs on that basis. Flexible budget revenue is still based on units – in this case, the aggregate of (standard selling price × actual sales volume) for all the individual cost units concerned.

⇨ Why is it preferable to flex the budget on the basis of standard, rather than actual hours of output?

If the budget were to be flexed using actual hours, then the flexible budget would be distorted by differences between the standard and actual levels of efficiency, which would result in budget-holding managers being 'penalised' for better-than-standard efficiency and 'rewarded' for lower-than-standard efficiency. We will use the information in Exhibit 13.8 to illustrate how this would happen.

Standard v actual hours as flexing basis

A budget centre which produces several different types of cost unit provides the following data for Periods 7 and 8 of the current accounting year:

	Period 7	Period 8
Standard hours' output achieved	7,000	5,000
Actual hours worked	8,000	4,000
Standard variable cost per hour	£6	£6

EXHIBIT **13.8 Alternative flexing bases**

⇨ Calculate the flexible budget variable cost for each of Periods 7 and 8 using

1 standard hours; and
2 actual hours as the flexing basis.

For each period, the flexible budget variable cost will be:

	Period 7		Period 8	
		£		£
Standard hours	(7,000 × £6)	42,000	(5,000 × £6)	30,000
Actual hours	(8,000 × £6)	48,000	(4,000 × £6)	24,000

In Period 7, actual efficiency was lower than standard (because 8,000 actual hours were required to produce 7,000 standard hours' worth of output); using actual hours as the flexing basis, this is 'rewarded' by a higher flexible budget allowance for variable cost, thereby artificially reducing the flexible budget variance by removing efficiency differences from its calculation. Conversely, in Period 8, use of actual hours as the flexing basis will incur the 'penalty' of a lower flexible budget allowance for variable cost, thereby artificially increasing the flexible budget variance. In both cases, use of actual hours will give an unrealistic view of actual performance against budget and should therefore be avoided.

Multiple flexing bases

Use of standard hours to flex the budget will only be practical where variable costs vary with hours (whether labour or machine hours). If you look again at the data in Exhibit 13.2, you will see that such an approach would not be possible in PTB Ltd's case where labour is a fixed cost (as is often the case) and where variable costs vary with the number of cost units. Had the company produced more than one type of EPOS equipment, then a unitary flexible (and fixed) budget could only be produced by aggregating the flexible (and fixed) budget allowances for each kind of cost unit. As an additional complication, variable costs need not necessarily vary in relation to the same measure of activity: for example, direct materials could vary relative to the number of cost units, with variable overhead varying according to the number of direct labour hours. Here, it would be necessary to ensure that the correct activity measure was used both to prepare the fixed budget and to flex the budget for control purposes. Thus, a degree of care is necessary in selection of the activity measure to be used but, once identified, different activity measures are easily incorporated into fixed and flexible budget calculations.

DETERMINING THE SIGNIFICANCE OF VARIANCES

We said earlier that one of the principles of exceptions reporting is that managerial action is triggered by significant variances from budget and we must now discuss how the significance of variances might be determined.

Absolute amount approach

If this method were adopted, a variance's significance would be measured with reference to a set monetary amount. For example, PTB Ltd might stipulate that every variance in excess of £5,000 (favourable *and* adverse) should be investigated, which is a simple enough rule to apply.

⇨ What is the weakness of investigating all variances in excess of an absolute monetary amount?

The problem with investigating every variance in excess of, say, £5,000 is that such an absolute measure does not, in fact, reflect significance. We may say that £5,000 is a large amount of money and that this is sufficient to warrant the time, effort (and possibly cost) involved in investigating variances in excess of £5,000. But consider the following:

Budgeted expenditure (£)	Actual expenditure(£)	Variance(£)
4,000	8,000	4,000A
4,000,000	4,006,000	6,000A

Applying our absolute amount rule of investigating every variance in excess of £5,000 means that only the second of the above variances will be investigated. A variance of £4,000 relative to a budget of £4,000 is clearly significant – but £6,000 against a budget of £4 million? Application of the absolute amount rule may commit valuable managerial time and resources to investigation of insignificant variances, thereby negating the principle of exceptions reporting. Although it can be argued that elimination of a variance such as the £6,000A (even when it relates to a large budgeted/actual amount) will have the effect of improving profit, it is questionable whether this can be achieved without breaching the cost/benefit criterion.

Percentage of budget approach

We can overcome the problem just described by expressing variances *relative* to the budget: that is, as a percentage of budget, rather than as an absolute amount, so that the criterion for significance may be stated as something like: 'investigate every variance in excess of 5% of flexible budget'. Like the absolute amount approach, this method is easy to apply, but the problem here lies in determining the most appropriate percentage to use. A frequently-quoted 'rule-of-thumb' is 5 per cent, but it has no objective or mathematical justification, and a different percentage (e.g. 10 per cent) could as easily be used and justified, as could use of different percentages for different budget items. And if the measure of significance is open to debate, then the credibility of the control process may be questionable.

Statistical definition of significance

Statistics may be able to provide an objective test of the significance of variances. If, say, usage of direct materials is normally distributed, and if the standard cost is the mean value (i.e. average) of this distribution, then it is possible to use statistical theory to set *control limits*. Given the normal distribution referred to, we can predict, for example, that approximately 95 per cent of output should use direct materials falling within limits of ± two standard deviations of the mean value (i.e. of the standard direct materials usage) and that roughly 99 per cent of output should have direct material usage falling within limits of ± 3 standard deviations of the mean value etc. Control limits may then be set at the desired level of statistical tolerance (e.g. ± 1 or 2 standard deviations of the mean) and a *statistical control chart*, as in Figure 13.2, can be prepared.

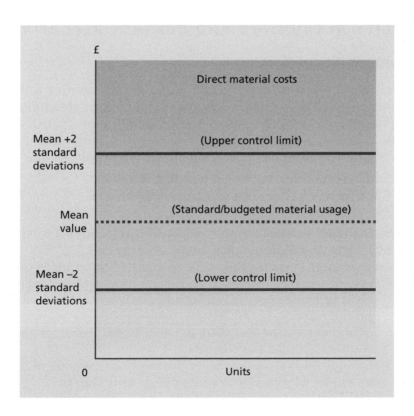

FIGURE 13.2
Statistical
control chart

In Figure 13.2, the control limits have been set at mean value ± 2 standard deviations. All material usage which falls inside these control limits will be deemed to be 'in control', whereas all material usage falling outwith the control limits will be considered 'out of control' and therefore worthy of investigation. If more than 5 per cent of actual material usage falls outside the control limits, then either there is a problem with material usage and/or the standard needs to be revised. This kind of approach may be useful for repetitive tasks, but is reliant on the accuracy of the mean and standard deviation being used. Since these will be based on past observations, the assumption is being made that the past is a reliable guide to the future. In addition, it will only really be applicable to situations where tolerance levels can be set with reasonable accuracy and where actuals are controllable. This may be true for material usage, but may not hold for material price, which could be determined by external factors not under management's control.

Surveys of practice by Puxty and Lyall (1989) and by Drury *et al.* (1993) strongly suggest that significance appears to be largely a matter of managerial judgement and that many organisations employ more than one criterion in assessing the significance of variances. This same research indicates that statistical approaches are very rare, with the most common methods (listed in decreasing order of frequency) being:

■ managerial judgement;
■ absolute amount method; and
■ percentage approach.

RESPONSIBILITY ACCOUNTING AND CONTROL REPORTING

Responsibility accounting

Operation of a system of budgetary planning and control within a particular organisation will be determined by that organisation's structure, most often following lines of managerial responsibility. In all but the smallest organisations, decision making is delegated and the principle of **responsibility accounting** is that financial control procedures should reflect this delegation of authority. In other words, authority to make decisions confers responsibility for the financial consequences of those decisions on the managers concerned. In broad terms, a system of responsibility accounting possesses the following features:

1 The organisation is divided into **responsibility centres** (i.e. budget centres), of which there are five main types:
   (a) **cost centre**: budgeted and actual costs are recorded and compared;
   (b) **revenue centre**: budgeted and actual revenues are recorded and compared;
   (c) **profit centre**: budgeted and actual costs, revenues and profit are recorded and compared;
   (d) **investment centre**: budgeted and actual costs, revenues and capital expenditure are recorded and compared;
   (e) **strategic business unit**: this is effectively an investment centre which has the additional authority to determine its own strategy.

All five may co-exist within the same organisation, although, for the moment, our primary concern will be with cost (and to a lesser extent profit) centres. We will take an in-depth look at investment centres and strategic business units in Chapter 15.

2 An individual manager is delegated the authority and responsibility for running each responsibility centre, for meeting and (in most cases) participating in setting that responsibility centre's budget.

3 Control reports comparing budget and actual for each responsibility centre are prepared periodically and passed upwards through the organisational hierarchy.

Responsibility accounting has a twofold objective: first, to enhance planning, control and decision making for a responsibility centre (and for the organisation overall) by delegating these functions to the manager 'at the sharp end', who understands the centre's functions and operations, along with their financial consequences; second, to improve **goal congruence**. Involving managers in planning, control and decision making (via delegation) should reduce the possibility that those managers will act in a manner which is inconsistent with the organisation's overall objectives (i.e. will reduce the incidence of **dysfunctional** decisions).

Control reporting

We have said that control reports for each responsibility centre should be periodically prepared and passed upwards through the organisational hierarchy, and it is now necessary to give some consideration to the frequency and content of such reports. Since control reports are supposed to monitor the extent to which budgets are being achieved, their frequency should fit the broader framework of the budget period. We described budget periods in the last chapter and stated that, for tactical budgets, this will be one year, and, for strategic budgets, it may range from three to (say) five years.

▷ Exhibit 13.7 could be viewed as a control report for PTB Ltd covering the tactical budget period of one year. Why would it generally be unwise to prepare control reports *only* at the end of the budget period?

If an organisation were to wait until the end of the budget period to prepare control reports, then *ongoing* monitoring of the extent to which budgets are being achieved would not be possible. It is thus unlikely that any major problems would come to light until the end of the budget period concerned (by which time it will be too late to take any action in response). In extreme circumstances, this could even lead to failure of the business. It is therefore advisable to split each budget period into shorter control periods: for example, for tactical budgets, the budget period could be split into 12 calendar months or into 13 periods of four weeks (to prevent any distortion of variances caused by months of differing length); and strategic budgets may be split into annual (or possibly six-monthly) control periods to allow assessment of progress towards strategic objectives. 'Real time' – i.e. produced simultaneously with the processes to which they relate – control statistics (e.g. input/output quantities) are an increasingly common feature of automated and computerised production systems.

Control periods of different length to those we have suggested are possible, and the frequency of control reporting should ultimately suit the specific circumstances of the organisation. However, care must be exercised in this respect. Control periods which are too infrequent may defeat the objective of allowing ongoing monitoring of budget and actual, but too frequent control periods may run the risk of 'swamping' managers in paperwork, with the result that reports may not be properly followed up.

The content of control reports also merits careful consideration. The level of detail, for example, may have an important bearing on the extent to which control reports are read, understood and acted on. Exhibit 13.7 may contain sufficient detail for consideration by PTB Ltd's senior management, but might be insufficiently detailed for managers in charge of individual responsibility centres. In general, the lower the managerial level being reported to, the greater the relevant detail necessary to allow effective response to control reports. Conversely, the higher the managerial level being reported to, the lower the amount of detail, until, at the most senior level, a summarised statement, such as that contained in Exhibit 13.7, will probably suffice. Again, the precise detail contained in control reports to each management level should be governed by specific circumstances, but the principle being followed is the same in all situations: that is, that 'lower-level' control reports are combined and their key elements summarised in 'higher-level' reports. In addition to the kind of information shown in Exhibit 13.7, budget control reports may show information such as year-to-date totals for actual and budget, or state variances as a percentage of budget (as well as giving the absolute monetary amount), and, where feasible, variable and fixed costs should be distinguished. Items deemed fully controllable by the responsible manager should be separated from those only partly controllable (or uncontrollable) – a vexed issue which we shall discuss in more detail later in the chapter.

ACTIVITY-BASED CONTROL

Our discussion of control has so far concentrated on controlling particular categories of financial item (e.g. cost of direct materials or of direct labour). In Chapters 4 and 12 we described, respectively, activity-based costing (ABC) and activity-based budgeting (ABB); in the earlier chapter, we mentioned the use of activity-based principles as an aid to control, often termed **activity-based management (ABM)** or **activity-based cost management (ABCM)**. You will recall from our earlier discussion that the major features of an activity-based approach are:

- identifying key organisational activities;
- setting up a cost pool for each of these activities;
- identifying the **cost driver** for each activity (i.e. the main underlying cause of the associated costs); and
- determining unit costs on the basis of each unit's usage of the various cost drivers identified.

ABCM applies these principles to the control (and/or reduction) of costs, regardless of whether unit costs are determined on an activity basis. If key activities and their related cost drivers can be identified, then controlling/reducing the incidence of the cost driver should control/reduce the associated cost. It is also argued that identification, measurement and control of cost drivers (within a system of ABB) will provide additional and valuable control information, thereby attempting to address the possible problem of overemphasising financial control measures (which we shall discuss below). And, by identifying key organisational activities, ABCM should enhance management's ability to 'home in' on activities which are especially important, or which require particular attention. The benefit of ABCM in this context is that it should allow management to distinguish between **value-added activities** and **non-value-added activities**: that is, between those activities which enhance customer perception of the 'value' of the product/service being offered and those which do not (such as the cost of storing stock of raw materials and finished goods). If non-value-added activities and their cost drivers can be identified, then control of inessential costs and competitiveness may be enhanced through use of activity-based techniques within a cost reduction scheme of the sort we shall describe later in the chapter.

However, the requirement to compare budget and actual, identify variances and take action on the basis of those variances which are significant remains fundamental to ABCM. In addition, the extent to which activity-based approaches (whether ABC, ABB or ABCM) can be successfully applied is heavily dependent on the organisation's ability to correctly identify its main activities and, more problematically (as we saw in Chapter 4), their associated cost drivers. It might also be said that, if a system of 'conventional' responsibility centres has been carefully designed, then these will be a reflection of key activities within the organisation. We could also argue that any attempt to control/reduce costs (irrespective of the use of activity-based methodology) should involve consideration of the underlying cause of the cost(s) concerned. In some circumstances, the 'pooling' of activity-based costs and the identification of a single cost driver for every cost pool may even hamper effective control if the cost driver is not strictly applicable to every cost within that particular pool. As we suggested in Chapter 4, some subjectivity may exist with cost drivers as with apportionment bases.

FINANCIAL CONTROL: POSSIBLE PROBLEM AREAS

The essence of financial control – budget/actual comparison and investigation/action on the basis of significant variances – may appear to be a straightforward matter. However, there are certain potential problem areas which, if not borne in mind, may utterly defeat attempts at financial control.

Cost control v performance appraisal

Budget/actual comparisons of the type we have been describing are primarily intended as cost control aids. But it is often the case that they are also used to assess managerial performance. There are many instances where management bonuses are linked to their responsibility centre's performance against budget, and it is certainly true that variances from budget can provide some indication of performance.

⇨ Can you see any dangers in using only financial budget variances to measure managers' performance?

Using financial budget variances as the sole measure of performance will almost certainly represent a dangerous oversimplification and may result in some or all of the adverse consequences which we discussed below.

Non-financial aspects of performance underemphasised or ignored

When we described total quality management in Chapter 2, we emphasised the importance of the quality of products/services. If financial measures are the main (or only) measure of performance, then this crucial aspect of organisational activity may be overlooked, with managers concentrating their efforts on achievement of financial targets to the exclusion of virtually everything else. It could even be suggested that budget variances of the type we calculated in Exhibit 13.7 are irrelevant in a total quality context because:

- they do not reflect quality of product/service (although this might be said to be reflected indirectly in sales and contribution variances);
- they do not reflect the cost of attempting to achieve quality (e.g. internal and external failure costs of the kind we described in Chapter 2); and
- they are primarily internal comparisons.

A **target costing** approach (see Chapter 8) suggests that financial control be exercised with an outward-looking perspective, namely:

- a selling price consistent with the market and desired market share is set;
- the required profit return is deducted from sales; and
- the residual after deducting required return from sales represents the target cost.

This is certainly consistent with strategic considerations and with the market orientation of total quality management, placing selling considerations first and working backwards to cost. However, control of *individual* costs (e.g. materials or labour) could be difficult using this system because budgeted cost is a 'global' residual after application of target costing principles. So some sort of subdivision of this residual may be necessary: in effect, standard costs might need to be developed.

The implication of total quality management is that if the organisation is 'getting it right first time all of the time', then variances will not arise. But it is debatable whether, even under the most favourable circumstances and given the utmost emphasis on quality, operations will always be 'right first time' – so variances will inevitably arise. As a minimum, it will probably be necessary to monitor the budgeted and actual costs of trying to achieve quality: for example, by comparing budgeted and actual internal failure costs. In addition to budget variances, it may be advisable to examine a range of performance indicators encompassing both financial and non-financial considerations. We shall discuss performance appraisal and the need to look at a range of measures in Chapter 15.

The budget may inhibit managers

If the financial control aspect of budgets is overemphasised, managers may come to view budgets as constraints on their activities and as an attempt to 'fix blame', rather than as the aid they are intended to be. Whilst some form of financial constraint is obviously necessary, it should not be so tight that it prevents managers from suggesting new or radical ideas on the grounds that these would 'breach the budget' or 'cost too much' – some freedom to make decisions is necessary within the budget system.

Pressure to take panic action

Stemming from the previous two points, overemphasising financial performance against budget may have the effect of 'pressuring' managers into taking precipitate control action. For example, a significant adverse cost variance may result in an attempt to cut costs unnecessarily. Variances may indicate the possible existence of a problem, but control action in the form of cost reduction should only follow investigation of the cause of any significant variances. There is a danger that the need to investigate significant variances could be overshadowed by the very existence of what appears to be an adverse performance indicator. There may, however, be a perfectly valid reason for the existence of an adverse cost variance (e.g. random or uncontrollable factors of the sort we shall describe below). Misplaced control action of this kind may have severe non-financial implications (e.g. for quality), and might adversely affect the strategic dimension.

If financial variances are to be used as performance indicators – and it is perfectly reasonable that they should be used in this way – then it is important that they be used sensibly, and preferably in conjunction with other measures of the kind we shall discuss in Chapter 15.

In addition to the problems which could stem from use of control measures to assess performance, there are further, more general, difficulties.

Random factors

The need for careful investigation of significant variances is underlined by the impact on actual performance of random factors not foreseen at the time the budget was prepared.

⇨ In Exhibit 13.7, the flexible budget variance for direct materials was £51,840*F*. Assuming that the materials concerned are imported, can you suggest *two* random factors that might underlie this variance (or part of it) and which may not have been foreseen at the time the original budget was prepared?

There are many possible random factors which may have affected the actual direct materials cost: for example, fluctuations in the exchange rate, unforeseen loosening of import/export regulations, changes in the domestic situation in the country of origin of the materials, and so forth. The point about such random factors is that they will affect the budget variance reported and, because they were neither foreseen when the budget was originally prepared nor were they under managerial control, their effect on the variance concerned should really be eliminated for the purposes of cost control comparison. In the next chapter, we shall see how the impact of such random factors may be dealt with by calculating planning and operational variances, along with the extent to which this approach is successful in dealing with the problem.

Allowing for the impact of inflation

In Chapter 3, we saw the potential impact of inflation on estimates of future costs, and suggested that it would be unwise to omit its effect from such estimates. Clearly, inflation has a bearing on the budgetary planning/control process. Although inflation may have been allowed for in preparation of a budget, it can be argued that any difference between the rate of inflation foreseen when the budget was prepared and that which actually applied within a control period represents a random and uncontrollable factor of the type described above, and that its impact should be allowed for in calculation of variances. Exhibit 13.9 contains further information about PTB Ltd's actual and budgeted material costs for the year. Because of the difference between the anticipated and actual rates of inflation, the flexible budget variance will be distorted because, in essence, we are not comparing like with like.

PTB Ltd: inflation and material costs

PTB Ltd's budget specified a standard direct materials cost of £100 per unit, based on an expected average inflation rate of 5 per cent for the year concerned. In the event, the actual inflation rate was only 3 per cent. Before adjusting for inflation, comparison of flexible budget and actual revealed the following:

	Flexible budget	Flexible budget variance	Actual
Direct material cost	£864,000	£51,840F	£812,160

EXHIBIT **13.9 Inflation and financial control**

⇨ In Exhibit 13.9, will the difference between inflation rates cause a favourable or an adverse distortion in the flexible budget variance?

Because we are dealing with a cost and because the actual inflation rate was lower than anticipated, the distortion to the flexible budget variance will be favourable: that is, the effect is to overstate the budgeted amount. To make a true comparison, we can remove this inflationary distortion, by **deflating** the flexible budget prior to comparison:

$$\text{deflated flexible budget: } £864,000 \times \frac{1.03}{1.05} = £847,543 \text{ (rounded)}$$

which gives an amended flexible budget variance of:

$$(£847,543 - £812,160) = £35,383F.$$

Deflating the budget in this way allows us to compare like with like: that is, budget and actual both incorporate the same rate of inflation. Had the actual inflation rate been higher than budgeted, then the effect of our adjustment would be to **inflate** the budget. Whether inflating or deflating the budget, the general adjustment to apply is:

$$\frac{1 + \text{actual inflation rate}}{1 + \text{budgeted inflation rate}}$$

Comparison of the deflated variance (£35,383*F*) with that reported in Exhibit 13.7 (£51,840*F*) illustrates just how great can be the impact of differences between budgeted and actual inflation. (The difference between these two variances might be treated as a planning variance of the type we shall discuss in the next chapter.)

Controllability of budget items

In an ideal world, control reports submitted to managers in respect of their responsibility centre should reflect only those revenues/costs over which direct and complete control can be exercised at responsibility centre level. Unfortunately, this is rarely the case. Budget control reports will almost invariably contain items for which the locus of control is 'grey', or shared, or items whose genuine controllability in the short term is questionable.

⟹ We said earlier that the flexible budget variance for direct materials reflects differences between standard and actual price and/or usage. How might responsibility for such a variance be unclear?

If purchasing and usage fall within the remit of different responsibility centres (e.g. buying and production), then responsibility for the materials' flexible budget variance may be shared between these centres. To complicate matters further, there may well be a link between the price and usage elements of the flexible budget variance. For example, purchase of cheaper-than-standard materials may result in a favourable price element, but this may be offset by an adverse usage element resulting from poorer-than-standard quality. Problems of this sort may be partly solved by subdividing flexible budget variances in the manner we shall describe in the next chapter – but even this does not solve the difficulties caused by interrelationships between variances and of dual responsibility.

A second area of possible control difficulty arises in the case of cost **apportionments**: for example, front-line responsibility centres may receive a 'charge' for central support services (e.g. administration, computer services). Whilst it may occasionally be possible to base such a charge entirely on usage, it is more likely that some element of apportionment will be present. Showing such charges on responsibility centres' control reports (even when based wholly on apportionment) can be justified in terms of providing some indication of the cost of supporting the activities of front-line centres and of making clear that central support services are not 'free'. Even though front-line managers may be unable to directly control support service costs, they may nevertheless be able to exert pressure on support service managers to control costs in the event that apportioned charges appear to be rising to unacceptably high levels. Alternatively, it might be said, particularly by managers of responsibility centres receiving charges of this sort, that their inclusion is unwarranted on the basis that the underlying costs cannot be directly controlled. In such a case, serious disputes about controllability versus responsibility may arise, to the detriment of working relationships within the organisation and, ultimately, of the organisation itself. If apportionments are to be shown on budget control reports, then the fact that certain figures *are* apportionments should be made clear. Moreover, the apportionment bases should be as objective as practicable, should be applied consistently to all relevant responsibility centres, and should not be changed without prior warning.

One final problem area under the general heading of 'controllability' concerns the nature of certain costs being reported on. The fundamental tenet of exceptions reporting, feedback and feedforward control and responsibility accounting is that significant variances, once identified, give rise to management action to control the situation. For those costs which reflect a tangible input/output relationship (**engineered costs**) – such as PTB Ltd's direct material costs – this may be a relatively straightforward matter; but there are two categories of cost which present something of a difficulty where *short-term* control action is required.

Committed costs

We first encountered this term in Chapter 7 when we discussed the concept of relevant costs and revenues for decision making, stating that they were irrelevant to the financial analysis as they would be incurred regardless of the decision under consideration. A similar type of argument may be made in the control context. Once certain strategic decisions have been made (e.g. about the scale of organisational operations), then a certain level of costs will be unavoidable in the short term if the predetermined strategy is to be achieved. This being the case, financial control exercises must attempt to recognise the extent to which some variances (e.g. relating to building occupancy costs, or to certain elements of direct labour) may not be amenable to short-term control measures without prejudice to strategic aims.

Discretionary costs

A **discretionary cost**, as the term implies, is one over the amount of which management has discretion. In an emergency, it would theoretically be possible to reduce such costs to zero without adversely affecting the short-term wellbeing of the organisation. Much advertising and promotional expenditure, training costs and a certain proportion of legal and accountancy costs, possibly along with items such as the level of staff bonuses, would fall into the category of discretionary costs. The hallmark of discretionary costs is their 'black box' nature: that is, the fact that there is no definable relationship between input (the amount of expenditure) and output (the benefit derived from that expenditure). This makes discretionary costs very difficult to budget (e.g. what is the 'correct' amount of budgeted expenditure on advertising?) and to control.

⇨ A firm's budget/actual comparison for advertising costs reveals the following:

Flexible budget	Actual
£3 million	£2 million

Is the £1 million favourable variance 'good' or 'bad'?

The £1 million favourable variance could be considered a 'good' sign, in that actual expenditure was lower than budgeted by that amount. On the other hand, the same variance could be viewed as 'bad', since it might represent a missed opportunity to improve sales or organisational profile. The point is, we cannot be sure, and the result of such uncertainty is often a feeling that budgets for discretionary costs should be 'spent to the hilt', regardless of inability to define the resulting benefits with any precision.

Unclear input/output relationships of this sort can pose a particular problem in service and some non-profit organisations. Given the intangible, heterogeneous and perishable nature of most services which we discussed in Chapter 2, the proportion of discretionary costs may be higher here than in the manufacturing sector, with greater attendant planning and control problems. It may be, therefore, that in such organisations, supplementing financial control/performance measures with non-financial indicators may have particular significance – a point which we shall consider further in Chapter 15. Irrespective of the organisation, planning and control of discretionary costs must be undertaken with care to prevent their spiralling out of control.

Measurement errors

In addition to random factors such as exchange rate fluctuations and the impact of inflation, budgetary control exercises must also attempt to recognise the fact that errors do occur. Whilst most arithmetic errors relating to financial data may be corrected within a computerised accounting system, wide scope still exists for incorrect recording of data such as actual direct labour hours, or usage of materials – a fact which should be borne in mind when interpreting budget control reports.

Tactical v strategic control

In addition to the dangers discussed above, overemphasising the control aspect of annual tactical budgets (e.g. by using budget variances as the main indicator of managerial performance) may have the effect of concentrating managerial attention on a continual 'annual financial firefighting' exercise, in an attempt to keep strictly within budget limits. Where these limits are significantly breached, the result may be the sort of panic cost-cutting reaction we described earlier: not only might this have implications for quality, but also the tactical benefit of such measures may be more than offset by their adverse impact on achievement of strategic plans. When considering or implementing control action, management must be aware of the potential time lag which could exist between the taking of action and the appearance of its benefits and/or costs, and should beware of the 'ripple effect' of ad hoc tactical control into the strategic arena.

Outdated control information

We suggested earlier that control reports should be produced periodically within the budget period to which they relate – say, monthly or four-weekly (or even fortnightly/weekly). For organisations which operate within the sort of advanced manufacturing technology (AMT) framework we described in Chapter 2, reports prepared on this sort of basis might be too infrequent for them to be effective. For example, where automated output processes produce 'real time' control data, financial measures may be relegated to the position of confirming that which is already known. This may be particularly true where manufacturing processes are heavily oriented towards the just-in-time (JIT) approach. In fact, budget reports based on absorption costing may even conflict with JIT principles – as we illustrated in Chapter 4, unwarranted increases in stocks of finished goods may be 'rewarded' by unrealistically high profit figures. In such environments, control reports may therefore be required in good time and very much more frequently than might be necessary in more 'traditional' situations, and the value of absorption costing for internal purposes may be called even more into question.

It is even debatable whether budgetary control has much relevance in AMT environments, where control is likely to be heavily dependent on product/technology design and controllability will reflect management's ability to influence these factors.

Fixed/variable cost analysis

Our flexible budget analysis of PTB Ltd in Exhibit 13.7 was based on marginal costing principles, but you will recall from Chapters 3 and 5 that there may be problems with this approach in terms both of separating fixed from variable costs and of the predominantly fixed nature of many organisations' cost structures. Although it is true that, in practice, marginal costing in the 'pure' form set out in Exhibit 13.7 is somewhat unlikely, it is important that the principle of flexible budgeting be applied: that is, to recognise, as part of the financial control exercise (and as far as practicable, given the cost/benefit criterion), the fact that certain budget items will react to volume changes. Even if such changes are limited to revenue and step increases in some fixed costs, flexing the budget is still desirable, if only as an enhancement of control reports.

Means – end confusion

In the last chapter, we observed that budget systems may suffer from bureaucratic 'overkill'; this may be particularly evident in the context of budgetary control, with the control exercise coming to be viewed as an end in its own right, rather than as a means to an end (i.e. achievement of objectives). This is inconsistent with the need for managerial and organisation flexibility and also conflicts with strategic considerations.

COST REDUCTION

Cost *control* and cost *reduction* should not be confused. **Cost control**, as should be evident from the preceding discussion, means attempting to keep costs within pre-determined limits. **Cost reduction**, on the other hand, involves the reduction of costs from previous levels, *without adverse impact on the quality of product/service being provided*. Although it is often possible to achieve marked cost reductions by taking a common-sense view of the situation, or perhaps by application of activity-based cost management, there are other techniques available, the more important of which are described briefly below.

Where an organisation employs target costing (*see* Chapter 8), cost reduction techniques may be of particular relevance.

Value analysis (value engineering)

Value analysis is a systematic attempt to remove inessential aspects of a product or service and would normally be undertaken both prior to that product/service being offered for sale (i.e. at the design stage, or possibly as the result of market testing) and also at regular intervals throughout the product/service's life cycle. The analysis is normally carried out by a team consisting of technical and accounting personnel, who pose and attempt to answer such questions as:

■ Can a product/service's essential function be achieved differently, using less expensive methods/materials etc.?
■ Is every proposed product/service function essential, or can some be eliminated without prejudice to quality?
■ To what extent is it possible to standardise a new product/service with existing products/services?

If applied thoroughly and on a continuous basis, value analysis should result in a planned, ongoing search for cost reductions.

Variety reduction

As the name suggests, variety reduction involves examination of the range of products/services offered for sale, or of the types and sources of materials/labour/machinery used in provision of these products/services. The objective is to reduce costs by reducing variety – in essence, by standardising wherever possible, again without adversely affecting quality. Variety reduction may be particularly effective in manufacturing organisations, where standardisation may allow longer and less complex production runs involving fewer products, which could significantly reduce costs.

Work study

Slack *et al.* (1995) define work study as: 'a generic term for those techniques, particularly method study and work measurement, which are used in the examination of human work in all its contexts, and which lead systematically to investigation of all the factors which affect the efficiency and economy of the situations being reviewed in order to effect improvements'.

The techniques referred to are aimed at determining the most efficient methods of utilising labour, materials and machinery and may be applied across a wide spectrum of organisational activities, ranging from the design of forms, office layout and telephone systems (method study) to the establishment of standard labour times for employees to carry out specified tasks at a predetermined efficiency level (work measurement). Sensible application of the different specific techniques which fall under the general heading of 'work study' can result in significant cost reductions, especially when applied to major areas of expenditure such as administration.

Business process re-engineering and benchmarking

Although these are more wide-ranging in their application than simply as cost reduction techniques, they are often employed in the context of a cost reduction programme. Business process re-engineering attempts to improve organisational performance by simplifying/improving procedures, reducing costs and enhancing quality. Business process re-engineering's underlying principle is that operations should be based on the processes which add value to output, rather than on the functions which comprise these processes – a view which is consistent with ABC and ABCM. The move by many manufacturing businesses to a just-in-time basis may be the result of business process re-engineering.

Benchmarking involves identification of the best method of undertaking an organisation's main functions. 'Best practice' is often defined in terms of an external organisation that has achieved 'world class' status in respect of a particular activity, and whose methods can then be used as a target for internal performance. We shall have more to say about benchmarking in Chapter 15.

Potential problems with cost reduction schemes

A well-planned cost reduction scheme is an important management tool, but such schemes are not without their difficulties. Exhibit 13.10 highlights the fact that there is a trade-off between cost reduction and the quality of product/service being offered. A narrow or ad hoc view of cost reduction may mean that, as with cost control, quality or wider-ranging criteria may suffer. (Note that the strategic implications of the reductions are indirectly referred to in Exhibit 13.10 – 'likely to go on rising as a result of staff reductions.')

OMBUDSMAN SAYS WHITEHALL CUTS THREATEN STANDARDS

Mr William Reid, the parliamentary ombudsman, yesterday claimed that standards of service to the public were being threatened by large-scale reductions in Whitehall funding.

In his annual report to parliament, Mr Reid also said complaints against government bodies – already running at record levels – were likely to go on rising as a result of staff reductions . . .

Source: James Blitz, *Financial Times*, 21 March 1996.

Exhibit **13.10 A possible problem with cost reductions?**

⇨ Standardisation of products/services may offer scope for cost reductions. Can you envisage a sales-related problem which may possibly result from a programme of standardisation?

Standardisation of products/services may well yield cost reductions, but there is a danger that these could be more than counterbalanced by loss of sales revenue or customer loyalty – particularly where there is extensive interdependence between sales of different products/services within the range currently offered by the organisation. It can also happen that an organisation deliberately markets a wide range of what are basically similar products, possibly to maintain market share or to deter would-be entrants to their market. This sort of approach is taken by some manufacturers of soap powders and detergents. The marketing implications of a variety reduction scheme would thus require careful consideration before such a scheme were to be implemented.

Cost reduction schemes may also have undesirable behavioural consequences. Staff may feel threatened or pressurised by cost reduction programmes and could resist their introduction, or even attempt to sabotage their effective operation. The need for objectivity in cost reduction schemes means that they may often be devised by external consultants, which might cause resentment amongst the organisation's own staff, with possibly similar behavioural results. In addition, any cost reduction scheme must itself meet the cost/benefit criterion – design and implementation of cost reduction schemes can be costly, especially where external consultants are extensively used.

So, although an organisation may reap considerable benefit from a cost reduction scheme, such a scheme should not be hurried through in the hope of gaining some narrow or short-term benefit, nor should the behavioural implications be ignored.

SUMMARY

In this chapter, we have examined the principles of financial control and illustrated that, although these principles may be straightforward enough, their application has many potential problem areas. We have seen that:

- Financial controls are **administrative controls**, which consist of rules and regulations and output controls.

- Financial control is based on **exceptions reporting**: that is, the triggering of management action by significant variances between two sets of outcomes.

- **Feedback control** is retrospective. Budget is compared with actual and appropriate control action taken (amending budget and/or actual) where significant variances arise.

- **Positive feedback** attempts to maximise the benefit of any favourable variances; **negative feedback** attempts to minimise the undersirable impact of any adverse variances.

- **Feedforward control** compares desired outcomes with predicted outcomes and attempts to exert control (amend desired and/or predicted outcomes) in advance to remedy any significant variances.

- A **flexible budget** recognises the impact on revenue and certain costs of changes in the volume of activity.

- A **fixed budget** is based on a single volume of activity and cannot therefore accommodate the effects of changes in the volume of activity.

- Flexible budgets may be used as a form of sensitivity analysis by preparing budgets based on different volume levels.

- Where actual volume differs from that originally budgeted, the budget should be flexed on the basis of actual volume to permit a valid like-with-like comparison.

- Differences between the fixed and flexible budget are *volume* variances, reflecting the revenue, cost and profit impact of differences between budgeted and actual volume.

- Differences between flexible budget and actual are **flexible budget variances**, reflecting differences between standard and actual price/usage/rate/efficiency.

- The flexing basis may be the cost unit, the number of standard hours produced (for budgets covering multiple products/services), or there may be several flexing bases (where variable items vary with different measures of activity).

- The significance of variances may be stated in terms of their absolute amount, as a percentage of budget, or using statistical theory.

- **Responsibility accounting** is a control framework within which the organisation is divided into a number of **responsibility centres**, in respect of each of which responsibility is delegated to a stated manager and budgets/control reports prepared.

■ Control reports should be prepared for each **control period** within a given budget period and should contain adequate detail to permit effective control at the relevant organisational level.

■ **Activity-based cost management (ABCM)** attempts to control the cost of activities, rather than control individual costs.

■ Financial control has several problem areas, which may be summarised under the following headings:
  – cost control -v- performance appraisal;
  – random factors;
  – controllability of budget items;
  – tactical v strategic control;
  – fixed/variable cost analysis;
  – allowing for the impact of inflation;
  – measurement errors;
  – outdated control information; and
  – means-end confusion.

■ **Cost reduction** is aimed at reducing costs from their previous level, without adversely affecting the quality of the product service. Some major cost reduction techniques are: value analysis, variety reduction, and work study.

In the next chapter, we shall illustrate how budget variances may be further analysed, and discuss the benefits which this might offer and the extent to which such analysis could potentially augment the problems of financial control above.

FURTHER READING

Daniel, W. and Terrell, J., *Business Statistics for Management and Economics*, 7th edn, Houghton Mifflin, 1995. Chapter 17 describes statistical control charts.

Doyle, D., *Cost Control: A strategic guide*, CIMA, 1994. This comparatively short text places cost control in its strategic context.

Drury, C., Braund, S., Osborne, P. and Tayles, M., *A Survey of Management Accounting Practices in UK Manufacturing Companies*, CACA, 1993.

Hopwood, A., *Accounting and Human Behaviour*, Prentice-Hall, 1974.

Morrow, M. and Ashworth, G., 'An evolving framework for activity-based approaches', in *Management Accounting,* February 1994, CIMA.

Otley, D. and Berry, A., *Control, Organisation and Accounting,* in Accounting, Organisations and Society, Vol. 5 No. 2, 1980.

Puxty, A. and Lyall, D., *Cost Control into the 1990s: A survey of standard costing and budgeting practices in the UK*, CIMA, 1989.

Slack, N., Chambers, S., Harland, C., Harrison, H. and Johnston, R., *Operations Management*, Pitman Publishing, 1995. Chapter 9 deals with work study and more general issues of job design.

Self-test questions

13.1 During Period 4, the following information applied to one of a firm's products:

Budgeted output: 10,000 units
Actual output: 9,000 units
Standard direct material cost per unit: £40
Actual direct material cost for period: £342,000

What was the flexible budget variance for direct materials in Period 4?

A £18,000 adverse
B £18,000 favourable
C £58,000 adverse
D £58,000 favourable

13.2 FMR Ltd, a firm specialising in provision of risk management consultancy, provides the following information relating to operations in the last control period:

Budgeted standard hours' work:	3,500 hours
Actual hours' work:	4,000 hours
Standard direct expenses per standard hour of work:	£6
Actual direct expenses cost for the period:	£25,200

Work actually performed in one hour during the period represents 90 per cent of standard.

What was the flexible budget variance for direct expenses for the period?

A £1,200 adverse
B £3,600 adverse
C £4,200 adverse
D £6,300 adverse

13.3 A hospital's boiler house has a total budget cost allowance for next year of £600,000, based on a budgeted level of operation of 80 per cent of maximum. Of the budgeted costs, 60 per cent are wholly fixed irrespective of the level of operation, the remaining 40 per cent being variable with the level of operation. What will be the boiler house's total budget cost allowance for a level of operation of 84 per cent of maximum?

A £612,000
B £618,000
C £624,000
D £630,000

13.4 Tick the appropriate box to indicate whether each of the following statements is true or false.

True   *False*

(a) Use of actual hours as the flexing basis will distort the budget by incorporating actual inefficiencies. ☐ ☐

(b) Investigation of every variance in excess of a given monetary amount will ensure that only significant variances are acted on by management. ☐ ☐

CHAPTER 13 • BUDGETARY CONTROL

(c) Feedforward control is based on comparison of actual and budgeted outcomes. ☐ ☐

(d) Discretionary costs display no tangible input/output relationship. ☐ ☐

(e) Committed costs are readily controllable in the short term. ☐ ☐

(f) Differences between fixed budget and actual are termed volume variances. ☐ ☐

(g) A flexible budget may be used as a form of sensitivity analysis during the planning process. ☐ ☐

13.5 Complete the following paragraph by inserting the appropriate word/phrase from those provided.

Overemphasis of budget variances as .... may result in ....
measures being ignored, may .... managerial freedom, and may panic
management into an .... cost-cutting response. In addition, the
.... of budget items by various managers requires careful consideration:
there may be problems with ...., the possible inclusion of cost
.... in budget control reports, along with the difficulty of exercising genuine short-term control over .... costs.

dual responsibility   *controllability*
unnecessary   *restrict*
quality and non-financial   *committed and discretionary*
managerial performance measures   *apportionments*

QUESTIONS WITH ANSWERS

13.6 This question tests whether you can:

- prepare flexible cost budgets for three different volumes of possible activity;

- distinguish between engineered, committed and discretionary costs, citing an example of each from given data; and

- appreciate the potential problems of using flexible budgets in a service organisation.

ACI Ltd is a credit reference agency and the standard and budgeted costs of providing the service next year are provided below.

Variable costs per credit enquiry	
Computing	£0.75
Direct expenses	£0.30
Semi-variable cost	
Direct labour	£0.15 per enquiry + £300,000 fixed for the year
Fixed costs	
General administration	£220,000
Computing	£130,000
Building occupancy	£40,000
Promotional	£100,000

It is anticipated that somewhere between 50,000 and 75,000 credit enquiries will be handled next year.

Requirements

(a) Prepare flexible cost budgets for ACI Ltd for each of the following volumes of business:

> 50,000 enquiries
> 65,000 enquiries
> 75,000 enquiries

(Your flexible budgets should clearly distinguish between variable and fixed costs and should show the total cost of each level of activity.)

(b) From the data in the question, provide *one* example of each of the following: engineered cost; committed cost; and discretionary cost.

(c) Briefly discuss possible difficulties which may be faced by ACI Ltd in the operation of a flexible budgeting system.

13.7 This question tests whether you can:

- prepare budgeted and actual profit statements showing fixed and flexible budgets, with volume and flexible budget variances identified;

- comment on a business's financial performance in light of the budget/actual comparison above; and

- appreciate the potential impact of inflation on the budget/actual comparison and suggest how this might be overcome.

The following information relates to production and sale of snare drums by CMC (Musical Instruments) Ltd:

Standard per drum	£
Selling price	170
Variable costs:	
Direct material	30
Direct labour	15
Selling	5

Budget per annum	
Sales/production volume	15,000 units
Fixed costs:	£
Production overhead	450,000
Administration overhead	288,000
Selling overhead	180,000

Actuals for March 19X5	
Sales/production	1,120 units
	£
Sales revenue	201,600
Direct materials	35,840
Direct labour	20,160
Variable selling costs	6,300
Production overhead	34,000
Administration overhead	25,000
Selling overhead	9,000

For budget control purposes, CMC Ltd divides the annual budget period into 12 calendar months. You may assume that budgeted sales and fixed costs are expected to arise evenly during the year and that each calendar month is of equal length.

Requirements

(a) Prepare CMC Ltd's budgeted and actual profit statements for March 19X5 using marginal costing principles and showing fixed budget, flexible budget and actuals, with volume and flexible budget variances identified.

(b) Provide a brief commentary on the company's financial performance during March as revealed by your answer to (a).

(c) Explain how a difference between the rate of inflation incorporated into the budget and that which actually occurred would distort the budget/actual comparison and suggest how such a distortion might be overcome.

13.8 This question tests whether you can:

■ prepare a budget control report by application of a stated approach to determining the budget for a control period;

■ appraise the approach adopted above and suggest an improved method; and

■ appreciate the issue of controllability as it affects the financial items in the control report prepared.

Cornton Town Council operates a system of responsibility accounting, within which the office of the town's Registrar of Births, Marriages & Deaths is treated as a responsibility centre. The following budgeted, standard and actual information is available:

Budgeted for 19X2	
Total number of registrations	13,000
	£
Total registration fees	182,000
Fixed costs for year:	
Administration	26,000
Occupancy	65,000
Apportionment of Council HQ costs	52,000
Direct labour	58,500
Total variable costs for year:	
Stationery	11,700
Other	3,900
Actuals for Period 4 19X2	
Total number of registrations	1,650
	£
Total registration fees	23,040
Administration costs	2,400
Occupancy costs	5,100
Apportionment of Council HQ costs	4,800
Direct labour	5,200
Stationery costs	1,700
Other variable costs	1,080

It is the Council's current policy to compare responsibility centres' actuals for each four-week control period to one-thirteenth of their annual budget.

Requirements

(a) Prepare a control report for Period 4 19X2 , comparing one-thirteenth of the Registrar's Office budget for the year with the actuals for the period and identifying all variances for income, costs and operating surplus/deficit.

(b) Evaluate the approach taken in (a) and suggest an improved methodology, explaining your reasoning.

(c) As far as the information permits, assess the extent to which the various financial items in the control report in (a) might be controllable by the Registrar's Office.

QUESTIONS WITHOUT ANSWERS

13.9 As part of its fund-raising effort and to provide employment for some of its beneficiaries, a national charity operates a small factory which produces and sells items of furniture. The following information relates to the quarter just ended:

Budgeted and standard
Budgeted sales revenue: £400,000 per month
Variable costs:
   20% of revenue up to and including sales of £400,000
   15% of revenue if sales exceed £400,000

Fixed/step costs (per month):
Direct labour:
   £80,000 up to and including sales of £450,000
   £90,000 up to and including sales of £500,000
Production overheads:
   £20,000 up to and including sales of £375,000
   £24,000 if sales fall between £375,000 and £425,000
   £30,000 if sales exceed £425,000
General overheads:
   £26,000 fixed for all foreseeable sales volumes

Actuals

	Month 1 (£000)	Month 2 (£000)	Month 3 (£000)
Revenue	320	390	460
Variable costs	80	90	92
Contribution	240	300	368
Fixed costs:			
Direct labour	78	78	94
Production overheads	40	60	100
General overheads	25	25	40
Profit	97	137	134

Requirements

(a) For *each* of Months 1–3, prepare a budget control report showing the flexible budget and actual profit statement, with variances identified.

(b) As far as the information permits, comment on the factory's financial performance during the quarter and explain how the results in (a) could be used by management in a feedforward control exercise.

13.10 BH plc is a large conglomerate business operating in a variety of different markets. As head of the company's Technical Support Section, you have received the following memorandum from the newly appointed Financial Controller.

Memorandum

To: Head of Section, Technical Support

From: Financial Controller

Budget overspend for 6 months to 30 September 19X1

As you are aware, this company operates a system where section heads are responsible for meeting their section's budget. Given below is a budget/actual comparison for your section's operations, covering the six months just ended.

	Budget	*Actual*	*Variance*
Standard hours' work performed	10,000	12,250	
Staff costs:	£	£	£
Section head	25,000	27,250	2,250A
Technical	75,000	81,750	6,750A
Clerical	22,000	33,980	11,980A
Overtime	nil	8,700	8,700A
Computing costs:			
Purchase of hardware	10,000	13,600	3,600A
Charge for use of Head Office mainframe	4,000	6,100	2,100A
Purchase of software	9,000	7,450	1,550F
Other costs:			
Stationery etc.	3,000	5,400	2,400A
Travel and subsistence	5,000	18,700	13,700A
Sundries	2,000	1,000	1,000F
Apportionment of Head Office running costs	6,000	7,700	1,700A
	161,000	211,630	50,630A

I am sure you will agree that the picture these figures paint is far from rosy and would appreciate your response as soon as possible.

(signed)

Financial Controller

The following additional information is available:

1 The apportionment of Head Office costs is made to sections on an arbitrary basis.

2 The budgeted figure for purchase of hardware were based on an anticipated inflation rate of 1 per cent. In the event, actual inflation turned out to be 5 per cent.

3 Budgeted staff costs do not take account of a pay rise of 9 per cent awarded to the section head and of 4 per cent to all other staff in August and backdated to the start of the six-month period. The budgeted cost of clerical staff excludes payment to additional temporary workers who completed 1,000 standard hours' worth of work in 1,250 actual hours, the standard cost of which is £6 per hour. Because of the higher-than-expected workload, 500 standard hours of work had to be performed in overtime, although this actually required 870 hours' work, which were paid for at the standard overtime rate of £10 per hour.

4 The charge for use of the Head Office mainframe is made on the basis of the time logged on by each section. For the Technical Support Section, the standard hours logged on is reckoned to be 80 per cent of the total standard hours of work performed. For each standard hour logged on, sections are charged £0.50.

5 Of the actual travel and subsistence costs, some 70 per cent arose because of an emergency request for assistance from one of BH plc's overseas branches.

6 Subject to Head of Section's approval, software, stationery and sundries' costs are incurred on a discretionary basis by section staff.

Requirements

As Head of the Technical Support Section, prepare a draft response to the Financial Controller. As part of your response, redraft the budget control report in a manner which you consider provide a more representative picture of actual financial performance.

13.11 Prayton Farm Park has been operating as a commercial concern for roughly six years. Mr and Mrs Stillworth, the Park's owners, have just negotiated an increased overdraft facility with their bank. One of the conditions attaching to this increase is that a suitable system of financial control be instituted, and you have been requested to provide advice as to how this might be achieved. Details of the Park's operations are as follows:

■ The Farm Park offers the following facilities to visitors:
  – access to animal pens, barns and enclosures;
  – adventure playground (outdoor);
  – play barn (indoor);
  – golf driving range;
  – Farm Shop; and
  – Farmhouse Cafeteria.

■ Tickets covering admission to the Farm Park's animal enclosures, adventure playground and play barn are available from the Farm Shop. Use of the golf driving range requires purchase of a separate ticket – either instead of, or in addition to, the basic admission ticket.

■ The Farm Park has a workforce of 16 in addition to Mr and Mrs Stillworth. Two of these employees are permanently assigned to the Farm Shop and two to the Farmhouse Cafeteria, with the others undertaking work on all the remaining operational areas as required. Mrs Stillworth supervises the Farm Shop and Farmhouse Cafeteria, Mr Stillworth dealing with the other facilities.

- Although the Farm Park is open from February to October, business is highly seasonal, with the highest number of visitors in June, July and August. September is also fairly busy, but there are few visitors in February, March and October.

- Mrs Stillworth is in charge of the Farm Park's financial records, which consist of a computerised cash book, where receipts and payments are entered as they arise. The cash book is usually updated on an ad hoc basis as pressure of other work permits. Entries in the cash book are periodically reconciled with the Farm Park's monthly bank statements – but there is often a two- or three-month delay before this reconciliation occurs, and the records are only brought fully up to date after the end of each accounting year for the purpose of completing the Stillworths' income tax return.

Requirement

Prepare a report for Mr and Mrs Stillworth, explaining how a system of financial control might be implemented at Prayton Farm Park, explaining the advantages and possible drawbacks of such a system.

13.12 The Wheatdale Group has recently completed a major corporate restructuring, which involved disposal of all 'non-core' business activities, 'core' activities being defined as provision of financial services. Nevertheless, Stock Exchange concerns about profit projections continue, partly fuelled by a series of adverse press reports describing labour relations problems stemming from the restructuring. Faced with this situation, Wheatdale Group's board is proposing to embark on a cost reduction programme.

Some relevant details about the Group's 'core' business (i.e. after restructuring) are as follows:

- *Insurance* The Group offers a wide range of personal, commercial, property, vehicle and 'special case' policies to clients. It is reckoned that some 80 per cent of policies offered by Wheatdale are 'tailored' to client requirements in some way. Whilst the ability to offer insurance to meet specific needs represents a major selling point to existing and prospective clients, provision of such policies is very resource-intensive and therefore less profitable than 'standard' insurances.

- *Risk management* Allied to its insurance services, Wheatdale undertakes risk management consultancy work, whereby the Group's team of specialists visits clients in order to assess various types of risk, recommending appropriate methods of reducing exposure (often including referral to the Group's Insurance Division to arrange cover).

- *Other services* These services are extremely diverse in nature: personal pensions, investment analysis and advice, portfolio management for both the Group's own funds and on behalf of corporate and private clients, accounting and tax services, and management consultancy.

Requirement

With respect to the proposed cost reduction programme, discuss:

1 Possible approaches which Wheatdale Group might take to effect the desired cost reductions.

2 Factors which should be accorded particular consideration in the design and/or implementation of such a programme.

CHAPTER 14

Analysis of variances

TWO LEAVE HUNTING AFTER COST OVERRUNS

Hunting, the aviation, defence and oil group, yesterday said two senior executives had left the company after failing to detect cost overruns in its aircraft interiors subsidiary.

Shares in the company fell 10p to 202p after it warned that profits at Hunting Aviation were unlikely to show any improvement on last year's £2.6m.

Mr Ken Miller, chief executive, blamed the problems on additional costs incurred on a contract for de Havilland of Canada, which has ordered Hunting interiors for its Dash-8 aircraft. 'Our managers are paid to know where we are on contracts. If they don't, we clearly have serious difficulties.'

Source: Tim Burt, *Financial Times*, 21 May 1996.

EXHIBIT **14.1** Could this situation have been avoided by analysing budget variances?

INTRODUCTION

When we introduced the concept of standard costing in Chapter 12, we said that one of its purposes was to permit more detailed analysis of variances. In the last chapter, we suggested that flexible budget variances, whilst of considerable use for tactical control purposes, may still be too aggregated to permit effective pinpointing of problems and of managerial responsibility (i.e. to permit effective operational control). In this chapter, we will demonstrate how the 'global' budget variances can be analysed into their constituent elements and how this may enhance financial control – which may have helped the situation referred to in Exhibit 14.1. We will also illustrate how these variances can be presented so as to reconcile budgeted and actual profit, and discuss the extent to which detailed variance analysis might aggravate the argued weaknesses of standard costing and 'conventional' budgetary control.

OBJECTIVES   When you have completed this chapter, you will be able to:

- appreciate the potential enhancement of financial control which may result from availability of detailed variance information;

- for each element of cost and for sales, calculate budget variances and subdivide these into their constituent elements;

- prepare an operating statement incorporating variances and reconciling budgeted and actual profit;

- distinguish between operational and planning variances;

- understand the potential benefits and weaknesses of using a planning/operational approach to variance analysis; and

- appreciate how a system of detailed variance analysis may exacerbate the argued 'general' shortcomings of standard costing and budget variance analysis.

WHY ANALYSE BUDGET VARIANCES?

You will recall from the last chapter that our flexible budget/actual comparison revealed variances such as:

Materials   £5,000 adverse

This undoubtedly indicates that actual spending on materials was £5,000 higher than the budget based on an identical output volume, but does it tell us anything about what aspect of material cost may be causing problems, or about where, within a responsibility accounting system, the locus of managerial responsibility might lie?

⇨ State *two* general reasons why actual and budgeted material cost might differ.

In general, actual and budgeted material cost may differ because either or both of the purchase cost and/or usage differ, and it is these differences which a 'global' flexible budget variance such as '£5,000 adverse' cannot reflect. Suppose, in addition, that, within a responsibility accounting system, purchase of materials is the responsibility of the Buyer whereas usage is the responsibility of, say, the Operations Manager – subdivision of the flexible budget variance into price and usage elements may help decide to whom the respective variances should be reported. But, as we shall discover later, this is not the same as suggesting that the Buyer and Operations Manager are responsible, respectively, for the price and usage elements of the budget variance. This is an important point. Variances (regardless of their level of detail) are merely indicative of possible problem areas, but without further investigation do not constitute conclusive evidence of personal responsibility or of anything else. What we are suggesting is that reporting detailed variances may help identify the individual who is in the best position to investigate and perhaps to suggest or initiate corrective action. It is worth repeating the point made in the last chapter that a budget system which is used (or thought to be used) as some form of managerial witchhunt is unlikely to find much support amongst managers, and, as a consequence, is unlikely to work particularly well. We shall return to this issue when we discuss the behavioural aspects of management accounting in Chapter 16.

SUBDIVIDING BUDGET VARIANCES

If, as we have just suggested, there may be a case for further analysis of budget variances, how can this be achieved? The prerequisite is existence, within the budget system, of standard costing data such as the estimated material usage per unit of output and the estimated cost per unit of material. Without the existence of such information in a reasonably formal way, it is hard to see how meaningful budgets can be prepared, let alone analysis of budget variances undertaken.

We shall use the data in Exhibit 14.2 to illustrate how an organisation's budget variances may be analysed in detail.

AMC Laundry Services Ltd

AMC Ltd undertakes bulk contract laundries for various organisations. The work is highly standardised: each of the company's clients provides laundry in 100 kg batches, and every batch receives identical cleaning treatment. A single grade of labour is employed and the materials used to process each batch of laundry are pre-packaged units of detergent, conditioner, etc. Budgeted, standard and actual data for the month just ended are as follows:

Standard per 100 kg batch	£	
Selling price	35	
Direct material (2 units @ £4)	8	
Direct labour (1.5 hours @ £6)	9	
Output-related overhead:		
Variable (1.5 direct labour hours @ £2)	3	
Fixed (1.5 direct labour hours @ £4)	6	
Variable distribution overhead	1	

	Budget for the month	Actual for the month
Number of batches processed	16,000	14,400
	£	£
Sales revenue		532,800
Direct materials purchased/used (29,600 units)		112,480
Direct labour (25,600 hours)		133,120
Output-related overhead:		
Variable		46,100
Fixed	96,000	101,000
Variable distribution overhead		12,000
Fixed administration overhead	60,000	63,400

EXHIBIT **14.2: Data for variance analysis**

Before commencing our analysis of AMC Ltd's variances, it might be useful to present a statement of the company's fixed and flexible budgets for the month, along with actuals and variances. This is done in Exhibit 14.3, employing the same format and construction as were used in the last chapter.

Although the business appears to be performing well in budget/actual terms, there may nevertheless be areas of weakness which are 'masked' by the aggregate nature of the variances in Exhibit 14.3. Before proceeding, it is also worth stating that the extent (if any) to which budget variances are analysed should depend on the precise circumstances: for example, if materials form a small proportion of total cost, further analysis of budget variances may not be worthwhile in cost/benefit terms.

AMC Ltd: fixed and flexible budgets, actuals and variances for the month

	Fixed budget	Volume variances	Flexible budget	Flexible budget variances	Actual variances
Output/sales volume (batches)	16,000	1,600A	14,400	nil	14,400
	£	£	£	£	£
Sales revenue	560,000	56,000A	504,000	28,800F	532,800
Variable costs:					
Direct material	128,000	12,800F	115,200	2,720F	112,480
Direct labour	144,000	14,400F	129,600	3,520A	133,120
Output-related overhead	48,000	4,800F	43,200	2,900A	46,100
Distribution overhead	16,000	1,600F	14,400	2,400F	12,000
	336,000	33,600F	302,400	1,300A	303,700
Contribution	224,000	22,400A	201,600	27,500F	229,100
Fixed costs:					
Output-related overhead	96,000	nil	96,000	5,000A	101,000
Administration overhead	60,000	nil	60,000	3,400A	63,400
	156,000	nil	156,000	8,400A	164,400
Net profit	68,000	22,400A	45,600	19,100F	64,700

EXHIBIT **14.3** Fixed and flexible budgets, actuals and variances

Materials' variances

Flexible budget (total) material variance

In the last chapter and in Exhibit 14.3, we compute this variance by comparing flexible budget and actual figures:

Actual output *should* have a material cost of:

	£	
(14,400 batches ×£8)	115,200	(AO × SMCU)
Actual output *did* have a direct materials' cost of	112,480	(TAMC)
Flexible budget variance	2,720F	

'F' representing a favourable variance, since actual cost is lower than flexible budget. It is possible to compress the variance calculation into a formula:

$$\{(AO \times SMCU) - TAMC\}$$

where: AO represents actual output;
SMCU is the standard materials' cost per unit of output; and
TAMC is the total actual materials' cost.

Thus (AO × SMCU) is the flexible budget cost, and you will see that the formulaic version is merely an alternative presentation of the 'narrative' calculation, with both methods being equally acceptable.

▷ Insert the appropriate data from Exhibit 14.2 into the formula and obtain the flexible budget variance for materials.

The formula gives:

$$\{(14,400 \times £8) - £112,480\} = £2,720F$$

The flexible budget variance for materials can be subdivided as follows:

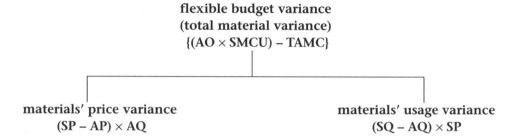

We will explain the formulae for price and usage variances below.

Material price variance

This shows the extent to which the flexible budget variance is due to differences between the actual and standard cost of materials. The actual cost per unit of direct material is not given in Exhibit 14.2, but can easily be determined as:

$$\frac{\text{total actual materials' cost}}{\text{actual materials purchased}} = \frac{£112,480}{29,600} = £3.80$$

	£	
One unit of direct material *should* cost	4.00	(SP)
One unit of direct material *did* cost	3.80	(AP)
Difference per unit of material	0.20F	
Actual units of material purchased were	29,600	(AQ)
Material price variance	£5,920F	

Since the actual cost per unit of material is less than standard, we have a favourable price variance. As a formula, the price variance can be expressed as:

$$(SP - AP) \times AQ$$

where: SP represents the standard purchase price per unit of material;
AP is the actual purchase price per unit of material; and
AQ is the actual purchase quantity of material.

⇨ Insert AMC Ltd's data from Exhibit 14.2 into the price variance formula and compute the variance for the month.

Using the formula, we have:

$$(£4 - £3.80) \times 29,600 \text{ units} = £5,920F$$

In this particular example, purchase and usage quantities are identical. Had they been different, we would have based the price variance on the *purchase* quantity. Determining variances at the earliest identifiable point in the business cycle is necessary to enable effective control action to be taken if needed: that is, if material purchases are placed in store prior to use, there may be a marked time lag between purchase and usage. However, waiting until materials are used before extracting the price variance could mean that action cannot be taken to avoid future adverse variances or to perpetuate favourable ones (e.g. because firm orders have already been placed).

⇨ Can you suggest *two* possible reasons for the price variance calculated?

One possibility is that inferior quality (and cheaper) materials have been purchased. Or AMC Ltd may have changed to a cheaper supplier, or might have negotiated a quantity discount from the existing supplier. Perhaps there has been a slump in demand for the particular materials concerned, resulting in a lowering of the market price. In the absence of additional information, however, we can only speculate. Hence the need for further investigation if the variance is significant enough to warrant it.

Material usage variance

This measures the extent to which the flexible budget variance is due to differences between actual and standard usage of materials: that is, the extent to which we have used more or less materials for the output achieved than envisaged in the standard. The usage variance is:

	Units	
Actual output *should* use (14,400 batches × 2)	28,800	(SQ)
Actual output *did* use	29,600	(AQ)
Difference in units used	800A	
Per unit, this difference should have cost	£4.00	(SP)
Material usage variance	£3,200A	

'A' indicating that the variance is adverse. Actual output required more direct materials than the standard allowed.

As a formula, the usage variance is:

$$(SQ - AQ) \times SP$$

where: SQ represents the standard quantity of materials allowed *for actual output;*
AQ is the actual quantity of materials used; and
SP is the standard purchase price per unit of material.

497

Standard price is employed in the usage variance because, had actual price been substituted, the resulting variance would have been due partly to usage and partly to price factors – giving an unclear control 'signal' to management.

⇨ Use the data in Exhibit 14.2 to determine AMC Ltd's material usage variance for the month by formula.

AMC Ltd's usage variance is:

$$\{(14,400 \times 2 \text{ units}) - 29,600 \text{ units}\} \times £4 = £3,200A$$

Since the price and usage variances represent subdivisions of the flexible budget variance, we can check the arithmetic integrity of our calculations:

	£
Price variance	5,920 F
Usage variance	3,200 A
Flexible budget variance	2,720 F

⇨ Can you suggest *two* possible reasons for the usage variance?

Since actual usage exceeded standard, it may be that there has been some laxity in handling of materials by the company's operatives. Or it may be that purchase of inferior or different materials has caused problems in their use. You will see that the last two reasons we have suggested were also suggested in respect of the price variance: that is, there may be a link between the favourable price variance arising from, say, purchase of inferior, cheaper materials and resultant problems in usage of these materials. We shall return to the problem of *interdependence of variances* later in the chapter.

Labour variances

Flexible budget (total) variance

This is determined as follows:

	£	
Actual output *should* have a direct labour cost of (14,400 batches × £9)	129,600	(AO × SLCU)
Actual output *did* have a direct labour cost of	133,120	(TALC)
Flexible budget variance	3,520 A	

As a formula, the total variance is:

$$\{(AO \times SLCU) - TALC\}$$

where: AO represents actual output;
       SLCU is the standard labour cost per unit of output; and
       TALC is the total actual labour cost.

☞ Use the formula to determine AMC Ltd's flexible budget variance for direct labour.

Using the formula gives:

$$\{(14,400 \times £9) - £133,120\} = £3,520A$$

The flexible budget variance for direct labour can be subdivided in a manner very similar to that adopted with the material budget variance:

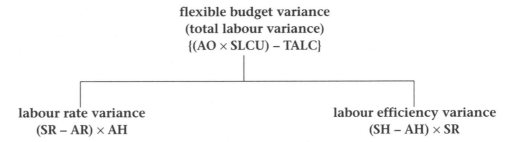

flexible budget variance
(total labour variance)
$\{(AO \times SLCU) - TALC\}$

labour rate variance
$(SR - AR) \times AH$

labour efficiency variance
$(SH - AH) \times SR$

Labour rate variance

This variance assesses the extent to which the flexible budget variance arises because of differences between standard and actual rates of pay per hour. As with the actual direct material cost, we need to calculate the actual labour rate per hour from Exhibit 14.2:

$$\frac{\text{actual direct labour cost}}{\text{actual direct labour hours}} = \frac{£133,120}{25,600} = £5.20$$

	£	
Direct labour rate per hour *should* have been	£6.00	(SR)
Direct labour rate per hour *was*	£5.20	(AR)
Difference per hour	£0.80F	
Actual hours paid for were	25,600	(AH)
Labour rate variance	£20,480F	

Converting the rate variance to a formula:

$$(SR - AR) \times AH$$

where: SR represents the standard rate of pay per hour;
　　　AR is the actual hourly rate of pay; and
　　　AH is the actual number of hours.

The favourable rate variance might have arisen because a different, less well paid, grade of labour has been employed to that which was incorporated in the standard. However, a more probable explanation is that a pay rise envisaged when the standard was set has either not been paid or was lower than anticipated.

Labour efficiency variance

This variance reflects the extent to which the flexible budget labour variance arises because of differences between standard and actual labour efficiency:

	Hours	
Actual output *should* take (14,400 batches × 1.5 hours)	21,600	(SH)
Actual output *did* take	25,600	(AH)
Difference in hours	4,000A	
Standard rate per hour	£6	(SR)
Labour efficiency variance	£24,000A	

As a formula, the efficiency variance is:

$$(SH - AH) \times SR$$

where: SH represents the standard hours allowed *for actual output;*
      AH is the actual hours; and
      SR is the standard rate of pay per hour.

The standard rate per hour is used in the efficiency variance for the same reason that standard price was used in the material usage variance: that is, to prevent distortion of the efficiency variance by rate differences.

Using the data from Exhibit 14.2, gives an efficiency variance of:

$$\{(14,400 \text{ units} \times 1.5 \text{ hours}) - 25,600 \text{ hours}\} \times £6 = £24,000A$$

Again, we can check the arithmetic accuracy of our labour variance calculations:

	£
Labour rate variance	20,480 *F*
Efficiency variance	24,000 *A*
Labour flexible budget variance	3,520 *A*

Here we have a situation where a relatively small budget variance 'hides' rate and efficiency elements which are almost certainly significant enough to warrant investigation.

⮕ Can you see a possible interrelationship between the rate and efficiency variances above?

We suggested earlier that the favourable rate variance may have arisen because a pay rise anticipated in the standard had not been paid in full (or at all), and this may have had a bearing on the lower-than-expected efficiency. Perhaps making a lower-than-anticipated pay award has had some effect on worker motivation. Once more, we are faced with the possibility of interdependence between variances – but beware the danger of leaping to quickfire cause/effect conclusions.

Variable overhead variances

Flexible budget (total) variance

The important computational aspect of all variable overhead variances is that we are dealing with a *variable* cost (which also happens to be indirect).

⇨ Use the data in Exhibit 14.2 to complete the calculation below.

	£
Actual output *should* have incurred variable overhead of	
(............................@..............................)	....
Actual output *did* incur variable overhead of	....
Flexible budget variance	....

The completed variance calculation is:

	£	
Actual output *should* have incurred variable overhead of		
(14,400 batches @ £3)	43,200	(AO × SVOU)
Actual output *did* incur variable overhead of	46,100	(AVO)
Flexible budget variance	2,900A	

As a formula, we have:

$$\{(AO \times SVOU) - AVO\}$$

where: AO represents actual output;
SVOU is standard variable overhead per unit of output; and
AVO is the actual variable overhead cost.

Applying the formula gives:

$$\{(14,400 \text{ units} \times £3) - £46,100\} = £2,900A$$

The flexible budget variable overhead variance can be split into an expenditure variance and, where the overhead varies with labour hours, into an efficiency variance:

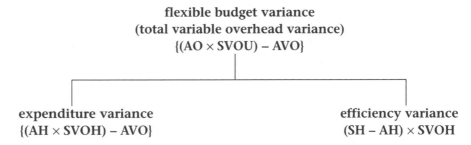

flexible budget variance
(total variable overhead variance)
$$\{(AO \times SVOU) - AVO\}$$

expenditure variance
$$\{(AH \times SVOH) - AVO\}$$

efficiency variance
$$(SH - AH) \times SVOH$$

Variable overhead expenditure variance

This shows the extent to which the total variance is due to differences between budgeted and actual expenditure. In AMC Ltd's case, variable overhead varies with the number of direct labour hours, which form the basis for calculating the standard cost allowed. Where variable overhead varies with the number of units of output, this will replace actual hours in the variance calculation:

	£	
Actual labour hours *should* incur variable overhead of		
(25,600 @ £2)	51,200	(AH × SVOH)
Actual labour hours did incur variable overhead of	46,100	(AVO)
Variable overhead expenditure variance	5,100F	

As a formula:

$$\{(AH \times SVOH) - AVO\}$$

where: AH is the actual hours;
         SVOH is the standard variable overhead rate per hour; and
         AVO is the actual variable overhead cost.

⇨ Use the formula to confirm AMC Ltd's variable overhead expenditure variance.

The expenditure variance is:

$$\{(25,600 \text{ hours} \times £2) - £46,100\} = £5,100F$$

Variable overhead efficiency variance

Where variable overhead varies with labour hours, part of the flexible budget variance may arise because of differences between standard and actual efficiency:

	Hours	
Actual output *should* take		
(14,400 batches × 1.5 hours)	21,600	(SH)
Actual output *did* take	25,600	(AH)
Difference in hours	4,000A	
Standard variable overhead per hour	£2	(SVOH)
Variable overhead efficiency variance	£8,000A	

You will see that the variance is essentially the same as that for direct labour efficiency, the only difference being that the standard variable overhead rate per hour replaces the standard labour rate.

In formulaic layout:

$$(SH - AH) \times SVOH$$

where: SH represents the standard hours allowed for actual output;
         AH is the actual hours worked; and
         SVOH is the standard variable overhead rate per hour.

Application of the formula gives a variance of:

$$\{(14,400 \text{ units} \times 1.5 \text{ hours}) - 25,600 \text{ hours}\} \times £2 = £8,000A$$

In situations where variable overhead varies with the number of units of output, an efficiency variance will not be calculated and the expenditure variance will equal the flexible budget variance.

⇨ Is there a possible link between the variable overhead efficiency and labour rate variances?

Since, in this example, variable overhead varies with direct labour hours, any factors which affect labour efficiency will also affect variable overhead efficiency. This variance, like the labour efficiency variance, may be linked to the favourable labour rate variance: that is, a lower-than-anticipated pay award may have had an adverse effect on efficiency. It is quite possible for interdependence to affect different elements of cost as well as separate subvariances of the same cost element.

Fixed overhead variances

You will recall from Chapter 5 that fixed production overhead receives different treatment in absorption costing (where it is included in unit costs) and marginal costing (where it is not included in unit costs, but is written off in full to the relevant period's profit statement). In describing the variances relating to fixed production overhead, we must therefore distinguish between marginal and absorption costing.

Fixed overhead variances: marginal costing

Fixed overhead expenditure variance

In a marginal costing system, the only variance for fixed overhead is an expenditure variance reflecting the difference between budgeted and actual cost:

	£	
Budgeted fixed overhead cost was	96,000	(BFO)
Actual fixed overhead cost was	101,000	(AFO)
Expenditure variance	5,000A	

As a formula, the fixed overhead expenditure variance is thus:

$$(BFO - AFO)$$

where: BFO is the budgeted fixed overhead cost; and
AFO is the actual fixed overhead cost.

A glance at Exhibit 14.3 shows that the expenditure variance is also, in marginal costing, the flexible budget variance.

⇨ Why might expenditure variance such as the £5,000 A for fixed overhead and £5,100F for variable overhead prove unsatisfactory for cost control purposes?

The expenditure variance is likely to be of limited value since, in most cases, the terms 'fixed overhead' and 'variable overhead' are generic descriptions of several costs sharing the same behaviour pattern relative to volume of output. Before any control action can be taken, it will normally be necessary to investigate budget and actual for each individual cost which, in total, comprise 'fixed overhead' or 'variable overhead'. If such investigation reveals some (or possibly all) of the overheads to be committed costs then, as we said in the last chapter, they may not be susceptible to short-term control action by management.

Fixed overhead variances: absorption costing

Here, variances for fixed production overhead are complicated by their absorption into the cost per unit of output, and it is important to realise that the additional variances we are about to discuss all derive from the process of absorption.

Fixed overhead total variance

Exhibit 14.2 indicates that AMC Ltd absorbs fixed output-related overhead at £4 per *standard* direct labour hour. In Chapter 12, we saw that the standard labour hour is a measure of work (i.e. output) and we know (from Chapter 4) that overhead is absorbed on the basis of actual output. A distinction must therefore be drawn between actual *input hours* (25,600 in Exhibit 14.2) and the output which actually resulted from this number of hours:

$$(14,400 \text{ batches} \times 1.5 \text{ standard hours per batch}) = 21,600 \text{ standard hours}$$

Fixed overhead absorbed for the month will therefore be:

$$(21,600 \text{ standard hours} \times £4 \text{ per standard hour}) = £86,400$$

Since AMC Ltd's output consists of identical batches, we can obtain the same result by using actual unit output in batches and the fixed overhead absorbed per unit:

$$(14,400 \text{ batches} \times £6 \text{ per batch}) = £86,400$$

£6 per batch being equivalent to (1.5 standard hours per batch × £4 per hour).

The fixed overhead total variance measures the difference between the amount absorbed and the amount incurred:

	£	
Fixed overhead absorbed by actual output	86,400	(AO × FOPU)
Actual fixed overhead	101,000	(AFO)
Total variance	14,600*A*	

Stated as a formula:

$$\{(AO \times FOPU) - AFO\}$$

where: AO is actual output in units;
   FOPU is the fixed overhead per unit of output; and
   AFO is the actual fixed overhead cost.

You should be careful, when calculating the total fixed overhead variance, that the overhead rate employed is a rate per cost unit. In situations such as AMC Ltd's, where overhead is absorbed other than by a cost unit rate, it is easy to fall into the error of using the wrong rate – AMC Ltd's unit rate is (1.5 standard hours × £4) = £6.

▷ What does the fixed overhead total variance represent?

Calculation of the total variance involves comparison of overhead absorbed with overhead incurred, so we are indicating overabsorption (favourable total variance) and underabsorption (adverse total variance). The total variance may be subdivided as follows:

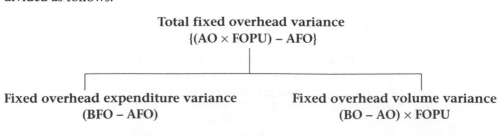

Total fixed overhead variance
$$\{(AO \times FOPU) - AFO\}$$

Fixed overhead expenditure variance
(BFO – AFO)

Fixed overhead volume variance
(BO – AO) × FOPU

The expenditure variance is exactly the same as that which we calculated for marginal costing, but the total and volume variances *do not exist in marginal costing*, as they derive from absorption of fixed overhead (which does not occur in marginal costing).

In Chapter 4, we saw that a predetermined overhead absorption rate derives from estimates of overhead expenditure and of volume, over- and underabsorption occurring because either or both of these estimates differ from actual. It is the impact of such differences which the expenditure and volume variances represent.

Fixed overhead volume variance

This variance indicates the extent to which the total variance is due to differences between budgeted and actual volumes of output:

	Batches	
Budgeted output was	16,000	(BO)
Actual output was	14,400	(AO)
Difference	1,600*A*	
Fixed overhead per unit	£6	(FOPU)
Fixed overhead volume variance	£9,600*A*	

As a formula:

$$(BO - AO) \times FOPU$$

where: BO represents budgeted output in units;
AO is actual output in units; and
FOPU is the fixed overhead absorption rate per cost unit.

AMC Ltd's volume variance for the month is:

$$(16,000 \text{ batches} - 14,400 \text{ batches}) \times £6 = £9,600A$$

▷ Why is the volume variance of £9,600 adverse?

The volume variance is adverse because actual output was 1,600 batches lower than budget for the month, and, to this extent, an underabsorption of fixed overhead has arisen. The volume variance may be of particular interest to management of organisations where there is a heavy investment in technology, with high related fixed costs. In these circumstances, volume, and the extent to which it does/does not recover fixed costs, can be a major consideration in judging whether or not resources are being effectively and efficiently used. Where absorbing fixed overhead through volume is especially important (e.g. in high-technology set-ups, with a large proportion of fixed costs), the volume variance may be subdivided into a fixed overhead efficiency variance and a fixed overhead capacity variance. The efficiency variance reflects the extent to which differences between budgeted and actual volume are due to labour efficiency, while the capacity variance reflects the impact on volume of other factors (e.g. unexpected machine downtime).

However, care is needed in use of the volume variance (and its subvariances), as there is a danger that it might be confused with expenditure and mislead managers into taking inappropriate control action.

Reconciling the expenditure and volume variances with the total variance, we get:

	£
Fixed overhead expenditure variance	5,000*A*
Fixed overhead volume variance	9,600*A*
Total fixed overhead variance	14,600*A*

Variances for selling, distribution and administration costs

Because of the discretionary nature of many of the costs which fall under this general heading, close monitoring of actual expenditure against budget is particularly important. However, it will rarely be possible to calculate more than the flexible budget or expenditure variance, given the nature of the costs concerned. Looking at Exhibit 14.2, we can calculate variances for the distribution and administration overhead as follows.

Variable distribution overhead

The flexible budget variance is:

	£	
Actual sales *should* have a distribution cost of		
(14,400 batches × £1)	14,400	(FBC)
Actual sales *did* have a distribution cost of	12,000	(AC)
Flexible budget variance	2,400*F*	

By formula:

$$(FBC - AC)$$

where: FBC is the flexible budget cost; and
AC is the actual cost.

Where output and sales volumes differ, you should be careful to flex the budget on the correct volume (i.e. sales).

⇨ Why might the favourable variance for distribution costs cause concern to management?

The favourable variance, which, on the face of things, should please management, might be a mixed blessing. There may, for example, be a relationship between distribution expenditure and sales volume such that a reduction in actual expenditure may have had an adverse effect on sales.

Fixed administration overhead

We can compute an expenditure variance for this cost:

	£	
Budgeted administration overhead was	60,000	(BC)
Actual administration overhead was	63,400	(AC)
Expenditure variance	3,400*A*	

As a formula, the variance is:

$$(BC - AC)$$

where: BC is the budgeted cost; and
AC is the actual cost.

➲ Even in an absorption costing system, a total and volume variance for fixed administration overhead are unlikely; why is this?

Fixed overheads which are not related to output, such as administration, selling and distribution, are not normally absorbed into unit costs (*see* Chapter 4), except for specific purposes such as setting selling prices. Calculation of a total or a volume variance (both deriving from overhead absorption) would therefore be irrelevant.

Sales variances

Selling price variance

This measures the difference between the standard and the actual selling price per unit. Actual selling price per batch must be calculated from the information in Exhibit 14.2:

$$\frac{\text{actual sales revenue}}{\text{actual sales volume}} = \frac{£532,800}{14,400 \text{ batches}} = £37$$

The selling price variance is:

	£	
Selling price per batch *should* have been	35	(SSP)
Selling price per batch *was*	37	(ASP)
Difference in selling price per batch	2F	
Actual sales volume	14,400 batches	(AS)
So selling price variance	£28,800F	

As a formula, the variance is:

$$(SSP - ASP) \times AS$$

where: SSP is the standard selling price per unit;
ASP is the actual selling price per unit; and
AS is the actual sales volume in units.

Remember that, for sales, an actual in excess of budget/standard is a favourable variance.

Sales volume variance

This variance indicates the effect on budgeted contribution/gross profit/revenue of differences between the budgeted and actual sales volumes. Before computing this variance for AMC Ltd, we must determine the standard contribution and gross profit per batch of output:

	£	£
Selling price		35
Direct materials	8	
Direct labour	9	
Variable output-related overhead	3	
Variable distribution overhead	1	21
Contribution per batch		14

⇨ What will the standard *gross* profit per batch be?

In Chapter 5, we saw that absorption costing gross profit is (sales *less* output-related costs), which, for AMC Ltd, gives:

	£	£
Selling price		35
Direct materials	8	
Direct labour	9	
Variable output-related overhead	3	
Fixed output-related overhead	6	26
Gross profit per batch		9

We can now compute the sales volume variance. Using marginal costing principles, we get:

	Batches	
Budgeted sales volume was	16,000	(BS)
Actual sales volume was	14,400	(AS)
Difference in sales volume	1,600A	
Standard contribution per batch	£14	(SCU)
Sales volume variance	22,400A	

⇨ What is the sales volume variance based on absorption costing?

In the absorption costing variance, standard gross profit per batch replaces standard contribution:

	Batches	
Budgeted sales volume was	16,000	(BS)
Actual sales volume was	14,400	(AS)
difference in sales volume	1,600A	
Standard gross profit per batch	£9	(Sπ)
Sales volume variance	14,400A	

A third variant of the sales volume variance uses standard selling price per unit:

	Batches	
Budgeted sales volume was	16,000	(BS)
Actual sales volume was	14,400	(AS)
Difference in sales volume	1,600*A*	
Standard selling price per batch	£35	(SSP)
Sales volume variance	56,000*A*	

You will notice that each version is valued in standard terms. This prevents distortion of the sales volume variance by other variances, (i.e. for costs and selling prices).

As a formula, the sales volume variance is:

$$(\text{BS} - \text{AS}) \times \text{SCU/S}\pi\text{/SSP}$$

where: BS is the budgeted sales volume in units;
AS is the actual sales volume in units;
SCU is standard contribution per unit;
Sπ is the standard gross profit per unit; and
SSP is standard selling price per unit.

Of these three approaches, the absorption costing basis is consistent with external reporting requirements for many organisations, but is somewhat distorted by absorption of fixed overheads. The marginal costing basis comes closest to reflecting the cash impact of additional/reduced sales against budget and may be the best approximation of the opportunity cost attaching to lost sales (or opportunity 'benefit' resulting from additional sales). Although the revenue-based sales volume variance excludes all costs in its calculation, it may nevertheless be of great interest to management in assessing factors such as lost/gained market share, or relative competitiveness.

⇨ How might interdependence present a particular problem in relation to the sales volume and selling price variances?

In Chapter 8 we introduced the concept of price elasticity of demand: that is, the notion that the higher the selling price, the lower the quantity demanded, and the lower the selling price, the higher the quantity demanded. In AMC Ltd's case, the actual selling price per 100 kg batch of laundry (£532,800/14,400 batches = £37) exceeds the standard selling price by £2 and it is possible that this may account for the lower-than-budgeted sales volume. So the problem of interdependence may make selling price and sales volume variances especially difficult to interpret.

RECONCILIATION OF BUDGETED AND ACTUAL PROFIT

We can prepare an operating statement which reconciles budgeted and actual profit, so as to provide an overview of financial performance during the control period. Such a statement for AMC Ltd (using marginal costing principles) is given below, showing appropriate variances from our earlier calculations:

AMC Ltd: operating statement for the month

	£	£
Original (fixed) budget contribution (16,000 batches @ £14)		224,000
Sales volume variance		22,400A
Flexible budget contribution (14,400 batches @ £14)		201,600
Budgeted fixed costs:		
Output-related overhead	96,000	
Administration	60,000	156,000
Flexible budget profit		45,600

Variances

	F(£)	A(£)	
Selling price	28,800		
Direct material price	5,920		
Direct material usage		3,200	
Direct labour rate	20,480		
Direct labour efficiency		24,000	
Variable overhead expenditure	3,500		
Variable overhead efficiency		6,400	
Fixed overhead expenditure		5,000	
Distribution overhead	2,400		
Administration overhead		3,400	
	61,100	42,000	19,100F
Actual profit (as per Exhibit 14.3)			64,700

Had absorption costing been used, some minor amendment to the presentation above would be necessary:

AMC Ltd: operating statement for the month

	£	£
Original (fixed) budget gross profit (16,000 batches @ £9)		144,000
Sales volume variance		14,400A
Flexible budget gross profit (14,400 batches @ £9)		129,600
Flexible budget distribution overhead (14,400 batches @ £1)	14,400	
Budgeted administration overhead	60,000	74,400
Flexible budget net profit		55,200

Variances

	F(£)	A(£)	
(As in the statement above, *except* that			
the fixed overhead volume		42,000	
variance of £9,600A is included.)		9,600	
	61,100	51,600	9,500F
Actual profit			64,700

In this particular example, output and sales are the same, so absorption and marginal costing will report the same net profit. You should bear in mind, however, that where stock increases or decreases occur during a period, the two systems will yield different net profit figures (*see* Chapter 5).

PLANNING AND OPERATIONAL VARIANCES

It may well have occurred to you during our detailed analysis of AMC Ltd's variances that one possible reason for some or all of the variances, in part or in whole, is error in the standards from which the budget and variances were both derived. To the extent that variances are the result of errors in setting standards, they may be misleading indicators of *operational* performance and valuable time and resources could be committed in an attempt to discover operational causes for what are essentially *planning* errors. It might therefore be desirable to further analyse variances to distinguish between their planning and operational elements, thereby allowing control activity to focus on operational aspects, while the planning variances may be used to assess the accuracy of the planning process with a view to improving future planning.

The variances we have so far examined are based on comparison of a predetermined standard (an **ex-ante standard**) with actual results. If the ex-ante standard is found to be incorrect, it can be revised with the benefit of hindsight into an **ex-post standard** (i.e. a standard which is set *after* the event). Planning and operational variances can then be calculated by making the following comparisons:

■ Planning variances: ex-ante standard with ex-post standard;
■ Operational variances: ex-post standard with actual results.

If you look at these two sets of comparisons, you should see that when planning and operational variances are taken together, the overall comparison is still between the ex-ante standard and actual results (just as it was for the 'conventional' variances we calculated earlier). In other words, planning and operational variances represent a further subdivision of the detailed variances we have already examined.

AMC Laundry Services Ltd: planning and operational variances

Selling price
The original standard selling price per 100 kg batch of laundry (£35) was based on a prediction about the degree of competition within the company's market which, in the event, was exaggerated. It is now recognised that a more realistic assessment of competitor activity would have resulted in a standard selling price of £38. In the event, the actual selling price was £37 per batch.

EXHIBIT **14.4 Error in standard-setting**

We will use the data in Exhibit 14.4 to illustrate how planning and operational variances might be applied to AMC Ltd's situation. If, as Exhibit 14.4 suggests, the original standard selling price was incorrect, then this error will be incorporated in the selling price and sales volume variances we calculated earlier. The planning variance can be isolated as follows:

	£
Original standard selling price per batch was	35
Revised standard selling price per batch is	38
Difference in standard selling price per batch	3F
Actual sales volume	14,400 batches
Planning variance	£43,200F

The planning variance is favourable because the effect of the revision to the standard is to increase budgeted revenue.

The operational selling price variance is now:

	£
Revised standard selling price per batch	38
Actual selling price per batch	37
Difference in selling price per batch	1A
Actual sales volume	14,400 batches
Operational selling price variance is	£14,400A

As you can see, the operational variance is computed using the approach described earlier in the chapter, but incorporating the revised standard selling price.

⇨ Comment on AMC Ltd's performance as revealed by the operational selling price variance in conjunction with the adverse sales volume variance reported in the operating statement above.

The selling price variance reported in the operating statement was £28,800 favourable. Removing the planning error paints an entirely different picture and, when this is considered in light of the adverse sales volume variance plus a less competitive market, there may be cause for concern. If AMC Ltd could have sold at £38 per batch in a less competitive market without affecting volume, questions need to be asked about why budgeted volume was not achieved.

The planning and operational variances can be reconciled with the original selling price variance of £28,800 favourable:

	£
Planning variance	43,200F
Operational variance	14,400A
'Conventional' variance	28,800F

A similar analysis is possible for any other of the original standards which are subsequently discovered to be incorrect.

Advantages and problems of planning and operational variances

We have seen that separation of 'conventional' variances into their planning and operational elements can have a dramatic effect on the portrayal of performance against budget. If planning errors are due to unforeseen or 'one-off' events (such as AMC Ltd's less competitive market), then they are not under management control and should be excluded from a budget/actual comparison. This should allow management to concentrate control effort on those factors which can be controlled, as reflected in operational variances. In addition, where planning variances arise from circumstances which might have been foreseen (e.g. the effect on material usage of a change in supplier/material), then this knowledge can be used to improve future standard-setting and budgeting. The fact that ex-ante standards are revised as part of the budgetary control exercise should help prevent them becoming outdated – an important consideration in a dynamic environment.

However, there are some problems:

1 It may be difficult in practice to decide what the ex-post standard should be and to assess possible interdependencies which may arise in variances as a consequence of revision of standards. For example, is £38 a reasonable ex-post standard for AMC Ltd's selling price? Even if it is, how would this interact with the budgeted sales volume, given that, at a £37 price, budgeted volume (ex-ante and ex-post) is not currently being achieved?

2 Following from the previous problem is the difficulty of who should set the ex-post standard. The simple answer would appear to be the manager with greatest influence over the particular aspect of performance for which the standard is being revised. But there is a danger here. If the ex-post standard is set by the manager who also has budget responsibility for variances, the temptation may exist to do this in such a way as to maximise the planning (uncontrollable) and minimise the operational (controllable) variances, so that operational performance acquires an unrealistic 'gloss' .

3 Interpretation of planning variances may cause confusion. AMC Ltd has a sales price planning variance of £43,200 favourable. Is this 'good' or 'bad'? It could be seen as good *and* bad: good in the sense that the planning error understated budgeted revenue, but bad when considered as an error of judgement about the competitiveness of the company's market.

4 Planning variances may be redundant, as thorough investigation of 'conventional' variances should reveal factors such as a market which is less competitive than was expected.

5 Compared to a system of 'conventional' variance reporting, a planning/operational approach may be more costly.

We have undertaken an extensive variance analysis exercise, and we can now discuss the extent to which detailed analysis of variances may reinforce some of the more general problems of budgetary control and standard costing.

VARIANCE ANALYSIS: REINFORCING SOME GENERAL PROBLEMS?

Potential for dysfunctional decisions

The main reason for undertaking the kind of detailed variance analysis which we have been describing is to help pinpoint potential problem areas in order to enhance control action and possibly identify managerial 'responsibility'. Whilst this may work perfectly well, there might be a risk that overemphasising the 'responsibility' aspect of budget subvariances could backfire in the form of dysfunctional decisions by managers. Suppose, for example, that AMC Ltd's Buyer has responsibility for the material price variance and that the Operations Manager has responsibility for the usage variance. We have already seen that these two variances may be interdependent: that is, that purchase of cheaper-than-standard materials (resulting in a favourable price variance) may result in an adverse usage variance (e.g. due to poorer quality materials). The problem with linking detailed variances to managerial responsibility is that this may encourage (or may 'pressure') managers into taking decisions which optimise the variance(s) for which they are 'responsible,' but which have an adverse effect on other managers' areas of responsibility and on the organisation as a whole. Thus AMC Ltd's Buyer may purchase cheaper-than-standard materials as a matter of optimising the price variance, but at the expense of an adverse usage variance.

Problems of this sort may be addressed by ensuring that managers are aware of the wider implications of their actions (as would be the case with a total quality management philosophy), or by placing less emphasis on the 'control' and 'responsibility' aspects of variances and more on their role as an *aid* to management. In some cases, interdependencies between budget subvariances may be so intricate that their report and investigation fails the cost/benefit test.

Interpretation and investigation of variances

As we mentioned at the start of this chapter, variances are indicative, but not conclusive. As a minimum, all significant variances should be investigated to establish likely cause and/or learn lessons. As well as the question of interdependence, this raises several issues which we discussed in detail in the last chapter, but which are important enough to warrant repetition in summary, as follows:

1 Defining what constitutes a 'significant' variance.
2 Assessing the impact on variances of random factors.
3 Making allowance for the effect of inflation, especially in volatile areas, such as some raw material markets.
4 Controllability of certain budget lines and their associated variances.
5 Impact of measurement errors.
6 Risk of stressing financial performance and control to the detriment or even exclusion of non-financial considerations.
7 Means-end confusion.

All of the concerns listed here are relevant to any form of variance analysis, regardless of level of detail, but the last three difficulties may be aggravated by reporting budget subvariances. The potential danger is that detailed calculations of the type we have just been undertaking may imply a spurious degree of controllability (e.g. overhead expenditure variances) and in no way reflect important factors such as quality of product/service (which we shall discuss in the next chapter). You will recall that we made this point in Chapter 13 when we compared an inwardly focused financial control system with an outward-looking, market-oriented **target costing** approach. You should also bear in mind the potential weaknesses of standard costing which we discussed in Chapter 12 (all of which have a bearing on variance analysis).

Misdirected emphasis?

When analysing AMC Ltd's budget variances, we calculated labour rate and efficiency variances. Reporting these variances might be appropriate in AMC's situation, where labour costs form a significant part of the budget, but for many organisations, labour costs are of far less importance relative to materials, machine and technology costs. Reporting detailed variances for labour or for any other costs which are comparatively immaterial could attach a 'weight' to them which they do not possess. This may, in turn, result in cost control or cost reduction effort which is misplaced in the context of organisations which are highly automated and which operate in highly competitive and increasingly 'global' markets. For example, adverse labour variances could be seen as suggestive of a 'quick fix' for cost problems, whereas a better solution in strategic terms may lie elsewhere. As Doyle (1994) puts it:

> Many corporate experts watching the events of the past decade are now convinced that the effort expended in appraising activities, devising downsizing plans and implementing them is misdirected. Their main fear is that company heads are being distracted by direct labour costs and in-house efficiencies to the detriment of what it really takes to be competitive in to-day's markets.

Standard costs and budget subvariances may have the effect of concentrating managerial attention on immediate and internal concerns (at the expense of strategic and external), simply because of their level of detail and 'demand' for speedy response. For example, highlighting comparison of actual costs with internally generated standards may obscure the need to compete in cost terms with external organisations operating in the same market. As we suggested in the last chapter, a strict interpretation of total quality management, with its emphasis on customer satisfaction, 'getting it right first time' and continuous improvement, would view the very existence of a standard costing and variance analysis system having an in-built allowance for anticipated inefficiencies as irrelevant (at best) or harmful (at worst).

Variance analysis has the potential to misdirect managerial attention in another way. Being essentially retrospective in nature, it could be detrimental to control at the design stage of products/services, encouraging the belief that design errors can somehow be rectified by addressing resultant variances. This may be of especial significance in organisations which employ advanced manufacturing technology (AMT): in this sort of environment, the major 'standard' is technological specification. Similarly, we suggested in Chapter 12 that one advantage of setting standards might be use of improved methods/materials. The opposite may equally be true, however: standard setting, with its 'after-the-event' control philosophy could induce an unhealthy rigidity in planning and design of products/services. For example, substitutability and flexibility of resource inputs might be subordinated to the short-term need for a minimum-cost solution.

Responsiveness to sudden change

Sudden and unforeseen changes in an organisation's operational environment may cause difficulty in the operation of a system of standard costing and variance analysis, and may increase pressure on managers to react to financial control measures in a dysfunctional manner. Suppose, for example, that volume of output must be increased to meet a quite unexpected upsurge in demand. Meeting such an increase in demand may be in the long-term interest of the organisation (if sustained), but may give rise to adverse variances in the short term.

⇨ How might a sudden, unexpected increase in demand give rise to adverse variances?

If the rise in demand is sufficiently large, additional resources will be required, almost certainly at short notice: for instance, labour may need to work overtime and emergency orders for materials placed with suppliers. There is a strong likelihood that acquiring resources at short notice will attract a penalty such as premium payments for overtime working and increased material purchase costs. Such penalties will not have been included in the determination of standards for labour and materials, thus giving rise to adverse variances. In other words, the very need to respond to a dynamic environment may give rise to adverse variances. Reporting variances which arise due to this kind of situation raises two issues:

1 To what extent are the variances genuinely controllable?
2 What is the likelihood of such variances prompting inappropriate responses from management (e.g. failure to react to a change in demand because of adverse short-term consequences)?

If there is a danger that detailed variance analysis might inhibit managerial action, then we have another argument either for a more flexible approach, or for a more radical solution, such as adoption of the planning/operational methodology, or even complete abandonment.

SUMMARY

Our discussion of variance analysis suggests that it may be a useful tool, but that it may also aggravate certain potential weaknesses of 'conventional' financial control mechanisms. Care is therefore needed if its use is to enhance, rather than hinder, managerial and organisational activity. We have seen that:

- Budget variances, because of their 'global' nature, may mask important aspects of performance which merit investigation.

- Analysis of budget variances requires the existence of a standard costing system.

- A formulaic approach to variance analysis gives the following:

Materials	
Flexible budget variance	$\{(AO \times SMCU) - TAMC\}$
Price variance	$(SP - AP) \times AQ$
Usage variance	$(SQ - AQ) \times SP$
Labour	
Flexible budget variance	$\{(AO \times SLCU) - TALC\}$
Rate variance	$(SR - AR) \times AH$
Efficiency variance	$(SH - AH) \times SR$

Variable overhead

Flexible budget variance	$\{(AO \times SVOU) - AVO\}$
Expenditure variance	$\{(AH \times SVOH) - AVO\}$
Efficiency variance	$(SH - AH) \times SVOH$

Fixed overhead

Total variance	$\{(AO \times FOPU) - AFO\}$
Expenditure variance	$(BFO - AFO)$
Volume variance	$(BO - AO) \times FOPU$

Sales

Selling price variance	$(SSP - ASP) \times AS$
Sales volume variance	$(BS - AS) \times S\pi/SCU/SSP$

■ Operating statements can be prepared to reconcile budgeted and actual cost and profit based on marginal or absorption costing principles.

■ In a marginal costing system, there are no variances for total fixed overhead or fixed overhead volume, and the sales volume variance is based on standard unit contribution.

■ Where the original (**ex-ante**) standards prove to be incorrect, the effect of this can be separated from operational factors by calculating **planning** and **operational variances**, planning variances being based on comparison of the ex-ante standard and a revised (**ex-post**) standard.

■ Planning and operational variances may help management to concentrate control effort on operational factors and may also enhance the planning process, but there are some problems:
  – deciding on an appropriate ex-post standard;
  – who sets the ex-post standard;
  – interpretation of planning variances;
  – potential redundancy of planning variances; and
  – possibility of extra cost.

■ In addition to the potential weaknesses of standard costing and budget variances described in Chapters 12 and 13, detailed variance analysis may:
  – increase the chance of dysfunctional decisions by managers;
  – have a large element of interdependence and pose problems in interpretation and investigation;
  – misdirect managerial attention, especially in the context of a total quality environment; and
  – cause problems in a dynamic environment.

In the next chapter, we shall discuss further measures of performance – both financial and non-financial.

FURTHER READING

Doyle, D., *Cost Control, A Strategic Guide*, CIMA, 1994. This book places cost control in its strategic perspective.

Drury, C., *Management and Cost Accounting*, 4th edn, International Thomson Business Press, 1996. Chapter 20 provides further discussion of planning/operational variances, along with additional analysis of materials' variances. Chapter 19 contains examples of fixed overhead efficiency and capacity variances.

Ezzamel, M. and Hart, H., *Advanced Management Accounting: An Organisational Emphasis*, Cassell, 1992. Chapter 14 contains a discussion of more advanced aspects of standard costing and variance analysis.

Sᴇʟꜰ-ᴛᴇꜱᴛ Qᴜᴇꜱᴛɪᴏɴꜱ

The following information is to be used for Questions 14.1 and 14.2.

A sewage treatment plant adds a series of chemicals to raw sewage. Budgeted, standard and actual data in respect of one of these chemicals for the month of June was:

Actual price per kg: £15
Standard price per kg: £16
Actual quantity purchased: 19,200 kg
Actual quantity used: 18,400 kg
Standard usage: 0.4 kg per 50 litres of untreated sewage
Budgeted throughput of untreated sewage: 2,000,000 litres
Actual throughput of untreated sewage: 2,206,250 litres

14.1 What was the sewage treatment plant's material price variance for June?

A £16,480 *F*
B £17,000 *F*
C £18,400 *F*
D £19,200 *F*

14.2 What was the sewage treatment plant's material usage variance for June?

A £12,000 *A*
B £21,000 *A*
C £22,400 *A*
D £30,720 *A*

14.3 For each of the following statements, tick the appropriate box to indicate whether it is true or false.

	True	False
(a) If actual output is lower than budgeted output, the fixed overhead volume variance will be favourable.	☐	☐
(b) Where variable overhead varies with direct labour hours, an efficiency variance may be calculated for this cost.	☐	☐
(c) Planning variances are based on comparison of ex-ante and ex-post standards.	☐	☐

(d) Expressing the sales volume variance in revenue terms provides the best approximation of the cash effect involved. ☐ ☐

(e) In a marginal costing system, only the fixed overhead expenditure variance is calculated. ☐ ☐

(f) Actual material losses which are unexpected will have a favourable impact on the usage variance. ☐ ☐

14.4 MVF Ltd's variable overhead varies with labour hours and data for last month are as follows:

Budgeted variable overhead cost: £38,000
Actual cost: £40,000
Standard variable overhead per labour hour: £5
Standard labour hours per unit of output: 0.25
Budgeted output: 30,400 units
Actual output: 32,000 units
Actual labour hours: 7,000

What is MVF Ltd's variable overhead expenditure variance?

A £2,000A
B £3,000A
C £5,000A
D £8,000A

14.5 SC Ltd uses a standard marginal costing system for internal reporting and control purposes and the following information relates to August:

Budgeted sales: 4,000 units
Standard selling price per unit: £40
Actual sales: 4,600 units
Actual selling price per unit: £36
Budgeted output: 4,300 units
Standard variable cost per unit: £22
Actual output: 4,400 units
Actual variable cost per unit: £24

What is SC Ltd's sales volume variance for August?

A £4,200F
B £7,200F
C £10,800F
D £18,400F

14.6 APF Ltd's standard absorption costing system reported the following fixed overhead variances last month:

Total variance £16,000 A
Volume variance £7,000 F

What was the company's fixed overhead expenditure variance for the month?

A £9,000A
B £9,000F
C £23,000F
D £23,000A

QUESTIONS WITH ANSWERS

14.7 This question tests whether you can:

- compute detailed labour variances; and

- assess the consistency of explanations offered with the variances calculated.

HCR Ltd, a printer, has two operational cost centres, Printing and Binding. For May, the following information relating to Binding is available:

Standard direct labour time per binding operation	2 minutes
Standard direct labour rate per hour	£9
Actual number of binding operations during month	33,000
Actual direct labour cost (1,400 hours)	£11,760

Requirements

(a) Calculate variances for May in respect of labour rate and efficiency.

(b) State, with supporting explanation, whether each of the following claims by the Binding cost centre's manager is consistent with the variances calculated in (a):

(i) unforeseen repair work in the Printing cost centre affected Binding's productivity for the month;

(ii) a batch of substandard binding materials adversely affected the efficiency of Binding's direct labour;

(iii) payment of a wage rise, originally scheduled to occur in June, was brought forward to May.

14.8 This question tests whether you can:

- compute detailed variances for labour, variable and fixed overhead;

- explain the meaning of the fixed overhead volume variance; and

- comment on a suggestion that the workforce be reduced.

IB Ltd provides a specialised electronic bulletin board to registered clients, who pay a fee per 'downloading session': that is, for each occasion spent transferring information from IB Ltd's computer to their own. The following information relates to March:

Downloading

Budgeted number of downloading sessions	15,000
Actual number of downloading sessions	13,100

Standard operating costs per client downloading session

	£
System operators' time (10 minutes @ £12 per hour)	2.00
Variable overhead	3.00
Fixed overhead	1.00
	6.00

Budgeted and actual costs

System operators:	actual – 1,800 hours costing £25,200
Variable overhead:	actual – £42,000
Fixed overhead:	actual – £13,000
	budgeted – £15,000.

Requirements

(a) Compute the following variances and present them in an operating statement which reconciles budgeted and actual total cost for March:

    (i) labour rate and efficiency;

    (ii) variable overhead expenditure; and

    (iii) fixed overhead volume and expenditure.

(b) Explain the meaning of the fixed overhead volume variance.

(c) The Managing Director has suggested that the number of system operators should be reduced, as some of their time is 'unproductively' spent advising clients on how to 'navigate' IB Ltd's complex database. The potential benefits of this course of action are seen as twofold: a reduction in labour costs, coupled with an increase in revenue, as clients will require more downloading sessions to capture the data they require. Comment on the Managing Director's suggestion.

14.9 This question tests whether you can:

■ compute detailed variances for direct material, direct labour, variable and fixed overhead, along with selling price and sales volume;

■ incorporate these variances in an operating statement reconciling budgeted and actual profit;

■ evaluate the frequency of an organisation's variance reporting; and

■ illustrate interdependence between variances.

PTP & Co manufactures a standard type of alloy garden storage unit and it is the firm's practice to extract a detailed variance report and operating statement at the end of every accounting year. The information given below relates to the accounting year ending 31 March 19X5:

Standard data per unit

Direct materials:	
Alloy	5 metres^2 @ £2.65
Fixings	14 units @ £1.70
Direct labour:	4 hours @ £7.20
Variable overhead:	4 hours @ £3.60
Fixed overhead:	4 hours @ £0.85
Selling price:	£110

Budgeted data for 19X5

Output/sales:	50,000 units
Fixed overhead:	£170,000

Actual data for 19X5

Output/sales:	47,000 units
Sales revenue:	£4,935,000
Direct labour:	192,000 hours costing £1,363,200
Direct materials purchased/used:	
Alloy	256,000 metres^2 @ £2.50
Fixings	641,000 units @ £1.76
Variable overhead:	£750,000
Fixed overhead:	£165,000

Requirements

(a) Compute the following variances:

    (i)   price and usage for each direct material;

    (ii) direct labour rate and efficiency;

    (iii) variable overhead expenditure and efficiency;

    (iv) fixed overhead expenditure and volume; and

    (v) selling price and sales volume.

(b) Present an operating statement detailing the variances calculated in (a) and reconciling budgeted with actual profit for 19X5.

(c) Explain your view of the adequacy or otherwise of PTP & Co's control mechanisms as suggested by the firm's practice of extracting detailed variances on an annual basis.

(d) Indicate *two* possible interdependencies which may exist between the variances in (a), providing a brief justification for your answer.

14.10 This question tests whether you can:

■ calculate detailed variances for costs and sales; and

■ explain the concept of planning and operational variance reporting, and link this to the concepts of feedback and feedforward control introduced in the last chapter.

OV Ltd is a privately owned training company, specialising in provision of a two-day management skills course. The standard variable cost per student attending this course was as follows last year:

	£
Direct material (computer consumables)	10
Direct labour: 20 hours @ £15	300
Variable overhead: 20 hours @ £0.75	15
	325

Budgeted data for the year:

Number of students attending the course	3,500
Fee per student per course	£450
Fixed costs	£87,500

The actual results were:

Number of students attending the course	3,100
	£
Total revenue	1,271,000
Direct materials cost	30,600
Direct labour (59,000 hours @ £18)	1,062,000
Variable overhead	46,300
Fixed overhead	82,000

Requirements

(a) Present a detailed analysis of OV Ltd's variances for the year.

(b) Explain how planning and operational variances may be used to enhance both *feedback control* and *feedforward control*.

QUESTIONS WITHOUT ANSWERS

14.11 MM Ltd, a manufacturer of duvets, operates a computerised standard costing system and a virus has recently caused the loss of some key data. The following fragmentary information is available:

Variances

Direct material price variance	£1,572 A
Direct material usage variance	£2,640 F
Direct labour rate varience	£2,050 F
Direct labour efficiency variance	£3,900 A
Variable overhead expenditure variance	£3,400 A

Actual data

Output	12,000 units
Direct materials:	
Used	26,200 kg
Cost	£90,652
Direct labour cost:	
Worked	10,250 hours
Cost	£59,450
Variable overhead:	£49,525.

Your investigations have also revealed that the actual rate of pay for direct labour was £0.20 per hour lower than the standard, and that the material price variance is extracted when materials are issued to production from stores.

Requirements

(a) Using the information given, prepare a statement showing the standard variable cost per unit along with the standard resource inputs for each of direct labour, direct materials and variable overhead.

(b) From a cost control standpoint, evaluate MM Ltd's policy of extracting the material price variance at point of issue from stores to production.

14.12 The following operating statement relates to TRN Ltd, a manufacturer of cardboard packaging, for last year:

	F(£)	A(£)	£
Original (fixed) budgeted profit			4,500,000
Sales volume variance			1,200,000A
Flexible budget profit			3,300,000
Variances	*F(£)*	*A(£)*	
Selling price:		600,000	
Direct material:			
Price		70,000	
Usage	30,000		
Direct labour:			
Rate	104,000		
Efficiency		116,000	
Fixed overhead:			
Expenditure	400,000		
Volume		14,000	
Selling and distribution costs	300,000		
	834,000	800,000	34,000A
Actual profit			3,266,000

Additional information

1 Management has expressed satisfaction that, faced with difficult trading conditions, actual profit was roughly in line with budget.

2 During the year to which the operating statement refers, the company underwent a major cost-cutting and downsizing exercise, which is reflected in the variances for labour rate, fixed overhead expenditure, and selling and distribution costs.

Requirement

Draft a report to TRN Ltd's Chief Executive analysing the company's performance (as far as the information permits), and indicating any areas of possible concern.

CHAPTER 15

Performance appraisal

P & O TO GO FOR HIGHER RETURNS

P & O announced yesterday that it planned to increase its return on capital to 15 per cent in the medium term. The target comes after several analysts had criticised the low returns the group makes from some of its core businesses, such as containers, which have received significant capital investment in recent years. Lord Sterling, chairman, said that higher returns were needed if the group was to meet its capital expenditure requirements, which were £505m last year, and to increase dividends. The return on capital was 11 per cent last year . . .

The containers division continued to suffer from market deregulation and declining rates, with profits falling from £63.2m to £40.9m. The return on capital was 6 per cent.

Responding to criticisms of the division's returns, Lord Sterling said: 'If we cannot find an answer in a reasonable period of time, then the business will leave the group.'

Source: Geoff Dyer, Financial Times, 27 March 1996.

EXHIBIT **15.1 Return on capital: an important financial performance measure**

INTRODUCTION

In the course of the last two chapters, we have discussed financial control and said that, whilst budget variances (and their subdivisions) may provide some indication of performance, it would be unwise to emphasise this aspect of variances to the extent that other measures of equal or greater importance are overlooked. The importance of performance measures is well illustrated by the quote from Lord Sterling in Exhibit 15.1: 'If we cannot find an answer [to an unacceptably low return on capital] in a reasonable period of time, then the business will leave the group.' Understanding such measures is therefore vital – and an appreciation of their calculation, their strengths and their weaknesses is a major element in the current chapter. However, this is only part of the story. Performance has many facets, such as quality, which may be difficult to express in financial terms, so we must also consider the important topic of non-financial and qualitative measures. Our discussion will not encompass stock market indicators such as earnings per share and dividend yield, but you should appreciate that performance is not neatly compartmentalised and that these measures depend to some extent on perceptions of the kind of measures we are about to describe.

Initially, we shall consider performance evaluation in divisionalised organisations, before broadening our discussion to cover more general performance indicators, both financial and non-financial. Finally, we will examine the problems of performance appraisal which might arise in non-profit and public sector organisations.

OBJECTIVES

When you have completed this chapter, you will be able to:

- appreciate the advantages and potential problems of divisionalisation;

- calculate return on capital employed and residual income;

- understand the general strengths and weaknesses of return on capital employed and residual income and in particular the possibility of dysfunctional decisions resulting from their use;

- appreciate the existence, calculation and significance of a range of other financial measures applicable to cost, profit and investment centres;

- suggest non-financial and qualitative performance measures for an organisation (or organisational subunit);

- understand the concept of benchmarking and its role in performance appraisal;

- describe the concept of value for money, and the use of value-for-money audits; and

- explain the particular performance appraisal problems which may be faced by non-profit and public sector organisations, being aware of possible solutions along with their merits and drawbacks.

Divisionalisation

In the previous two chapters, our discussion has centred almost exclusively on cost centres and profit centres. We must now broaden this discussion to include investment centres: that is, organisational subunits to which revenues, costs and capital investment are all traced. Organisations which have a structure of investment centres are often described as *divisionalised* (or *segmented*), but terminology can be confusing. Although investment centres are often referred to as 'divisions' or 'segments', they may also, for example, be separate companies within a group, different branches/ departments of the same company, 'strategic business units' or 'divisions of service' in public sector organisations, and other definitions are also encountered. The strategic business unit (SBU) is an important development of the investment centre: here, in addition to costs, revenues and capital investment, the subunit has responsibility for determining its own strategy – in effect, is virtually independent of central control.

Furthermore, it is quite feasible for large investment centres and SBUs (e.g. separate companies within a group) to be subdivided into their own profit and cost centres. Regardless of the label(s) applied by a particular organisation, its subunits can only be said to be investment centres if costs, revenues and some/all of the related capital investment are attributed to it *and* if management has some degree of control over these items. Genuine *divisionalisation* will thus only be practical in larger organisations, where overall capital investment is substantial enough to be meaningfully split into areas of divisional responsibility. In smaller organisations, responsibility and authority may be devolved to cost or profit or revenue centres based on functional or departmental lines.

It is also necessary to realise that divisionalisation, like the principles of decentralisation and delegation upon which it is based, is not an absolute, but a matter of degree, which should be judged solely in light of an organisation's specific circumstances. Similarly, the strengths and weaknesses of a divisionalised structure are effectively the same as those attaching to the broader principles of decentralisation and delegation.

Benefits of divisionalisation

Exhibit 15.2 contains some general information about HTM plc, from which it is easy to see that the very size and diversity of a company could justify a divisionalised structure.

HTM plc: general information

HTM plc is a large conglomerate company with widely diversified operations, ranging from management consultancy to civil engineering, from manufacture of aircraft components to freight transport and oil exploration. Although company headquarters is based in the UK, HTM plc is a multinational organisation, with trading being carried out by subsidiary companies in the UK and 14 other countries.

EXHIBIT **15.2 A multinational conglomerate**

⇨ What potential benefits could divisionalisation offer to HTM plc?

The main benefits of divisionalisation are discussed below; some are fairly obvious, others perhaps less so:

1 *Taking advantage of localised or specialist knowledge* Use of investment centres is based on devolving a degree of authority and responsibility to divisional management, who will almost certainly possess the greatest knowledge of the operational conditions faced by their divisions. A corporate structure which allows this knowledge to be brought to bear on planning, control and decision making could help avoid costly errors in these functions which might result from their implementation at a distance (e.g. by headquarters staff).

2 *Speed of reaction* Because authority to make decisions is localised at divisional level, it is likely that reaction to change will be quicker than it would be if all decisions were taken centrally. Ability to react quickly is a vital ingredient of success in a rapidly changing environment.

3 *Offers enhanced training opportunities* Because divisional management is to some extent independent of central control, greater scope may exist for training executives than might be the case in a more centralised organisation. Depending on the degree of divisional independence, the benefit of this may be particularly evident at the strategic level. In a centralised structure, trainees may have little opportunity either to observe or participate in strategic processes: for example, because it is not practicable due to the sheer number of trainees.

4 *Avoiding management 'bottlenecks' at the centre* Headquarters staff and senior management will be freer to consider issues of wider significance than the operational situation of individual investment centres (e.g. corporate strategy in the 'global market place'). There is the danger that, with a highly centralised corporate structure, such issues may be submerged by a tidal rush of operational minutiae submitted to the centre. In extreme cases, the sheer volume and detail might strangle effective management and/or cause an increase in the cost of central functions quite disproportionate to any benefit derived.

5 *Behavioural benefits* Divisionalisation may confer on divisional managers the benefit of what Horngren (1982) has described as 'first class citizenship': that is perceptions of status and individual value may be enhanced by added authority and responsibility. Motivation and commitment could be improved by participation in the planning, control and decision-making processes. We will discuss these (and other) behavioural issues in the next chapter. It is also possible that headquarters staff could benefit in behavioural terms: for example, by a reduction in time pressure with consequent lessening of related stress levels.

6 *Easier organisational expansion/contraction* An organisation with a divisionalised structure may find it simpler to expand or contract in the face of changing circumstances. Expansion, for example, could be more straightforward administatively and structurally (compared to expansion from within) if it can be achieved by purchase of an existing business which is then designated a division. Exhibit 15.1 suggests a similar advantage may exist in the case of organisational contraction.

7 *Managing by numbers* The task of senior executives might be eased by delegation of a wide range of planning, control and decision-making functions. If you look again at Exhibit 15.1, you might see why this could be so: from a senior management perspective, it is comparatively easy to set a target return for divisions

where the ways and means of achieving that target are principally matters of divisional responsibility. The appeal of this kind of 'management by numbers' is not hard to understand.

The benefits of divisionalisation can be significant, especially in a strategic context, offering a more flexible, adaptable organisation. But there are some problems.

Problems of divisionalisation

1 *Duplication of work* In a divisionalised organisation, some duplication of work between head office and divisions is inevitable, with administrative functions being particularly prone to unnecessary duplications. For example, computer systems at headquarters may be exactly replicated at divisions – but is this absolutely necessary? This aspect of divisionalisation requires careful monitoring, as the associated cost could be substantial.

2 *Flow of information* It is particularly important to consider the management information flowing (in both directions) between divisions and the centre – this should be sufficient for the circumstances. For example, too high a volume may cause overload at both ends of the information chain and may be resented by divisional managers as a compromise to their authority, whilst too low a volume will provide (at best) an incomplete picture of divisional and organisation-wide activities. It seems to be the case that, where information flows of this type are concerned, organisations tend to 'err' on the side of caution, requiring more rather than less information from divisions. Inappropriate information flows will result in ineffective planning, control and decision making at both divisional and organisational levels, and the related rectification costs may be prohibitive.

3 *Dysfunctional behaviour* It is possible that divisionalisation may have dysfunctional effects: that is, may encourage divisional managers to act in a manner which is not consistent with the wider organisational interest. For example, divisional management may interpret delegation as effectively freeing them from central control and may consequently pursue narrow divisional interests at the expense of the organisation generally. Or disputes may arise between divisions, especially where a buyer/seller relationship exists, or where separate divisions compete with each other in external markets, the result in both cases probably being pursuit of divisional interest as the overriding priority.

4 *Lack of functional expertise* There is a possibility that the level of expertise in a particular area (e.g. marketing) may be diluted in a divisional structure. Adequate knowledge may exist for divisional purposes, but is this sufficient for the organisation as a whole?

Divisionalisation may therefore have a harmful, fragmentary effect on the organisation. A careful and ongoing cost/benefit 'balancing act' is necessary to avoid the organisational sprawl and sloth which may arise if divisionalisation is allowed to evolve from circumstance, rather than design.

Given the extent of delegation which exists within divisionalised organisations, adequate performance appraisal measures are essential. The two measures which we are about to discuss – return on capital employed and residual income – both attempt to reflect the major financial elements of delegation: sales revenue, costs and capital employed.

RETURN ON CAPITAL EMPLOYED (ROCE)

Return on capital employed (ROCE), also referred to as **return on investment (ROI)**, is a financial performance indicator which links the key accounting measures of profit and capital:

$$\frac{\text{operating profit}}{\text{capital employed}} \times 100\%$$

As was the case with P & O in Exhibit 15.1, ROCE can be calculated for the entire organisation and for individual divisions. To illustrate divisional calculations, we shall use the further information about HTM plc given in Exhibit 15.3.

HTM plc: further information

KK Division, based in the USA, provides management consultancy services, whilst TM Division, based in Germany, is a light engineering operation. Summarised data relating to each division for the control period just ended is given below.

	KK Division (£m)	TM Division (£m)
Sales revenue	3.0	8.0
Divisional operating profit	0.4	3.3
Capital employed	1.6	25.0

HTM plc has a target return of 12 per cent.

EXHIBIT **15.3 Data for calculation of financial performance measures**

⇨ Use the formula above to determine the ROCE for each division. Can any conclusions be drawn from the results?

The divisional ROCEs are:

$$\text{KK Division:} \quad \frac{£0.4 \text{ million}}{£1.6 \text{ million}} \times 100\% = 25\%$$

$$\text{TM Division:} \quad \frac{£3.3 \text{ million}}{£25.0 \text{ million}} \times 100\% = 13.2\%$$

It is tempting to conclude from these two figures that KK Division has 'outperformed' TM Division, but this conclusion is highly suspect, for reasons which we shall discuss shortly. The most which can be said on the basis of the very limited information available is that KK Division has exceeded the target return of 12 per cent by a larger margin than TM.

It is possible to subdivide ROCE into the following percentage measures:

$$\text{divisional profit : sales percentage} \quad \frac{\text{divisional profit}}{\text{sales revenue}} \times 100\%$$

$$\text{sales : capital employed} \quad \frac{\text{sales revenue}}{\text{capital employed}} \times 100\%$$

Multiplication of these two percentages will yield the ROCE, since the two 'sales revenues' will cancel out. In addition to performing an arithmetic check on our ROCE figure, we may also obtain some useful additional pointers about financial performance not directly revealed by ROCE: for instance, about profitability in the case of the profit percentage, and possibly about the intensity with which assets have been used to generate revenue in the case of sales : capital employed.

⇨ From the data in Exhibit 15.3, determine the profit and sales : capital employed percentages for each division.

The subdivisions of each of the previously calculated ROCEs are:

KK Division:

$$\text{profit : sales} \quad \frac{£0.4\text{m}}{£3.0\text{m}} \times 100\% = 13.33\%$$

$$\text{sales : capital employed} \quad \frac{£3.0\text{m}}{£1.6\text{m}} \times 100\% = 187.50\%$$

TM Division:

$$\text{profit : sales} \quad \frac{£3.3\text{m}}{£8.0\text{m}} \times 100\% = 41.25\%$$

$$\text{sales : capital employed} \quad \frac{£8.0\text{m}}{£25.0\text{m}} \times 100\% = 32.00\%$$

Using TM Division's figures for illustration, the 13.2 per cent ROCE obtained earlier can be checked:

$$(\text{profit : sales} \times \text{sales : capital employed}) = (0.4125 \times 0.3200) = 13.2\%$$

Again, we might be tempted to jump to conclusions about the two divisions' comparative performance, but again, this would be dangerous. Before discussing why this might be so, we shall describe one further measure of financial performance.

RESIDUAL INCOME (RI)

Residual income (RI) is defined as: divisional operating profit *less* interest on capital employed. The interest on capital employed is a notional (i.e. imaginary) charge determined by application of an appropriate cost of capital to the amount of capital invested in the division. Referring to Exhibit 15.3, and assuming that HTM plc's 12 per cent target return is appropriate, KK Division's RI is:

	£m
Divisional operating profit	0.400
less Interest on capital employed (12% × £1.6 million)	0.192
Residual income	0.208

RI therefore provides an *absolute* measure of financial performance, whereas ROCE is *comparative*.

⇨ Use the 12 per cent target return along with the other data in Exhibit 15.3 to determine TM Division's RI.

TM Division's RI is:

	£
Divisional operating profit	3.3
less Interest on capital employed (12% (£25 million)	3.0
Residual income	0.3

Once again, a rash judgement about performance should be avoided, but you should note the contradiction between residual income (TM Division higher) and ROCE (KK Division higher); we will return to this point shortly.

ROCE AND RI: STRENGTHS AND WEAKNESSES

Strengths

Both measures possess the same strengths:

1 They are simple to calculate and understand, although RI may be slightly less 'accessible' due to the inclusion of a notional charge.
2 They are based on profit and capital – accounting data which are readily available from the organisation's accounting records.

Despite these fairly compelling practical considerations, ROCE and RI possess some serious limitations.

Weaknesses

Absolute v comparative measure?

Like the internal rate of return which we described in Chapter 10, ROCE, being merely a percentage, does not, on its own, reflect the size of investment, nor does it indicate how much 'better' or 'worse off' is the organisation as a result of a particular division's operations. RI, as an absolute measure, can certainly address the latter shortcoming, but does not itself show the size of investment. On the other hand, ROCE, being a percentage (i.e. a comparative measure), provides a better basis for comparisons of financial performance. Thus neither ROCE nor RI is clearly superior in all circumstances.

Target return/cost of capital

As we saw in Chapter 11, determination of an appropriate cost of capital (or target return) can be problematic. The problems described there in the context of capital investment appraisal apply equally to performance appraisal, and may become particularly acute when comparing two or more divisions.

⇨ In Exhibit 15.3, HTM plc applies a target rate of return of 12 per cent to both KK and TM divisions. Why might this be inappropriate?

HTM plc's two divisions are operating in markedly different economic sectors and geographic locales, and may be subject to different degrees of risk. A different cost of capital may therefore be validly applicable to each in order to reflect these differences. If a single cost of capital is to be applied across the entire organisation, its suitability to all divisions must be assessed with care. Perhaps, in HTM plc's case, 12 per cent is a company-wide figure, reflecting the company's *general* situation, but which might be too low when applied to the specific circumstances of KK Division and too high relative to TM Division.

One reason for the applicability of different target returns to different divisions would be the risk attaching to their operations – a high-risk division having a higher target than a low-risk (*see* Chapter 11). One of the dangers of applying the same target to all divisions is that it might be too high in relation to low-risk divisions, tempting them to pursue high-risk (and therefore high-return) opportunities as the only way of meeting their target. The effect of this is likely to be an increase in risk for the organisation as a whole.

So the apparent disparity in the extent to which the two divisions exceed target ROCE may be due, in part, to shortcomings in the target. In a very diverse organisation such as HTM plc, it might be better to apply target returns specific to each division. Comparisons in performance (if desired) could then be made by comparing the extent to which divisions had succeeded in outperforming their own target. But even this approach is not without problems. By calculating a separate cost of capital for a large number of divisions, we could multiply the general problems discussed in Chapter 11 and, where divisions have no issued capital distinct from the organisation as a whole (i.e. no shares and debentures of their own), we may be forced into an unacceptably subjective assessment.

Use of accounting figures in calculation of ROCE and RI

Although accounting profit and capital employed (the key elements of both ROCE and RI) are readily available figures, their use leads to some difficulties.

Accounting concepts

Profit and capital employed are calculated after application of accounting concepts such as prudence, money measurement and periodicity. Prudence may be difficult to apply objectively and consistently across different divisions: for example, should the same allowance be made for bad debts in every division?

Money measurement will exclude non-monetary items. For example, KK Division's largest asset is likely to be the expertise of its staff, a fact only very incompletely reflected in the accounts via salaries and other staff costs. Compare this with TM Division, which will have a large investment in plant and equipment recorded in its accounts. Thus comparison of the two divisions' performance may be distorted by differences in the type and amount of assets employed and the extent to which the accounts can reflect these differences.

Periodicity stipulates the periodic reporting of accounting information – for example, accounts are typically published annually – but use of one target return to cover a whole accounting year (even where a separate rate is used for individual divisions) may distort performance appraisal by masking seasonal fluctuations. In the longer term, cyclical fluctuations may be hidden by the need for annual figures, resulting in the kind of questionable target referred to in Exhibit 15.4.

ROLLS-ROYCE

The good news from Rolls-Royce is that it has set itself a target of doubling return on capital over the next five years [to 16per cent] . . . the aero-engine industry is extremely cyclical . . . Five years from now may well be the peak of the current cyclical upswing, after which profitability could plummet. In order to cover its cost of capital, Rolls needs to earn an average return of 12 per cent over the cycle. If it only makes 16 per cent at the peak, the prospects of doing so are not great.

Source: Lex Column, *Financial Times*, 30 August 1996.

EXHIBIT **15.4 Cyclical business and financial performance**

Accounting policies

These are the different acceptable methods which may be used to calculate figures such as depreciation. Where divisions keep their own accounting records (e.g. where they are subsidiary companies within a group), differences in their methodology may exist, perhaps reflecting different national accounting requirements. To the extent that such differences exist, divisional figures will need to be standardised before valid interdivisional comparison can be made, and this may have cost implications.

Historic cost accounts

Accounting records are conventionally based on historic transactions. Fixed assets such as plant and equipment, for example, will normally be stated in the balance sheet at their acquisition cost less depreciation written off to date. Using historic costs has the merit of rendering accounting figures accessible to verification by audit, but it can cause problems in performance appraisal exercises. Consider Exhibit 15.5, which provides some additional information about HTM plc.

HTM plc: light engineering divisions

In addition to TM, HTM plc has a second light engineering division in Germany, BW Division. Summarised data for each division for the control period just ended is given below.

	TM Division	BW Division
Divisional operating profit	£3.3m	£3.3m
Capital employed	£25.0m	£40.0m
ROCE	13.20%	8.25%
Residual income	£0.3m	(£1.5m)

The two divisions are identical in every respect save the age of their operational fixed assets – plant, machinery and premises – BW Division's being of considerably more recent date than TM Division's.

EXHIBIT **15.5 Two 'identical' divisions**

⇨ Comment on the difference in ROCE and residual income reported by the two divisions.

Since the two divisions are stated to be identical in every respect save the age of their operational fixed assets, the reason for the difference in ROCE and residual income must lie here. TM Division's older assets will be recorded in the accounts at a lower amount than the newer assets of BW. This is due in part to the write-off of a higher amount of depreciation over their longer working life to date, and in part to the lower acquisition cost of the older assets. Moreover, assuming that all other factors are identical, the annual depreciation charge on the newer assets will be higher than that on the older because of the higher acquisition cost of the former. So our inter-divisional comparison is further distorted.

To overcome this, we might, for performance evaluation purposes, restate divisional assets at their full acquisition cost (rather than at acquisition cost less depreciation to date). Alternatively, we could use current replacement cost, or even disposal value. Although this kind of adjustment might help reduce the distortionary effect of different asset age profiles, it has practical limitations. For example, how likely is it that assets in different divisions will be identical? Can exact replacements be found for assets currently in use? Complete elimination of this problem is therefore unlikely to be possible.

Impact of inflation

Inflation can have quite marked implications for profit and capital employed which have been calculated using the historic cost approach. Consider first the effect of inflation on the profit and loss account: sales are stated at their current value, but costs are almost exclusively based on historic amounts. Thus, if the rate of inflation is high, there may be a severe 'mismatch' of costs and revenues with profit being overstated in *real terms*. Turning to the balance sheet, assets employed will be 'valued' at their historic cost (less any amounts written off for depreciation). If costs are rising, assets employed (and hence capital) will be understated in real terms. Taken together, the effect of inflation on profit and capital will mean an artificial boost for ROCE and RI. Add to this the likely non-uniformity of the rate of increase affecting different costs and between different locations, and we have another potentially serious distortionary influence. Attempts to incorporate the effect of general and specific price changes in accounting statements have been dogged by practical and theoretical problems – for instance, determination of the appropriate inflation rate(s) to apply – and similar attempts in the context of performance appraisal may prove equally controversial.

Definition of 'profit' and 'capital'

As we saw in Chapter 10 when we discussed accounting rate of return, 'profit' and 'capital' are capable of different definition: for example, profit before/after tax/interest, capital including debentures and overdrafts or equity capital plus reserves only? Consequently, comparisons – especially between different organisations – must be viewed with caution: valid comparison requires that the same definitions be used. Ideally, the profit figure used for performance appraisal purposes should be 'finance neutral', i.e. should not be affected by the source(s) from which operations are financed (e.g. payments of debenture interest). We should therefore try, wherever possible, to use operating profit in our evaluation; in other words profit earned by the division's normal trading activities.

Controllability of items included in calculation of ROCE and RI

We discussed this potentially contentious issue relative to financial control in Chapter 13, and the issues raised there are also applicable to performance evaluation, especially where *managerial* performance is being judged on the basis of *divisional* performance (a practice we will discuss shortly). Exhibit 15.6 provides summary profit statements for two of HTM plc's divisions.

HTM plc: summary divisional profit statements

Given below are the control period's summary profit statements, capital employed, ROCE and residual income for KK and TM divisions.

	KK Division (£m)	TM Division (£m)
Sales revenue	3.0	8.0
Divisional costs:		
variable	0.2	0.6
fixed	2.0	3.3
Apportionment of Head Office costs	0.4	0.8
Divisional operating profit	0.4	3.3
Capital employed	1.6	25.0
ROCE	25.0%	13.2%
Residual income	£0.208m	£0.300m

Head Office costs are apportioned to divisions on the basis of each division's sales revenue.

EXHIBIT **15.6 Divisional profit statements**

⟜ Comment on the controllability at divisional level of the items in the summary profit statements in Exhibit 15.6.

Although it may be beneficial to apportion Head Office costs to divisions (to give divisional management an idea of the cost of supporting their activities), it is unlikely that Head Office costs will be under the control of divisional management and should thus be excluded from ROCE/RI computations. The summary profit statements can be redrafted to reflect this:

Summary profit statements

	KK Division (£m)	*TM Division* (£m)
Sales revenue	3.0	8.0
Divisional costs:		
Variable	0.2	0.6
Fixed	2.0	3.3
Controllable divisional operating profit	0.8	4.1
Apportionment of Head Office costs	0.4	0.8
Divisional operating profit	0.4	3.3

In addition, different costs, even though attributable to a specific division, may be subject to differing degrees of short-term control depending on the cost and/or the division concerned. For example, depreciation of some/all divisional fixed assets may be determined according to Head Office policy, and to that extent will not be strictly controllable at divisional level. A similar argument may be advanced in respect of any element of capital employed that is determined centrally. On the other hand, an organisation may take the view that issues of controllability are irrelevant to the question of divisional performance.

For the purpose of *management* performance appraisal using profit-based measures, however, exclusion of non-controllable items is desirable, if only to minimise the chance of dispute and dissatisfaction. Using the controllable operating profit determined above, and assuming all other items to be controllable by divisional managers, the revised ROCE and RI are:

	KK Division	*TM Division*
ROCE	50%	16.4%
Residual income	£0.608m	£1.1m

In this case, there is no change to the relative position of the two divisions. KK's ROCE still exceeds the 12 per cent target by more than TM's, while TM's residual income is still higher than KK's. But suppose management bonuses are linked to divisional ROCE in excess of the target 12 per cent. Use of the revised ROCEs would lead to a significant increase compared to what would have been receivable had the original figures (25 per cent and 13.2 per cent for KK and TM respectively) been used as the basis of bonus calculations.

Divisional v managerial performance

Not only is it desirable to exclude uncontrollable items from management performance appraisal schemes, but it is also necessary to make a *general* distinction between the two. It would be inequitable to assume that a poorer-than-expected ROCE or RI is a sure-fire indicator of poor management, and, like variances, this should prompt investigation rather than instigate a managerial 'blame-fixing' exercise. Many aspects of sound management, such as good employee relations or strategic orientation, may not be immediately (or ever) apparent from ROCE/RI. Different divisions, even if they operate within the same economic sector, may be faced with different local conditions, may have products/services which are at different stages in their life cycle, or may be well-established or growing organisations. As parts of a larger whole, divisions may have different strategic roles – ROCE/RI, being short-term measures with a largely inward-looking perspective, cannot adequately reflect strategic issues (let alone differences in strategy between divisions).

Conflict between performance appraisal and decision making

In Chapter 10, we discussed the use of net present value (NPV) to assess capital investment proposals and saw that it is a discounted cash-flow technique which allows for the time value of money over a proposal's life. Because ROCE and RI are primarily *annual* measures and are non-discounted, a conflict may arise between the investment decision suggested by the long-term decision criterion (NPV) and that suggested by the short-term performance evaluation criteria (ROCE/RI). If a conflict like this arises and if the decision indicated by ROCE/RI is pursued, then the decision concerned is dysfunctional: that is, it is not in the interest of the organisation as a whole. We will use the data in Exhibit 15.7 to illustrate.

HTM plc: capital investment decision by TM Division

KK Division is considering the acquisition of a new computer network next period:

- Initial purchase cost   £125,000
- Estimated life   5 years
- Estimated residual value   nil
- Annual depreciation   £25,000
- Annual net cash inflow Years 1–5 inclusive   £35,000

12 per cent is deemed by HTM plc to be an appropriate cost of capital for appraisal of such purchase decisions. KK Division's budgeted data for next period (*excluding* profit and capital implications of the proposed purchase) is:

Operating profit	£500,000
Capital employed	£1.6m

EXHIBIT 15.7 Performance appraisal v decision making

At the required cost of capital, the proposal's net present value is shown in Table 15.1. Since the net present value is positive, the proposal should be accepted. But how will acceptance affect ROCE?

⇨ Using the data in Exhibit 15.7, determine KK Division's ROCE at the end of next period assuming:

1 that the new equipment in not purchased; and
2 that the new equipment is purchased.

TABLE 15.1 NPV of new equipment

Year	Cash flow	Amount (£)	Discount factor	Present value (£)
0	Initial cost	(125,000)	1.000	(125,000)
1–5	Net cash inflow	35,000	3.605	126,175

| | | | NPV | 1,175 |

KK's ROCE without the new equipment is:

$$\frac{£0.5m}{£1.6m} \times 100\% = 31.25\%$$

If the new equipment is purchased, we must adjust both profit and capital elements of the ROCE calculation and, since we are calculating divisional ROCE at the end of the period, we must also make allowance for the year's depreciation in both of these adjustments. The requisite figures are:

	Profit (£)	Capital (£m)
Without purchase	500,000	1.600
add		
Initial cost		0.125
Cash flow for year	35,000	
less Additional depreciation	25,000	0.025
	510,000	1.700

giving a revised ROCE of:

$$\frac{£0.51m}{£1.70m} \times 100\% = 30.00\%$$

⇨ On the basis of ROCE, what is divisional management's likely reaction to the proposed purchase?

If performance is being assessed using ROCE and if divisional management is acting in an economically rational manner, the proposal will very likely be rejected, despite its positive net present value, as acceptance will reduce the division's budgeted ROCE next period (albeit by a small margin).

Another way of looking at the same situation is to compare the accounting rate of return offered by the proposed acquisition (i.e. the *proposal's* 'ROCE') with divisional ROCE:

$$\text{proposal accounting rate of return:} \quad \frac{\text{average annual profit}}{\text{initial investment}} \times 100\%$$

$$= \frac{(\pounds35{,}000 - \pounds25{,}000)}{\pounds125{,}000} \times 100\% = 8\%$$

which is lower than divisional ROCE of 31.25 per cent and would thus be rejected. If we look at the proposal's impact on divisional residual income, we get:

	Without proposal (£)	*With proposal (£)*
Divisional operating profit	500,000	510,000
less Interest on capital employed (12% × £1.6/£1.7 million)	192,000	204,000
Residual income	308,000	306,000

Since the proposal reduces next period's divisional RI, rejection would be a distinct possibility.

In this particular case, ROCE and RI *both* point to a decision at odds with that indicated by net present value. But to complicate matters further, it is quite possible to encounter a situation where ROCE conflicts with both residual income *and* net present value. Suppose, for example, that the annual cash inflow from KK Division's proposed acquisition was £38,000 (all other factors remaining as stated in Exhibit 15.7), residual income with the proposal would now be:

	£
Divisional operating profit without proposal	500,000
add Cash flow from proposal	38,000
less Depreciation on proposal	25,000
Revised divisional operating profit	513,000
less Interest on capital (12% × £1.7 million)	204,000
Residual income	309,000

which is higher than the RI without the new equipment, implying an 'accept' decision consistent with that indicated by net present value. (Note that the increased net cash inflow will improve the original NPV as calculated in Table 15.1.)

As we have said, the reason for possible conflict between net present value and ROCE/RI lies in the essentially short-term nature of the latter measures. However, if we look at ROCE and RI each year over the life of the proposal (assuming acceptance and no change to any factors other than those relating to the new equipment), a different view of its acceptability emerges, as Table 15.2 illustrates using the original figures from Exhibit 15.7.

TABLE **15.2** **Divisional RI and ROCE over life of proposed equipment**

Year	1 £	2 £	3 £	4 £	5 £
Operating profit	510,000	510,000	510,000	510,000	510,000
Int. on capital	204,000	201,000	198,000	195,000	192,000
Residual income	306,000	309,000	312,000	315,000	318,000
Capital employed	£1.7m	£1.675m	£1.65m	£1.625m	£1.6m
ROCE	30.00%	30.45%	30.91%	31.38%	31.90%

Note: Interest on capital is calculated as (12% × capital employed) each year.

As you can see, compared to the values resulting from rejection, acceptance improves RI from Year 2 onwards, and ROCE from Year 4 onwards. Viewed in this light, management might be less inclined to reject the proposal than if only the Year 1 figures were examined. However, this does not eliminate the very real danger of dysfunctional decisions. If, for example, KK Division's management were served a warning about return on capital of the type quoted in Exhibit 15.1, it is easy to imagine the temptation to reject a project which, although financially viable over its life span, nevertheless has an adverse impact on short-term performance measures.

Interdivisional trading and ROCE/RI

When we discussed the problems of divisionalisation, we mentioned the potential for dispute between divisions which trade with each other. Concentration on ROCE and RI as divisional performance measures may aggravate such disputes and persuade divisional managers to make dysfunctional decisions. The problem here is the effect on divisional profit (hence on ROCE and RI) of the **transfer price** (i.e. the interdivisional selling price). Consider the information in Exhibit 15.8.

HTM plc: trading between KK and TM divisions

Next period, TM Division requires consultancy services which KK has offered to perform, using some of its anticipated spare capacity. KK has suggested that this work be charged to TM at the same rate per hour (£150) as that which is charged to clients external to HTM plc. Each hour's work has an associated variable cost to KK of £30 and no additional fixed costs would be incurred.

A firm of consultants unconnected with HTM plc has offered to undertake the same work as KK Division, but at a cost to TM Division of only £120 per hour.

EXHIBIT **15.8** **Interdivisional trading**

▷ All other things being equal, which offer will be most beneficial in terms of TM Division's ROCE and RI? Will acceptance of this offer be in the best interests of HTM plc?

TM Division's profit-based performance measures will benefit from accepting the lower-cost offer – that is, the offer made by the external firm of consultants – and acceptance of their offer is a perfectly rational decision from TM Division's standpoint (assuming freedom from Head Office instruction to the contrary and unwillingness by KK to reduce its price). But such a decision is not in HTM plc's interest. Leaving aside the possible cost attaching to unused capacity at KK, there is the issue of the relevant cost to *HTM plc* of each option open to TM Division:

	£
Relevant cost per hour if work done by KK Division (= variable cost per hour)	30
Relevant cost per hour if work done by outside firm	120

Thus a rational decision taken by TM in order to minimise its cost (hence optimising its ROCE/RI) is dysfunctional, costing HTM plc an additional £90 per hour. The seeds of dispute are well sown. Head Office might instruct TM to accept KK Division's offer to perform the work at a price of £150 per hour, or might require KK to reduce its price to £120 (or lower), or a compromise solution may be sought. Regardless of the ultimate course of action pursued, divisional autonomy may be undermined, and either or both of the divisions may be aggrieved by the profit impact of what is likely to be (from their point of view) a less-than-ideal solution. Such friction may be extremely damaging to an organisation and a less profit-oriented approach to performance evaluation (e.g. supplementing ROCE with non-financial measures) might help reduce its incidence.

Lack of strategic orientation

ROCE and RI may not only encourage 'short-termism', as suggested by Table 15.1, but may also obscure important strategic considerations, and, in particular, divisions' ability to exploit the strategic advantage of, for example, their size. Similarly, use of percentage figures such as ROCE may mask potential/actual growth. Reduction in capital employed may improve ROCE, but may also stunt growth.

Like variances, ROCE and RI can be useful indicators of financial performance, but awareness of their weaknesses is important – especially given the wide use in practice of ROCE and budgets. A 1993 study by Drury *et al.* found that, of the manufacturing companies who responded to a survey, more than half reported return on capital and 'staying within budget' as being regularly used evaluative measures. One possible reason for the popularity of ROCE is that it facilitates comparisons. Another reason might be that percentages and ratios are commonly used by parties external to the organisation in assessing its performance. It could also be the case that percentage-type measures have a 'convenience' value to managers.

So far, we have discussed performance appraisal in the context of divisionalised organisations (although ROCE and RI can also be calculated for organisations as a whole). We shall now broaden our discussion to deal with financial performance measures with wider applicability, before considering non-financial performance indicators.

OTHER FINANCIAL MEASURES

In addition to ROCE, RI and variances, there are other measures of financial performance which can be used and we shall discuss the more common of these below.

Target profit

The extent to which target profit is achieved is an important indicator of financial health for commercial organisations and may be applied to both profit and investment centres (this importance is reflected in the study by Drury *et al.* mentioned above, where some two thirds of respondents used target profit). But its use may be problematic if performance comparisons are being made. Exhibit 15.9 provides some information which we shall use to illustrate this point.

HTM plc: divisional performance against target profit

For the control period just ended, KK and TM divisions' target and actual profit figures were:

	KK Division (£m)	TM Division (£m)
Target profit for the period	0.3	2.2
Target sales revenue for the period	2.0	7.85
Actual profit for the period	0.4	2.5
Actual sales revenue for the period	3.0	8.0

EXHIBIT **15.9 Target profit**

⇨ On the basis of the figures in Exhibit 15.9, which division has the better performance?

Both divisions have managed to exceed target profit, and, to that extent, both have performed well. We could also claim that, since KK has exceeded target by some 33 per cent compared to TM's 12 per cent, KK's performance is better, but this may be misleading. Comparison of divisional profit performance is shown in a different light if we relate target and actual profit to the related sales effort:

	KK Division (%)	TM Division (%)
Increase over target profit	33.00	13.06
Target profit : target sales	15.00	28.03
Actual profit : actual sales	13.33	31.25

What these figures suggest is that, relative to target, KK's profit increase has been achieved at a proportionally higher cost, whereas the cost to TM has been proportionally lower. This is revealed by comparison of the change in each division's target and actual profit : sales percentages.

Use of profit in this way raises many of the same issues (e.g.controllability and definition) discussed in relation to ROCE and RI.

Target cash flow

Important as profit undoubtedly is, liquidity is also a prime concern for most organisations, and you will recall from Chapter 12 that profitability does not necessarily equate with the availability of cash. Cash flow targets may be set for cost, profit, revenue and investment centres, although in the case of cost centres, these would be stated in terms of cash outflows only (since sales are not attributed to cost centres). One possible benefit of using cash flows to measure financial performance is that they apply to all organisations, regardless of the type of activity undertaken, and removal of profit from the assessment means that cash flows may be particularly appropriate for non-profit organisations.

Target contribution

We saw in Chapter 5 that contribution is (sales *less* all variable costs). As such, it may be a useful indicator in terms of monitoring profitability relative to the volume of sales, without the potential distortion which might be caused if profit (i.e. contribution after deduction of fixed costs) were used. In the same way as for target profit, comparisons of performance in contribution terms really require a relative (i.e. percentage) approach – in this instance, use of the contribution : sales ratio.

Variable costs may be more susceptible to short-term managerial control than fixed costs, so use of target contribution might be seen as a superior performance measure. The danger of using contribution in this way is that fixed costs may be overlooked, or receive less attention than variable – and in many organisations, fixed costs represent the major part of total cost. The financial press contains frequent references such as, 'X Division's contribution to Group profit was £.......', but instead of meaning marginal costing contribution, 'divisional profit attributable to the group' would be a more accurate description.

Other financial measures

A vast array of financial measures is possible – being primarily numerical in nature, accounting information naturally lends itself to 'neat' performance indicators. For example:

- individual categories of cost : sales (profit and investment centres);
- individual categories of cost : total cost (cost centres);
- gross profit : sales (profit and investment centres); and
- sales : fixed assets employed (investment centres).

For divisions which produce their own annual profit and loss account and balance sheet (typically subsidiary companies within a group), even more measures are possible. For example:

- current assets : current liabilities;
- creditors' turnover (i.e. period of credit taken by the division from suppliers of goods and services); and
- debtors' turnover (i.e. period taken by the division to receive payment of debts due to it).

And there are many others, all of which can provide useful information about different aspects of financial performance.

What should be clear is that no single measure is capable of adequately reflecting all aspects of financial performance, nor are all financial measures appropriate to every situation. In addition there are facets of performance which such indicators are incapable of addressing. It is to this area of performance evaluation that we now turn.

Non-FINANCIAL MEASURES

The emergence of the total quality management (TQM) and world class manufacturing philosophies described in Chapter 2 has meant that organisations have become increasingly aware of the importance of measures of non-financial performance, and of quality in particular. In this context, 'quality' refers not only to the product/service being delivered to customers, but also to the quality of inputs used (e.g. raw materials and a well-trained workforce). It should also be evident from the preceding discussion that financial measures, on their own, cannot adequately reflect performance.

The **balanced scorecard** advocated by Kaplan and Norton (1992, 1993) is aimed at encouraging an holistic view of performance, suggesting that, *in addition* to financial aspects, the following areas of performance be examined:

1 customer-focused measures;
2 internal indicators; and
3 indicators of innovation and learning.

We shall discuss each of these categories below.

Customer-focused measures of performance

One of the major benefits of the total quality management attitude of 'get it right first time all the time' has been to emphasise the importance of customer satisfaction – an importance which has added force in light of world class organisations operating in a global market.

▷ Suggest *three* customer-focused performance measures which might be used.

There are many possible customer-oriented measures, such as:

- complaints as percentage of total sales volume;
- average time required to deal with customer queries;
- average time required to deliver customer orders;
- items returned by customers;

- new customer accounts opened;
- repeat business from existing customers; and
- market penetration.

Measures like those above can be plotted over time, so that trends can be seen: that is, the extent to which performance is improving or deteriorating, and the cost of poorer-than-expected performance monitored, for example by keeping records of **external failure costs** (see Chapter 2). Measures of the sort we have quoted above have the advantage of being fairly easy to quantify, assuming adequate records are kept. As with financial measures such as variances and ROCE, however, their interpretation should follow investigation. In addition, many organisations attempt to gauge customer satisfaction by means of questionnaires. A bank, for example, might use this approach to assess customer perception of branch staff's politeness, time waiting for service in branches, intelligibility of communications, and so forth. The collated results of such questionnaires will provide a profile of customer perceptions and may be used as the basis for activities such as future staff training. Although much valuable information may be obtained in this way, there are some problems:

- low response rate such that interpretation is difficult;
- cost involved (e.g. printing and distributing questionnaires); and
- designing the questionnaire (e.g. ensuring the questions asked address issues crucial to both the organisation and its customers).

Internal indicators

Total quality is as much about internal as about external factors and organisations may wish to measure performance in areas such as:

- percentage rejects in production;
- returns to suppliers;
- machine downtime and idle time; and
- staff turnover, etc.

Organisations may also monitor aspects of performance such as health and safety or staff welfare, and may seek staff views about various issues of importance.

Indicators of innovation and learning

In a dynamic environment, organisational flexibility and development are essential, and one of the key facets of TQM is the need for properly trained staff. An organisation may therefore have a policy of ongoing staff training, which should be monitored (e.g. proportion of staff attending relevant training courses within a specified period). 'Learning' could also be reflected in the extent to which new production technologies and work methods are successfully adopted (e.g. robotics and 'dedicated cell' production).

Development and introduction of new products/services should also be monitored. For example:

- proportion of new products/services successfully brought to the market;
- time from inception to market introduction of new products/services; and
- number of developments currently under way, etc.

Kaplan and Norton (1992, 1993) argue that the balanced scorecard offers two major advantages:

1 Its four categories of performance – financial, internal, customer, innovation – span key areas of organisational activity.
2 Consideration of performance under four broad headings should allow management to assess whether improvement in one aspect has been achieved at the expense of deterioration in another.

Non-financial indicators can also have an impact and immediacy not possible with financial measures. For example, target and actual market penetration figures are likely to be more significant to sales staff than ROCE. However, non-financial measures can present problems of their own:

1 *Identification problems* It may not always be apparent which non-financial measure(s) are most appropriate to a particular organisation's circumstances, and the comparative weighting which they receive may differ between organisations. New product development, for instance, may be the lifeblood of a firm which operates in a high-tech market such as computer software, but may be of much less significance than training to a firm providing legal services.
2 *Quantification problems* Some measures of non-financial performance may be difficult to quantify objectively and directly. 'Customer satisfaction', for example, may be assessed by a number of different measures, but the tendency is for these to be indirect. Figures such as customer complaints and number of returns provide useful information, but to what extent can they be taken as indicative of *general* customer satisfaction? Without additional evidence, inferring an improvement in overall customer satisfaction from a reduction in the number of complaints received is debatable.
3 *Interpretation problems* For some non-financial measures, identification of cause and effect may be problematic, causing difficulty in interpretation. We may, for example, strongly suspect that improved training has led to a lowering of the reject rate, or that a reduction in staff turnover is due to better welfare facilities – but how sure can we be?

BENCHMARKING

How can an organisation assess the 'success' of its performance? Trends in different measures may be monitored, or target and actual indicators compared. If the latter approach is adopted, **benchmarking** provides an invaluable method of setting performance targets. Scott (1996) makes the key point that benchmarking 'is about practices or *how* things are done at least as much as *what* level of performance is achieved'. The starting-point in a benchmarking exercise is often the setting of internally generated targets ('benchmarks') against which actual performance and methods can be compared. Internal benchmarking often develops into external, whereby an organisation is identified – preferably one which is not in direct competition – whose performance/method in a particular area is considered to be 'world class', and this is adopted as the target to be achieved.

Information for benchmarking exercises may be derived from a variety of sources such as the published accounts of the world class organisation concerned, the financial press or trade journals, Government statistical sources, or through an interfirm comparison scheme (IFC). IFCs are operated in several economic sectors roughly along the following lines: participating organisations provide key statistics to a central agency (funded by levy on participators in the scheme), which then, under conditions of anonymity and confidentiality, produces periodic listings of appropriate indicators. The Association of British Insurers, for example, produces a quarterly *Statistical Bulletin* of claims results against which an individual insurance company might compare its own claims for major categories of hazard.

⇨ Can you foresee any potential problems in setting performance targets by means of benchmarking?

Setting targets by means of benchmarking provides an organisation with vital information about its performance relative to other, similar organisations – but the process should be undertaken with care. Except possibly in the case of IFCs (although there may be problems even here, as, for example, ensuring uniformity of submission between participating organisations), benchmarking may be fraught with difficulty. In particular, it will be necessary to ensure that the data being used to provide the benchmark is as complete and relevant as possible – which might be problematic where figures are industry-wide averages. Failure to do so may result in damagingly inappropriate targets being set. Moreover, where no IFC exists, commercial confidentiality will curtail the availability and quality of benchmarking information.

VALUE FOR MONEY

What has emerged from our discussion so far is the need for organisations to employ a range of performance indicators, both financial and non-financial, and there is a danger that performance appraisal could become fragmented by an artificial division between the two broad categories of performance measure. Assessment of the extent to which an organisation has achieved **value for money (VFM)** adopts a more overtly integrative view of performance. The basis of VFM is that operations should be *economic, efficient* and *effective* – the 'three Es'. Although these terms are often employed almost interchangeably, there are differences in precise meaning:

- *Economic* Acquisition of resources of the appropriate quality and provision of product/service to the appropriate standard at the lowest cost.
- *Efficient* Achieving maximum output from a given set of inputs.
- *Effective* Extent to which objectives are achieved.

You should note that VFM is a relative concept: that is, it requires comparison of the existing state of things with an alternative, which may well be provided by benchmarking. This comparison is achieved by means of a performance review (or 'management audit'), which will encompass not only inputs and outputs, but also the management information system, asking questions such as:

- Is too much being spent on certain areas relative to their importance in achieving objectives?
- Has money been spent which does not help to achieve objectives?
- Is there a better way of doing things?
- Are controls adequate?

Systematically and regularly assessing an organisation's operations in light of the 'three Es' may possess the benefit of balancing apparently disparate financial and non-financial considerations, and, by including objectives in the review, should help ensure consistency between tactical and strategic performance. But there is a danger that the 'value' and tactical/strategic aspects of VFM may be submerged by the relentless pressure to cut costs, and that the 'three Es' could be assessed on the basis of inappropriate cost data. VFM may also be criticised on the grounds that 'value' is not clearly defined.

NON-PROFIT AND PUBLIC SECTOR ORGANISATIONS

Non-profit and public sector organisations face particular difficulties in the area of performance evaluation, which can be summarised under the following broad headings:

1 *Lack of profit measure* Where an organisation is not intended to make a profit, or where it has no sales, indicators such as ROCE and RI are meaningless.
2 *Nature of service provided* Many non-profit and public sector organisations provide services which defeat simple cost unit measurement: for instance, the 'output' of a local fire service is not readily quantifiable. Although this problem also affects commercial service providers, problems of performance evaluation are eased (if not solved) by the existence of a profit measure.
3 *Financial constraints* Although every organisation operates under financial constraints, these are more pronounced in non-profit and public sector situations. For example, a commercial organisation's borrowing power is effectively limited by managerial prudence and the willingness of lenders to lend, but a local authority's ability to raise finance (whether by borrowing or via local taxes) is subject to strict control by central government.
4 *Political, social and legal considerations* Public sector bodies are subject to political influences in a way not experienced by commercial organisations. For example, local authorities must carry out policies determined by central government and will, in addition, have their own (possibly conflicting) policies to carry out. Because of their nature, public sector and non-profit organisations may be subject to more exacting public expectations and judgement than their commercial counterparts. Thus closure of a local hospital on cost-cutting grounds may be less acceptable than closure of a local factory on the same basis. Public sector bodies are also subject to detailed legal requirements in respect of performance indicators, while private organisations are subject to much less onerous requirements.

These factors have meant that, traditionally, performance in public sector and non-profit bodies was defined almost exclusively in terms of *inputs* – that is, of keeping actual expenditure within budget – but, for all its importance, this is now recognised as inadequate, since it ignores the output side of the equation. It is possible to incorporate 'outputs' in a number of ways, and the influence of commercial practice is very evident. We discuss some of the major developments in this area below.

Introduce the profit measure

One problem was stated to be lack of a profit measure. If this were to exist, then conventional financial measures such as ROCE could be applied. For example, the National Health Service's *internal market* aims to provide just such a measure by subdividing what were formerly unitary health authorities into a number of 'provider' and 'user' subunits which 'buy' and 'sell' various elements of health care services, with target returns (akin to the commercial ROCE) being set for each subunit involved. Although this type of approach may permit application of profit-based performance measures and of quasi-commercial operational and performance criteria, it has been suggested that the subdivisions which have occurred lead to unnecessary duplication, bureaucracy and cost, and that, in any case, a 'profit' motive is inappropriate to a public service such as the NHS.

Value for money

The external auditors of public sector bodies have a statutory obligation to attend to value-for-money issues, and value-for-money studies are normal elements of the annual audit process, the intention being to improve accountability. In non-profit organisations outwith the public sector, VFM is less rigorously applied, but is no less important.

Quantity of 'output'

One way of addressing the traditionally input-based performance evaluation philosophy is to devise performance measures relating to 'output'. A charity, for example, might report on the range of its activities and show the cost of delivering a stated quantity of benefit to an individual recipient or group of recipients. A school may report exam passes by grade and level and calculate pupil:teacher ratios.

Quality of 'output'

Because of the nature of the services provided by many public sector and non-profit organisations, quality is of prime concern. Some quantitative measures (e.g. exam passes in schools) could be viewed as being also measures of the quality of provision. Similarly, the percentage of crimes solved could indicate the quality of policing. Quality assessment can pose particular difficulty to public sector and non-profit bodies. In almost every commercial situation, the consumer is the ultimate arbiter of quality – poor quality products/services will be reflected in falling sales and profits. However, many public sector bodies are in an effective monopoly position (e.g. police provision), so quality issues may be reflected more through public reaction and political debate than through performance measures.

The necessity for reporting performance on a wide front is exemplified by the local authority indicators published by the Audit Commission (*Local Authority*

Performance Indicators). Financial measures include a league table of per capita council expenditure. Quantitative and qualitative output measures are numerous and varied, as the following selection relating to housing suggests:

- average time taken to relet council houses;
- percentage of tenants in arrears of 13 weeks or more;
- rent collected as percentage of rent due;
- percentage of householder planning applications processed in 8 weeks;
- percentage of housing benefit claims processed within 14 days; and
- average length of stay of homeless families in bed-and-breakfast accommodation.

A year-on-year comparison of the first two years' Audit Commission local authority statistics (1994/5 and 1995/6) suggests that the 'poorest' authorities (as measured by the reported indicators) have generally improved performance in the second year, so it might not be far-fetched to suggest that, for these authorities, the need to calculate and report a range of performance measures may have had a beneficial impact. However, the Audit Commission concedes that the measures may mask differences between authorities and that the performance of many authorities ranked as 'average' in 1994/5 has remained fairly static in 1995/6. It may be that the reporting of fairly 'broad-brush' statistics encompassing authorities operating in diverse environments offers little real incentive to 'average' performers.

Measures of the kind listed above suffer from all the same problems of identification, quantification and interpretation as do their equivalents in the commercial sector. These problems may be intensified by the statutory requirement for public sector bodies to produce certain specified performance measures. Laudable though such reporting may be, it can also be argued that 'imposed' measures of this sort (and their implicit uniformity) can mask very real differences between reporting bodies. And the publication of 'league tables' (e.g. of school exam results) could be seen as encouraging dubious comparisons or of fostering a 'competitive' spirit at odds with the nature of many of the services being provided.

Summary

In our discussion of performance appraisal, we have suggested that there is no all-embracing or flawless indicator – perhaps this is as it should be, given the diversity and imperfection of what we are attempting to reflect. We have seen that:

- The main potential benefits of divisionalisation are:
  - taking advantage of specialist or localised knowledge;
  - avoiding management bottlenecks at the centre;
  - speed of reaction;
  - enhanced training opportunities;
  - behavioural.
  - easier organisational expansion/contraction; and
  - managing by numbers.

- A divisionalised structure's major potential weaknesses may relate to:
  - duplication of work;
  - flow of information;

- dysfunctional decisions; and
- lack of functional expertise.

■ **Return on capital employed** (ROCE) is an important indicator of financial performance and is calculated as:

$$\frac{\text{operating profit}}{\text{capital employment}} \times 100\%$$

■ Financial performance may also be assessed using **residual income**, which is defined as:

(operating profit *less* interest on capital employed at an appropriate cost of capital)

■ Return on capital and residual income have a number of drawbacks, which can be summarised as:
- absolute v comparative measure;
- target return/cost of capital;
- use of accounting figures in calculation;
- controllability of items included in calculation;
- divisional v managerial performance; and
- conflict between performance appraisal and decision making.

■ A range of additional financial indicators may be used, including items such as target profit, target cash flow, target contribution and cost : sales percentages.

■ The **balanced scorecard** suggests the following categories of performance be appraised:
- financial measures;
- customer-focused measures;
- internal indicators; and
- measures of innovation and learning.

■ Non-financial indicators may suffer from problems of identification, quantification and interpretation.

■ **Benchmarking** is the process of setting internal performance standards based on best practice by external organisations.

■ **Value for money** reflects the extent to which performance has been economic, efficient and effective.

■ The performance of non-profit and public sector bodies is subject to the following pressures:
- lack of profit measure;
- nature of the service provided;
- financial constraints; and
- political, social and legal considerations.

■ In addition to input-based control of costs, public sector and non-profit 'output' may be measured by:

- introducing the profit measure;
- using value-for-money studies;
- indicating the quantity of output; and
- assessing the quality of output.

In our final chapter, we shall look at the behavioural aspects of management accounting: that is, the extent to which management accounting may affect people's behaviour and how that behaviour may affect management accounting.

FURTHER READING

Cave, M., Kogan, M. and Smith, R. (eds), *Output and Performance Measurement in Government: The state of the art*, Jessica Kingsley Publishers, 1990. Chapters 1–4 contain an in-depth discussion of public sector performance appraisal, and some interesting case studies are provided in chapters 5–9.

Drury, C., *Management and Cost Accounting*, 4th edn, International Thomson Business Press, 1996. Chapter 27 discusses the issue of transfer pricing within divisionalised organisations.

Drury, C., Braund, S., Osborne, P. and Tayles, M., *A Survey of Management Accounting Practices in UK Manufacturing Companies*, CACA, 1993.

Ezzamel, M. and Hart, H., *Advanced Management Accounting: An organisational emphasis*, Cassell, 1987. Chapter 12 discusses divisional performance appraisal with the organisational perspective very much in view.

Horngren, C., *Cost Accounting, a Managerial Emphasis*, Prentice-Hall, 1982.

Jones, R. and Pendlebury, M., *Public Sector Accounting*, 4th edn, Pitman Publishing, 1996. Chapter 12 discusses public sector performance indicators and VFM audit.

Kaplan, R. and Norton, D., 'The balanced scorecard – measures that drive performance', in *Harvard Business Review*, January–February 1992.

Kaplan, R. and Norton, D., 'Putting the balanced scorecard to work', in *Harvard Business Review*, September–October 1993.

Scott, P., 'Benchmarking', in *Management Accounting*, July–August 1996, CIMA.

SELF-TEST QUESTIONS

The following data should be used to answer questions 15.1 and 15.2.

KH Group's Automotive Parts Division reported the following results last period:

	£
Sales revenue	600,000
Contribution	400,000
Operating profit	200,000
Capital employed	2,000,000

The Group's cost of capital is 8 per cent.

15.1 What was the Automotive Division's return on capital for the period?

    A 8%

    B 10%

    C 20%

    D 25%

15.2 What was the Automotive Division's residual income for the period?

    A £40,000

    B £240,000

    C £440,000

    D £1,840,000

15.3 Place a tick in the appropriate box to indicate whether each statement is true or false.

	True	False
(a) Inflation will have the effect of overstating capital as measured by the historic cost accounting convention.	☐	☐
(b) A comparative measure such as ROCE does not indicate the size of investment involved.	☐	☐
(c) Differences in the age and type of assets employed by divisions can distort comparison of those divisions' ROCE and residual income.	☐	☐
(d) In a value-for-money context, efficiency reflects the extent to which objectives are achieved.	☐	☐
(e) Target cash flow may be used as a performance indicator in both profit and non-profit organisations.	☐	☐
(f) A capital investment proposal with a positive net present value must also cause an increase in short-term residual income.	☐	☐
(g) Circumstances may arise where different divisions within the same organisation may each have a different cost of capital.	☐	☐

15.4 Northern Division of BHG Ltd is considering acquisition of an operating fixed asset with the following characteristics:

Initial cost	£500,000
Estimated life	5 years
Annual depreciation	£100,000
Annual cash inflow	£160,000

Without allowing for the impact of the acquisition, the division has budgeted operating profit of £1,488,000 and capital employed of £12,500,000. Using year-end values, what will be Northern Division's budgeted ROCE if the asset is acquired?

    A 4%

    B 12%

    C 15%

    D 20%

15.5 State, and discuss briefly, the argued advantages and disadvantages of a divisionalised organisation structure.

QUESTIONS WITH ANSWERS

15.6 This question tests whether you can:

■ substantiate the calculation of given ROCEs, explain their weakness and recalculate them;

■ calculate divisional residual income and make appropriate performance-related comment; and

■ prepare a range of additional financial indicators and analyse divisional performance.

Northern and Southern Divisions of AAM plc produce roughly the same kind of output – packaging material – and it is therefore considered appropriate by headquarters to compare their performance. For the accounting period just ended, finance staff at headquarters have prepared the following summarised information:

	Northern Division £	Southern Division £
Sales:		
External customers	2,000,000	150,000
Other divisions of AAM plc	60,000	1,800,000
	2,060,000	1,950,000
Variable costs:		
Production	370,800	234,000
Selling and distribution	160,000	78,000
	530,800	312,000
Contribution	1,529,200	1,638,000
Fixed costs:		
Production*	300,000	720,000
Selling and distribution	200,000	110,000
Administration	240,000	160,000
Apportionment of headquarters costs	150,000	280,000
	890,000	1,270,000
Divisional operating profit	639,200	368,000
Divisional capital employed	3,196,000	4,600,000
Return on capital employed	20%	8%

(*Note:* * fixed production costs include depreciation on plant and equipment)

Concern has been expressed at the poor ROCE achieved by Southern Division, especially in light of the recent major investment in new plant and equipment undertaken there, and also compared to the return achieved by Northern Division with very much older operating assets. AAM plc's target return/cost of capital is 10 per cent.

Requirements

(a) Demonstrate how the ROCE for each division has been calculated and suggest an improved approach, explaining your reasoning. As far as the figures permit, restate the divisional ROCEs on the basis of your suggested improvement.

(b) Calculate each division's residual income and comment on divisional performance as revealed by this measure.

(c) For each division, determine the following additional indicators of financial performance:

  (i)   variable production costs : sales percentage;
  (ii)   variable selling and distribution costs : sales percentage;
  (iii)   contribution : sales percentage;
  (iv)   fixed production costs : sales percentage;
  (v)   fixed selling and distribution costs : sales percentage;
  (vi)   fixed administration costs : sales percentage;
  (vii)   controllable operating profit : sales percentage; and
  (viii) sales : capital employed percentage.

(d) Using your answers to (a), (b) and (c), and any other relevant information from the question, analyse the financial performance of the two divisions.

15.7 This question tests whether you can:

■ prepare a range of performance measures relating to a primary school; and

■ analyse the school's performance as revealed by these measures, explaining any reservations about the measures used.

Melthorpe Council is concerned about the performance of Hougham School, one of the primary schools within its jurisdiction and, in order to substantiate this concern, the Council's Education Department has collected the following information regarding the last two school years:

Hougham School	19X3/X4	19X4/X5
School roll (no. of pupils)	502	584
Teaching staff complement	22	21
Support/janitorial staff complement	6	6
Number of classes:	20	20
Teaching days in year:		
Possible	290	290
Actual	279	282
Total pupil absences (in pupil teaching days)	2,259	3,066
Total teaching staff absences (in pupil teaching days)	132	189
Total expenditure:		
Budget for year	£2,400,000	£2,600,000
Actual for year	£2,200,000	£2,900,000

Requirements

(a) Calculate the following performance indicators for Hougham School for *each* of the last two years:

- (i) total pupil teaching days (possible and actual);
- (ii) actual:possible total pupil teaching days (percentage);
- (iii) pupil absences as percentage of total actual pupil teaching days;
- (iv) staff absences as percentage of total actual pupil teaching days;
- (v) pupil:teacher ratio;
- (vi) pupil:non-teaching staff ratio;
- (vii) average class size (number of pupils);
- (viii) total expenditure per pupil (budgeted and actual); and
- (ix) total expenditure variance.

(Express your answers to two decimal places.)

(b) Based on your answer to (a), analyse the school's performance and explain any reservations you may have about use of these indicators as the sole measures of performance.

15.8 This question tests whether you can:

■ calculate divisional ROCE and residual income with and without the effect of proposed capital expenditure projects;

■ assess the acceptability of capital expenditure proposals based on their impact on divisional ROCE and residual income; and

■ assess the extent to which goal congruence is likely to exist between divisions and group in respect of the acceptability of capital expenditure proposals.

The Microprocessor Division of TNF Group is assessing the desirability of three capital investment proposals, details of which are given below.

Proposal A	
Initial cost	£300,000
Estimated life	4 years (zero scrap value)
Annual cash inflow	£100,000
Annual depreciation	£75,000
Proposal B	
Initial cost	£200,000
Estimated life	3 years (£50,000 scrap value)
Annual cash inflow	£90,000
Annual depreciation	£50,000
Proposal C	
Initial cost	£500,000
Estimated life	6 years (£20,000 scrap value)
Annual cash inflow	£95,000
Annual depreciation	£80,000

The Microprocessor Division's operating profit and capital employed (excluding the proposals above) are, respectively, £600,000 and £2,500,000. TNF Group's cost of capital is 12 per cent.

Requirements

(*Note*: In determination of ROCE and residual income, year-end values for capital employed should be used and you should deal with each proposal individually.)

(a) Assuming that divisional performance (and associated managerial bonuses) are assessed on the basis of ROCE, provide calculations to indicate the likely acceptability of each of the three capital investment proposals to the Microprocessor Division's management.

(b) Would the acceptability of each of the three proposals to the Microprocessor Division's management be altered if residual income were the main indicator of divisional performance? Provide supporting calculations.

(c) For *each* of (a) and (b), demonstrate (with supporting numerical evaluation) whether goal congruence would be likely to exist between the Microprocessor Division and TNF Group in respect of each project's acceptability. Explain the reason for any potential conflict between divisional and group viewpoints.

QUESTIONS WITHOUT ANSWERS

15.9 Due to the high level of customer dissatisfaction in the previous year, PG Insurance has tightened quality control procedures within its Motor Vehicle Claims Department during the year which has just ended. Comparative data relating to standard claims for the two years is supplied below. A standard claim is one for £200 or less, and which does not involve any question of liability or coverage.

| | Standard motor insurance claims | | | |
| | Previous year | | Year just ended | |
	Budget	Actual	Budget	Actual
Number of claims submitted	6,000	5,400	6,800	8,100
Total value of claims submitted	£0.8m	£1.1m	£1.2m	£1.8m
Total payouts on claims submitted	£0.7m	£1.0m	£1.0m	£1.6m
Claims settled within:				
5 working days of submission	4,000	4,100	6,120	6,885
10 working days of submission	1,000	200	680	486
30 working days of submission	1,000	800	nil	700
60 working days of submission	nil	250	nil	26
unsettled and in dispute	nil	50	nil	3
Average administrative cost per claim settled:				
within 5 working days	£10	£12	£14	£15
within 10 working days	£25	£28	£30	£32
within 30 working days	£30	£36	n/a	£38
within 60 working days	n/a	£80	n/a	£86
unsettled and in dispute	n/a	£100	n/a	£110

Requirement

Prepare a report analysing the Motor Vehicle Claims Department's performance over the two-year period. Your report should contain a range of appropriate financial and other indicators and should assess the extent to which the tightening of quality control has been successful.

15.10 FDS plc has recently acquired a wholly owned subsidiary company, NJ Ltd, and proposes to use ROCE to assess this subsidiary's performance. For the forthcoming year, FDS plc has set NJ Ltd's target return at 20 per cent (which is FDS plc's cost of capital), and managerial bonuses at the subsidiary will be dependent on the extent to which this target is exceeded.

Requirement

Draft a report to the Board of FDS plc evaluating the proposed performance appraisal scheme and suggesting (with supporting reasons) any improvements which might be made.

Behavioural considerations

MARKS & SPENCER ENDS PERKS FOR WORKERS

Marks & Spencer is to revolutionise its century-old tradition of paternalism in July when it stops providing free breakfasts for staff and abolishes the notion of the full-time employee . . .

Marks & Spencer is widely regarded as one of the country's best employers. For example, it runs a non-contributory pension scheme and provides reduced rates for hairdressing and chiropody.

But it is also regarded as authoritarian. Shopworkers union USDAW says that when all benefits are taken into account, Tesco pays more to employees than M & S, and Woolworths is 'not far behind'.

An USDAW spokesman says: 'At least these companies negotiate and talk to the union. At Marks there is no one to talk to. An individual isn't able to carry much weight . . .

Source: Neasa MacErlean, *Observer,* 21 April 1996.

CAN CARING COMPANIES BEAT THE COLD-BLOODED COST-CUTTERS?

The slash-and-burn corporate leadership of the 1980s, with its concentration on cost-cutting and sackings, is out of date. Long live the caring corporation of the 1990s, whose priority is to develop loyalty among employees, customers and shareholders.

Such companies do much better for everyone in the long run – including their shareholders – than firms focused narrowly on financial measures of short-term profit . . .

These ideas are the central theme of a new book, *The Loyalty Effect,* by Frederick F Reichheld, a director of Bain & Co, one of the best-known US management consultancies . . .

Source: Peter Rodgers, *Independent,* 15 March 1996.

EXHIBIT **16.1 Different organisational cultures?**

INTRODUCTION

Numbers have played a central role in all the preceding chapters. They are, after all, the main medium of communication employed by management accounting. But important as numbers undoubtedly are, it is *people* who are at the very centre of management accounting. Their reaction to the numbers, to the system which generates them, and to the wider organisational setting – all of these are vitally important, and simply cannot be overlooked in the design, implementation and operation of a management accounting system. How, for example, might the different types of organisational culture and managerial style suggested by the two quotations in Exhibit 16.1 impact on operation of a system of responsibility accounting?

OBJECTIVES

When you have completed this chapter, you will be able to:

- appreciate the major influences on organisational culture, its diverse nature and potential impact on management accounting;

- outline the difference between 'theory X' and 'theory Y' styles of management and describe the contingency approach;

- provide an overview of Maslow's need hierarchy, Herzberg's hygiene theory and expectancy theory as views of motivation;

- discuss the behavioural aspects of using budgets and standards as targets;

- enumerate the potentially dysfunctional consequences of using accounting information as a managerial pressure device;

- differentiate between budget-constrained, profit-conscious and non-accounting styles of evaluation;

- distinguish between administrative, social and self controls;

- appreciate the main issues in the participation debate; and

- describe the types of problem which may face the users of management accounting information and suggest how these might be overcome.

ORGANISATIONAL 'CULTURE'

An organisation's culture determines how management accounting techniques are used, how they are perceived, and what patterns of behaviour are intended to result from their use. Unfortunately, a precise definition of organisational 'culture' is difficult to formulate, but it may be loosely expressed as the extent to which an organisation rests on shared value systems or systems of meaning. Imprecise though this may be, organisational culture, as Preston (1995) says, defines 'the limits of currently acceptable behaviour or of current practices and beliefs'; most often, it is unstated, is constantly developing and is all-pervasive within the organisation.

⇨ What sort of factors are likely to have an influence on organisational culture?

Many different influences may be traced, but amongst the most important are the following:

Country/countries within which the organisation operates

The perceived importance of this influence on organisational culture has been reflected in recent years in the way in which Japanese approaches have been extensively studied, and, to a lesser extent, emulated, by Western organisations seeking 'improvement'. Similarly, a slightly 'different' organisational attitude may often be noticed in multinational organisations when compared to single-country entities, which may be a reflection of the impact of several national cultures as against one only. The impact of national differences is nowhere more clearly illustrated than in management's attitude to control. The view in many Western countries is that it is necessary to motivate people to work hard in the interests of their employing organisation. In countries such as Japan, however, such motivation is presumed to be part of an individual's psychological make-up, so that management is less concerned with control and much more with *co-operation*. But we need to recognise that such fundamental differences of view may be largely the result of the way society in general has developed through time in the countries concerned. Attempting to graft a co-operative emphasis onto a traditionally control-oriented approach may thus be less than totally successful with both controllers and those whom they are attempting to control.

Size and diversity of the organisation and its outputs

An extremely large (possibly multinational) organisation and/or one which is widely diversified may exhibit a markedly 'looser' culture than one which is smaller and more narrowly focused. One way in which this sort of difference may be manifest is the 'placing' of an organisation on the centralised–decentralised continuum: that is, the degree of organisational segmentation and the independence of action permitted to segments. A high degree of segmentation *implies* delegation of authority and responsibility for planning, control and decision-making functions within the organisation; but this may occur at the expense of increased bureaucratisation, and managers at all but the very uppermost levels often feel that they have responsibility without the associated authority. Not only might this neutralise much of the benefit of delegation/decentralisation, but it could also reinforce the belief that control is of the utmost importance.

Managerial attitudes and beliefs

We shall discuss the issue of management 'style' shortly. At the moment, we need to be aware that management attitudes and beliefs are closely interrelated with organisational culture – each having a major bearing on the other. The factors which influence organisational culture must, in some measure, pass through the 'filter' of management before their effect on the organisation is apparent. A 'caring' organisation of the type referred to in Exhibit 16.1 may originate with the current 'dominant coalition': that is, the manager or group of managers whose beliefs and values predominate within the organisation. But neither the attitudes nor the membership of this dominant coalition is constant, so organisational culture will change according to who comprises the dominant coalition, what they believe, and how they feel this should shape the organisation.

Organisational culture is central to all aspects of operations. In a management accounting context, it may be reflected in the willingness of an organisation to adopt newer methodologies such as activity-based cost management, or in the degree of participation within the budget-setting process. However, such effects could be seen as rather passive (or even accidental). The notion of organisational culture may be more actively employed – as an impetus for change, for example in the case of Western organisations attempting to copy Japanese practices; or as an instrument of control, for example where operation of, and responses to, control mechanisms are framed in terms of what is considered to be organisationally desirable (or at least desirable to the dominant coalition). Issues of power structure are of crucial importance. It often happens that the 'dominant coalition' will attempt to use the management information system as a means of communicating its own power and influence with regard to the organisational 'ethos'.

The problem with attempting to employ organisational culture in this active way is the difficulty of precise definition. At one extreme, we could say that organisational culture consists of too many nebulous, contradictory and shifting value-sets to be an effective control 'tool'. On the other hand, we could take the view that, by limiting our interpretation of the term 'culture', it may usefully be employed to enhance organisational performance: for instance, by structuring personnel selection procedures so that employees' behavioural traits are broadly consistent with what is deemed to be organisationally desirable. Johnson and Gill (1993) summarise these issues neatly: 'Even if democratically inclined, thoughtful managers find that cultures as systems of control are not capable of being managed mechanistically in the manner of, say, the financial reward system.'

The variety of influences affecting organisational culture means that not only will this differ between organisations, but also *within* the same organisation: that is, 'subcultures' will exist. Whilst these may be beneficial to the organisation as a whole, and might arise in some cases as a matter of conscious policy, it is equally possible that they may operate against the wider organisational interest. Subcultures may, for example, spring from conflict between individual or group norms and those of the organisation (and its dominant coalition), or separate subcultures may conflict with each other. The major implication of this is that the sort of rationalistic organisation upon which much accounting data and its anticipated effect are predicated may bear only a tenuous relationship with reality.

⇨ In what way do the management accounting techniques we have described in this text assume that the organisation is rationalistic?

Implicit to many of the techniques we have discussed has been the existence of stated objectives, communicated effectively to all concerned via clearly defined channels, which also provide the conduit for two-way transmission of financial and other data relating to these objectives. Assessment of effectiveness, efficiency and economy tends to be predominantly one-dimensional: that is, mainly financial or quantitative. In reality, objectives may be ill-defined, may conflict, or may be assumed in a given situation (and thus be open to different interpretation); channels of communication may be blurred, or may be inappropriate to particular circumstances; subcultures may react to certain information in an unpredictable manner.

Perhaps the key aspect of objectives is that they are an attribute of *people* – organisations in and of themselves do not possess objectives. Power structures within the organisation (the dominant coalition) are therefore important with regard to both the setting and fulfilment of objectives. Given the personal nature of objectives, with its associated potential for diversity and conflict, perhaps the notion of goal congruence that we discussed in earlier chapters is unrealistic and the aim of management and management accounting should be *behavioural* congruence – which returns us to the importance of organisational culture in terms of organisationally 'desirable' behaviour. Even where objectives are sufficiently well defined and communicated, three important considerations remain:

1 How are objectives set (and by whom)?
2 How are objectives interpreted by those who set them as opposed to those tasked with fulfilling them?
3 How do we check that the objectives we are pursuing are the correct ones (and how do we amend them if they are not)?

The first two questions depend on the interaction of culture, management style and view of motivation within an organisation. For example, to what extent is participation encouraged? Which subculture(s) represent the dominant coalition? The second and third questions are more intractable. Morgan (1986) distinguishes between *single loop learning* and *double loop learning*, suggesting that correction of deviations from predetermined standards (single loop) may inhibit management's ability to question the validity of the objectives being pursued and to amend them where necessary (double loop). What Morgan is emphasising is, in effect, the need for both feedback and feedforward mechanisms (see Chapter 13).

MANAGEMENT 'STYLE'

Management style and the impact which this may have on relationships between individuals and subcultures is highly significant to management accounting, as it determines *how* organisational culture is applied to planning, control and decision making. Two schools of thought can be identified and these roughly equate with the recent chronology of management theory.

Characteristics of good leaders

Much effort has been devoted to attempting to identify the traits which comprise a 'good' manager – the underlying notion being that, if such characteristics can be successfully identified, then they can inform managerial selection and training processes. Many different definitions of the traits required have been suggested. The list proposed by Ghiselli (1971) is fairly typical: supervisory ability, occupational achievement, intelligence, self-assurance, decisiveness, lack of need for security, working-class affinity, initiative, and so on. The premise on which such lists are based is that there is an optimal set of characteristics which is applicable to almost every situation. This premise itself stems from the belief that the management–employee relationship can be defined in terms of making best possible use of an input resource (i.e. labour). And the question of how these desirable traits should be used depends on the view taken of the management–employee relationship. At one extreme, McGregor's 'theory X' postulates that employees are basically passive and resistant to organisational needs.

⇨ What sort of managerial style is suggested by 'theory X'?

'Theory X' suggests an authoritarian management style, based on a system of reward and punishment, coupled with a depersonalisation of employee–manager relationships. Such an approach might be expected to place heavy emphasis on personal responsibility for meeting financial targets, like budgets, and on the need for strong control action where these are not achieved.

At the other end of the spectrum is 'theory Y', which views employees as ambitious, responsible and responsive to a range of monetary and non-monetary stimuli. 'Theory Y' therefore implies a more relaxed, democratic, participative management style than does 'theory X'. There are two points which we can make about the theory X/theory Y approach:

1 These are the extremes on a range of views, with practice tending towards one or the other.
2 Management styles based largely (though not exclusively) on the theory X end of the spectrum are consistent with Western perception of the need to control individuals.

Contingency view of management

Rather than attempting to define a set of universally desirable managerial traits, contingency theory suggests that management style is a function of specific circumstances. For example, Fiedler (1967) developed a contingency model based on a manager's personality, combined with the degree to which a manager is able to exert influence and control in a given situation. Vroom and Yetton (1973) suggest that the characteristics of a specific problem will be an important determinant of managerial style; the hypothesis advanced is that, the more complex the problem, the more democratic should be management style, whereas an autocratic approach would be suitable to more straightforward problems. House (1971) linked task complexity to satisfaction: the more complex the task, the greater would be the satisfaction derived from performing it, and, in such circumstances, the 'consideration' shown by a manager to subordinates is virtually irrelevant. Empirical findings on contingency theory have been extremely contradictory, ranging from occasional full support (e.g. Chemers and Skrzypek, 1972), through partial support (e.g. Schneier, 1978) to flat contradiction (e.g. Utechet and Heier, 1976). But even if the evidence were fully supportive of contingency theory, there would still remain a practical problem, that of using the theory as a predictive tool to provide *guidance* to managers: that is, what particular style will prove most effective in given circumstances? (This weakness is of particular relevance to much of our discussion later in the chapter.)

THEORIES OF MOTIVATION

If the management accounting system, governed by culture and management style, aims to encourage behavioural congruence, then it is important that we are aware of the kind of factors which might influence the extent to which individuals/subcultures are likely to act in the desired manner. This is the realm of motivation.

Motivation and the hierarchy of needs

Although developed some time ago (1943, 1954), Maslow's view of motivation as the hierarchical satisfaction of needs remains an important milestone in the subject. Maslow's hierarchy is based on 'prepotency': that is, the lower a particular need in the hierarchy, the more important is its fulfilment. Figure 16.1 illustrates the five basic levels of Maslow's need hierarchy.

Self-actualisation needs (e.g. achieving one's potential)

Esteem needs (e.g. desire for prestige)

Love needs (e.g. group membership)

Security needs (e.g. safety)

Physiological needs (e.g. food)

Source: Adapted from Maslow, 1943, 1954

FIGURE **16.1**
Maslow's need hierarchy

Once a particular set of needs has been fulfilled, it will no longer act as a motivator, with the next set in ascending order providing the motivational stimulus, until the top level of the hierarchy has been reached. There have been many refinements of Maslow's hierarchy (e.g. by McClelland, 1975), all of which stem from the same idea – that motivation hinges on the hierarchical satisfaction of needs.

⇨ What implications for management generally might be derived from Figure 16.1?

If the hierarchical view is correct, then we might be able to suggest that motivation is a function of factors such as an individual's position in the organisation and of work conditions. Thus an improvement in physical working conditions may allow lower-level needs to be satisfied, thereby shifting the motivational emphasis to higher-level needs. Although compelling in its approach, the needs hierarchy has the crucial drawback of containing elements which are almost impossible to define and measure objectively.

Hygiene theory

One aspect of motivation which is not really addressed by the needs hierarchy approach is the cause(s) of job satisfaction and its link to motivation. Herzberg (1966, 1976) developed a theory which differentiated between factors causing positive and factors causing negative attitudes to work, as illustrated in Figure 16.2.

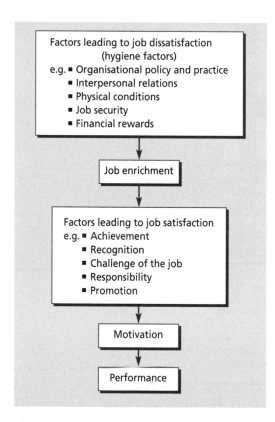

FIGURE 16.2
Herzberg's 'satisfiers' and 'hygiene' factors

The implication of Figure 16.2 is that improving hygiene factors will only prevent dissatisfaction – for motivation to exist, the 'satisfiers' must be addressed (e.g. by examining the intrinsic nature of the job). Like Maslow's hierarchy of needs, Herzberg's theory has had a fundamental impact on management thinking, with the notion of job enrichment assuming central importance. Research (e.g. Schwab *et al.*, 1971) seems to support the effect on performance of 'satisfiers' whilst at the same time casting doubt on that of hygiene factors.

Expectancy theory

Simply stated, expectancy theory proposes that an individual's actions are a function of his or her expectations about the outcome of these actions, coupled with the amount of effort the individual is prepared to expend in order to achieve this outcome (which is dependent on the perceived 'desirability' of the outcome concerned). It could be argued that awareness of expectancy theory may help highlight those factors which affect motivation – information which, if available, would clearly be of value to management. Whilst it is difficult to deny the logic of expectancy theory, this very logic may also be the theory's weakness, as it implies that individuals will act in a strictly rational and predictable manner. Behaviour which appears to an observer to be irrational or impulsive may, in fact, be based on perfectly rational (but internalised) expectancy reasoning – and, of course, there are occasions when behaviour *is* irrational and impulsive.

A prime example of how these views of motivation could affect management accounting can be seen in the operation of a system of budgetary planning and control. If such a system is operated in the overtly 'carrot and stick' way implied by 'theory X', undesirable behavioural consequences may result because:

■ the system threatens the fundamental security need in Maslow's hierarchy, without the satisfaction of which, higher-level needs will not be addressed;
■ the system represents one of Herzberg's hygiene factors and will cause dissatisfaction; and
■ expectations tend to concentrate on the 'stick' rather than the 'carrot'.

Which (if any) of these explanations is correct is debatable. It is probably more important to be aware of the influence on management accounting of such factors than it is to identify which specific factors are of more or less importance in a given situation. (The same point is equally relevant to organisational culture, management style and motivation, since these issues are so closely interwoven as to be almost inextricable.)

BUDGETS AND STANDARDS AS TARGETS

In Chapter 12, we said that one of the purposes of budgets and standards is to provide a target, and that the existence of such a target could have a beneficial effect on motivation. However, as we said at the end of the last section, these management accounting tools, if poorly designed/implemented, may have a demotivational effect. It could be said that, in order to fulfil their functions effectively, budgets should allow managers some freedom to fail without fear of recrimination: that is, to pursue courses of action which, if reality fails to live up to expectations, may cause budget overspends. The practical difficulty with such an approach, however, lies in balancing necessary management freedom against lax performance. It seems to be the case that most organisations find this balancing act virtually impossible to achieve, which, coupled with pressure to use scarce financial resources effectively, will cause adoption of a 'strict' approach to budgetary planning and control.

A further motivational aspect of budgets and standards lies in individual perceptions of their value as targets. 'Strictness' may certainly encourage managers to try and keep expenditure within budget, but this may have little to do with effective target-setting. One way to assess the effectiveness of budgets and standards as targets, is to examine them relative to a manager's **aspiration level**, which is the level of performance that an individual hopes, and will strive, to attain. Research by Stedry (1960) and Hofstede (1968) into the relationship between performance, budgets and aspiration levels suggests that worst performance results from an easy target and that best performance occurs relative to a difficult, but still credible target: in other words, a very 'loose' or very 'tight' budget is unlikely to improve performance. We can illustrate Hofstede's findings using Figure 16.3.

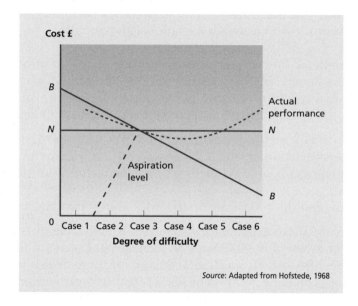

Source: Adapted from Hofstede, 1968

FIGURE **16.3**
Budgets and aspiration levels

In Figure 16.3, the line *NN* represents the level of costs which would occur if there were no budget and *BB* shows the different levels of budget which may be set, ranging from slack (Case 1) to very tight (Case 6). If a very slack budget is set, aspiration levels are low and, although better than budget, actual performance is worse than it would have been had no budget been set. At the opposite extreme, a very tight budget is viewed as impossible to achieve, and actual performance is worse than both budget and what would have resulted had no budget been set. When a budget is set which exactly matches a manager's aspiration level (Case 2), then the effect of the budget on performance is neutral: that is, is neither better nor worse than budget or what would have occurred if there was no budget. As the budget is tightened (Cases 3, 4 and 5), the aspiration level is revised below *NN*, but still in excess of budget, with optimal performance here occurring at Case 4, after which performance deteriorates as the budget's tightness begins to detract from its credibility as a target.

An important implication of this in light of what we said earlier about freedom to fail is that targets which are likely to improve performance will be difficult to achieve, so that adverse variances will frequently result in spite of such improvements. But perceptions of 'difficulty' vary from person to person, and may also vary between different levels within the organisation. Thus, where the person setting and attempting to fulfil budgets/standards is not one and the same, disputes may arise.

However, the imponderable remains. Are individuals 'motivated' by budgets and standards or is performance related to fear of failure (and its consequences)? Or, to apply Herzberg's terminology, are budgets and standards satisfiers or hygiene factors?

MANAGEMENT ACCOUNTING INFORMATION AND DYSFUNCTIONAL BEHAVIOUR

We have already discussed the possibility that behavioural congruence might be a more realistic expectation than goal congruence and suggested the potentially demotivational implications of a 'theory X' application of budgets. What we must now consider is how problems in these areas may be reflected in management actions.

⇨ What adverse behaviour could result from inappropriately designed/used management accounting systems?

Management accounting information is supposed to help managers to plan, control and take decisions. Perhaps the most obvious and general effect of a poorly designed/implemented management accounting system is that it could actually inhibit managers in these actions. Commentators such as Argyris (1954) and Hopwood (1970) suggest that using management accounting information (and budgets in particular) as a pressure device may have the following kinds of dysfunctional results.

1 *Projection* Essentially, this is blame-shifting. Rather than attempting to address any problems which may be revealed, managers will 'pass the buck', blaming other managers, 'the system', 'the computer' and so forth.
2 *Short-termism* Undue pressure on managers to meet financial targets may result in short-term action which improves a particular measure, but which is detrimental to the organisation in strategic terms. We saw one example of this in the last chapter when we illustrated how the impact on short-term ROCE could lead to rejection of a capital investment which, over its life, is financially viable.
3 *Aggression* This could manifest itself in the form of acrimonious disputes between managers about the allocation of budget resources, in the manipulation of accounting figures, or even in outright sabotage of the information system. It can also often be seen in conflict between the accounting and other organisational functions, stemming from the misconception that the purpose of accounting and accountants is to investigate errors and 'wield the big stick'.
4 *Slack* In Chapter 12, we defined budgetary slack as the difference between minimum necessary expenditure and actual/budgeted expenditure, observing at that point that it may arise as a consequence of using incremental budgets.

⇨ How might use of budgets as a managerial pressure device result in budgetary slack?

Managers may react to what they consider to be unduly tight targets by deliberately incorporating an element of slack into their budget estimates as a 'cushion' against unforeseen events and/or the possibility of future budget cuts.

(Production, by managers, of budget figures which are favourable to themselves is also referred to as budgetary 'bias'). Managers may also feel pressured into making impossibly optimistic estimates (e.g. for sales). Dependent on the amounts involved, serious misallocations of scarce budget resources could arise, or wrong decisions be made on the basis of unachievable budget estimates. Attempts to reduce the incidence of slack may, however, lead to major dispute. Evidence of the existence of budgetary slack may be seen in situations where unseemly and frantic efforts to spend money occur towards the end of a budget period, regardless of whether such expenditure is genuinely necessary. Although retaining some budget funds until the end of the financial year may be a matter of prudence, it could equally suggest that the budget was greater than absolutely necessary.

5 *Empire building* This is really an extreme form of budgetary slack, whereby managers attempt to protect themselves from budget pressure by augmenting the resources under their control: that is, a large budget will present more opportunity for future reduction. (Empire building may also result from managerial perceptions about increased status being associated with larger budgets.)

6 *Evasion* If managers view the formal system as being too restrictive or punitive, they may simply ignore it, preferring instead to rely on informal systems and channels of communication. In such circumstances, the formal system will be relegated to the role of routine, but comparatively unimportant, procedure. Another form of evasion is *displacement activity*: rather than spend time on, for example, budget preparation, a manager will undertake other (less essential) work instead.

7 *The ethical dimension* We are becoming increasingly conscious that organisational activities should be ethical. However ethics (like objectives) are not inherent to organisations, but to *people*. It is possible that in very extreme cases of real (or perceived) financial pressure, managers could pursue unethical courses of action. This need not imply that the managers concerned are themselves unethical, as the pressure to act may be so intense that even an overtly unethical action can be justified in terms of 'organisational best interest'. (Question 16.6 provides an illustration of a situation where unethical actions may be suggested in response to financial indicators).

Although they may be imperfect *per se*, the way we *use* accounting measures is most often a major contributory factor towards dysfunctional behaviour. In the last chapter, we suggested that a range of evaluative criteria be applied to performance. Ridgeway (1975) suggests a similar approach, whilst emphasising interrelationships between different measures. Use of financial criteria alone may not only provide a limited view of performance, but may also give rise to conflicts of purpose, and we might ask whether it is sensible to use the same budget for planning, control and performance evaluation. Further, it is debatable whether potentially contradictory and possibly ill-defined organisational objectives can be adequately translated into 'simple' financial expressions such as budgets. It is therefore likely that performance improvements – where they occur – will, at best, be limited when placed in relation to organisational objectives.

STYLES OF EVALUATION AND TYPES OF CONTROL

The requirement for evaluation and control is central to much of management accounting, so it is important that we consider these issues in a wider perspective than that which we have so far taken.

Styles of evaluation

A 1972 study by Hopwood identified three styles of evaluation: budget-constrained, profit-conscious and non-accounting. Budget constrained evaluation is based on achieving operational targets to the virtual exclusion of any other consideration; a profit-conscious style evaluates managers on the basis of their contribution to achievement of the organisation's long-term goals, with operational targets being seen as a means to this end; in non-accounting evaluation, budgets play a relatively unimportant role. Table 16.1 shows the results of Hopwoods's study.

TABLE **16.1 Hopwood's styles of evaluation (adapted from Hopwood, 1972)**

	Budget-constrained	*Profit-conscious*	*Non-accounting*
Involvement with costs	High	High	Low
Job-related tension	High	Medium	Medium
Manipulation of accounting reports	Extensive	Little	Little
Relations with supervisor	Poor	Good	Good
Relations with colleagues	Poor	Good	Good

What is clear from Table 16.1 is that a profit-conscious evaluation style is optimum in terms of all the variables examined, but Hopwood is careful to make the point that this may differ between organisations and between tasks within the same organisation. A similar study by Otley (1978) reported that accounting information was a preferable performance indicator, and that the style of evaluation had no material effect on job tension and performance. Otley reconciled this apparent contradiction in findings by distinguishing between style and context – style referring to the importance of accounting data in evaluation, and context relating to management interdependency and the uncertainty of the task being performed. The conclusion, supported by the work of, amongst others, Imoisili (1989), was that, in situations where managers felt they were in less than total control (e.g. in very uncertain situations), a budget-dominated approach was likely to be unsuitable.

Types of control

Since a large part of management accounting is aimed at control, we need to be aware of the different types of control which exist within an organisation, and how these might react with each other. Hopwood (1974) identified three control influences which we introduced briefly in Chapter 13 – administrative, social and self – and suggested that their interrelationship is a vital element of the control situation in any organisation.

Administrative control

Administrative control is that which is deliberately designed to control the behaviour of individuals, groups, and possibly other organisations.

⇨ What major contribution to administrative control does management accounting make?

573

Budgets, along with the detailed figures which support them, their emphasis on goal congruence, and the probability that they are operated within a responsibility accounting framework, can be seen as an important form of administrative control. Indeed, it is possible to argue that accounting (and accountants) have concentrated on this sort of technical control to such an extent that its interaction with other controls (and possibly even the existence of other controls) has been largely overlooked.

Every organisation has administrative controls – rules and regulations, as contained, for example, in the budget manual – and it is impossible to gainsay the need for such mechanisms. One problem with administrative controls is that adherence to their requirements (e.g. by remaining strictly within budget) may become an end in its own right, which could ultimately defeat the reason for their existence. Short-termism in the face of strict performance or budgetary criteria could be seen as an example of this. A further difficulty, as Perrow (1967) has observed, is that adherence to rules and regulations becomes an effective impossibility in uncertain or ambiguous situations, and the amount of discretion allowed to managers in applying rules and regulations should depend on the unpredictability of the situation. This could make assessment of the organisational 'desirability' of behaviour extremely difficult.

Less overt administrative controls may be employed in order to help ensure 'desirable' behaviour by managers: for example, use, during recruitment, of selection procedures which attempt to identify applicants whose behavioural traits are consistent with organisational norms. The provision of breakfasts by Marks & Spencer referred to in Exhibit 16.1 could be seen in this light. Training courses (especially in the early stages of employment) may be used to mould behaviour in the organisational interest.

Although most management accounting information may be viewed as overt administrative control, we could argue that the provision of information is itself a form of control. Remember that, in Chapter 1, we defined the overall purpose of management accounting as being the provision of useful information to management. It is possible that selective disclosure of information to and by management – whether in the form of budgets or more ad hoc reports – could enhance goal (or at least behavioural) congruence by raising awareness of the different problems being faced by the organisation. This is not to claim that information provision is a panacea, but it does suggest a degree of flexibility in our approach to who receives what information and under which circumstances.

Pervasive and important as they are, administrative controls do not exist in isolation – they exist to influence behaviour – so we must consider their interaction with social and self controls.

Social and self controls

The extent to which administrative controls are effective depends on our recognition of the fact that social relationships exist, and that individuals and groups of individuals have different values, expectations and motivations. The dividing line between the less overt administrative controls we described above and social controls is blurred, but is perhaps best characterised by the degree of consciousness and formality. Social controls, as exerted for example by the group to which an individual belongs, will tend to be less conscious and more informal than administrative controls. In general, what we need to appreciate about social controls is their complexity and the fact that they will affect all parties in a control situation. Consider the different views about Marks & Spencer expressed in Exhibit 16.1. Perceptions about whether the firm is a 'good' or 'authoritarian' employer may stem from the interaction between administrative and social controls. If, as seems probable, these opinions are held by different groups within the organisation, then it is not implausible to suggest that administrative controls might affect the behaviour of these groups in markedly different ways.

Self control, in an organisational context, can be defined as the extent to which an individual *internalises, identifies with or complies with* administrative and social controls: that is, adopts them as being personally desirable. Compliance, according to Kelman (1961), comes from the desire to obtain a reward or avoid a punishment; identification, from the desire to be like others who are significant to the individual; and internalisation, from the personal *adoption* of the values and norms held by these 'significant others'. The reaction of individuals to administrative and social controls is highly complex, comprising a blend of personal motivation and psychology, management style and organisational culture. Perhaps the best that can be said is that, even when individuals appear to be acting in harmony with administrative and social controls, their underlying state of mind may be quite different to that implied by their actions.

In the next section, we will discuss the question of participation, which arguably provides the potential for a subtle blend of administrative, social and self controls. Their diffuse and possibly conflicting interrelationship may go some way towards explaining contradictory findings about the effectiveness of participation.

THE PARTICIPATION DEBATE

The Maslow hierarchy of needs along with Herzberg's satisfier/hygiene factor analysis suggest a more democratic organisational culture and management style: that is, tending more towards McGregor's 'theory Y'.

⇨ How might a participative approach be consistent with Maslow's hierarchy of needs in Figure 16.1?

We could say that participation (e.g. in budget-setting) will help satisfy the higher-level needs in Maslow's hierarchy, such as love, esteem needs and possibly self-actualisation. We might even suggest that participation could be a form of job enrichment which, by mitigating the negative impact of Herzberg's hygiene factors, might strengthen the positive effect of satisfiers.

If we accept the proposition that participation may be motivationally beneficial, or may increase satisfaction at work, then we need to consider the factors which might have a bearing on effective participation:

1 *Organisational culture and structure* The 'strength' or 'weakness' of an organisation's culture may be reflected in the extent to which participation is actively encouraged. One way in which organisational culture may be expressed is through that organisation's structure. Thus, highly centralised or hierarchical organisations may have a 'stronger' culture than those which are more decen-

tralised or less pyramidal. Research by Bruns and Waterhouse (1975) suggests that managers in the latter type of organisation perceive their level of participation to be greater than that enjoyed by managers in more centralised structures.

2 *Nature of the task being performed* Tasks which are repetitive, standardised, are highly constrained (e.g. by technology), or which require speed and accuracy for effective performance may, as Hopwood (1974) has observed, be better suited to a more authoritarian approach than tasks which are open-ended, ad hoc or which require flexibility in approach. However, Hopwood does make the point that the benefit of participation in the latter case may be 'more immediate and more narrowly economic . . . than more authoritarian styles'. The force of this is that increased participation is not being equated automatically with improved motivation or satisfaction.

3 *Personality considerations* Certain individuals thrive on the challenges presented by participation, while others react in quite the opposite way: Vroom (1960) found that highly authoritarian individuals were not greatly affected by participative processes. We also need to consider the preference match between different subordinate/superior combinations: Hopwood (1974) makes the comment that satisfaction may be greater in situations where an authoritarian or participative superior is dealing with a like-minded subordinate.

But is participation effective in improving performance? Research findings are contradictory. Chenhall (1986) confirms the view that participation improves job satisfaction, but a 1988 study by Chenhall and Brownell suggests that this will not automatically result in improved performance. Locke (1967), on the other hand, found a negative correlation between participation and performance.

⇨ What kind of difficulties may arise if a participatory approach is implemented without adequate consideration of the factors discussed above?

Earlier in this chapter, we mentioned the possible use of organisational culture as a control device. This might be attempted by adding a participatory veneer to an authoritarian reality, the result being *pseudo-participation*: for example, meetings which can achieve little or nothing without authority from the top, and so degenerate into tortuous, unresolved discussion. The same sort of deadlock may arise if participation is applied in situations which do not really warrant it (e.g. where instant, decisive action is required), or where some/all of the individuals concerned either do not support it or believe that it is already adequate, as the quotation in Exhibit 16.2 illustrates.

Another potential problem with participation is that any improvement in motivation or satisfaction may be achieved at the cost of poorer performance, as managers incorporate slack into the targets which they participate in setting.

We shall leave Johnson and Gill (1993) to summarise the participation debate:

> The effects of participation are varied and very complex, since they are influenced by the interaction of an array of social, psychological and organisational factors. One thing, however, soon becomes apparent: it is naive to assume that the opportunity to participate in objective-setting will automatically result in the controlled becoming more highly motivated to achieve the resulting objective(s).

ACCOUNTING FOR TASTE

Temperatures are rising in the cool-headed world of accountancy. Scenes rarely witnessed among the nation's number-crunchers have been unfolding at Lincoln's Inn Fields, home to the ACCA, the body representing almost 50,000 certified accountants.

The trigger was the extraordinary general meeting of members just forced by dogged dissident professor Prem Sikka from the University of Essex. He's waging a strident campaign for greater democracy and – dare one say it – accountability within the organisation.

Bent on reform, Sikka would need a calculator to tot up his angry critics but with postal ballots heavily against him, the meeting should have allowed everyone to let off steam before tea and biscuits . . .

Source: 'Observer', *Financial Times*, 11 November 1996.

EXHIBIT **16.2 Participative conflict**

HUMAN INFORMATION PROCESSING (HIP)

Implicit in the provision of management accounting information is the belief that its recipients can use it effectively. Although there has been considerable interest in HIP relative to auditing, comparatively little has been done to date in a management accounting context. Yet, if management accounting information is to achieve its objective of being useful to management, we should be aware of the problems which may be experienced by the individuals who are trying to process it.

⇨ What aspects of management accounting information might cause problems to its users?

The main problems are as follows:

- volume of information;
- complexity of information; and
- need to apply personal judgement to information.

In addition, but not necessarily arising solely from management accounting information, will be the effect on its users of work pressures such as stress, crisis and conflict.

'Information overload' is a common managerial complaint, which seems to be heard increasingly often. In part, this is the result of the growing complexity of organisations' environments, and to this extent may be unavoidable. However, it may also be due partly to the increased *availability* of information. There may be a tendency to misuse improving information technology to produce additional information for no better reason than that it can be produced, irrespective of management requirements. It is also possible that use of information provision as a form of administrative control could have the perverse effect, through overprovision, of weakening such control. Unnecessary volume can prove confusing and might, in extreme cases, lead to the dysfunctional consequence of evasion. It is therefore important that management accounting information is to the point.

Management accounting information is potentially complex and there is a danger that it may therefore not be understood. Elimination of unnecessary volume may reduce complexity, as may imaginative presentation: Moriarity (1979) used schematic faces to represent 13 different financial variables, with each of the faces' features representing a different variable; and a study by Stock and Watson (1984) showed the performance of subjects using schematic faces to be superior to that of subjects using tabulated information. It is also important that the accountant acts as an educator, explaining the purpose and meaning of reports. If this is done well, it may enhance the value of accounting information by reducing the mystification and intimidation often experienced by non-accountants when faced with financial data.

Possibly the greatest problem faced by the user of management accounting information lies in the need to apply personal skill and judgement in its interpretation and use – even assuming the information is understood. Faced with a complex or uncertain situation, individuals will employ *heuristics* (i.e. 'rules of thumb') and biases in analysis. Accounting heuristics such as linear cost behaviour within the relevant range may transmit themselves to information recipients as statements of fact. This may either destroy the information's credibility or distort the recipient's own judgement. It may be helpful to explain what heuristics have been applied in a particular situation, so that information recipients are aware of the fact and can try to assess the resultant impact (training may be valuable here).

Work pressures will also have a bearing on how management accounting information is used. Time pressure, for example, might contribute to poor use of information every bit as much as lack of understanding. Other influences will be at play, too. For example, a study by Shapiro and Gilbert (1975) indicated that, when under stress, decision makers tend to consider a smaller range of alternatives.

What all of this suggests is that we cannot properly separate the users of management accounting information from provision of that information – a fact which should be borne very much in mind when designing information systems.

SUMMARY

In this chapter, we have discussed the organisational and behavioural context of management accounting. Although we have been able to provide only an overview of the issues involved, it should be clear that they are complex and frequently contradictory – but then, so are the people and organisations which we are attempting to describe. Perhaps the most important conclusion which can be drawn from our discussion is the need for a flexible approach. We have seen that:

■ Organisational culture is a nebulous concept, which is influenced by factors such as:
  – country within which the organisation operates;
  – size and diversity of the organisation and its outputs; and
  – managerial attitudes and beliefs.

■ Conflict between subcultures may mean that the rationalistic organisation assumed by management accounting techniques does not exist.

■ 'Theory-X' management is based on rewards and punishments, 'theory-Y' on democracy and participation.

■ The contingency approach to management is based on adapting managerial style to suit specific circumstances.

■ Maslow explains motivation in terms of satisfaction of a hierarchy of needs, ranging from physiological at the lower end to self-actualisation at the higher.

■ Herzberg attempts to assess job satisfaction in terms of satisfiers and hygiene factors.

■ Expectancy theory postulates that motivation stems from individual expectations about the outcome(s) of particular actions.

■ Use of the budget to 'reward' and 'punish' managers may inhibit their actions.

■ The extent to which budgets and standards are successful as targets depends on their relationship with an individual's **aspiration level**.

■ In addition to inhibiting managerial action, a 'theory-X' use of accounting measures may have other dysfunctional consequences:
  – projection;
  – short-termism;
  – aggression;
  – budgetary slack;
  – empire building;
  – evasion; and
  – potentially unethical actions.

■ Hopwood's three styles of evaluation are: budget-constrained; profit-conscious; and non-accounting. A budget-constrained style is unsuitable in uncertain situations.

■ Controls can be divided into administrative, social and self controls – the interaction of these must be recognised if control is to be effective.

■ Participation is not a cure-all and its effectiveness depends on factors such as:
  – organisational culture and structure;
  – nature of the task being performed; and
  – personality considerations.

■ Management accounting information should be guided by consideration of human information processing factors: that is, the potential difficulties which the recipient may experience when attempting to use information.

FURTHER READING & REFERENCES

Argyris, C., *The Impact of Budgets on People*, Controllership Foundation, 1954.

Ashton, D., Hopper, T. and Scapens, R. (eds), *Issues in Management Accounting*, 2nd edn, Prentice Hall International, 1995. In addition to the section by Preston (see below), chapters 3 and 11 are of particular relevance to our discussion in this chapter.

Bruns, W. and Waterhouse, J., 'Budgetary control and organisational structure', *Journal of Accounting Research*, Autumn 1975.

Chemers, M. and Skrzypek, G., 'Experimental test of the contingency model of leadership effectiveness', *Journal of Personality and Social Psychology*, 24, 1972.

Chenhall, R., 'Authoritarianism and participative budgeting: a dyadic analysis', *The Accounting Review*, 1986.

Chenhall, R. and Brownell, P., 'The effect of participative budgeting on job satisfaction and performance: role ambiguity as an intervening variable', *Accounting, Organisations and Society*, 13(3), 1988.

Emmanuel, C., Otley, D. and Merchant, K. (eds), *Readings in Accounting for Management Control*, Chapman & Hall, 1995. Chapters 1–7, along with chapters 10–12, contain some interesting discussion about organisational and behavioural aspects of management accounting.

Ezzamel, M. and Hart, H., *Advanced Management Accounting: An organisational emphasis*, Cassell, 1987.

Fiedler, F., *A Theory of Leadership Effectiveness*, McGraw-Hill, 1967.

Ghiselli, E., *Explorations in Management Talent*, Goodyear Publishing, 1971.

Herzberg, F., *Work and the Nature of Man*, World, 1966.

Herzberg, F., *The Managerial Choice: To be efficient and to be human*, Dow Jones–Irwin, 1976.

Hofstede, G., *The Game of Budget Control*, Tavistock, 1968.

Hopwood, A., 'Leadership climate and the use of accounting data in performance evaluation', in *Accounting Review*, July 1974.

House, R., 'A path–goal theory of leader effectiveness', *Administrative Science Quarterly,* 16, 1971.

Imoisili, O., 'The role of budget data in the evaluation of managerial performance,' in *Accounting Organisations & Society,* 14(4), 1989.

Johnson, P. and Gill, H., *Management Control and Organisational Behaviour*, Paul Chapman Publishing, 1993.

Kelman, H., 'The processes of opinion change', *Public Opinion*, 25, 1961.

Locke, E. and Bryan, J., *Goals and Intentions as Determinants of Performance Level*, American Institute for Research, 1967.

McClelland, D., *Power: The inner experience*, Irvington, 1975.

McGregor, D., *The Human Side of Enterprise*, McGraw-Hill, 1960.

Maslow, A., 'A theory of human motivation', *Psychological Review*, 50, 1943.

Maslow, A., *Motivation and Personality*, Harper & Row, 1954.

Morgan, G., *Images of Organisation*, Sage, 1986.

Moriarity, 'Communicating financial information through multi-dimensional graphics', *Journal of Accounting Research*, Spring 1979.

Otley, D., 'Budget use and managerial performance', in *Journal of Accounting Research,* 16(1), 1978.

Perrow, C., 'A framework for the comparative analysis of organisations', *American Sociological Review*, 32, 1967.

Preston, A., 'Budgeting, creativity and culture', in Ashton *et al.* (eds), *Issues in Management Accounting*, 2nd edn, Prentice Hall International, 1995.

Ridgeway, V., 'Dysfunctional consequences of performance measurement', *Information for Decision Making* (A. Rappaport, ed.), 1975.

Schneier, C., 'The contingency model of leadership: an extension to emergent leadership and leader's sex', *Organisational Behaviour and Human Performance*, 21, 1978.

Schwab, D., DeVitt, H. and Cummings, L., 'A test of the adequacy of the two-factor theory as a predictor of self-report performance effects', *Personnel Psychology*, 24, 1971.

Shapiro, H. and Gilbert, M., *Crisis Management: Psychological and sociological factors in decision making*, Human Sciences Research Inc., 1975.

Stedry, A., *Budget Control and Cost Behaviour*, Prentice-Hall, 1960.

Stock, D. and Watson, C., 'Human judgement accuracy, multidimensional graphics, and humans versus models', *Journal of Accounting Research*, Spring 1984.

Utechet, R. and Heier, W., 'The contingency model and successful military leadership', *Academy of Management Journal*, 1976.

Vroom, V., *Some Personality Determinants of the Effects of Participation*, Prentice-Hall, 1960.

Vroom, V. and Yetton, P., *Leadership and Decision Making*, University of Pittsburgh Press, 1973.

CHAPTER 16 • BEHAVIOURAL CONSIDERATIONS

SELF-TEST QUESTIONS

16.1 Statements I, II and III relate to budgets and aspiration levels:

I   Aspiration levels cannot be increased in the face of a strict budget.

II Aspiration levels can be increased to meet a strict, but credible budget.

III Setting the budget equal to aspiration levels implies that adverse variances will always arise.

Which of the statements above is true?

A I only
B II only
C I and III only
D II and III only

16.2 For each of the following statements, place a tick in the appropriate box to indicate whether it is true or false.

	True	False
(a) A 'theory-X' management style implies that employees are responsive and responsible.	☐	☐
(b) Improvement in the hygiene factors identified by Herzberg will improve satisfaction at work.	☐	☐
(c) A profit-conscious style of evaluation takes a broader and longer-term view than a budget-constrained style.	☐	☐
(d) A 'theory-Y' view implies that accounting information should be used as a managerial pressure device.	☐	☐
(e) Heuristics are used to simplify complex realities.	☐	☐
(f) Participation will not be effective in every situation.	☐	☐
(g) Expectancy theory would support the linking of promotion to consistent outperformance of financial targets.	☐	☐
(h) A contingency approach suggests unvarying application of predetermined administrative controls.	☐	☐

16.3 In the tenth month of the accounting year, a budget-holding manager, commenting on her budget, stated, 'We'd better spend it or we'll lose it.' Which of the following does this comment reflect?

A Budgetary slack
B Evasion
C Projection
D Aggression

16.4 From the list of words and phrases provided, complete the paragraph below.

Effective participation depends on organisational ...., the nature of the task being performed and the .... of the individuals concerned. In a highly .... situation, or in one where .... is vital, participation may be .... Moreover, if participation conflicts with organisational culture and/or management style, ... may occur, with .... consequences. Participation may be .... in situations characterised by a high degree of .... and where the individuals concerned are .... to a participative approach.

pseudo-participation	*effective*
personality	*responsive*
culture and structure	*dysfunctional*
uncertainty	*structured*
speed of action	*ineffective*

16.5 A Health Board has a Capital Projects Committee, at which the desirability – financial and otherwise – of various capital proposals is discussed and decided upon. More often than not, the committee's decisions are reversed by the Health Board's Chief Executive. In these circumstances, what do the deliberations and decisions of the Capital Projects Committee represent?

    A Empire building
    B Goal congruence
    C A Herzberg 'satisfier'
    D Pseudo-participation

QUESTIONS WITH ANSWERS

16.6 This question tests whether you can:

- appreciate the organisational and behavioural issues involved in use of an accounting measure of performance; and

- suggest how the chance of such situations might be avoided in future.

AMI plc operates a scheme which links divisional managers' bonus payments to achievement of budgeted return on capital. Towards the end of the current financial year, management at the company's Electrical Wholesale Division realise that their target return is unlikely to be achieved unless action is taken. At a meeting of the division's management team, all of whose bonuses depend on achieving budgeted return on capital, the following suggestions for remedying the situation are proposed.

Divisional General Manager's suggestion
'We are due to deliver a large consignment to a customer right at the start of next financial year. If we reschedule this delivery so that we can process the associated invoice in the current year, budgeted return will be achieved.'

Divisional Accountant's suggestion
'Head Office allows me considerable freedom to adopt the accounting policies most suitable to our division. If I change the method of depreciation used for our fixed assets and

reduce the provision for doubtful debts, profit will be increased sufficiently to achieve budgeted return. I can easily persuade Head Office that these changes are necessary, as no one there is sufficiently knowledgeable about our division's business to argue the point.'

Warehousing Manager's suggestion
'As you know, our Brinkley warehouse requires urgent repair work to its roof, but the tarpaulins seem to be holding reasonably well and I'm sure the work can wait until next financial year. The resulting water-damaged stock can be sold at a deep discount next year and, although the water leakage causes some difficulties for staff, I'm sure I can smooth this out.'

Requirements

(a) As a neutral observer at the meeting, draft a report to the Electrical Wholesale Division's General Manager outlining:

(i) the main organisational and behavioural issues involved; and

(ii) possible implications for the division and AMI plc if the proposals are implemented.

(b) What steps might be taken to reduce the possibility of such a situation arising in future? Explain the rationale for your suggestions.

16.7 This question tests whether you can explain how differing organisational and behavioural factors may result in different approaches to the use of management accounting information.

Highfield Building Society and the Holt Advertising Agency provide very different services to their clients, but both organisations make extensive use of management accounting information.

Requirement
Explain how organisational and behavioural factors might influence the building society to take a different approach in its use of management accounting information compared to that adopted by the advertising agency.

16.8 This question tests whether you can assess the dysfunctional potential of stated budget regulations.

The following quotations have been extracted from Bidebury Council's Budget Manual:

1 'Section heads are personally responsible for meeting their section's budget.'

2 'Budget performance reports will be prepared monthly by the Finance Department, and section heads must report personally to the Finance Director on any overspend in excess of £10,000 in a given month.'

3 'Approval of next year's budget estimates by the Council's Finance Committee depends upon adherence, as far as possible, to previous budgets; or, where such adherence has not been possible, upon adequate explanation of the reason(s).'

Requirement
Discuss the dysfunctional consequences which may result from the regulations quoted.

QUESTIONS WITHOUT ANSWERS

16.9 Requirements

(a) With reference to aspiration levels, discuss the performance implications of setting an ideal standard and an attainable standard.

(b) Discuss the extent to which participation in planning, control and decision making procedures may be beneficial.

16.10 Exhibit 16.3 shows a typical monthly budget control report produced by TMM Ltd's computerised management accounting system.

TMM Ltd: sample monthly budget control report

	Budget for year £	Actual: Month 9 For the month £	For the year to date £
Sales revenue:			
Home market	100,000,000	14,000,000	64,000,000
Export market	80,000,000	6,000,000	41,000,000
	180,000,000	20,000,000	105,000,000
Cost of sales	55,000,000	7,000,000	38,000,000
Administration expenses:			
Head Office	8,000,000	1,000,000	5,000,000
Northern Division	3,000,000	400,000	1,900,000
Southern Division	4,000,000	800,000	2,900,000
Selling expenses:			
Advertising	16,000,000	4,000,000	11,000,000
Promotional	5,000,000	300,000	4,100,000
Distribution	20,000,000	3,000,000	15,100,000
	111,000,000	16,500,000	89,000,000
Net profit before taxation	69,000,000	3,500,000	16,000,000

EXHIBIT **16.3** Monthly budget control report

The following additional information is available:

1 Each month, a report using the same format as that illustrated in Exhibit 16.3 is sent to every budget-holding manager within the company. This is the only financial information received by managers.

2 Functional budgets are prepared by the relevant managers and are then submitted to TMM Ltd's Finance Director, who makes whatever amendments he judges to be necessary before drafting a master budget for presentation to the company's board of directors. Once the board has made any additional amendments, the master budget

is approved, disaggregated into functional budgets by the Finance Director, and distributed to individual managers to implement.

3 Several members of the company's management team have expressed concern about operation of the budget system and have communicated their concern to the Chairman. Responding to the concerns expressed, the Chairman has asked you to investigate.

Requirement

Prepare a report for TMM Ltd's Chairman analysing the company's budgetary procedures and suggesting improvements which might be made.

16.11 Consider the press cutting in Exhibit 16.4.

CLUB MED TURNS ITS BACK ON IDEALISM OF THE PAST

Club Méditerranée, the French leisure group, reached the end of an era over the weekend as it closed the final chapter on its idealistic origins and began preparing for a future of tougher professional management.

Its new chief executive, Mr Philippe Bourguinon, who starts work this week, faces a challenge not unlike that in his current job as chairman of Euro Disney, the theme park outside Paris. He must steer a valuable brand through financial difficulties, preserving its qualities while adapting them to a different era.

The holiday village operator unveiled 1995–96 losses last week of FFr 743m (£130.3m) after taking provisions of FFr 820m to support a wide-ranging restructuring.

Mr Bourguignon takes over from Mr Serge Trigano, son of one of the founders of a business launched nearly 50 years ago, and which has become a central part of French culture and one of the country's best-known and most widely-copied exports . . .

Club Med's internal management has arguably evolved rather less rapidly than its activities – and was reluctant to risk souring the informal corporate atmosphere by taking sufficiently tough decisions at a time of intensifying competition and difficult economic conditions.

The convivial Mr Trigano himself encapsulates the Club's founding spirit. He has spent much of his career in the business, and managed to succeed his father in 1993 as chairman even though he owns no shares (and his father only 0.8 per cent). In a touching admission to journalists last Friday, he said: 'Perhaps I was not quick enough to take the necessary measures. Perhaps we should have closed [loss-making] villages more quickly. Philippe Bourguignon will bring more rigorous methods.'

Source: Andrew Jack, *Financial Times*, 24 February 1997.

EXHIBIT **16.4 Change of management personnel**

Requirement

Discuss the organisational and behavioural implications of Exhibit 16.4, with particular reference to how these could impact on the operation of the business's management accounting system.

GLOSSARY

A

Absorption costing Costing system which includes fixed and variable overhead in cost per unit.

Accounting rate of return Appraisal criterion for capital investment proposals:

$$\frac{\text{average annual profit}}{\text{initial capital cost}} \times 100\% \ or \ \frac{\text{average annual profit}}{\text{average capital cost}} \times 100\%$$

Activity based budgeting (ABB) Budget system based on activities and cost drivers.

Activity-based cost management (ABCM) Approach to financial control aimed at controlling cost of activities, rather than amount of individual costs.

Activity-based costing (ABC) Absorption of overhead based on activities' consumption of resources and output's consumption of activities.

Activity-based management Approach to management based on activities rather than departments or individual costs.

Actual absorption rate Overhead absorption rate derived from actual overhead cost and actual activity measure.

Algebraic reapportionment Algebraic approach to reapportionment of service/support cost centre overhead to front-line/production cost centres giving full recognition to reciprocal services.

Allocation Attribution of cost to a single cost objective.

AMT Advanced manufacturing technology.

Annual budgeted volume Volume of activity (e.g. output) upon which annual budget is based.

Annuity Equal annual cash flow over life of an investment.

Apportionment Splitting a common cost between the cost objectives to which it relates.

Apportionment basis Basis of apportioning a common cost between the cost objectives to which it relates.

Appraisal cost Cost incurred to ensure desired quality is achieved.

Aspiration level Performance level which an individual will strive to achieve.

Attention-directing Provision of reports on key aspects of operations.

Average capital cost Possible definition of capital for use in accounting rate of return:

$$\frac{(\text{initial cost} + \text{resale value})}{2}$$

B

Balanced scorecard Approach to performance appraisal advocated by Kaplan & Norton which suggests a range of indicators – financial, customer-focused, internal and innovation/learning.

Barriers to communication Factors which prevent effective communication of information.

Batch costing Costing methodology for batches of identical/similar items which may/may not be produced to customer specification.

Benchmarking Identification of performance target by reference to either internal or external criteria.

Beta (β) Measure of a security's systematic risk.

Blanket absorption rate *see* Plantwide absorption rate.

Breakeven chart Graphical representation of relationship between volume, revenue, total fixed cost and total cost, from which breakeven point can be determined.

Breakeven point Sales volume (units or revenue) at which profit is exactly zero:

$$\text{in units} = \frac{\text{total fixed costs}}{\text{contribution per unit}}$$

$$\text{in revenue} = \frac{\text{total fixed costs}}{\text{CS ratio}}$$

Budget A quantified plan aimed at achieving a particular objective.

Budget centre Organisational subunit for which a budget is prepared.

Budget committee Management group which deals with issues of budget implementation.

Budget manual Document containing procedural guidance on budget preparation.

Budget officer Provides budgetary liaison between different organisational functions.

Budget period Period to which budget is to apply.

Budget slack Difference between minimum necessary expenditure and actual/budgeted expenditure.

C

CS ratio *see* Contribution/sales ratio.

Capital asset pricing model (CAPM) Determines a security's required return with reference to the security market line.

Capital budget Budget which reflects long-term capital investment plans.

Combined probability *see* Joint probability.

Committed cost Cost which must be incurred if the organisation is to continue in existence.

Constant dividend stream Required return on ordinary shares based on constant future dividends

$$r = \frac{d}{P_0}.$$

Contingency approach Adaptation to meet specific circumstances.

Continuous allotment *see* Repeated distribution.

Continuous budget *see* Rolling budget.

Continuous operation costing Group of costing methodologies applicable to output of identical/similar products/services.

Contract costing Costing methodology for dissimilar cost units produced to customer requirements, where output designedly spans two/more accounting periods.

Contribution Sales revenue (or unit selling price) *less* total (unit) variable costs.

Contribution analysis Determination of product/department/division contribution to general costs.

Contribution chart Graphical representation of relationship between volume, revenue, total variable cost and total cost, from which breakeven point can be determined.

Contribution/sales ratio Total (or unit) contribution as a percentage of sales revenue (or unit selling price).

Control period Subdivision of budget period for control purposes.

Cost/benefit analysis Evaluation of capital investment proposal based on quantification of monetary and non-monetary outcomes.

Cost/benefit criterion Need for the benefit of an action to exceed the associated cost.

Cost centre Organisational subunit to which costs are attributed.

Cost control Keeping cost within predetermined limits.

Cost driver Underlying cause of cost.

Cost-effectiveness analysis Evaluation of capital investment proposal based on quantification of monetary outcomes and assessment of unquantified non-monetary outcomes.

Cost objective Target or purpose of a cost attribution exercise.

Cost of capital Minimum return required by investors in an organisation and from that organisation's own investments.

Cost reduction Reduction of cost from previous level without adverse effect on quality.

Cost unit Unit of product/service to which costs are attributed.

Cost/volume/profit (CVP) analysis Marginal costing technique analysing relationship between costs, volume and profit.

Coupon rate Rate of interest payable on debentures relative to their nominal value.

Cross elasticity of demand Relationship between demand for complementary/substitute products/services.

Currently attainable standard Cost/performance standard based on efficient operation under current conditions.

Cutoff rate Target rate of return.

D

Data Unprocessed information.

DCF yield *see* Internal rate of return.

Debenture Loan made to incorporated organisation (e.g. limited company).

Decision tree Schematic representation of the possible outcomes of a decision.

Deflating Removing inflation from series of costs/revenues so as to state them on a common basis.

Departmental absorption rate Overhead absorption rate based on cost centre overhead and activity measure.

Deterministic model Model which assumes certainty/perfect knowledge.

Differential cost/benefit/cash flow Difference in relevant cost/benefit/cash flow between alternative courses of action.

Direct cost Cost which can be unambiguously and quantifiably associated with a single cost objective.

Direct costing *see* Marginal costing.

Direct expenses Non-labour, non-materials cost allocable to a single cost objective.

Direct labour cost/hours Labour cost/hours allocable to a single cost objective.

Direct material cost/quantity Material cost/quantity allocable to a single cost objective.

Direct reapportionment Method of secondary overhead distribution which ignores reciprocal services.

Discounted cash flow (DCF) Future cash flow stated in today's terms after allowing for the time value of money; for £1 received at the end of n years from now at a cost of capital r, this is

$$\frac{1}{(1 + r)^n}$$

Discretionary cost Cost incurred at management's discretion.

Dividend growth model Required rate of return on ordinary shares based on constant growth in future dividends:

$$r = \frac{d(1 + g)}{P_0} + g$$

Dual price(s) Increase/decrease in objective function value resulting from gaining/losing one unit of scarce resource.

Dysfunctional Conflict between aims of individual managers/subunits and those of organisation overall.

E

Engineered cost Cost having a definable input/output relationship.

Engineering cost estimation Technical methods of cost estimation.

Ex-ante standard Standard set in advance of events to which it relates.

Exceptions reporting *see* Management by exception.

Expected value (EV) Weighted average outcome of a probability distribution:

$$\Sigma[x\{(p(x)\}]$$

Ex-post standard Standard set after the event to which it relates.

External failure cost Cost incurred as result of quality failure after output has reached end-user.

F

Feedback control Control exercised by retrospective comparison of standard/budget with actual.

Feedforward control Future-oriented control exercised by comparison of desired and budgeted outcomes.

Financial accounting Records monetary transactions of the organisation with principal aim of satisfying external users and requirements.

Fixed budget Budget prepared on basis of single volume prediction.

Fixed cost Cost whose total amount is unaffected by increases/decreases in the volume of activity.

Fixed overhead expenditure variance Difference between budgeted and actual fixed overhead cost.

Fixed overhead volume variance Difference between budgeted and actual unit output, multiplied by the unit fixed overhead absorption rate.

Flexible budget Budget which recognises impact of volume change on costs/revenues.

Functional budget Budget relating to an individual organisational function (e.g. production).

G

Gearing Existence in company's capital structure of prior charge capital.

Gearing ratio $\dfrac{\text{prior charge capital}}{\text{all long-term capital} + \text{reserves}}$

Goal congruence Convergence of individual managers' and subunits' aims with those of the organisation overall.

Gross redemption yield Discount/interest rate at which future interest payments plus loan repayment equate with current market value of debenture.

H

High–low analysis Cost estimation technique which takes the variable cost per unit of activity to be:

$$\frac{\text{(difference between total cost of high activity and total cost of low activity)}}{\text{(difference between high and low volumes of activity)}}$$

fixed cost being determined by substitution of this result into either of the high- or low-volume total cost.

Hurdle rate Target return from investment.

I

Ideal standard Performance/cost standard based on maximum efficiency.

Incremental budget Budget prepared by adjusting previous period's budget for expected future changes in conditions.

Incremental cost/benefit Additional cost/benefit resulting from an action.

Indirect cost Cost which is common to two or more cost objectives.

Inflating Adding inflation to a series of costs/revenues to restate them on a common basis.

Information Data which has been processed into a useful form.

Inspection of accounts Estimation technique based on inspection of past accounting records.

Internal failure cost Cost resulting from quality failure before output reaches end-user.

Internal rate of return Discount rate yielding zero net present value.

Investment centre Organisational subunit to which costs, revenues and capital investment are attributed.

Irredeemable debenture Debenture on which capital is not repaid, having cost of:

$$\frac{i}{P_0}$$

J

Job costing Costing methodology relevant to output of dissimilar units to customer requirement, the units being smaller than for contract costing.

Joint probability Probability of two independent events occurring simultaneously, calculated as the product of the probabilities attaching to each event.

Just-in-time (JIT) Purchase/production as close to point of use/sale as possible.

K

Key factor *see* Limiting factor.

L

Labour efficiency variance Difference between standard labour hours allowed for actual output and actual hours worked, multiplied by standard rate per hour.

Labour rate variance Difference between standard labour rate per hour and actual rate per hour, multiplied by number of hours actually paid for.

Learning curve Recognises that, up to certain point, average time per unit reduces as cumulative output increases, average time per unit (y) being ax^b.

Learning rate Percentage of previous level to which average time per unit falls when cumulative output doubles.

Leverage *see* Gearing.

Life cycle costing Tracking budgeted/actual costs and revenues over a product/service's entire lifespan.

Limiting factor Constraint on organisational activity.

Line-item budget Budget which classifies costs according to their nature.

Linear costs Cost behaviour pattern where the variable cost per unit of activity is constant at all volumes and/or the total fixed cost is the same for all volumes.

Linear programming Mathematical technique for optimising a given outcome, subject to constraints.

Linear regression analysis Mathematical technique for estimating straight line $y = a + bx$:

$$b = \frac{n\Sigma xy - \Sigma x \Sigma y}{n\Sigma x^2 - (\Sigma x)^2} \qquad a = \frac{\Sigma y}{n} - \frac{b\Sigma x}{n}$$

M

Management accounting Provision of useful information to help management in their planning, control and decision-making activities.

Management by exception Control principle whereby management action is triggered by significant exceptions to plan.

Management information system (MIS) Set of interrelated subsystems which processes and filters data from internal and external sources.

Margin *see* Profit margin.

Margin of safety Difference between budgeted/actual and breakeven sales in units, revenue, or as a percentage:

$$\frac{(\text{budgeted or actual sales} - \text{breakeven sales})}{\text{budgeted or actual sales}} \times 100\%$$

Marginal costing Costing system which attributes marginal/variable costs to units of output.

Mark-up Profit expressed in terms of cost.

Market portfolio Theoretical optimum mix of securities, from which unsystematic risk has been diversified away.

Market risk *see* Systematic risk.

Master budget Summary of functional and cash budgets.

Material price variance Difference between standard and actual purchase price of materials multiplied by actual purchase quantity.

Material usage variance Difference between standard material usage allowed for actual output and actual usage, multiplied by standard price per unit of material.

Maximax Financial decision criterion which postulates acceptance of the option having the optimum best possible outcome.

Maximin Financial decision criterion which postulates acceptance of the option with the best worst outcome.

Mission statement Statement of an organisation's desired economic/social role over the long term.

Mixed cost *see* Semi-variable cost.

Multiple regression analysis Analytical technique which recognises impact on target variable of several factors.

N

Negative feedback Control action intended to mitigate effect of adverse control comparisons.

Net present value (NPV) Sum of a capital investment proposal's discounted relevant cash inflows and outflows over its lifespan.

Noise Irrelevant/distracting information within communication system.

Nominal value Face value of shares/debentures.

Non-programmed decision Non-routine/non-recurrent decision – variables/outcomes subject to considerable uncertainty.

Non-value-added activity Activity which adds no worth to output in perceptions of its end-user.

Normal volume Medium-term average volume.

O

Objective classification Linkage between subjective classification and cost objective.

Objective function Mathematical statement of what a linear programming exercise is attempting to maximise/minimise.

Operational information Plans and resources which translate tactics into action.

Operational variance Difference between ex-post standard and actual performance.

Opportunity cost Benefit foregone as result of pursuing one course of action, rather than the best alternative course of action.

Ordinary shares Shares which confer 'ownership' of company.

Overabsorption Arises where overhead absorbed using predetermined rate exceeds overhead incurred.

Overhead Sum of all indirect costs.

Overhead absorption Practice of including overhead in unit cost.

Overhead absorption rate Mechanism for determining overhead cost per unit, taking the general form:

$$\frac{\text{estimated overhead cost}}{\text{estimated volume measure}} \quad or \quad \frac{\text{estimated overhead cost}}{\text{estimated units of cost driver}}$$

Overhead analysis sheet Presentation of primary and secondary distribution of overhead.

Overhead application *see* Overhead absorption.

Overhead cost pool Collection point for overheads relating to an activity.

Overhead recovery *see* Overhead absorption.

P

Payback Period (usually expressed in years) required for capital investment proposal's net cash inflows to equal its initial cost.

Perfect information Information which is error-free.

Planning variance Difference between ex-ante and ex-post standard performance.

Plantwide absorption Overhead absorption rate based on total, rather than departmental, overhead and activity/volume measure.

Positive feedback Control action intended to take advantage of favourable outcomes of control comparisons.

Post-audit *see* Project post-audit.

Post-completion audit *see* Project post-audit.

Practical capacity Volume measure based on maximum operational capability.

Predetermined absorption rate Overhead absorption rate based on estimated figures.

Preference share Fixed-dividend share taking payment precedence over ordinary share.

Present value Future expected cash flow stated in today's terms.

Prevention cost Cost incurred to prevent inferior quality.

Price elasticity of demand Relationship between selling price and quantity demanded.

Primary distribution of overhead Allocation and apportionment of overhead to cost centres.

Prime cost Sum of all direct costs.

Principal budget factor *see* Limiting factor.

Prior charge capital Capital which takes payment/repayment precedence over ordinary shares.

Probability distribution List of possible outcomes along with the associated probability of each.

Problem solving Quantification of costs/benefits of actions, often coupled with recommendation based thereon.

Process costing Costing methodology for output of identical/similar items by means of single process/sequence of processes.

Product line pricing Pricing a range of products so as to maximise profit from sale of whole range.

Profiled budget Budget structured in such a way as to reflect fluctuations within budget period (e.g. monthly cash flows within annual budget).

Profit centre Organisational subunit to which costs and revenues are attributed.

Profit margin Profit expressed relative to sales value.

Profit/volume chart Graphical representation of relationship between volume and profit, from which breakeven point can be determined.

Profit : volume ratio *see* Contribution:sales ratio.

Programme budget Budget which classifies costs according to the reason for their being incurred.

Programmed decision Routine decision with fairly predictable outcomes.

Project post-audit Monitoring a project/decision after implementation to ensure that financial and non-financial objectives are being met.

Q

Qualitative information Information which is not (or which cannot be) expressed in numerical form.

Quantitative information Information expressed in numerical form.

R

Reapportionment basis Basis for undertaking secondary distribution of overheads.

Reciprocal services Provision of service/support by one service/support cost centre to another.

Redeemable debenture Debenture on which capital is ultimately repaid, having cost equal to discount rate which equates present value of future interest plus capital repayment with current market value.

Relevant cost/revenue Future cash flow arising as result of a decision under consideration.

Relevant range Range of activity volumes and/or time horizon over which a particular assumption/set of assumptions is a reasonable approximation of reality.

Repeated distribution Method of secondary overhead distribution which fully recognises reciprocal services.

Residual income (RI) Divisional net profit *less* interest on capital employed.

Responsibility accounting Planning/control system based on assigning budget responsibility to individual managers.

Responsibility centre Budget centre within responsibility accounting system

Return on capital employed (ROCE)

$$\frac{\text{operating profit}}{\text{capital employed}} \times 100\%$$

Return on investment (ROI) *see* Return on capital employed.

Revenue budget Short term operational plan.

Rights issue Issue of new shares to existing shareholders in proportion to current shareholding.

Risk averse Risk profile which seeks the least-risk option, regardless of expected value.

Risk neutral Risk profile which seeks the option having the best expected value regardless of associated risk.

Risk premium Return required above the risk-free rate to compensate for a security's systematic risk.

Risk seeking Risk profile which seeks the option having the best potential outcome, regardless of associated 'downside' risk.

Rolling budget Budget which is updated on a continuous basis.

S

Sales price variance Difference between standard and actual unit selling prices, multiplied by actual unit sales volume.

Sales required for target profit Key cost/volume/profit indicator, calculated in units (revenue) as:

$$\frac{\text{total fixed costs} + \text{target profit}}{\text{contribution per unit (\textit{or} CS ratio)}}$$

Sales volume variance Difference between budgeted and actual sales volumes, multiplied by standard profit/contribution per unit.

Scattergraph Graphical cost estimation technique using a number of past costs plotted against volume of activity.

Scorekeeping Keeping tally of financial data as basis of provision of useful information.

Secondary distribution of overhead Reapportionment of service/support cost centres' overhead to production/front-line cost centres.

Security market line Relationship between different values of β and associated return required, having equation $R_x = R_f + \{(\beta_x(R_m - R_f)\}$

Semi-fixed cost *see* Semi-variable cost.

Semi-variable cost Cost which is partly variable, partly fixed.

Sensitivity analysis 'What-if' technique, examining the effect of changing one or more variables in a model.

Service costing Costing methodology for provision of service, rather than tangible output.

Shadow price(s) *see* Dual prices.

Shadow value(s) *see* Dual prices.

Simplex Iterative method of solving linear programming problems, normally computer-based.

Simulation Computerised technique for modelling complex uncertain situations, based on random numbers and probabilistic analysis.

Specific order costing Group of costing methodologies appropriate where work is carried out to customers' requirements.

Specified order of closing *see* Step reapportionment.

Stakeholders Those who have an interest in, or who are affected by, organisational activity.

Standard cost Predetermined unit specifications of resource inputs and associated costs.

Standard hour Amount of work which should be performed in one hour at standard efficiency.

Static budget *see* Fixed budget.

Step cost Cost whose total amount is fixed within a range of activity volumes, increasing/decreasing by a lump-sum amount above/below this range.

Step reapportionment Method of secondary overhead distribution which partially recognises reciprocal services.

Stochastic model Model which allows for impact of uncertainty.

Strategic information Relates to organisational objectives and the policies/resources required to achieve them.

T

Target cost(ing) Selling price/revenue *less* desired profit.

Target return Minimum return required from an investment.

Term loan Loan made for fixed period of time.

Three-level analysis Analyses uncertainty by considering three possible outcomes of a decision: the best possible, the worst possible and the most likely (often combined with probabilistic analysis).

Time value of money Phenomenon of £1 paid/received today having greater value than £1 paid/received at some point in future.

Total quality management (TQM) Management philosophy based on 'getting it right first time all of the time'.

Transfer price Price set for goods/services traded between different segments of the same organisation.

U

Underabsorption Arises where overhead absorbed using predetermined rate is less than overhead incurred.

Unique risk *see* Unsystematic risk.

Unsystematic risk Risk specific to an organisation.

V

Value-added activity Activity which adds worth to output in perception of its end-user.

Value analysis Cost reduction method aimed at elimination of inessential aspects of products/services/procedures.

Value for money (VFM) Economic, efficient and effective operation.

Value of perfect information Absolute maximum payable to obtain additional information – difference between best expected value achievable without information and that achievable with information.

Variable cost Cost whose total amount increases/decreases in line with increases/decreases in the volume of activity.

Variable costing *see* Marginal costing.

Variable overhead efficiency variance Difference between standard hours allowed for actual output and actual hours worked, multiplied by variable overhead rate per hour

Variable overhead expenditure variance Difference between flexible budget variable overhead allowed for actual hours/units and actual variable overhead.

Variance Difference between standard/budgeted and actual outcome.

W

Weighted average contribution Unit contributions (CS ratios) weighted by each individual product/service's proportion of overall sales mix.

Weighted average cost of capital (WACC) Company cost of capital determined by weighting cost of individual capital elements relative to their proportion of total capital.

World class manufacturing (WCM) Response to global and competitive markets which emphasises quality, lead time, adaptability and cost.

Y

Yield to maturity *see* Gross redemption yield.

Z

Zero-base budgeting (ZBB) Approach to budget preparation which assumes zero prior expenditure, with justification of budgeted costs required.

Overhead: secondary distribution

Introduction

In Chapter 4, we performed a primary distribution of Success Direct Ltd's overhead, allocating and apportioning this to each of the company's four cost centres. We also saw that the departmental totals arrived at after this exercise cannot readily be used for development of an overhead cost per unit of output. A **secondary distribution** is needed, whereby overhead for the support centres (Reprographic and Dispatch) are *reapportioned* to the centres through which units of output actually pass (i.e. Bookkeeping and Secretarial).

We therefore need to develop **reapportionment bases**, which must reflect the underlying cause of each support cost centre's overhead (i.e. the cost driver relating to the service being provided) if it is readily identifiable and quantifiable, failing which we should use the best available proxy. Exhibit A.1 summarises the results of the primary distribution and presents some additional information relating to Success Direct Ltd. From the information in Exhibit A.1, we can use the number of dispatches to reapportion Dispatch overhead and the number of reprographic requests for Reprographic.

Success Direct Ltd: additional information

	Cost centre			
	Bookkeeping	Secretarial	Reprographic	Dispatch
Departmental overhead from primary distribution (see Chapter 4)	£112,000	£136,700	£109,460	£75,840
Number of dispatches	800	1,000	200	nil
Number of reprographic requests	200	700	nil	100

EXHIBIT A.1

There is one final issue to consider before undertaking the secondary distribution: to what extent should we recognise reciprocal services (i.e. services performed by one service cost centre for another service cost centre)? We can ignore them totally (**direct reapportionment**), we can partially recognise them (**step reapportionment**), or we can recognise them fully (**repeated distribution/algebraic reapportionment**). You should note, however, that even full recognition of reciprocal services may still result in inaccurate departmental totals, as it does not allow for services performed by a service cost centre on its own behalf.

Direct reapportionment

This approach to secondary distribution reapportions support cost centres' overheads to front-line cost centres *only*. For Success Direct Ltd, this means that Reprographic and Dispatch overheads (£109,460 and £75,840 from Exhibit A.1) will be reapportioned to Bookkeeping and Secretarial on the basis of reprographic requests and number of dispatches in those two departments only: that is, we ignore the reprographic requests raised by Dispatch and the number of dispatches made for Reprographic.

From Exhibit A.1, the number of dispatches for each front-line cost centre is:

Bookkeeping	800	44%
Secretarial	1,000	56%
	1,800	100%

For reprographic requests, we get:

Bookkeeping	200	22%
Secretarial	700	78%
	900	100%

The departmental overhead resulting from primary distribution is the starting-point for our secondary distribution, shown in Table A.1 below.

TABLE A.1 Direct reapportionment

	Amount (£)	Reapportionment basis	Percentages	Bookkeeping (£)	Secretarial (£)	Reprographic (£)	Dispatch (£)
Totals from primary distribution	434,000			112,000	136,700	109,460	75,840
Dispatch overhead reapportioned	75,840	Number of dispatches	44%, 56%	33,370	42,470		(75,840)
Reprographic overhead reapportioned	109,460	Number of reprographic requests	22%, 78%	24,081	85,379	(109,460)	
Totals				169,451	264,549		

Step reapportionment

Also termed **specified order of closing**, step reapportionment starts either with the support cost centre having the highest departmental overhead total after primary distribution, or with that providing the greatest service to other cost centres. This cost centre's overhead is reapportioned to *all* other departments (including support cost centres), and the relevant column in the overhead analysis sheet is then 'closed off'. Moving to the next support cost centre in sequence (as determined by departmental overhead or extent of services provided), we reapportion this department's overhead to all other departments, excluding the support cost centre whose column has already been closed off. This procedure is repeated until all columns relating to support cost centres have been closed off.

When performing step reapportionments, two computational requirements should be borne in mind:

1 The percentages used to make the reapportionments should relate only to those cost centres receiving a share of the reapportioned cost.
2 For all service cost centres subsequent to the first, the amount of overhead being reapportioned will consist of that centre's total from the primary distribution *plus* a share of previously reapportioned service centres' overhead.

We shall begin our step reapportionment with Reprographic, since this centre has the higher of the two support departments' overhead totals. Reprographic requests is still the reapportionment basis, but we are now including those raised by Dispatch:

Bookkeeping	200	20%
Secretarial	700	70%
Dispatch	100	10%
	1,000	100%

For reapportionment of Dispatch, the percentages used are the same as for the direct method. This is because, having closed off the Reprographic column in the analysis sheet, only Bookkeeping and Secretarial receive a share of Dispatch overhead *plus* Dispatch's share of Reprographic. Table A.2 shows the step reapportionment.

TABLE A.2 Step reapportionment

	Amount (£)	Reapportionment basis	Percentages	Bookkeeping (£)	Secretarial (£)	Reprographic (£)	Dispatch (£)
Totals from primary distribution	434,000			112,000	136,700	109,460	75,840
Reprographic overhead reapportioned	109,460	Number of reprographic requests	20%, 70%,10%	21,892	76,622	(109,460)	10,946 / 86,786
Dispatch overhead reapportioned	86,786	Number of Dispatches	44%, 56%	38,186	48,600		(86,786)
Totals				172,078	261,922		

Reapportionment by repeated distribution

The **repeated distribution** (or **continuous allotment**) method gives full recognition to reciprocal services. Support cost centres' overhead is reapportioned in sequence to all other departments, including other support departments. Using this method, the sequence in which the support cost centres are reapportioned is unimportant, providing it is applied consistently to every 'repeated distribution'. Once this first 'round' of reapportionments has been completed, the column for the support cost centre which started the sequence will contain a figure which is used as the basis for a second 'round' of reapportionments; at the end of this 'round', another (smaller) figure will remain in the first support centre's column, which serves as the basis for another 'round' of reapportionments – and so on until the amount remaining in one of the support centre columns is too small to warrant detailed reapportionment, being split arbitrarily between the front-line cost centres.

The reapportionment bases are still reprographic requisitions and number of dispatches for Reprographic and Dispatch respectively. The percentages used should, as always, relate to those cost centres which are to receive part of the reapportioned support centres' overhead. In this example, Bookkeeping, Secretarial and Dispatch will receive a reapportionment of Reprographic overhead, so the relevant percentages derived from those centres' reprographic requests are 20%, 70% and 10% (as calculated for the step reapportionment above). For Dispatch overhead, Bookkeeping, Secretarial and Reprographic receive a reapportionment, so the relevant percentages based on number of dispatches (from Exhibit A.1) are:

Bookkeeping	800	40%
Secretarial	1,000	50%
Reprographic	200	10%
	2,000	100%

Table A.3 shows the resulting secondary distribution.

TABLE A.3 Reapportionment using repeated distribution

	Amount (£)	Reapportionment basis	Percentages	Bookkeeping (£)	Secretarial (£)	Reprographic (£)	Dispatch (£)
Totals from primary distribution	434,000			112,000	136,700	109,460	75,840
Dispatch overhead reapportioned	75,840	Number of dispatches	40%, 50%, 10%	30,336	37,920	7,584 / 117,044	(75,840)
Reprographic overhead reapportioned	117,044	Number of reprographic requests	20%, 70%, 10%	23,409	81,931	(117,044)	11,704
Dispatch overhead reapportioned	14,630	Number of dispatches	40%, 50%, 10%	4,682	5,852	1,170	(11,704)
Reprographic overhead reapportioned	1,170	Number of reprographic requests	20%, 70% 10%	234	819	(1,170)	117
Dispatch overhead reapportioned	117	Number of dispatches	40%, 50%, 10%	47	59	11	(117)
Reprographic overhead reapportioned	11	Arbitrary split	Not applicable	5	6	(11)	
Totals				170,713	263,287		

Algebraic reapportionment

Repeated distribution, whilst fully reflecting reciprocal services, can be unwieldy, as Table A.3 suggests. This may be avoided by adopting an algebraic approach to reapportionment. The first step is to express each support cost centre's overhead as an equation. Using Success Direct Ltd's data, we get:

$$R = £109,460 + 10\%D \qquad \text{(equation 1)}$$
$$D = £75,840 + 10\%R \qquad \text{(equation 2)}$$

where: R is total Reprographic overhead (including share of Dispatch overhead); and
D is total Dispatch overhead (including share of Reprographic overhead).

Note that the 10 per cent included in the expressions for R and D represent the proportion of dispatches and reprographic requests calculated for Reprographic and Dispatch as a preliminary to repeated distribution. We must now solve equations 1 and 2 to obtain a value for each of R and D. Rearranging gives:

$$R - 10\% D = £109,460 \qquad \text{(equation 3)}$$

and

$$D - 10\% R = £75,840 \qquad \text{(equation 4)}$$

Equation 3 multiplied by 10 is:

$$10R - D = £1,094,600 \qquad \text{(equation 5)}$$

Adding equations 4 and 5, we get:

$$D - 10\%R = £75,840$$
$$10R - D = £1,094,600$$
$$\overline{9.9R = £1,170,440}$$

R is therefore:

$$(£1,170,440 \div 9.9) = £118,226$$

Substituting this value into equation 2:

$$D = £75,840 + 10\% (£118,226)$$
$$\Rightarrow D = £75,840 + £11,823$$
$$\Rightarrow D = £87,663.$$

Finally, in Table A.4 we apportion these values for R and D to Bookkeeping and Secretarial.

Comparison of the departmental totals in Table A.4 with those obtained using repeated distribution in Table A.3 shows that, allowing for small rounding differences, they are the same. Although the algebraic approach may be less cumbersome than repeated distribution, the calculations involved can become complex where it is necessary to solve more than two simultaneous equations in order to obtain departmental overhead totals for support cost centres (i.e. where there are more than two support centres).

TABLE A.4 Reapportionment of algebraically determined support centre overhead

	Amount (£)	Reapportionment basis	Percentages	Bookkeeping (£)	Secretarial (£)
Totals				112,000	136,700
Reprographic overhead reapportioned	118,226	Number of reprographic requests	20%, 70%	23,645	82,758
Dispatch overhead reapportioned	90,656	Number of dispatches	40%, 50%	35,065	43,832
Totals				170,710	263,290

Secondary distribution: which method?

The overhead figures for each of Bookkeeping and Secretarial which result from the different methods of secondary distribution are:

	Bookkeeping (£)	Secretarial (£)
Direct reapportionment	169,451	264,549
Step reapportionment	172,078	261,922
Repeated distribution	170,713	263,287
Algebraic reapportionment	170,710	263,290

The differences in this particular case are extremely small and there would appear to be little justification for use of a more involved methodology where a simpler one produces substantively the same result. Additionally, it can be argued that, because of the subjectivity inherent to certain apportionment/reapportionment bases, the degree of accuracy implied by the repeated distribution or algebraic methods is misleading. As a general guide, the sophistication of secondary distribution should be governed by:

1 *The extent of reciprocal servicing* If negligible, complex secondary distribution is not warranted;
2 *The nature of reciprocal servicing* Some services may readily be translated into reapportionment bases, possibly rendering a more thorough approach viable;
3 *The cost/benefit criterion* The cost of obtaining additional information about reciprocal servicing sufficient to support its recognition in secondary distribution should not outweigh the benefit to be derived from more 'accurate' methodology.

However, it may be the case that increasing accessibility of suitable computer software (and spreadsheets in particular) will enhance recognition of reciprocal servicing where this may breach the cost/benefit criterion if done manually.

APPENDIX B

Present value tables

TABLE B.1 Present value of a single payment/receipt of £1 at the end of *n* years from now, discounted at *r*%

Years	1%	2%	3%	4%	5%	6%	7%	8%	9%	10%	11%	12%	13%	14%
1	0.990	0.980	0.971	0.962	0.952	0.943	0.935	0.926	0.917	0.909	0.901	0.893	0.885	0.877
2	0.980	0.961	0.943	0.943	0.907	0.890	0.873	0.857	0.842	0.826	0.812	0.797	0.783	0.770
3	0.971	0.942	0.915	0.889	0.864	0.840	0.816	0.794	0.772	0.751	0.731	0.712	0.693	0.675
4	0.961	0.924	0.889	0.855	0.823	0.792	0.763	0.735	0.708	0.683	0.659	0.636	0.613	0.592
5	0.952	0.906	0.863	0.822	0.784	0.747	0.713	0.681	0.650	0.621	0.594	0.567	0.543	0.519
6	0.942	0.888	0.838	0.790	0.746	0.705	0.666	0.630	0.596	0.565	0.535	0.507	0.480	0.456
7	0.933	0.871	0.813	0.760	0.711	0.665	0.623	0.584	0.547	0.513	0.482	0.452	0.425	0.400
8	0.924	0.854	0.789	0.731	0.677	0.627	0.582	0.540	0.502	0.467	0.434	0.404	0.376	0.351
9	0.914	0.837	0.766	0.703	0.645	0.592	0.544	0.500	0.460	0.424	0.391	0.361	0.333	0.308
10	0.905	0.820	0.744	0.676	0.614	0.558	0.508	0.463	0.422	0.386	0.352	0.322	0.295	0.270
11	0.896	0.804	0.722	0.650	0.585	0.527	0.475	0.429	0.388	0.351	0.317	0.288	0.261	0.237
12	0.887	0.789	0.701	0.625	0.557	0.497	0.444	0.397	0.356	0.319	0.286	0.257	0.231	0.208
13	0.879	0.773	0.681	0.601	0.530	0.469	0.415	0.368	0.326	0.290	0.258	0.229	0.204	0.182
14	0.870	0.758	0.661	0.578	0.505	0.442	0.388	0.341	0.299	0.263	0.232	0.205	0.181	0.160
15	0.861	0.743	0.642	0.555	0.481	0.417	0.362	0.315	0.275	0.239	0.209	0.183	0.160	0.140
16	0.853	0.728	0.623	0.534	0.458	0.394	0.339	0.292	0.252	0.218	0.188	0.163	0.142	0.123
17	0.844	0.714	0.605	0.513	0.436	0.371	0.317	0.270	0.231	0.198	0.170	0.146	0.125	0.108
18	0.836	0.700	0.587	0.494	0.416	0.350	0.296	0.250	0.212	0.180	0.153	0.130	0.111	0.095
19	0.828	0.686	0.570	0.475	0.396	0.331	0.277	0.232	0.195	0.164	0.138	0.116	0.098	0.083
20	0.820	0.673	0.554	0.456	0.377	0.312	0.258	0.215	0.178	0.149	0.124	0.104	0.087	0.073

Years	15%	16%	17%	18%	19%	20%	21%	22%	23%	24%	25%	30%	35%	40%
1	0.870	0.862	0.855	0.848	0.840	0.833	0.826	0.820	0.813	0.807	0.800	0.769	0.741	0.714
2	0.756	0.743	0.731	0.718	0.706	0.694	0.683	0.672	0.661	0.650	0.640	0.592	0.549	0.510
3	0.658	0.641	0.624	0.609	0.593	0.579	0.565	0.551	0.537	0.525	0.512	0.455	0.406	0.364
4	0.572	0.552	0.534	0.516	0.499	0.482	0.467	0.451	0.437	0.423	0.410	0.350	0.301	0.260
5	0.497	0.476	0.456	0.437	0.419	0.402	0.386	0.370	0.355	0.341	0.328	0.269	0.223	0.186
6	0.432	0.410	0.390	0.370	0.352	0.335	0.319	0.303	0.289	0.275	0.262	0.207	0.165	0.133
7	0.376	0.354	0.333	0.314	0.296	0.279	0.263	0.249	0.235	0.222	0.210	0.159	0.122	0.095
8	0.327	0.305	0.285	0.266	0.249	0.233	0.218	0.204	0.191	0.179	0.168	0.123	0.091	0.068
9	0.284	0.263	0.243	0.226	0.209	0.194	0.180	0.167	0.155	0.144	0.134	0.094	0.067	0.048
10	0.247	0.227	0.208	0.191	0.176	0.162	0.149	0.137	0.126	0.116	0.107	0.073	0.050	0.035
11	0.215	0.195	0.178	0.162	0.148	0.135	0.123	0.112	0.103	0.094	0.086	0.056	0.037	0.025
12	0.187	0.169	0.152	0.137	0.124	0.112	0.102	0.092	0.083	0.076	0.069	0.043	0.027	0.018
13	0.163	0.145	0.130	0.116	0.104	0.094	0.084	0.075	0.068	0.061	0.055	0.033	0.020	0.013
14	0.141	0.125	0.111	0.099	0.088	0.078	0.069	0.062	0.055	0.049	0.044	0.025	0.015	0.009
15	0.123	0.108	0.095	0.084	0.074	0.065	0.057	0.051	0.045	0.040	0.035	0.020	0.011	0.006
16	0.107	0.093	0.081	0.071	0.062	0.054	0.047	0.042	0.036	0.032	0.028	0.015	0.008	0.005
17	0.093	0.080	0.069	0.060	0.052	0.045	0.039	0.034	0.030	0.026	0.023	0.012	0.006	0.003
18	0.081	0.069	0.059	0.051	0.044	0.038	0.032	0.028	0.024	0.021	0.018	0.009	0.005	0.002
19	0.070	0.060	0.051	0.043	0.037	0.031	0.027	0.023	0.020	0.017	0.014	0.007	0.003	0.002
20	0.061	0.051	0.043	0.037	0.031	0.026	0.022	0.019	0.016	0.014	0.012	0.005	0.003	0.001

TABLE B.2 Present value of £1 paid/received at the end of *each* of *n* years from now, discounted at *r*%

Years	1%	2%	3%	4%	5%	6%	7%	8%	9%	10%	11%	12%	13%	14%
1	0.990	0.980	0.971	0.962	0.952	0.943	0.935	0.926	0.917	0.909	0.901	0.893	0.885	0.877
2	1.970	1.942	1.913	1.886	1.859	1.833	1.808	1.783	1.759	1.736	1.713	1.690	1.668	1.647
3	2.941	2.884	2.829	2.775	2.723	2.673	2.624	2.577	2.531	2.487	2.444	2.402	2.361	2.322
4	3.902	3.808	3.717	3.630	3.546	3.465	3.387	3.312	3.240	3.170	3.102	3.037	2.974	2.914
5	4.853	4.713	4.580	4.452	4.329	4.212	4.100	3.993	3.890	3.791	3.696	3.605	3.517	3.433
6	5.795	5.601	5.417	5.242	5.076	4.917	4.767	4.623	4.486	4.355	4.231	4.111	3.998	3.889
7	6.728	6.472	6.230	6.002	5.786	5.582	5.389	5.206	5.033	4.868	4.712	4.564	4.423	4.288
8	7.652	7.325	7.020	6.733	6.463	6.210	5.971	5.747	5.535	5.335	5.146	4.968	4.799	4.639
9	8.566	8.162	7.786	7.435	7.108	6.802	6.515	6.247	5.995	5.759	5.537	5.328	5.132	4.946
10	9.471	8.983	8.530	8.111	7.722	7.360	7.024	6.710	6.418	6.145	5.889	5.650	5.426	5.216
11	10.368	9.787	9.253	8.760	8.306	7.887	7.499	7.139	6.805	6.495	6.207	5.938	5.687	5.453
12	11.255	10.575	9.954	9.385	8.863	8.384	7.943	7.536	7.161	6.814	6.492	6.194	5.918	5.660
13	12.134	11.348	10.635	9.986	9.394	8.853	8.358	7.904	7.487	7.103	6.750	6.424	6.122	5.842
14	13.004	12.106	11.296	10.563	9.899	9.295	8.745	8.244	7.786	7.367	6.982	6.628	6.302	6.002
15	13.865	12.849	11.938	11.118	10.380	9.712	9.108	8.559	8.061	7.606	7.191	6.811	6.462	6.142
16	14.718	13.578	12.561	11.652	10.838	10.106	9.447	8.851	8.313	7.824	7.379	6.974	6.604	6.265
17	15.562	14.292	13.166	12.166	11.274	10.477	9.763	9.122	8.544	8.022	7.549	7.120	6.729	6.373
18	16.398	14.992	13.754	12.659	11.690	10.828	10.059	9.372	8.756	8.201	7.702	7.250	6.840	6.467
19	17.226	15.678	14.324	13.134	12.085	11.158	10.336	9.604	8.950	8.365	7.839	7.366	6.938	6.550
20	18.046	16.351	14.877	13.590	12.462	11.470	10.594	9.818	9.129	8.514	7.963	7.469	7.025	6.623

Years	15%	16%	17%	18%	19%	20%	21%	22%	23%	24%	25%	30%	35%	40%
1	0.870	0.862	0.855	0.847	0.840	0.833	0.826	0.820	0.813	0.806	0.800	0.769	0.741	0.714
2	1.626	1.605	1.585	1.566	1.547	1.528	1.509	1.492	1.474	1.457	1.440	1.361	1.289	1.224
3	2.283	2.246	2.210	2.174	2.140	2.106	2.074	2.042	2.011	1.981	1.952	1.816	1.696	1.589
4	2.855	2.798	2.743	2.690	2.639	2.589	2.540	2.494	2.448	2.404	2.362	2.166	1.997	1.849
5	3.352	3.274	3.199	3.127	3.058	2.991	2.926	2.864	2.803	2.745	2.689	2.436	2.220	2.035
6	3.784	3.685	3.589	3.498	3.410	3.326	3.245	3.167	3.092	3.020	2.951	2.643	2.385	2.168
7	4.160	4.039	3.922	3.812	3.706	3.605	3.508	3.416	3.327	3.242	3.161	2.802	2.508	2.263
8	4.487	4.344	4.207	4.078	3.954	3.837	3.726	3.619	3.518	3.421	3.329	2.925	2.598	2.331
9	4.772	4.607	4.451	4.303	4.163	4.031	3.905	3.786	3.673	3.566	3.463	3.019	2.665	2.379
10	5.019	4.833	4.659	4.494	4.339	4.192	4.054	3.923	3.799	3.682	3.571	3.092	2.715	2.414
11	5.234	5.029	4.836	4.656	4.486	4.327	4.177	4.035	3.902	3.776	3.656	3.147	2.752	2.438
12	5.421	5.197	4.988	4.793	4.611	4.439	4.278	4.127	3.985	3.851	3.725	3.190	2.779	2.456
13	5.583	5.342	5.118	4.910	4.715	4.533	4.362	4.203	4.053	3.912	3.780	3.223	2.799	2.469
14	5.724	5.468	5.229	5.008	4.802	4.611	4.432	4.265	4.108	3.962	3.824	3.249	2.814	2.478
15	5.847	5.575	5.324	5.092	4.876	4.675	4.489	4.315	4.153	4.001	3.859	3.268	2.825	2.484
16	5.954	5.668	5.405	5.162	4.938	4.730	4.536	4.357	4.189	4.033	3.887	3.283	2.834	2.489
17	6.047	5.749	5.475	5.222	4.990	4.775	4.576	4.391	4.219	4.059	3.910	3.295	2.840	2.492
18	6.128	5.818	5.534	5.273	5.033	4.812	4.608	4.419	4.243	4.080	3.928	3.304	2.844	2.494
19	6.198	5.584	5.584	5.316	5.070	4.843	4.635	4.442	4.263	4.097	3.942	3.311	2.848	2.496
20	6.259	5.929	5.628	5.353	5.101	4.870	4.657	4.460	4.279	4.110	3.954	3.316	2.850	2.497

APPENDIX C

Solutions to chapter-end questions

Chapter 1

1.1 Qualitative information is financial/non-financial information which is not, or cannot be, expressed in numerical form. Three examples relating to this particular decision are:

- The ability of employees to cope with the new system.
- Potential developments in KGK's market/services which could render the new system obsolete.
- Potential disruption to branch activity during installation of the new system. How will this affect the building society's clients?

1.2 (a) True (b) False (c) True (d) False (e) False (f) False (g) True

1.3 The three elements of the scenario are:

- *Strategic* Decision to enter into a joint venture to expand range of productions.
- *Tactical* Decision to produce two costume dramas and one documentary during first year of joint venture.
- *Operational* Seeking locations for first costume drama.

1.4 C III only

Published accounting information will not be sufficiently timely for management purposes, typically being produced on an annual basis. If management has to wait until some time after the end of the current accounting year before receiving financial information about operations, then effective action based on this information will not be possible. Costs may therefore spiral out of control, unknown to management, and opportunities may be missed through lack of information.

1.5 D II and III only

The information generated will incur costs which are explicit, such as stationery, and which are recorded in the accounts, plus costs which are implicit, and which are therefore not recorded in the accounts. The fact that managers must spend time gathering and interpreting the information (when they might be more gainfully employed on other tasks) is an example of the latter kind of cost.

1.6 (a) Five possible objectives are:

- To stage as wide a variety of productions as possible.
- To stage productions in as many different venues as possible.
- To raise awareness of contemporary theatrical output.

- To provide minimum-cost public access to theatre.
- To provide theatre workshops for drama students.

(b) Part (a) lists five possible objectives – and this is one possible problem: namely, that the organisation may have several objectives which could conflict with each other. 'Staging a wide variety of productions' might well conflict with 'raising awareness of contemporary theatrical output', and 'minimum-cost access' may be at variance with all of the others. In addition, objectives will change over time, partly as the result of the kind of environmental pressure discussed in (c) below and many objectives may be difficult to quantify (e.g. 'wide variety of productions').

Management accounting aims to provide useful information to help managers to plan, control and make decisions, all of which activities (and their supporting information) stem from the desire to achieve a given objective/objectives. If, however, objectives are contradictory, preparation of meaningful plans to achieve them will be difficult, to say the least, and may require (or result in) some form of prioritisation. Further, if objectives change over time, there is a danger that management accounting information may be geared towards outdated objectives. Finally, management accounting is principally a quantitative discipline and may therefore have problems providing information relative to unquantified (or unquantifiable) objectives.

(c) The theatre company is almost entirely dependent on funding from the Arts Council (i.e. from government). If government funding of the arts is reduced due, say, to political pressure to increase funding in other areas, then it may be necessary to revise (or even abandon) some of the objectives suggested in (a). If funding is reduced, then 'minimum-cost access' may not be a viable objective, and might be revised to read something like 'low-cost access'; other objectives could be similarly affected. It is possible that a new, explicitly financial, objective might be introduced (e.g. 'minimising the operating deficit'), such introduction being either explicit or implied. Even if existing objectives can be left largely unaltered by reduced funding, there may be additional conflict between objectives as they compete for a share of available resources.

1.7 **(a)** The statement presented in Exhibit 1.7 has almost no value for the purposes described because:

- It reflects only what *did* happen. In order to assess the extent of the quarter's profit shortfall, management also need to know what was *expected* to happen: that is, budgeted figures for the quarter should also be provided.
- It is based on figures for the entire store. This is unlikely to prove helpful either for investigating the poorer-than-expected profit or for deciding how to implement the promotional campaign. For example, management will need some information to support their decision about what specific areas should be promoted.
- The figures are quarterly, which may not be timely enough to allow proper assessment or effective action by management.

(b) Subject to the cost/benefit criterion, the following improvements could be made:

- Provide budgeted and actual figures.
- Classify costs/revenues in a manner which reflects managerial responsibilities and in sufficient detail to permit informed evaluation (e.g. on a departmental basis).
- Provide reports more frequently (e.g. monthly), so that potential problems can be spotted sooner, thereby improving the chance of effective remedial action.

- Institute *ad hoc* reports, which should be useful in consideration of decisions such as the promotional campaign.

1.8   Memorandum

To: Chairman, Telec plc

From:

New management accounting system

The aim of management accounting is to provide useful information to help management to plan, control and make decisions. Although these activities could be said to constitute the fundamentals of management, it is doubtful whether management accounting can (or should) attempt to 'tell managers everything they need to know'. The reasons for this are as follows:

- Management accounting's main medium of communication is quantitative, with the majority of the information being financial. Managers need more than this. For instance, possible action by competitors is an important consideration which may not be readily incorporated into management accounting reports.
- Attempting to tell managers everything may seriously breach the cost/benefit criterion, even if it is possible to determine what constitutes 'everything' and obtain relevant data.
- Attempting to be comprehensive in provision could cause information overload.
- Management accounting is not intended to act as a surrogate, but as a support for managerial judgement. Ability to 'hide behind' figures could erode this judgement, and might be encouraged by overprovision.

What the company requires is an effective management information system, with management accounting forming one part of a wider, integrated whole.

Signed

Chapter 2

2.1   D £400,000

Prime cost refers to the total of all direct costs; in TG's case, this is:

direct labour	£150,000
direct expenses	£250,000
prime cost	£400,000

2.2   C I and III only

As the volume of output increases, the total amount of royalty paid to the patent holder will likewise increase, so the cost is variable. Since the £10 royalty payment can be traced to a single cost objective (unit of output in this example), it is also a direct cost. Note that, although the *total cost* is variable, the royalty cost *per unit* is fixed.

2.3   D £10.00

The process's total cost for the month was (£60,0000 + £14,000 + £6,000) = £80,000. This must be averaged over the number of litres of good output during the period:

that is, (input *less* losses) = (10,000 – 2,000). Cost per litre of good output was thus (£80,000 ÷ 8,000 litres) = £10 per litre.

2.4 (a) False (b) False (c) True (d) False (e) True (f) False

2.5 **B** Job costing

The firm will undertake jobs to customer specification and each will be different. Relative to contract costing, the size of job will be small. Job costing is therefore appropriate. Had the firm specialised in industrial (rather than domestic) work, where the jobs could be very large, then contract costing might have been appropriate.

2.6 (a) *Payment to insurance company* Figure 2.8 (c): this is a variable cost relative to volume of policies sold, but the cost per policy is not constant. The fact that the slope of the total cost line in Figure 2.8 (c) has three progressively less steep gradients indicates that there are three levels of cost per unit.

Payments to sales staff Figure 2.8 (a): up to a certain volume, this cost is fixed (the annual salary of £10,000, which is paid irrespective of volume). Once this volume is exceeded, the cost becomes semi-variable, the variable element representing the £20 per policy commission on all sales above the target number.

Administration costs Figure 2.8 (b): administration costs are semi-variable at all volumes. At zero volume, £60,000 will still have to be paid in respect of premises and full-time staff (assuming PP remains in business). On top of this amount, £5 per policy is payable, meaning that the total cost will increase above £60,000 in line with the volume of sales.

(b) Figure C 2.1 illustrates the revised behaviour of each cost. Figure C2.1(a) represents the payment to the insurance company, which is now a linear variable cost, being a flat-rate £3 per policy sold. Payments to sales staff are shown in Figure C2.1(b): since commission is now payable on *all* policies sold, the variable element of this cost commences immediately volume exceeds zero. Within a one-year time span, the administration cost is wholly fixed for all foreseeable volumes, as illustrated in Figure C2.1(c); outside the relevant range – one year and 'foreseeable volume' in this instance – administration cost will probably exhibit step behaviour.

(c) Preparation of tolerably realistic budgets requires some knowledge about how costs are likely to be affected by the volume of activity upon which the budget is based. Budgets may be prepared for a variety of different volumes, the purpose of this being primarily to assess the impact of different volumes on costs/revenues/profit.

Financial control is typically exercised by comparing budgeted and actual costs. If these two sets of costs are based on different volumes of activity, part of the difference may arise because of this difference in volume, rather than because of efficiency/cost factors. For a more meaningful control exercise, the impact on budgeted/actual costs of such volume differences must be appreciated.

Decisions involve choice between alternatives. Analysing the financial implications of different alternatives requires an awareness of how costs are likely to react to each course of action being considered. This will be particularly true when the decision concerned affects volume of activity: for example, should a component be made in-house or subcontracted to an external supplier?

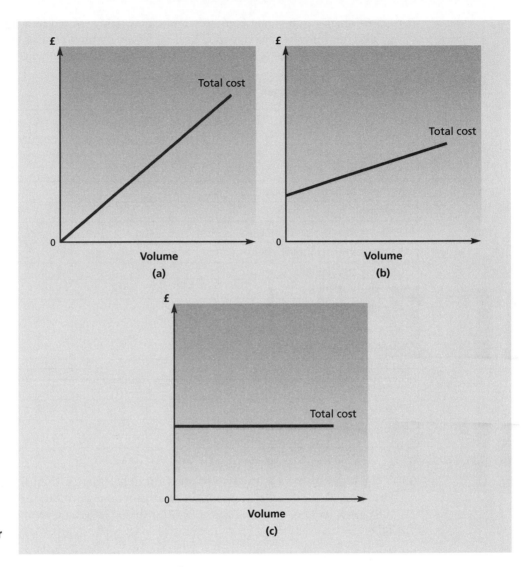

FIGURE C2.1
Sketch graphs
of revised
cost behaviour
patterns

2.7 **(a)** The suggested costing methodology for each organisation is:

- Northfields Passenger Transport Ltd   Service costing
- Dinnie, Kerr & Co   Service costing
- NPP plc*   Process *or* batch costing
- Northfields Electrical & Plumbing   Job costing
- NF Engineering Ltd*   Job *or* batch costing
- CRE Courier Services   Service costing
- Window Systems Ltd*   Job *or* batch costing
- Fit Feet   Service costing
- Maritime Projects Ltd*   Job *or* contract costing

*Note:** For these businesses, it is not possible to be precise without additional information. For example, for Maritime Projects Ltd: What is the magnitude/duration of the work undertaken? If small and large orders are produced, then it is possible that the company will use both job and contract costing.

(b) Costs which can be unambiguously and quantifiably related to a single cost objective (cost unit here) are classified as direct. Costs which cannot be related in this way are indirect. Table C2.1 shows the classification of the given costs.

TABLE **C2.1 Cost classification**

Cost	Direct Labour	Direct Materials	Direct Expenses	Indirect Labour	Indirect Materials	Indirect Expenses
Depreciation of assembly machinery						✓
Insurance of factory premises						✓
Advertising costs						✓
UPVC for double glazing units		✓				
Wages of shop floor operatives	✓					
Assembly and finishing supervisory salaries				✓		
Salaries of office staff				✓		
Depreciation of office equipment						✓
Telephone and postage costs						✓
Office stationery					✓	
Shatter-proof glass		✓				
Factory rent and rates						✓
Royalty payment to designers			✓			

(c) If the cost objective is the two production departments, then the Assembly and Finishing Departments' supervisory salaries would become direct, since we can trace each to its related cost objective. All other costs would remain as classified in Table C2.1.

(d) A just-in-time system aims to purchase/produce as close to the point of production/sale as possible. This may already occur to some extent at Window Systems Ltd, as production will generally occur in response to customer orders with output of completed double-glazing units being held 'in stock' for a very short while pending installation at customers' premises. We cannot tell from the question whether, or to what extent, JIT purchasing is in use by the company.

The main benefit of adopting JIT would be reduction in the costs associated with stockholding, such as storage, or the cost of damage/deterioration. In addition, less of the company's capital would be 'tied up' unnecessarily, releasing it for use in other, potentially profitable, ways. The success of JIT is, however, heavily contingent on the suppliers' ability to supply what is required when it is required, and to the desired specification. Similarly, Window Systems' production facilities must be sufficiently flexible to respond at short notice to fluctuations in demand. If there is a problem with either suppliers or production facilities, the benefit of JIT may be lost (and additional costs may even be incurred). It is also possible that a change in the pattern of raw materials' purchasing (i.e. from a few large orders to many small orders) may result in an increase in the cost of materials due, for example, to loss of quantity discounts. Before implementing such a system, management must carefully weigh the associated costs and benefits.

2.8 Report

To: General Manager, Seaforth Nursing Home

From:

Provision of financial information for internal uses

Information is currently geared to meet external requirements. This has several weaknesses:

1 The uses for which the information is principally intended are those of parties external to the organisation, which will generally differ from management's requirements. The nursing home's owners, for example, will use the accounting information to assess the performance of their investment and the success with which management has acted as 'steward' of this investment; management will require information to permit them to perform this 'stewardship' role: that is, to help them plan, control and make decisions.

2 Financial information provided to external parties will be mostly historic in nature and based on transactions, which permits independent audit of the figures reported. Management's prime concern is with the future – planning and decision making are both future-oriented – so historic information will have very limited value.

3 The classification of costs and revenues may be inappropriate to management's requirements. For example, for decision making, costs and revenues should be classified into relevant/irrelevant, which may not be possible from existing accounting records, where the classification is principally along functional lines.

4 There may be a problem with the timeliness of existing information provision: management may require information much more quickly than external users.

Overall, the financial problems being experienced, such as budget overspends, may be largely attributable to an inherent conflict between external/internal information requirements. But it is worth observing that this may not be the only reason, and some investigation is merited before major changes are made.

Nevertheless, improvements can be made to the accounting system. The most radical step would be to report internal and external accounting information quite separately. This would allow the problems outlined above to be addressed in full, but may incur costs which are unjustifiable. In addition, the changeover period may result in confusion, which may be perpetuated by the operation of what is, effectively, a dual system. Alternatively, the existing system could be modified so as to give better recognition to management's requirements, which is essentially a matter of building in greater flexibility: for example, allowing for the provision of detailed and timely analysis of costs and revenues for internal use, or the ability to generate *ad hoc* reports.

Regardless of how the system is amended, the associated costs and benefits should be carefully considered.

Signed

Chapter 3

3.1 C £4.00

The high and low volumes occur in Periods 1 and 3 respectively, giving the following differences in total overhead cost and output:

	Total overhead cost (£)	Output (units)
High volume	156,000	19,000
Low volume	140,000	15,000
Difference	16,000	4,000

The variable overhead cost per unit is:

$$\frac{\text{difference in total cost}}{\text{difference in activity}} = \frac{£16,000}{4,000} = £4$$

3.2 (a) False (b) False (c) True (d) False (e) True (f) True

3.3 If an 80 per cent learning curve applies, then the average time per unit will fall to 80 per cent of its previous amount with each successive doubling of cumulative output:

Cumulative output	Average hours per unit		Total hours
1	140		140.0
2	(80% × 140)	= 112.0	224.0
4	(80% × 112)	= 89.6	358.4
8	(80% × 89.6)	= 71.68	573.44
16	(80% × 71.68)	= 57.34	917.44
32	(80% × 57.34)	= 45.87	1,467.84
64	(80% × 45.87)	= 36.70	2,348.80

3.4 Bearing in mind the cumulative nature of inflation, we get:

19X6: (£4,000,000 × 1.028)	£4,112,000
19X5: (£3,400,000 × 1.035 × 1.028)	£3,617,532
19X4: (£3,200,000 × 1.047 × 1.035 × 1.028)	£3,564,759

Note that the inflation applicable to each year is already contained within the actual cost stated for that year, so there is no need to adjust, say, the 19X6 cost for 19X6 inflation.

3.5 The point where the estimated total cost line in Figure 3.9 intersects the vertical axis represents the estimated fixed cost. Substituting this value into the total cost given in the question allows us to obtain an estimate of the variable selling cost per unit:

	£
given total cost	660,000
less fixed element	200,000
variable element	460,000

The variable selling cost per unit is therefore:

$$\frac{\text{variable element}}{\text{unit sales volume}} = \frac{£460,000}{200,000} = £2.30$$

3.6 **(a)** The high and low volumes occur in 19X7 and 19X4 respectively, giving differences in total cost and output of:

	Total production cost (£)	Output (units)
High volume	1,850,000	1,800,000
Low volume	250,000	200,000
Difference	1,600,000	1,600,000

The variable cost per unit is:

$$\frac{\text{difference in total cost}}{\text{difference in activity}} = \frac{£1,600,000}{1,600,000} = £1$$

Substituting into either the high volume or low volume total cost will give the fixed cost. Using the high volume total cost gives:

	£
total cost	1,850,000
less variable element (1,800,000 @ £1)	1,800,000
fixed element	50,000

Tabulating the appropriate values for x (number of units) and y (total cost) will allow us to perform a regression analysis.

x	y	xy	x^2
000	000		
400	520	208,000	160,000
200	250	50,000	40,000
600	710	426,000	360,000
520	680	353,600	270,400
1,800	1,850	3,330,000	3,240,000
440	600	264,000	193,600
$\Sigma 3,960$	$\Sigma 4,610$	$\Sigma 4,631,000$	$\Sigma 4,264,000$

Total cost is given by the expression $y = a + bx$. From our tabulation, we can obtain the value of b (variable cost per unit):

$$b = \frac{n\Sigma xy - \Sigma x \, \Sigma y}{n\Sigma x^2 - (\Sigma x)^2} = \frac{6(4,631,000) - (3,960 \times 4,610)}{6(4,264,000) - 3,960^2}$$

$$= \frac{27,786,000 - 18,255,600}{25,584,000 - 15,681,600}$$

$$= \frac{9,530,400}{9,902,400}$$

$$= £0.96 \text{ (rounded)}.$$

Total fixed cost *a* is:

$$\frac{\Sigma y}{n} - \frac{b\Sigma x}{n} = \frac{4,610}{6} - \frac{0.96(3,960)}{6} = 768.33 - 633.60 = 134.73$$

that is, £134,730, remembering that values for *x* and *y* are stated in thousands.

(b) Estimated total production cost for 19X9 using the results of high–low analysis is:

	£
variable element (560,000 @ £1)	560,000
fixed element	50,000
total production cost	610,000

Using the regression results gives:

	£
variable element (560,000 @ £0.96)	537,600
fixed element	134,730
total production cost	672,330

Comment: There is a difference of some £62,000 between the two estimates, but the problem lies in deciding which should be used. Regression analysis may provide greater *mathematical* accuracy, but this is no guarantee of a more accurate *estimate*.

(c) The management accountant is presumably concerned by the fact that both the high and low volumes given are significantly different, both from the other past volume levels and from the estimated volume for 19X9. The danger of using such widely separated volumes in a high–low analysis is that there may well be a step (or even more than one) in the fixed element of total production cost. It may also be the case that the variable cost per unit is different at these two extreme volume levels from what it is likely to be at more 'normal' volumes. In other words, there is a risk that the *relevant range* is being breached by using such widely differing volumes as the basis of the estimation exercise. Because it assumes linear cost behaviour (i.e. that the variable cost per unit is constant and that the fixed cost is unchanging), high–low analysis is unable to make allowance for the potential changes in cost behaviour suggested above, with the consequence that the resulting cost estimate may be seriously distorted.

A possible solution might be to omit these two extreme volumes from the calculation, or to undertake further investigation of the costs so as to determine whether there is a significant impact on cost structure of operating at very high and very low volumes.

3.7 (a) The past costs are inflated as follows:

Year	Adjustment	Inflated amount (£)
19X3	(£133,000 × 1.07 × 1.05 × 1.06 × 1.04 × 1.05)	172,963
19X4	(£150,000 × 1.05 × 1.06 × 1.04 × 1.05)	182,309
19X5	(£120,000 × 1.06 × 1.04 × 1.05)	138,902
19X6	(£163,000 × 1.04 × 1.05)	177,996
19X7	(£170,000 × 1.05)	178,500

(b) The high and low volumes occur in 19X7 and 19X5 respectively, giving the following differences in total cost and volume:

	Volume of work (hours' processing time)	Total cost (£)
High volume	63,680	£178,500
Low volume	32,000	£138,902
Difference	31,680	£ 39,598

The variable cost per hour of processing time is:

$$\frac{\text{difference in total cost}}{\text{difference in activity}} = \frac{£39,598}{31,680} = £1.25 \text{ (rounded)}$$

Substituting into either the high or low volume total cost gives the fixed cost; using the high volume gives:

	£
total cost	178,500
less variable element (63,680 @ £1.25)	79,600
fixed element	98,900

(c) The estimated total cost for 19X8 is:

	£
variable cost (68,000 hours @ £1.25)	85,000
fixed cost	98,900
total cost	183,900

The charge to be made to each user department will therefore be:

$$(1/10 \times £98,900) + £1.25 \text{ per processing hour}$$
$$= £9,890 + £1.25 \text{ per processing hour}$$

(d) Two factors which may have a bearing on the Computer Services Department's 19X8 costs are:

■ *Changes in technology* These changes occur very rapidly and might mean that new hardware and/or software must be bought, so that the department's costs are likely to change as a result.

■ *Type of work performed* This will not necessarily be the same in 19X8 as it has been in the past, which could be reflected in the 19X8 costs.

3.8 **(a)** Applying a 75 per cent learning rate to tradesmen's time gives:

Cumulative output	Average hours per caravan		Total hours
1	60		60
2	(75% × 60)	= 45.00	90
4	(75% × 45)	= 33.75	135
8	(75% × 33.75)	= 25.31	202
16	(75% × 25.31)	= 18.98	304
32	(75% × 18.98)	= 14.24	456

For unskilled workers, the learning rate is 90 per cent, giving the following times:

Cumulative output	Average hours per caravan		Total hours
1	30		30
2	(90% × 30)	= 27.00	54
4	(90% × 27)	= 24.30	97
8	(90% × 24.30)	= 21.87	175
16	(90% × 21.87)	= 19.68	315
32	(90% × 19.68)	= 17.71	567

(b) The total cost of producing 32 static caravans is:

	£
Pre-fabricated parts, etc (32 @ £1,600)	51,200
Direct labour:	
tradesmen (456 hours @ £8)	3,648
unskilled (567 hours @ £4)	2,268
Direct labour-related costs:	
(25% of {£3,648 + £2,268})	1,479
Sundry costs (32 @ £500)	16,000
Total cost	74,595

(c) If the client's suggestion means that 16 of the caravans are to be produced this year and 16 next year, then the break in production will almost certainly result in some loss of the learning effect, as the learning curve is based on continuous production. Since the break may be lengthy, it is possible that, for the second batch of caravans, all of the benefit of learning will be lost.

This could be addressed in the computations by applying the learning curve to cumulative output of 16 caravans (the first batch) and using the resulting labour time for the second batch also. From the calculations above, this would give, for tradesmen, total hours of 304 per batch (i.e. 608 for 32 caravans); for unskilled workers, we would have 315 hours per batch – i.e. 630 for 32 caravans. (Hours required have been taken from workings in (a) above.)

Chapter 4

4.1 A £1.20

The absorption rate is calculated as:

$$\frac{\text{estimated overhead cost}}{\text{estimated machine hours}} = \frac{£156,000}{130,000} = £1.20 \text{ per machine hour.}$$

4.2 D £43,200 underabsorbed

Using the absorption rate calculated in Question 4.1, we can compare overhead absorbed with overhead incurred:

	£
Absorbed (120,000 machine hours @ £1.20)	144,000
Incurred	187,200
Underabsorption	43,200

4.3 (a) False (b) True (c) True (d) False (e) True (f) False (g) True

4.4 Examination of the data in the question suggests that Production is heavily machine-intensive and that Installation is labour-intensive, so a machine hour and direct labour hour rate would be appropriate, respectively, for the cost centres. A unit rate is inappropriate here, because the question states that a *range* of decoders is produced and installed: that is, cost units are not uniform (which would be the implication of using a unit rate). The absorption rates are:

Production

$$\frac{\text{estimated overhead cost}}{\text{estimated machine hours}} = \frac{£240,000}{48,000} = £5 \text{ per machine hour.}$$

Installation

$$\frac{\text{estimated overhead cost}}{\text{estimated direct labour hours}} = \frac{£330,000}{15,000} = £22 \text{ per direct labour hour.}$$

4.5 B £8

The cost per unit is built up as follows:

	£
Total direct cost	5
Production overhead (0.5 machine hours @ £4)	2
Inspection and packing overhead (0.1 direct labour hours @ £10)	1
	8

Remember that, for stock valuation purposes, selling and distribution costs are not absorbed.

4.6 (a) The blanket rate is:

$$\frac{\text{estimated overhead cost}}{\text{estimated number of client/hours}} = \frac{£306,000}{40,000} = £7.65 \text{ per client/hour.}$$

The estimated overhead cost is the total of the various overhead costs given separately in the question and total client hours is the total for the three cost centres.

(b) Table C4.1 is CD & Co's overhead analysis sheet.

It is possible to apportion general overhead on the basis of the number of junior partners/employees, in which case the cost-centre totals will be different to those shown in Table C4.1.

The absorption rates are still based on the number of client/hours, but, rather than the total used in part (a), we now use the client/hours for each cost centre:

TABLE C4.1 Overhead analysis sheet

Overhead cost	Amount (£)	Apportionment basis	Percentages	Civil (£)	Criminal (£)	Property (£)
Senior partner's salary	210,000	Not applicable	Allocated	70,000	80,000	60,000
Rates etc.	26,000	No. of offices	50%, 30%, 20%	13,000	7,800	5,200
Employee benefits	50,000	No. of junior partners/employees	48%, 36%, 16%	24,000	18,000	8,000
General	20,000	No. of client/hours	35%, 40%, 25%	7,000	8,000	5,000
Totals	306,000			114,000	113,800	78,200

$$\text{Civil:} \quad \frac{£114,000}{14,000} = £8.14 \text{ (rounded)}$$

$$\text{Criminal:} \quad \frac{£113,800}{16,000} = £7.11 \text{ (rounded)}$$

$$\text{Property:} \quad \frac{£78,200}{10,000} = £7.82$$

(c) Departmental absorption rates are almost certainly better for CD & Co, as their use gives some recognition to the different pattern of resource consumption necessary to support the work of each 'front-line' cost centre. However, given that each cost centre's work is based on client hours, use of a blanket rate may not, in these circumstances, cause too severe a distortion in unit costs.

4.7 (a) (i) *Annual budgeted volume*

The absorption rate is:

$$\frac{£600,000}{250,000} = £2.40 \text{ per machine hour.}$$

(ii) *Practical capacity*

Budgeted volume equals 80 per cent of current maximum operational (i.e. practical) capacity, so practical capacity is:

$$\frac{250,000 \text{ machine hours}}{0.8} = 312,500$$

Using this activity volume as the denominator gives an absorption rate of:

$$\frac{£600,000}{312,500} = £1.92 \text{ per machine hour}$$

(iii) *Normal volume*

Average annual machine hours per annum over the six-year period is:

$$\frac{250,000 + 340,000 + 370,000 + 260,000 + 350,000 + 380,000}{6} = 325,000$$

This gives an absorption rate of:

$$\frac{£600,000}{325,000} = £1.85 \text{ (rounded)}.$$

(b) Comparison of overhead absorbed and overhead incurred based on each of the rates in (a) gives:

	Budgeted volume (£)	Practical capacity (£)	Normal volume (£)
Overhead absorbed:			
260,000 @ £2.40/£1.92/£1.85	624,000	499,200	481,000
Overhead incurred	595,000	595,000	595,000
(Over-)/underabsorbed	(29,000)	95,800	114,000

(c) In broad terms, use of either practical capacity or normal volume results in a significant underabsorption of overhead, which suggests that the overhead charge per unit might be unrealistically low, resulting in understated unit costs. If unit costs are used as the basis of selling prices, then the company may also be underpricing: that is, losing revenue and profit unnecessarily.

The £95,800 underabsorption resulting from use of practical capacity could be viewed as a measure of the 'cost' of failing to achieve maximum operational capacity, but is maximum capacity a realistic basis upon which to set the absorption rate?

Use of normal volume may cause some problems in the specific circumstances. The question states that a substantial investment in increased operating capacity is envisaged at the start of Year 2. This will almost certainly have the effect of increasing overhead costs. It is therefore possible to suggest that the 325,000 machine hour normal volume is 'mismatched' with the Year 1 overhead cost and that this causes a distortion in the absorption rate. In addition, examination of the six-year plan's volumes indicates that HPW Ltd's business is cyclical and the accuracy of the volume estimates may be questioned.

In the absence of additional information, annual budgeted volume would seem the best option for the Year 1 absorption rate, possibly followed by a change to normal volume in Years 2–6.

4.8 **(a)** Each cost centre's overhead is:

	£
Laundry (70% × £400,000)	280,000
Transport (30% × £400,000)	120,000

Existing absorption rates are:

Laundry

$$\frac{\text{estimated cost centre overhead}}{\text{estimated number of cost units}} = \frac{£280,000}{48,000} = £5.83 \text{ per cost unit.}$$

Transport

$$\frac{\text{estimated cost centre overhead}}{\text{estimated transport km}} = \frac{£120,000}{100,000} = £1.20 \text{ per transport km.}$$

(b) Before calculating the ABC absorption rates, we need to determine the amount of overhead in each of the specified cost pools:

Cost pool	Overhead cost
Collection and delivery	$(15\% \times £400,000) = £60,000$
Loading/unloading of vans	$(10\% \times £400,000) = £40,000$
Laundry	$(30\% \times £400,000) = £120,000$
Drying	$(25\% \times £400,000) = £100,000$
Steam pressing	$(20\% \times £400,000) = £80,000$

Applying the given quantity of cost driver for each cost pool gives the following absorption rates:

$$\text{Collection and delivery } \frac{£60,000}{100,000} = £0.60 \text{ per transport km}$$

$$\text{Loading/unloading } \frac{£40,000}{8,000} = £5.00 \text{ per transport run}$$

$$\text{Laundry } \frac{£120,000}{300,000} = £0.40 \text{ per kg dry weight}$$

$$\text{Drying } \frac{£100,000}{400,000} = £0.25 \text{ per kg wet weight}$$

$$\text{Steam pressing } \frac{£80,000}{48,000} = £1.67 \text{ per cost unit}$$

(c) (i) Using NLS Ltd's existing absorption rates, the charge to the two sample contracts will be:

	Hillsmere Hospital (£)	Goreton Prison (£)
Transport (6,000/8,000 transport km @ £1.20)	7,200	9,600
Laundry (9,000/2,000 cost units @ £5.83)	52,470	11,660
Overhead charge	59,670	21,260

(ii) Applying the ABC absorption rates gives:

	Hillsmere Hospital (£)	Goreton Prison (£)
Collection and delivery:		
(6,000/8,000 transport km @ £0.60)	3,600	4,800
Loading/unloading:		
(1,200/300 transport runs @ £5.00)	6,000	1,500
Laundry:		
({9,000 × 4 kg dry weight} @ £0.40)	14,400	
({2,000 × 2 kg dry weight} @ £0.40)		1,600
Drying:		
({9,000 × 5.3 kg wet weight} @ £0.25)	11,925	
({2,000 × 3.3 kg wet weight} @ £0.25)		1,650
Steam pressing:		
(9,000/2,000 cost units @ £1.67)	15,030	3,340
Overhead charge	50,955	12,890

(d) The overhead charges calculated in (c) may support the idea of a change to ABC, since the departmental approach could well mask the usage of resources on different contracts. For example, the existing absorption method cannot explicitly or with any reasonable accuracy absorb overhead in a way which recognises the fact (important to the Laundry part of NLS Ltd's operation) that the dry weight per cost unit for the Hillsmere contract is twice that of the Goreton contract. ABC, however, charges the Hillsmere job twice as much Laundry overhead as the Goreton job because the importance of cost units' dry weight as a cost driver is recognised. On the face of it, changing to ABC would appear beneficial to NLS Ltd. This assumes that the cost drivers have been correctly identified and quantified and that the activities specified in the question are, in fact, the main ones constituting the company's operation. The potential cost of changing to, and operating, the new system should also be borne in mind.

Chapter 5

5.1 C £204,000

Contribution per tree is (selling price – variable cost) = (£40 – £6) = £34.

Total contribution is thus (units sold × contribution per unit) = (6,000 × £34) = £204,000.

5.2 C I and III

When production exceeds sales, there will be an increase in stock, and, because absorption costing stock values are higher than marginal costing, absorption costing will report the higher net profit. Statement II is incorrect because, where sales exceed production, marginal costing will report the higher net profit (which is not the case here).

5.3 (a) True (b) False (c) False (d) True (e) False (f) True

5.4 C £1,100

The contribution per passenger/kilometre is:

	£
Average fare per passenger/kilometre	0.30
Variable cost per passenger/kilometre	0.08
	0.22

Total passenger/kilometres from 10 additional journeys: (10 × 500) = 5,000.
Increase in profit = increase in total contribution = (5,000 × £0.22) = £1,100.

5.5 D Decrease of £16,000

If the sportswear department is closed, sales revenue (£30,000) will be lost, and only the cost of sales (£14,000) will be avoided. Staff wages and general store running costs will continue to be incurred whether the sportswear department is closed or not and therefore have no bearing on the profit effect of the decision.

5.6 **(a)** **(i)** *Absorption costing*

The absorption rate is $\dfrac{\text{estimated overhead cost}}{\text{estimated unit volume}} = \dfrac{£300,000}{25,000} = £12$ per unit.

Production cost per unit is:

	£
Direct materials	20
Direct labour	10
Direct expenses	6
Fixed production overhead	12
	48

Comparison of overhead absorbed with overhead incurred reveals the following:

	£
Overhead absorbed (26,000 units × £12)	312,000
Overhead incurred	324,000
Underabsorption	12,000

The absorption costing profit statement is as follows:

FDS Ltd: absorption costing profit statement for year just ended

	£	£
Sales (24,000 @ £90)		2,160,000
Cost of sales:		
Opening stock (2,000 @ £48)	96,000	
add Cost of production (26,000 @ £48)	1,248,000	
	1,344,000	
less Closing stock (4,000 @ £48)	192,000	
	1,152,000	
add Underabsorbed overhead	12,000	1,164,000
Gross profit		996,000
Selling overhead:		
variable (24,000 @ £4)	96,000	
fixed	110,000	
Administration overhead	80,000	286,000
Net profit		710,000

(The underabsorption is *added* to costs, because the company's predetermined absorption rate has absorbed less than the actual amount incurred.)

(ii) *Marginal costing*

The marginal production cost per unit is (£48 – the fixed production overhead per unit) = £36.

FDS Ltd: marginal costing profit statement for year just ended

	£	£
Sales		2,160,000
Cost of sales		
Opening stock (2,000 @ £36)	72,000	
add Marginal cost of production		
(26,000 @ £36)	936,000	
	1,008,000	
less Closing stock (4,000 @ £36)	144,000	
	864,000	
Variable selling overhead	96,000	960,000
Contribution		1,200,000
Fixed costs:		
Production overhead	324,000	
Selling overhead	110,000	
Administration overhead	80,000	514,000
Net profit		686,000

(Remember that *all* variable costs are deducted from sales in computation of contribution.)

(b) The two systems report a different net profit because there has been a stock movement during the year. In this instance, stock has increased by 2,000 units and, because the absorption costing stock values will include fixed production overhead (and will therefore be higher than the marginal costing equivalents), absorption costing net profit will be the higher to the extent of the fixed production overhead absorbed by the stock increase. A reconciliation of the profit figures can be effected as follows:

	£
Absorption costing net profit	710,000
Marginal costing net profit	686,000
Difference	24,000
Fixed production overhead absorbed by	
stock increase (2,000 × £12)	24,000

(c) The Operations Manager's claim is incorrect: marginal costing net profit will only fluctuate in relation to fluctuations in sales volume; absorption costing profit will react to changes in both sales and production volumes. Consider the effect on the net profit reported in each of the statements in (a) of a production volume of 27,000 units relative to unchanged sales and opening stock of 24,000 and 2,000 units respectively:

> Marginal costing: no change
> Absorption costing: increase of £12,000

(You may wish to check this; note that we are assuming that the change in production volume has no effect on costs.)

5.7 **(a)** Before preparing the marginal costing statement, we can separate wages and selling costs into their specific and general elements:

	£
Wages:	
General (40% of £112,000)	44,800
Specific:	
House insurance (60% of £28,000)	16,800
Car insurance (60% of £50,000)	30,000
Commercial insurance (60% of £34,000)	20,400

Selling costs	£
General (70% of £56,000)	39,200
Specific:	
House insurance (30% of £12,000)	3,600
Car insurance (30% of £30,000)	9,000
Commercial insurance (30% of £14,000)	4,200

MP & Co: contribution analysis of business

	House insurance £	Car insurance £	Commercial insurance £	Total £
Revenue	80,000	220,000	105,000	405,000
Specific costs:				
Variable	16,000	90,000	40,000	146,000
Wages	16,800	30,000	20,400	67,200
Selling	3,600	9,000	4,200	16,800
	36,400	129,000	64,600	230,000
Contribution to general costs	43,600	91,000	40,400	175,000
General costs:				
Administration				24,000
Wages				44,800
Selling costs				39,200
Net profit				67,000

(b) Comparison of the additional revenue and costs relating to the proposed sales campaign will permit assessment of the proposal's financial viability:

	£
Additional revenue (30% × £80,000)	24,000
less Additional variable costs (15% × £16,000)	2,400
Additional specific selling costs	10,000
Additional contribution to general costs	11,600

Since the proposal offers an increase in house insurance's contribution to the firm's general costs (hence in overall profit), it is financially worthwhile and the sales campaign should be undertaken.

5.8 (a) Of the cost of sales:

(20% of [£100,000 + £170,000 + £104,000]) = £74,800

is general. Amounts specific to each model are:

XX/3l (80% of £100,000) = £80,000
YY/7k (80% of £170,000) = £136,000
ZZ/4t (80% of £104,000) = £83,200.

Selling and distribution overhead:

	£
Total (£30,000 + £96,000 + £48,000)	174,000
General (20%)	34,800
Specific to:	
Model XX/3l (40%)	69,600
Model YY/7k (20%)	34,800
Model ZZ/4t (20%)	34,800

Administration overhead:

	£
Total (£30,000 + £30,000 + £30,000)	90,000
General (40%)	36,000
Specific to:	
Model XX/3l (40%)	36,000
Model YY/7k (10%)	9,000
Model ZZ/4t (10%)	9,000

PM Ltd: profit statement for last year

	Model XX/3l £	Model YY/7k £	Model ZZ/4t £	Total £
Sales	180,000	360,000	228,000	768,000
Specific costs:				
Cost of sales	80,000	136,000	83,200	299,200
Selling and distribution overhead	69,600	34,800	34,800	139,200
Administration overhead	36,000	9,000	9,000	54,000
	185,600	179,800	127,000	492,400
Contribution to general costs	(5,600)	180,200	101,000	275,600
General costs:				
Cost of sales				74,800
Selling and distribution overhead				34,800
Administration overhead				36,000
Net profit				130,000

(b) If Model XX/3l were dropped from the sales mix, a negative contribution to general costs would be avoided, and overall profit would have increased by £5,600 had this been done last year.

(c) The analysis in (b) is based on the following crucial assumptions:

1 Costs which are specific to Model XX/3l will be avoided if it is dropped from the sales mix.
2 General costs will not be affected by the change in sales mix.
3 Last year's figures are a reasonable indication of continued future unprofitability.
4 Dropping Model XX/3l from the sales mix will not have any adverse effect on sales of other models.

Chapter 6

6.1 (a) True (b) False (c) False (d) True (e) False

6.2 C £15,000

The CS ratio is:

$$\frac{\text{contribution}}{\text{selling price}} = \frac{(£15 - £6)}{£15} = 0.6$$

which gives a breakeven point of:

$$\frac{\text{total fixed cost}}{\text{CS ratio}} = \frac{(£6,000 + £3,000)}{0.6} = £15,000$$

6.3 B £42,000

Margin of safety is:

$$\frac{(\text{estimated or actual sales} - \text{breakeven sales})}{\text{estimated/actual sales}} \times 100\%$$

Inserting the values given in the question, we get:

$$\frac{(£70,000 - \text{breakeven sales})}{£70,000} = 40\%$$

Rearranging:

$$(£70,000 - \text{breakeven sales}) = 40\% \times £70,000$$
$$\text{i.e. } (£70,000 - \text{breakeven sales}) = £28,000$$

Breakeven sales are therefore £42,000.

6.4 (a) Option A (b) Option A (c) Option B (d) Option A (e) Option A

6.5 The completed paragraph reads as follows:

The assumption of linear costs means that unit variable cost is *constant* at all *volumes* and that total fixed cost is not *stepped*. In reality, the impact of *economies/ diseconomies of scale* means that costs will more likely be *curvilinear*. This discrepancy can be overcome by application of the concept of *relevant range* which limits *time and volume* to operational possibilities. This approach is consistent with the *short term* information requirements of management.

6.6   **B** 12,000

Unit sales required to earn a target profit are:

$$\frac{(\text{total fixed cost} + \text{target profit})}{\text{unit contribution}}$$

Inserting the values given in the question into this formula gives:

$$\frac{(\text{total fixed cost} + £150,000)}{£15} = 22,000 \text{ units}$$

In order to determine the breakeven point, we require a value for total fixed cost, which we can obtain by rearranging the formula above:

$$(\text{total fixed cost} + £150,000) = 22,000 \text{ units} \times £15$$
$$\text{i.e. } (\text{total fixed cost} + £150,000) = £330,000$$

Total fixed cost is thus £180,000, which allows us to obtain the breakeven point:

$$\frac{\text{total fixed cost}}{\text{contribution per unit}} = \frac{£180,000}{£15} = 12,000 \text{ units}$$

6.7   **(a)**   (i)   The breakeven point is:

$$\frac{\text{total fixed cost}}{\text{contribution per unit}} = \frac{(£80,000 + £60,000)}{(£600 - £250)} = 400 \text{ programs.}$$

(ii)   Margin of safety as a percentage of estimated sales:

$$\frac{(\text{estimated sales} - \text{breakeven sales})}{\text{estimated sales}} \times 100\% = \frac{(640 - 400)}{640} \times 100\% = 37.5\%$$

(b) Sales required to earn a target profit of £56,000 are:

$$\frac{(\text{total fixed cost} + \text{target profit})}{\text{contribution per unit}} = \frac{(£140,000 + £56,000)}{(£650 - £250)} = 560 \text{ programs}$$

Estimated sales volume (640 programs) will therefore yield profit in excess of the target. The amount of this excess is:

$$(\text{estimated volume} - \text{target volume}) \times \text{unit contribution}$$
$$= (640 - 560) \times £350 = £28,000.$$

(c) Figure C6.1 is BX Ltd's breakeven chart.

This breakeven chart is based on an assumed maximum volume of 700 programs, which is sufficiently high to cover both the breakeven and estimated sales volumes. You may have selected a different maximum for your chart.

The following key values have been used to plot the breakeven chart:

Total fixed cost: (£80,000 + £60,000) = £140,000 at all volumes.
Total cost:
  At zero volume: £140,000 (= total fixed cost)
  At 700 programs:

total variable cost (700 @ £250)	£175,000
total fixed cost	£140,000
	£315,000

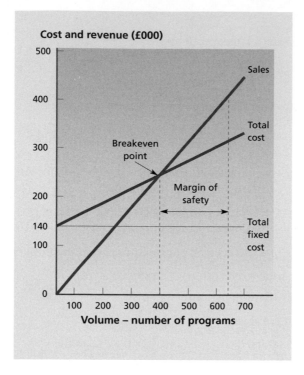

FIGURE C6.1
BX Ltd breakeven chart

Sales

At zero volume: zero
At 700 programs: (700 @ £600) = £420,000

(d) If the overseas contract is won, annual volume will increase by more than 350 per cent of its estimated level for next year. This means that the expanded volume will almost certainly lie outside BX Ltd's relevant range. In addition, the five-year time period is greater than that which applies to the model used in the earlier parts of the question. Given these two factors, the assumptions underlying cost/volume/ profit analysis are most unlikely to hold true. For example, such a large increase in volume will likely result in an increase in fixed costs; unit variable cost may be affected – especially if the company changes production methods in order to deal with the greater volume; and the sales price relating to the contract might be different to that which applies to domestic sales, meaning that the company is effectively selling two products.

If the company wishes to undertake a cost/volume/profit analysis of the situation which might result from winning the contract, the model used in (a)–(c) above will not apply, and would give seriously misleading results were the company to use it. Sensitivity analysis would need to be employed to allow for the impact on the model's variables of the potential significant change in the business.

6.8 (a) (i) Breakeven point in occupied stall days is:

$$\frac{\text{total fixed cost}}{\text{contribution per unit}} = \frac{\text{£46,000}}{(\text{£30} - \text{£5})} = 1,840$$

Before we can calculate the margin of safety, we must determine the estimated number of occupied stall days (i.e. estimated sales) for the period under review. This will be:

$$(\text{number of stalls} \times \text{number of days available} \times \text{occupancy rate})$$
$$= (20 \times 365 \times 80\%) = 5,840.$$

(ii) Margin of safety:

$$\frac{(\text{estimated sales} - \text{breakeven sales})}{\text{estimated sales}} \times 100\% = \frac{(5,840 - 1,840)}{5,840} \times 100\% = 68.5\%$$

(b) If the proposed reduction in charge per day occurs, the stable will effectively be offering two services, so a weighted average approach will need to be adopted in breakeven calculations. The weightings will be based on the estimated 'mix' of 60 per cent of estimated occupied stall days being charged at the full rate of £30 per day and 40 per cent being charged at the reduced rate of £21.

6.9 (a) The weighted average CS ratio can be determined from total sales revenue and total contribution:

	£
Total sales	
Car hire (10,000 @ £30)	300,000
Minibus hire (4,000 @ £50)	200,000
Van hire (8,000 @ £37.50)	300,000
	800,000
Total contribution	
Car hire (10,000 @ {£30 – £4})	260,000
Minibus hire (4,000 @ {£50 – £25})	100,000
Van hire (8,000 @ {£37.50 – £12.50})	200,000
	560,000

Weighted average CS ratio:

$$\frac{\text{total contribution}}{\text{total sales}} = \frac{£560,000}{£800,000} = 0.7$$

The company's breakeven point is:

$$\frac{\text{total fixed cost}}{\text{weighted average CS ratio}} = \frac{£420,000}{0.7} = £600,000$$

(b) The company's profit/volume chart is shown in Figure C6.2. Since the profit/volume chart illustrates a three-service business, the horizontal axis must be scaled in terms of revenue rather than units. Figure C6.2 uses £800,000 as the maximum value on the horizontal axis, which is based on the estimated sales given in the question, for which we calculated the revenue in (a). You may have chosen a different maximum value.

To plot the profit/loss line, we need to know the loss at zero volume plus the profit/loss at some volume greater than zero:

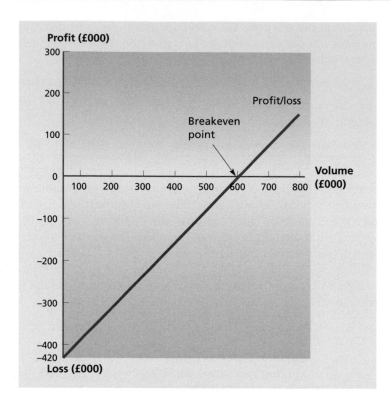

Profit (£000)

Volume (£000)

Breakeven point

Profit/loss

Loss (£000)

FIGURE **C6.2**
**Speedi Ltd
profit/volume chart**

at zero volume, loss = total fixed cost = £420,000
at £600,000 volume (i.e. breakeven point), profit/loss = 0

Joining these two points and extending upwards as far as £800,000 volume provides us with the profit/loss line.

6.10 (a) Since no unit data are given, breakeven calculations must be based on the contribution/sales ratio. We can determine the existing CS ratio from the marginal costing profit statement given:

$$\frac{\text{total contribution}}{\text{total sales}} = \frac{£198,000}{£440,000} = 0.45$$

CM Ltd's breakeven point is:

$$\frac{\text{total fixed cost}}{\text{CS ratio}} = \frac{£90,000}{0.45} = £200,000$$

Margin of safety must likewise be based on revenue:

$$\frac{(\text{estimated sales} - \text{breakeven sales})}{\text{estimated sales}} \times 100\% = \frac{(£440,000 - £200,000)}{£440,000} \times 100\% = 54.5\%$$

Managing director's suggestion

If total material cost reduces to £80,000 from its present level of £102,000, total contribution will increase by a corresponding amount: that is, from £198,000 to £220,000, giving a revised CS ratio of:

$$\frac{£220,000}{£440,000} = 0.5$$

The revised breakeven point, allowing for the £24,000 increase in total fixed cost, will be:

$$\frac{(£90,000 + £24,000)}{0.5} = £228,000$$

Margin of safety:

$$\frac{(£440,000 - £228,000)}{£440,000} \times 100\% = 48.2\%$$

Sales director's suggestion

If sales volume increases and there is no increase in variable costs as a proportion of sales, the CS ratio under this option will be the same as for the original data: that is, 0.45. However, total fixed cost will increase, resulting in a revised breakeven point of:

$$\frac{(£90,000 + £45,000)}{0.45} = £300,000$$

Margin of safety will be affected not only by the revised breakeven point, but also by the increase in estimated sales volume from £440,000 to (£440,000 × 1.2) = £528,000:

$$\frac{(£528,000 - £300,000)}{£528,000} \times 100\% = 43.2\%$$

(b) A summary of the indicators calculated in (a) is given below:

	Original estimates	Managing director's suggestion	Sales director's suggestion
Breakeven point	£200,000	£228,000	£300,000
Margin of safety	54.5%	48.2%	43.2%

In purely financial terms, the original estimates are best: the breakeven point is lowest, which makes it the easiest to achieve, and the margin of safety is the highest, which means that profit under this option is less vulnerable to a drop in demand than under the other two options.

(c) The sort of factor which management should consider includes:

- The possibility of reducing costs other than materials. For example, can fixed costs be reduced?
- Reduction in selling price(s) in order to stimulate demand, which may avoid the need for a costly advertising campaign.
- The accuracy of the estimates which have been used. The difference between the original estimates and the managing director's suggestion is not wide; if there is serious inaccuracy in the original estimates, it may be that this suggestion is better on financial grounds.

■ What developments are likely to occur in CM Ltd's market in the period under review? Is competition likely to stay much the same, increase or decrease? Are there any opportunities which could be exploited, or possible threats which need to be countered?

■ If changes were made next year, how consistent are these with the company's longer-term strategy?

You may have mentioned different factors. The important point, however, is that management would be ill-advised to take a final decision based solely on the very limited analysis in (a) and (b).

Chapter 7

7.1 **B** Sunk cost

Although the loan repayment is a future cash flow, it is one which arises because of a different decision to the one under consideration and is therefore a sunk cost.

7.2 **D** Net relevant benefit of £600

The hardware's original cost of £900 is a historic cost and is therefore a sunk cost (irrelevant). The engineer will be paid £10 per hour for the time required to modify the hardware, irrespective of whether modification work is done, so this cost is also irrelevant.

7.3 **D** £10,000

The sales of £10,000 will be lost if the special order is accepted – a relevant cost of accepting. The wages cost of £7,000 will be incurred irrespective of whether the special order is accepted, and so is irrelevant. The sales value of the special order is relevant to the decision about whether or not to accept, but *not* to calculation of the opportunity cost of acceptance.

7.4 **C** £350

The original purchase cost of the soil is irrelevant; its alternative uses are:

■ use on another job, saving £300 in purchases; or
■ sell to a client, which will yield a benefit of:

	£
Sales value	450
less Delivery charge	100
	350

Of these alternatives, sale to a client is therefore better, which defines the opportunity cost of using the topsoil as being £350.

7.5 (a) False: this will be paid irrespective of *who* undertakes the work.

(b) True: this will be paid as the result of a previous decision to employ the staff member concerned, and will be unaffected by this decision.

(c) True: this type of factor cannot readily be incorporated into an analysis of relevant costs/benefits.

(d) False: this extra cost will be incurred irrespective of *who* undertakes the work, and is thus irrelevant.

(e) False: the wages clerk's salary will be paid irrespective of who undertakes the work, and is irrelevant.

7.6 (*Note*: In this, and the answers which follow, we have adopted the tabular approach to analysis used in Chapter 7. You need not have done this, providing you have tested all financial items against each criterion for relevance.)

(a) Table C7.1 tests all the financial data from the question against each of the criteria for relevance. Relevant items have a tick in each of the three 'criteria' columns.

TABLE C7.1

Item	Future?	Cash?	Differs?	Amount (£)
Total funds raised – Venue A	✓	✓	✓	300,000
Fund-raising Manager's travel and accommodation	✓	✓	✓	1,600
Transport:				
Original cost		✓		60,000
Depreciation	✓			10,000
Hire cost	✓	✓	✓	4,000
Rent of premises	✓	✓	✓	10,000
Refreshments	✓	✓	✓	2,000
Total funds raised – Venue B	✓	✓	✓	280,000
Purchase of materials	✓	✓		30,000
Salary of Fund-raising Manager	✓	✓		1,500
Printing	✓	✓		6,000

Assumptions

1 The purchase cost of materials, the Fund-raising Manager's salary and the printing of promotional posters are costs which will arise irrespective of the venue chosen and are thus irrelevant.

2 All items identified as relevant in Table C7.1 are cash flows.

3 Estimates are accurate.

4 No relevant costs/benefits exist, apart from those listed in the question.

(b) The net relevant benefit of holding the fund-raising event at Venue A is:

	£	£
Relevant benefits		
Additional funds raised (£300,000 – £280,000)		20,000
Relevant costs		
Fund-raising Manager: travel etc.	1,600	
Hire of transport	4,000	
Rent of premises	10,000	
Refreshments	2,000	17,600
Net relevant benefit		2,400

Note that, of the funds raised, £280,000 is irrelevant, as this amount will be raised irrespective of which venue is used for the event.

As it yields a net relevant benefit of £2,400, Venue A is better on financial grounds.

7.7 **(a)** Financial items having a tick in each of the three 'criteria' columns in Table C7.2 are relevant to the decision.

TABLE C7.2

Item	Future?	Cash?	Differs?	Amount (£)
Sales revenue	✓	✓	✓	7,000
Purchase cost of materials in stock		✓		1,200
Purchase cost of additional materials	✓	✓	✓	2,200
Cost of 200 hours of skilled labour	✓	✓		1,100
Cost of 50 hours of semi-skilled labour	✓	✓	✓	175
Production manager's overtime		✓		300
Hire of special machine	✓	✓	✓	1,000
Original cost of plant and equipment		✓		60,000
Depreciation of plant and equipment	✓			2,000
Fixed overhead at £12 per labour hour	✓		✓	3,000
Variable overhead at £6 per labour hour	✓	✓	✓	1,500

(b) The net relevant benefit of accepting the special order are:

	£	£
Relevant benefits		
Payment by building firm (100 @ £70)		7,000
Relevant costs		
Purchase of additional materials	2,200	
Casual semi-skilled labour (50 hours @ £3.50)	175	
Hire of plant (2 months @ £500)	1,000	
Variable overhead (250 hours @ £6)	1,500	4,875
Net relevant benefit		2,125

Note that the variable overhead will relate to *all* labour hours: that is, 200 skilled plus 50 semi-skilled.

As acceptance yields a net relevant benefit, the special order would be accepted on financial grounds.

(c) Qualitative factors which may be relevant to this situation include:

1 The possibility of receiving repeat orders from the same source in future.

2 Potential improvement in workforce morale as a result of the extra work – skilled labour is stated to be 'not particularly busy'.

3 How quickly does the building firm require the padlocks? Can the order be completed in time?

7.8 (a) Financial data relevant to the decision are identified in Table C7.3 by a tick under each 'criterion' heading.

TABLE C7.3

Item	Future?	Cash?	Differs?	Amount (£)
Purchase cost of chemicals:				
CF Ltd	✓	✓	✓	432,000
If GP Ltd stores	✓	✓	✓	360,000
Maintenance costs:				
Apportionment of operative's salary	✓		✓	800
Materials' purchase	✓	✓	✓	1,200
Sales value of temperature equipment	✓	✓		1,800
Stock of fuel:				
Original purchase cost		✓		400
Sales value	✓	✓	✓	350
Purchase saving	✓	✓	✓	500
Storekeeper:				
Present salary	✓	✓		15,000
Casual employee	✓	✓	✓	8,000
Leasehold payment	✓	✓		4,000
Insurance premium				
Operate store	✓	✓	✓	2,000
Close store	✓	✓	✓	800
Overheads:				
£0.80 per kg material stored	✓	✓	✓	57,600
apportionment of general costs	✓			2,400

Note that only the *additional* purchase cost of £1.00 per kg is relevant to the decision; £5 per kg will be paid irrespective of the course of action adopted. The sale proceeds from temperature and humidity control equipment are irrelevant, as they will either be received now, or in one year's time: that is, irrespective of the decision about *when* the secure store should be closed.

The opportunity 'benefit' attaching to the stock of fuel is determined by its best alternative use, which is to use elsewhere, saving purchase costs of £500.

£800 of the insurance premiums is irrelevant, as it will be paid irrespective of the decision: although the store may be closed, it will nevertheless require to be insured against, for instance, fire.

The net relevant cost of closure now is:

	£
Relevant benefits	
Purchase of maintenance parts avoided	1,200
Fuel purchase avoided	500
Employment of casual labour avoided	8,000
Saving in insurance premiums	1,200
Saving in variable overheads	57,600
	68,500
Relevant cost	
Additional purchase cost of chemicals (£432,000 – £360,000)	72,000
Net relevant cost	3,500

On financial grounds, the secure store should be kept open for the year, as immediate closure yields a net relevant cost.

(b) The practical difficulties involved in incorporating opportunity cost into analyses such as that in (a) are:

1 It may be very difficult to identify viable alternative courses of action; and even if these can be identified, it may be equally difficult to quantify the 'benefit foregone' as a result of not pursuing the best alternative.

2 Opportunity costs may therefore contain a large element of subjectivity, which is undesirable. For example, in GP Ltd's case, how sure are we that the alternatives identified for use of the fuel stock are viable, and, if viable, how accurate are the monetary amounts attaching to them?

7.9 (a) The relevant financial data for this decision are identified in Table C7.4.

	£
Sales revenue lost	26,000
less Associated costs saved: expenses	6,000
	20,000

The associated labour cost of £8,000 will be incurred irrespective of the decision under consideration and the fixed overhead absorbed is not a cash flow: both are therefore irrelevant.

(b) The net relevant benefit of completing the research is:

	£	£
Relevant benefit		
Payment by prospective client		35,000
Relevant costs		
Material purchases	2,000	
Opportunity cost of labour	20,000	
Additional fixed overheads	5,000	27,000
Net relevant benefit		8,000

As this course of action yields a net relevant benefit, it is better on financial grounds.

The opportunity cost of using MCM & Co's labour to complete the research is:

TABLE C7.4

Item	Future?	Cash?	Differs?	Amount (£)
Offer by prospective client	✓	✓	✓	35,000
Costs of research to date		✓		50,000
Payment by original client		✓		15,000
Cost of senior partner's time		✓		1,300
Materials to complete:				
Already purchased		✓		3,000
Special purchases	✓	✓	✓	2,000
Labour cost:				
Lost sales revenue	✓	✓	✓	26,000
Associated labour cost	✓	✓		8,000
Associated expenses cost	✓	✓	✓	6,000
Associated fixed overhead absorbed	✓		✓	4,000
Fixed overheads for completion of research:				
Additional	✓	✓	✓	5,000
Absorbed at 50% of labour cost	✓		✓	4,000

7.10 (a) Relevant financial data are identified in Table C7.5. All the costs and revenues relating to 'normal' business during the period will arise irrespective of the decision and are therefore irrelevant. The sale proceeds of the old kitchen equipment will likewise be received irrespective of the decision (either now or in January) and are also irrelevant. However, the *extra* installation cost is relevant, as offering the two-night holidays requires that installation be brought forward to October, thereby incurring the additional cost.

The net relevant benefit of offering the two-night holidays is:

	£	£
Relevant benefits		
Additional revenue from room lettings		24,000
Additional revenue from bar and restaurant		
(£88,000 – £72,000)		16,000
		40,000
Relevant costs		
Additional variable costs:		
Room lettings	1,200	
Bar and restaurant	9,000	
Additional wages and salaries	8,000	
Additional administrative costs	3,000	
Additional installation cost	1,500	22,700
Net relevant benefit		17,300

Note that it is the *incremental* (i.e. additional) costs/benefits which are relevant. Costs/revenues associated with 'normal' business will arise regardless of the decision and are therefore irrelevant.

TABLE C7.5

Item	Future?	Cash?	Differs?	Amount (£)
Room lettings:				
Revenue – 'normal'	✓	✓		12,500
Revenue – 2-night	✓	✓	✓	24,000
Variable costs – 'normal'	✓	✓		625
Variable costs – 2-night	✓	✓	✓	1,200
Bar and restaurant:				
Revenue – 'normal' only	✓	✓		72,000
Revenue – with 2-night	✓	✓	✓	88,000
Variable costs – 'normal' only	✓	✓		43,000
Variable costs – with 2-night	✓	✓	✓	52,000
Staff wages and salaries:				
Permanent staff	✓	✓		14,000
With 2-night	✓	✓	✓	22,000
Administrative costs:				
'Normal' only	✓	✓		16,000
With 2-night	✓	✓	✓	19,000
Rates and insurance	✓	✓		5,000
Absorption of fixed overheads:				
Per single room	✓		✓	14
Per double room	✓		✓	20
New equipment:				
Purchase cost	✓	✓		20,000
Additional installation cost	✓	✓	✓	1,500
Old equipment:				
Purchase cost		✓		4,000
Sales proceeds	✓	✓		800

On financial grounds, the two-night holidays should be offered, as a net relevant benefit results.

(b) Assumptions in (a):

1 'Normal' business will be unaffected by the two-night holidays, which means that all costs and revenues relating to 'normal' business have been omitted from the analysis as irrelevant. However, had some of the 'normal' business transferred to the two-night holidays, the analysis would have to allow for the consequent reduction in *revenue* associated with 'normal' business (the related variable costs would presumably still be incurred).

2 The hotel has sufficient capacity to deal with the expected volume of two-night holidays *and* with 'normal' business. If it has not, the revenue and variable costs associated with either or with both types of business would have to be reduced accordingly. Linked to this is an assumption that the new kitchen equipment can be installed in time for the start of the period during which two-night holidays are to be offered.

3 There are no additional costs involved in offering the two-night holidays: advertising them, for example, or costs arising because the new kitchen equipment is

not installed in time. If there are any such costs, they would need to be included in the analysis as relevant.

4 All the relevant costs and benefits are cash flows.

(c) If the decision related to a possible discontinuation of room-letting during the off-peak season, the following items would be treated differently in the financial analysis:

1 Revenue and variable costs relating to 'normal' room lettings, would, respectively, become a relevant cost (revenue lost) and a relevant benefit (cost avoided), and, as such, would need to be included in the analysis.

2 A reduction in the revenue and variable costs relating to 'normal' business in the bar and restaurant would need to be included as a relevant cost and benefit, respectively. Note, however, that these would only *reduce* if room lettings were discontinued, since non-residents would presumably still use the bar and restaurant.

Other financial data which we treated as irrelevant in (a) may also become relevant: there may, for example, be a reduction in administrative and permanent staff costs.

Chapter 8

8.1 D £0.880

Kg per brick is:

$$\frac{\text{direct material cost per brick}}{\text{cost per kg of material}} = \frac{£0.05}{£0.20} = 0.25$$

Contribution per brick is:

	£	£
Selling price		0.40
less Variable costs:		
Direct materials	0.05	
Direct labour	0.10	
Variable selling costs	0.03	0.18
		0.22

Contribution per kg of materials is:

$$\frac{\text{contribution per brick}}{\text{kg per brick}} = \frac{£0.22}{0.25} = £0.88$$

8.2 D £0.40

The relevant cost per brick to make is:

	£
Direct materials	0.05
Direct labour	0.10
	0.15

(Note that the variable selling cost is not a cost of *making*, but of selling, and will be incurred irrespective of who makes the bricks. It is therefore irrelevant.)

The additional cost per brick to subcontract is (£0.25 – £0.15) = £0.10 and the additional cost to subcontract per kg of material is:

$$\frac{\text{additional cost per brick}}{\text{kg per brick}} = \frac{£0.10}{0.25} = £0.40$$

8.3 **B** The area bounded by B, C, D, 0

The feasible region for '≤' constraints lies to their left, and must be such that *all* constraints are satisfied. The area B, C, D, 0 is the only one in Figure 8.3 which meets this criterion: that is, which lies to the left of all constraint functions.

8.4 **C** £108

Target cost is calculated as: (selling price – required profit). Required profit here is 10 per cent of sales. At a selling price of £120, this is:

$$(10\% \times £120) = £12$$

Target cost is therefore:

$$(£120 – £12) = £108.$$

8.5 (a) False (b) True (c) True (d) False (e) True

8.6 (a) The limiting factor in this example is the number of machine hours available. Machine hours per unit for each style is calculated as:

$$\frac{\text{production overhead per unit}}{\text{production overhead per machine hour}}$$

	Style 1	Style 2	Style 3	Style 4
Production overhead per unit (£)	20	25	35	40
Production overhead per machine hour (£)	5	5	5	5
Machine hours per unit	4	5	7	8

Although it is not strictly necessary in order to answer the question, we can confirm that the 100,000 machine hours available in the forthcoming period are insufficient to meet projected demand in full for all four products:

Style 1: maximum demand = 8,000, requires (8,000 × 4)   32,000 hours
Style 2: maximum demand = 6,500, requires (6,500 × 5)   32,500 hours
Style 3: maximum demand = 4,800, requires (4,800 × 7)   33,600 hours
Style 4: maximum demand = 3,200, requires (3,200 × 8)   25,600 hours

Total machine hours required to meet demand in full   123,700

There is thus a shortfall of 23,700 hours.

The four products must be ranked according to their respective contribution per machine hour, with the highest contribution per hour being ranked first. Contribution per machine hour is:

$$\frac{\text{contribution per unit}}{\text{machine hours per unit}}$$

Contribution per unit requires deduction from unit selling price of all variable costs. The variable selling overhead is £4 per unit for all products; the variable production overhead must, however, be calculated:

Variable overhead per unit: (machine hours per unit × £2)

£

Style 1: (4 hours × £2) =   8
Style 3: (7 hours × £2) = 14
Style 2: (5 hours × £2) = 10
Style 4: (8 hours × £2) = 16

Calculation of unit contribution, contribution per machine hour and rankings are given below:

	Style 1	Style 2	Style 3	Style 4
	£	£	£	£
Selling price per unit	80	110	145	170
Variable costs per unit:				
Direct materials	12	30	35	40
Direct labour	16	20	15	20
Production overhead	8	10	14	16
Selling overhead	4	4	4	4
	40	64	68	80
Contribution per unit	40	46	77	90
Machine hours per unit	4	5	7	8
Contribution per machine hour (£)	10.00	9.20	11.00	11.25
Ranking	III	IV	II	I

Producing/selling according to the rankings above gives:

	Hours
Produce/sell 3,200 Style 4 uses	25,600
Produce/sell 4,800 Style 3 uses	33,600
Produce/sell 8,000 Style 1 uses	32,000
Total hours used	91,200

There are therefore (100,000 – 91,200) = 8,800 machine hours available for production of Style 2. However, we know from our earlier calculation that, in order to fully satisfy demand for this product, we need 32,500 hours. Therefore, some demand for this product will be unsatisfied, as we can only produce/sell a quantity sufficient to utilise the remaining 8,800 hours. This quantity can be calculated as:

$$\frac{\text{hours remaining}}{\text{hours per unit of Style 2}} = \frac{8,800}{5} = 1,760 \text{ units.}$$

Thus the full production/sales plan is:

Units
Style 1: 8,000
Style 2: 1,760
Style 3: 4,800
Style 4: 3,200

(b) Where more than one resource constraint exists, analysis based on contribution per unit of limiting factor cannot be used. Instead, we must employ *linear programming*, a mathematical technique for optimising some outcome (total contribution in this case) subject to a number of constraints (shortage of machine hours and labour hours here). Mathematical expressions for total contribution (the *objective function*) and the constraints will be formulated and the contribution-maximising output/sales mix determined by *Simplex*. (A graphical approach cannot be used in this example because there are more than two products, each of which requires its own axis on a graphical representation of the problem.) Simplex works by trying successive solutions until the optimum is found: that is, it is an *iterative* process, normally requiring computer software.

(c) Two solutions to the shortage of machine hours might be:

- *Acquire additional machinery* This should certainly solve the problem, but may be costly if the machines are to be bought. Also, should demand subsequently fall, the company may find itself in the equally undesirable position of having surplus capacity.
- *Subcontract production which cannot be undertaken in-house* This may be cheaper than acquiring additional machinery and avoids the possibility of surplus capacity if demand should fall. However, there may be problems ensuring consistency of quality between subcontracted items and those produced in-house, with resulting cost implications (e.g. for inspection or for customer returns).

8.7 **(a)** Before we can determine the shortfall in theatre hours, we need to calculate the average theatre hours per procedure for each of the four categories:

$$\frac{\text{variable theatre cost per procedure}}{\text{variable cost per theatre hour}}$$

General: $\dfrac{\text{£}60}{\text{£}25} = 2.4$ hours/procedure

Orthopaedic: $\dfrac{\text{£}75}{\text{£}25} = 3.0$ hours/procedure

Renal: $\dfrac{\text{£}120}{\text{£}25} = 4.8$ hours/procedure

Coronary: $\dfrac{\text{£}170}{\text{£}25} = 6.8$ hours/procedure

Theatre hours required to fully meet each medical specialty's anticipated requirements in the period can now be determined and compared to theatre hours available in order to determine the extent of the shortfall:

		Hours
General: 3,500 procedures require	$(3,500 \times 2.4)$	8,400
Orthopaedic: 2,400 procedures require	$(2,400 \times 3)$	7,200
Renal: 1,800 procedures require	$(1,800 \times 4.8)$	8,640
Coronary: 1,200 procedures require	$(1,200 \times 6.8)$	8,160
Theatre hours required		32,400
Theatre hours available (4 suites $\times$ 16 hours $\times$ 365 days)		23,360
Shortfall in theatre hours is thus		9,040

(b) The direct labour costs relate to permanent staff whose salaries will be paid irrespective of where the procedures are performed. The apportionment of general overhead is not a cash flow and the underlying cost is assumed to be unaffected by the rankings and potential related decisions. Both of these items are therefore irrelevant. Calculation of the relevant extra cost per procedure and per theatre hour for each category of procedure is shown below:

	General £	Orthopaedic £	Renal £	Coronary £
Surgical and medical supplies	102	120	160	180
Variable theatre costs	60	75	120	170
Relevant cost per procedure	162	195	280	350
Cost per procedure at Southford Royal Infirmary	558	600	760	1,302
Extra cost per procedure	396	405	480	952
Theatre hours per procedure	2.4	3.0	4.8	6.8
Extra cost per hour (£)	165	135	100	140
Ranking	IV	II	I	III

(c) Three problems likely to arise if the ranking in (b) is implemented are as follows:

- Can Southford Royal Infirmary cope with the type and quantity of procedures transferred?
- Would medical emergencies override the rankings? Or is there a danger of the rankings prevailing at the expense of medical necessity?
- Who will make the decision about which specific cases to transfer? Will this be a medical or an administrative decision?

8.8 The following are some circumstances in which selling price lower than cost may be acceptable:

- market recession;
- attempt to gain market penetration;
- provide a barrier to entry for a potential new competitor;
- loss leader pricing;
- to utilise spare capacity;
- to obtain an order; and
- stage in its life cycle reached by a product/service may require such a price to be set.

(For more detail, refer to Chapter 8.)

8.9 **(a)** In this example, profit is stated in terms of sales value: that is, as a margin. Since we are working towards selling price from cost, an adjustment is necessary. If profit is 25 per cent of sales value, then (sales value – profit) = 25 per cent of sales value: that is, total cost is equal to 75 per cent of sales value. Sales value is therefore (total cost ÷ 0.75).

The selling price which results from the company's 'cost +' formula is:

	£
Direct costs	230
Production overhead (14 hours @ £7.50)	105
Non-production costs	67
Total cost per unit	402
Selling price per unit (£402 ÷ 0.75)	536

This is higher than the selling price of £492 required to achieve the 20 per cent increase in sales volume, so it seems unlikely that the 'cost +' price will achieve the desired increase, since the higher the selling price, the lower is demand.

(b) Target cost is:

$$(\text{selling price} - \text{required profit})$$

giving:

$$(£492 - \{25\% \times £492\}) = £369$$

(c) The existing overhead costs per unit are based on a volume of 5,000 units; the total estimated overhead cost from which these unit costs derive is:

$$(\text{unit volume} \times \text{overhead cost per unit})$$

giving:

Production overhead (5,000 × £77) = £525,000
Non-production costs (5,000 × £67) = £335,000.

Revised overhead absorption rates per unit are:

$$\frac{\text{overhead cost}}{\text{number of units}}$$

giving production overhead:

$$\frac{£525,000}{6,000} = £87.50 \text{ per unit.}$$

and non-production costs:

$$\frac{£335,000}{6,000} = £56 \text{ per unit.}$$

(d) The revised cost per unit is:

	£
Direct costs (unchanged)	230.00
Production overhead (from (c))	87.50
Non-production costs (from (c))	56.00
Total cost per unit	373.50

In (b), the target cost was calculated as £369, so we can conclude that the target cost will not be achieved.

8.10 Report

To: Management, DSC Partnership

From: Financial Adviser

Quotation to Ministry of Agriculture and Fisheries

The lowest quotation which is financially viable is based on the relevant costs of undertaking the work: that is, the future cash flows which differ depending on whether or not the work is performed. Table C8.1 lists all the financial items potentially concerned and identifies those which meet the criteria for being treated as relevant to this decision. Only those items having a tick in each of the three columns in Table C8.1 are relevant, and these are listed along with the associated amounts.

TABLE **C8.1**

Item	Future?	Cash?	Differs?	Amount (£)
Saving in feed purchase	✓	✓	✓	4,000
Disposal of feed	✓	✓	✓	1,600
Storage of equipment	✓	✓	✓	750
Saving in refurbishment	✓	✓	✓	200
Labour costs:				
Payment for 300 hours	✓	✓		1,200
Cost of other work not done:				
scrubland	✓	✓	✓	2,000
repairs	✓	✓	✓	2,800*
Travel and subsistence cost	✓	✓	✓	2,200
Payment to chargehand	✓	✓	✓	400
Fixed costs for period	✓	✓		28,000
Extra fixed costs	✓	✓	✓	2,700

Note: * Subcontracting cost saved (£3,400) *less* material cost incurred (£600).

Quotation

	£	£
Relevant benefits:		
Saving in feed purchase costs	4,000	
Saving in refurbishment costs	200	4,200
Relevant costs:		
Disposal of existing feed	1,600	
Equipment storage	750	
Opportunity cost of labour*	2,800	
Travel and subsistence costs	2,200	
Payment to chargehand	400	
Extra fixed costs	2,700	10,450
Net relevant cost		6,250

Note: *Opportunity cost of labour:* an opportunity cost is defined as the benefit foregone as a result of pursuing one course of action rather than the best alternative; if the ministry's work is undertaken, the workers will be unable to perform one of the stated other tasks:

- clear scrubland, saving £2,000; or
- undertake repairs, saving (£3,400 − £600) = £2,800.

The amount of the opportunity cost involved is defined by the best of these alternatives – that is, undertaking repairs to save £2,800 – so this amount has been included in the costing above.

Minimum quotation price

The calculations above suggest that a quotation of £7,000 or less is financially viable, subject to an absolute minimum of £6,250. Any quotation of less than this is not financially worthwhile.

Other factors

Other factors which may have a bearing on the decision about the quotation price include:

- the possibility of future work from this source;
- accuracy of the cost estimates involved;
- likelihood of an upturn in market conditions; and
- possibility of other, more profitable, work.

Chapter 9

9.1 A risk-neutral decision maker would be likely to choose Option B, as this has the highest expected value of total contribution. Although it also appears to be the riskiest of the four options (it has the lowest 'worst outcome'), a risk-neutral view concentrates on the expected value of return, regardless of any associated risk. A risk-averse approach would be to choose Option A, since the total contribution offered by this option's 'worst outcome' is the highest. Conversely, a risk-seeking view would accept Option D, since the 'best outcome' associated with this option is the highest.

9.2 Expected value is calculated as $\Sigma[x\{p(x)\}]$ where x is each predicted outcome, p is its related probability and Σ is the symbol for 'sum of'. The expected value of the number of repairs next year is:

$$(8,000 \times 0.15) + (10,000 \times 0.25) + (14,000 \times 0.30)$$
$$+ (17,000 \times 0.20) + (20,000 \times 0.10)$$
$$= 13,300$$

9.3 (a) Expected unit demand is:

$$(16,000 \times 0.4) + (22,000 \times 0.6) = 19,600$$

(b) Expected unit variable cost is:

$$(£10 \times 0.3) + (£12 \times 0.4) + (£14 \times 0.3) = £12$$

9.4 **(a)** Expected value of unit contribution is:

(unit selling price – expected value of unit variable cost)

$$= (£35 - £12) = £23$$

(b) Expected value of total contribution is:

(expected demand × expected unit contribution)

$$= (19,600 \times £23) = £450,800$$

9.5 The joint probability of two independent events, A and B is $p(A) \times p(B)$.

(a) Probability of demand = 16,000 units is 0.4, and of unit variable cost = £12 is 0.4, so the joint probability of these two events is $(0.4 \times 0.4) = 0.16$.

(b) Probability of demand = 22,000 units is 0.6, and of unit variable cost = £14 is 0.3, so the joint probability of these two events is $(0.6 \times 0.3) = 0.18$.

9.6 **(a)** False **(b)** True **(c)** False **(d)** True **(e)** True

9.7 **(a)** The schedule of possible total contribution figures is shown in Table C9.1.

TABLE **C9.1**

Unit demand	Unit selling price (£)	Unit variable cost (£)	Unit contribution (£)	Total contribution (£)
4,000	220	80	140	560,000
4,000	220	140	80	320,000
4,000	220	100	120	480,000
10,000	220	80	140	1,400,000
10,000	220	140	80	800,000
10,000	220	100	120	1,200,000

(b) We saw in Chapter 6 that breakeven point is calculated as:

$$\frac{\text{total fixed cost}}{\text{contribution per unit}}$$

(i) Using the lowest unit contribution gives:

$$\frac{£210,000}{£80} = 2,625 \text{ units}$$

(ii) The highest unit contribution gives:

$$\frac{£210,000}{£140} = 1,500 \text{ units}$$

(iii) And the most likely contribution gives:

$$\frac{£210,000}{£120} = 1,750 \text{ units}$$

(c) The analysis has some limited value insofar as it recognises that more than one outcome is possible. This is reflected in the calculations of total contribution in (a) and in the range of breakeven points in (b). But the range of possible outcomes is wide and the analysis does not quantify the extent of uncertainty: that is, how likely is it that a particular demand volume or unit variable cost will occur? The analysis would therefore be improved if probabilities were assigned to the uncertain variables so that uncertainty is quantified. This would also help assess the risk attendant upon launch of the new software.

9.8 (a) The expected values of leakage as (i) a percentage of throughput and (ii) throughput in litres are as follows:

(i) $(10\% \times 0.1) + (20\% \times 0.6) + (30\% \times 0.3) = 22\%$

(ii) $(800 \times 0.2) + (600 \times 0.5) + (350 \times 0.3) = 565$ million litres

(iii) Expected leakage in litres is:

(expected throughput in litres × expected leakage as a percentage of throughput)

$$= (565 \text{ million} \times 22\%) = 124.3 \text{ million litres.}$$

(b) The total cost associated with leakages next year is:

	£m
Fixed cost	3.000
Variable cost (124.3 million litres @ £0.02)	2.486
Expected total cost	5.486

(c) Table C9.2 is the completed version of Table 9.6. Reading down the total cost and joint probability columns in this table, we can extract the following total costs of less than or equal to £5 million, along with their associated joint probabilities:

TABLE C9.2 Table of outcomes and probabilities

Throughput (million litres)	Leakage as % of throughput	Leakage (million litres)	Total variable cost (£m)	Total fixed cost (£m)	Total cost (£m)	Probability (throughput)	Probability (leakage %)	Joint probability
800	10	80	1.6	3.0	4.6		0.1	0.02
	20	160	3.2	3.0	6.2	0.2	0.6	0.12
	30	240	4.8	3.0	7.8		0.3	0.06
600	10	60	1.2	3.0	4.2		0.1	0.05
	20	120	2.4	3.0	5.4	0.5	0.6	0.30
	30	180	3.6	3.0	6.6		0.3	0.15
350	10	35	0.7	3.0	3.7		0.1	0.03
	20	70	1.4	3.0	4.4	0.3	0.6	0.18
	30	105	2.1	3.0	5.1		0.3	0.09

Total cost (£m)	Joint probability
4.6	0.02
4.2	0.05
3.7	0.03
4.4	0.18

The probability that the budget allowance will not be exceeded is therefore:

$$(0.02 + 0.05 + 0.03 + 0.18) = 0.28.$$

9.9 (a) As the first stage in determining expected profit, we need to obtain the expected value both of total contribution for each proposed charge rate and of specific fixed costs.

£30 charge per hour
EV of revenue: (£800,000 × 0.15) + (£420,000 × 0.30) + (£570,000 × 0.55)
            = £559,500

EV of total contribution = (EV of revenue × contribution/sales ratio)
                        = (£559,500 × 90%) = £503,550

£40 charge per hour
EV of revenue: (£660,000 × 0.10) + (£360,000 × 0.35) + (£500,000 × 0.55)
            = £467,000

EV of total contribution = (£467,000 × 90%) = £420,300

The expected value of fixed costs, which is independent of revenue, is

(£280,000 × 0.2) + (£200,000 × 0.2) + (£230,000 × 0.6) = £234,000.

Expected profit at each charge rate is thus:

	£30 per hour £	£40 per hour £
EV of total contribution	503,550	420,300
less EV of fixed costs	234,000	234,000
EV of profit	269,550	186,300

In order to maximise expected profit, the charge rate should be set at £30 per hour.

(b) The implied attitude is *risk neutral*. Management will adopt the option having the higher expected value of profit, irrespective of any attendant risks.

(c) Probabilities would be attached to uncertain events and each uncertain event would then be assigned a series of random numbers, depending on its probability of occurrence. Computer software would be used to generate random numbers corresponding to each uncertain variable in turn and would 'simulate' the situation by calculating the resulting total contribution after each complete 'run' of uncertain variables.

This might improve the analysis by allowing for a greater number of uncertain variables: for example, more than three revenue and fixed cost estimates along with several C/S ratios could be incorporated. The simulation would be run a large number of times and the software could extract a summary of the results, perhaps in the form of a probability distribution. Thus the scope of the analysis would be broadened and its results potentially rendered more useful to management.

9.10 Figure C9.1 is a decision tree of the problem faced by the Board of Management. Note that there are three options available – place a high volume, a low volume, or a medium volume contract – so there will be three expected values.

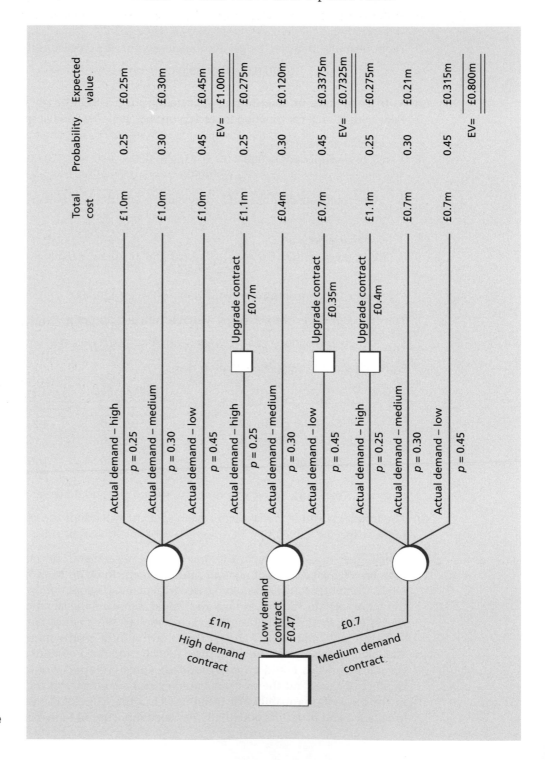

FIGURE C9.1
Decision tree
of problem

(b) Based on the data in Figure C9.1, the board of management should place the initial contract for low volume demand, as this has the lowest expected value of total cost (£732,500).

(c) If the Board of Management has 100 per cent accurate advance information about the level of actual demand, the initial contract will be placed on the basis of minimum total cost:

- If the advance information predicts high demand, the minimum cost option is to place a high volume initial contract (cost £1,000,000).
- If the advance information predicts medium demand, the minimum cost option is to place a medium demand initial contract (cost £700,000).
- If the advance information predicts low demand, the least cost option is to place a low demand contract (cost £400,000).

Since the advance information is 100 per cent accurate, the probability that it will predict a particular market state is the same as the probability of that market state actually occurring, as follows:

	Probability
High demand	0.25
Low demand	0.30
Medium demand	0.45

EV of total cost with perfect information is therefore:

$$(0.25 \times £1,000,000) + (0.30 \times £400,000) + (0.45 \times £700,000) = £685,000.$$

The minimum expected value of total cost without perfect information was £737,500, so the value of perfect information is (£737,500 – £685,000) = £52,500. In other words, obtaining the information will reduce the expected value of total cost by £52,500. Since it will cost £60,000 to obtain this information, we can conclude that the adviser's offer should be rejected.

(d) Three possible factors are:

- The quality of service being provided.
- The ability of the contractor to cope with a sudden upgrade in contract size.
- The possibility of negotiating a 'downgrade' option.

Chapter 10

10.1 **(a)** False **(b)** True **(c)** True **(d)** False **(e)** False **(f)** True **(g)** True **(h)** False

10.2   £

(a)	(£750,000 × 0.665)	= 498,750
(b)	(£20,000 × 6.142)	= 122,840
(c)	(£250,000 × 1.000)	= 250,000
(d)	(£8,000 × 3.837)	= 30,696
(e)	(£12,000 × 0.191)	= 2,292

10.3 Average annual profit is:

$$\frac{\text{total profit from proposal}}{\text{number of years of proposal life}}$$

$$= \frac{(4 \text{ years} \times £12,000) + (4 \text{ years} \times £16,000) + (4 \text{ years} \times £20,000)}{12 \text{ years}} = £16,000$$

Average capital cost is:

$$\frac{(\text{initial capital cost} + \text{resale value})}{2}$$

$$= \frac{(£110,000 + £6,000)}{2} = £58,000$$

(a) Accounting rate of return based on initial capital cost

$$\frac{\text{average annual profit}}{\text{initial capital cost}} \times 100\%$$

$$= \frac{£16,000}{£110,000} = \times 100\% = 14.55\%$$

(b) Accounting rate of return based on average capital cost

$$\frac{\text{average annual profit}}{\text{average capital cost}} \times 100\%$$

$$= \frac{£16,000}{£58,000} = \times 100\% = 27.59\%$$

Using initial capital cost, the proposal has a return which is lower than the target of 20 per unit (not acceptable), but if average capital cost is used, the return exceeds target (proposal acceptable). The acceptability of this proposal therefore depends on the definition of accounting rate of return: this is unsatisfactory.

10.4 By the end of the firm's target payback period of three years, the new coach will have recovered only (£15,000 + £20,000 + £20,000) = £55,000 of its initial cost. As its payback period exceeds the target, the proposal is unacceptable using this criterion. The payback period can be estimated more precisely as follows: by the end of the third year, the coach still requires to recover (£60,000 – £55,000) = £5,000 of its initial cost; assuming even cash inflows, this will take:

$$\frac{\text{cash flow required}}{\text{total cash flow for year}} = \frac{£5,000}{£24,000} = 0.21 \text{ of Year } 4$$

Payback is thus approximately 3.21 years.

10.5 Note that the estimated cash inflow each year is identical, so we can use the annuity factor from Appendix B to discount this particular cash flow. The equipment's NPV is set out in Table C10.1.

TABLE C10.1

Year	Cash flow	Amount (£)	Discount factor	Present value (£)
0	Initial cost	(80,000)	1.000	(80,000)
1–5	Net cash inflow	20,000	3.791	75,820
5	Resale value	3,000	0.621	1,863
			NPV	(2,317)

Since NPV is negative, the proposal to acquire the new equipment is not acceptable on financial grounds.

10.6 (a) Purchase of a minibus has the NPV set out in Table C10.2.

TABLE C10.2

Year	Cash flow	Amount (£)	Discount factor	Present value (£)
0	Initial cost	(22,000)	1.000	(22,000)
1	Saving in hire costs	6,000		
	Running costs	(3,000)		
	Net cash inflow	3,000	0.926	2,778
2	Saving in hire costs	10,000		
	Running costs	(3,000)		
	Net cash inflow	7,000	0.857	5,999
3	Saving in hire costs	15,000		
	Running costs	(3,800)		
	Net cash inflow	11,200	0.794	8,893
4	Saving in hire costs	15,000		
	Running costs	(4,400)		
	Resale value	2,000		
	Net cash inflow	12,600	0.735	9,261
			NPV	4,931

(b) Since the proposal has a positive NPV at the college's 8 per cent cost of capital, the cash flows will need to be discounted at a higher rate in order to obtain the IRR. At 20 per cent, the proposal's NPV is as set out in Table C10.3. The proposal's IRR must therefore lie between 8 per cent and 20 per cent. Interpolating between these two values, we get:

TABLE C10.3

Year	Cash flow	Amount (£)	Discount factor	Present value (£)
0	Initial cost	(22,000)	1.000	(22,000)
1	Saving in hire costs	6,000		
	Running costs	(3,000)		
	Net cash inflow	3,000	0.833	2,499
2	Saving in hire costs	10,000		
	Running costs	(3,000)		
	Net cash inflow	7,000	0.694	4,858
3	Saving in hire costs	15,000		
	Running costs	(3,800)		
	Net cash inflow	11,200	0.579	6,485
4	Saving in hire costs	15,000		
	Running costs	(4,400)		
	Resale value	2,000		
	Net cash inflow	12,600	0.482	6,073
			NPV	(2,085)

$$\text{IRR} = 8\% + \left[\frac{4{,}931}{(4{,}931 + \pounds 2{,}085)} \times (20\% - 6\%) \right] = 16.43\% \text{ approximately}$$

(Your estimate of IRR may be slightly different if you used a second discount rate different to 20%.)

(c) The proposed minibus purchase has a positive NPV at the college's cost of capital and also has an IRR in excess of this rate. It is therefore acceptable when judged by both of these criteria.

(d) Report

To: Principal

From:

Evaluation of capital investment proposals

Whilst the DCF techniques of net present value and internal rate of return are both preferable to non-DCF techniques such as accounting rate of return, net present value is preferable to internal rate of return for the following reasons:

- IRR can rarely be determined exactly

- IRR cannot cope with changes in discount rate during the life of a proposal

- Some proposals may have a single IRR, some may have no IRR, and some may have several – depending on the overall pattern of cash inflows and outflows

- IRR does not reflect the size of investment required, nor the increase/decrease in wealth resulting from undertaking it, and is therefore of little use for comparisons of competing proposals.

Should you require clarification or amplification of any of these points, please let me know.

Signed

(Refer to Chapter 10 for full discussion of the points mentioned above.)

10.7 (a) By the end of the fifth year, the proposal has paid back:

£40,000 + £2,000 + £50,000 + £70,000 + £90,000 + £60,000 = £312,000

By the end of the fourth year, £252,000 of the initial cost of £260,000 has been paid back; the remaining £8,000 required will take:

$$\frac{£8,000}{£60,000} = 0.13 \text{ of Year 5}$$

so payback will occur in approximately 4.13 years. Note that the sale proceeds of the existing equipment (£2,000) have been included in the payback calculation.

The proposal's NPV at the firm's 15 per cent cost of capital is (£45,340). As this is negative, the discount rate must be reduced in order to obtain a positive NPV. At 8 per cent, the proposal's NPV is £3,232. IRR must therefore lie between 15 per cent and 8 per cent:

$$8\% + \left[\frac{£3,232}{(£3,232 + £45,340)} \times (15\% - 8\%) \right] = 8.47\% \text{ approximately}$$

(Your estimate may be slightly different depending on the second discount rate used in the trial and error process.)

NPV calculations are shown in Table C10.4.

TABLE C10.4

Year	Cash flow	Amount (£)	Discount factor (15%)	Discount factor (8%)	Present value (£) (15%)	Present value (£) (8%)
0	Initial cost	(260,000)	1.000	1.000	(260,000)	(260,000)
1	Sale of existing equipment	2,000				
	Net cash inflow	40,000				
		42,000	0.870	0.926	36,540	38,892
2	Net cash inflow	50,000	0.756	0.857	37,800	42,850
3	Net cash inflow	70,000	0.658	0.794	46,060	55,580
4	Net cash inflow	90,000	0.572	0.735	51,480	66,150
5	Net cash inflow	60,000	0.497	0.681	29,820	40,860
6	Net cash inflow	10,000				
	Resale value	20,000				
		30,000	0.432	0.630	12,960	18,900
				NPV	(45,340)	3,232

(b) Before we can calculate accounting rate of return, we must convert the proposal's cash flows to *profit* by deducting annual depreciation of £40,000 from the net cash inflows:

Year 1 (£40,000 + £2,000 – £40,000)   = £2,000 profit
Year 2 (£50,000 – £40,000)   = £10,000 profit
Year 3 (£70,000 – £40,000)   = £30,000 profit
Year 4 (£90,000 – £40,000)   = £50,000 profit
Year 5 (£60,000 – £40,000)   = £20,000 profit
Year 6 (£10,000 – £40,000)   = £30,000 *loss*

Average annual profit is:

$$\frac{£2,000 + £10,000 + £30,000 + £50,000 + £20,000 - £30,000}{6 \text{ years}} = £13,667$$

The average capital cost of the proposal is:

$$\frac{(£260,000 + £20,000)}{2} = £140,000$$

The question does not specify whether initial or average capital cost should be used in the accounting rate of return calculation, so either is acceptable.

(i) Accounting rate of return based on initial capital cost:

$$\frac{£13,667}{£260,000} \times 100\% = 5.26\%$$

(ii) Accounting rate of return based on average capital cost:

$$\frac{£13,667}{£140,000} \times 100\% = 9.76\%$$

(c) Judged against each of the four criteria calculated in (a) and (b), the proposal's acceptability is as follows:

(i) payback: shorter than target, therefore acceptable;

(ii) NPV: negative at firm's cost of capital, therefore unacceptable;

(iii) IRR: lower than cost of capital, therefore unacceptable;

(iv) accounting rate of return: lower than cost of capital, irrespective of capital base used, therefore unacceptable.

Unless there are very compelling non-financial reasons for acquiring the new equipment, the proposal should be rejected, as it has a negative NPV. For financial evaluation, NPV is superior to the other criteria, since it not only allows for the time value of money, but is also preferable to IRR, which has certain weaknesses in comparison.

(d) These two appraisal criteria assume that cash flows arising at different points in time have the same value in today's terms, which ignores the time value of money. This reflects lost interest on capital funds used in a project, and organisations' liquidity preference. The further into the future a stream of cash flows extends, the greater will be the impact on those cash flows of the factors just mentioned, and hence the lower will be their value in today's terms. It can therefore be argued that, before they can validly be added/subtracted, proposal cash flows must be expressed on a common basis, so as to remove the differing effects of the time value of money.

10.8 (a) You should note at the outset that the £10,000 removal cost of existing machinery will arise irrespective of which option is selected and is thus irrelevant to the appraisal.

By the end of Year 3, Option A will have paid back:

$$(£180,000 + £140,000 + £120,000) = £440,000.$$

£80,000 requires to be paid back in the third year of the proposal's life, which will take:

$$\frac{£80,000}{£120,000} = 0.67 \text{ of that year}$$

Payback therefore occurs in 2.67 years.

By the end of Year 5, Option B will have paid back:

$$(£50,000 + £50,000 + £150,000 + £200,000 + £320,000) = £770,000.$$

The £190,000 required from the Year 5 cash flow will take:

$$\frac{£190,000}{£320,000} = 0.59 \text{ of that year}$$

Payback therefore occurs in 4.59 years.

Each option's NPV at PTK Ltd's 12% cost of capital is calculated in Table C10.5.

TABLE C10.5

Year	Cash flow	Amount (£) Option A	Amount (£) Option B	Discount factor	Present value (£) Option A	Present value (£) Option B
0	Initial cost	(400,000)	(640,000)	1.000	(400,000)	(640,000)
1	Net cash inflow	180,000	50,000	0.893	160,740	44,650
2	Net cash inflow	140,000	50,000	0.797	111,580	39,850
3	Net cash inflow	120,000	150,000	0.712	85,440	106,800
4	Net cash inflow	80,000	200,000	0.636	50,880	127,200
5	Net cash inflow	80,000	320,000	0.567	45,360	181,440
6	Net cash inflow	40,000	430,000	0.507	20,280	218,010
				NPV	74,280	77,950

(b) The results of (a) are summarised below:

	Payback	NPV
Option A	2.67 years	£74,280
Option B	4.59 years	£77,950

Therefore, using payback as the criterion, Option A is preferable, whereas based on NPV, Option B is better. Unless there are reasons for adopting A which are not revealed by the financial analysis (e.g. a liquidity crisis, which might add extra weight to an earlier payback), then Option B should be adopted, as it has the higher positive NPV.

The two criteria differ in their indication of the desirability of each option because:

1 Payback ignores the time value of money, giving the same weight to all cash flows, irrespective of when they arise.

2 Payback will tend to suggest acceptance of proposals with heavier cash inflows in earlier, rather than later years, irrespective of the *overall* financial desirability of a proposal; Option A has heavier cash inflows in its earlier years, but is not as financially viable as Option B when considered over the *full* time horizon involved.

10.9 (a) The differential cash flows are the differences between the cash flows associated with retaining the existing turntable ladder and replacing it. In this example, the reduction in annual maintenance cost is treated as a cash inflow associated with purchase of the new ladder. The differential NPV is calculated below in Table C10.6.

TABLE C10.6

Year	Cash flow	Amount (£)	Discount factor	Present value (£)
0	Purchase of new ladder Sale of existing ladder	(180,000) 10,000		
	Differential cash flow	(170,000)	1.000	(170,000)
1	Purchase of new ladder Maintenance saving	(180,000) 30,000		
	Differential cash flow	(150,000)	0.952	(142,800)
2	Maintenance saving Overhaul saving	35,000 5,000		
	Differential cash flow	40,000	0.907	36,280
3	Maintenance saving	36,000	0.864	31,104
4	Maintenance saving Overhaul saving	45,000 6,000		
	Differential cash flow	51,000	0.823	41,973
5	Maintenance saving	54,000	0.784	42,336
6	Maintenance saving Overhaul saving	62,000 14,000		
	Differential cash flow	76,000	0.746	56,696
7	Maintenance saving	70,000	0.711	49,770
8	Maintenance saving Resale value	76,000 7,000		
	Differential cash flow	83,000	0.677	56,191
			NPV	1,550

As the NPV is positive, the new turntable ladder should be acquired.

(b) Qualitative factors which may be relevant include:

1 Safety factor: if the new ladder is acquired, is there any chance that lives may be put at risk while training in its use is undertaken?

2 What is the likelihood that the existing ladder will actually last another eight years in use?

3 How accurate are the estimated cash flows? – the proposal is only marginally acceptable, so a small error in estimation would affect its financial viability.

10.10 (a) Before determining the proposal's NPV, it is necessary to isolate the relevant cash flows. (Depreciation and apportioned general overheads are irrelevant to the decision, as is the projected annual increase in the latter.) The relevant cash inflow and outflows are from operation of the canteen presently:

	£	£
Income		20,000
less: Cost of food purchases	19,200	
Power for equipment	3,000	22,200
Net cash outflow		2,200

This net cash flow will improve by {£2,000 – (£800 + £800)} = £400 in each of Years 1–4: that is, to an outflow of £1,800 in Year 1, £1,400 in Year 2, £1,000 in Year 3 and £600 in Year 4.

The NPV calculations in Table C10.7 are based on the differential cash flows associated with subcontracting canteen provision, although it would be possible to

TABLE **C10.7**

Year	Cash flow	Amount (£)	Discount factor	Present value (£)
0	Redundancy payments	(12,000)	1.000	(12,000)
1	Net cash outflow avoided	1,800		
	Rental from subcontractor	6,000		
	Differential cash flow	7,800	0.893	6,965
2	Net cash outflow avoided	1,400		
	Rental from subcontractor	6,000		
	Differential cash flow	7,400	0.797	5,898
3	Net cash outflow avoided	1,000		
	Rental from subcontractor	6,000		
	Differential cash flow	7,000	0.712	4,984
4	Net cash outflow avoided	600		
	Rental from subcontractor	6,000		
	Differential cash flow	6,600	0.636	4,198
			NPV	10,045

separately discount all the relevant cash flows attaching to both options and to compare the resultant NPVs.

Since subcontracting canteen provision has a positive NPV, the proposal is financially worthwhile.

(b) Management would be advised to consider the following points before making a final decision:

1 Reaction of employees to the change – especially since redundancies are involved. Is there a potential industrial relations problem?
2 Will the quality and price of food provided by the subcontractor be comparable to that presently provided?
3 What will happen to canteen provision after the four-year period?

Although it is not a qualitative factor, it is also worth pointing out that once irrelevant costs are removed, then the loss suffered by the canteen is fairly small and, if projections are reasonably accurate, breakeven should be achieved in about five and a half years from now, with the loss reducing each year until then.

Chapter 11

11.1 D 30%

The cost of ordinary shares, r, is defined as:

$$\frac{d\,(1 + g)}{P_0} + g$$

d being the most recent dividend, P_0 the current market price (ex-div) and g the rate of expected future growth in dividends. Inserting the values from the question gives:

$$\frac{19\,(1 + 0.05)}{79.8} + 0.05 = 0.3.$$

11.2 D 20.64%

Bearing in mind that retained profit 'belongs' to the ordinary shareholders, then the WACC is:

Cost of ordinary shares: $\dfrac{(50 + 4)}{75} \times 24\%$		17.28
Cost of 10% debentures: $\dfrac{21}{75} \times 12\%$		3.36
WACC		20.64

11.3 C 17%

The CAPM defines the cost of capital as

$$R_x = R_f + [\beta_x(R_m - R_f)]$$

From the question, we have values of 8 per cent, 1.5 and 14 per cent for R_f, β_x and R_m respectively, giving a cost of ordinary shares of:

$$8\% + \{1.5(14\% - 8\%)\} = 17\%.$$

11.4 (a) False (b) True (c) False (d) False (e) True (f) False (g) True

11.5 D 30%

The gearing ratio is:

$$\frac{\text{prior charge capital}}{\text{all long term capital + reserves}}$$

Both the 15 per cent preference shares and 10 per cent debentures are prior charge capital, so TRA plc's gearing ratio is:

$$\frac{£5,000,000 + £7,000,000}{£40,000,000} = 0.3$$

11.6 (a) We can obtain a value for β by applying the regression analysis formula:

$$\frac{n\Sigma\, xy - \Sigma\, x \Sigma\, y}{n\, \Sigma\, x^2 - (\Sigma x)^2}$$

where: n is the number of past observations being used; and
x and y are returns from the average market investment and from the security respectively.

Tabulating the figures from the question lets us determine the values we need for the formula above:

x	y	xy	x^2
2.2	1.6	3.52	4.84
2.8	2.1	5.88	7.84
2.0	1.5	3.00	4.00
1.8	1.0	1.80	3.24
1.2	0.6	0.72	1.44
0.7	0.0	0.00	0.49
0.3	−0.8	−0.24	0.09
0.8	0.1	0.08	0.64
$\Sigma 11.8$	$\Sigma 6.1$	$\Sigma 14.76$	$\Sigma 22.58$

This gives a value for β of:

$$\frac{n\Sigma xy - \Sigma x \Sigma y}{n\Sigma x^2 - (\Sigma x)^2} = \frac{8(14.76) - (11.8 \times 6.1)}{8(22.58) - 11.8^2}$$

$$= \frac{118.08 - 71.98}{180.64 - 139.24} = 1.11$$

(b) The weaknesses of regression analysis as an estimation technique are as follows:

- It assumes a linear relationship between variables (between returns from GM plc's ordinary shares and the market portfolio).
- It assumes the past is a reasonable guide to the future.

- It assigns equal weight to all past observations, and the more observations which are used, the more statistically valid is the result.
- Statistical validity may be confused with predictive accuracy.

(c) The CAPM will value the cost of GM plc's ordinary shares as:

$$R_f + \{\beta_x(R_m - R_f)\} = 8\% + \{1.11(14\% - 8\%)\} = 14.66\%$$

(For ease of discounting calculations, this would probably be rounded to 15%.)

(d) One way in which the answer to (c) could be adjusted to reflect the specific project's additional risk is by increasing the value of β. If the project is thought to be twice as risky as GM plc's normal operations, we could set β at twice its value in (c): that is, at 2.22. This would give a revised cost of ordinary shares of:

$$8\% + \{2.22(14\% - 8\%)\} = 21.32\%$$

Increasing the cost of ordinary shares in this way reflects the general principle that the higher the perceived risk, the higher should be the associated return. However, determining β for a specific proposal with any degree of accuracy is likely to be extremely difficult.

11.7 (a) Application of the dividend growth model gives a cost of ordinary shares of:

$$\frac{d(1+g)}{P_0} + g = \frac{30(1+0.025)}{415} + 0.025 = 0.099 \text{ (say 10\%)}$$

(b) In order to determine the cost of NBV plc's redeemable debentures, we need to estimate the discount rate at which the discounted expected future cash flows (interest *plus* repayment of loan principal) equate to the current market price of the debentures. Treating the debentures as a capital investment 'proposal' with 'initial outlay' equal to the current market value and discounting first at the debentures' interest rate (15 per cent), we reach the NPV illustrated in Table C11.1. Since a 15 per cent discount rate yields a negative net present value, we need to reduce the rate used. Discounting at 8 per cent gives the NPV shown in Table C11.2.

TABLE C11.1 NPV of redeemable debentures at 15 per cent

Year	Cash flow	Amount (£)	Discount factor	Present value (£)
0	Initial cost	(130.00)	1.000	(130.00)
1–15	Annual interest	15.00	5.847	87.71
15	Loan repayment	100.00	0.123	12.30
			NPV	(29.99)

TABLE C11.2 NPV of redeemable debentures at 8 per cent

Year	Cash flow	Amount (£)	Discount factor	Present value (£)
0	Initial cost	(130.00)	1.000	(130.00)
1–15	Annual interest	15.00	8.559	128.39
15	Loan repayment	100.00	0.315	31.50
			NPV	29.89

The IRR/cost of redeemable debentures is:

$$8\% + \left[\frac{29.89}{29.89 + 29.99} \times (15\% - 8\%) \right] = 11.49\%$$

(If a second discount rate other than 8 per cent is used, then the resulting IRR will be slightly different, and this will also affect the calculations in (c).)

(c) (i) Using balance sheet values, the weighted cost of ordinary shares is:

$$\frac{\text{ordinary shares} + \text{retained profit}}{\text{total capital}} \times \text{cost of ordinary shares}$$

$$= \frac{£25m + £5}{£40m} \times 10\% = 7.5\%$$

The weighted cost of the redeemable debentures is:

$$\frac{\text{debentures}}{\text{total capital}}$$

$$= \frac{£10m}{£40m} \times 11.49\% = 2.87\%$$

The weighted average cost of capital is thus:

$$(7.5\% + 2.87\%) = 10.37\%$$

(ii) We can restate the balance sheet figures for ordinary shares and debentures in terms of market values:

	£
Ordinary shares (25m shares @ 415p)	103,750,000
Debentures ([£10m ÷ £100] @ £130)	13,000,000
	£116,750,000

(Remember that the retained profit is allowed for in the market value of the company's ordinary shares.)

The weighted cost of ordinary shares is therefore:

$$\frac{£103.75m}{£116.75m} \times 10\% = 8.89\%$$

For debentures, we get:

$$\frac{£13m}{£116.75m} \times 11.49\% = 1.28\%$$

The WACC using market values is therefore:

$$(8.89\% + 1.28\%) = 10.17\%$$

(d) Several views of the appropriateness of the WACC may be taken:

- It is inappropriate, since funding for the proposal comes from a single, identifiable source with an 8 per cent cost of capital and this is the rate which should be used to discount proposal cash flows.

- It is inappropriate because funding the proposal by means of additional borrowing will alter the company's capital structure for the duration of the proposal, and we should use a cost of capital which reflects this revised capital structure.
- It may be inappropriate due to a significant difference in risk between the proposal and the company's existing operations.

Alternatively, we could take a rather more pragmatic view. Providing the WACC is sufficient to allow for payment of interest and capital on the debt which funds it, and providing it is high enough to meet shareholder requirements under the altered circumstances brought about by the proposal's adoption, then it is as accurate a discount rate as we can reasonably expect to obtain.

11.8 (a) (i) The gearing ratio is:

$$\frac{\text{prior charge capital}}{\text{all long-term capital + reserves}}$$

For the existing capital structure, the gearing ratio is:

$$\frac{\pounds 22\text{m}}{\pounds 80\text{m}} = 0.28$$

If the expansion programme is funded by issuing ordinary shares, the numerator in the gearing ratio will be unchanged, but the denominator will increase by the amount of the additional ordinary shares:

$$\frac{\pounds 22\text{m}}{\pounds 80\text{m} + \pounds 20\text{m}} = 0.22$$

If either preference shares or debentures are used as the source of finance, both numerator and denominator will increase by £20m:

$$\frac{\pounds 22\text{m} + \pounds 20\text{m}}{\pounds 80\text{m} + \pounds 20\text{m}} = 0.42$$

(ii) Table C11.3 shows the profit available for ordinary shareholders under each capital structure. Note that, under the existing structure, profit will remain at £10 million.

(iii) The market value of AFG plc's existing capital is:

	£	%
Ordinary shares (50,000,000 @ 540p)	270,000,000	91.77
Debentures {(£22,000,000 ÷ £100) @ £110}	24,200,000	8.23
	294,200,000	100.00

If additional ordinary shares are issued, this changes to:

	£	%
Ordinary shares (70,000,000 @ 560p)	392,000,000	94.19
Debentures {(£22,000,000 ÷ £100) @ £110}	24,200,000	5.81
	416,200,000	100.00

TABLE C11.3 Profit available for ordinary shareholders

	Existing capital structure (£)	Issue 20 million ordinary shares (£)	Issue 20 million 10% preference shares (£)	Issue £20 million of 8% debenture stock (£)
Profit before interest and taxation	10,000,000	14,000,000	14,000,000	14,000,000
less Debenture interest	1,760,000	1,760,000	1,760,000	3,360,000[2]
Taxable profit	8,240,000	12,240,000	12,240,000	10,640,000
Tax @ 35%	2,884,000	4,284,000	4,284,000	3,724,000
Profit after tax	5,356,000	7,956,000	7,956,000	6,916,000
less Preference dividends	nil	nil	2,000,000[1]	nil
Profit available for ordinary shareholders	5,356,000	7,956,000	5,956,000	6,916,000
Number of ordinary shares	50,000,000	70,000,000	50,000,000	50,000,000
Profit per share	£0.11	£0.11	£0.12	£0.14

Notes:

[1] The preference dividend is (£20,000,000 × 10%).

[2] Debenture interest will consist of:

	£
Existing debentures (8% × £22,000,000)	1,760,000
New debentures (8% × £20,000,000)	1,600,000
	3,360,000

Issue of preference shares will result in a market value of:

	£	%
Ordinary shares (50,000,000 @ 580p)	290,000,000	86.05
Debentures {(£22,000,000 ÷ £100) @ £110}	24,200,000	7.18
Preference shares (20,000,000 @ 114p)	22,800,000	6.77
	337,000,000	100.00

If additional debentures are issued, the market value will be:

	£	%
Ordinary shares (50,000,000 @ 600p)	300,000,000	86.87
Debentures {(£42,000,000 ÷ £100) @ £108}	45,360,000	13.13
	345,360,000	100.00

The appropriate formulae for determination of the cost of each element of capital are:

$$\text{Ordinary shares:} \quad \frac{d(1+g)}{P_0} + g$$

$$\text{Preference shares:} \quad \frac{d}{P_0}$$

$$\text{Debentures:} \quad \frac{i}{P_0}$$

Inserting the values relating to the present capital structure, we get:

$$\text{Ordinary shares:} \quad \frac{20p(1+0.025)}{540p} + 0.025 = 0.063$$

$$\text{Debentures:} \quad \frac{(8\% \times £100)}{£110} = 0.07$$

Using the weightings calculated above, the WACC is:

$$(91.77\% \times 0.063) + (8.23\% \times 0.07) = 6.36\%$$

For a rights issue, we get:

$$\text{Ordinary shares:} \quad \frac{20p(1+0.035)}{560p} + 0.035 = 0.07$$

$$\text{Debentures:} \quad \frac{(8\% \times £100)}{£110} = 0.07$$

The WACC is therefore 7%.

If preference shares are issued:

$$\text{Ordinary shares:} \quad \frac{20p(1+0.04)}{580p} + 0.04 = 0.08$$

$$\text{Debentures:} \quad \text{unchanged at } 0.07$$

$$\text{Preference shares:} \quad \frac{(10\% \times £1)}{114p} = 0.09$$

The WACC is:

$$(86.05\% \times 0.08) + (7.18\% \times 0.07) + (6.77\% \times 0.09) = 7.99\%$$

If debentures are issued:

$$\text{Ordinary shares:} \quad \frac{20p(1+0.05)}{600p} + 0.05 = 0.09$$

$$\text{Debentures:} \quad \frac{(8\% \times £100)}{£108} = 0.07$$

giving a WACC of:

$$(86.87\% \times 0.09) + (13.13\% \times 0.07) = 8.74\%$$

(b) If the proposed expansion scheme proceeds, then a cost of capital based on AFG plc's existing capital structure is inappropriate for discounting purposes; one based on the structure which will apply should expansion occur is preferable. However, the accuracy of the cost of capital calculations in (a) is heavily dependent on the accuracy with which the various estimates in the question have been made (e.g. about the impact of different sources of funds on the market value of ordinary shares).

Although there is little difference between the cost of capital figures calculated in (a), no more than a small change in discount rate may be required to render a marginally acceptable proposal unacceptable, or a marginally unacceptable proposal acceptable. In such circumstances, the cost of capital may have an impact, not only on the specific proposal but also, potentially, on the company's strategic direction.

(c) The major strengths and weaknesses of the sources of funding may be summarised as follows:

Rights issue

The advantages are:

- May be less expensive than issue of preference shares or debentures.
- No need to make set interest/dividend payments, nor to repay principal as in the case of debentures.

The problems are:

- May upset balance of voting power if significant number of existing shareholders decline to exercise their rights.
- Market confidence in the company may be damaged if existing shareholders are unenthusiastic about exercising their rights.

Preference shares and debentures

The advantages are:

- Holders not normally entitled to vote at company meetings.
- Fixed rate of dividend/interest.
- Dividend/interest may be lower than payable on ordinary shares.
- Debenture interest is a tax-deductible expense, which may benefit ordinary shareholders.

The problems are:

- Need to pay fixed dividend/interest may cause liquidity problems, and may, in periods of fluctuating profit, threaten the amount of profit available to ordinary shareholders.
- The amount of principal will need to be repaid if debentures are issued, which may also give rise to liquidity problems.
- Debentures will probably be secured on some/all of the company's assets, which may restrict their use and reduce the possibility of capital repayment to ordinary shareholders in the event of the company being wound up.

(The additional risk posed to ordinary shareholders by the issuing of preference shares and, more particularly, of debentures, may be one of the reasons underlying the increased cost of capital attaching to these two methods of finance compared to that which relates to a rights issue.)

Chapter 12

12.1 C Actual output was 1,400 standard hours lower than budgeted.

Actual and budgeted output in standard hours are determined by summing (output × standard hours per unit):

	Units	
	Budgeted output	*Actual output*
Product A (10,000/9,000 × 1)	10,000	9,000
Product B (14,000/16,000 × 1.5)	21,000	24,000
Product C (17,000/12,000 × 2)	34,000	24,000
Product D (15,000/18,000 × 2.2)	33,000	39,600
	98,000	96,600

Actual output is therefore 1,400 standard hours lower than budgeted.

12.2 B £54,400

Cash receipts in April will consist of the following:

	£
10% of May's rent due	6,000
60% of April's rent due	33,600
20% of March's rent due	11,600
5% of February's rent due	3,200
	54,400

12.3 B 59,000 × 250 ml containers and 24,000 × 500 ml containers

The production budget for next year is:

	250 ml containers	*500 ml containers*
Production required for sales	60,000	25,000
add Desired closing stock	5,000	1,500
	65,000	26,500
less Opening stock	6,000	2,500
Production required	59,000	24,000

12.4 D 10,700,000 ml

The usage budget will be determined by the budgeted production quantities from question 12.3:

Bonding agent used in production of:	
250 ml containers (59,000 × 100 ml)	5,900,000
500 ml containers (24,000 × 200 ml)	4,800,000
Budgeted usage	10,700,000

(Note that the stocks of bonding agent mentioned in the question are not relevant.)

12.5 (a) True (b) True (c) False (d) True (e) False (f) False (g) True (h) False

12.6 (a) Table C12.1 shows the Alexandra Nursery's cash budget for each of the months of January–April.

TABLE **C12.1 Alexandra Nursery: cash budget**

	January (£)	February (£)	March (£)	April (£)
Opening balance	(4,000)	(22,800)	300	80
add Cash receipts:				
Loan				5,000
Sale of unwanted toys etc.		500		
40% of outstanding fees	19,200	19,200		
18% of outstanding fees			8,640	
20% of current month's fees	11,600	12,000	13,200	11,800
50% of last month's fees		29,000	30,000	33,000
28% of two months ago's fees			16,240	16,800
	26,800	37,900	68,380	66,680
less Cash payments:				
Payment of creditors	12,000			
Purchase of equipment			28,000	22,000
Purchase of consumables		2,000	2,500	2,200
Building renovations:				
70% in month due	8,400	11,200	14,000	17,500
30% in month after due		3,600	4,800	6,000
Insurance		2,800		
Telephone	1,200			1,400
Sundry overheads	6,000	7,000	7,000	7,000
Rent and rates	3,000			3,000
Taxation	8,000			
Wages and salaries	11,000	11,000	12,000	12,000
	49,600	37,600	68,300	71,100
Closing balance	(22,800)	300	80	(4,420)

(b) (i) If fees are raised by 10 per cent effective from 1 January, and assuming that all other factors remain as stated, then cash receipts in respect of next year's fees will increase by 10 per cent. Note that fee payments relating to the current year which are received next year are *not* affected by the 10 per cent increase. A restated, summarised cash budget is presented in Table C12.2.

TABLE **C12.2** **Alexandra Nursery: revised cash budget**

	January (£)	February (£)	March (£)	April (£)
Opening balance	(4,000)	(21,640)	5,560	11,284
add Cash receipts:				
Loan				5,000
Sale of unwanted toys etc		500		
40% of outstanding fees	19,200	19,200		
18% of outstanding fees			8,640	
20% of current month's fees	12,760	13,200	14,520	12,980
50% of last month's fees		31,900	33,000	36,300
28% of two months ago's fees			17,864	18,480
	27,960	43,160	79,584	84,044
less Cash payments:				
As in cash budget in (a)	49,600	37,600	68,300	71,100
Closing balance	(21,640)	5,560	11,284	12,944

(ii) As can be seen from Table C12.2, increasing fees has the effect of markedly improving the nursery's cash flow position over the four-month period. However, this assumes that the *volume* of business will be unaffected by the fee increase. Price elasticity may have the effect of reducing demand for places at the nursery if fees are increased, and it is possible that such a reduction in demand could cause a deterioration in the cash-flow position revealed in Table C12.1.

Possible alternatives include:

■ Attempting to collect fees more quickly.
■ Selling more redundant equipment.
■ Raising a larger loan, or arranging for a bank overdraft (but remember that any loan will incur interest payments and will ultimately have to be repaid).
■ Reducing cash payments – purchases of machinery and building renovations in particular. If these cannot be reduced, can the amount be spread over a longer period? Or can the equipment be acquired by a method other than purchase?

(c) Tables C12.1 and 12.2 are manual spreadsheets and a computerised version can be used in any 'row and column' situation, such as a cash budget. A computer spreadsheet approach to cash budgeting requires the user to specify, first, whether the contents of specific 'cells' are numeric or descriptive, and second, any mathematical relationships between the contents of different cells. For example, the first cell in each row of the cash budget will be designated as descriptive (i.e. will contain the headings), and the sum of the cells containing cash payments each month is deducted from the sum of the cells containing cash receipts to produce the closing balance.

    The major benefit offered by such an approach is the complex *sensitivity analysis* which may be undertaken. Part (b) is just such an analysis, and is somewhat cumbersome to perform manually. Once the mathematical relationships within a computer spreadsheet have been specified, it is a simple matter to interrogate the spreadsheet program about the effect of changing the value of one or more of the variables involved.

12.7 (a) (i) LGP Ltd: Sales budget

	£
3 metre ladders (20,000 × 1.2): 24,000 units @ £30	720,000
5 metre ladders (same as current year): 15,000 units @ £58	870,000
10 metre ladders (10,000 × 0.9): 9,000 units @ £95	855,000
Total sales revenue	2,445,000

(ii) LGP Ltd: Production budget

	Units		
	3 metre	5 metre	10 metre
Required for sales	24,000	15,000	9,000
add Desired closing stock[1]	3,000	1,500	600
	27,000	16,500	9,600
less Opening stock	4,000	2,000	800
Production required	23,000	14,500	8,800

Note: [1] Closing stock is to be 25 per cent lower than the level anticipated at the end of the current year.

(iii) LGP Ltd: Material usage budget

	Aluminium (metres)	Fixings (units)
Required for production of:		
3 metre ladders (23,000 × 3.5m/100 units)	80,500	2,300,000
5 metre ladders (14,500 × 6 metres/200 units)	87,000	2,900,000
10 metre ladders (8,800 × 12 metres/400 units)	105,600	3,520,000
Total usage	273,100	8,720,000

(iv) LGP Ltd: Material purchases budget

	Aluminium (metres)	Fixings (units)
Usage in production	273,100	8,720,000
add Desired closing stock[1]	12,000	45,000
	285,100	8,765,000
less Opening stock	16,000	60,000
Purchases required	269,100	8,705,000
Purchase cost per metre/unit	£2.00	£0.01
Total purchase cost	£538,200	£87,050
Overall total purchase cost	£625,250	

Note: [1] Closing stock is to be 25 per cent lower than the level anticipated at the end of the current year.

(v)   LGP Ltd: Direct labour hours and manpower budget

	Hours
Required for production of:	
3 metre ladders (23,000 × 0.1 hours)	2,300
5 metre ladders (14,500 × 0.5 hours)	7,250
10 metre ladders (8,800 × 1.0 hour)	8,800
Total direct labour hours required	18,350
Productive hours per annum per worker {(35 × 0.75) × 48 weeks}	1,260
Direct workers required	14.56 (say 15)

(b) The principal budget factor is not explicitly identified, but is assumed to be sales demand.

(c) Machine utilisation will be based on the budgeted production quantities in (a), in conjunction with the standard machining time per unit of each product from the question.

LGP Ltd: Machine Utilisation Budget

	Machine hours
Required for production of:	
3 metre ladders (23,000 × 4 hours)	92,000
5 metre ladders (14,500 × 6 hours)	87,000
10 metre ladders (8,800 × 10 hours)	88,000
Total machine hours required	267,000
Hours available per machine	8,000
Number of machines required	33.375 (say 34)

Machines available next year will be the existing 30 plus the two additional specified in the capital budget. Thus there will be insufficient machine capacity to meet budgeted production requirements. This shortfall may be overcome by:

- *Purchasing additional machines* LGP Ltd will own the machines and have control over the quality of output, but this is a costly option, especially if production is likely to fall after next year.
- *Lease additional machines* This is likely to be cheaper than purchase, and will confer all the benefits of ownership. But the machines will not actually be owned, and the lessor may place some restriction on their use.
- *Subcontract some output* Avoids the need for additional machinery, but may raise problems of compatibility with LGP Ltd's own output and incur quality-related costs such as inspection.
- *Reduce output to suit the availability of machine capacity* This is really a 'last-ditch' remedy, and would only be advisable if it proved impossible to overcome the shortage of machine hours. Sales would be lost in the short term, and there may also be an adverse effect on longer-term sales.

12.8 (a) Table C12.3 gives the Home Help Section's budgets for next year. Note that the current year's budget requires to be adjusted for inflation (with the exception of depreciation) as well as for each of the different levels of service provision.

TABLE C12.3 Home Help Section's expenditure budgets

| | Service level relative to current year | | |
	(i) Same (£)	(ii) Minimum (£)	(iii) Improved (£)
Employee costs:			
Wages and salaries (614 × 1.02) × 1/0.8/1.2	626,280	501,024	751,536
Wage-related costs (128 × 1.02) × 1/0.8/1.2	130,560	104,448	156,672
Employee benefits (10 × 1.02) × 1/0.8/1.2	10,200	8,160	12,240
Transportation:			
Vehicle running costs (86 × 1.05) × 1/0.8/1.2	90,300	72,240	108,360
Vehicle depreciation [27 × 1/0.8/1.2]	27,000	21,600	32,400
Vehicle maintenance (34 × 1.05) × 1/0.8/1.2	35,700	28,560	42,840
IT costs:			
Depreciation of equipment [8 × 1/0.8/1.2]	8,000	6,400	9,600
Running & maintenance (12 × 1.06) × 1/0.8/1.2	12,720	10,176	15,264
Consumables (15 × 1.06) × 1/0.8/1.2	15,900	12,720	19,080
Other costs:			
Sundry administration (50 × 1.1) × 1/0.8/1.2	55,000	44,000	66,000
Property-related (30 × 1.1) × 1/0.8/1.2	33,000	26,400	39,600
Insurances (6 × 1.1) × 1/0.8/1.2	6,600	5,280	7,920
Gross expenditure	1,051,260	841,008	1,261,512
Expenditure recovered through grants (6%)	63,076	50,460	75,691
Net expenditure	988,184	790,548	1,185,821

(b) Splitting the annual expenditure from Table C12.3 according to the quarterly percentages given in the question gives the profiled expenditure budget in Table C12.4.

(c) The budgets exhibit incremental characteristics in that next year's budget is based on an amended version of this year's. Zero-base influence can be seen in the provision of a budget for three levels of service, which could be viewed as incremental decision packages for the Home Help Section.

TABLE C12.4 Home Help Section's profiled expenditure budget

	Quarter I (35%) (£)	Quarter II (30%) (£)	Quarter III (20%) (£)	Quarter IV (15%) (£)
Employee costs:				
Wages and salaries (£626,280 × %s)	219,198	187,884	125,256	93,942
Wage-related costs (£130,560 × %s)	45,696	39,168	26,112	19,584
Employee benefits (£10,200 × %s)	3,570	3,060	2,040	1,530
Transportation:				
Vehicle running costs (£90,300 × %s)	31,605	27,090	18,060	13,545
Vehicle depreciation (£27,000 × %s)	9,450	8,100	5,400	4,050
Vehicle maintenance (£35,700 × %s)	12,495	10,710	7,140	5,355
IT costs:				
Depreciation of equipment (£8,000 × %s)	2,800	2,400	1,600	1,200
Running and maintenance (£12,720 × %s)	4,452	3,816	2,544	1,908
Consumables (£15,900 × %s)	5,565	4,770	3,180	2,385
Other costs:				
Sundry administration (£55,000 × %s)	19,250	16,500	11,000	8,250
Property-related (£33,000 × %s)	11,550	9,900	6,600	4,950
Insurances (£6,600 × %s)	2,310	1,980	1,320	990
Gross expenditure	367,941	315,378	210,252	157,689
Expenditure recovered through grants (6%)	22,077	18,923	12,615	9,461
Net expenditure	345,864	296,455	197,637	148,228

Chapter 13

13.1 B £18,000 favourable

The flexible budget cost for direct material is:

(actual output × standard direct material cost per unit)
= (9,000 units × £40) = £360,000

Thus, the flexible budget variance is:

(flexible budget direct material cost – actual material cost)
= (£360,000 – £342,000) = £18,000F.

13.2 B £3,600 adverse

The flexible budget should be based on *standard hours*. As demonstrated in the chapter, flexing the budget on actual hours will, in this example, 'reward' actual inefficiency. In fact, 4,000 actual hours worked at 90 per cent of standard efficiency represents (90% × 4,000) = 3,600 standard hours of work. The flexible budget for direct expenses is:

(standard hours of work actually performed × standard direct expenses per hour)
= (3,600 × £6) = £21,600

The flexible budget variance is therefore:

(flexible budget direct expenses cost – actual direct expenses cost)
= (£21,600 – £25,200) = £3,600A

13.3 **A** £612,000

Bearing in mind that only the *variable* element of total cost will react to volume changes, we need to identify both variable and fixed components of the total cost quoted in the question. At 80 per cent capacity, 60 per cent of total cost is wholly fixed: that is, (60% × £600,000) = £360,000, and (£600,000 – £360,000) = £240,000 is therefore the variable cost of 80 per cent of maximum capacity. For capacity of 84 per cent of maximum, the budgeted total cost allowance is:

	£
Fixed element	360,000
Variable element (84/80 × £240,000)	252,000
Total cost	612,000

13.4 **(a)** True **(b)** False **(c)** False **(d)** True **(e)** False **(f)** False **(g)** True

13.5 The completed paragraph reads as follows:

Overemphasis of budget variances as *managerial performance measures* may result in *quality and non-financial* measures being ignored, may *restrict* managerial freedom, and may panic management into an *unnecessary* cost-cutting response. In addition, the *controllability* of budget items by various managers requires careful consideration: there may be problems with *dual responsibility*, the possible inclusion of cost *apportionments* in budget control reports, along with the difficulty of exercising genuine short-term control over *committed and discretionary* costs.

13.6 **(a)** The flexible budget amount for the different variable costs at each level of activity in Table C13.1 is:

(budgeted number of credit enquiries × standard variable cost per enquiry)

Fixed costs will remain at the same amount regardless of the number of enquiries handled.

(b) An engineered cost is one where a tangible input/output relationship exists, as will often be the case with variable costs such as ACI Ltd's computing cost: that is, £0.75 of computing (input) is required for each credit enquiry (output). Such costs may be more amenable to short-term control measures than either discretionary or committed costs.

A discretionary cost is one over the amount of which management can exercise discretion and which could be eliminated without harm to the organisation in the short term. These costs do not have any definable input/output relationship. ACI Ltd's promotional costs fall into this category. It is difficult to link the amount of expenditure precisely to the benefit derived and management could probably decide to dispense with such expenditure without damaging the firm's short-term business position. (But note that elimination of discretionary costs may have adverse medium- and long-term effects.)

TABLE C13.1 ACI Ltd: flexible cost budgets

	Number of enquiries		
	50,000	65,000	75,000
Variable costs:			
	£	£	£
Computing	37,500	48,750	56,250
Direct expenses	15,000	19,500	22,500
Direct labour	7,500	9,750	11,250
	60,000	78,000	90,000
Fixed costs:			
	£	£	£
Direct labour	300,000	300,000	300,000
General administration	220,000	220,000	220,000
Computing	130,000	130,000	130,000
Building occupancy	40,000	40,000	40,000
Promotional	100,000	100,000	100,000
	790,000	790,000	790,000
Total cost	850,000	868,000	880,000

A committed cost is one which must be incurred if the organisation is to continue in the short term, and is therefore effectively unavoidable and unresponsive to short-term control measures. ACI Ltd's building occupancy costs will fall into this category, as it would be very difficult for the company to substantially reduce them in the short term (e.g. by moving to different premises). Some or all of the general administration and fixed computing costs may also be committed, since some or all of these costs are necessarily incurred in order to allow the firm to operate.

(c) As well as the problems of assessing future cost and revenue patterns and of estimating volume of activity, service organisations such as ACI Ltd have additional problems stemming from the heterogeneity and perishability of their operations. (We discussed these terms in Chapter 2 – simultaneity is rather less of a problem for ACI Ltd, since the answer to an enquiry would not be provided at the same time as the enquiry itself.)

The flexible budgets in (a) are based on the assumption of identical cost units, each consuming identical resources in their provision. But credit enquiries may not be identical (heterogeneity), and some may require significantly higher expenditure than others – not because of inefficiency or poor cost control, but simply because of the nature of the enquiry concerned. In addition, periods of peak activity cannot be prepared for by building up 'stocks' of responses to enquiries – these can only be made after ACI Ltd receives the enquiry (simultaneity).

Therefore, use of flexible budgets such as those in (a) may be problematic, since the assumptions underpinning the budgets do not tally with the reality of operations. If such budgets were to be operated by ACI Ltd, budget/actual comparisons would need to be made with this discrepancy very much in mind.

13.7 (a) The budget statement is given in Table C13.2 and the following brief notes relate to its construction.

1. *Monthly budget amounts* The budgeted fixed costs, along with the fixed budget sales/production volume, represent 1/12 of the annual figures given in the question.

2. *Budget revenue/variable costs* These are calculated as: (fixed/flexible budget volume × standard amount per unit).

3. *Budgeted fixed costs* Fixed and flexible budget amounts are the same, since the fixed costs are assumed to be unaffected by the volume difference.

4. *Variance signs* A distinction should be made between variances relating to costs and to revenue/contribution/profit, as the 'signs' are opposite. For example, flexible budget revenue, contribution and profit lower than fixed budget – adverse variances; flexible budget variable costs lower than fixed budget – favourable variances.

TABLE **C13.2 CMC Ltd: budgeted and actual profit statements, March 19X5**

	Fixed budget	Volume variances	Flexible budget	Flexible budget variances	Actual
Sales/production (units)	1,250	130A	1,120	nil	1,120
	£	£	£	£	£
Sales revenue	212,500	22,100A	190,400	11,200F	201,600
Variable costs:					
Direct materials	37,500	3,900F	33,600	2,240A	35,840
Direct labour	18,750	1,950F	16,800	3,360A	20,160
Selling	6,250	650F	5,600	700A	6,300
	62,500	6,500F	56,000	6,300A	62,300
Contribution	150,000	15,600A	134,400	4,900F	139,300
Fixed costs:					
Production overhead	37,500	nil	37,500	3,500F	34,000
Administration overhead	24,000	nil	24,000	1,000A	25,000
Selling overhead	15,000	nil	15,000	6,000F	9,000
	76,500	nil	76,500	8,500F	68,000
Profit	73,500	15,600A	57,900	13,400F	71,300

(b) Any comment on performance which is based solely on the content of Table C13.2 will, at best, be indicative, and further investigation will be required before firm conclusions can be arrived at.

■ *Sales* Actual sales volume was lower than budget, but this was more than offset by an actual selling price in excess of budget (as revealed by the flexible budget variance for revenue). Possibly the two are linked due to price elasticity of demand: that is, a higher-than-standard selling price has resulted in a lower-than-budgeted sales volume.

- *Variable costs* Actual variable costs were higher than the budget allowance for the volume of output achieved, perhaps due to price rises unforeseen when the standards were set or due to inefficient purchasing and/or usage.
- *Fixed costs* Substantial savings appear to have been made in production and selling overhead. Has there been a change in production methods? Is the reduction in actual selling overhead linked in any way to the lower-than-budgeted sales volume?
- *Contribution/profit* These are both markedly in excess of the budgeted amounts for the actual sales volume achieved, due to the higher actual selling price more than compensating for higher actual variable costs, and also to savings in production and selling overhead.

(c) If the actual rate of inflation were different to that envisaged in the budget, then it would mean that the flexible budget variances would be due (in part at least) to this difference. If we assume that the actual inflation rate were greater than budget, the impact on cost variances would be adverse. Since the inflation rate is not under managerial control, a fairer budget/actual comparison would be achieved if the effect of inflation were removed from both sets of figures by stating them on a common basis, exclusive of the inflationary element (i.e. by deflating them). Note, however, that such an adjustment would only be appropriate when the unforeseen price increase could not be countered by management (as it might have been in the case of direct materials by changing to a cheaper supplier).

13.8 (a) The budgeted amounts for Period 4 in Table C13.3 are 1/13 of the annual budget given in the question.

TABLE **C13.3 Registrar's Office: control report for Period 4 19X2**

	Budget	Actual	Variance
Number of registrations	1,000	1,650	650F
	£	£	£
Registration fees	14,000	23,040	9,040F
Fixed costs:			
Administration	2,000	2,400	400A
Occupancy	5,000	5,100	100A
Apportionment of HQ costs	4,000	4,800	800A
Direct labour	4,500	5,200	700A
	15,500	17,500	2,000A
Variable costs:			
Stationery	900	1,700	800A
Other	300	1,080	780A
	1,200	2,780	1,580A
Total costs	16,700	20,280	3,580A
Surplus/(deficit)	(2,700)	2,760	5,460F

(b) The budget/actual comparison in (a) is flawed because of the way the budget for the control period has been prepared. Simply dividing the annual amounts by 13 does not allow for the impact of volume differences on registration fees and on variable costs. It also makes the somewhat simplistic assumption that fixed costs are the same in every control period. The reported variances are therefore likely to be misleading. A better approach would be to flex the budget: that is, base registration fees and variable costs on the actual number of registrations during the period; and to *profile* fixed cost expenditure: that is, allow for uneven fixed cost expenditure within the budget period.

(c) Although the information in the question is limited, it seems likely that few of the items in the control report in (a) are genuinely under the short-term control of the Registrar's Office. Inclusion of items such as the apportionment of HQ costs in the report without any additional comment may *suggest* that they are somehow controllable by the Registrar's Office. Occupancy, administration and labour costs may likewise be subject to little short-term control. Variable costs, however, may be controllable, but before assessing the extent to which control of these has been effective, the budget must be flexed. Registration fees are outwith the control of the Registrar's Office, depending on natural phenomena such as birth and death rates. Moreover, if variable costs vary relative to the number of registrations, little control may be possible here either.

Chapter 14

Note: In the answers which follow, we have adopted the formulaic approach to calculation. You may have used the narrative method, which is equally acceptable. Both methods yield the same answers.

14.1 D £19,200F

The price variance is:

$$(SP - AP) \times AQ$$

Bearing in mind that 'AQ' refers to purchase quantity, we have:

$$(£16 - £15) \times 19,200 \text{ kg} = £19,200F$$

14.2 A £12,000A

The usage variance is calculated as:

$$(SQ - AQ) \times SP$$

Bearing in mind that 'SQ' is the standard quantity of materials allowed for actual output (throughput of untreated sewage here), the usage variance is:

$$\{(\frac{2,206,250 \text{ litres}}{50} \times 0.4 \text{ kg}) - 18,400 \text{ kg}\} \times £16 = £12,000A$$

14.3 (a) False (b) True (c) True (d) False (e) True (f) False

14.4 C £5,000A

The variable overhead expenditure variance is computed as:

$$\{(AH \times SVOH) - AVO\}$$
$$\{(7,000 \text{ hours} \times £5) - £40,000\} = £5,000A$$

14.5 C £10,800F

Standard contribution per unit is:

$$(£40 - £22) = £18$$

The sales volume variance is:

$$(BS - AS) \times SCU$$
$$= (4,000 \text{ units} - 4,600 \text{ units}) \times £18 = £10,800F$$

14.6 D £23,000A

We can obtain the expenditure variance by working backwards from the variances given:

$$\text{volume} + \text{expenditure variances} = \text{total variance}$$
$$= £7,000F + \text{expenditure variance} = £16,000A$$
$$= £7,000F + £23,000A \qquad = £16,000A$$

14.7 (a) Labour rate variance:

$$(SR - AR) \times AH$$
$$= \left(£9 - \frac{£11,760}{1,400 \text{ hours}}\right) \times 1,400 \text{ hours}$$
$$= £840F$$

Efficiency variance:

$$(SH - AH) \times SR$$
$$= \{(33,000 \times 2 \text{ minutes}) - 1,400 \text{ hours}\} \times £9$$
$$= £2,700A$$

(b) (i) This statement is consistent with the efficiency variance. Unforeseen idle time in Binding would result in an adverse efficiency variance; Binding operatives presumably cannot work without input from Printing.

(ii) This statement is consistent with the efficiency variance, which indicates lower-than-standard efficiency. Substandard materials may be harder to bind, increasing the time needed to produce a given number of bound volumes.

(iii) This statement is inconsistent with the favourable rate variance, which indicates that the actual rate of pay was lower than standard. This suggests either that the rise has not yet been paid or that a rise in excess of that which was actually awarded has been incorporated in the standard rate per hour.

14.8 (a) The variance calculations are as follows:

(i) *Labour rate*: $(SR - AR) \times AH$

$$= \left(£12 - \frac{£25,000}{1,800}\right) \times 1,800$$
$$= £3,600A$$

Labour efficiency: $(SH - AH) \times SR$

$$= \frac{\{(13{,}100 \text{ sessions} \times 10 \text{ minutes}) - 1{,}800 \text{ hours}\}}{60 \text{ minutes}} \times £12$$

$$= £4{,}600F$$

(ii) *Variable overhead expenditure:* $\{(AO \times SVOU) - AVO\}$

$$= \{(13{,}100 \text{ sessions} \times £3) - £42{,}000\} = £2{,}700A$$

(*Note:* Variable overhead in this example varies with the number of cost units – that is, downloading sessions – so 'AO' (actual output) replaces actual hours in the expenditure variance and an efficiency variance is not calculated.)

(iii) *Fixed overhead volume:* $(BO - AO) \times FOPU$

$$= (15{,}000 - 13{,}100 \text{ sessions}) \times £1 = £1{,}900A$$

Fixed overhead expenditure: $(BFO - AFO)$

$$= (£15{,}000 - £13{,}000)$$
$$= £2{,}000F$$

(b) The fixed overhead volume variance, which exists only in an absorption costing system, indicates the extent to which the total variance for fixed overhead (i.e. under- or overabsorption) arises due to differences between budgeted and actual volumes of output. This variance may be significant in assessing the effectiveness with which productive assets are utilised and the recovery of fixed overheads, but it has no relevance to cost control, which is monitored via the expenditure variance.

(c) The Managing Director's comment about 'unproductive' use of system operators' time is not borne out by the efficiency variance, so presumably the standard time of 10 minutes per downloading session includes an allowance for this element of their work. Although the suggestion may indeed reduce costs and increase revenue, it is possible that these benefits will be short-term. For example, clients may object to the proposed lack of help in 'navigating' the database and take their business elsewhere (note that the actual volume of sessions was lower than budget, which might suggest an existing marketing/sales problem); there may be an adverse effect on the efficiency of the systems operators remaining after the proposed reduction, as they may feel insecure in their jobs; a staff reduction may also lead to a situation where IB Ltd cannot cope with an increase in demand or leave themselves with insufficient expertise to cope with technological change. Overall, the company would be unwise to base this decision purely on financial criteria.

14.9 (a) The required variances are as follows:

(i) *Material price:* $(SP - AP) \times AQ$

Alloy $(£2.65 - £2.50) \times 256{,}000 \text{ m}^2 = £38{,}400F$
Fixings $(£1.70 - £1.76) \times 641{,}000 \text{ units} = £38{,}460A$

Material usage: $(SQ - AQ) \times SP$

Alloy $([47{,}000 \times 5 \text{ m}^2] - 256{,}000 \text{ m}^2) \times £2.65 = £55{,}650A$
Fixings $\{(47{,}000 \times 14 \text{ units}) - 641{,}000 \text{ units}\} \times £1.70 = £28{,}900F$

(ii)   *Direct labour rate*: (SR – AR) × AH

$$\left(£7.20 - \frac{£1,363,200}{192,000 \text{ hours}}\right) \times 192,000 \text{ hours} = £19,200F$$

Direct labour efficiency: (SH – AH) × SR

$$\{(47,000 \times 4 \text{ hours}) - 192,000 \text{ hours}\} \times £7.20 = £28,800A$$

(iii)   *Variable overhead expenditure*: {(AH × SVOH) – AVO}

$$\{(192,000 \text{ hours} \times £3.60) - £750,000\} = £58,800A$$

Variable overhead efficiency: (SH – AH) × SVOH

$$\{(47,000 \times 4 \text{ hours}) - 192,000 \text{ hours}\} \times £3.60 = £14,400A$$

(iv)   *Fixed overhead expenditure*: (BFO – AFO)

$$= (£170,000 - £165,000) = £5,000F$$

Fixed overhead volume: (BP – AP) × FOPU

$$= (50,000 \text{ units} - 47,000 \text{ units}) \times (4 \text{ hours @ } £0.85) = £10,200A$$

(v)   *Selling price*: (SSP – ASP) × AS

$$= \left(£110 - \frac{£4,935,000}{47,000 \text{ units}}\right) \times 47,000 \text{ units} = £235,000A$$

Sales volume: (BS – AS) × Sπ

The fact that fixed overhead is absorbed into unit costs indicates that an absorption costing system is in operation; therefore the sales volume variance is based on standard unit profit:

	£	£
Standard selling price		110.00
Standard direct materials:		
alloy – 5 m² @ £2.65	13.25	
fixings – 14 units @ £1.70	23.80	
Standard direct labour – 4 hours @ £7.20	28.80	
Standard variable overhead – 4 hours @ £3.60	14.40	
Standard fixed overhead – 4 hours @ £0.85	3.40	83.65
Standard gross profit		26.35

This gives a sales volume variance of:

$$(50,000 \text{ units} - 47,000 \text{ units}) \times £26.35 = £79,050A$$

(b) PTP & Co: operating statement for the year ending 31 March 19X5

		£
Original (fixed) budget gross profit (50,000 units @ £26.35)		1,317,500
Sales volume variance		79,050A
Flexible budget gross profit (47,000 units @ £26.35)		1,238,450

Variances

	F(£)	A(£)	
Material price			
Alloy	38,400		
Fixings		38,460	
Material usage			
Alloy		55,650	
Fixings	28,900		
Labour rate	19,200		
Labour efficiency		28,800	
Var. overhead expenditure		58,800	
Var. overhead efficiency		14,400	
Fixed overhead expenditure	5,000		
Fixed overhead volume		10,200	
Selling price		235,000	
	91,500	441,310	349,810A
Actual profit			888,640

(c) Extracting variances annually suggests that the firm's control mechanisms are inadequate. Unless variance information is gathered on an interim basis (e.g. monthly), then management will not be in a position to take timely control action. It may be that the large variances reported in the statement in (b) have, in part, arisen because management has been unaware of the situation until the year-end – by which time it is too late to exploit favourable variances or to mitigate the effect of adverse variances.

(d) Interdependence may exist between the favourable price variance for alloy and the adverse usage variance for the same material. If the favourable price variance has arisen because of purchase of a different, or poorer, quality of alloy from that specified in the standard data, then there might have been a knock-on effect in terms of increased wastage in use.

A second possible interdependence may exist between the adverse alloy usage variance and the adverse labour (and variable overhead) efficiency variance. Increased wastage of material in production could mean that labour time per unit of output is greater than standard.

14.10 (a) Because the standard cost per student excludes a charge for fixed overhead, we know that marginal costing is in operation and that the sales volume variance should be stated in terms of standard contribution. Similarly, we know from this that a fixed overhead volume variance will not be required. The required variances are as follows:

Direct labour rate: $(SR - AR) \times AH$

$$= (£15 - £18) \times 59,000 \text{ hours} = £177,000A$$

Direct labour efficiency: $(SH - AH) \times SR$

$$\{(3,100 \text{ students} \times 20 \text{ hours}) - 59,000 \text{ hours}\} \times £15 = £45,000F$$

Sales volume: $(BS - AS) \times SCU$

$$= (3,500 - 3,100) \times (£450 - £325) = £50,000A$$

Selling price: $(SSP - ASP) \times AS$

$$\left(£450 - \frac{£1,271,000}{3,100 \text{ students}}\right) \times 3,100 \text{ students} = £124,000A$$

Variable overhead expenditure: $\{(AH \times SVOH) - AVO\}$

$$\{(59,000 \text{ hours} \times £0.75) - £46,300\} = £2,050A$$

Variable overhead efficiency: $(SH - AH) \times SVOH$

$$= \{(3,100 \text{ students} \times 20 \text{ hours}) - 59,000 \text{ hours}\} \times £0.75 = £2,250F$$

Fixed overhead expenditure: $(BFO - AFO)$

$$= (£87,500 - £82,000) = £5,500F$$

(b) Feedback control involves comparison of actual with plan, and taking control action where significant variances exist. Planning and operational variances may enhance this process by helping to ensure that managerial control 'effort' is concentrated on areas which are genuinely controllable, rather than being wasted on uncontrollable planning errors. Feedforward control involves setting objectives, preparing a plan, and amending the plan and/or objectives where a significant difference exists between the two. Planning/operational variances might enhance this process by helping to ensure that objectives are realistic and that the plan is not based on out-of-date information.

Chapter 15

15.1 **B** 10%

The Automotive Parts Division's ROCE is:

$$\frac{\text{operating profit}}{\text{capital employed}} \times 100\% = \frac{£200,000}{£2,000,000} \times 100\% = 10\%$$

15.2 **A** £40,000

Residual income is calculated as (operating profit *less* interest on capital employed). For the Automotive Parts Division, this gives:

	£
Operating profit	200,000
less Interest on capital employed (8% × £2,000,000)	160,000
Residual income	40,000

15.3 **(a)** False **(b)** True **(c)** True **(d)** False **(e)** True **(f)** False **(g)** True

15.4 **B** 12%

Divisional profit and capital employed must be revised to allow for the impact of the proposed asset's acquisition:

	£
Profit	
Budgeted without acquisition	1,488,000
add Cash inflow from new asset	160,000
less Depreciation on new asset	100,000
Revised profit	1,548,000

	£
Capital	
Budgeted without acquisition	12,500,000
add Cost of new asset	500,000
less Depreciation on new asset	100,000
Revised capital	12,900,000

ROCE is thus:

$$\frac{\text{operating profit}}{\text{capital employed}} \times 100\% = \frac{£1,548,000}{£12,900,000} \times 100\% = 12\%$$

15.5 The main advantages/disadvantages of a divisionalised structure are:

Advantages
- Specialised local knowledge
- Avoiding management bottlenecks at the centre
- Speed of reaction
- Enhanced training opportunities
- Behavioural benefits
- Ease of acquisition/disposal
- Managing by numbers

Disadvantages
- Duplication of work
- Problems with information flow
- Potential for dysfunctional decisions
- Lack of functional expertise

These points are more fully discussed in Chapter 15.

15.6 (a) The quoted ROCEs have been calculated as follows:

Northern Division

$$\frac{\text{operating profit}}{\text{capital employed}} \times 100\% = \frac{£639,200}{£3,196,000} \times 100\% = 20\%$$

Southern Division

$$\frac{\text{operating profit}}{\text{capital employed}} \times 100\% = \frac{£368,000}{£4,600,000} \times 100\% = 8\%$$

The ROCEs above have been calculated on the basis of divisional operating profit: that is, after deduction of the apportionment of headquarters costs. It may be argued that deduction of these costs in the context of performance appraisal is inequitable because:

- there will be an element of subjectivity in the apportionment exercise; and
- the level of headquarters costs is not strictly under the control of divisional management.

It may therefore be preferable to restate divisional ROCE on the basis of operating profit *before* deduction of the headquarters cost apportionment. Increasing each division's net profit by the amount apportioned gives revised returns of:

Northern Division

$$\frac{£639,200 + £150,000}{£3,196,000} \times 100\% = 24.69\%$$

Southern Division

$$\frac{£368,000 + £280,000}{£4,600,000} \times 100\% = 14.09\%$$

Note that these calculations assume that all other items in the profit statement and capital figures are controllable at divisional level. In fact, this may not be the case: for example, headquarters may control a certain part of divisional capital investment decisions (say, for particularly large amounts).

(b) Applying AAM plc's cost of capital to divisional capital employed and deducting interest on capital from *controllable* divisional profit (i.e. excluding the apportionment of headquarters costs) gives:

	Northern Division £	Southern Division £
Operating profit	639,200	368,000
add Apportionment of headquarters costs	150,000	280,000
Controllable divisional profit	789,200	648,000
less Interest on capital employed		
(10% × £3,196,000/£4,600,000)	319,600	460,000
Residual income	469,600	188,000

Residual income suggests the same relative position between the two divisions as does ROCE: that is, that Northern Division has 'outperformed' Southern. However, a 'snap' judgement like this could be misleading, as it is based on very limited information. Further investigation/analysis is required.

(c) The additional financial indicators are

	Northern Division	Southern Division
Variable production costs : sales %	$\dfrac{£370,800}{£2,060,000}$	$\dfrac{£234,000}{£1,950,000}$
	18%	12%
Variable selling and distribution costs : sales %	$\dfrac{£160,000}{£2,060,000}$	$\dfrac{£78.000}{£1,950,000}$
	7.77%	4%

	Northern Division	Southern Division
Contribution : sales %	$\dfrac{£1,529,200}{£2,060,000}$	$\dfrac{£1,638,000}{£1,950,000}$
	74.23%	84%
Fixed production costs : sales %	$\dfrac{£300,000}{£2,060,000}$	$\dfrac{£720,000}{£1,950,000}$
	14.56%	36.92%
Fixed selling and distribution costs : sales	$\dfrac{£200,000}{£2,060,000}$	$\dfrac{£110,000}{£1,950,000}$
	9.71%	5.64%
Fixed administration costs : sales %	$\dfrac{£240,000}{£2,060,000}$	$\dfrac{£160,000}{£1,950,000}$
	11.65%	8.21%
Controllable operating profit : sales %	$\dfrac{£789,200}{£2,060,000}$	$\dfrac{£648,000}{£1,950,000}$
	38.31%	33.23%
Sales : capital employed	$\dfrac{£2,060,000}{£3,196,000}$	$\dfrac{£1,950,000}{£4,600,000}$
	64.46%	42.39%

(d) Northern Division's performance *appears* superior to Southern's based on comparison of ROCE, residual income, fixed production costs : sales percentage, controllable operating profit : sales percentage, and sales : capital employed percentage. However, this comparison is not altogether valid because of the difference in asset ages between the two divisions. Equalising fixed asset values and depreciation charges (which are presumably considerably higher in Southern than in Northern) – for example, by basing both on current replacement cost – may go a long way towards removing the apparent discrepancy in performance revealed by these measures. Comparison of the two divisions' sales : capital employed percentage may also suggest that the new assets at Southern Division are not yet fully operational.

The difference in asset base between the two divisions may also be reflected in the variable production costs : sales percentage. In this case, the lower percentage for Southern Division could reflect the lower operating cost of the newer, more efficient operating assets. Variable and fixed selling and distribution costs, along with fixed administration costs as percentages of sales, are all lower in Southern than in Northern division. This may be due to poor cost control in the latter division, but may also be connected with the balance of internal : external sales in each division – Northern's preponderance of external sales may need higher selling, distribution and administration costs compared to Southern's mainly internal sales. However, it may be the case that Southern's internal sales are made at a lower price than the external sales in order to reflect the associated cost savings, in which case that division's cost advantage may be somewhat negated. But you should note that Southern Division's contribution : sales ratio is markedly higher than Northern's, so that if Southern's internal sales are made at a lower price than that which would apply for external, then Southern's success in variable cost terms is even greater.

So, despite the similarity of the two divisions' output, comparison of their relative financial performance is fraught with anomaly and potentially incorrect analysis if based solely on the figures provided.

15.7 (a)

| | | *Hougham School* | |
		19X3/X4	*19X4/X5*
(i)	*Total pupil teaching days*		
	(school roll × teaching days in year)		
	Possible	(502×290)	(584×290)
		145,580	169,360
	Actual	(502×279)	(584×282)
		140,058	164,688
(ii)	*Actual : possible total pupil teaching days (percentage)*	140,058	164,688
		145,580	169,360
	Actual: possible %:	96.21%	97.24%
(iii)	*Pupil absences as percentage of total actual*	2,259	3,066
	pupil teaching days	140,058	164,688
		1.61%	1.86%
(iv)	*Staff absences as percentage of total actual*	132	189
	pupil teaching days	140,058	164,688
		0.1%	0.1%
(v)	*Pupil : teacher ratio*	$(502:22)$	$(584:21)$
		$22.82:1$	$27.81:1$
(vi)	*Pupil : non-teaching staff ratio*	$(502:6)$	$(584:6)$
		$83.67:1$	$97.33:1$
(vii)	*Average class size (school roll ÷ number of classes)*	502	584
		20	20
		25.10	29.20
(viii)	*Total expenditure per pupil*:		
	Budgeted	£2,400,000	£2,600,000
		502	584
		£4,780.88	£4,452.05
	Actual	£2,200,000	£2,900,000
		502	584
		£4,382.47	£4,965.75
(ix)	*Total expenditure variance*	(£2.4m–£2.2m)	(£2.6m–£2.9m)
		£200,000F	£300,000A

(b) In certain respects, the school's performance has been fairly consistent over the two-year period. Staff and pupil absences as a percentage of total actual pupil teaching days have deteriorated marginally, whilst actual : possible total pupil teaching days has shown a slight improvement. The major area of difference (and possibly concern) is the number of pupils on the school roll (roughly 16 per cent higher in 19X4/X5 than in the previous year), and the impact that this may have had on performance. Pupil : teaching staff, pupil : non-teaching staff ratios, and average class size have all worsened markedly. Whether this is sufficient to prejudice quality of provision, it is impossible to say without further investigation. Expenditure per pupil has fallen but this is a function of increased pupil numbers. The large swing in expenditure variance may result from poor cost control, but may also stem from attempts to cope with an unexpected rise in pupil numbers. Overall, it is not really possible to arrive at firm conclusions about the school's performance, partly because of lack of data from the school, and partly because of lack of data from other schools against which to compare it.

15.8 (a) The effect of the three proposals on the Microprocessor Division's net profit and capital employed will be:

	Proposal A £	Proposal B £	Proposal C £
Operating profit without proposal	600,000	600,000	600,000
add Cash inflow from proposal	100,000	90,000	95,000
less Depreciation on proposal	75,000	50,000	80,000
Revised operating profit	625,000	640,000	615,000
Capital employed without proposal	2,500,000	2,500,000	2,500,000
add Cost of proposal	300,000	200,000	00,000
less Depreciation on proposal	75,000	50,000	80,000
Revised capital employed	2,725,000	2,650,000	2,920,000

The acceptability of the proposals to management at the Microprocessor Division is likely to depend on the effect of each on ROCE without the proposals, which is:

$$\frac{\text{operating profit}}{\text{capital employed}} \times 100\% = \frac{£600,000}{£2,500,000} \times 100\% = 24\%$$

Acceptance of each proposal individually will change this to:

$$\text{Accept Proposal A:} \quad \frac{£625,000}{£2,725,000} \times 100\% = 22.94\%$$

$$\text{Accept Proposal B:} \quad \frac{£640,000}{£2,650,000} \times 100\% = 24.15\%$$

$$\text{Accept Proposal C:} \quad \frac{£615,000}{£2,920,000} \times 100\% = 21.06\%$$

Since Proposal B improves ROCE, this is likely to be the only proposal acceptable to management of the Microprocessor Division.

(b) Acceptability will again be contingent on each proposal's effect on residual income:

	Without Proposals £	*Accept Proposal A* £	*Accept Proposal B* £	*Accept Proposal C* £
Capital employed	2,500,000	2,725,000	2,650,000	2,920,000
Operating profit	600,000	625,000	640,000	615,000
Interest on capital at 12%	300,000	327,000	318,000	350,400
Residual income	300,000	298,000	322,000	264,600

Based on residual income, B offers an improvement, and so, as in (a), B would be the only proposal likely to be acceptable to Microprocessor Division management.

(c) TNF Group is likely to assess the desirability of the three proposals on the basis of their net present value, which is calculated in Table C15.1.

TABLE C15.1 NPV of three proposals

Year	Cash flow	Amount: A £	Amount: B £	Amount: C £	Discount factor	PV – A £	PV – B £	PV – C £
0	Initial cost	(300,000)	(200,000)	(500,000)	1.000	(300,000)	(200,000)	(500,000)
1–3	Cash inflow		90,000		2.402		216,180	
1–4	Cash inflow	100,000			3.038	303,800		
1–6	Cash inflow			95,000	4.112			390,640
3	Scrap value		50,000		0.712		35,600	
6	Scrap value			20,000	0.507			10,140
					NPV	3,800	51,780	(99,220)

For Proposals B and C, goal congruence is likely to exist between the Microprocessor Division and TNF Group, ROCE, residual income and NPV all suggesting acceptance and rejection of B and C respectively. However, there is the real possibility of a dysfunctional decision regarding Proposal A, where a positive NPV indicates acceptability, but ROCE and residual income both suggest rejection.

▍Chapter 16

16.1 **B** II only

Aspiration levels can be increased to meet a strict, but credible budget. The key word here is 'credible' – statement I would apply if the budget were perceived as too strict to represent a credible target. If the budget is set at a level equal to aspiration levels, the implication is that the budget will be achieved – no more, no less.

16.2 (a) False (b) False (c) True (d) False (e) True (f) True (g) True (h) False

16.3 A Budgetary slack

The manager's comment suggests that at least some part of the budget is 'unnecessary' and that conscious effort should be made to spend it. Budgetary slack is the difference between the minimum necessary expenditure and the budgeted expenditure: that is, the 'unnecessary' element of the budget referred to.

16.4 The completed paragraph, with the missing words highlighted, reads as follows:

Effective participation depends on organisational *culture and structure*, the nature of the task being performed and the *personality* of the individuals concerned. In a highly *structured* situation, or in one where *speed of action* is vital, participation may be *ineffective*. Moreover, if participation conflicts with organisational culture and/or management style, *pseudo-participation* may occur, with *dysfunctional* consequences. Participation may be *effective* in situations characterised by a high degree of *uncertainty* and where the individuals concerned are *responsive* to a participatory approach.

16.5 D Pseudo-participation

The actions of the Chief Executive in frequently reversing decisions made by the Capital Projects Committee suggest a conflict between a participatory approach and either/both the Chief Executive's view or/and the organisational culture/structure. It is possible that the Health Board's structure is extremely pyramidal or bureaucratic, in which case, active participation may well prove a somewhat alien concept.

Note: the answers to Questions 16.6, 16.7 and 16.8 are not intended to be exhaustive but are indicative of the main issues raised

16.6 (a)

Report

To: General Manager, Electrical Wholesale Division

From:

Issues arising from management meeting

It appears that the target return on capital is being used as a device to pressure divisional management, which is leading to dysfunctional behaviour, as the three suggestions clearly show. Your own and the Warehousing Manager's suggestions are examples of short-termism, and all three could be viewed as highly unethical, given their possible future effects on both the division and company overall. The impression is that divisional management are unhappy with the target return, which raises three questions:

1 To what extent does the company encourage effective participation in the setting of such targets?
2 What is divisional management's view of the 'strictness' and achievability of the targets set?
3 Is achievement of target return the only performance criterion applied by the company?

If any of the suggestions is adopted, possible consequences might be as follows:

- *Your own suggestion* Although this may have the desired effect in the short term, have the reactions of the customer been considered? Will rescheduling delivery incur any additional costs? If the customer is displeased, then this might sour future relations, with a possible effect on future sales. Furthermore, incurring additional costs merely to achieve bonus is unethical.
- *Divisional Accountant's suggestion* 'Massaging' the figures as suggested is not only unethical, but may result in a seriously misleading effect at Head Office. If, as claimed, no one at Head Office is sufficiently knowledgeable about the division's business, then a dialogue is suggested, rather than unilateral and covert action.
- *Warehousing Manager's suggestion* This will incur additional costs in the form of the deep discounts and perhaps also in terms of additional damage to the building's fabric. Postponing the work may also have a detrimental effect on staff morale in the warehouse concerned and might cause a deterioration in staff/management relations. Even more importantly, allowing water damage to electrical goods which are for sale may open the company to claims for damages resulting from sale of faulty goods. Ingress of water may also represent a health and safety risk to employees in the warehouse.

None of the suggestions is therefore in the interest of either the division or company as a whole.

(b) Steps which might be taken include the following:

- Involve divisional managers in the setting of target return (if this does not already happen). This could help avoid the possibility of targets being viewed as 'unrealistic' by divisional managers, and might improve motivation to achieve targets.
- Use a range of performance criteria. Basing bonuses solely on achievement of target return may cause managers to focus on performance in too narrow a sense.
- Run short training courses for divisional managers to explain how the financial evaluation system operates and to stress the need for dialogue between divisions and Head Office. By explaining the nature and purpose of what the company is doing, and by encouraging communication, the possibility of conflict may be reduced.

16.7 The main differences between the two organisations may be as follows:

1 *Organisational structure* This is likely to be fairly hierarchical in the building society, but 'flatter' in the advertising agency.
2 *Organisational culture* 'Strong' and comparatively bureaucratic in the case of the building society, but less rigid in the advertising agency.
3 *Management style* Possibly tending more towards 'theory-X' in the building society and towards 'theory-Y' in the advertising agency.
4 *Nature of the work* Relatively structured and certain in the building society, but much less so in the advertising agency.

These differences would suggest that we might expect to see a more budget-constrained style of evaluation in the building society than in the advertising agency. This may be true, but budgets will be every bit as important in both organisations, and it is therefore perfectly possible that a budget-constrained style may exist in both. However, non-accounting evaluation may be more prominent in the advertising agency, which may also adopt a more participative approach (because of the less structured work) and may place less emphasis on administrative controls than does the building society. A word of warning, however. Though we may expect the sort of general difference outlined, based on the very limited information available, reality is not black and white, nor need it conform to our expectation.

16.8 The regulations quoted might, together or in isolation, cause or reinforce the following kinds of dysfunctional behaviour:

- *Budget slack* To protect themselves against what they may perceive as adverse consequences of breaching their budget, section heads may introduce an element of slack.
- *Inhibition of action* Section heads may be unwilling to pursue certain courses of action simply because of the strictness with which the budget appears to be enforced.
- *Projection* The ethos of personal responsibility for budgets and the need to gain approval of future budgets may result in 'buck-passing' exercises, with the true cause of problems becoming obscured.
- *Aggression* Far from encouraging goal congruence, the strict budgetary regime may result in disputes over budget allocations, with the largest allocations being made to the most strident section heads, regardless of economic necessity. The problem of aggression may be worsened by projection and empire building.
- *Empire building* Section heads may view the size of their budgets, or their success in defending their section's budgetary interests, as of greater concern than the overall good of the council.
- *Evasion* Section heads may be tempted to bypass formal budgetary procedures, relying instead on informal systems, or indulging in unauthorised virement.
- *Short-termism* Because of the strict monitoring of actual against budget, section heads may defer or cancel expenditures which have strategic importance to the section and/or the council.

INDEX